Introduction to
Emergency Management

Introduction to Emergency Management
Third Edition

George D. Haddow
Jane A. Bullock
Damon P. Coppola

AMSTERDAM • BOSTON • HEIDELBERG • LONDON
NEW YORK • OXFORD • PARIS • SAN DIEGO
SAN FRANCISCO • SINGAPORE • SYDNEY • TOKYO
Butterworth-Heinemann is an imprint of Elsevier

Acquisitions Editor: Pamela Chester
Marketing Manager: Marissa Hederson
Project Manager: Jeff Freeland
Designer: Joanne Blank
Compositor: SPI Technologies India Pvt. Ltd.
Cover Printer: Phoenix Color Corp.
Text Printer/Binder: Sheridan Books

Butterworth-Heinemann is an imprint of Elsevier
30 Corporate Drive, Suite 400, Burlington, MA 01803, USA
Linacre House, Jordan Hill, Oxford OX2 8DP, UK

Recognizing the importance of preserving what has been written, Elsevier prints its books on acid-free paper
whenever possible.

∞ **Library of Congress Cataloging-in-Publication Data**
Haddow, George D.
    Introduction to emergency management / George Haddow, Jane Bullock, Damon Coppola.–3rd ed.
        p. cm.
    Includes bibliographical references and index.
    ISBN-13: 978-0-7506-8514-6 (hardcover : alk. paper) 1. Emergency management. 2. Emergency
management–United States. I. Bullock, Jane A. II. Coppola, Damon P. III. Title.
    HV551.2.H3 2007
    363.34′80973–dc22

                                                                                    2007019634

British Library Cataloguing-in-Publication Data
A catalogue record for this book is available from the British Library.

ISBN: 978-0-7506-8514-6

For information on all Butterworth–Heinemann publications
visit our Web site at www.books.elsevier.com

Printed in the United States of America
    08 09 10 11 12   10 9 8 7 6 5 4 3 2

Working together to grow
libraries in developing countries

www.elsevier.com | www.bookaid.org | www.sabre.org

ELSEVIER   BOOK AID
            International   Sabre Foundation

Dedication

This book is dedicated to Lacy Suiter. Lacy taught us all the responsibility, privilege, and honor of serving people as emergency managers. He singlehandedly made emergency management an important discipline to the safety of our citizens. He was a gentleman, mentor, teacher, cheerleader, and impromptu singer. But most of all he was the best friend anyone could ever have.

Table of Contents

Foreword

In 1993, when I took over leadership of the Federal Emergency Management Agency (FEMA), emergency management was not a very well known or respected discipline. Many in the profession were hold-overs from the days of civil defense and most elected officials did not see the value of emergency management until they had a major disaster in their community; and even then the value was transitory. Throughout the 1990s, as the United States and the world experienced an unprecedented number of severe disasters, the critical role emergency management plays in protecting the social and economic stability of our communities was evidenced. Emergency management began to grow beyond the response environment and focus on risk analysis, communications, risk prevention/mitigation, and social and economic recovery. This required a new skill base for emergency managers, and colleges and universities added courses and degrees in emergency management to their offerings. This resulted in a better educated, multidisciplinary, proactive approach to emergency management. Emergency managers were valued members of a community's leadership. Emergency management became an important profession. It allowed me as Director of FEMA, to work with our State, local and private partners to build one of the most respected emergency management systems in the world.

As the tragic outcome of Hurricane Katrina so vividly demonstrated, a strong emergency management system is vital to the safety of all of our citizens. There is no time in our recent history when the need for and understanding of the discipline of emergency management have been more important. The current risk environment we live in, from potential bioterrorist threats, increasingly severe hurricanes and floods, and more frequent wildfires, has dramatically increased the skills and knowledge required to be an effective emergency manager in today's world.

Introduction to Emergency Management is the authoritative guide on today's discipline of emergency management. It takes the reader through the historical context of emergency management to the present day evolution into the world of homeland security. The book focuses on the elements of an emergency management process while providing the policy underpinnings that support that process. It provides a comprehensive case study that examines the events and issues surrounding Hurricane Katrina. While focusing on the current changes happening to United States system for emergency management, it provides readers with a solid background in international practices and policies for disaster management/homeland security. The book gives the reader practical, real world experiences through documented case studies and provides extensive references and internet sites for follow up research.

My philosophy about emergency management has always been that we need to take a common-sense, practical approach to reducing the risks we face and protecting our citizens and our communities. We need to identify our risks, educate and communicate to our people about those risks, prepare as best we can for the risks, and then, together, form partnerships to take action to reduce those risks. This approach applies whether we are dealing with a flood, a tornado, a hazardous materials spill, a wildfire, a potential suicide bomb explosion, or a pandemic flu outbreak. The authors of this book were my Deputy Chief of Staff and my Chief of Staff, respectively, when I was Director of FEMA. Together we worked to apply this approach to making our citizens and communities more disaster resistant and safer throughout the world. As you read and learn from this book, I hope you will keep those ideals in mind.

—James Lee Witt, James Lee Witt Associates

Acknowledgments

This book could not have been completed without the assistance of a series of valuable partners. First, we would like to thank Wayne Blanchard, whose vision, encouragement, and insights on effective education in emergency management have improved our work and the work of emergency managers everywhere. Second, the authors are grateful to the Institute for Crisis, Disaster, and Risk Management at The George Washington University and its co directors, Dr. Jack Harrald and Dr. Joseph Barbera, for their support. The Institute's Greg Shaw's humor helped us keep things in perspective. The third group includes the many professors, students and practitioners who have talked with us about different aspects of the book and provided suggestions to make the text more relevant and useful. Finally, the authors wish to thank their respective spouses, Kim Haddow and Mary Gardner Coppola, for their enduring good humor and patience.

Introduction

No country, no community, and no person is immune to the impact of disasters. Disasters, however, can be and have been prepared for, responded to, recovered from, and had their consequences mitigated to a certain degree. The profession and the academic discipline that addresses this "management" of disasters is called *emergency management*. This book, *Introduction to Emergency Management*, is designed to provide the reader with a comprehensive foundation on the background, components, and systems involved in the management of disasters and other emergencies. Herein are detailed current practices, strategies, and the key players involved in emergency management both within the United States and around the world. The intent is to provide the reader with a working knowledge of how the functions of emergency management operate and the influence they can have on everyday life.

This edition of the textbook is very different from the previous editions, because it reflects the experience of Hurricane Katrina, which demonstrated that the system of emergency management in the United States is broken. The devastating results of the government's failure to respond to Hurricane Katrina can be summarized in the over 1,800 lives lost and billions of dollars in property destroyed. The failure of FEMA and state and local emergency management and the political leadership at all levels in New Orleans, Louisiana, and Washington, D.C., was witnessed by millions of people around the world. A national system of emergency management that was once regarded as one of the most effective and emulated systems in the world proved incompetent in responding to an event that had been long predicted, planned for, and studied. Even now, two years after the Category 3 storm made landfall, the recovery has been equally ineffective and characterized by political and bureaucratic bungling. Unlike the sudden attacks of September 11, a Category 3 hurricane was something that emergency management should have been able to handle, something for which the system had been training and exercising. However, changes made to the system in the aftermath of September 11, 2001, directly contributed to the debacle of Katrina. This edition looks more closely at the changes to emergency management in the post-September 11 environment, discusses how these changes may have contributed to the events of Hurricane Katrina, and suggests some options for future directions in emergency management in the United States. Because of the impact of the event, a special case study focuses solely on Hurricane Katrina, but we include the impact and implications of the Katrina experiences in each of the chapters as appropriate.

While the book emphasizes the U.S. domestic system of emergency management, many of the experiences in the face of disasters across the globe are discussed. Lessons learned and emerging trends are replicable to emergency management systems around the world. Emergency management in the United States has experienced every form of disaster: natural, human-made, and political. The lessons learned from these experiences, the changes made in response to these events, and how the system continues to evolve in the aftermath of Katrina and because of new threats provide a solid landscape to examine what emergency management is or could be.

However, this book is not exclusively focused on FEMA. State and local emergency management organizations are the subjects of many of the included case studies, and their collaborative affiliations with FEMA are discussed at length throughout the text. In fact, the states are given responsibility for public health and safety under the U.S. Constitution. The federal government becomes involved only after the state government has requested assistance or when it is apparent that the state agencies are or will be unable to fulfill their basic functions. The federal government is the primary source of the funding for public health and safety programs, with the states and communities as the primary recipients, resulting in a strong federal presence in emergency management. The competition for oftentimes scarce resources, coupled with the immediate priorities of state and local governments, has ensured a strong federal influence in emergency management—a trend that may be changing, as we discuss in later chapters.

A comprehensive chapter is included that describes emergency management activities in the international sector. When the ability of an individual nation or a region as a whole to respond to a disaster is exceeded, the world's nations must join together to intervene and assist to manage the event. With greater frequency, events such as the 2004 Asian earthquake and tsunami highlight the need for a more robust international emergency management system, and governments across the globe have focused more attention on the issue. A detailed case study of the response to the 2001 earthquake in Gujarat, India, is provided to illustrate these systems.

A brief summary of the contents and special features of this edition follows:

- Chapter 1, The Historical Context of Emergency Management, includes a brief discussion of the historical, organizational, and legislative evolution of emergency management in the United States by tracing the major changes triggered by disasters or other human or political events, including the creation of the Department of Homeland Security. The chapter includes an analysis of the organizational, legislative, and policy changes made in emergency management both before and after Hurricane Katrina.
- Chapter 2, Natural and Technological Hazards and Risk Assessment, identifies and defines the hazards confronting emergency management.
- Chapter 3, The Disciplines of Emergency Management: Mitigation, discusses the function of mitigation and the strategies and programs applied by emergency management or other disciplines to reduce the impact of disaster events.

- Chapter 4, The Disciplines of Emergency Management: Response, focuses on the essential functions and processes of responding to a disaster event.
- Chapter 5, The Disciplines of Emergency Management: Recovery, describes the broad range of government and voluntary programs available to assist individuals and communities in rebuilding in the aftermath of a disaster.
- Chapter 6, The Disciplines of Emergency Management: Preparedness, catalogues the broad range of programs and processes that constitute the preparedness function of modern emergency management.
- Chapter 7, The Disciplines of Emergency Management: Communications, breaks from the more traditional approach to emergency management and focuses on why communication with the public, the media, and partners is critical to emergency management in the twenty-first century.
- Chapter 8, International Disaster Management, provides an overview of current activity in international emergency management through an examination of selected international organizations.
- Chapter 9, Emergency Management and the New Terrorist Threat, describes how the events of September 11 altered the traditional perceptions of emergency management.
- Chapter 10, The Future of Emergency Management, looks at the post-September 11, post-Katrina environment and provides insights, speculations, recommendations, and three options on where emergency management is or should be headed in the future.
- A special case study on Hurricane Katrina that provides an in-depth analysis and discussion of the hurricane, including detailed timelines, statistics, and experiences of the event. This case study includes analysis of the reports and commentaries by congressional committees, the Bush administration, and others about what happened in Katrina and discusses the diverse and numerous recommendations put forth to correct the problems experienced in Katrina.
- Supplements for this book are available online at: books.elsevier.com/companions/ 9780750685146

Our goal in writing this book was to provide readers with an understanding of emergency management, insight into how events have shaped the discipline, and thoughts about the future direction of emergency management. The events of September 11 and the failures of Hurricane Katrina demonstrate the critical need for and value of emergency management. The evolving threats, the realities of global climate change, and our changing social, economic, and political environment demand innovative approaches and leadership. We hope this text will motivate each reader to accept the challenge.

1

The Historical Context of Emergency Management

What You Will Learn

- The early roots of emergency management.
- The modern history of emergency management in the United States.
- How FEMA came to exist, and how it evolved during the 1980s, 1990s, and the early twenty-first century.
- The sudden changes to modern emergency management that have resulted from the September 11 terrorist attacks and Hurricane Katrina.

Introduction

Emergency management has ancient roots. Early hieroglyphics depict cavemen trying to deal with disasters. The Bible speaks of the many disasters that befell civilizations. In fact, the account of Moses parting the Red Sea could be interpreted as the first attempt at flood control. As long as there have been disasters, individuals and communities have tried to do something about them; however, organized attempts at dealing with disasters did not occur until much later in modern history.

The purpose of this chapter is to discuss the cultural, organizational, and legislative history of modern emergency management in the United States. Some of the significant events and people that shaped the emergency management discipline over the years are reviewed. Understanding the history and evolution of emergency management is important because, at different times, the concepts of emergency management have been applied differently. The definition of *emergency management* can be extremely broad and all-encompassing. Unlike other more structured disciplines, it has expanded and contracted in response to events, congressional desires, and leadership styles.

In the most recent history, events and leadership, more than anything else, have brought about dramatic changes to emergency management in the United States. The terrorist attacks of September 11, 2001, led to massive organizational changes and programmatic shifts in emergency management. Many believe that these changes undermined the effective national system of emergency management that had evolved during the 1990s and led to the profound failure of all levels of emergency management in response to Hurricane Katrina in 2005.

A simple definition is that *emergency management* is the discipline dealing with risk and risk avoidance. Risk represents a broad range of issues and includes an equally diverse set of players. The range of situations that could possibly involve emergency management or the emergency management system is extensive. This supports the premise that emergency management is integral to the security of everyone's daily lives and should be integrated into daily decisions and not just called on during times of disasters.

Emergency management is an essential role of government. The Constitution tasks the states with responsibility for public health and safety—hence the responsibility for public risks—with the federal government in a secondary role. The federal role is to help when the state, local, or individual entity is overwhelmed. This fundamental philosophy continues to guide the government function of emergency management.

Based on this strong foundation, the validity of emergency management as a government function has never been in question. Entities and organizations fulfilling the emergency management function existed at the state and local level long before the federal government became involved. But, as events occurred, as political philosophies changed, and as the nation developed, the federal role in emergency management steadily increased.

In the aftermath of the failed response to Hurricane Katrina, extensive discussion has centered about emergency management, particularly the response and recovery functions. An ever-increasing presence of nonprofit organizations delivering support to their particular constituencies after Katrina has given rise to interest on the part of the nonprofit community to take on increased responsibility for disaster response. This interest can best be attributed to the underlying belief that the federal government no longer can be relied on in disaster response and recovery. Both the actions of Congress and potential changes in the political leadership at the federal level may have a very strong influence on how this plays out in the near future.

Early History: 1800–1950

In 1803, a congressional act was passed to provide financial assistance to a New Hampshire town that had been devastated by fire. This is the first example of the federal government becoming involved in a local disaster. It was not until the administration of Franklin Roosevelt began to use government as a tool to stimulate the economy that a significant investment in emergency management functions was made by the federal government.

During the 1930s, both the Reconstruction Finance Corporation and the Bureau of Public Roads were given authority to make disaster loans available for repair and reconstruction of certain public facilities after disasters. The Tennessee Valley Authority was created during this time to produce hydroelectric power and, as a secondary purpose, reduce flooding in the region.

A significant piece of emergency management legislation was passed during this time. The Flood Control Act of 1934 gave the U.S. Army Corps of Engineers increased authority to design and build flood control projects. This act had a significant and long-lasting impact on emergency management in this country. The act reflected a philosophy that humans could control nature, thereby eliminating the risk of floods. Although this program would promote economic and population growth patterns along the nation's rivers, history has proven that this attempt at emergency management was shortsighted and costly.

The Cold War and the Rise of Civil Defense: 1950s

The next notable time frame for the evolution of emergency management occurs during the 1950s. The era of the Cold War presented the principal disaster risk as the potential for nuclear war and nuclear fallout. Civil defense programs proliferated across communities during this time. Individuals and communities were encouraged to build bomb shelters to protect themselves and their families from nuclear attack from the Soviet Union.

Almost every community had a civil defense director, and most states had someone who represented civil defense in their state government hierarchy. By profession, these individuals usually were retired military personnel, and their operations received little political or financial support from their state or local governments. Equally often, the civil defense responsibility was in addition to other duties.

Federal support for these activities was vested in the Federal Civil Defense Administration (FCDA), an organization with little staff or financial resources, whose main role was to provide technical assistance. In reality, the local and state civil defense directors were the first recognized face of emergency management in the United States.

A companion office to the FCDA, the Office of Defense Mobilization, was established in the Department of Defense (DoD). The primary functions of this office were to allow for quick mobilization of materials and production and stockpiling of critical materials in the event of a war. It included a function called *emergency preparedness*. In 1958, these two offices were merged into the Office of Civil and Defense Mobilization.

The 1950s were a quiet time for large-scale natural disasters. Hurricane Hazel, a Category 4 hurricane, inflicted significant damage in Virginia and North Carolina in 1954; Hurricane Diane hit several mid-Atlantic and northeastern states in 1955; and Hurricane Audrey, the most damaging of the three storms, struck Louisiana and North Texas in 1957. Congressional response to these disasters followed a familiar pattern of ad hoc legislation to provide increased disaster assistance funds to the affected areas.

As the 1960s started, three major natural disaster events occurred. In a sparsely populated area of Montana, the Hebgen Lake earthquake, measuring 7.3 on the Richter scale, brought attention to the fact that the nation's earthquake risk went beyond the California borders. Also in 1960, Hurricane Donna hit the west coast of Florida, and Hurricane Carla blew into Texas in 1961. The incoming Kennedy administration decided to make a change to the federal approach. In 1961, it created the Office of Emergency Preparedness inside the White House to deal with natural disasters. Civil defense responsibilities remained in the Office of Civil Defense within the DOD.

Natural Disasters Bring Changes to Emergency Management: 1960s

As the 1960s progressed, the United States would be struck by a series of major natural disasters. The Ash Wednesday storm in 1962 devastated more than 620 miles of shoreline on the East Coast, producing more than $300 million in damages. In 1964, an earthquake measuring 9.2 on the Richter scale in Prince William Sound, Alaska, became front-page news throughout America and the world. This quake generated a tsunami that affected beaches as far down the Pacific Coast as California and killed 123 people. Hurricane Betsey struck in 1965, and Hurricane Camille in 1969, killing and injuring hundreds of people and causing hundreds of millions of dollars in damage along the Gulf Coast.

As with previous disasters, the response was passage of ad hoc legislation for funds; however, the financial losses resulting from Hurricane Betsey's path across Florida and Louisiana started a discussion of insurance as a protection against future floods and a potential method to reduce continued government assistance after disasters. Congressional interest was prompted by the unavailability of flood protection insurance on the standard homeowner policy. Where this type of insurance was available, it was cost prohibitive. These discussions eventually led to passage of the National Flood Insurance Act of 1968, which created the National Flood Insurance Program (NFIP).

Congressman Hale Boggs of Louisiana is appropriately credited with steering this unique legislation through Congress. Unlike previous emergency management/disaster legislation, this bill sought to do something about the risk before the disaster struck. It brought the concept of *community-based mitigation* into the practice of emergency management. In simple terms, when a community joined the NFIP, in exchange for making federally subsidized, low-cost flood insurance available to its citizens, the community had to pass an ordinance restricting future development in its floodplains. The federal government also agreed to help local communities by producing maps of their community's floodplains.

The NFIP began as a voluntary program as part of a political compromise that Boggs reached with then-Senator Tom Eagleton of Missouri. As a voluntary program, few communities joined. After Hurricane Camille struck the Louisiana, Alabama, and Mississippi coasts in 1969, the goals of the NFIP to protect people's financial investments and reduce government disaster expenditures were not being met. It took Hurricane Agnes devastating Florida for a change to occur.

George Bernstein, brought down from New York by President Nixon to run the Federal Insurance Administration (FIA) within the Department of Housing and Urban Development (HUD), proposed linking the mandatory purchase of flood insurance to all homeowner loans backed by federal mortgages. This change created an incentive for communities to join the NFIP because a significant portion of the home mortgage market was federally backed. This change became the Flood Insurance Act of 1972.

It is important to note how local and state governments choose to administer this flood risk program. Civil defense departments usually had responsibility to deal with risks and disasters. Although the NFIP dealt with risk and risk avoidance, responsibilities for the NFIP were sent to local planning departments and state departments of natural resources. This reaction is one illustration of the fragmented and piecemeal approach to emergency management that evolved during the 1960s and 1970s.

Critical Thinking

Can you think of any positive or negative aspects of disaster-driven evolutionary changes in the United States' emergency management system? What about for changes that occur in the absence of initiating disaster events?

The Call for a National Focus on Emergency Management: 1970s

In the 1970s, responsibility for emergency management functions was evident in more than five federal departments and agencies, including the Department of Commerce (weather, warning, and fire protection), the General Services Administration (continuity of government, stockpiling, and federal preparedness), the Treasury Department (import investigation), the Nuclear Regulatory Commission (power plants), and HUD (flood insurance and disaster relief).

With passage of the Disaster Relief Act of 1974, prompted by the previously mentioned hurricanes and the San Fernando earthquake of 1971, HUD possessed the most significant authority for natural disaster response and recovery through the NFIP under the FIA and the Federal Disaster Assistance Administration (disaster response, temporary housing, and assistance). On the military side, there existed the Defense Civil Preparedness Agency (nuclear attack) and the U.S. Army Corps of Engineers (flood control); however, taking into account the broad range of risks and potential disasters, more than 100 federal agencies were involved in some aspect of risk and disasters.

This pattern continued down to the state and, to a lesser extent, local levels. Parallel organizations and programs added to confusion and turf wars, especially during disaster response efforts. The states and the governors grew increasingly frustrated over this fragmentation. In the absence of one clear federal lead agency in emergency management, a group of state civil defense directors, led by Lacy Suiter of Tennessee and Erie Jones of Illinois, launched an effort through the National Governor's Association to consolidate federal emergency management activities in one agency.

With the election of a fellow state governor, President Jimmy Carter of Georgia, the effort gained steam. President Carter came to Washington committed to streamlining all government agencies and seeking more control over key administrative processes. The state directors lobbied the National Governor's Association (NGA) and Congress for a consolidation of federal emergency management functions. When the Carter administration proposed such an action, it met with a receptive audience in the Senate. Congress already had expressed concerns about the lack of a coherent federal policy and the inability of states to know to whom to turn in the event of an emergency.

The federal agencies involved were not as excited about the prospect. A fundamental law of bureaucracy is a continued desire to expand control and authority, not to lose control. In a consolidation of this sort, there would be losers and winners. There was a question of which federal department or agency should house the new consolidated structure. As the debate continued, the newly organized National Association of State Directors of Emergency Preparedness championed the creation of a new independent organization, an idea that was quickly supported by the Senate.

In the midst of these discussions, an accident occurred at the Three Mile Island Nuclear Power Plant in Pennsylvania that added impetus to the consolidation effort. This accident brought national media attention to the lack of adequate off-site preparedness around commercial nuclear power plants and the role of the federal government in responding to such an event.

On June 19, 1978, President Carter transmitted to the Congress the Reorganization Plan Number 3 (3 CFR 1978, 5 U.S. Code 903). The intent of this plan was to consolidate emergency preparedness, mitigation, and response activities into one federal emergency management organization. The president stated that the plan would establish the Federal Emergency Management Agency (FEMA) and that the FEMA director would report directly to the president.

Reorganization Plan Number 3 transferred the following agencies or functions to FEMA: National Fire Prevention Control Administration (Department of Commerce), Federal Insurance Administration (HUD), Federal Broadcast System (Executive Office of the President), Defense Civil Preparedness Agency (DoD), Federal Disaster Assistance Administration (HUD), and the Federal Preparedness Agency (GSA).

Additional transfers of emergency preparedness and mitigation functions to FEMA were

- Oversight of the Earthquake Hazards Reduction Program (Office of Science and Technology Policy).
- Coordination of dam safety (Office of Science and Technology Policy).
- Assistance to communities in the development of readiness plans for severe weather-related emergencies.
- Coordination of natural and nuclear disaster warning systems.
- Coordination of preparedness and planning to reduce the consequences of major terrorist incidents.

Reorganization Plan Number 3 articulated several fundamental organizational principles:

> *First, Federal authorities to anticipate, prepare for, and respond to major civil emergencies should be supervised by one official responsible to the President and given attention by other officials at the highest levels. Second, an effective civil defense system requires the most efficient use of all available resources. Third, whenever possible, emergency responsibilities should be extensions of federal agencies. Fourth, federal hazard mitigation activities should be closely linked with emergency preparedness and response functions.*

Subsequent to congressional review and concurrence, the Federal Emergency Management Agency was officially established by Executive Order 12127 of March 31, 1979 (44 FR 19367, 3 CFR, Comp., p. 376). A second Executive Order, 12148, mandated reassignment of agencies, programs, and personnel into the new entity FEMA.

Creating the new organization made sense, but integrating the diverse programs, operations, policies, and people into a cohesive operation was a much bigger task than realized when the consolidation began. It would take extraordinary leadership and a common vision. The consolidation also created immediate political problems. By consolidating these programs and the legislation that created them, FEMA would have to answer to 23 committees and subcommittees in Congress with oversight of its programs. Unlike most other federal agencies, it would have no organic legislation to support its operations and no clear champions to look to during the congressional appropriations process.

In addition, President Carter had problems finding a director for this new organization. No large constituent group was identified with emergency management. Furthermore, the administration was facing major problems with Congress and the public because of the Iranian hostage crisis. President Carter finally reached into his own cabinet and asked John Macy, then head of the Office of Personnel Management (OPM), to become director of FEMA.

John Macy's task was to unify an organization that was not only physically separated—parts of the agency were located in five different buildings around Washington—but also philosophically separate. Programs focused on nuclear war preparations were combined with programs focused on a new consciousness of the environment and floodplain management. Macy focused his efforts by emphasizing the similarities between natural hazards preparedness and civil defense by developing a new concept called the *integrated emergency management system* (IEMS). This system was an all-hazards approach that included direction, control, and warning as functions common to all emergencies from small, isolated events, to the ultimate emergency of nuclear attack.

For all his good efforts, FEMA continued to operate as individual entities pursuing their own interests and answering to their different congressional bosses. It was a period of few major disasters, so virtually nobody noticed this problem of disjointedness.

Civil Defense Reappears as Nuclear Attack Planning: 1980s

The early and mid-1980s saw FEMA facing many challenges but no significant natural disasters. The absence of the need for a coherent federal response to disasters, as was called for by Congress when it approved the establishment of FEMA, allowed FEMA to continue to exist as an organization of many parts.

In 1982, President Reagan appointed Louis O. Guiffrida as director of FEMA. Guiffrida, a California friend of Ed Meese, one of the president's closest advisors, had a background in training and terrorism preparedness at the state government level. General Guiffrida proceeded to reorganize FEMA consistent with administration policies and his background. Top priority was placed on government preparedness for a nuclear attack. Resources within the agency were realigned, and additional budget authority was sought to enhance and elevate the national security responsibilities of the agency. With no real role for the states in these national security activities, the state directors who had lobbied for the creation of FEMA saw their authority and federal funding decline.

Guiffrida also angered one of the only other visible constituents of the agency, the fire services community. Guiffrida diminished the authority of the U.S. Fire Administration by making it part of FEMA's Directorate of Training and Education. The newly acquired campus at Emmetsburg, Maryland, was intended to become the preeminent National Emergency Training Center (NETC).

During Guiffrida's tenure, FEMA faced several unusual challenges that stretched its authority, including asserting FEMA into the lead role for continuity of civilian government in the aftermath of a nuclear attack, managing the federal response to the contamination at Love Canal and Times Beach, Missouri, and the Cuban refugee crisis. Although Guiffrida managed to bring the agency physically together in a new headquarters building in southwest Washington, severe morale problems persisted.

Dislike of Guiffrida's style and questions about FEMA's operations came to the attention of U.S. Representative Al Gore of Tennessee, who then served on the House Science and Technology Committee. As the congressional hearings proceeded, the Department of Justice and a grand jury began investigations of senior political officials at FEMA. These inquiries led to the resignation of Guiffrida and top aides in response to a variety of charges, including misuse of government funds, but the shake-up marked a milestone of sorts: FEMA and emergency management had made it into the comic strip *Doonesbury*.

President Reagan then selected General Julius Becton to be director of FEMA. General Becton was a retired military general and had been the director of the Office of Foreign Disaster Assistance in the State Department. General Becton is credited uniformly with restoring integrity to the operations and appropriations of the agency. From a policy standpoint, he continued to emphasize the programs of his predecessor but in a less visible manner. Becton expanded the duties of FEMA when he was asked by the DoD to take over the program dealing with the off-site cleanup of chemical stockpiles on DoD bases. This program was fraught with problems, and bad feelings existed between the communities and the bases over the funds available to the communities for the cleanup. FEMA had minimal technical expertise to administer this program and was dependent on the DoD and the Army for the funding. This situation led to political problems for the agency and did not lead to significant advancements in local emergency management operations, as promised by the DoD.

At one point in his tenure, General Becton ranked the programs in FEMA by level of importance. Of the more than 20 major programs, the earthquake, hurricane, and flood programs ranked near the bottom. This priority seems logical, based on the absence of any significant natural hazards, but this situation is noteworthy in the context that it continued the pattern of isolating resources for national security priorities without recognizing the potential of a major natural disaster.

This issue was raised by then Senator Al Gore in hearings on FEMA's responsibilities as lead agency for the National Earthquake Hazards Reduction Program (NEHRP). Senator Gore, reacting to a scientific report that said there could be up to 200,000 casualties from an earthquake occurring on the New Madrid fault, believed that FEMA's priorities were misplaced. The legislation that created the NEHRP called on FEMA to develop a plan for how the federal government would respond to a catastrophic earthquake. This Federal Response Plan would later become the operating Bible for all the federal agencies response operations. Senator Gore concluded that FEMA needed to spend more time working with its federal, state, and local partners on natural hazards planning.

An Agency in Trouble: 1989–1992

As Congress debated, and finally passed, major reform of federal disaster policy as part of the Stewart McKinney–Robert Stafford Act, the promise of FEMA and its ability to support a national emergency management system remained in doubt.

As the 1980s closed, FEMA was an agency in trouble. It suffered from severe morale problems, disparate leadership, and conflicts with its partners at the state and local level over agency spending and priorities.

With a new administration being formed, President George H. W. Bush named Wallace Stickney as director of FEMA. Stickney was from New Hampshire and a friend of John Sununu, who was then President George H. W. Bush's chief of staff. Stickney came to the director's position having been a staff person at the New England Regional Office of the Environmental Protection Agency and a volunteer fireman. His emergency management credentials were minimal, and his selection was poorly received by many of the state directors. At the same time, the political appointees named to FEMA's regional director positions—the first line of FEMA's response system—were equally lacking in emergency management experience. These appointments would prove to have dire consequences for FEMA and the American public.

In 1989, two devastating natural disasters called the continued existence of FEMA into question. In September, Hurricane Hugo slammed into North Carolina and South Carolina after first hitting Puerto Rico and the Virgin Islands. It was the worst hurricane in a decade, with more than $15 billion in damages and 85 deaths. FEMA was slow to respond, waiting for the process to work and the governors to decide what to do. Senator Ernest Hollings (D-SC) personally called the FEMA director and asked for help, but the agency moved slowly. Hollings went on national television to berate FEMA in some of the most colorful language ever, calling the agency the "sorriest bunch of bureaucratic jackasses."

Less than a month later, the Bay Area of California was rocked by the Loma Prieta earthquake as the 1989 World Series got under way in Oakland Stadium. FEMA was not prepared to respond, but it was lucky. Although FEMA had spent the last decade focused on nuclear attack planning, FEMA's state partners in emergency management, especially in California, had been preparing for a more realistic risk, an earthquake. Damages were high, but few lives were lost. This outcome was a testament to good mitigation practices in building codes and construction that were adopted in California, and some good luck relative to the time when the earthquake hit.

A few years later, FEMA was not so lucky. In August 1992, Hurricane Andrew struck Florida and Louisiana and Hurricane Iniki struck Hawaii within months of each other. FEMA was not ready, and neither were FEMA's partners at the state level. The agency's failure to respond was witnessed by Americans all across the country as major news organizations followed the crisis. The efficacy of FEMA as the national emergency response agency was in doubt. President Bush dispatched then secretary of transportation Andrew Card to take over the response operation and sent in the military.

It was not just FEMA that failed in Hurricane Andrew, it was the process and the system. In Hurricane Andrew, FEMA recognized the need to apply all its resources to the response and began to use its national security assets for the first time in a natural disaster response—but it was too late. Starting with Hurricane Hugo, public concern over natural disasters was high. People wanted and expected the government to be there to help in their time of need. FEMA seemed incapable of carrying out the essential government function of emergency management.

In the aftermath of Hurricanes Andrew and Iniki, there were calls for abolishing FEMA. Investigations by the General Accounting Office (GAO) and other government and nongovernment watchdog groups called for major reforms. None of this was lost on the incoming Clinton administration. As governor of Arkansas, President Clinton had experience responding to several major flooding disasters and realized how important an effective response and quick recovery were to communities and voters. At his side throughout these disasters was James Lee Witt, former county judge and administrator of Yell County and, later, the state director for Emergency Management in Arkansas.

The Witt Revolution: 1993–2001

When President Clinton nominated James Lee Witt to be director of FEMA, he breathed life back into FEMA and brought a new style of leadership to the troubled agency. Witt was the first director of FEMA with emergency management experience. He was from the constituency that had played a major role in creating FEMA but had been forgotten—the state directors. With Witt, President Clinton had credibility and, more important, a skilled politician who knew the importance of building partnerships and serving customers.

Witt came in with a mandate to restore the trust of the American people that their government would be there for them during times of crisis. He initiated sweeping reforms inside and outside the agency. Inside FEMA, he reached out to all employees, implemented customer service training, and reorganized the agency to break down bottlenecks. He supported application of new technologies to the delivery of disaster services and focused on mitigation and risk avoidance. Outside the agency, he strengthened the relationships with state and local emergency managers and built new ones with Congress, within the administration, and with the media. Open communications internally and externally was one of the hallmarks of the Witt years at FEMA.

Witt's leadership and the changes he made were quickly tested as the nation experienced an unprecedented series of natural disasters. The Midwest floods in 1993 resulted in major disaster declarations in nine states. The Midwest floods called into question the value of some of the flood control measures initiated long ago as part of the 1930s Army Corps of Engineers' legislation. FEMA's successful response to these floods brought the opportunity to change the focus of postdisaster recovery by initiating the largest voluntary buyout and relocation program to date in an effort to move people out of the floodplain and out of harm's way.

The Northridge, California earthquake quickly followed the Midwest floods in 1994 (Figures 1–1 and 1–2). Northridge tested all the new streamlined approaches and technology advancements for delivery of services and created some more. Throughout the next several years, FEMA and its state and local partners would face every possible natural hazard, including killer tornadoes, ice storms, hurricanes, floods, wildfires, and drought.

FIGURE 1–1 Midwest floods, June 1994. Homes, businesses, and personal property were all destroyed by the high flood levels. A total of 534 counties in nine states were declared for federal disaster aid. As a result of the floods, 168,340 people registered for federal assistance. FEMA News Photo.

FIGURE 1–2 Northridge, California, earthquake, January 17, 1994. Many roads, including bridges and elevated highways, were damaged by the 6.7 magnitude earthquake. Approximately 114,000 residential and commercial structures were damaged and 72 deaths were attributed to the earthquake. Damage costs were estimated at $25 billion. FEMA News Photo.

When President Clinton elevated Witt as director of FEMA to be a member of his cabinet, the value and importance of emergency management was recognized. Witt used this promotion as an opportunity to lobby the nation's governors to include their state emergency management directors in their cabinets.

The Oklahoma City bombing in April 1995 represented a new phase in the evolution of emergency management. This event, following the first bombing of the World Trade Center in New York City in 1992, raised the issue of America's preparedness for terrorism events. Because emergency management responsibilities are defined by risks and the consequences of those risks, responding to terrorist threats was included. The Oklahoma City bombing tested this thesis and set the stage for interagency disagreements over which agency would be in charge of terrorism.

The Nunn-Lugar legislation of 1995 left the question open as to who would be the lead agency on terrorism. Many people fault FEMA leadership for not quickly claiming that role, and the late 1990s were marked by several different agencies and departments having a role in terrorism planning. The question of who is the first responder to a terrorism incident—fire, police, emergency management, or emergency medical services—was closely examined, with no clear answers. The state directors were looking for FEMA to claim the leadership role. In an uncharacteristic way, the leadership of FEMA vacillated on this issue. Terrorism was certainly part of the all-hazards approach to emergency management championed by FEMA, but the resources and technologies needed to address specific issues such as biochemical warfare and weapons of mass destruction events seemed well beyond the reach of the current emergency management structure.

FIGURE 1–3 Franklin, Virginia, September 21, 1999. Hurricane Floyd left the downtown section of Franklin under six feet of water. The water had begun to recede, as shown by the high-water marks, but hazards still included propane tanks, gas tanks, chemical barrels, and pesticides. Photo by Liz Roll/FEMA News Photo.

While this debate continued, FEMA took an important step in its commitment to disaster mitigation by launching a national initiative to promote a new community-based approach, Project Impact: Building Disaster-Resistant Communities. This project was designed to mainstream emergency management and mitigation practices into every community in America. It went back to the roots of emergency management. It asked a community to identify risks and establish a plan to reduce those risks. It asked communities to establish partnerships that included all the local stakeholders, including, for the first time, the business sector.

The goal of Project Impact was to incorporate decisions about risk and risk avoidance into the community's everyday decision-making processes. By building a disaster-resistant community, the community would promote sustainable economic development, protect and enhance its natural resources, and ensure a better quality of life for its citizens. Project Impact had ambitious goals and was well received by the communities and Congress. It was designed to create a broader constituency, a grassroots campaign, for emergency management issues.

As the decade ended without any major technological glitches from Y2K, FEMA was recognized as the preeminent emergency management system in the world. It was emulated in other countries, and Witt became an ambassador for emergency management overseas. Hurricane Mitch saw a change in American foreign policy toward promoting and supporting community-based mitigation projects. State and local emergency management programs had grown and their value recognized and supported by society. Private-sector and business continuity programs were flourishing.

The role and responsibility and the partnerships supporting emergency management had significantly increased, and its budget and stature had grown. Good emergency management became a way to get economic and environmental issues on the table; it became a staple of discussion relative to a community's quality of life.

The profession of emergency management was attracting a different type of individual. Political and management skills were critical, and candidates for state, local, and private emergency management positions were now being judged on their training and experience rather than their relationship to the community's political leadership. Undergraduate and advanced degree programs in emergency management were flourishing at more than 65 national colleges and universities. It was now a respected, challenging, and sought-after profession.

Terrorism Becomes the Major Focus: 2001

With the election of George W. Bush, a new FEMA director, Joe Allbaugh, was named to head the agency. As a former chief of staff to Governor Bush in Texas and President Bush's campaign manager in the 2000 presidential race, Allbaugh had a close personal relationship with the president. As demonstrated by Witt and Clinton, this was viewed as a positive for the agency. His lack of emergency management background was not an issue during his confirmation hearings.

Allbaugh got off to a rocky start when the administration decided to eliminate funding for the popular Project Impact. Immediately after this decision was announced, the 6.8 magnitude Nisqually earthquake shook Seattle, Washington. Seattle happened to be one of the most successful Project Impact communities. The mayor of Seattle appeared on national television and credited Project Impact as responsible for why there was almost no damage from the quake. Later that evening, Vice President Dick Cheney was asked why the program was being eliminated, and he replied by saying there were questions about its effectiveness. As FEMA's budget proceeded through the appropriations process, Congress put funding back into the Project Impact.

As part of major reorganization of the agency, Allbaugh recreated the Office of National Preparedness (ONP). This office was first established in the 1980s during the Guiffrida reign, for planning for World War III, and eliminated by Witt in 1992. This action raised some concerns among FEMA's constituents and FEMA staff members. However, this time the mission of the office was focused on terrorism.

In a September 10, 2001, speech, Director Allbaugh spoke about his priorities as being firefighters, disaster mitigation, and catastrophic preparedness. These words seem prophetic in light of the events of September 11. As the events of that tragic day unfolded, FEMA activated the Federal Response Plan and response operations proceeded as expected in New York and Virginia. Most of the agency's senior leaders, including the director, were in Montana attending the annual meeting of the National Emergency Management Association (NEMA), an organization that represents state emergency management directors. The strength of the U.S. emergency management system was proven; however, as hundreds of response personnel initiated their operations within just minutes of the onset of events.

The Creation of the Department of Homeland Security: 2001–2005

Almost immediately following the terrorist attacks, the president created by executive order the Office of Homeland Security within the White House. The same day that announcement was made, Pennsylvania governor Tom Ridge was sworn in to lead the office with the rank of assistant to the president. The office had only 120 employees and what was derided as a prohibitively small budget in light of the gravity of the events the nation had just witnessed and began to be seen as just another government bureaucracy.

In March of 2002, President Bush signed Homeland Security Presidential Directive-3 (HSPD-3), which stated that

> *The Nation requires a Homeland Security Advisory System to provide a comprehensive and effective means to disseminate information regarding the risk of terrorist acts to Federal, State, and local authorities and to the American people. Such a system would provide warnings in the form of a set of graduated "Threat Conditions" that would increase as the risk of the threat increases. At each Threat Condition, Federal departments and agencies would implement a corresponding set of "Protective Measures" to further reduce vulnerability or increase response capability during a period of heightened alert.*
>
> *This system is intended to create a common vocabulary, context, and structure for an ongoing national discussion about the nature of the threats that confront the homeland and the appropriate measures that should be taken in response. It seeks to inform and facilitate decisions appropriate to different levels of government and to private citizens at home and at work.*

What resulted was the widely recognizable five-color coded homeland security advisory system. The homeland security advisory system repeatedly has raised and lowered the nation's alert levels between elevated (yellow) and high (orange) several times since the system's inception but has done so with less frequency as standards for such movements have been established.

On November 25, 2002, President Bush signed into law the Homeland Security Act of 2002 (HS Act; Public Law 107-296), and announced that former Pennsylvania governor Tom Ridge would become secretary of a new Department of Homeland Security (DHS) to be created through this legislation. This act, which authorized the greatest federal government reorganization since President Harry Truman joined the various branches of the armed forces under the Department of Defense, was charged with a threefold mission of protecting the United States from further terrorist attacks, reducing the nation's vulnerability to terrorism, and minimizing the damage from potential terrorist attacks and natural disasters.

The sweeping reorganization into the new department, which officially opened its doors on January 24, 2003, joined together over 179,000 federal employees from 22 existing federal agencies under a single, cabinet-level organization. The legislation also included several changes within other federal agencies that were only remotely affiliated with DHS.

The creation of DHS was the culmination of an evolutionary legislative process that began largely in response to criticism that increased federal intelligence interagency cooperation could have prevented the September 11 terrorist attacks. Both the White House and Congress recognized that a Homeland Security czar would require both a staff and a large budget to succeed and so began deliberations to create a new cabinet-level department that would fuse many of the security-related agencies dispersed throughout the federal government.

For several months during the second half of 2002, Congress jockeyed between different versions of the Homeland Security bill in an effort to establish legislation that was passable yet effective. Lawmakers were particularly mired on the issue of the rights of employees—an issue that prolonged the legal process considerably. Furthermore, efforts to incorporate many of the intelligence-gathering and investigative law enforcement agencies, namely the National Security Agency (NSA), the Federal Bureau of Investigation (FBI), and the Central Intelligence Agency (CIA), into the legislation failed.

Despite these delays and setbacks, after the 2002 midterm elections, the Republican seats gained in both the House and Senate gave the president the leverage he needed to pass the bill without further deliberation (H.R., 299–121 on November 13, 2002; Senate, 90–9 on November 19, 2002). Although the passage of this act represented a significant milestone, the implementation phase presented a tremendous challenge, a concern expressed by several leaders from the agencies that were to be absorbed. On November 25, 2002, President Bush submitted his reorganization plan (as required by the legislation), which mapped out the schedule, methodology, and budget for the monumental task.

Beginning March 1, 2003, almost all the federal agencies named in the act began their move, whether literally or symbolically, into the new department. Those remaining followed on June 1, 2003, with all incidental transfers completed by September 1, 2003. Although a handful of these agencies remained intact after the move, most were fully incorporated into one of four new directorates: Border and Transportation Security (BTS), Information Analysis and Infrastructure Protection (IAIP), Emergency Preparedness and Response (EP&R), and Science and Technology (S&T). A fifth directorate, Management, incorporated parts of the existing administrative and support offices within the merged agencies.

Secretary Ridge was given exactly one year to develop a comprehensive structural framework for DHS and to name new leadership for all five directorates and other offices created under the legislation.

In addition to the creation of the Department of Homeland Security, the HS Act made several changes to other federal agencies and their programs and created several new programs. A list of the most significant is presented below:

- Established a National Homeland Security Council within the Executive Office of the President, which assesses U.S. objectives, commitments, and risks in the interest of Homeland Security; oversees and reviews federal homeland security policies; and makes recommendations to the president.

- Transferred the Bureau of Alcohol, Tobacco, and Firearms (ATF) from the Department of the Treasury to the Department of Justice (DOJ).

- Explicitly prohibits both the creation of a national ID card and the proposed Citizen Corps Terrorism Information and Prevention System (Operation TIPS, which encouraged transportation workers, postal workers, and public utility employees to identify and report suspicious activities linked to terrorism and crime). The act also reaffirmed the Posse Comitatus Act, which prohibits the use of the Armed Forces in law enforcement activities except under constitutional or congressional authority (the Coast Guard is exempt from this act).

- The Arming Pilots against Terrorism Act, incorporated into the HS Act, allows pilots to defend aircraft cockpits with firearms or other "less-than-lethal weapons" against acts of criminal violence or air piracy and provides antiterrorism training to flight crews.

- The Critical Infrastructure Information Act (2002), incorporated in the HS Act, exempts certain components of critical infrastructure from Freedom of Information Act (FOIA) regulations.
- The Johnny Michael Spann Patriot Trusts, created to provide support for surviving spouses, children, or dependent parents, grandparents, or siblings of various federal employees who die in the line of duty as result of terrorist attacks, military operations, intelligence operations, or law enforcements operations.

On March 1, 2003, Joe Albaugh, in a memo to the FEMA staff, announced that he was resigning as FEMA director. Michael Brown, formerly general counsel to FEMA and acting deputy director was named as the acting director of FEMA within the DHS Emergency Preparedness and Response Directorate. Mike Brown came to FEMA because of his long, personal friendship with Albaugh. His academic training was in law, and prior to coming to FEMA, he had been the executive director of the Arabian Horse Association based in Colorado. On his resume, Brown indicated that he had experience in local emergency management, which would come under question in the aftermath of Hurricane Katrina.

With the DHS establishment moving forward, FEMA entered a 2004 hurricane season that was marked by four major hurricanes impacting the state of Florida. Because of that election year's overall political nature and with the state of Florida being regarded as key in deciding the outcome of the presidential election (as well as the fact that the sitting president's brother, Jeb Bush, was the state's governor), a great deal of effort was expended to ensure that the federal response to these hurricanes appeared to go well. However, it also was recognized that the state of Florida has one of the most effective state emergency management systems in the country and this state-level organization actually was "calling the shots." The senior political management at DHS worked with the Florida governor's office to ensure the response and recovery went smoothly, but the loss of resources, departure of experienced staff members, and lack of effective leadership was steadily eroding the FEMA structure. In fact, many long-time professional FEMA staff members commented, after the 2004 hurricane season that year, that each subsequent hurricane would draw media attention away from any failures or mistakes before they became public. However, subsequent to the 2004 presidential election, several investigative press reports and the DHS Office of Inspector General would document and criticize abuses in excess delivery of financial assistance to nonvictims of the hurricanes, particularly in Miami and Dade County (DHS Office of the Inspector General, "Audit of FEMA's Individuals and Households Program in Miami-Dade County, Florida, for Hurricane Frances," OIG-05-20, available at http://www.dhs.gov/xoig/assets/mgmtrpts/OIG_05-20_May05.pdf).

On November 30, 2004, following the presidential election, DHS secretary Ridge announced his resignation. Former mayor Rudy Giuliani, a star of the September 11 response, recommended the nomination of NYPD commissioner Bernard Kerik for the position. His nomination was withdrawn quickly due to questions about an undocumented immigrant he employed at his home, Federal Judge Michael Chertoff was named to lead the agency. On February 16, 2005, Michael Chertoff was unanimously confirmed by the Senate to lead the Department of Homeland Security.

On July 13, 2005, DHS secretary Michael Chertoff released a six-point agenda that would be used to guide a reorganization of the department aimed at streamlining its efforts. The agenda followed an initial review that Chertoff initiated immediately on assuming the leadership position. The review was designed to closely examine the department to discover ways in which leadership could better manage risk in terms of threat, vulnerability, and consequence; set priorities on policies and operational missions according to this risk-based approach; and establish a series of preventive and protective steps that would increase security at multiple levels. According to the six-point agenda, changes at the DHS would focus on

- Increasing overall preparedness, particularly for catastrophic events.
- Creating better transportation security systems to move people and cargo more securely and efficiently.
- Strengthening border security and interior enforcement and reforming immigration processes.
- Enhancing information sharing (with partners).
- Improving financial management, human resource development, procurement, and information technology within the department.
- Realigning the department's organization to maximize mission performance.

As part of the proposed reorganization, virtually all the remaining preparedness capabilities in FEMA, including the U.S. Fire Administration, would be moved to the new Office of Preparedness. The exception was the Emergency Management Institute (EMI). Although the EMI training function always was considered part of preparedness, senior level FEMA officials argued that its courses supported the response and recovery functions of FEMA. The new FEMA office would focus exclusively on response and recovery.

Under the initial DHS organization (Figure 1–4), the Emergency Preparedness and Response directorate contained most of the pre-DHS FEMA functions and staff. Under the Chertoff reorganization, EP&R was eliminated and the director of FEMA, formerly the undersecretary for EP&R, now became an office director. The reorganization was somewhat unclear regarding who actually would be in charge in a disaster, since responsibility for the new national incident management system (NIMS) is vested in the director of operations coordination.

The reorganization raised several policy issues, including whether the "all hazards" approach had been abandoned in exchange for a focus on catastrophic events, such as a nuclear war, as evidenced through the creation of a domestic nuclear detection office. Mitigation, the cornerstone of emergency management, was not even recognized, although the National Flood Insurance Program and the other natural hazards mitigation efforts would be part of the FEMA office.

Under this Chertoff reorganization, the structure of federal emergency management and disaster assistance functions were returned to the pre-FEMA status. The responsibilities and capabilities for mitigation, preparedness, response, and recovery were now spread out among several entities within the Department of Homeland Security. Policy decisions had been exercised to focus most of the human and financial resources on catastrophic threats of bioterrorism, and terrorism.

This situation was very similar to the one that existed prior to the creation of FEMA in 1979: Federal emergency management and disaster assistance capabilities were located in numerous federal departments and agencies scattered across the federal

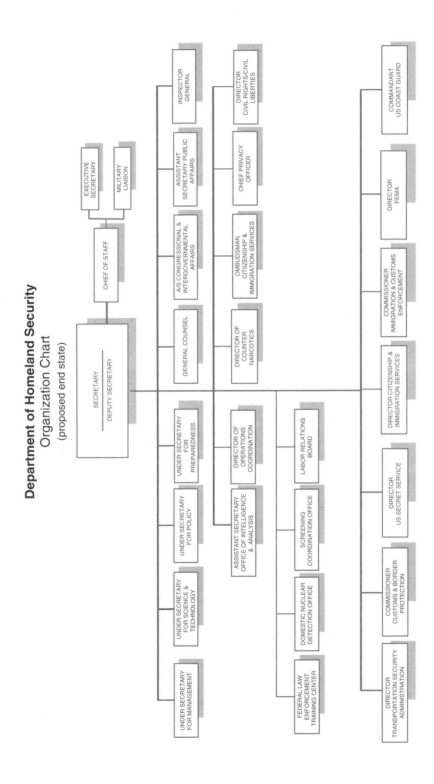

FIGURE 1–4 Department of Homeland Security organizational chart, depicting the projected end state following Secretary Chertoff's reorganization. *Source:* www.dhs.gov.

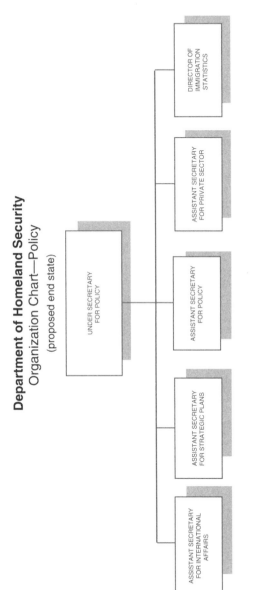

Department of Homeland Security
Organization Chart—Policy
(proposed end state)

UNDER SECRETARY FOR POLICY

ASSISTANT SECRETARY FOR INTERNATIONAL AFFAIRS

ASSISTANT SECRETARY FOR STRATEGIC PLANS

ASSISTANT SECRETARY FOR POLICY

ASSISTANT SECRETARY FOR PRIVATE SECTOR

DIRECTOR OF IMMIGRATION STATISTICS

Homeland Security

FIGURE 1-4 *(Cont'd)*

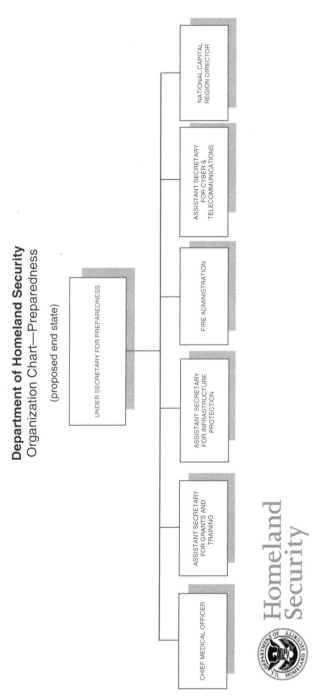

Department of Homeland Security
Organization Chart—Preparedness

(proposed end state)

FIGURE 1-4 (Cont'd)

government and in the White House. In this case, instead of being scattered across the federal government, they were scattered within the fledgling Department of Homeland Security. Before this reorganization, FEMA programs were constantly being tasked and taxed to provide financial and human resources to support higher priority programs in DHS. By taking apart the core programs of FEMA, it became even easier to reassign its resources and diminish its mission within DHS.

Mike Brown's role in this reorganization has never been fully illuminated. At the time, on paper, he was on a par with other undersecretaries within DHS. However, having no personal connections with Secretary Chertoff and no political clout within the administration, because his connection had departed with Joe Albaugh, he apparently chose not to fight to keep FEMA together. He did argue that the FEMA name should remain just like the Coast Guard was able to keep its name, however.

The Hurricane Katrina Debacle: 2005

As Secretary Chertoff was proceeding with his reorganization, scientists like Max Mayfield (the director of the National Hurricane Center) and renowned hurricane experts such as Dr. William Gray were predicting another active hurricane season. As with any hurricane season, the greatest concern was a major storm hitting the Gulf Coast, particularly low-lying New Orleans.

Under James Lee Witt, the risk of a Category 5 hurricane impacting New Orleans was considered one of the three possible worst case disaster scenarios. In fact, since the 1980s, FEMA funds had been used to contract multiple evacuation studies of the New Orleans area. In 1995, a national exercise of the federal response plan, entitled "Response 95," used a New Orleans hurricane scenario. This particular exercise was never completed because on the first day of play, a major flood event impacted the Gulf Coast (including the site of the exercise play, New Orleans) and abruptly ended the exercise.

As the nation would discover in the aftermath of Katrina, another disaster exercise, termed "Hurricane Pam," was convened and completed in July 2004, with appropriate follow-up requirements to correct the problems and deficiencies discovered during the exercise recorded. Unfortunately, the funding to support these corrective actions, adequately budgeted by FEMA, became part of a funding reallocation requested of FEMA by DHS management to support other DHS priorities.

The Senate report on Katrina best describes what occurred during those fateful hours and days in late August. The specific danger that Katrina posed to the Gulf Coast became clear on the afternoon of Friday, August 26, when forecasters at the National Hurricane Center and the National Weather Service saw that the storm was turning west. First in phone calls to Louisiana emergency management officials and then in their 5 PM EDT Katrina forecast and accompanying briefings, they alerted both Louisiana and Mississippi that the track of the storm was now expected to shift significantly to the west of its original track to the Florida panhandle. The National Hurricane Center warned that Katrina could be a Category 4 or even 5 by landfall. By the next morning, Weather Service officials directly confirmed to the governor of Louisiana and other state and local officials that New Orleans was squarely at risk.

Over the weekend, there continued a drumbeat of warnings: FEMA held video-teleconferences on both days, in which the danger of Katrina and the particular risks to

New Orleans were discussed; Max Mayfield of the Hurricane Center called the governors of the affected states, something he had done only once before in his 33-year career; and President Bush took the unusual step of declaring a disaster in advance of an emergency event for the states in the projected impact zone.

But, however vigorous these preparations, ineffective leadership, poor advance planning, and an unwillingness to devote sufficient resources to emergency management over the long term doomed them to fail when Katrina struck. Despite the understanding of the Gulf Coast's particular vulnerability to hurricane devastation, officials braced for Katrina with full awareness of critical deficiencies in their plans and gaping holes in their resources. While Katrina's destructive force could not be denied, state and local officials did not marshal enough of the resources at their disposal. Adding to these shortfalls, years of inadequate funding of federal, state, and local emergency functions left them incapable of fully carrying out their missions to protect the public and care for victims. (Senate Committee on Homeland Security and Governmental Affairs, "Hurricane Katrina: A Nation Still Unprepared," available at http://hsgac.senate.gov/_files/Katrina/ExecSum.pdf, 2006).

More than 1,800 people died. As a result of Hurricane Katrina, tens of thousands were displaced and suffered for days in places like the Superdome, on freeway ramps, and on tops of roofs while waiting for rescue. Thousands lost their homes and were separated from loved ones. The dislocation, chaos, and desperation that lingered for days and weeks after the storm was a direct result of the failure of government at all levels to plan, prepare for, and respond aggressively to the storm. Failure can be assessed at all levels, but when President Bush signed the federal declaration of disaster and announced it in the Rose Garden, *before* Katrina actually made landfall, the federal government through DHS/FEMA took the primary responsibility for the stewardship of the response to this storm's aftermath. And, by any objective evaluation of the response, it was a colossal failure.

The Lead-up to the Katrina Debacle

In many respects, FEMA's Katrina failures were a predictable outgrowth of steps that were taken over the course of the Bush administration. First, in the aftermath of September 11, FEMA lost its status as an independent agency—and its direct access to the president—when it was absorbed into the newly created Department of Homeland Security. The director of FEMA was no longer on a par with the cabinet secretaries FEMA had to task and direct during disasters. At the state level, many states created their own offices of homeland security that subsumed emergency management or were competitive structures, further complicating emergency response organization.

Second, FEMA personnel and funds, including money for preparedness and mitigation intended for state and local agencies, were redistributed to support other higher priorities within DHS. The result of these actions was that the agency was even further hollowed out.

Third, the federal response plan was restructured into the national response plan to accommodate the new DHS arrangements and the operational oversight role of the department's secretary. A new level of bureaucracy was added with the creation of the principal federal official (PFO) as the new coordinator in a disaster. Where previously the director of FEMA had maintained a clear line of authority and accountability, the existence of a new PFO created confusion over who would be in charge in a disaster. As a result, the necessary civilian and military assets were not deployed to facilitate the evacuations and provide supplies to the evacuation shelters before Katrina hit. FEMA also failed to work with the governors on how to use the National Guard. These problems were exacerbated by the inexperience of both brand-new DHS Secretary Chertoff and the relatively new FEMA director, Michael Brown.

A fourth factor was the dramatic post-September 11 change from a focus on "all-hazards" management, in which responders prepare for calamities according to plans that apply regardless of their precise nature, to a focus on terrorism that led to significantly weakened national capabilities. At all levels of government, approximately 75 percent of available resources for emergency management activities were applied to terrorism. Preparing, mitigating, or responding to natural disasters like floods, tornadoes, or hurricanes was subordinated to a narrow, if understandable, focus on terrorism. That reprioritization depleted capabilities to respond to disasters at all levels of government.

A final factor to be considered is the political philosophy of the Bush administration about the role of government. Early in his tenure as director of FEMA, Joe Albaugh referred to FEMA as a "bloated agency" and compared the disaster programs to an entitlement program. It was his philosophy that disasters were state and local issues. Since Albaugh was a close friend and advisor to President Bush and had served as his chief of staff while Bush was governor of Texas, his thoughts probably reflect somewhat on the Bush philosophy. In addition, reflecting back on the rapid response to the 2004 Florida hurricanes, one could draw the conclusion that the administration just did not care about the people of New Orleans. In any event, the failure of the political leadership at all levels, particularly in Louisiana, which is continuing in a very slow-moving recovery, needs to be considered as a fundamental cause for the problems of Katrina.

Post-Katrina Changes

In the rush to examine and investigate what went wrong, and take corrective actions, both the U.S. House of Representatives and the U.S. Senate engaged in extensive hearings and investigations. The White House dispatched Frances Townsend, assistant to the president for Homeland Security, to conduct a thorough review of what went wrong and to generate corrective recommendations. The administration's report, "The Federal Response to Hurricane Katrina: Lessons Learned," was released in February 2006. It was a weighty document, which included 125 recommendations and 11 critical actions that needed to be completed by June 1, the start of the 2006 hurricane season. However, the report, just like the Hurricane Katrina event, reflected the administration's lack of understanding and lack of accountability for disaster response and recovery.

These organizational and leadership issues were not easily swept away. Senators Clinton and Mikulski introduced legislation to restore FEMA to its independent status and make the director's position a cabinet member. This legislation went nowhere. Powerful forces on the Senate Committee on Homeland Security blocked these efforts, particularly Senator Joe Lieberman who had been instrumental in DHS's creation and clearly did not want his creation tampered with. Senator Lieberman was joined by Republican Committee chair Susan Collins, who would not even consider moving FEMA out. After a series of hearings and investigations both the House and Senate Committees on Homeland Security issued reports, all of which are detailed in later chapters.

Supported by these reports and a public demanding action, the 109th Congress passed revised federal emergency management policies that vested more power in the president, reorganized the Federal Emergency Management Agency, and enhanced and clarified the mission, functions, and authorities of both the agency and its parent organization, the Department of Homeland Security.

Six statutes enacted by the 109th Congress are notable in that they contain changes that apply to future federal emergency management actions. These public laws include the following:

- The Post-Katrina Emergency Management Reform Act of 2006.
- The Security and Accountability for Every Port Act of 2005, known as the SAFE Port Act.
- The Pets Evacuation and Transportation Standards Act of 2006.
- The Federal Judiciary Emergency Special Sessions Act of 2005.
- The Student Grant Hurricane and Disaster Relief Act.
- The John Warner National Defense Authorization Act for Fiscal Year 2007.

Most of these statutes contain relatively few actual changes to federal authorities related to emergencies and disasters. The Post-Katrina Act, however, contains many changes that have long-term consequences for FEMA and other federal entities. That statute reorganizes FEMA, expands its statutory authority, and imposes new conditions and requirements on the operations of the agency. In addition to the public laws noted already, Congress enacted supplemental appropriations, one-time waivers of requirements, and temporary extensions solely associated with Hurricanes Katrina, Rita, and Wilma. (Congressional Research Service, "Federal Emergency Management Policy Changes after Hurricane Katrina, a Summary of Statutory Provisions," available at http://www.fas.org/sgp/crs/homesec/RL33729. pdf, December 15, 2006).

The Post-Katrina Act requires that the DHS reconsolidate all the emergency management functions (including preparedness) into FEMA, elevates the status of FEMA within the department, protects the FEMA assets from reassignment within the DHS, and gives FEMA enhanced organizational autonomy. In addition, the Act provides for FEMA to maintain 10 regional offices. It adds to FEMA a National Advisory Council, Regional Advisory Councils, a disability coordinator, a small state and rural advocate, and regional strike teams. They provide autonomy for the FEMA administrator (formerly director) to communicate directly with Congress.

As this edition is being written, the DHS and FEMA are working on implementing all these changes along with undertaking another major revision on the national response plan. After the resignation (or firing) of Mike Brown shortly after Katrina hit, David Paulison was nominated and confirmed as FEMA director, now administrator. Paulison had been serving as the U.S. fire administrator and has had a long and distinguished career in the fire service in Florida. His elevation to the top position was well received by the fire service constituencies, who long felt that they had not received their due within FEMA and the emergency management community. As with fire and police, the emergency management community has had an uneasy relationship with the fire community, which they view as a competitor for resources. Whether Paulison has the leadership skills or the political clout to resurrect FEMA remains to be seen.

Critical Thinking

What do you think could have been done in the years preceding Hurricane Katrina to better prepare the states to deal with this kind of event? Do you think that this event was so large that only a federal response could have managed it? Explain your answer.

The Future Environment of Emergency Management

In previous editions of this text, we talked about the consequences of moving FEMA into the Department of Homeland Security, focusing emergency management on terrorism at the cost of natural and other hazards, and the importance of supportive political leadership at the highest levels, including the presidency, as bellwethers for effective emergency management. We, unfortunately, predicted the failure that was evidenced in Hurricane Katrina.

The changes required by Congress in the Post-Katrina legislation do not correct many of the flaws that led to the failures of the Katrina response. This legislation may improve the climate, but it does not correct systemic problems in the federal system nor does it address the critical resource shortfall that has forever plagued the emergency management discipline. It focuses emergency management on preparedness, that is, evacuation and response. The long-term strategy of mitigation of the risks and using long-term recovery as a means toward improved mitigation are largely forgotten.

The legislation also fails to address some of the societal changes this nation has undergone, which warrant that a new examination of our disaster assistance programs and delivery systems be made. For example, the designation of "head of household" as the recipient of disaster assistance is ambiguous and not reflective of current societal trends. It is not likely that DHS/FEMA will take the initiative to look into these issues.

It can be safely said that the future of emergency management, at least at the federal level, remains uncertain. More and more the states are assuming, in regard to disaster response, that they will be on their own. Two bright notes of Hurricane Katrina were the leadership of Governor Haley Barbour of Mississippi in leading his state into recovery and the celebrated response carried out in Alabama, a state with an excellent emergency management organization. However, the strong partnership of federal and state emergency management organizations that had existed unfortunately remains broken.

The last chapter of this text looks at several new approaches to emergency management. Perhaps, it is time to reexamine the emergency management cycle of preparedness, response, recovery, and mitigation that was established in the National Governors Association study of the early 1960s. Perhaps, we need to look at new organizations to assume the emergency management mantle, nonprofits and private organizations. Perhaps, a new generation of individuals committed to the principles of emergency management can design and implement a new approach. Perhaps, the time is right for a seismic change in our approach to emergency management at all levels of government.

IMPORTANT TERMS

- Emergency management
- Civil defense
- Federal Emergency Management Agency
- Department of Homeland Security

Self-Check Questions

1. What are some of the first examples of emergency management?
2. According to the Constitution, does the federal government have a primary or secondary role in managing public risks?
3. What is the first example of the federal government becoming involved in a local disaster? What was provided?
4. What is the significance of the Flood Control Act of 1934?
5. How did the Cold War era contribute to the evolution of modern emergency management?
6. What disaster led to the creation of the National Flood Insurance Program?
7. Describe the events of the 1970s that led to the creation of FEMA.
8. Why was FEMA an agency in trouble at the close of the 1980s?
9. How did James Lee Witt improve FEMA?
10. What changes did the creation of the Department of Homeland Security bring about for the federal emergency management capacity?
11. List the steps involved in the creation of the Department of Homeland Security.
12. Why was the response to Hurricane Katrina so ineffective?
13. How did the poor response to the Hurricane Katrina disaster change emergency management in the United States?

Out of Class Exercise   Investigate how civil defense and emergency management evolved in your state or city. Look at such factors as when it was created, what was its original purpose, and what did it do. Find out how this organization changed following the creation of FEMA. Determine who is your local or state emergency manager, and where this person falls within the organizational diagram of your municipal or state leadership. Is there an online profile or biography for this person? If so, what emergency management experience does he or she have to qualify for the job?

2

Natural and Technological Hazards and Risk Assessment

What You Will Learn

- The range of natural hazards that affect the United States.
- Scales and systems used to measure the magnitude of hazards and disasters.
- Technological hazards and their causes and effects.
- The terrorist threat, including weapons of mass destruction.
- How hazard risks are assessed.
- Social and economic risk factors, and how they influence a community's risk profile.

Introduction

A *hazard* is defined as a "source of danger that may or may not lead to an emergency or disaster and is named after the emergency/disaster that could be so precipitated." *Risk* is defined as "susceptibility to death, injury, damage, destruction, disruption, stoppage, and so forth." *Disaster* is defined as an "event that demands substantial crisis response requiring the use of government powers and resources beyond the scope of one line agency or service" (National Governors Association, 1982).

Hazard identification is the foundation of all emergency management activities. When hazards react with the human or built environments, the risks associated with that hazard can be assessed. Understanding the risk posed by identified hazards is the basis for preparedness planning and mitigation actions. Risk, when realized, such as in the event of an earthquake, tornado, flood, and so on, becomes a disaster that prompts emergency response and recovery activities. All emergency management activities are predicated on the identification and assessment of hazards and risks.

This chapter discusses the full range of existing hazards, both natural and technological. For each hazard, a brief description of the hazard and its effects is provided. Also included in this chapter is a discussion of risk assessment.

Much of the information for this chapter was acquired from the U.S. Federal Emergency Management Agency Web site, www.fema.gov, and FEMA's book *Multi-Hazard*

Identification and Risk Assessment: A Cornerstone of the National Mitigation Strategy. Included in the supplements at the companion Web site for this book are organizations' Web site addresses to reference for more in-depth information on a particular hazard. (See the URL for the companion Web site in the *Introduction.*)

Natural Hazards

Natural hazards are those that exist in the natural environment and pose a threat to human populations and communities. Human development often has exacerbated natural hazards. Building communities in the floodplain or on barrier islands increases the potential damage caused by flooding and storm surge. Building a school on a known earthquake fault increases the potential that the school will be destroyed by an earthquake. How humans can better live with hazards is the principal topic of Chapter 3, The Disciplines of Emergency Management: Mitigation.

Floods

Floods can be slow or fast rising but generally develop over a period of days. Floods usually occur from large-scale weather systems generating prolonged rainfall or onshore winds. Other causes of flooding include locally intense thunderstorms, snowmelt, ice jams, and dam failures. Floods are capable of undermining buildings and bridges, eroding shorelines and riverbanks, tearing out trees, washing out access routes, and causing loss of life and injuries. Flash floods usually result from intense storms dropping large amounts of rain within a brief period. Flash floods occur with little or no warning and can reach full peak in only a few minutes (see Figure 2–1).

FIGURE 2–1 Midwest floods, June 1994. Homes, businesses, and personal property were destroyed by the high flood levels. A total of 534 counties in nine states were declared for federal disaster aid. As a result of the floods, 168,340 people registered for federal assistance. FEMA News Photo.

Floods are the most frequent and widespread disaster in many countries around the world. Historically, human development has congregated around rivers and ports, and transportation of goods has been most commonly conducted by water. This relationship has resulted in greater exposure to floods. For example, FEMA estimates that more than 9 million households and $390 billion in property are at risk from flooding in the United States alone. Flood losses paid by FEMA's National Flood Insurance Program in the 1990s totaled in the billions of dollars (see Table 2–1).

Governments in many countries maintain river and stream gauges to measure floodwater elevations and provide information on rising water for use in sandbagging and dyke construction and to warn populations of an impending flood.

Table 2–1   Top Ten U.S. Flood Disasters, 1900–2007

Event	Date	# Paid Losses	Amount of Paid Losses
Hurricane Katrina	Aug. 2005	164,713	$15,633,231,066
Hurricane Ivan	Sept. 2004	27,274	$1,506,620,582
Tropical Storm Allison	June 2001	30,626	$1,100,825,754
Louisiana Flood	May 1995	31,343	$585,072,008
Hurricane Isabel	Sept. 2003	19,681	$473,549,744
Hurricane Floyd	Sept. 1999	20,438	$462,178,153
Hurricane Rita	Sept. 2005	9,301	$439,813,073
Hurricane Opal	Oct. 1995	10,343	$405,528,543
Hurricane Hugo	Sept. 1989	12,843	$376,494,566
Hurricane Wilma	Oct. 2005	9,504	$353,625,980

Source: www.fema.gov.

☐ ☐ ☐ ▄▄▄

The Great Midwest Floods of 1993: Recovery Costs

- A total of 534 counties in nine states were declared for federal disaster aid for the 1993 Midwest floods. As a result of the floods, 168,340 people registered for federal assistance.
- According to the Galloway Report in June 1994, estimated federal response and recovery costs included more than $4.2 billion in direct federal assistance, $1.3 billion in federal flood insurance payments, and more than $621 million in federal loans to individuals, businesses, and communities.

Of those totals, an estimated $1.69 billion was provided by the USDA for food stamps/commodities, crop loss payments, and other emergency farm grant and loan programs; $597 million by the Small Business Administration (SBA) for loans to homeowners, renters, and businesses; $500 million by Housing and Urban Development (HUD) for housing and community grants; $200 million by the Department of Commerce (DOC) for economic development programs;

$253 million by the Army Corps of Engineers (USACE) for flood control and other emergency operations; $75 million by the Department of Health and Human Services (HHS) for various public health services; $100 million by the Department of Education (DOE) for schools and student aid; $64.6 million by the Department of Labor (DOL) for employment training and temporary job assistance; $146.7 million by the Department of Transportation (DOT) for federal highway repairs, rail freight assistance, and other transportation and emergency services; $34 million by the Environmental Protection Agency (EPA) for environmental abatement, control, and cleanup projects; and $41.2 million by the Department of the Interior (DOI) for various construction, survey, and cultural restoration programs.

FEMA's costs currently total $1.17 billion, including $371 million in grants to individuals and families for temporary housing, home repairs, unemployment payments, and other disaster-related expenses; $539.5 million to states and local governments for public property restoration and cleanup work; $167.6 million for property acquisitions and other hazard mitigation projects; and $29.2 million to other federal agencies for delivery of emergency supplies and other mission-assigned work.

Note: All funding amounts are in current FY2000 dollars, unadjusted for inflation.
Source: FEMA, www.fema.gov.

Earthquakes

An earthquake is a sudden, rapid shaking of the earth caused by the breaking and shifting of rock beneath the earth's surface. This shaking can cause buildings and bridges to collapse; disrupt gas, electric, and phone service; and sometimes trigger landslides, avalanches, flash floods, fires, and huge, destructive ocean waves (tsunamis). Buildings with foundations resting on unconsolidated landfill, old waterways, or other unstable soil are most at risk. Earthquakes can occur at any time of the year (see Figure 2–2).

Specific active seismic zones have been identified around the globe. Millions of people live in these seismic zones and are exposed to the threat of an earthquake daily. The damage caused by an earthquake can be extensive, especially to incompatible building types and construction techniques. Also, earthquakes usually ignite fires, which can spread rapidly among damaged buildings if the water system has been disabled and fire services lack access to the site of the fire. Thousands of residents of Kobe, Japan, perished in the fires caused by the 1995 earthquake in that city because fire trucks and personnel were unable to get to the fires because of debris from fallen and damaged buildings blocked the streets (see Table 2–2).

Earthquakes are sudden events, despite scientists' and soothsayers' best efforts to predict when they will occur. Seismic sensing technology can track seismic activity but has yet to accurately predict when a major seismic shift will occur that causes an earthquake. The effects of earthquakes are commonly described by the Richter scale.

FIGURE 2–2 Northridge, California, earthquake, January 17, 1994. Buildings, cars, and personal property were destroyed when the earthquake struck. Approximately 114,000 residential and commercial structures were damaged, and 72 deaths were attributed to the earthquake. Damage costs were estimated at $25 billion. FEMA News Photo.

Table 2–2   Estimated Earthquake Losses, 1987–1997

Date	Location	Amount
November 24, 1987	Southern California	$4 million
October 18, 1989	Northern California	$5.6 million
February 28, 1990	Southern California	$12.7 million
April 25, 1991	Northern California	$66 million
June 28, 1992	Southern California	$92 million
January 17, 1994	Southern California	$13–20 billion

Source: United States Geological Survey (USGS).

The Richter and Modified Mercalli Scales

Earthquakes usually are measured according to either the Richter scale or the modified Mercalli intensity scale—or both. The Richter scale, designed by Charles Richter in 1935, assigns a single number to quantify the overall magnitude of an earthquake based on the strength of ground waves (as measured by a seismograph). Magnitudes are logarithmic and have no upper limit. The modified Mercalli scale also measures the effects of earthquakes, but rather than applying a single value to the event, it allows for site-specific evaluation according to the observed severity of the quake at each location. The Mercalli scale rates the intensity on a Roman numeral scale that ranges from I to XII and generally is determined according to reports by people who felt the event and observations of damages sustained by structures.

Modified Mercalli	Damage Sustained	Richter Scale
I–IV Instrumental to moderate	No damage.	≤4.3
V Rather strong	Damage negligible. Small, unstable objects displaced or upset; some dishes and glass broken.	4.4–4.8
VI Strong	Damage slight. Windows, dishes, glassware broken. Furniture moved or overturned. Weak plaster and masonry cracked.	4.9–5.4
VII Very strong	Damage slight to moderate in well-built structures; considerable in poorly built structures. Furniture and weak chimneys broken. Masonry damaged. Loose bricks, tiles, plaster, and stones will fall.	5.5–6.1
VIII Destructive	Structural damage considerable, particularly to poorly built structures. Chimneys, monuments, towers, elevated tanks may faill. Frame houses moved. Trees damaged. Cracks in wet ground and steep slopes.	6.2–6.5
IX Ruinous	Structural damage severe; some buildings will collapse. General damage to foundations. Serious damage to reservoirs. Underground pipes broken. Conspicuous cracks in ground; liquefaction.	6.6–6.9
X Disastrous	Most masonry and frame structures/foundations destroyed. Some well-built wooden structures and bridges destroyed. Serious damage to dams, dikes, embankments. Sand and mud shifting on beaches and flat land.	7.0–7.3
XI Very disastrous	Few or no masonry structures remain standing. Bridges destroyed. Broad fissures in ground. Underground pipelines completely out of service. Widespread earth slumps and landslides.	7.4–8.1
XII Catastrophic	Damage nearly total. Large rock masses displaced. Lines of sight and level distorted.	>8.1

Source: FEMA, www.femagov.

Critical Thinking

It is possible to assign modified Mercalli intensity values to historical earthquakes, but Richter magnitudes cannot be retroactively assigned. Why do you think this is true? Which of these scales is more useful in terms of disaster planning? Why?

Hurricanes

All hurricanes start as tropical waves that grow in intensity and size to tropical depressions, which in turn grow to be tropical storms. A tropical storm is a warm-core tropical cyclone in which the maximum sustained surface wind speed ranges from 39 miles per hour (mph) to less than 74 mph. Tropical cyclones are defined as a low-pressure area of closed-circulation winds that originates over tropical waters. Winds rotate counterclockwise in the northern hemisphere and clockwise in the southern hemisphere.

A hurricane is a tropical storm with winds that have reached a constant speed of 74 mph or more. Hurricane winds blow in a large spiral around a relatively calm center known as the *eye*. The eye generally is 20 to 30 miles wide, and the storm may extend outward for 400 miles. As a hurricane approaches, the skies begin to darken and winds strengthen. As a hurricane nears land, it can bring torrential rains, high winds, and storm surges. A single hurricane can last for more than two weeks over open waters and can run a path across the entire length of the eastern seaboard (see Figure 2–3).

Hurricane season runs annually from June 1 through November 30. August and September are peak months during the hurricane season. Hurricanes are commonly described using the Saffir-Simpson scale.

FIGURE 2–3 Hurricane Andrew, Florida, August 24, 1992. An aerial view showing damage from one of the most destructive hurricanes in America's history. One million people were evacuated and 54 died in this hurricane. FEMA News Photo.

☐ ☐ ☐ ▬▬▬▬▬▬▬▬▬▬▬▬▬▬▬▬▬▬▬▬▬▬▬▬▬▬▬▬▬▬▬

The Saffir-Simpson Scale

1. Wind speed: 74–95 mph
   Storm surge: 4–5 feet above normal
   Primary damage to unanchored mobile homes, shrubbery, and trees. Some coastal flooding and minor pier damage. Little damage to building structures.

2. Wind speed: 96–110 mph
   Storm surge: 6–8 feet above normal
   Considerable damage to mobile homes, piers, and vegetation. Coastal and low-lying areas escape routes flood 2–4 hours before arrival of hurricane center. Buildings sustain roofing material, door, and window damage. Small craft in unprotected mooring break moorings.

3. Wind speed: 111–130 mph
   Storm surge: 9–12 feet above normal
   Mobile homes destroyed. Some structural damage to small homes and utility buildings. Flooding near coast destroys smaller structures; larger structures damaged by floating debris. Terrain continuously lower than 5 feet above sea level (ASL) may be flooded up to six miles inland.

4. Wind speed: 131–155 mph
   Storm surge: 13–18 feet above normal
   Extensive curtain-wall failures, with some complete roof structure failure on small residences. Major erosion of beaches. Major damage to lower floors of structures near the shore. Terrain continuously lower than 10 feet ASL may flood (and require mass evacuations) up to six miles inland.

5. Wind speed: Over 155 mph
   Storm surge: Over 18 feet above normal
   Complete roof failure on many homes and industrial buildings. Some complete building failures. Major damage to lower floors of all structures located less than 15 feet ASL and within 500 yards of the shoreline. Massive evacuation of low-ground, residential areas may be required.

Source: FEMA.

▬▬▬▬▬▬▬▬▬▬▬▬▬▬▬▬▬▬▬▬▬▬▬▬▬▬▬▬▬▬ ☐ ☐ ☐

Hurricanes are capable of causing great damage and destruction over vast areas. Hurricane Floyd in 1999 first threatened the states of Florida and Georgia, made landfall in North Carolina, and damaged sections of South Carolina, North Carolina, Virginia, Maryland, Delaware, New Jersey, New York, Connecticut, Massachusetts, and Maine. The damage was so extensive in each of these states that they all qualified for federal disaster assistance. Single hurricanes can affect several countries, as was the case with Hurricane Mitch, which brought death and destruction to Nicaragua, Guatemala, El Salvador, and Honduras.

The costliest disaster in U.S. history in pure dollar figures (approximately $80 billion) and one of the deadliest in terms of lives lost and injuries sustained (1,836 killed) was Hurricane Katrina. Katrina reached Category 5 status with sustained winds of over 175 mph—making it the fourth strongest hurricane recorded at the time—before making landfall as a Category 3 hurricane along the Gulf of Mexico coast. With strong winds and a storm surge reaching 28 feet, Katrina devastated coastal communities in Alabama, Florida, Mississippi, and Louisiana. Flooding and near total destruction was sustained in almost 80 percent of New Orleans and much of Biloxi/Gulfport, Mississippi. The storm went on to cause further destruction in several other states as it made its way north toward Canada. Two years later, many of the Gulf Coast areas are still reeling from this disaster event, with full recovery years or even decades away.

In recent years, significant advances have been made in hurricane tracking technology and computer models. The National Hurricane Center in Miami, Florida, now tracks tropical waves from the moment they form off the coast of West Africa through their development as a tropical depression. Once the tropical depression grows to the strength of a tropical storm, the Hurricane Center assigns the storm a name. Once the sustained wind speed of the tropical storm exceeds 74 mph, it becomes a hurricane. The Hurricane Center uses aircraft to observe and collect meteorological data on the hurricane and track its movements across the Atlantic Ocean. It also uses several sophisticated computer models to predict the storm's path. These predictions are used by local and state emergency officials to make evacuation decisions and to predeploy response and recovery resources (see Table 2–3).

Table 2–3 Top Ten Costliest Hurricanes in the United States, 1900–2006, Ranked by FEMA Relief Costs

Hurricane	Year	Category	Damage
Hurricane Katrina AL, LA, MS	2005	4	$7.2 billion
Hurricane Georges AL, FL, LA, MS, PR, VI	1998	4	$2.255 billion
Hurricane Ivan AL, FL, GA, LA, MS, NJ, NY, NC, PA, TN, WV	2004	3	$1.947 billion
Hurricane Andrew FL, LA	1992	5	$1.814 billion
Hurricane Charley FL, SC	2004	4	$1.559 billion
Hurricane Francis FL, GA, NY, NC, OH, PA, SC	2004	4	$1.425 billion
Hurricane Jeanne DE, FL, PR, VI, VA	2004	3	$1.407 billion
Hurricane Hugo NC, SC, PR, VI	1989	4	$1.307 billion
Hurricane Floyd CT, DE, FL, ME, MD, NH, NJ, NY, NC, PA, SC, VT, VA	1999	3	$1.054 billion
Hurricane Fran MD, NC, PA, SC, VA, WV	1996	3	$620.9 million

Source: www.fema.gov.

Historically, storm surge and high winds have been the principal contributors to the loss of life and injuries and the property and infrastructure damage caused by hurricanes. In recent years, inland flooding caused by hurricane rainfall has resulted in loss of life and severe property damage. Hurricanes also cause significant damage to the natural environment. Storm surge from hurricanes can result in severe beach erosion on barrier islands. Inland flooding from Hurricane Floyd inundated waste ponds on hog farms in North Carolina, washing the hog waste into the Cape Fear River, which eventually dumped these materials into the ocean. The storm surge created by Hurricane Katrina also had a profound impact on the environment, in some cases completely devastating coastal areas. Dauphin Island was actually pushed toward the land by the force of the surge, and the Chandeleur Islands were completely destroyed. Breton National Wildlife Refuge, one of 16 wildlife refuges damaged by the storm, lost over half of its area. Much of this land lost served as breeding grounds for marine mammals, reptiles, birds, and fish.

Storm Surges

A storm surge is a mass of water pushed toward the shore by the force of an oncoming storm or other force. Storm surges are most commonly seen in the approach of or during hurricane strikes. The advancing surge of water is combined with the normal tides, resulting in a rise in sea level that can reach several dozen feet under the right conditions. In addition, wind-driven waves become superimposed on the storm tide. This rise in water level can cause severe coastal flooding, erosion, and is often what is behind many of the injuries, deaths, and structural damages associated with hurricanes, cyclones, nor'easters, and other coastal storms.

Because much of the United States' densely populated Atlantic and Gulf Coast coastlines lie less than 10 feet above mean sea level, the storm surge risk is extreme. One of the greatest examples of the destructive force of a hurricane storm surge is the surge associated with Hurricane Katrina. After crossing southern Florida, Katrina followed a westward track across the Gulf of Mexico before turning to the northwest toward the Gulf Coast. Hurricane Katrina made its second landfall as a strong Category 4 hurricane in Plaquemines Parish, Louisiana, on August 29, 2005. When the storm made its third and final landfall along the Mississippi/Louisiana border, its hurricane-force winds extended up to 190 miles from the center of the storm and tropical storm-force winds extended for approximately 440 miles. The strength and wide geographical area affected by the storm resulted in a surge greater than anything previously recorded along the Gulf Coast. The combination of a 30-foot storm surge, very strong wave action, and constant high winds resulted in destruction of buildings and roads observed in the affected areas. The surge placed inordinate pressure on the levee system protecting New Orleans, resulting in numerous breaches that ultimately led to the flooding of the city under up to 20 feet of water. FEMA has since developed detailed maps that illustrate localized storm surge effects resulting from Hurricane Katrina, which can be accessed on FEMA's Web site at http://www.fema.gov/hazard/flood/recoverydata/katrina/katrina_about.shtm.

The National Hurricane Center operates a computerized model, called SLOSH (Sea, Lake and Overland Surges from Hurricanes), to estimate storm surge heights and winds resulting from historical, hypothetical, or predicted hurricanes. SLOSH takes into account several factors in its calculations, including

- Pressure
- Size
- Forward speed
- Track
- Winds

The model's output is a color coded map indicating storm surge heights for defined areas in feet above the model's reference level. These calculations are applied to a specific locale's shoreline, incorporating the unique bay and river configurations, water depths, bridges, roads, and other physical features. When SLOSH is used to estimate storm surge from predicted hurricanes, forecast data is entered every 6 hours over a 72-hour period and updated as new forecasts become available. SLOSH is accurate within a range of ±20 percent of what actually is observed. The model accounts for astronomical tides, but does not consider rainfall, river flow, or wind-driven waves. However, this information can be combined with the model's output to create a more accurate analysis of at-risk areas.

Tornadoes

A tornado is a rapidly rotating vortex or funnel of air extending groundward from a cumulonimbus cloud. Approximately 1,000 tornadoes are spawned by thunderstorms each year. Most tornadoes remain aloft, but the danger is when they touch the ground. A tornado can lift and move huge objects, destroy or move whole buildings long distances, and siphon large volumes from bodies of water. Tornadoes follow the path of least resistance. People living in valleys have the greatest exposure to damage.

For more than three decades (since 1971), tornadoes have been measured using the Fujita-Pearson tornado scale. In 2006, after research indicated that much weaker winds than previously thought could generate the most powerful tornadoes, the National Weather Service created the enhanced Fujita-Pearson tornado scale. The new scale, which began to be used in January 2007, expands on the original system's measure of damage to homes by adding 18 new indicators including trees, mobile homes, and several other structures (giving a total of 28 indicators studied in the classification of a tornado). Unlike before, a tornado that does not affect houses still can be classified according to the system.

□ □ □ ▬▬▬▬▬▬▬▬▬▬▬▬▬▬▬▬▬▬▬▬▬

The Fujita-Pearson Tornado Scale

The Old Fujita-Pearson Tornado Scale

F-0: 40–72 mph, chimney damage, tree branches broken.

F-1: 73–112 mph, mobile homes pushed off foundation or overturned.

F-2: 113–157 mph, considerable damage, mobile homes demolished, trees uprooted.

F-3: 158–205 mph, roofs and walls torn down, trains overturned, cars thrown.

F-4: 207–260 mph, well-constructed walls leveled.

F-5: 261–318 mph, homes lifted off foundations and carried considerable distances, autos thrown as far as 100 meters.

(Continued)

The Enhanced Fujita-Pearson Tornado Scale
   F-0: 65–85 mph
   F-1: 86–110 mph
   F-2: 111–135 mph
   F-3: 136–165 mph
   F-4: 166–200 mph
   F-5: Over 200 mph

In the United States, the most susceptible states to tornadoes are Texas, Oklahoma, Arkansas, Missouri, and Kansas (see Table 2–4). Together these states occupy what is commonly known as *tornado alley*. In recent years, however, tornadoes have struck in cities that are not regularly frequented by tornadoes, including Miami, Nashville, and Washington, D.C. Tornado season is generally March through August, although tornadoes can occur at any time of the year. They tend to occur in the afternoon and evening: More than 80 percent of all tornadoes strike between noon and midnight.

Table 2–4   The 25 Deadliest U.S. Tornadoes

Date	Place	Deaths
1. March 18, 1925	Tri-State (MO, IL, IN)	689
2. May 6, 1840	Natchez, MS	317
3. May 27, 1896	St. Louis, MO	255
4. April 5, 1936	Tupelo, MS	216
5. April 6, 1936	Gainesville, GA	203
6. April 9, 1947	Woodward, OK	181
7. April 24, 1980	Amite, LA; Purvis, MS	143
8. June 12, 1899	New Richmond, WI	117
9. June 8, 1953	Flint, MI	115
10. May 11, 1953	Waco, TX	114
11. May 18, 1902	Goliad, TX	114
12. March 23, 1913	Omaha, NE	103
13. May 26, 1917	Mattoon, IL	101
14. June 23, 1944	Shinnston, WV	100
15. April 18, 1880	Marshfield, MO	99
16. June 1, 1903	Gainesville and Holland, GA	98
17. May 9, 1927	Poplar Bluff, MO	98
18. May 10, 1905	Snyder, OK	97
19. April 24, 1908	Natchez, MS	91
20. June 9, 1953	Worcester, MA	90
21. April 20, 1920	Starkville, MI; Waco, AL	88
22. June 28, 1924	Lorain and Sandusky, OH	85
23. May 25, 1955	Udall, KS	80
24. September 29, 1927	St. Louis, MO	79
25. March 27, 1890	Louisville, KY	76

Source: National Storm Prediction Center, NOAA.

Tornadoes can have winds of up to 300 mph and possess tremendous destructive force. Damage is incurred only when the tornado touches down, but tornadoes can touch down in more than one place. The tornado that struck the Washington, D.C., metropolitan area in 2001 first touched down in Alexandria, Virginia, just south of the District of Columbia, went airborne over the district, and touched down again in College Park, Maryland, just north of the district (see Figure 2–4).

Building collapse and flying debris are the principal causes of death and injuries by tornadoes. Early warning is the key to surviving in the path of a tornado. Doppler radar and other meteorological tools are improving the amount of advance warning time available before a tornado strikes. Improved communications and new technologies have also been critical to giving people advance warning of a tornado.

Buildings that are directly in the path of a tornado have little chance of surviving; however, new "safe room" technology developed by FEMA and Texas A&M University offers families and communities a method for surviving the tornado even if their homes or community facilities do not. A safe room can be built into an existing or new home for a small cost (estimated between $3,000 to $5,000) that will survive a tornado's high winds and flying debris. The home may be destroyed, but anyone in the safe room would survive. Similar technology is being developed for community shelters.

Although reducing the loss of life and injuries is the principal goal of tornado preparedness and mitigation activities, new technologies in building design and construction are being developed by FEMA and others to reduce the damage to buildings and structures not located directly in the path of a tornado. Some of the same wind-resistant construction techniques used effectively in high-risk hurricane areas are being incorporated into building renovation and construction in tornado-prone areas.

FIGURE 2–4 College Park, Maryland, September 25, 2001. Rescue workers clean up the debris left by the tornado that killed two people and left more than $16.5 million in damages. Photo by Jocelyn Augustino/FEMA News Photo.

Wildfires

Wildland fires are classified into three categories: (1) a *surface fire* is the most common type and burns along the floor of a forest, moving slowly and killing or damaging trees; (2) a *ground fire* usually is started by lightning and burns on or below the forest floor; and (3) a *crown fire* spreads rapidly by wind and moves quickly by jumping along the tops of trees. Wildland fires usually are signaled by dense smoke that fills the area for miles around.

As residential areas expand into relatively untouched wildlands, people living in these communities increasingly are threatened by forest fires. Protecting structures in the wildland from fire poses special problems and can stretch firefighting resources to the limit. If heavy rains follow a fire, other natural disasters can occur, including landslides, mudflows, and floods. Once ground cover has been burned away, little is left to hold soil in place on steep slopes and hillsides. A major wildland fire can leave a large amount of scorched and barren land. These areas may not return to prefire conditions for decades. If the wildland fire destroyed the ground cover, then erosion becomes one of several potential problems.

Types of wildland fires include the following:

- *Wildland fires*. Fueled almost exclusively by natural vegetation, they typically occur in national forests and parks, where federal agencies are responsible for fire management and suppression.
- *Interface or intermix fires*. Urban/wildland fires in which vegetation and the built environment provide fuel.
- *Firestorms*. Events of such extreme intensity that effective suppression is virtually impossible, firestorms occur during extreme weather and generally burn until conditions change or the available fuel is exhausted.
- *Prescribed fires and prescribed natural fires*. Fires that are intentionally set or selected natural fires that are allowed to burn for beneficial purposes.

Severe drought conditions and the buildup of large quantities of dead trees and vegetation on the forest floors recently have led to a significant increase in wildfires in the United States. In summer 2002, several major wildfires raged across the country, principally in the western states. These fires consumed approximately 6 million acres of forestland, and 20 firefighters lost their lives fighting these fires.

Landslides

Landslides occur when masses of rock, earth, or debris move down a slope. Landslides may be very small or very large, and they can move at slow to very high speeds. Many landslides have been occurring over the same terrain since prehistoric times. They are activated by storms and fires and by human modification of the land. New landslides occur as a result of rainstorms, earthquakes, volcanic eruptions, and various human activities.

Mudflows (or debris flows) are rivers of rock, earth, and other debris saturated with water. They develop when water rapidly accumulates in the ground, such as during heavy rainfall or rapid snowmelt, changing the earth into a flowing river of mud or "slurry." A slurry can flow rapidly down slopes or through channels and can strike with little or no warning at avalanche speeds. A slurry can travel several miles from its source, growing in size as it picks up trees, cars, and other materials along the way.

Lateral spreads are large elements of distributed, lateral displacement of materials. They occur in rock, but they also can occur in fine-grained, sensitive soils such as quick clays. Loose granular soils commonly produce lateral spreads through liquefaction. Liquefaction can occur spontaneously, presumably because of changes in pore-water pressures or in response to vibrations such as those produced by strong earthquakes.

Falls occur when masses of rock or other material detach from a steep slope or cliff and descend by freefall, rolling, or bouncing. Topples consist of the forward rotation of rocks or other materials about a pivot point on a hill slope.

Tsunamis

A tsunami is a series of waves generated by an undersea disturbance such as an earthquake. Tsunamis also can be caused by volcanic eruptions and landslides. From the area of the disturbance, the waves travel outward in all directions, much like the ripples caused by throwing a rock into a pond. As the waves approach the shallow coastal waters, they appear normal and the speed decreases. Then, as the tsunami nears the coastline, it may grow to great height and smash into the shore, causing much destruction.

Areas at greatest risk are less than 50 feet above sea level and within one mile of the shoreline. Tsunamis arrive as a series of successive "crests" (high water levels) and "troughs" (low water levels). These successive crests and troughs can occur anywhere from 5 to 90 minutes apart. They usually occur 10 to 45 minutes apart. The wave speed in the open ocean will average 450 miles per hour. Tsunamis reaching heights of more than 100 feet have been recorded. Most deaths during a tsunami are a result of drowning. Associated risks include flooding, polluted water supplies, and damaged gas lines.

□ □ □ ▬▬▬▬▬▬▬▬▬▬▬▬▬▬▬▬▬▬▬▬▬▬▬▬▬▬▬▬▬▬▬▬▬▬▬

2004 Indian Ocean Tsunami

On December 26, 2004, following an earthquake off the coast of the Banda Aceh region of Indonesia that measured 8.9 on the Richter scale, a series of tsunamis devastated vast coastal regions in 11 countries as far away as East Africa. The earthquake was the most powerful to have occurred in four decades and generated waves that reached heights as tall as 60 feet on coastal shorelines. The devastation from this event, in regard to the geographical range and number of people affected within the brief time frame, is virtually unprecedented in modern history.

Due to an almost complete lack of tsunami warning systems, no advance notice of the presence or severity of these impending waves was possible for the local populations, many of whom included foreign tourists. As a result, most people had no opportunity to move to higher ground, an action that surely would have prevented injuries and the loss of so many lives. Although the exact number of people killed will never be known, it is assumed to be greater than 150,000 and possibly more than 200,000. Over 500,000 people were injured and 10 times that many left homeless.

The reconstruction period for this disaster is expected to last for many years. Countries from around the world provided rescue personnel, equipment, and billions of dollars in relief funding. For information on the U.S. involvement in this event, see Figure 2–5 or visit www.usaid.gov.

▬▬▬▬▬▬▬▬▬▬▬▬▬▬▬▬▬▬▬▬▬▬▬▬▬▬▬▬▬▬▬▬▬▬▬ □ □ □

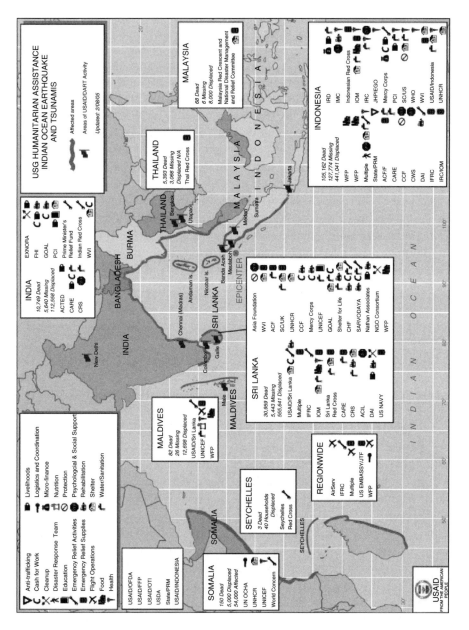

FIGURE 2-5 U.S. government humanitarian assistance following the Indian Ocean earthquake and tsunamis. *Source:* United States Agency for International Development (http://www.usaid.gov/locations/asia_near_east/tsunami/02.11.05-Tsunami_USAID_Program_Map.pdf).

□ □ □ ▬▬▬▬▬▬▬▬▬▬▬▬▬▬▬▬▬▬▬▬▬

2004 Indian Ocean Tsunami Q&A

Question: Why was the recent earthquake in Sumatra and the resulting tsunami so destructive?

Answer: The reason is actually a combination of factors, including the following: It was generated by an extremely large earthquake; it occurred within the Indian Ocean, which is essentially a basin surrounded by very heavily populated areas; there was no warning system in place in the Indian Ocean basin; and the event occurred on a Sunday morning of what was, for some, a holiday weekend when many were at the beach.

Question: Could the tsunami disaster that has occurred in Indonesia and the Indian Ocean region happen in the United States?

Answer: Yes, although the probability of tsunami is significantly less than other coastal hazards such as hurricanes and storms. However, even though they are rare, as shown in the recent event, the consequences are large enough that they can pose a significant risk. Tsunamis can occur along any coastline, although they occur mostly along the Pacific coastline because of the more frequent seismic hazard. Since they occur so infrequently, the probability is considered too remote to address this hazard in normal building code requirements.

One significant difference between the Indian Ocean and the Pacific Ocean is that the National Oceanic and Atmospheric Administration (NOAA) has a tsunami warning system in place and partner agencies such as FEMA are working with states and local communities to help establish local warning systems and evacuation plans and to raise tsunami awareness among residents and visitors.

Question: What is the greatest tsunami risk to the United States?

Answer: Probably the greatest risk to the United States is believed to be a tsunami that would be generated by an earthquake along the Cascadia subduction zone off the coast of Washington, Oregon, and northern California. Similar to the northern coast of Sumatra, a Cascadia earthquake would be very large, would result in a tsunami, and would give only a few minutes of warning time to the residents along the Pacific Northwest coastline, in many cases not enough time to allow for evacuation, especially during vacation season. This fault last generated an estimated magnitude 9.0–9.5 earthquake and tsunami on January 26, 1700. Although there is Native American folklore and geologic evidence, such as sand deposits, to prove the impact of the tsunami, the actual date has been confirmed from Japanese tsunami records. Although an Atlantic Coast tsunami would certainly cause tremendous amounts of damage, the probability of such an event is smaller than a Pacific event.

Question: Has there been a tsunami that has caused fatalities in the United States?
Answer: Yes, several.

On April 1, 1946, a magnitude 7.8 earthquake near Uminak Island in Alaska's Aleutian Islands destroyed a steel reinforced concrete U.S. Coast Guard lighthouse on Uminak Island, killing all five occupants. The tsunami hit Hawaii five hours later, destroying the Hilo waterfront and killing a total of 165 people, including children

(Continued)

at a school on Laupahoehoe Point. It was because of this event that the United States established the Pacific Tsunami Warning Center, now part of NOAA.

On May 22, 1960, a magnitude 9.5 subduction zone earthquake off the coast of Chile resulted in a tsunami that affected the entire Pacific Rim, including Hilo, Hawaii, where it killed 61 people.

On March 28, 1964, the magnitude 9.2 Anchorage earthquake generated a tsunami that caused damage in southeast Alaska, Vancouver Island, Washington, California, and Hawaii. Hardest hit by the tsunami was Crescent City, California, where the tsunami reached 30 feet and destroyed half of the waterfront district. A total of 120 people were killed by the tsunami.

Question: Is a tsunami possible in the Atlantic Ocean?

Answer: Yes. In 1755, an earthquake off the coast of Lisbon, Portugal, reportedly killed thousands along the coast of Portugal, Spain, and North Africa. More recently, a moderate tsunami struck the northwest coast of Puerto Rico in 1918 as a result of an offshore earthquake along the North Atlantic and Caribbean Plate boundary. Also, an earthquake on November 18, 1929, in the Grand Banks of Newfoundland, generated a tsunami that caused considerable damage and loss of life at Placentia Bay, Newfoundland, and resulted in waves that were observed along much of the East Coast of the United States.

Although there is the potential for seismic activity in the Caribbean, the Atlantic Ocean generally does not have the type or number of earthquake faults capable of generating a tsunami with the frequency and severity of those in the Pacific. However, there are other potential hazards that could also trigger a tsunami, including volcanic activity along the mid-Atlantic ridge and slumping from pockets of methane hydrate recently found off the coast of South Carolina. Though the probability of such an Atlantic Ocean tsunami is considered rare, a tsunami striking the east coast of the United States or almost anywhere else along the Atlantic Ocean shoreline would result in significant damage and loss of life.

Question: Do we have any quantified tsunami risk assessment information?

Answer: Part of the National Oceanic and Atmospheric Administration (NOAA)-led National Tsunami Hazard Mitigation Program (NTHMP) (www.pmel.noaa.gov/tsunami-hazard) includes a program of developing tsunami inundation maps that show the extent of inundation for the affected area for the Pacific Northwest, Alaska, and Hawaii. These NOAA tsunami inundation maps are now being used at the state and community level to plan for tsunami response and evacuations.

In addition, the FEMA National Flood Insurance Program (NFIP) (www.fema.gov/fima/nfip.shtm) considered tsunami wave heights during the development of its Flood Insurance Rate Maps in areas of Hawaii and the West Coast where tsunamis were considered a significantly probable flood threat. In addition, FEMA recently funded a NOAA pilot project under its NFIP Flood Map Modernization Program to develop improved maps and tsunami probabilities, using Seaside, Oregon, as a pilot project.

However, we do not have any reliable risk assessment data, such as information that would be available through HAZUS, FEMA's standardized loss estimation software program. Some interest has been expressed in developing a HAZUS tsunami model that could be based on these inundation maps, but funding has not been available.

Question: Can planning for a large disaster event such as a tsunami make a difference?
Answer: Although a tsunami can generate forces that can overwhelm the best-constructed buildings, planning for such an event can make a difference. A comparison between the 1993 tsunami of Aonae, Japan, and the 1998 tsunami of Warapu, Papua, New Guinea, demonstrates how planning can make a difference. Although both events were triggered by earthquakes of similar magnitudes and impacted areas of roughly similar population, the first event killed 15 percent of the population, the second event killed 40 percent of the population. The primary difference was that Japan has a strong program for tsunami public education, awareness, and a warning system that allowed people to get to high ground, whereas Warapu did not. FEMA is aware that public education, awareness, and a warning system can make a real difference in community disaster resistance, and supports continued improvement of community tsunami preparedness, plans, and activities.

Question: Is there anything individuals can do to reduce their vulnerability to the tsunami hazard?
Answer: Residents and visitors to coastal communities should take the time to learn the local evacuation routes and safe areas (visitors' centers often have tsunami evacuation maps and information) and be prepared with emergency supplies that will help them deal with any emergency. Strong ground shaking near the ocean may be the only clue to the arrival of a tsunami within minutes. If shaking is felt, or if you see the ocean suddenly begin to recede, you should go to high ground immediately and wait for further instructions from local officials about when it is safe to return. Tsunami waves can last for hours. Also, subsequent sets of waves are usually the most dangerous, as they can often be higher and contain debris generated from the initial waves.

Question: Is there a federal program that addresses the tsunami hazard?
Answer: Yes, the National Tsunami Hazard Mitigation Program (NTHMP) is a federal/state program formed to address the tsunami hazard, improve tsunami warning, develop tsunami inundation mapping, and mitigate its effects. The program is led by the National Oceanic and Atmospheric Administration (NOAA), which is part of the Department of Commerce, and includes FEMA, which is part of the Department of Homeland Security, along with the U.S. Geological Survey (USGS) and the National Science Foundation (NSF) as the participating federal agencies. The NTHMP also includes state emergency management and geoscience agencies from five states (Alaska, California, Hawaii, Oregon, and Washington). NOAA, FEMA, USGS, and the five states make up the steering committee for the NTHMP.

FEMA and the states are involved primarily in the emergency management and mapping issues, NOAA with tsunami modeling and warning system issues, and USGS with seismic system issues. Together, the agencies have developed many products and activities for West Coast communities that have increased their readiness for both long distance and local tsunamis. Future work will continue to improve the level of readiness.

(Continued)

Since tsunami is an earthquake-generated hazard, it is also referenced in the National Earthquake Hazard Reduction Program (NEHRP), which was established by Congress to reduce the risk posed by earthquakes. FEMA is responsible for implementation of the NEHRP, and we have sought to work with NOAA to coordinate activities between the two programs.

Additional information on the NTHMP can be found on the NOAA Web site, (www.pmel.noaa.gov/tsunami-hazard), and on the FEMA/NEHRP Web site.

Question: Are there any early lessons we can gain from this disaster?

Answer: This disaster demonstrates the importance of tsunami mapping and preparedness activities and the need for tsunami awareness in the United States. The NOAA-led NTHMP is a federal and state program that has several components to address the tsunami hazard, primarily in our Pacific coastal states. NOAA's primary focus has been on developing a tsunami warning system, which is an important component of an overall tsunami program. FEMA has been working in partnership with other federal and state emergency management and science agencies to improve the level of tsunami hazard awareness, planning, and preparedness.

Question: Are there any examples or demonstration projects of tsunami identification and mitigation on a local community level?

Answer: FEMA, through the National Flood Insurance Program (NFIP), NOAA, and USGS are cofunding a $540,000 pilot project to develop risk identification products that will help communities understand their actual level of risk from tsunami in a way that could be conveyed on our existing flood maps. The goal of the project is to develop techniques that can be used to determine the probability and magnitude of tsunami in other communities along the West Coast of the United States. The location of the pilot project is Seaside, Oregon. FEMA's NFIP is involved because FEMA is responsible for mapping areas subject to flooding in order to properly rate flood insurance policies and provide risk assessment information to states and local communities.

Question: Is there a program that communities can participate in to reduce their risk from tsunami?

Answer: FEMA supports and promotes NOAA's TsunamiReady Program (www. prh.noaa.gov/ptwc/tsunamiready/tsunamiready.htm) because it includes the same important emergency planning elements that FEMA promotes in all predisaster preparedness activities. Currently, there are 11 TsunamiReady communities located in the Pacific Northwest. The criteria for being recognized as a TsunamiReady community includes establishing an Emergency Operating Center, warning systems, a community preparedness program, identification of their hazard zone, and establishing evacuation routes and safe areas. Also required is the establishment of plans and drills for schools in the hazard zone, by which the community protects its most precious commodity—its children, its hope, and its lifeblood for the future. This kind of planning, preparedness, and mitigation changes the impact that earthquakes and tsunamis have on communities, and results in a community that is safer and more disaster resistant.

Question: Is it possible to build a structure that would be capable of resisting the extreme forces of a tsunami?

Answer: This question takes on a greater significance because there are several coastal communities along our nation's West Coast that are vulnerable to tsunami triggered by an earthquake on the Cascadia subduction zone. An earthquake along this fault could potentially generate a tsunami within minutes, similar to what happened on the north end of Sumatra. Given that many of these coastal communities are located in areas that would be impossible to evacuate in time, which could result in a significant loss of life, FEMA and its mitigation partners at the federal, state, and local levels are looking for alternatives. The only feasible alternative would be vertical evacuation, providing such a structure could be constructed to resist tsunami loads.

For the average structure, generally it would not be economically feasible to construct to withstand the extreme loads of a tsunami. However, we believe it would be possible that a specially designed structure could be built to withstand at least specific tsunami loads without collapse for the purposes of providing community shelter for vertical evacuation. Similarly, the same criteria could possibly be used if the structure was to house a large occupancy load (such as some larger seaside resorts).

Question: Are there any current FEMA design guidance documents that provide design criteria on tsunami?

Answer: FEMA's most recent study of coastal seismic and tsunami loads was done in association with the *FEMA Coastal Construction Manual* (FEMA-55). This manual was developed to provide design and construction guidance for structures built in coastal areas throughout the United States. The *Coastal Construction Manual* (CCM) addresses seismic loads for coastal structures and provides information on the tsunami hazard and associated loads. The conclusion of the CCM's authors is that tsunami loads are far too great and that, in general, it is not feasible or practical to design normal structures to withstand these loads. It should be noted that the study was for conventional construction and did not take into account the possibility of special design and construction details that would be possible for critical facilities.

Question: Is there any work currently under way to develop tsunami design criteria for shelters or critical facilities?

Answer: Yes, there is a joint National Oceanic and Atmospheric Administration (NOAA)/FEMA-funded effort currently under way to do just that. Given the significant level of risk that exists for the residents of the certain coastal communities in the Pacific Northwest, Alaska, and Hawaii, the cofunded FEMA/NOAA work for the development of guidance for the design of structures that could be used for vertical evacuation will be a significant step toward improving the protection of the residents of these communities.

The first phase of this effort is being managed by the state of Washington under a $100,000 grant from NOAA under the NTHMP. In Phase 1, data regarding tsunamis and their potential forces on structures was collected. The Phase 1 work was preceded by a workshop held in 2003 and attended by engineers from the

(Continued)

different affected states. A report on this workshop has been issued by the NTHMP. The overall Phase 1 work is complete and the report is being finalized.

The second phase will determine whether it is possible to design and build a structure to withstand specific tsunami loads, and if so, to develop a technical design and construction guidance document for special facilities that would allow for vertical evacuation from tsunami conditions. This work would continue and build on the work started in Phase 1. Funding for this two-year $400,000 effort will be equally divided between FEMA, the National Earthquake Hazards Reduction Program (NEHRP), and NOAA, through the NTHMP.

The Phase 2 work will be done with input from the engineering and design communities and the states to research and produce the construction design guidance for a tsunami shelter structure capable of withstanding both the severe ground shaking expected during a design earthquake and specific velocities and water pressure from a tsunami that would impact structures. This is a significant challenge since current design practice takes into account earthquake or coastal storm surge but does not address stronger forces that a tsunami would generate. The project will work with Oregon State University's improved tsunami testing basin, recently funded by the National Science Foundation's Network for Earthquake Engineering Simulation (NEES). The project is being done under contract to the Applied Technology Council, and is just getting under way.

A third phase is planned, where information for states and local communities on how this tsunami design guidance can be utilized will be developed. This information will especially be critical for low-lying communities that lack evacuation access to high ground following a local earthquake and that may have to rely on vertical evacuation in existing buildings. Funding is anticipated to be $100,000, also equally divided between NOAA and FEMA.

Source: www.fema.gov.

□ □ □

Volcanic Eruptions

A volcano is a mountain that opens downward to a reservoir of molten rock below the surface of the earth. Unlike most mountains, which are pushed up from below, volcanoes are built up by an accumulation of their own eruptive products—lava, ash flows, and airborne ash and dust. When pressure from gases and the molten rock becomes strong enough to cause an explosion, eruptions occur. Gases and rock shoot up through the opening and spill over or fill the air with lava fragments. Volcanic products are used as building or road-building materials, as abrasive and cleaning agents, and as raw materials for many chemical and industrial uses. Lava ash makes soil rich in mineral nutrients.

Volcanic ash can affect people hundreds of miles away from the cone of a volcano. Several of the deaths from the Mount St. Helens volcano in 1980 were attributed to inhalation of ash. Volcanic ash can contaminate water supplies, cause electrical storms, and collapse roofs. An erupting volcano can also trigger tsunamis, flash floods, earthquakes, rock falls, and mudflows.

Sideways-directed volcanic explosions, known as *lateral blasts*, can shoot large pieces of rock at very high speeds for several miles. These explosions can kill by impact, burial, or heat. They have been known to knock down entire forests. Most deaths attributed to the Mount St. Helens volcano were a result of lateral blast and trees that were blown down.

Severe Winter Storms

Severe winter storms consist of extreme cold and heavy concentrations of snowfall or ice. A blizzard combines heavy snowfall, high winds, extreme cold, and ice storms. In the United States, the origins of the weather patterns are from four sources:

1. In the Northwestern states, cyclonic weather systems from the North Pacific Ocean or the Aleutian Island region sweep massive low-pressure systems with heavy snow and blizzards.
2. In the Midwestern and Upper Plains states, Canadian and Arctic cold fronts push ice and snow deep into the interior region and, in some instances, all the way down to Florida.
3. In the Northeast, lake-effect snowstorms develop from the passage of cold air over the relatively warm surfaces of the Great Lakes, causing heavy snowfall and blizzard conditions.
4. The Eastern and Northeastern states are affected by extra-tropical cyclonic weather systems in the Atlantic Ocean and Gulf of Mexico that produce snow, ice storms, and occasional blizzards.

Beginning on January 1, 2006, the federal government began using a new scale to measure severe winter storms similar to the scales used to measure the magnitude and intensity of hurricanes and tornadoes. The Northeast Snowfall Impact Scale (NESIS) provides a numerical value to storms based on the geographical area affected, the amount of snow accumulation, and the number of people affected. The minimum threshold for a storm's inclusion in the scale is 10 inches of snow falling over a wide area.

NESIS values range from 1 to 5 and include associated descriptors (from most to least severe) of extreme, crippling, major, significant, and notable (see Table 2–5). The NESIS scale differs from other meteorological indices in that it considers population data. Using the following formula,

$$n = 30$$
$$\text{NESIS} = S[n/10(A_n/A_{mean} + P_n/P_{mean})]$$
$$n = 4$$

where A equals the area affected and P equals the population affected. Using this formula, the categories in Table 2–5 are assigned to severe winter storms.

Droughts

Drought is defined as a water shortage caused by a deficiency of rainfall. Drought differs from other natural hazards in three ways: (1) A drought's onset and end are difficult to determine because the effects accumulate slowly and may linger even after the apparent termination of an episode; (2) the absence of a precise and universally accepted definition adds to the confusion about whether a drought exists and, if it does, the degree of severity; and (3) drought effects are less obvious and spread over a larger geographic area.

Table 2–5   NESIS Values

Category	NESIS Value	Description
1	1–2.499	Notable
2	2.5–3.99	Significant
3	4–5.99	Major
4	6–9.99	Crippling
5	10.0+	Extreme

Source: NOAA, 2006 (http://www.ncdc.noaa.gov/oa/climate/research/snow-nesis).

Extreme Heat

Extreme heat is defined as temperatures that hover 10 degrees or more above the average high temperature for the region and last for several weeks. Humid or muggy conditions, which add to the discomfort of high temperatures, occur when a "dome" of high atmospheric pressure traps hazy, damp air near the ground. Excessively dry and hot conditions can provoke dust storms and low visibility. Droughts occur when a long period passes without substantial rainfall. A heat wave combined with a drought is a very dangerous situation.

Coastal Erosion

Coastal erosion is measured as the rate of change in the position or horizontal displacement of a shoreline over a period of time. It generally is associated with storm surges, hurricanes, windstorms, and flooding hazards and may be exacerbated by human activities such as boat wakes, shoreline hardening, and dredging.

Thunderstorms

Thunderstorms can bring heavy rains (which can cause flash flooding), strong winds, hail, lightning, and tornadoes. Thunderstorms are generated by atmospheric imbalance and turbulence caused by the combination of conditions: (1) unstable warm air rising rapidly into the atmosphere; (2) sufficient moisture to form clouds and rain; and (3) upward lift of air currents caused by colliding weather fronts (cold and warm), sea breezes, or mountains.

Thunderstorms may occur singly, in clusters, or in lines. Therefore, it is possible for several thunderstorms to affect one location in the course of a few hours. Some of the most severe weather occurs when a single thunderstorm affects one location for an extended period.

Lightning is a major threat during a thunderstorm. In the United States, between 75 and 100 Americans are killed by lightning each year. A thunderstorm is classified as severe if its winds reach or exceed 58 mph, it produces a tornado, or it drops surface hail at least 0.75 inch in diameter.

Significant airplane disasters often are associated with thunderstorms and lightning. It is a myth that lightning never strikes twice in the same place. In fact, lightning will strike several times in the same place in the course of one discharge. A bolt of lightning reaches a temperature approaching 50,000° Fahrenheit in a split second.

Hailstorms

Hailstorms are an outgrowth of a severe thunderstorm, in which balls or irregularly shaped lumps of ice greater than 0.75 inch in diameter fall with rain. Hailstorms occur more frequently during late spring and early summer, when the jet stream migrates northward across the Great Plains. Hailstorms cause nearly $1 billion in property and crop damage annually.

Snow Avalanches

A snow avalanche is sliding snow or an ice mass that moves at high velocities. It can shear trees, completely cover entire communities and highway routes, and level buildings. Natural and human-induced snow avalanches most often result from structural weaknesses within the snowpack. The potential for a snow avalanche increases with significant temperature influences.

The primary threat is loss of life of backcountry skiers, climbers, and snowmobilers as a result of suffocation when buried in an avalanche. Around 10,000 avalanches are reported each year. Since 1790, an average of 144 persons have been trapped in avalanches annually: On average, 14 were injured and 14 died. The estimated annual average damage to structures is $500,000.

Land Subsidence

Land subsidence is the loss of surface elevation caused by the removal of subsurface support; it ranges from broad, regional lowering of the land surface to localized collapse. The primary cause of most subsidence is human activities: underground mining of coal, groundwater or petroleum withdrawal, and drainage of organic soils. The average annual damage from all types of subsidence is conservatively estimated to be at least $125 million (see Table 2–6).

Expansive Soils

Soils and soft rock that tend to swell or shrink because of changes in moisture content are commonly known as *expansive soils*. Changes in soil volume present a hazard primarily to structures built on top of expansive soils. The most extensive damage occurs to highways and streets. Two major groups of rocks that are prone to expansiveness and that occur more commonly in the West than East are aluminum silicate minerals (i.e., ash, glass, and rocks of volcanic origin) and sedimentary rock (i.e., clay minerals, shale).

Dam Failures

Dam failures are potentially the worst flood events. A dam failure is usually the result of neglect, poor design, or structural damage caused by a major event such as an earthquake. When a dam fails, a gigantic quantity of water is suddenly let loose downstream, destroying anything in its path.

Table 2–6   Top 10 Natural Disasters Ranked by FEMA Relief Costs, 1900–2007

Event	Year	FEMA Funding
Hurricane Katrina (AL, LA, MS)	2005	$7.2 billion
Northridge Earthquake (CA)	1994	$6.961 billion
Hurricane Georges (AL, FL, LA, MS, PR, VI)	1998	$2.251 billion
Hurricane Ivan (AL, FL, GA, LA, MS, NC, NJ, NY, PA, TN, WV)	2004	$1.947 billion
Hurricane Andrew (FL, LA)	1992	$1.813 billion
Hurricane Charley (FL, SC)	2004	$1.559 billion
Hurricane Frances (FL, GA, NC, NY, OH, PA, SC)	2004	$1.425 billion
Hurricane Jeanne (DE, FL, PR, VI, VA)	2004	$1.407 billion
Tropical Storm Allison (FL, LA, MS, PA, TX)	2001	$1.375 billion
Hurricane Hugo (NC, SC, PR, VI)	1989	$1.307 billion

Source: www.fema.gov.

Critical Thinking

- What hazards does your community face?
- Have any of your community's natural hazards resulted in a major disaster?
- Do any natural hazards affect your community routinely? What actions has the community taken to mitigate these recurrent hazards? Have these actions been successful in reducing the consequences or likelihood of the hazards?
- Are there any natural hazards that you or your community can ignore because your geographic location preclude you from risk? Which hazards, and why can you ignore them?

Technological Hazards

Fires

Fires can be triggered or exacerbated by lightning, high winds, earthquakes, volcanoes, and floods. Lightning is the most significant natural contributor to fires affecting the built environment. Buildings with rooftop storage tanks for flammable liquids are particularly susceptible.

Where Fires Occurred—2005

There were 1,602,000 fires in the United States (see Table 2–7). Of these,

- 50.0 percent were outside and other fires.
- 31.9 percent were structure fires.
- 18.1 percent were vehicle fires.

Residential fires represented 24.7 percent of all fires and 77.5 percent of structure fires. Of all civilian fire fatalities, 82.4 percent occurred in the home, where *home* is defined as one- and two-family dwellings and apartments. Of those, approximately 84.8 percent occurred in single-family homes and duplexes. Intentionally set structure fires represented 7.2 percent of all structure property loss. In 2005, 21,000 intentionally set vehicle

Table 2–7   U.S. Fire Losses, 1991–2005

Year	Fires	Deaths	Injuries	Losses (in $ millions)
1991	2,041,500	4,465	29,375	$10,906
1992	1,964,500	4,730	28,700	$9,276
1993	1,952,500	4,635	30,475	$9,279
1994	2,054,500	4,275	27,250	$8,630
1995	1,965,500	4,585	25,775	$9,182
1996	1,975,500	4,990	25,550	$9,406
1997	1,795,000	4,050	23,750	$8,525
1998	1,755,000	4,035	23,100	$8,629
1999	1,823,000	3,570	21,875	$10,024
2000	1,708,000	4,045	22,350	$11,207
2001	1,734,500	6,199/3,745*	21,100/20,300**	$44,023/10,583***
2002	1,687,500	3,380	18,425	$10,337
2003	1,584,500	3,925	18,125	$12,307
2004	1,550,500	3,900	17,785	$9,794****
2005	1,602,000	3,675	17,925	$10,672

Source: www.usfa.dhs.gov.

*This number, 3,745, does not include the deaths associated with the September 11, 2001, terrorist attacks. Including those events, there were 6,196 fire-related deaths in 2001.

**This number, 20,300, does not include the injuries associated with the September 11, 2001, terrorist attacks. Including those events, there were 21,100 fire-related injuries in 2001.

***This number, $10,583 million does not include the losses associated with the September 11, 2001, terrorist attacks. Including those events, there were $44,023 million in fire-related losses in 2001.

****The decrease in direct dollar loss in 2004 reflects the Southern California wildfires with an estimated loss of $2,040 million that occurred in 2003.

fires occurred, causing an estimated $113 million in property damage. (*Source:* National Fire Protection Association, "Fire Loss in the U.S. during 2005," abridged report.)

Hazardous Materials Incidents

Hazardous materials are chemical substances that, if released or misused, can pose a threat to the environment or health. These chemicals are used in industry, agriculture, medicine, research, and consumer goods. Hazardous materials come in the form of explosives, flammable and combustible substances, poisons, and radioactive materials. These substances most often are released as a result of transportation accidents or because of chemical accidents in plants. Hazardous materials in various forms can cause death, serious injury, long-lasting health effects, and damage to buildings, homes, and other property. Many products containing hazardous chemicals are routinely used and stored in homes. These products also are shipped daily on the nation's highways, railroads, waterways, and pipelines. Varying quantities of hazardous materials are manufactured, used, or stored at an estimated 4.5 million facilities in the United States, from major industrial plants to local dry cleaning establishments or gardening supply stores.

CHLORINE FACT SHEET

What chlorine is
- Chlorine is an element used in industry and found in some household products.
- Chlorine sometimes is in the form of a poisonous gas. Chlorine gas can be pressurized and cooled to change it into a liquid so that it can be shipped and stored. When liquid chlorine is released, it quickly turns into a gas that stays close to the ground and spreads rapidly.
- Chlorine gas can be recognized by its pungent, irritating odor, which is like the odor of bleach. The strong smell may provide an adequate warning to people that they have been exposed.
- Chlorine gas appears to be yellow-green in color.
- Chlorine itself is not flammable, but it can react explosively or form explosive compounds with other chemicals such as turpentine and ammonia.

Where chlorine is found and how it is used
- Chlorine was used during World War I as a choking (pulmonary) agent.
- Chlorine is one of the most commonly manufactured chemicals in the United States. Its most important use is as a bleach in the manufacture of paper and cloth, but it is also used to make pesticides (insect killers), rubber, and solvents.
- Chlorine is used in drinking water and swimming pool water to kill harmful bacteria. It also is used as part of the sanitation process for industrial waste and sewage.
- Household chlorine bleach can release chlorine gas if it is mixed with other cleaning agents.

How people can be exposed to chlorine
- People's risk for exposure depends on how close they are to the place where the chlorine was released.
- If chlorine gas is released into the air, people may be exposed through skin or eye contact. They may also be exposed by breathing air that contains chlorine.
- If chlorine liquid is released into water, people may be exposed by touching or drinking water that contains chlorine.
- If chlorine liquid comes into contact with food, people may be exposed by eating the contaminated food.
- Chlorine gas is heavier than air, so it would settle in low-lying areas.

How chlorine works
- The extent of poisoning caused by chlorine depends on the amount of chlorine a person is exposed to, how the person was exposed, and the length of time of the exposure.
- When chlorine gas comes into contact with moist tissues such as the eyes, throat, and lungs, an acid is produced that can damage these tissues.

Immediate signs and symptoms of chlorine exposure
- During or immediately after exposure to dangerous concentrations of chlorine, the following signs and symptoms may develop:

- ◦ Coughing.
- ◦ Chest tightness.
- ◦ Burning sensation in the nose, throat, and eyes.
- ◦ Watery eyes.
- ◦ Blurred vision.
- ◦ Nausea and vomiting.
- ◦ Burning pain, redness, and blisters on the skin if exposed to gas, skin injury similar to frostbite if exposed to liquid chlorine.
- ◦ Difficulty breathing or shortness of breath (may appear immediately if high concentrations of chlorine gas are inhaled or may be delayed if low concentrations of chlorine gas are inhaled).
- ◦ Fluid in the lungs (pulmonary edema) within two to four hours.
- • Showing these signs or symptoms does not necessarily mean that a person has been exposed to chlorine.

What the long-term health effects are

- • Long-term complications from chlorine exposure are not found in people who survive a sudden exposure unless they suffer complications such as pneumonia during therapy. Chronic bronchitis may develop in people who develop pneumonia during therapy.

How people can protect themselves, and what they should do if they are exposed to chlorine

- • Leave the area where the chlorine was released and get to fresh air. Quickly moving to an area where fresh air is available is highly effective in reducing exposure to chlorine.
  - ◦ If the chlorine release was outdoors, move away from the area where the chlorine was released. Go to the highest ground possible, because chlorine is heavier than air and will sink to low-lying areas.
  - ◦ If the chlorine release was indoors, get out of the building.
- • If you think you may have been exposed, remove your clothing, rapidly wash your entire body with soap and water, and get medical care as quickly as possible.
- • *Removing and disposing of clothing:*
  - ◦ Quickly take off clothing that has liquid chlorine on it. Any clothing that has to be pulled over the head should be cut off the body instead of pulled over the head. If possible, seal the clothing in a plastic bag. Then seal the first plastic bag in a second plastic bag. Removing and sealing the clothing in this way will help protect you and other people from any chemicals that might be on your clothes.
  - ◦ If you placed your clothes in plastic bags, inform either the local or state health department or emergency personnel on their arrival. Do not handle the plastic bags.
  - ◦ If you are helping other people remove their clothing, try to avoid touching any contaminated areas, and remove the clothing as quickly as possible.

(Continued)

CHLORINE FACT SHEET—Cont'd

- *Washing the body:*
  - ○ As quickly as possible, wash your entire body with large amounts of soap and water. Washing with soap and water will help protect people from any chemicals on their bodies.
  - ○ If your eyes are burning or your vision is blurred, rinse your eyes with plain water for 10 to 15 minutes. If you wear contacts, remove them before rinsing your eyes, and place them in the bags with the contaminated clothing. Do not put the contacts back in your eyes. You should dispose of them even if you do not wear disposable contacts. If you wear eyeglasses, wash them with soap and water. You can put the eyeglasses back on after you wash them.
- If you have ingested (swallowed) chlorine, do not induce vomiting or drink fluids.
- Seek medical attention right away. Dial 911 and explain what has happened.

How chlorine exposure is treated
- No antidote exists for chlorine exposure. Treatment consists of removing the chlorine from the body as soon as possible and providing supportive medical care in a hospital setting.

How people can get more information about chlorine
People can contact one of the following:
- Regional poison control center (1-800-222-1222)
- Centers for Disease Control and Prevention
  - ○ Public Response Hotline (CDC)
    - ○ English (888) 246–2675
    - ○ Español (888) 246–2857
    - ○ TTY (866) 874–2646
  - ○ Emergency Preparedness and Response Web site: E-mail inquiries: cdcresponse@ashastd.org
  - ○ Mail inquiries:
    Public Inquiry c/o BPRP
    Bioterrorism Preparedness and Response Planning
    Centers for Disease Control and Prevention
    Mailstop C-18
    1600 Clifton Road
    Atlanta, GA 30333
- Agency for Toxic Substances and Disease Registry (ATSDR) (1-888-422-8737)
  - ○ E-mail inquiries: atsdric@cdc.gov
  - ○ Mail inquiries:
    Agency for Toxic Substances and Disease Registry
    Division of Toxicology
    1600 Clifton Road NE, Mailstop E-29
    Atlanta, GA 30333
- Centers for Disease Control and Prevention (CDC), National Institute for Occupational Safety and Health (NIOSH), *Pocket Guide to Chemical Hazards.*

Nuclear Accidents

The potential danger from an accident at a nuclear power plant is exposure to radiation. This exposure could come from the release of radioactive material from the plant into the environment, usually characterized by a plume (cloudlike) formation. The area the radioactive release may affect is determined by the amount released from the plant, wind direction and speed, and weather conditions (e.g., rain, snow) that would quickly drive the radioactive material to the ground, hence causing increased deposition of radio nuclides. Radioactive materials are composed of atoms that are unstable. An unstable atom gives off its excess energy until it becomes stable. The energy emitted is radiation. The process by which an atom changes from an unstable state to a more stable state by emitting radiation is called *radioactive decay* or *radioactivity*.

Since 1980, each utility that owns a commercial nuclear power plant in the United States has been required to have both on-site and off-site emergency response plans as a condition of obtaining and maintaining a license to operate that plant. On-site emergency response plans are approved by the Nuclear Regulatory Commission (NRC). Off-site plans (which are closely coordinated with the utility's on-site emergency response plan) are evaluated by FEMA and provided to the NRC, which must consider the FEMA findings when issuing or maintaining a license.

Radioactive materials, if handled improperly, or radiation accidentally released into the environment can be dangerous because of the harmful effects of certain types of radiation on the body. The longer a person is exposed to radiation and the closer the person is to the radiation, the greater the risk. Although radiation cannot be detected by the senses (e.g., sight, smell), it is easily detected by scientists with sophisticated instruments that can detect even the smallest levels of radiation.

Terrorism

Terrorism is the use of force or violence against persons or property in violation of the criminal laws of the United States for purposes of intimidation, coercion, or ransom. Terrorists often use threats to create fear among the public, to try to convince citizens that their government is powerless to prevent terrorism, and to get immediate publicity for their causes.

Before the September 11, 2001, attacks on New York and the Pentagon, most terrorist incidents in the United States have been bombing attacks, involving detonated and undetonated explosive devices, tear gas, and pipe and fire bombs. The effects of terrorism can vary significantly from loss of life and injuries to property damage and disruptions in services such as electricity, water supply, public transportation, and communications.

One way governments attempt to reduce people's vulnerability to terrorist incidents is by increasing security at airports and other public facilities. The U.S. government also works with other countries to limit the sources of support for terrorism. The Federal Bureau of Investigations (FBI) categorizes terrorism in the United States as one of two types: domestic terrorism or international terrorism. Domestic terrorism involves groups or individuals whose terrorism activities are directed at elements of government or population without foreign direction. International terrorism involves groups or individuals whose terrorist activities are foreign based or directed by countries or groups outside the United States or whose activities transcend national boundaries.

Weapons of Mass Destruction

The U.S. military defines weapons of mass destruction (WMD) as the broad family of weapons, including conventional, biological, chemical, nuclear, or other advanced weapons, that are characterized by their broad-sweeping intended effects, such as inflicting mass casualties or physical destruction. There are many different ways that WMDs are categorized. One of the more common categorizations, which include chemical, biological, nuclear, and radiological agents, is referred to by the acronym CBRN. Although these weapons are considered WMDs because of their potential for creating such widespread destruction, it should be noted that they can be distributed in such a way as to harm or kill only one or a very few individuals but still maintain that potential—and, as such, still be considered weapons of mass destruction.

Chemical warfare agents are poisonous vapors, aerosols, liquids, or solids that have toxic effects on people, animals, or plants (see text box). They can be released by bombs; sprayed from aircraft, boats, or vehicles; or used as a liquid to create a hazard to people and the environment. Some chemical agents may be odorless and tasteless. They can have an immediate effect (a few seconds to a few minutes) or a delayed effect (several hours to several days). Although potentially lethal, chemical agents are difficult to deliver in lethal concentrations. Outdoors, the agents often dissipate rapidly. Chemical agents are also difficult to produce.

There are six types of agents:

1. Pulmonary or "choking" agents.
2. Blood agents.
3. Vesicants or blister agents.
4. Nerve agents.
5. Incapacitating agents.
6. Riot-control agents or "irritants."

□ □ □ ▬▬▬▬▬▬▬▬▬▬▬▬▬▬▬▬▬▬▬▬▬▬▬▬▬▬▬▬▬

List of Chemical Agents

Compiled by the Centers for Disease Control
  Abrin
  Adamsite (DM)
  Agent 15
  Ammonia
  Arsenic
  Arsine (SA)
  Benzene
  Bromobenzylcyanide (CA) **NEW! Aug 1, 2003**
  BZ
  Cannabinoids
  Chlorine (CL)
  Chloroacetophenone (CN) **NEW! Aug 1, 2003**
  Chlorobenzylidenemalononitrile (CS) **NEW! Aug 1, 2003**
  Chloropicrin (PS) **NEW! Aug 1, 2003**

Cyanide
Cyanogen Chloride (CK)
Cyclohexyl Sarin (GF)
Dibenzoxazepine (CR) **NEW! Aug 1, 2003**
Diphenylchloroarsine (DA)
Diphenylcyanoarsine (DC)
Diphosgene (DP)
Distilled Mustard (HD)
Ethyldichloroarsine (ED)
Ethylene Glycol
Fentanyls and Other Opioids
Hydrofluoric Acid
Hydrogen Chloride
Hydrogen Cyanide (AC)
Lewisite (L, L-1, L-2, L-3)
LSD
Mercury
Methyldichloroarsine (MD)
Mustard Gas (H) (Sulfur Mustard)
Mustard/Lewisite (HL)
Mustard/T
Nitrogen Mustard (HN-1, HN-2, HN-3)
Nitrogen Oxide (NO)
Paraquat
Perflurorisobutylene (PHIB)
Phenodichloroarsine (PD)
Phenothiazines
Phosgene (CG)
Phosgene Oxime (CX)
Phosphine
Potassium Cyanide (KCN)
Red Phosphorous (RP)
Ricin
Sarin (GB)
Sesqui Mustard
Sodium Azide
Sodium Cyanide (NaCN)
Soman (GD)
Stibine
Strychnine
Sulfur Mustard (H) (Mustard Gas)
Super Warfarin
Sulfur Trioxide-Chlorosulfonic Acid (FS)
Tabun (GA)

(Continued)

Teflon and Perflurorisobutylene (PHIB)
Thallium
Titanium Tetrachloride (FM)
Unidentified Chemical
VX
White Phosphorus
Zinc Oxide (HC)

Source: http://www.bt.cdc.gov/agent/agentlistchem.asp.

Biological agents are organisms or toxins, either naturally occurring or genetically engineered, that can kill or incapacitate people, livestock, and crops. Three basic groups of biological agents would likely be used as weapons:

1. Bacteria
2. Viruses
3. Toxins

Most biological agents are difficult to grow and maintain. Although many of these agents decay rapidly when exposed to sunlight and other environmental factors, others such as anthrax spores (see text box, pp. 61–64) can be very resilient and survive for decades or longer. Biological agents can be dispersed by aerosolization (spraying them in the air), by human-to-human or animal-to-human infection, and through food and water contamination. Human-to-human transmission has been the primary source of infection in past epidemics that involved pathogens capable of use as a biological weapon, including smallpox, plague, and the Lassa virus.

List of Biological Agents

Compiled by the Centers for Disease Control
Anthrax (*Bacillus anthracis*)
Bacillus anthracis (anthrax)
Botulism (*Clostridium botulinum* toxin)
Brucella species (brucellosis)
Brucellosis (*Brucella* species)
Burkholderia mallei (glanders)
Burkholderia pseudomallei (melioidosis)
Chlamydia psittaci (psittacosis)
Cholera (*Vibrio cholerae*)
Clostridium botulinum toxin (botulism)
Clostridium perfringens (Epsilon toxin)
Coxiella burnetii (Q fever)
E. coli O157:H7 (*Escherichia coli*)

Emerging infectious diseases such as Nipah virus and hantavirus

Epsilon toxin of *Clostridium perfringens*

Escherichia coli O157:H7 (*E. coli*)

Food safety threats (e.g., *Salmonella* species, *Escherichia coli* O157:H7, *Shigella*)

Francisella tularensis (tularemia)

Glanders (*Burkholderia mallei*)

Melioidosis (*Burkholderia pseudomallei*)

Plague (*Yersinia pestis*)

Psittacosis (*Chlamydia psittaci*)

Q fever (*Coxiella burnetii*)

Ricin toxin from *Ricinus communis* (castor beans)

Rickettsia prowazekii (typhus fever)

Salmonella species (salmonellosis)

Salmonella typhi (typhoid fever)

Salmonellosis (*Salmonella* species)

Shigella (shigellosis)

Shigellosis (*Shigella*)

Smallpox (variola major)

Staphylococcal enterotoxin B

Tularemia (*Francisella tularensis*)

Typhoid fever (*Salmonella typhi*)

Typhus fever (*Rickettsia prowazekii*)

Variola major (smallpox)

Vibrio cholerae (cholera)

Viral encephalitis (alphaviruses; e.g., Venezuelan equine encephalitis, eastern equine encephalitis, western equine encephalitis)

Viral hemorrhagic fevers (filoviruses, e.g., Ebola, Marburg; and arenaviruses, e.g., Lassa, Machupo)

Water safety threats (e.g., *Vibrio cholerae, Cryptosporidium parvum*)

Yersinia pestis (plague)

Source: http://www.bt.cdc.gov/agent/agentlist.asp.

◻ ◻ ◻

ANTHRAX FACT SHEET

Anthrax: What You Need to Know

What is anthrax?
Anthrax is a serious disease caused by *Bacillus anthracis*, a bacterium that forms spores. A bacterium is a very small organism made up of one cell. Many bacteria can cause disease. A spore is a cell that is dormant (asleep) but may come to life with the right conditions.

(Continued)

ANTHRAX FACT SHEET—Cont'd

There are three types of anthrax:

1. Skin (cutaneous)
2. Lungs (inhalation)
3. Digestive (gastrointestinal)

How do you get it?

Anthrax is not known to spread from one person to another.

> *Anthrax from animals.* Humans can become infected with anthrax by handling products from infected animals or by breathing in anthrax spores from infected animal products (like wool, for example). People also can become infected with gastrointestinal anthrax by eating undercooked meat from infected animals.
>
> *Anthrax as a weapon.* Anthrax also can be used as a weapon. This happened in the United States in 2001. Anthrax was deliberately spread through the postal system by sending letters with powder containing anthrax. This caused 22 cases of anthrax infection.

How dangerous is anthrax?

The Centers for Disease Control and Prevention classify agents with recognized bioterrorism potential into three priority areas (A, B, and C). Anthrax is classified a Category A agent. Category A agents

- Pose the greatest possible threat for a bad effect on public health.
- May spread across a large area or need public awareness.
- Need a great deal of planning to protect the public's health.

In most cases, early treatment with antibiotics can cure cutaneous anthrax. Even if untreated, 80 percent of people who become infected with cutaneous anthrax do not die. Gastrointestinal anthrax is more serious because between one fourth and more than half of cases lead to death. Inhalation anthrax is much more severe. In 2001, about half of the cases of inhalation anthrax ended in death.

What are the symptoms?

The symptoms (warning signs) of anthrax are different depending on the type of the disease:

- *Cutaneous.* The first symptom is a small sore that develops into a blister. The blister then develops into a skin ulcer with a black area in the center. The sore, blister, and ulcer do not hurt.
- *Gastrointestinal.* The first symptoms are nausea, loss of appetite, bloody diarrhea, and fever, followed by bad stomach pain.
- *Inhalation.* The first symptoms of inhalation anthrax are like cold or flu symptoms and can include a sore throat, mild fever, and muscle aches. Later symptoms include cough, chest discomfort, shortness of breath, tiredness, and muscle aches. (Caution: Do not assume that just because a person has cold or flu symptoms that he or she has inhalation anthrax.)

How soon do infected people get sick?

Symptoms can appear within seven days of coming in contact with the bacterium for all three types of anthrax. For inhalation anthrax, symptoms can appear within a week or can take up to 42 days to appear.

How is anthrax treated?

Antibiotics are used to treat all three types of anthrax. Early identification and treatment are important.

- *Prevention after exposure.* Treatment is different for a person who is exposed to anthrax but is not yet sick. Health-care providers use antibiotics (such as ciprofloxacin, doxycycline, or penicillin) combined with the anthrax vaccine to prevent anthrax infection.
- *Treatment after infection.* Treatment is usually a 60-day course of antibiotics. Success depends on the type of anthrax and how soon treatment begins.

Can anthrax be prevented?

There is a vaccine to prevent anthrax, but it is not yet available for the general public. Anyone who may be exposed to anthrax, including certain members of the U.S. armed forces, laboratory workers, and workers who may enter or reenter contaminated areas, may get the vaccine. Also, in the event of an attack using anthrax as a weapon, people exposed would get the vaccine.

What should I do if I think I have anthrax?

If you are showing symptoms of anthrax infection, call your health-care provider right away.

What should I do if I think I have been exposed to anthrax?

Contact local law enforcement immediately if you think that you may have been exposed to anthrax. This includes being exposed to a suspicious package or envelope that contains powder.

What is the CDC doing to prepare for a possible anthrax attack?

The CDC is working with state and local health authorities to prepare for an anthrax attack. Activities include

- Developing plans and procedures to respond to an attack using anthrax.
- Training and equipping emergency response teams to help state and local governments control infection, gather samples, and perform tests. Educating health-care providers, the media, and the general public about what to do in the event of an attack.
- Working closely with health departments, veterinarians, and laboratories to watch for suspected cases of anthrax. Developing a national electronic database to track potential cases of anthrax.
- Ensuring that there are enough safe laboratories for quickly testing suspected anthrax cases.
- Working with hospitals, laboratories, emergency response teams, and health-care providers to make sure they have the supplies they need in case of an attack.

A *radiation* threat, commonly referred to as a *dirty bomb* or *radiological dispersion device* (RDD), is the use of common explosives to spread radioactive materials over a targeted area. Radiological weapons are distinct from nuclear blasts. In a radiological attack, the force of the explosion and radioactive contamination is much more localized. Although the blast is immediately obvious, the presence of radiation is not be clearly defined until trained personnel with specialized equipment arrive and monitor environmental conditions. The radioactive material is harmful to those exposed and may be very difficult to remove or contain. The terror (fear) effect of a radiological attack, however, is expected to be more of a threat than the actual physical consequences that result.

RADIATION FACT SHEET

Frequently Asked Questions (FAQs) About a Radiation Emergency

What is radiation?
- Radiation is a form of energy present all around us.
- Different types of radiation exist, some of which have more energy than others.
- Amounts of radiation released into the environment are measured in units called *curies*. However, the dose of radiation that a person receives is measured in units called *rem*.

For more information about radiation, check the following Web sites: www.epa.gov/radiation, www.orau.gov/reacts/define.htm.

How can exposure occur?
- People are exposed to small amounts of radiation every day, both from naturally occurring sources (such as elements in the soil or cosmic rays from the sun), and human-made sources. Human-made sources include some electronic equipment (such as microwave ovens and television sets), medical sources (such as X-rays, certain diagnostic tests, and treatments), and from nuclear weapons testing.
- The amount of radiation from natural or human-made sources to which people are exposed usually is small; a radiation emergency (such as a nuclear power plant accident or a terrorist event) could expose people to small or large doses of radiation, depending on the situation.
- Scientists estimate that the average person in the United States receives a dose of about one third of a rem per year. About 80 percent of human exposure comes from natural sources and the remaining 20 percent comes from human-made radiation sources, mainly medical X-rays.
- *Internal exposure* refers to radioactive material that is taken into the body through breathing, eating, drinking, or injection for medical reasons.
- *External exposure* refers to an exposure to a radioactive source outside of our bodies.
- *Contamination* refers to particles of radioactive material that are deposited anywhere that they are not supposed to be, such as on an object or on a person's skin.

For more information about radiation, check the following Web sites: www.epa.gov/radiation, www.orau.gov/reacts/define.htm.

What happens when people are exposed to radiation?

- Radiation can affect the body in a number of ways, and the adverse health effects of exposure may not be apparent for many years.
- These adverse health effects can range from mild effects, such as skin reddening, to serious effects, such as cancer and death, depending on the amount of radiation absorbed by the body (the dose), the type of radiation, the route of exposure, and the length of time a person was exposed.
- Exposure to very large doses of radiation may cause death within a few days or months.
- Exposure to lower doses of radiation may lead to an increased risk of developing cancer or other adverse health effects later in life.

For more information about health effects from radiation exposure, check the following Web sites:

- www.epa.gov/radiation.
- www.orau.gov/reacts/injury.htm.
- www.bt.cdc.gov/radiation/healthfacts.asp.

What types of terrorist events might involve radiation?

- Possible terrorist events could involve introducing radioactive material into the food or water supply, using explosives (like dynamite) to scatter radioactive materials (a "dirty bomb"), bombing or destroying a nuclear facility, or exploding a small nuclear device.
- Although introducing radioactive material into the food or water supply most likely would cause great concern or fear, it probably would not cause much contamination or increase the danger of adverse health effects.
- Although a dirty bomb could cause serious injuries from the explosion, it most likely would not have enough radioactive material in a form that would cause serious radiation sickness among large numbers of people. However, people who were exposed to radiation scattered by the bomb could have a greater risk of developing cancer later in life, depending on their dose.
- A meltdown or explosion at a nuclear facility could cause a large amount of radioactive material to be released. People at the facility probably would be contaminated with radioactive material and possibly injured if there was an explosion. Those people who received a large dose might develop acute radiation syndrome. People in the surrounding area could be exposed or contaminated.
- Clearly, an exploded nuclear device could result in a lot of property damage. People would be killed or injured from the blast and might be contaminated by radioactive material. Many people could have symptoms of acute radiation syndrome. After a nuclear explosion, radioactive fallout would extend over a large region far from the point of impact, potentially increasing people's risk of developing cancer over time.

(Continued)

RADIATION FACT SHEET—Cont'd

For more information about radiation terrorist events, check the following Web sites:

- www.bt.cdc.gov/radiation/terrorismqa.asp.
- www.orau.gov/reacts.
- www.nrt.org.
- www.energy.gov.
- www.nrc.gov.
- www.epa.gov.

What preparations can I make for a radiation emergency?

- Each community should have a plan in place in case of a radiation emergency. Check with community leaders to learn more about the plan and possible evacuation routes.
- Check with a child's school, the nursing home of a family member, and one's employer to see what their plans are for dealing with a radiation emergency.
- Develop a family emergency plan so that every family member knows what to do.
- At home, put together an emergency kit that would be appropriate for any emergency. The kit should include the following items:
  - A flashlight with extra batteries.
  - A portable radio with extra batteries.
  - Bottled water.
  - Canned and packaged food.
  - A hand-operated can opener.
  - A first-aid kit and essential prescription medications.
  - Personal items such as paper towels, garbage bags, and toilet paper.

For more information about preparing for a radiation emergency event, check the following Web sites:

- ww.fema.gov.
- www.redcross.org/services/disaster/beprepared.
- www.epa.gov/swercepp/.
- www.ojp.usdoj.gov/bja.

How can I protect myself during a radiation emergency?

- After a release of radioactive materials, local authorities will monitor the levels of radiation and determine what protective actions to take.
- The most appropriate action depends on the situation. Tune to the local emergency response network or news station for information and instructions during any emergency.
- If a radiation emergency involves the release of large amounts of radioactive materials, people may be advised to "shelter in place," which means to stay in a home or office, or they may be advised to move to another location.
- If advised to shelter in place, do the following:
  - Close and lock all doors and windows.
  - Turn off fans, air conditioners, and forced-air heating units that bring in fresh air from the outside. Use units only to recirculate air that is already in the building.

- ○ Close fireplace dampers.
- ○ If possible, bring pets inside.
- ○ Move to an inner room or basement.
- ○ Keep a radio tuned to the emergency response network or local news to find out what else to do.
- • If advised to evacuate, follow the directions that local officials provide. Leave the area as quickly and orderly as possible. In addition,
  - ○ Take a flashlight, portable radio, batteries, first-aid kit, supply of sealed food and water, hand-operated can opener, essential medicines, and cash and credit cards.
  - ○ Take pets only if you are using a vehicle and going to a place that will accept animals. Emergency vehicles and shelters usually will not accept animals.

For more information about emergency response, check the following Web sites:

- • www.fema.gov.
- • www.redcross.org/services/disaster/beprepared.
- • www.epa.gov/swercepp.
- • www.ojp.usdoj.gov/bja.

Should I take potassium iodide during a radiation emergency?
- • Potassium iodide (KI) should be taken only in a radiation emergency that involves the release of radioactive iodine, such as an accident at a nuclear power plant or the explosion of a nuclear bomb. A "dirty bomb" most likely will not contain radioactive iodine.
- • A person who is internally exposed to radioactive iodine may experience thyroid disease later in life. The thyroid gland absorbs radioactive iodine and may develop cancer or abnormal growths later on. KI saturates the thyroid gland with iodine, decreasing the amount of harmful radioactive iodine that can be absorbed.
- • KI protects only the thyroid gland and does not provide protection from any other radiation exposure.
- • Some people are allergic to iodine and should not take KI. Check with your doctor about any concerns you have about potassium iodide.

For more information about KI, check the following Web sites:

- • www.bt.cdc.gov/radiation/ki.asp.
- • www.fda.gov/cder/drugprepare/KI_Q&A.htm.
- • www.fda.gov/cder/guidance/4825fnl.htm.

A *nuclear* blast is an explosion with intense light and heat, a damaging pressure wave, and widespread radioactive material that can contaminate the air, water, and ground surfaces for miles around. The detonation of a nuclear weapon involves the release of great amounts of destructive energy resulting from an intentional initiation of a chain fission or fusion nuclear reaction. A highly refined, weapons-grade nuclear fuel is required for a reaction of this kind. Although experts may predict at this time that a nuclear attack is less likely than other types, terrorism by its nature is unpredictable.

Sources: www.ready.gov, www.dhs.gov.

Critical Thinking

- What technological hazards affect your community? What are the sources of those hazards?
- Society accepts certain technological hazards because they enjoy the benefits associated with the action or process that causes the hazard. For instance, nuclear power plants produce inexpensive electricity with very little emissions. However, in the event of an accident, a major disaster could result. What benefits does your community enjoy despite the existence of associated technological hazards, and what are those hazards?

Risk Assessment

Most practitioners and academics refer to the term *risk assessment* as a process or methodology that can be used for evaluating risk. In this context, *risk* is defined as (1) the probability and frequency of a hazard occurring, (2) the level of exposure of people and property to the hazard, and (3) the effects or costs, both direct and indirect, of this exposure. There are various approaches to developing a risk assessment methodology, ranging from qualitative to quantitative, as well as several computer-based models for natural hazard risk assessment, currently in use in the United States and Japan.

The validity and use of any risk assessment is determined by the quality and availability of data. Because these two factors are still unknown and will not be determined until the in-country risk templates have been compiled, the determination of the most effective approach will not be made until the data have been collected and reviewed; however, a general discussion of the suggested approach will be undertaken.

As mentioned previously, various accepted methodologies could be applied. These include the risk matrix approach that is qualitative and designed to support risk management planning and decision making. The composite exposure indicator (CEI) approach is based on the effects of a single or multiple hazards on a series of indicator variables focused primarily on infrastructure, such as roads, pipelines, hospitals, and public water supply. The CEI is a measure of exposure of 14 variables to produce a number that is then correlated to the population affected. Numerous approaches result in vulnerability analyses that have been applied to earthquake and hurricane (coastal) hazards. The differences between these approaches often relate to *how* direct costs or *if* indirect costs are measured. Internal to the World Bank, several individuals have developed methodologies to assess environmental risks, health risks, and other hazards. Common to most of these methodologies is a series of essential elements or steps that must be undertaken. In general, these steps are as follows:

1. *Identify and characterize the hazard.* What are the characteristics of the hazard (e.g., high-velocity winds, ground shaking)? What causes the hazard event, and how does it trigger or relate to other hazards?
2. *Evaluate each hazard for the severity and frequency.* What is the probability of a hazard event happening annually, every 10 years, once a century? What factors enhance or deter the probabilities? What measurements or scales can be applied to determine severity? Could other factors influence severity and frequency (e.g., El Niño, global warming)?

3. *Estimate the risk*. Identify and quantify what will be affected by the hazard event. This step imposes the human and built environment that could be affected, damaged, or disrupted by a hazard event. Included in the analysis would be the general building stock (commercial and residential), inventories of lifelines, and essential, critical facilities. Population and development concentrations would be included.

4. *Determine the potential societal and economic (direct) effects and the indirect effects or costs*. In estimating direct economic losses, data that would be included are the cost of repair or replacement of damaged structures or lifelines, nonstructural damage, loss of contents and business inventory, and related loss of function costs. Agricultural (crop) losses figure prominently in this category. Other costs could be income loss, relocation costs, and rental losses that occur as a consequence of the event.

   Social costs are predominantly categorized as casualties, injuries, displaced households, and the cost of sheltering. Indirect effects and costs are more difficult to calculate and the data more difficult to obtain. Examples of indirect economic effects can include increase in unemployment, business interruption and loss of production, reduction in demand and consumer spending, and tax base losses. Indirect losses are more easily calculated at the local and regional levels because the information needed relative to population, employment, and tax base and the nature of the economy and businesses is more easily identified.

   The costs to federal, state, and local governments; individuals; and businesses of responding to disaster events often are not incorporated into the cost-effect equation, but in many cases these costs have a significant effect on agencies' budgets and should be considered.

   Two other steps should be included in looking at a risk assessment methodology:

5. *Determine the acceptable level of risk*. An analysis is undertaken of the information or data assembled in steps 1 to 4 to establish an acceptable level of risk. This means simply: What level of damage or impact will be tolerated? Societal effects and the less tangible, direct, and indirect costs make this evaluation a more difficult part of the process. Compounding this difficulty are the public perception of risk and the political consequences of taking or not taking action to address the risks.

6. *Identify risk-reduction opportunities*. This critical step takes the risk assessment methodology beyond process to decision making and action. At this point, cost-effective actions that reduce or mitigate unacceptable risks should be identified and implemented. A variety of structural and nonstructural alternatives can be combined with technology, legislation, and other solutions to design a risk-reduction implementation plan consistent with the degree of risks.

Technology

The nation's ability to identify hazards and quantify risk has significantly improved in the last 15 years. Technological advances refined the ability to identify and understand the nature of hazards and develop better risk assessment methods. Recent technological advances include the use of satellite imagery and radar to map ever-changing floodplains and areas of coastal erosions, the FEMA-developed HAZUS loss estimation model that provides us with loss estimates from various earthquake scenarios, and the technology that created safe rooms for homes in tornado-prone areas. The research and scientific agencies of the federal government and the university community continue to develop new approaches to measuring, mapping, and predicting natural hazards. With the reality of September 11, technology is focusing on new methods to detect, prevent, or provide an antidote for the various biological and chemical agents that could be used in a terrorist event.

Social and Economic Risk Factors

It has long been known that a strong correlation exists between disasters and poverty. Because of several factors, including the inability to afford preparedness and mitigation measures, the lower rental and purchase costs associated with of high-risk land, and a general lack of knowledge concerning risk and its sources, the poor are more vulnerable to disasters and therefore find themselves repeatedly subject to them. While this fact is much more apparent in the developing countries, where the bulk of annual disaster deaths occur, risk factors based on poverty and social conditions also exist within countries.

In the United States, little has been done to address the social and economic factors of risk that make one group more vulnerable than another. Risk assessments generally consider populations to be homogeneous for risk planning purposes, thereby neglecting to address individual problems of certain social and economic groups that may not benefit as much or at all from the plans and capacities developed. Social advocacy groups have been working for years to raise awareness the increased disaster vulnerability of "special populations" (which include, among others, the disabled, the elderly, the poor, children, and immigrants) with mixed success. However, Hurricane Katrina brought the reality of the socioeconomic vulnerability divide into every living room in the country via the mass media. Numerous social and political groups contend that poverty was what caused Katrina's high number of victims and the poor shouldered an undue portion of the region's risk while the wealthy escaped relatively unharmed (a claim that later was refuted). Others called it a race disaster, claiming that the government neglected to bring about a more significant immediate response because a majority of the victims were African American. Regardless of the validity of these claims, it is clear that the majority of the people who failed to evacuate from New Orleans did so because they had no access to transportation, were afraid to leave their meager possessions behind, or had no resources with which to shelter themselves away from the risk zone. And in the aftermath of this disaster, it has become painfully apparent that these same social and economic risk factors further hamper the poorer victims as they attempt recovery. A study conducted by Columbia University one year after the hurricane found that the poorest victims continue to suffer from significant income loss, a higher than normal incidence of chronic illnesses, and a proportionally higher rate of mental health problems in children.

The social makeup of a population is based on a diverse set of factors that includes education, culture, local government, social interaction, values, laws, beliefs, and other aspects of society. Within most communities, the vulnerability of different groups varies due to a range of sociocultural factors that help or prevent individuals from being able to protect themselves from disasters. The prevalence of epidemics, in particular, are heavily influenced by the social factors that vary from one country to another. Certain religious, cultural, or traditional practices and beliefs can help or hinder disaster management practices. Although it may not be evident to the people practicing such behavior, their practices may have been a product of adjustment to a hazard. Disaster managers must be able to recognize when social interactions are helping or hindering people in reducing their vulnerability to hazards and must recognize what aspect of that social process cause the alteration. Examples of factors that disaster managers must consider when examining social vulnerability include

- Religion.
- Age.
- Gender.
- Literacy.
- Health.
- Politics.
- Security.
- Human rights.
- Government and governance (including social services).
- Social equality and equity.
- Traditional values.
- Customs.
- Culture.

Financial status also deeply affects a population's and individuals' abilities to protect themselves from the consequences of disaster. Financial well-being, however, does not indicate that they *will* protect themselves; rather, it is just a measure of their ability to do so. Other factors may be learned from this economic profile. Trends and tendencies associated with wealth, or the lack thereof, can be deduced. For instance, the poor are often marginalized and forced to live on more dangerous land. Their housing is more likely to be constructed of materials that are unable to withstand environmental pressures. They are more likely to have zero tolerance to delays in basic necessities that often follow disasters. Factors involved in the economic profile that affect vulnerability include

- Debt.
- Access to credit.
- Insurance coverage.
- Sources of income.
- Funds reserved for disasters.
- Social distribution of wealth.
- Business continuity planning.

When considering the definition of a disaster and the concept of vulnerability, it is easy to understand why the poor are more vulnerable. Because an event becomes a disaster only when the capacity to respond to the event is exceeded, requiring external assistance to manage the consequences, the poor—who survive on the brink of disaster each day—are much quicker to exhaust their resources when unforeseen events arise.

Critical Thinking

- Select a hazard that affects you or your community. Describe the characteristics of the hazard (with what mechanisms would affect you or the community, including strong winds, ground shaking, etc.). Assess the risk associated with this hazard for you or your community, including the frequency of the hazard affecting you and the consequences if a disaster were to occur.
- What aspects of a community's geographic profile influence the hazards they face (e.g., proximity to a coast, slope of terrain)? What human practices influence these hazards (e.g., damming of rivers, filling in wetlands)? What natural processes influence these hazards (e.g., annual rainfall, temperature)?

Conclusion

In the process by which hazard risks are managed, often called *hazards risk management*, the identification of hazards is the key factor that determines what preparative and preventive measures will be taken by the community. In other words, a community needs to know its risks to manage them.

Through monitoring hazards, emergencies, and disaster throughout the world and research conducted into the mechanism by which natural, technological, and intentional hazards operate, a greater understanding of risk is being achieved. Without this valuable information that is collected, societies would be much less able to manage the consequences of the low-incidence, high-catastrophe events, such as tsunamis or weapons of mass destruction, which traditionally have gone unaddressed or addressed in a haphazard manner. In sum, information is power, and with information about hazards, societies have the power to act effectively to reduce or eliminate their risk.

Of course, with increased knowledge comes increased responsibility. The provision of hazard information and management tools to states and communities is but one necessary step in the risk reduction process. Success of these efforts requires that those states and communities assume responsibility and take appropriate action. Emergency management provides the impetus for incorporating these considerations into the planning and governing of our communities.

Hazards will persist. Some, particularly technological hazards, may be reduced by our efforts, but our ability to control or eliminate natural hazards is questionable. Recent efforts to undo some of the former channelization and flood control projects undertaken by the U.S. Army Corps of Engineers, once thought to be an effective measure to eliminate flood risk, are vivid examples of our inability to control nature. However, there is still a strong argument for an increased emphasis on improved science in hazard identification and increased financial support for hazards mapping, both of which have been effective components in community hazards risk management efforts.

As our knowledge about hazards continues to expand, the economic and social logic of applying long-term solutions for reducing the risks posed by these hazards through mitigation and preparedness gain momentum. The cost-to-benefit ratios of mitigation and preparedness efforts will become more attractive to local political bodies, and eventually, disaster losses will begin to fall substantially. However, all of these local successes are wholly dependent on the leadership potential and motivational abilities of an emergency management professional, who will be the driving force behind any such positive momentum that exists.

IMPORTANT TERMS

- Risk
- Disaster
- Natural hazard
- Technological hazard
- Flood
- Earthquake
- Hurricane
- Tropical storm
- Tropical cyclone
- Storm surge
- Tornado
- Safe room
- Wildland fire or wildfire
- Landslide
- Mudflow
- Lateral spread
- Fall
- Tsunami
- Volcano
- Severe winter storm
- Blizzard
- Drought
- Extreme heat
- Coastal erosion
- Thunderstorm
- Hailstorm
- Avalanche
- Subsidence
- Expansive soil
- Dam failure
- Hazardous materials
- Terrorism
- Weapon of mass destruction
- Risk assessment

Self-Check Questions

1. How is a hazard different than a disaster?
2. What is the most frequent and widespread disaster-causing hazard?
3. What scale is commonly used to describe the effects of earthquakes?
4. How are earthquakes measured?
5. Describe the process by which hurricanes form.
6. What scale is used to describe the intensity of hurricanes?
7. What are the various ways that hurricanes cause damages to a community?
8. What is a SLOSH model used to measure?
9. Why was the Fujita-Pearson tornado scale updated in 2006, and what changes were made?
10. What are the three categories of wildland fires?
11. How are severe weather storms measured?
12. What single disaster type caused 9 of the top 10 natural disasters ranked by FEMA relief costs?
13. What is the source of most hazardous materials incidents?
14. List and describe four categories of weapons of mass destruction.

15. What six steps are common to most risk assessment methodologies?

16. Name several of the social factors emergency managers must consider when assessing a community's risk.

17. What are some of the factors that make up a community's economic profile? How do these factors influence that community's disaster risk?

Out of Class Exercise   Visit FEMA's disaster declaration archive (http://www.fema. gov/news/disaster_totals_annual.fema). View the disaster declarations for your state. Beginning with 1998 and moving forward to the present time, view the disaster declarations to determine what disasters affected your county. What hazards affected your county during this time? How many times did each occur? If possible, determine what assistance the federal government provided in response to the disaster.

3

The Disciplines of Emergency Management: Mitigation

What You Will Learn

- The variety of mitigation tools available to planners.
- Impediments to mitigation and other associated problems.
- Federal and nonfederal mitigation programs.
- Mitigation methods in practice.

Introduction

Disasters are a reality of living in the natural world. Despite humans' attempts to control nature, dating back to the early Egyptians and continuing to this century's massive flood control efforts, natural hazards continue.

Over the last decade, the social and economic costs of disasters to the United States and throughout the world have grown significantly. From the period 1990 to 1999, FEMA spent more than $25.4 billion to provide disaster assistance in the United States. During the 1990s, the economic toll of natural disasters topped $608 billion worldwide, more than the previous four decades combined. The causes of this growth are myriad. Climatological changes such as El Niño, global warming, and sea level rise are one factor. Add to these changes the effects of societal actions such as increased development, deforestation and clear-cutting, migration of population to coastal areas, and filling in of floodplains and a recipe for disaster results.

The discipline of mitigation provides the means for reducing these impacts. *Mitigation* is defined as a sustained action to reduce or eliminate risk to people and property from hazards and their effects. This discussion of mitigation focuses on natural hazards mitigation efforts and programs in the United States. Techniques for mitigation of technological hazards are referenced, but the body of knowledge and applications in this area are still evolving; however, many of the successful natural hazards techniques such as building codes have applicability to technological hazards.

The function of mitigation differs from the other emergency management disciplines because it looks at long-term solutions to reducing risk as opposed to preparedness for hazards, the immediate response to a hazard, or the short-term recovery from a hazard event. Mitigation usually is not considered part of the emergency phase of a disaster as in response or part of emergency planning, as in preparedness. The definition lines get a little blurred regarding recovery. As discussed in Chapter 5, applying mitigation strategies should be a part of recovery from disaster; however, even in this context, these are actions that reduce the impacts, or risks, over time.

The recovery function of emergency management still represents one of the best opportunities for mitigation, and until recently, this phase in a disaster plan provided the most substantial funding for mitigation activities. Recently, there has been a trend toward greater federal spending on predisaster mitigation, which is discussed later in this chapter.

Another difference sets mitigation apart from the other disciplines of emergency management. Implementing mitigation programs and activities requires the participation and support of a broad spectrum of players outside of the traditional emergency management circle. Mitigation involves, among others, land-use planners, construction and building officials (both public and private), business owners, insurance companies, community leaders, and politicians.

The skills and tools for accomplishing mitigation (i.e., planning expertise, political acumen, marketing and public relations, and consensus building) are different from the operational, first responder skills that more often characterize emergency management professionals. In fact, historically, emergency management professionals have been reluctant to take a lead role in promoting mitigation. A state director of emergency management once said words to the effect: "I will never lose my job for failing to do mitigation, but I could lose my job if I mess up a response."

With the exception of the fire community, who were early leaders in the effort to mitigate fire risks through support for building codes, code enforcement, and public education, the emergency management community has remained focused on response and recovery obligations; however, this trend is changing for several reasons. Leadership at the federal level, larger disasters, substantial increases in funding, and more value and professionalism in emergency management have resulted in greater acknowledgment of the importance of mitigation.

This chapter discusses the tools of mitigation, the impediments to mitigation, federal programs that support mitigation, and several case studies that demonstrate how these tools have been applied to successfully reduce various risks.

Tools for Mitigation

Over the years, the United States has made great strides in reducing the number of deaths that occur in natural disasters. Through building codes, warning systems, and public education, the number of deaths and casualties from natural disasters in the last century has declined significantly; however, the economic effects and property damages have escalated. Many people believe that these costs are preventable and the tools exist to dramatically reduce these costs.

Technological disasters such as the Oklahoma City bombing and the terrorist attacks of September 11, 2001, are not as easy to analyze. There is much speculation about how improved intelligence and security could reduce the human effects of these disasters. From a property perspective, many people believe that some reduction in impacts could be achieved through application of traditional mitigation techniques such as improved building construction for blast effects. Other technological disasters such as the Valdez oil spill and the Three Mile Island emergency could have been prevented through better inspections, training, education, and exercises. These measures reflect good preparedness activities more than mitigation. In any case, further research and analyses are needed to answer the questions posed by the effects of terrorist events and similar technological hazards.

Most practitioners agree that the primary intent of mitigation is to ensure that fewer communities and individuals become victims of disasters. The goal of mitigation is to create economically secure, socially stable, better built, and more environmentally sound communities that are out of harm's way.

The following widely accepted mitigation tools are used to reduce risk:

- Hazard identification and mapping.
- Design and construction applications.
- Land-use planning.
- Financial incentives.
- Insurance.
- Structural controls.

Hazard Identification and Mapping

This is the most obvious tool for mitigation. You cannot mitigate a hazard if you do not know what it is or whom it affects. The most essential part of any mitigation strategy or plan is an analysis of what the hazards are in a particular area. The resources for hazards identification are numerous. The federal government has extensive programs that map virtually every hazard, and these products are available to communities. FEMA's National Flood Insurance Program (NFIP) provides detailed flood maps and studies, and the U.S. Geological Survey (USGS) provides extensive earthquake and landslide studies and maps. Many state agencies have refined the products for hazard identification. For example, special soil stability studies and geological investigations, which are required in some parts of California, further refine this analysis.

Geographic information systems (GIS) have become ubiquitous and staples for all local planning organizations. What is often missing from the available tools is the ability to superimpose the human and built environment onto the hazards, thereby providing a quantified level of risk. FEMA developed one such tool, called HAZUS, a nationally applicable methodology for estimating losses from earthquakes at the community or regional level. FEMA currently is expanding HAZUS to cover hurricane or wind losses and floods.

Design and Construction Applications

The design and construction process provides one of the most cost-effective means of addressing risk. This process is governed by building codes, architecture and design criteria, and soils and landscaping considerations. Code criteria that support risk reduction usually apply only to new construction, substantial renovation, or renovation to change the type or use of the building. Enactment of building codes are the responsibility of the states, and most state codes are derivatives of one of the three model codes, which reflect geographical differences across the United States. Some states delegate code adoption responsibility to more local government authorities. Because of cost, codes that require rehabilitation of existing potentially hazardous structures rarely have been implemented. The Los Angeles seismic retrofit ordinance is a rare example. The case study of the Virgin Islands at the end of this chapter illustrates the importance of building codes to mitigation.

The construction process offers other opportunities. For example, using fire-retardant building materials such as slate instead of wood for roofing is important in areas of wildland/urban interface such as Oakland, California. Constructing houses on pilings allows for uninterrupted flow of high-velocity waves in coastal areas.

Landscaping is particularly critical in areas of potential wildfires because vegetation close to structures can become fuel for a fire. Clearing, grading, and siting all have potential impacts to soil stability and erosion and can be included as part of a design or building permit review process.

The federal government made a significant investment in developing technical guidance for improving the building and construction of structures in hazard areas, particularly earthquake-, wind-, and flood-prone areas. There has been some discussion of developing a national code to support mitigation efforts. Because the constitutional responsibility for public health and safety resides with the states, a national code developed by the federal government is not politically feasible or practical.

Land-use Planning

Mitigation programs are most successful when undertaken at the local level, where most decisions about development are made. The strategies for land-use planning offer many options for effecting mitigation, including acquisition, easements, storm water management, annexation, environmental review, and floodplain management plans. It also encompasses a myriad of zoning options such as density controls, special uses permits, historic preservation, coastal zone management, and subdivision controls.

Land-use planning was one of the earliest tools used to encourage mitigation. In 1968, Congress passed the National Flood Insurance Act that established the NFIP. This act required local governments to pass a floodplain management ordinance in return for federally backed, low-cost flood insurance being available to the community. This act started one of the largest federal mapping efforts because the government promised local governments that it would provide them the technical tools to determine where the floodplains were in their communities, so they could steer development away from these areas. A more complete discussion of the NFIP can be found later in this chapter.

Moving structures out of harm's way through property acquisition is clearly the most effective land-use planning tool, but it is also the most costly. Following the Midwest floods of 1993, FEMA worked with Congress to make property acquisition more feasible by providing a substantial increase in funding for acquisition after a disaster. The case study on Missouri at the end of this chapter provides documentation on how well an acquisition strategy can work.

There are many other examples of how land-use planning and ordinances can promote risk reduction. The North Carolina coastal setback ordinance seeks to preserve the fragile and eroding coastlines of its barrier islands. The Alquist-Priola Act in California limits development near known earthquake faults.

Financial Incentives

This is one of the emerging areas for promoting mitigation. Among the approaches being used by localities to reduce risk are creation of special tax assessments, passage of tax increases or bonds to pay for mitigation, relocation assistance, and targeting of federal community development or renewal grant funds for mitigation.

The economic effects of repetitive flooding led the citizens of Napa, California, and Tulsa, Oklahoma, to pass small tax increases to pay for flood-mitigation activities. In both cases, the tax had minimal effect on the community citizens but a major effect in reducing the potential economic losses from future floods. Berkeley, California, has passed more than 10 bond issues to support seismic retrofit of public buildings, schools, and private residences.

Funding from the Community Development Block Grant (CDBG), a HUD program, has been used extensively to support local efforts at property acquisition and relocation. These funds have been used to meet the nonfederal match on other federal funding, which has often been a stumbling block to local mitigation. Other federal programs of the Small Business Administration (SBA) and the Economic Development Administration provide financial incentives for mitigation.

Other emerging areas of financial tools include special assessment districts, impact fees, and transfer of development rights. All these tools provide either incentives or penalties to developers as a means of promoting good risk-reduction development practices.

Insurance

Some people would argue with the inclusion of insurance as a mitigation tool. Their reasoning is that insurance by itself really provides only a transfer of the risk from the individual or community to the insurance company. Although this is true, the NFIP is the prime example of how, if properly designed, the insurance mechanism can be a tool for mitigation. The NFIP is considered to be one of the most successful mitigation programs ever created.

The NFIP was created by Congress in response to the damages from multiple, severe hurricanes and inland flooding and the rising costs of disaster assistance after these floods. At that time, flood insurance was not readily available or affordable through the private insurance market. Because many of the people being affected by this flooding were low-income residents, Congress agreed to subsidize the cost of the insurance so the premiums would be affordable. The idea was to reduce the costs to the government of disaster assistance through insurance. The designers of this program, with great insight, thought the government should get something for its subsidy. So in exchange for the low-cost insurance, they required that communities pass an ordinance directing future development away from the floodplain.

The NFIP was designed as a voluntary program and, as such, did not prosper during its early years, even though flooding disaster continued. Then in 1973, after Hurricane Agnes, the legislation was modified significantly. The purchase of federal flood insurance became mandatory on all federally backed loans. In other words, anyone buying a property with a Veterans Administration (VA) or Federal Housing Administration (FHA) loan had to purchase the insurance. Citizen pressure to buy the insurance caused communities to pass ordinances and join the NFIP. The NFIP helped the communities by providing them with a variety of flood hazard maps to define their flood boundaries and set insurance rates.

The 1993 Midwest floods triggered another major reform to the NFIP. This act strengthened the compliance procedures. It told communities that, if they did not join the program, they would be eligible for disaster assistance only one time. Any further request would be denied. As a positive incentive, the act established a Flood Mitigation Assistance (FMA) fund for flood planning, flood mitigation grants, and additional policy coverage for meeting the tougher compliance requirements such as building elevation.

Over the years, the NFIP has created other incentive programs such as the Community Rating System. This program rewards those communities that go beyond the minimum floodplain ordinance requirements with reduced insurance premiums. The NFIP represents one of the best public/private partnerships. Through the Write Your Own Program, private insurers are given incentives to market and sell flood insurance.

Today, more than 20,000 communities in the NFIP have mitigation programs in place. Other attempts have been made to duplicate this program for wind and earthquake hazards, but these have not received the support necessary to pass in the Congress. If another major earthquake occurs, the issue of creating a federally supported earthquake or all-hazards insurance will resurface.

Major disasters commonly instigate changes within the national and international private insurance industries, as firms attempt to adjust operations such that they are able to continue profitable operations according to newly acquired hazard information. Industry changes resulting from the September 11 terrorist events, which focused solely on damages caused by a perceived "long-shot" subsequent terrorism incident, focused on the availability of specialized terrorism insurance (and affected mainly a business clientele). However, Hurricane Katrina, which ranked as the costliest U.S. disaster, with between $40 to $55 billion in insured losses, resulted in new changes whose impacts are just beginning to be understood and which are expected to profoundly affect the ever-growing coastal populations that depend on insurance coverage for financial security.

The insurance industry was lambasted during the recovery from Hurricane Katrina, when it was reported that victims often faced long delays in receiving their insurance checks or, worse yet, were informed that their insurance coverage did not apply to the type of damage that was caused by the hurricane (many victims found themselves without coverage when it was determined that their damages were not caused by wind, which was covered in their policies, but rather by the excluded storm surge hazard). Class action lawsuits brought about some recourse for many of these Gulf Coast victims but in turn caused the insurance industry to reconsider whether risk assessments of coastal areas are still valid if insurers are being mandated to pay damages on events their original calculations did not consider. As a result, the insurance industry has steadily withdrawn its coverage from many Gulf Coast areas and coastal areas as far away as Connecticut, Rhode Island, and Massachusetts, claiming that new conditions brought about by the lawsuits would require them to raise premiums to unaffordable levels. State Farm Insurance, the nation's largest residential insurer and one of the largest companies operating on the Gulf Coast (which paid over $1 billion in claims in Mississippi alone following Katrina), refused to renew policies that cover homes within 1,000 feet of the water. Allstate Insurance company canceled or refused renewed coverage in a dozen coastal states.

However, residents in coastal areas are not the only people who will feel the ramifications from such costly megaevents. Industry experts predict that policy premiums will rise, even if slightly, in all "catastrophe-prone" areas regardless of risk level, to ensure ample backing of all policies within the risk pool. In Louisiana, the state Insurance Rating Commission approved premium rate increases of over 23 percent in some cases. Many may even find it difficult to acquire insurance as companies pull out of these areas in favor of low risk, "safe" markets (where policies may even decrease due to competition for low-risk policies). Those living in areas where no company will provide coverage traditionally have been able to find policies under state-provided "pools," such as the Mississippi Wind Pool. However, even those resources are experiencing rate hikes over 250 percent. With no insurance options, many people in these affected areas are choosing to rebuild elsewhere, in places where they are able to better protect themselves.

Some states are in the early stages of developing a hurricane insurance program they hope will expand nationally like the National Flood Insurance Program. Florida was the first to approve a measure that would lower insurance premiums by pledging up to $32 billion of state money to back insurers of homeowners whose houses have been damaged or destroyed by a hurricane. The money for this "state catastrophic fund," they determined, will come from increased taxes on houses, automobiles, and on other types of insurance policies sold in Florida. Florida state officials, recognizing that, unlike floods, not all states are affected by hurricanes, appealed to their neighbor states who share similar risk to join the program and make it more effective in the event of a future event as destructive as Katrina.

Structural Controls

Structural controls are controversial as a mitigation tool. Structural controls usually have been used to protect existing development. In doing so, they can have both positive and negative effects on the areas they are not protecting. In addition, as the name implies, they are used to control the hazard, not reduce it. Invariably, as was seen so graphically in the Midwest floods, the structures lose control and nature wins; however, in some circumstances, structural controls are the only alternative.

The most common form of structural control is the levee. The U.S. Army Corps of Engineers designed and built levees as flood control structures across the United States. Levees are part of the aging infrastructure of America. As mitigation tools, they have obvious limitations. They can be overtopped or breached, as in the 1993 Midwest floods; they give residents a false sense of safety that often promotes increased development; and they can exacerbate the hazard in other locations. After the 1993 floods, a major rethinking of dependency on levees occurred. Efforts are being made to acquire structures built behind the levees, new design criteria are being considered, and other more wetland-friendly policies are being adopted. For a city like New Orleans, however, which is built below sea level and where relocation is impractical, levees can be used effectively to protect flood-prone areas.

Other structural controls are intended to protect along coastal areas. Seawalls, bulkheads, breakwaters, groins, and jetties are intended to stabilize the beach or reduce the impacts of wave action. These structures are equally controversial because they protect in one place and increase the damage in another. The shore of New Jersey is a prime example of the failure of seawalls as a solution to shoreline erosion problems. Cape May, New Jersey, where cars used to be raced on the beach, lost all of its beachfront. An ongoing beach replenishment project is the only thing that has brought some of it back.

Critical Thinking

- What mitigation measures are best suited to address the hazards you face as an individual?
- What mitigation measures are best suited to address the hazards faced by your community?
- Do you feel that more should be done to address your community's hazards? If so, what could or should be done?

Impediments to Mitigation

If so many tools can be applied, why have risk-reduction and mitigation programs not been more widely applied? There are several factors, including denial of the risk, political will, costs and lack of funding, and the taking issue. Despite the best technical knowledge, historic occurrence, public education, and media attention, many individuals do not want to recognize that they or their communities are vulnerable. Recognition requires action and it could have economic consequences as businesses decide to locate elsewhere if they find the community is at risk. Some people are willing to try to beat the odds, but if a disaster strikes, they know the government will help them out. Gradually, attitudes are changing. Potential liability issues are making communities more aware, media attention to disasters has brought public pressure, and the government has provided both incentives for, and penalties for not, taking action.

As previously mentioned, mitigation provides a long-term benefit. The U.S. political system tends to focus on short-term rewards. Developers are large players in the political process and often are concerned that mitigation means additional costs. Mitigation strategies and actions require political vision and will. As Tip O'Neill, former speaker of the U.S. House of Representatives, said, "All politics is local." Well, so is mitigation. Local elected officials are the individuals who have to promote, market, and endorse adopting risk reduction as a goal. For many elected officials, the development pressures are too much, funding is lacking, and other priorities dominate their agendas; however, with the increasing attention to the economic, social, and political costs of not dealing with their risks, more elected officials are recognizing that they cannot afford to *not* take action.

Mitigation costs money. Most mitigation of new structures or development can be passed on to the builder or buyer without much notice. Programs to retrofit existing structures or acquisition and relocation projects are expensive and almost always beyond the capacity of the local government. Funding for mitigation comes primarily from federal programs that need to be matched with state or local dollars. As state and local budgets constrict, their ability to match is reduced. Strong arguments can be made that it is in the best financial interest of the federal government to support mitigation. These arguments and a series of large disasters resulted in substantial increases in federal funding, including new monies for predisaster mitigation, but the fact remains that mitigation needs far outweigh mitigation funding.

Many mitigation actions involve privately owned property. A major legal issue surrounding this is the taking issue. The Fifth Amendment to the U.S. Constitution prohibits the taking of property without just compensation. What constitutes a taking, under what circumstances, and what is just compensation have been the focus of numerous legal cases. Several have dealt with the use of property in the floodplain and the use of oceanfront property on a barrier island. The decisions have been mixed, and taking will continue to be an issue in implementing mitigation programs and policies.

Counterproductive Mitigation Measures

Mitigation measures function by decreasing either the consequence or the likelihood factors of hazards. However, they are rarely able to fully eliminate the hazard's risk. If a hazard event is so large as to overwhelm the mitigation measures implemented, then the resulting disaster can strike with even greater consequences than if no mitigation measure were built in the first place. The primary reason why this phenomenon occurs is that people develop a false or inaccurate sense of security from specific hazards that they would not normally enjoy in the mitigation measure's absence. The classic example is that of the levee.

Before levees are built, the flood stage for a river is essentially the elevation of its banks. Once the river level exceeds that elevation, homes in the floodplain are flooded. With the introduction of levees, the flood level is increased more and more with each foot that the levee is raised above the elevation of the original river banks. This is accompanied by a decrease in likelihood of flooding caused by more routine flooding events, such as the 1 year (100 percent likelihood in a given year) to 100 year (1 percent likelihood in a given year) floods. However, levees have their limits and are designed and built to withstand only a maximum flood height, beyond which their effectiveness falls to zero (due to overtopping and breaching). Unfortunately, despite the continued flood risk, the decreased likelihood often generates increased development behind the levees due to a sense of absolute security. The result of this phenomenon is that, when a major flood occurs and the levees are overwhelmed, a greater number of victims lie in its path than would have had the mitigation measure never been built in the first place.

Other mitigation measures can have the same effect. Buildings have been constructed to be fireproof, or earthquake proof, only to topple in events stronger than anticipated. Unsinkable ships have been overloaded and sunk. Oceanfront developments are regularly washed away in hurricanes and other storms despite elaborate seawalls. And homes built deeper and deeper beyond the urban/wildland interface (where houses and the forest meet or mix) have led to costlier wildland fires each year despite the use of special building materials and landscaping practices. With these, and all mitigation measures, users and benefit recipients must be fully aware of their limits to prevent even greater disasters from resulting.

Federal Mitigation Programs

FEMA is responsible for most of the programs of the federal government that support mitigation; this section focuses on these programs. As noted earlier, the SBA, Economic

Development Administration (EDA), and HUD have policies that support mitigation. The PATH program at HUD supports incorporating mitigation into public housing. The Environmental Protection Agency (EPA) has several programs in floodplain management and, in 2002, initiated a pilot program for national watersheds. The National Earthquake Hazards Reduction Program, which is described in a following section, includes several other federal agencies; however, the predominant federal agency involved in disaster mitigation is FEMA. FEMA's programs include the NFIP (described earlier in the chapter), the Hazard Mitigation Grant Program (HMGP), the Pre-Disaster Mitigation (PDM) Program, the National Earthquake Hazard Reduction Program (NEHRP), the National Hurricane Program, the National Dam Safety Program, and the Fire Prevention and Assistance Grant Program.

In 2000, Congress passed the Disaster Mitigation Act of 2000 (DMA2000). DMA2000 amended the Robert T. Stafford Disaster Relief and Emergency Assistance Act in an effort to encourage mitigation planning at the state and local levels, requiring that states maintain mitigation plans as a prerequisite for certain federal mitigation funding and disaster assistance programs. The program also provided incentives to states that could show increased coordination and integration of mitigation activities by establishing two different levels of state plan certification: "standard" and "enhanced." States that demonstrated what was considered "an increased commitment to comprehensive mitigation planning" through the development of an approved enhanced state plan could increase the amount of funding they received through the Hazard Mitigation Grant Program, described next. DMA2000 also established a new requirement for local mitigation plans and authorized up to 7 percent of HMGP funds available to a state to be used for development of state, tribal, and local mitigation plans.

The Hazard Mitigation Grant Program

HMGP is the largest source of funding for state and local mitigation activities. This program provides grants to state and local governments to implement long-term hazard mitigation programs after a major disaster has been declared by the president. HMGP projects must reduce the risk, and the benefits of the project must exceed the costs.

Examples of activities supported by HMGP include the following:

- Acquisition of property on a voluntary basis and commitment to open use of the property.
- Retrofitting of structures and lifelines.
- Elevation of structures.
- Vegetation management programs.
- Building code enforcement.
- Localized flood-control projects.
- Public education and awareness.

This program was enacted by Congress in 1988 as part of the Robert T. Stafford Act, which was a major reworking of federal disaster policy. In addition to creating the HMGP, it established a cost sharing of disaster assistance by the states. At the time, the formula for state HMGP funding was 15 percent of the public assistance costs, and it had a 50 percent federal, 50 percent state cost share.

From the period 1988 to 1993, many states did not take advantage of the HMGP funding because it was difficult to meet the matching requirements, even though the 15 percent cap was often not very much. After the devastation of the 1993 Midwest floods, Congressman Volkmer from Missouri championed a change to the legislation that would significantly increase the states' ability to mitigate. Congress amended the legislation to allow for a 75 percent federal, 25 percent state match and dramatically increased the amount of funding to 15 percent of the total disaster costs. The rationale for these changes was to work aggressively to move people and structures out of the floodplain. As the Missouri case study at the end of this chapter documents, the rationale was sound.

HMGP allowed states to hire staff to work on mitigation and required development of a state Hazard Mitigation Plan as a condition of funding. This program brought about a change in the emergency management community at the state and local levels. With adequate funding, states and localities began to hire staff designated to work on mitigation.

HMGP has its detractors and, in 2002, the federal Office of Management and Budget (OMB) proposed that this program be eliminated in favor of a new predisaster competitive grant program. However, as of fiscal year 2007, this program still was available for disaster-stricken communities.

Pre-Disaster Mitigation Program

Through the Disaster Mitigation Act of 2000, Congress approved creation of a national Pre-Disaster Mitigation Program to provide mitigation funding not dependent on a disaster declaration. The genesis of PDM was an initiative of the Clinton administration called Project Impact: Building Disaster-Resistant Communities. Project Impact grew out of the devastating disasters of the 1990s. Many of the communities hit by these disasters took months and even years to recover emotionally and financially. James Lee Witt, then director of FEMA, questioned the wisdom of spending more than $2.5 billion per year on disaster relief and not a penny to reduce disasters before they happen. The mitigation tools and techniques were available, so why not work to prevent individuals and communities from becoming victims of disasters? With a small amount of seed money, FEMA launched Project Impact in 1997 in seven pilot communities.

The concept behind the initiative was simple. The mitigation activities had to be designed and tailored to the hazards in that community, and all sectors of the community had to become involved for it to be effective and sustainable. Project Impact brought the business community under the emergency management umbrella. Communities were asked to achieve the following four goals:

1. Build a community partnership.
2. Assess the risks.
3. Set priorities on risk-reduction actions.
4. Build support by communicating these actions.

By 2001, more than 200 communities were participating in Project Impact, and Congress had appropriated $25 million to the initiative. Seattle, Washington, was one of the original pilot communities. In 2002, when a 6.8 earthquake struck Seattle, the mayor attributed the success of the Project Impact activities for the minimal damages and prompt recovery. The Tulsa case study provides an example of a Project Impact community.

In 2002, the Bush administration decided to drop the Project Impact name and concept in exchange for a competitive grant program as its approach to PDM. The program's original budget request was $300 million, and it was proposed that PDM replace both Project Impact and the HMGP.

As designed, PDM is designed to provide "funds to states, territories, Indian tribal governments, communities, and universities for hazard mitigation planning and the implementation of mitigation projects prior to a disaster event." The program requires jurisdictions to submit applications for a competitive grant selection.

Since its inception, the amount of funding provided for the program has varied significantly from year to year. Fiscal year (FY) 2003 was the first year grants were awarded, with $150 million appropriated to fund the program's initiation and to cover $13.7 million in noncompetitive grants (awarded to all U.S. states and territories) and $131.5 million in competitive grants. These funding levels were continued through FY 2004, but increased in FY 2005 to $255 million. In FY 2006, PDM's appropriation decreased over 80 percent from FY 2005 to $50 million, its lowest level yet. Actual grant awards from FY 2006 totaled only $26 million, which represents an 88 percent drop from the previous year, presumably reflective of the federal government's continued focus on homeland security spending. However, in FY 2007, funding levels were increased twofold to $100 million (with a minimum of $500,000 reserved for each state), still far short of FY 2005 levels.

As of FY 2007, there are some changes to the program, including a significant eligibility requirement that local applicant communities maintain an approved FEMA Hazard Mitigation Plan in place as required by the Disaster Mitigation Act of 2000. Many of the original mechanisms remain the same, however, such as the 25 percent commitment that must be covered by the local applicant and that the state office of emergency management serve as grantee while local agencies apply to the state.

The National Earthquake Hazard Reduction Program

The National Earthquake Hazard Reduction Program is a federal government effort focused on reducing the risks to life and property from future earthquakes in the United States. Congress established the program in 1977 (Public Law 95–124) as a long-term, nationwide program to reduce the risks to life and property in the United States resulting from earthquakes. This is accomplished through the establishment and maintenance of an effective earthquake hazards reduction program.

The NEHRP works to improve understanding, characterization, and prediction of hazards and vulnerabilities; improve model building codes and land-use practices; reduce risk through postearthquake investigations and education; develop and improve design and construction techniques; improve mitigation capacity; and accelerate application of research results. The NEHRP provides funding to states to establish programs that promote public education and awareness, planning, loss estimation studies, and some minimal mitigation activities. FEMA also supports state and local governments by providing HAZUS, a computer risk modeling tool for communities to use for estimating potential losses from natural hazards.

The primary NEHRP program agencies are

- Federal Emergency Management Agency (FEMA).
- National Institute of Standards and Technology (NIST).
- National Science Foundation (NSF).
- United States Geological Survey (USGS).

Since NEHRP's inception, Congress has reviewed and reauthorized it every two or three years. Congress recently completed a thorough two-year review of NEHRP, resulting in enactment of the NEHRP Reauthorization Act of 2004 (P.L. 108–360), which the president signed into law on October 25, 2004. Public Law 108–360 designates NIST as the lead agency for NEHRP, transferring that responsibility from FEMA, which filled that role since the program's inception. The NIST director chairs the NEHRP Interagency Coordinating Committee, which comprises the directors of the primary program agencies, the White House Office of Science and Technology Policy (OSTP), and the Office of Management and Budget. In addition, the law assigns NIST significant new research and development responsibilities to close the research-to-implementation gap and accelerate the use of new earthquake risk mitigation technologies based on the earth sciences and engineering knowledge developed through NEHRP efforts.

The specific roles of each of the agencies within NEHRP are summarized:

- FEMA is responsible for emergency response and management, estimation of loss potential, and implementation of mitigation actions.
- NIST conducts applied earthquake engineering research to provide the technical basis for building codes, standards, and practices and provides the NEHRP lead agency function.
- NSF conducts basic research in seismology, earthquake engineering, and social, behavioral, and economic sciences and operates the Network for Earthquake Engineering Simulation (which includes the tsunami wave basin research facility and supporting tsunami research).
- USGS operates the seismic networks, develops seismic hazard maps, coordinates postearthquake investigations, and conducts applied earth sciences research (which includes tsunami research and risk assessment).
- NSF and USGS jointly support the Global Seismographic Network (GSN), the main facility for pinpointing earthquakes in real time.

The NEHRP Reauthorization Act of 2004 authorized $900 million to be spent during the period from 2004 to 2009. The law also authorizes the spending of $72.5 million, over a three-year period, for the creation of a National Windstorm Impact Reduction Program, which will be modeled according to the NEHRP model, to study the impact of wind-related hazards on structures and the mitigation of these consequences.

Source: Information from www.bfrl.nist.gov.

The National Hurricane Program

This FEMA program supports activities at the federal, state, and local levels that focus on the physical effects of hurricanes, improved response capabilities, and new mitigation techniques for the built environment. The program has done significant work in storm surge modeling and evacuation planning, design and construction of properties in hurricane-prone areas, and public education and awareness programs for schools and communities. The amount of funding that FEMA receives for this program is in the range of $3 million annually, which is clearly not commensurate with the risk.

The National Dam Safety Program

The National Dam Safety Program Act of 1996 formally established the National Dam Safety Program and named the director of FEMA as its coordinator. Initiatives under the act include funding to the states to establish and maintain dam safety programs, training for state dam safety staff and inspectors, technical and archival research in dam safety, education of the public in the hazards of dam failure and related matters, the establishment of the National Dam Safety Review Board, and support for the Interagency Committee on Dam Safety. This act, which is part of the Water Resources Development Act of 1996, expired in fiscal year 2002.

The Fire Prevention and Assistance Act

This program was created in 2001 to address the needs of the nation's paid and volunteer fire departments and to support prevention activities. Congress had longstanding concerns about status of this first responder community. New threats from potential biochemical terrorism, increasing wildfire requirements, and a stagnant search and rescue capability provided the rationale for funding this program. This multimillion-dollar grant program provides competitive grants to fire companies throughout the United States. In the wake of the September 11 events, the appropriations for this program tripled in 2002.

□ □ □ ▬▬▬▬▬▬▬▬▬▬▬▬▬▬▬▬▬▬▬▬▬▬▬▬▬▬▬

FEMA'S Assistance to Firefighters Grant Program

The purpose of the program is to award one-year grants directly to fire departments of a state to enhance their abilities with respect to fire and fire-related hazards. This program seeks to identify departments that lack the basic tools and resources necessary to protect the health and safety of the public and their firefighting personnel. The primary goal is to provide assistance to meet these needs. The program originally provided grants in four program areas, including fire operations and firefighter safety, fire prevention, firefighting vehicles, and emergency medical services (EMS). However, in FY 2004, emergency medical services activities were removed as an independent program area and incorporated into the appropriate activities under the Operations and Firefighter Safety Program activity.

Assistance to Firefighters Grant Program: FY 2002 Award Recipients
(through August 12, 2002)

Category	Number of Awards		Amount of Awards	
	2002	2003	2002	2003
Fire operations and firefighter safety	4,731	7,014	$281,091,066	$502,157,331
Fire prevention	215	294	$10,926,998	$14,070,509
Firefighting vehicles	315	1,374	$39,277,630	$185,113,255
Emergency medical services	53	68	$3,069,736	$4,547,325
Total	**5,314**	**8,753**	**$334,365,430**	**$705,888,420**

Source: http://www.firegrantsupport.com/af.

Critical Thinking

- Should mitigation funding from the federal government be tied to individual disasters, like it is with the Hazard Mitigation Grant Program, or should it be independent of disasters altogether, as it is with the Pre-Disaster Mitigation Program? Explain your answer.
- What are the advantages of having a hazard-specific grant program, such as the National Earthquake Hazard Reduction Program? Are there any disadvantages?

Nonfederal Mitigation Grant Programs

Virtually all mitigation funding in the United States comes from federally funded grant programs. Nongovernmental programs, whether private, nonprofit, or public, also provide the monetary, material, and technical assistance that individuals, businesses, and communities require to mitigate their hazard risks. The Institute for Business and Home Safety (IBHS), for example, creates guidance documents that illustrate various structural and nonstructural mitigation techniques. IBHS employees work with various entities, such as day care centers, to help them reduce hazard vulnerabilities. Another program administered by a public-private partnership in Florida, provides grant money to homeowners that wish to structurally mitigate their homes from storm damage. Rebuild Northwest Florida approves grants to qualified homeowners that help them improve the strength of their houses through such mitigation measures as creating secondary water barriers, improving roofing and roof decks, bracing gable ends, applying tie-down ("hurricane") straps, reinforcing wall-to-wall connections, and much more. The success of this particular program is already spawning similar programs throughout the state and, it is hoped, throughout the country.

Conclusion

Disasters occur in every state. The direct costs of these events are staggering, but the indirect effects to the economy and the social fabric of communities is even worse. Mitigation works. The case studies included in this chapter are just a few examples of successful, sustained programs that reduce risk and make communities safer. Mitigation programs exist at all levels of government, and there is a growing interest in the private sector for taking mitigation actions to reduce their risk exposure. To many people, even in a time when terrorism preoccupies the emergency management psyche, mitigation is—and should be—the future direction of emergency management.

CASE STUDY

Mitigating the Tornado Hazard in Kansas Schools

Wichita, Kansas, lies right in the heart of tornado alley—the area cutting across the center of the United States where tornadoes are most likely to strike. When strong tornadoes strike homes and buildings, the result almost always is disastrous. When they strike schools, where all the children of the community may be gathered at once, the physical and emotional loss can be confounded tenfold. On May 3, 1999, that is exactly what happened.

Luckily, when Chisholm Life Special Education School for teenagers to young adults and Greiffenstein Special Education Center were severely damaged by a pack of tornadoes, the schools were closed and no students were present. Although the county office of emergency management had conducted a hazard assessment in recognition of the tornado threat and identified areas of safe refuge within both structures, major damage occurred in several of these identified areas, where students surely would have congregated. The significance of these findings was not lost on community members, who recognized that they may not be as lucky the next time tornadoes strike.

Using all the information gathered in the postevent investigation relating to the schools, the state of Kansas used funding from several federal sources (including the Hazard Mitigation Grant Program and a supplemental appropriation from Congress) to identify and build additional protection measures for schoolchildren in the state. The Kansas Division of Emergency Management and the Kansas Hazard Mitigation Team decided to construct in-school tornado shelters with the funds and ensure that shelters be included in any new school construction or renovation project.

In Wichita, two safe room projects were initiated within the public school district, which by design will serve approximately 7,800 of the district's 9,000 students. The facilities also will protect many more community members, who use the facilities extensively for various activities including precinct voting, church worship services, and community outreach and recreation, such as the Boy Scouts and Girl Scouts. The structural mitigation components have been accompanied by associated processes and procedures, such as

- The creation of a shelter management team.
- The creation of shelter maintenance procedures and schedules.
- Shelter warning, training, and drill procedures and schedules.
- Weather monitoring.
- Shelter access inspections.
- The creation of shelter activation procedures, including head count, shelter security, in-shelter monitoring of weather, and stand-down procedures.

Sedgwick County Emergency Management continues to work closely with the Wichita Public School District to evaluate areas of refuge in the schools. Evaluators identify the schools' safest areas and make recommendations that instruct school administrators in the best methods for increasing occupant safety. Using this evaluation, the school district officials are able to determine the most appropriate and practical means of creating the shelter (which may include constructing an entirely new school, building an addition on to the existing structure, or retrofitting an identified area).

Today, all newly approved shelter construction carried out in the Wichita program meets the criteria presented in the FEMA publication *Design and Construction Guidance for Community Shelters.* In addition, all shelter construction projects are inspected by a trained team that assists in determining the best location for shelter areas, identifying areas that need improvement, and determining how to resolve any structural concerns.

Tulsa Safe Room Program

Tulsa, Oklahoma, lies in the heart of tornado alley. Tornadoes with major damage have hit Tulsa on an average of every four or five years. The May 3, 1999, tornadoes killed 44 people and decimated communities throughout Oklahoma. As a result of these storms, the president declared a major disaster. Oklahoma was provided the opportunity to take advantage of new construction technology to mitigate the effects of tornadoes. The concept of "safe room" construction was developed and pilot tested in 1998 by the Wind Engineering Research Center of Texas Tech University with financial support from FEMA. Safe rooms are anchored and armored rooms that provide shelter during tornadoes, even above ground. Tulsa proposed to FEMA that it use its HMGP funding provided through the president's declaration to provide grants to homeowners to build safe rooms in their homes (see Figure 3–1).

FIGURE 3–1 November 23, 2001, Tulsa, Oklahoma (disaster alley in the Eastland Mall). A safe room wall section is shown here. The insulated concrete form is cut away to show reinforcing steel. The cavity is filled with concrete. Photo by Kent Baxter/FEMA News Photo.

(Continued)

CASE STUDY—Cont'd

Under their Project Impact designation, Tulsa formed a coalition of partners, including FEMA, Oklahoma State Emergency Management, Home Builders of Greater Tulsa, Tulsa Public Works, State Farm Insurance, and other community partners. This coalition then agreed on building and construction standards, permitting, certification and compliance procedures, and public education and awareness programs. This coalition set as their goal to build a tornado safe room in every newly constructed and existing home by the year 2020. This program was supported through a variety of public and private funding, but the major key to its success was the partnership of the building and construction community (see Figure 3–2).

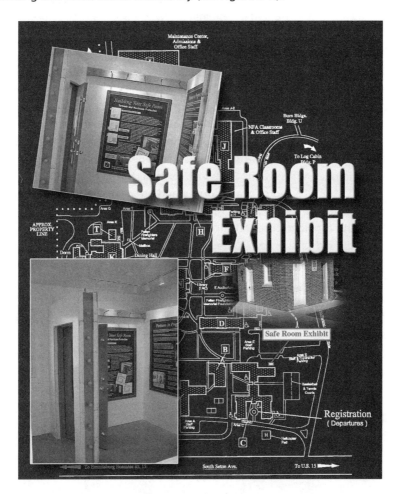

FIGURE 3–2 Exhibit of techniques for a tornado safe room. FEMA Photo.

Tulsa builders embraced the safe room concept and quickly made it a positive marketing tool for their business. The city continued to encourage growth of the program by providing certain financial incentives. Eleven major Tulsa builders launched the first safe room subdivision in a new upscale residential area of Tulsa. It is believed to be the first safe room subdivision in Oklahoma, and perhaps the first in the nation, financed entirely by private builders.

The program continues to expand not just within Tulsa and Oklahoma, but to other states and communities in tornado alley as well. Within Tulsa, wheelchair-accessible safe rooms have been designed and built. The next step is building safe rooms in public buildings and schools. The technology exists, but the societal questions of size, access, quantity of space, and related issues are still being worked on.

The Tulsa safe room project provides an excellent example of taking advantage of the opportunity afforded in the postdisaster climate. Its success provides an even better example of how building coalitions, particularly with the private sector, ensures sustainability of the mitigation program.

The Castaic Union School District

The Castaic Union School District, located in southern California, is a case study that demonstrates the threat from multiple hazards. After the 1994 Northridge earthquake, the Castaic Union School District conducted a study of the earthquake-related risks that threatened their elementary and middle schools and administration buildings. The assessment revealed that earthquake-related structural damage was not the only risk the school district faced.

The district maintained and operated 63 buildings (77,000 square feet of usable space) in northern Los Angeles County, which consisted of a mix of permanent and portable structures with construction dates as far back as 1917. These structures service approximately 1,200 students and 115 staff members. The San Andreas and San Gabriel fault systems, two of the most active faults in the country, pass through the area in which the district is located. In addition, the USGS has concluded that significant new earthquake activity may occur along both the San Andreas and San Gabriel systems.

These factors led the Castaic Union School District to conclude in its study that the probability of a large earthquake affecting the facilities was high. The district also learned, however, that the risk went well beyond possible damages caused by ground shaking. Along with the expected seismic damage, the study revealed two additional threats: flooding from the Castaic Dam and fire or explosion from a rupture in nearby oil pipelines.

The district's risk assessment study indicated that the school buildings were located within the inundation area of the Castaic Dam (located only 1.7 miles upstream). If the dam were to fail, the school buildings and their occupants would be inundated with catastrophic flooding. The 2,200-acre reservoir above the dam could release nearly 105 billion gallons of water, inundating the area below the dam with 50 feet of water. In 1992, the California Department of Water Resources (DWR) reexamined the seismic performance of the dam. Based on the analyses, the DWR considers the dam to meet all current safety requirements and to be able to resist failure caused by the maximum credible earthquake; however, the district's risk assessment concluded the probability the Castaic Dam will fail is never zero.

(Continued)

CASE STUDY—Cont'd

Along with the threat posed by the Castaic Dam, the study also revealed that the buildings were at high risk of damage from both fire and explosion if nearby pipelines failed. Two high-pressure crude oil pipelines currently cross the campus (a 1925 gas-welded pipeline and a 1964 modern arc-welded steel pipeline), both of which could rupture during ground shaking or ground displacement in earthquakes. An analysis of the lines and the fault conditions near the district indicated a 35 percent chance of failure somewhere in the Castaic area as a result of any large earthquake.

This information caused alarm about the safety of the district's facilities. In the event of a pipeline failure, a fire or explosion could result from the ignition of the released oil, putting both facilities and people at great risk. Additionally, the ability to prevent a nearby fire from spreading would be limited by the decreased reliability of water lines and hydrants, as well as the increased demands on emergency fire services after an earthquake.

Using the results of the district's risk analysis, it was determined that the potential economic costs from either a dam failure or oil pipeline break following an earthquake were enormous. The first potential cost to the school district would be incurred from both building and content damage. Replacement of the school buildings would cost an estimated $7.7 million. Second, if such an earthquake occurred, alternate school facilities would have to be located and rented at an estimated cost of more than $500,000 per year. Third, the community would have to absorb the costs of losing the educational services provided by the district in the time period between the actual loss of the facilities and the relocation to temporary facilities. The school district calculated the cost of the lost public services based on the operating expenses required to provide the services. The daily cost of lost educational services was estimated at $28,601.

In addition to these direct and indirect financial losses, the risk of earthquake-related casualties in the district's facilities was determined to be significant. In an earthquake-induced dam failure, the predicted speed of inundation on the campus caused the risk of casualties to be very high. When calculating this risk, a casualty rate of 250 individuals was determined based on the average hourly rate of campus usage in a typical week. In the event of a dam failure during school hours, the loss of life could be as high as 1,200 students and 115 faculty members. In an earthquake-induced potential pipeline failure, the district calculated a casualty rate of 9 individuals and injury rate of 45 individuals. Once again, the actual number of casualties increases dramatically if the earthquake and pipeline failure occurs during school hours.

Through the cost-benefit analysis, the district determined that the most feasible method to reduce its risks would be to condemn the structures on the old, high-risk site and relocate the campus to a low-risk area. Given the nature and severity of the potential hazards, mitigation options other than relocation were judged infeasible.

Once the decision was made to relocate, the district went to work to identify an alternate site for the school facilities. The selected location for the campus was completely out of the dam inundation area and far removed from the high-pressure oil pipelines. Thus, the risk posed by the dam and oil pipelines hazards would be eliminated.

Although the campus would still be within an active earthquake fault area, the new campus buildings would be constructed to fully conform to 1995 building code provisions, making them more resistant to seismic damage than the buildings being replaced.

The district then agreed to turn the land over to the Newhall County Water District as soon as the relocation effort was under way. The old school property is located above two active wells, which the water district can use to supply their customers in Castaic. In doing so, they changed the property deed to restrict human habitation and development and to return the site to natural open space.

The Castaic School District financed the relocation effort through a combination of grant money from FEMA and the sale of bonds. The district applied for and received a $7.2 million grant through FEMA's Hazard Mitigation Grant Program for the market value of the property, including the existing structures and infrastructure. The district used this funding, plus $20 million generated by school bonds, to rebuild the elementary school, district office, and middle school, and to relocate the elementary school students into temporary buildings during the construction of the new facilities. The new middle school opened in the fall of 1996 and the new elementary school opened in August 1997.

Virgin Islands Building Code

On September 18, 1989, Hurricane Hugo, a Category 4 storm, passed over the Virgin Islands with sustained winds of 130 mph, leaving near-total devastation in its wake. Losses of $1.5 billion included damage or destruction of 95 percent of the buildings and 90 percent of the power supply. Almost all public buildings, including hospitals, schools, and shelters, sustained major damage or were destroyed. The tourist industry was in a shambles. All communications with Puerto Rico and the mainland were severed. A presidential disaster declaration was announced.

The government of the Virgin Islands, with support from FEMA, began an immediate effort to identify measures to mitigate damage from future storms. Projects identified included upgrading the building codes and building practices, training building inspectors, initiating projects to harden the power grid, and establishing public education programs to show residents how to perform simple mitigation measures and their value.

With technical assistance from FEMA, a new building code was written and implemented. The code required anchoring systems, hurricane clips, shutters, and other measures to hold buildings together and reduce flying debris. Piers, water production, distribution, and oil storage facilities were strengthened. A massive public education program was launched.

When Hurricane Marilyn hit, the public buildings performed well, but most single-family homes lost their roofs. Once again, the building codes were amended to strengthen the quality of residential construction. The governor's office initiated a comprehensive program to repair damaged roofs. The Home Protection Roofing Program provided more than 350 homeowners with roofs to withstand a Category 2 storm.

Hurricane Georges, occurring in September 1998, packing winds of more than 100 mph, put these measures to the test. The results were excellent. Public and private efforts had retrofitted or rebuilt most of the structures on the island by

(Continued)

CASE STUDY—Cont'd

September 1998. Damage to homes was limited to less than 2 percent of the islands. All hotels survived with little or no damage. Power was interrupted to 15 percent of the island but was fully restored within two weeks. Schools and other public structures were undamaged and provided safe havens for the residents to ride out the storm. Officials attribute the reduction in damages not just to the stronger code but also to the intensive education effort for building officials, contractors, and building owners about proper building practices and other mitigation strategies (Figure 3–3 shows an example).

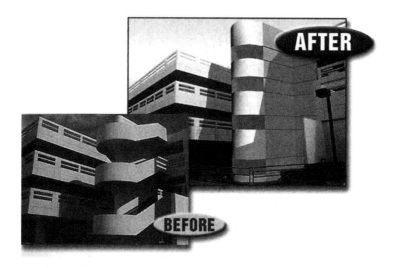

FIGURE 3–3 Guam Memorial Hospital before and after rebuilding and adding mitigation techniques for high wind. FEMA Photo.

Arnold, Missouri

The city of Arnold, Missouri, is located about 20 miles southwest of St. Louis at the confluence of the Meramec and Mississippi Rivers. The geography of Arnold causes it to be affected by backwaters from the Mississippi and direct flooding of the Meramec and its tributaries. The floodplains of both rivers had experienced extensive development. Because of these concerns, Arnold adopted a floodplain management program in 1991; however, it had no storm water management program.

The Midwest floods of the spring and summer of 1993 resulted in record flood losses and damages totaling between $12 to $16 billion. Nine states, 532 counties, and more than 55,000 homes were flooded. The 1993 floods had a devastating effect on the 18,000 residents of Arnold. Approximately 250 structures were under water, and more than 528 households applied for disaster assistance, which amounted to more than $2 million. The city had to operate more than 60 sandbag sites to hold off the waters. Parts of the town were under water for up to two weeks.

When the water receded, the city of Arnold started an aggressive program to voluntarily buy out properties in the floodplain. It proposed the purchase of single-family homes, commercial structures, and mobile homes. It developed a plan to turn the purchased land into an open space greenway along the west banks of the Meramec and Mississippi Rivers (see Figure 3–4). It initiated a public education campaign for the purchase of flood insurance, because only 208 of the 908 floodplain properties had flood insurance.

FIGURE 3–4 An example of relocation of homes out of the floodplain. FEMA Photo.

Although it was unable to implement the 1991 floodplain management plan, its commitment to mitigation paid off. Arnold received significant HMGP funding for the buyout because of its commitments. By combining HMGP, a community development block grant, and other HUD funding, it proceeded with the buyout program. Initial estimates put the program costs at $3.5 million, but in the end it would cost $7.3 million.

In the midst of this effort, Arnold experienced another major flood in 1995. The 1995 flood was the fourth largest flood in Arnold's history, but this time the results were dramatically different. Only four sandbag sites were needed, only 26 households applied for assistance, and the damage costs were less than $40,000.

Arnold continued its buyout program into 1996, working to obtain funding to remove the last 34 properties. The city continues to make other structural changes, including bridge elevations to restore the floodplain to its natural state and to provide a buffer for any future flooding.

IMPORTANT TERMS

- Mitigation
- Hazard identification
- Building codes
- Land-use planning
- Structural controls

Self-Check Questions

- How does the function of mitigation differ from other emergency management disciplines?
- Which other emergency management function offers the best opportunities for mitigation?
- Why is it more difficult to analyze, and therefore mitigate, the effects of terrorism?
- How have geographic information systems (GIS) aided the practice of mitigation?
- Why have building codes that require rehabilitation of existing potentially hazardous structures rarely been implemented?
- At what government level are mitigation programs most effective, and why?
- What is the most effective, but also the most expensive land-use planning tool? Why is it so effective?
- How has the Community Development Block Grant served to help communities perform local mitigation?
- Why do some people consider insurance to not be a proper mitigation method?
- Why are structural controls a controversial mitigation tool? How can structural mitigation negatively affect the areas they are presumably protecting?
- What are some impediments faced by communities wishing to perform hazard mitigation?
- Name the primary Federal mitigation programs, and explain how they serve to reduce hazard risk.
- Do non-Federal mitigation programs exist?

Out of Class Exercises

- Get a copy of your community's hazard mitigation plan from your local office of emergency management. Create a mitigation plan for yourself that addresses the hazards identified in the community plan as they affect you on a personal level. Determine if there are any hazards that you face as an individual that are not covered by the plan, and describe what mitigation measures you can take or have taken to address those hazards.
- Contact your State's office of emergency management, and find out what mitigation programs are currently offered. Are they all Federally-funded, or are there any programs funded by the State or other entity? Find out if your local government participates in any of these programs, or if they offer any additional programs funded by other sources. Do you believe that your community is taking advantage of every mitigation program that it is able to, or do you feel more could be done with what is currently offered?
- The Institute for Business and Home Safety (IBHS) has developed a mitigation guide for daycare centers (http://www.ibhs.org/docs/childcare.pdf). Using this guide, assist a daycare center in your community to perform the mitigation techniques suggested in the guide.

4

The Disciplines of Emergency Management: Response

What You Will Learn

- The roles and responsibilities of local first responders and emergency managers.
- How states are involved in emergency management.
- The contribution of volunteer organizations to disaster response efforts.
- What the incident command system is, and how it functions.
- The presidential disaster declaration process.
- How the federal government provides assistance in the aftermath of a declared disaster.
- The National Response Plan, its affiliated agencies, and how it functions.
- How response agencies communicate with each other.

Introduction

When a disaster event such as a flood, earthquake, or hurricane occurs, the first responders to this event are always local police, fire, and emergency medical personnel. Their job is to rescue and attend to those injured, suppress fires, secure and police the disaster area, and begin the process of restoring order. They are supported in this effort by local emergency management personnel and community government officials.

If the size of the disaster event is so large that the capabilities of local responders are overwhelmed and the costs of the damage inflicted exceeds the capacity of the local government, the mayor or county executive will turn to the governor and state government for assistance in responding to the event and in helping the community to recover. The governor will turn to the state's emergency management agency and possibly the state National Guard and other state resources to provide this assistance to the stricken community.

If the governor decides, based on information generated by community and state officials, that the size of the disaster event exceeds the state's capacity to respond, he or she will make a formal request to the president for a presidential major disaster declaration. This request is prepared by state officials in cooperation with regional staff from FEMA. The governor's request is analyzed first by the FEMA regional office then forwarded to FEMA headquarters in Washington, D.C. FEMA headquarters staff members review and evaluate the governor's request and forward their analysis and recommendation to the president. The president considers FEMA's recommendation then decides to grant the declaration or turn it down.

If the president grants a major disaster declaration, FEMA activates the National Response Plan (NRP) and proceeds to direct 32 federal departments and agencies, including the American Red Cross, in support of state and local efforts to respond to and recover from the disaster event. The presidential declaration also makes available several disaster assistance programs through FEMA and other federal agencies designed to assist individuals and communities to begin the process of rebuilding their homes, their community infrastructure, and their lives.

When a major disaster strikes in the United States, the aforementioned chronology describes how the most sophisticated and advanced emergency management system in the world responds and begins the recovery process. This system is built on coordination and cooperation among a significant number of federal, state, and local government agencies, volunteer organizations, and more recently, the business community.

In the 1990s, the emergency management system in the United States was tested repeatedly by major disaster events such as the 1993 Midwest floods; the 1994 Northridge, California, earthquake; and a series of devastating hurricanes and tornadoes. In each instance, the system worked to bring the full resources of the federal, state, and local governments to produce the most comprehensive and effective response possible. The system also leveraged the capabilities and resources of America's cadre of volunteer organizations to provide immediate food and shelter. In recent years, government officials and agencies at all levels have begun to reach out to the business community to both leverage their response capabilities and work closer with them in the recovery effort.

The September 11 terrorist attacks caused all levels of government to reevaluate response procedures and protocols. The unusual loss of so many first responders to this disaster event resulted in numerous after-action evaluations that likely will lead to changes in the procedures and protocols for first responders in the future. Additionally, the possibility of future terrorism attacks has focused attention on how best to protect first responders from harm in future attacks. These issues are discussed in detail in Chapter 9.

This chapter describes how local, state, and federal government officials and their partners respond to disasters in this country. The chapter includes sections discussing local response, state response, volunteer groups response, the incident command system, the FRP, and communications among responding agencies.

Local Response

Minor disasters occur daily in communities around the United States. Local fire, police, and emergency medical personnel respond to these events usually in a systematic and well-planned course of action. Firefighters, police officers, and emergency medical technicians respond to the scene. Their job is to secure the scene and maintain order, rescue and treat those injured, contain and suppress fire or hazardous conditions, and retrieve the dead.

The types of minor disasters responded to at the community level include hazardous materials transportation and storage incidents, fires, and localized flooding. Local officials also are the first responders to major disaster events such as large floods, hurricanes, and major earthquakes, but in these instances, their efforts are supported, on request by community leaders, by state government and, by request of the governor and approval of the president, by the federal government.

The actions of local first responders are driven by procedures and protocols developed by the responding agency (i.e., fire, police, and emergency medical). Most communities in the United States have developed communitywide emergency plans that incorporate these procedures and protocols. These community emergency plans also identify roles and responsibilities for all responding agencies and personnel for a wide range of disaster scenarios. These plans also include copies of the statutory authorities that provide the legal backing for emergency operations in the community.

In the aftermath of the September 11 terrorist events, many communities are reviewing and reworking their community emergency plans to include procedures and protocols for responding to all forms of terrorist attacks, including bioterrorism and weapons of mass destruction.

First Responder Roles and Responsibilities

The roles and responsibilities of first responders are often detailed in the community emergency plan. A review of the Madison County, North Carolina, All-Hazard Plan provides a typical example of the contents of community emergency plans and the designation of roles and responsibilities among local first responders.

□ □ □ ▬▬▬▬▬▬▬▬▬▬▬▬▬▬▬▬▬▬▬▬▬▬▬▬▬▬▬▬▬▬

Contents of Madison County (North Carolina) All-Hazard Plan

- Instructions for Use
- Basic Plan
- Glossary
- Acronyms and abbreviations
- Laws and Ordinances
- Madison County Emergency Management Ordinance
- Madison County State of Emergency Ordinance
- Proclamation of State of Emergency
- Proclamation of Terminating
- Mutual Aid
- Madison County Operation Plan (assignment of responsibilities)
  - Chairperson, County Commissioners
  - County Manager
  - Finance
  - Emergency Management Coordinator
  - Radiological Officer
  - Damage Assessment Officer (Tax Assessor)
  - Sheriff
  - Towns
  - County Fire Marshal and Fire Chiefs
  - Incident Commander

(Continued)

- ◦ EMS Coordinator
- ◦ Social Services Director
- ◦ Amateur Radio Emergency Service
- ◦ Health Director
- ◦ Medical Center Disaster Coordinator
- ◦ Medical Examiner
- ◦ Mental Health Coordinator
- ◦ Superintendent of Schools
- ◦ American Red Cross
- ◦ Public Works
- ◦ Salvation Army
- Direction and Control
- Communications
- Notification and Warning
- Emergency Public Information
- Law Enforcement
- Fire and Rescue
- Public Work/Landfill
- Health and Medical Services
- Evacuation and Transportation
- Shelter and Mass Care, Including Red Cross
- Damage Assessment/Recovery
- Radiological Protection
- Resource Management
- Nuclear Threat/Hazard
- Hazardous Materials Southern Railway (ATT) EOC
- Hurricanes and Flooding
- Transportation Accidents
- Mass Casualties
- Winter Storms
- Tornadoes
- Civil Disorders
- Dam Failure
- Major Incidents at Public Schools
- I-40 Detour Traffic
- Search and Rescue Plan
- 911 Failure
- Power Failure Countywide
- Formation of LEPC
- Contingency Plan
- (ATT) EOC—Federal Response Plan—Southern Railroad/HAZ Plan

Source: Madison County (NC) All-Hazard Plan.

Local Emergency Managers

It usually is the responsibility of the designated local emergency manager to develop and maintain the community emergency plans. This individual often holds one or more other positions in local government, such as fire or police chief, and serves only part-time as the community's emergency manager. The profession of local emergency management has been maturing since the 1980s. There are now more opportunities for individuals to receive formal training in emergency management in the United States. Currently, more than 80 junior college, undergraduate, and graduate programs offer courses and degrees in emergency management and related fields. Additionally, FEMA's Emergency Management Institute (EMI) located in Emmitsburg, Maryland, offers emergency management courses on campus and through long-distance learning programs. EMI has also worked closely with junior colleges, colleges and universities, and graduate schools to develop coursework and curriculums in emergency management. More information on EMI and other emergency management education programs can be found in Chapter 6.

☐ ☐ ☐ ▬▬▬▬▬▬▬▬▬▬▬▬▬▬▬▬▬▬▬▬▬▬▬▬▬▬▬▬

The Certified Emergency Manager Program

The International Association of Emergency Managers (IAEM) created the Certified Emergency Manager (CEM) Program to raise and maintain professional standards. It is an internationally recognized program that certifies achievements within the emergency management profession.

CEM certification is a peer review process administered through the International Association of Emergency Managers. One need not be an IAEM member to be certified, although IAEM membership does offer a number of benefits that can assist one through the certification process. Certification is maintained in five-year cycles.

The CEM program is served by a CEM Commission composed of emergency management professionals, including representatives from allied fields, education, the military, and private industry. Development of the CEM program was supported by FEMA, the National Emergency Management Association, and a host of allied organizations.

Source: IAEM, www.iaem.org.

▬▬▬▬▬▬▬▬▬▬▬▬▬▬▬▬▬▬▬▬▬▬▬▬▬▬▬▬ ☐ ☐ ☐

☐ ☐ ☐ ▬▬▬▬▬▬▬▬▬▬▬▬▬▬▬▬▬▬▬▬▬▬▬▬▬▬▬▬

Roles and Responsibilities of the Emergency Management Coordinator in the Madison County All-Hazard Plan

Emergency management coordinator

1. Performs assigned duties according to state statutes and local ordinances.
2. Is responsible for planning in accordance with federal and state guidelines and coordinating of emergency operations within the jurisdiction.

(Continued)

3. Maintains current inventories of public information resources.
4. Ensures regular drills and exercises are conducted to test the functions of the EOP annually.
5. Identifies resources, county and private, and maintains current inventories of county-owned resources, including sources and quantities, and develop mutual aid agreements to control these resources.
6. Requests funding for maintaining equipment for radiation hazard evaluation and exposure control.
7. Establishes and equips the county Emergency Operating Center (EOC) to include primary and backup radio communications (fixed and mobile) and provide for operations on a continuous basis as required.
8. Ensures adequate training for the emergency management organization.
9. Ensures means are available within the jurisdiction to gather necessary information (i.e., fuel storage facilities, major distributors, and end-user status), during the energy emergency status.
10. Provides emergency information materials for the public including non-English-speaking groups.
11. Prepares written statements of agreements with the media to provide for dissemination of essential emergency information and warning to the public, including the appropriate protective actions to be taken.
12. Coordinates exercises and tests of emergency systems within the jurisdiction.
13. Maintains liaison with utility companies to arrange for backup water, power, and telephone service during emergencies.
14. Maintains working relationships with the media and a current list of radio stations, television stations, and newspapers to be used for public information releases.
15. Is alert and activated, as required by the county Emergency Management Organization, when informed of an emergency within the county.
16. Receives requests for assistance from municipalities within the county and direct aid to areas where needed.
17. Coordinates disaster assessment teams conducting field surveys.
18. Conducts a public information campaign to disseminate disaster assistance information as necessary.
19. Maintains listing of medical facilities.
20. Collects data and prepare damage assessment reports.
21. Provides for the storage, maintenance, and replenishment/replacement of essential equipment and materials (e.g., medical supplies, food and water, radiological instruments).
22. Develops a schedule for testing, maintaining, and repairing EOC and other emergency equipment.
23. Develops and maintains the EOC Standard Operating Guides, including an activation checklist and notification/recall roster.
24. Establishes and maintains coordination with other jurisdictional EOCs as appropriate.

25. Provides for adequate coordination of recovery activities among private, state, and federal agencies and organizations.

26. Develops procedures to warn areas not covered by existing warning systems.

27. Coordinates warning resources with neighboring counties.

28. Develops and maintains a public information and education program.

29. Assists the public information officer (PIO) in disseminating public information and education program.

30. Identifies and develops procedures for potential evacuation areas in accordance with the county's hazard analysis.

31. Identifies population groups requiring special assistance during evacuation (e.g., senior citizens, the very ill and disabled, nursing home residents, prison population) and assures that they have evacuation procedures in place.

32. Establishes disaster assistance centers if appropriate.

33. Initiates the return of the population as soon as conditions are safe at the direction of the chairman, Board of County Commissioners.

34. Initiates the crisis upgrading and marking of shelters.

35. Identifies and surveys congregate care shelter facilities that have lodging and mass feeding capabilities.

36. Develops procedures to activate and deactivate shelters and ensure that American Red Cross and DSS develop shelter SOGs.

37. Establishes public information and education programs on sheltering.

38. Assists with designating facilities and arranging for the shelter needs of institutionalized or special needs groups.

39. Designates shelter facilities in the reception area with the shortest commuting distance to the hazardous area for essential workers and their families.

40. Appoints a damage assessment officer to coordinate overall damage assessment operations.

41. Recruits damage assessment team members.

42. Secures resources to support and assist with damage assessment activities (e.g., maps, tax data, cameras, identification, report forms).

43. Establishes a utilities liaison to coordinate information flow between the EOC and affected utilities.

44. Assists with identification and notification of applicants that may be eligible for public assistance programs.

45. Develops a flood warning system for areas in the county subject to frequent flooding.

46. Appoints a radiological officer or performs the duties of that office.

47. Acquires and provides radiological monitoring equipment.

48. Coordinates overall radiological protection activities.

49. Coordinates resource use under emergency conditions and provides a system to protect these resources.

50. Supports the Local Emergency Planning Council (LEPC) in maintaining liaison with facility emergency coordinators to ensure availability of current information concerning hazards and response to an incident.

(Continued)

51. Ensures a critique of incident responses to assess and update procedures as needed.

52. Serves as the community emergency coordinator as identified in SARA, Title Jill.

53. Assists the area staff and the energy policy council in obtaining the essential data for implementation of contingency plans.

54. Assures coordination of planning efforts among jurisdictions (e.g., municipalities, counties, facilities), including the development of notification/ warning, response, and remediation procedures for covered facilities.

55. Ensures serviceability of radiological monitoring instruments.

56. Alerts all emergency support services to the dangers associated with technological hazards and fire during emergency operations.

57. Advises decision makers on the hazards associated with hazardous materials.

Source: Madison County All Hazard Plan.

More and more communities have designated emergency managers responsible for guiding response and recovery operations. Training and education programs in emergency management are expanding dramatically, resulting in a growing number of professionally trained and certified local emergency managers. The maturing of this profession can lead only to more effective and efficient local responses to future disaster events.

State Response

Each of the 50 states and six territories that constitute the United States maintains a state government office of emergency management. The names of the office vary from state to state. For example, in California it is called the Office of Emergency Services (OES), in Tennessee it is the Tennessee Emergency Management Agency (TEMA), in North Carolina it is the Department of Emergency Management, and in Florida it is the Florida Division of Emergency Management. A full list of state emergency management organizations is presented in the supplements at the companion Web site for this book. (See the URL for the companion Web site in the *Introduction*.)

Also, where the emergency management office resides in state government varies from state to state. In California, OES is located in the office of the governor; in Tennessee, TEMA reports to the adjunct general; and in Florida, the emergency management function is located in the office of community affairs. National Guard adjutant generals manage state emergency management offices in more than half the 56 states and territories. The remaining state emergency management offices are led by civilian employees.

Funding for state emergency management offices comes principally from FEMA and state budgets. For years, FEMA has provided up to $175 million annually to states to fund state and local government emergency management activities. This money is used by state emergency management agencies to hire staff, conduct training and exercises, and purchase equipment. A segment of this funding is targeted for local emergency management operations as designated by the state. State budgets also provide funding for emergency management operations, but this funding historically has been inconsistent, especially in those states with minimal annual disaster activity.

The principal resource available to governors in responding to a disaster event in their state is the National Guard. The resources of the National Guard that can be used in disaster response include personnel, communications systems and equipment, air and road transport, heavy construction and earth-moving equipment, mass care and feeding equipment, and emergency supplies such as beds, blankets, and medical supplies.

In early 2007, with the passing of the John Warner National Defense Reauthorization Act (PL 109–364), the authority of governors to deploy the National Guard was severely eroded. In Section 1076 of this Act, the president is given the authority to effectively commandeer total control of this invaluable response resource. It is believed that the provision was a reaction to sentiments that the federal government should have taken over the response to the Katrina Disaster and that the military would have been best suited to manage in that case. The National Governors Association, an organization representing the interests of the leadership of all 50 states, immediately voiced the governors' opposition to the inclusion of such a provision in the legislation, as they felt it undermined their authority over the National Guard and therefore further limited their ability to assure the safety of their constituents. The governors wrote: "By granting the President specific authority to usurp the Guard during a natural disaster or emergency without the consent of a governor, Section 1076 could result in confusion and an inability to respond to residents' needs because it calls into question whether a governor or the President has primary responsibility during a domestic emergency" (National Governors Association, 2007).

Response capabilities and capacities are strongest in those states and territories that experience high levels of annual disaster activity. North Carolina is one of those states, with high risk of hurricanes and floods. How the North Carolina Department of Emergency Management describes its response process on its Web site provides an example of state response functions.

□ □ □ ▬▬▬▬▬▬▬▬▬▬▬▬▬▬▬▬▬▬▬▬▬▬▬▬▬▬▬▬▬▬▬▬▬

Response by the North Carolina Department of Emergency Management

The division's emergency response functions are coordinated in a proactive manner from the State Emergency Operations Center located in Raleigh. Proactive response strategies used by the division include

- Area commands that are strategically located in an impacted region to assist with local response efforts using state resources.
- Central warehousing operations managed by the state that allow for immediate delivery of bottled water, ready-to-eat meals, blankets, tarps, and the like; field deployment teams manned by division and other state agency personnel that assist severely impacted counties coordinate and prioritize response activity.
- Incident action planning that identifies response priorities and resource requirements 12 to 24 hours in advance.

(Continued)

The State Emergency Response Team (SERT), which consists of top-level management representatives of each state agency involved in response activities, provides the technical expertise and coordinates the delivery of the emergency resources used to support local emergency operations.

When resource needs are beyond the capabilities of state agencies, mutual aid from other unaffected local governments and states may be secured using the Statewide Mutual Aid Agreement or Emergency Management Assistance Compact. Federal assistance may also be requested through the Federal Emergency Response Team, which collocates with the SERT during major disasters.

Source: North Carolina Department of Emergency Management, www.dem.dcc.state.nc.us.

Volunteer Group Response

Volunteer groups are on the front line of any disaster response. National groups such as the American Red Cross and the Salvation Army roster maintain local chapters of volunteers who are trained in emergency response. These organizations work with local, state, and federal authorities to address the immediate needs of disaster victims. These organizations provide shelter, food, and clothing to disaster victims who have lost their homes to disasters large and small.

In addition to the Red Cross and the Salvation Army, numerous volunteer groups across the country provide aid and comfort to disaster victims. The National Volunteer Organizations Active in Disaster (NVOAD) consists of 34 national member organizations, 52 state and territorial VOADs, and a growing number of local VOADs involved in disaster response and recovery operations around the country and abroad. Formed in 1970, NVOAD helps member groups at a disaster location coordinate and communicate to provide the most efficient and effective response. A list of the NVOAD member organizations is provided on pp. 109–110.

Hurricane Katrina changed the landscape in terms of the involvement of voluntary agencies, nongovernmental organizations (NGOs), and the private sector in disaster response. The size of Katrina required resources and capabilities beyond the usual government programs. The massive evacuation in advance of the hurricane created an extraordinary demand for shelters, medicine, food, and temporary housing. NGOs and the private sector provided many of the support services to help Katrina victims to get back on their feet. Over 5,000 children were separated from their parents in the evacuations, and the NGO National Center for Missing and Exploited Children helped successfully reunite every one of these children with their families. The private sector helped raise over $1 billion for the response and supported a number of activities not covered by government relief programs. For example, Chevron worked with the Early Childhood Institute at Mississippi State University and Save the Children to rebuild and resupply child care centers across the three Mississippi coastal counties. A list of the many NGOs that joined the NVOAD members in responding to Katrina and details on the donations made by the private sector to the response are included in *Katrina: A Case Study.*

▢ ▢ ▢ ▬▬▬▬▬▬▬▬▬▬▬▬▬▬▬▬▬▬▬▬▬

List of NVOAD Member Organizations

Adventist Community Services
American Baptist Men USA
American Disaster Reserve
American Radio Relay League
American Red Cross
America's Second Harvest
Ananda Marga Universal Relief Team
Catholic Charities USA
Center for International Disaster Information
Christian Disaster Response
Christian Reformed World Relief Committee
Church of the Brethren Emergency Response
Church World Service
Churches of Scientology Disaster Response
Convoy of Hope
Disaster Psychiatry Outreach
Episcopal Relief and Development
Feed the Children
Friends Disaster Service
Hope Coalition America (Operation Hope)
Humane Society of the United States
International Aid
International Critical Incident Stress Foundation (ICISF)
International Relief and Development, Inc. (IRD)
International Relief Friendship Foundation
Lutheran Disaster Response
Mennonite Disaster Services
Mercy Medical Airlift
National Association of Jewish Chaplains
National Emergency Response Team
National Organization for Victim Assistance
Nazarene Disaster Response
Operation Blessing
Northwest Medical Teams International
The Phoenix Society for Burn Survivors
Points of Light Foundation and National Volunteer Center Network
The Presbyterian Church (USA)
REACT International
Samaritan's Purse
Save the Children
Society of St. Vincent De Paul

(Continued)

Southern Baptist Convention
The Salvation Army
Tzu Chi Foundation
United Church of Christ
United Jewish Communities
United Methodist Committee on Relief
United Way of America
Volunteers of America
World Vision

Source: National Volunteer Organizations Active In Disasters.

German Salvationists Provide Aid to Flood Victims

August 15, 2002. Salvationists in Dresden, Germany, have been working tirelessly to help people affected by the flooding that has brought chaos to the city and much of the surrounding area. The River Elbe is already at its highest point since the mid-nineteenth century and water levels are still rising. More than 3,000 people have so far been forced to evacuate their homes.

When the flooding started, Salvationists from the Salvation Army center in Dresden immediately offered support to the emergency workers, as no official supplies were then being provided to fire and ambulance personnel. However, the main focus of attention quickly shifted to the victims of the flooding.

The Salvation Army Corps (church) building in Dresden is located on high ground and, unlike many buildings in the city, still has power, so cooking and food preparation are possible. More than 2,000 meals have been provided so far. Local hotels and a bakery are assisting with preparation and two Salvation Army mobile kitchens are being used to deliver food.

There is great concern for the many elderly people who are unable to leave their properties but who now have no power for cooking or heating. In addition to providing hot soup, consideration is being given to assisting these elderly people to find alternative, temporary accommodation. Many offers of help have come in, including from a nurse who put herself forward to provide assistance after the hospital she was working in was evacuated.

Donations of clothing and supplies, up to now, have had to be turned down because of a lack of storage space. The Salvation Army's International Emergency

(Continued)

Services Office has arranged for US$25,000 to be sent out from International Headquarters and these funds will be used, among other things, to hire a suitable warehouse where donations can be stored.

Source: Salvation Army.

□ □ □

Incident Command System

A difficult issue in any response operation is determining who is in charge of the overall response effort. The incident command system (ICS) was developed after the 1970 fires in southern California. Duplication of efforts, lack of coordination, and communication hindered all agencies responding to the expanding fires. The main function of ICS is to establish a set of planning and management systems that would help the agencies responding to a disaster to work together in a coordinated and systematic approach. The step-by-step process enables the numerous responding agencies to effectively use resources and personnel to respond to those in need.

There are multiple functions in the ICS. They include common use of terminology, integrated communications, a unified command structure, resource management, and action planning. A planned set of directives includes assigning one coordinator to manage the infrastructure of the response, assigning personnel, deploying equipment, obtaining resources, and working with the numerous agencies that respond to the disaster scene. In most instances, the local fire chief or fire commissioner is the incident commander.

For the ICS to be effective, it must provide for effective operations at three levels of incident character: (1) single jurisdiction or single agency, (2) single jurisdiction with multiple agency support, and (3) multijurisdictional or multiagency support. The organizational structure must be adaptable to a wide variety of emergencies (i.e., fire, flood, earthquake, and rescue). The ICS includes agency autonomy, management by objectives, unity integrity, functional clarity, and effective span of control. The logistics, coordination, and ability of the multiple agencies to work together must adhere to the ICS so that efficient leadership is maintained during the disaster. One of the most significant problems before the ICS was that agencies that responded to major disasters would assign their own commander and there would be power struggles, miscommunication, and duplication of efforts (Irwin, 1980).

There are five major management systems within the ICS: command, operations, planning, logistics, and finance.

1. The *command section* includes developing, directing, and maintaining communication and collaboration with the multiple agencies on site, working with the local officials, the public, and the media to provide up-to-date information regarding the disaster.
2. The *operations section* handles the tactical operations, coordinates the command objectives, and organizes and directs all resources to the disaster site.
3. The *planning section* provides the necessary information to the command center to develop the action plan to accomplish the objectives. This section also collects and evaluates information as it is made available.

4. The *logistics section* provides personnel, equipment, and support for the command center. It handles the coordination of all services involved in the response, from locating rescue equipment to coordinating the response for volunteer organizations such as the Salvation Army and the Red Cross.

5. The *finance section* is responsible for accounting for funds used during the response and recovery aspect of the disaster. The finance section monitors costs related to the incident and provides accounting procurement time recording cost analyses.

In today's world, the public, private, and political values at risk in major emergencies demand the most efficient methods of response and management. Meeting this demand when multiple and diverse agencies are involved becomes a difficult task. The unified command concept of ICS offers a process that all participating agencies can use to improve overall management, whether their jurisdiction is of a geographical or functional nature (Irwin, 1980).

The unified command is best used when there is a multiagency response. Because of the nature of the disaster, multiple government agencies need to work together to monitor the response and manage the large number of personnel who respond to the scene (see Figure 4–1). It allows for the integration of the agencies to operate under one overall response management.

☐ ☐ ☐ ━━━━━━━━━━━━━━━━━━━━━━━━━━━━━━━━━━━━━━

Procedures for an Incident Command System

For an ICS to be effective, procedures need to be followed closely:

- A command post needs to be established.
- Proper equipment, such as computers, radios, and telephone lines, need to be installed and in working order.
- A media/press area needs to be established.
- Topographic maps need to be located and posted. After tornadoes, street signs or other identifying landmarks are destroyed and rescue personnel are unable to use traditional road maps.
- A missing persons list needs to be located or prepared.
- The movement and location of triage areas and transportation of victims must be monitored.
- The ability is needed to maintain continuous communication with local hospitals to monitor the number of victims received.
- The search area must be established and a grid prepared.
- Based on the type of disaster, such as flooding, responders may have to use boats to search for and rescue victims.
- What resources are available within the local area and what ones are being deployed must be determined.
- As the response system expands, the tasks that need to be performed must be reevaluated and new tasks developed.

Source: Irwin, 2002.

━━━━━━━━━━━━━━━━━━━━━━━━━━━━━━━━━━━━━━ ☐ ☐ ☐

FIGURE 4–1 New York, New York, October 30, 2001. FEMA/NY state disaster field office personnel meet to coordinate federal, state, and local disaster assistance programs. Photo by Andrea Booher/FEMA News Photo. Photo by Dave Gatley/FEMA News Photo.

The incident commander (IC) prepares to delegate responsibilities as needed to maintain focus on the overall situation. The IC needs to assign positions, such as debriefers, coordinators, and unit leaders, to manage the command center. As the response and recovery process proceeds, the IC needs to have an ongoing dialogue with staff members and officials to monitor and manage the response. The IC needs to evaluate the continuing needs of the responders and determine if additional resources are needed. In the after-action reports, discussion and evaluation of the disaster determines the success based on the initial competence and effectiveness of the incident commander and the center.

Federal Response

Once the governor has determined that a disaster event has overwhelmed the capacity of state and local governments to effectively respond and subsequently fund the recovery effort, the governor forwards a letter to the president requesting a presidential disaster declaration. This is the first step toward involving federal officials, agencies and departments, and resources in a disaster event (see Figure 4–2). If the event is declared a major disaster by the president, 32 federal departments and agencies, including the American Red Cross, work together to support the efforts of state and local officials.

The Department of Homeland Security, through FEMA, is responsible for coordinating all federal activities in support of state and local response and recovery efforts in a presidentially declared disaster. In such an instance, FEMA activates the National Response Plan. FEMA also manages several programs that provide disaster assistance to individuals and affected communities. These programs are discussed in detail in Chapter 5.

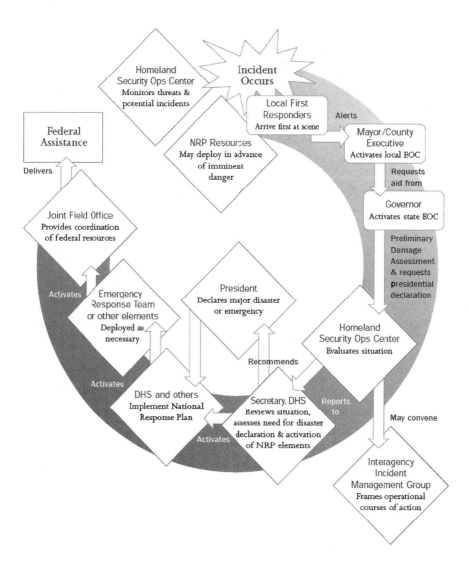

FIGURE 4–2 Flow of initial national-level incident management actions. *Source:* DHS National Response Plan.

Presidential Disaster Declaration Process

The presidential disaster declaration makes available the resources of the federal government to the disaster area. Although a formal declaration does not have to be signed for the federal government to respond, the governor must make a formal request for assistance and specify in the request the specific needs of the disaster area. The presidential major disaster declaration process is provided as follows:

☐ ☐ ☐ ▬▬▬▬▬▬▬▬▬▬▬▬▬▬▬▬▬▬▬▬▬▬▬▬▬▬▬▬▬

Presidential Major Disaster Declaration Process

A disaster declaration should include the following guidelines:

- Contact is made between the affected state and the FEMA regional office. This contact may take place before or immediately following the disaster.
- If it appears the situation is beyond state and local capacity, the state requests FEMA to conduct a joint preliminary damage assessment (PDA). Participants in the PDA include FEMA, state, local government, and other federal agency representatives.
- Based on the PDA findings, the governor submits a request to the president through the FEMA regional director for either a major disaster or an emergency declaration and identifying the counties affected.
- The FEMA regional office submits a summary of the event and a recommendation based on the results of the PDA to FEMA headquarters, along with the governor's request.
- On receipt of these documents, headquarters senior staff convenes to discuss the request and determine the recommendation to be made to the president.
- FEMA's recommendation is forwarded to the White House for review.
- The president declares a major disaster or an emergency.

Source: FEMA, 1999.

▬▬▬▬▬▬▬▬▬▬▬▬▬▬▬▬▬▬▬▬▬▬▬▬▬▬▬▬▬ ☐ ☐ ☐

Federal, state, local, tribal, private-sector, and nongovernmental organizations report threats, incidents, and potential incidents using established communications and reporting channels. The Homeland Security Operations Center (HSOC) receives threat and operational information regarding incidents or potential incidents and makes an initial determination to initiate the coordination of federal information-sharing and incident management activities.

The decision to make a disaster declaration is completely at the discretion of the president. There are no set criteria to follow and no government regulations to guide which events are declared by the president and which events are not. FEMA developed several factors it considers in making its recommendation to the president, including individual property losses per capita, level of damage to existing community infrastructure, and insurance coverage. In the end, however, the decision to make the declaration is the president's alone.

A presidential disaster declaration can be made in as short a time as a few hours, as was the case in the 1994 Northridge earthquake and the 1995 Oklahoma City bombing.

Sometimes, it takes weeks for damages to be assessed and the capability of state and local jurisdictions to fund response and recovery efforts to be evaluated. If the governor's request is turned down by the president, the governor has a right to appeal and can be successful, especially if new damage data become available and are included in the appeal.

Presidential declarations are routinely sought for such events as large floods, hurricanes, earthquakes, and big tornadoes. In recent years, governors have become more inventive and requested presidential disaster declarations for snow removal, drought, West Nile virus, and economic losses caused by failing industries such as the Northwest salmon spawning decline.

Since 1976, there have been 1,179 presidential disaster declarations, averaging 38 declarations per year (see Table 4–1). As an example of disaster declaration activity in a single year, in 2006, there were 52 major disaster declarations in 33 states (see Table 4–2).

Table 4–1 Total Major Disaster Declarations, 1976–2006

Year	Total Disaster Declarations	Number above or (below) Average
1976	30	(8)
1977	22	(16)
1978	25	(13)
1979	42	4
1980	23	(15)
1981	15	(23)
1982	24	(14)
1983	21	(17)
1984	34	(4)
1985	27	(11)
1986	28	(10)
1987	23	(15)
1988	11	(27)
1989	31	(7)
1990	38	0
1991	43	5
1992	45	7
1993	32	(6)
1994	36	(2)
1995	32	(6)
1996	75	37
1997	44	6
1998	65	27
1999	50	12
2000	45	7
2001	45	7
2002	49	11
2003	56	18
2004	68	30
2005	48	10
2006	52	14
Total	1,179	
Average	38.0	

Source: www.fema.gov.

Table 4–2   FEMA Major Disaster Activity, January 1, 2006, to December 31, 2006

Date	State	Title
12/29	Missouri	Severe winter storms
12/29	Oregon	Severe storms, flooding, landslides, and mudslides
12/12	Washington	Severe storms, flooding, landslides, and mudslides
12/12	New York	Severe storms and flooding
12/08	Alaska	Severe storms, flooding, landslides, and mudslides
11/02	Louisiana	Severe storms and flooding
11/02	Missouri	Severe storms
10/27	Alaska	Fire
10/24	New York	Severe storms and flooding
10/17	Hawaii	Earthquake
10/16	Alaska	Severe storms, flooding, landslides, and mudslides
10/06	Indiana	Severe storms and flooding
09/22	Virginia	Severe storms and flooding, including severe storms and flooding associated with Tropical Depression Ernesto
09/07	Arizona	Severe storms and flooding
08/30	New Mexico	Severe storms and flooding
08/15	Texas	Flooding
08/04	Alaska	Snow melt and ice jam flooding
08/01	Ohio	Severe storms, straight line winds, and flooding
07/13	Virginia	Severe storms, tornadoes, and flooding
07/05	Delaware	Severe storms and flooding
07/07	New Jersey	Severe storms and flooding
07/02	Maryland	Severe storms, flooding, and tornadoes
07/02	Ohio	Severe storms, tornadoes, straight line winds, and flooding
07/01	New York	Severe storms and flooding
06/30	Pennsylvania	Severe storms, flooding, and mudslides
06/05	Minnesota	Flooding
06/05	South Dakota	Severe winter storm
06/05	California	Severe storms, flooding, landslides, and mudslides
06/05	North Dakota	Severe storms, flooding, and ground saturation
05/25	Maine	Severe storms and flooding
05/25	New Hampshire	Severe storms and flooding
05/25	Massachusetts	Severe storms and flooding
05/17	Washington	Severe storms, flooding, tidal surge, landslides, and mudslides
05/02	Hawaii	Severe storms, flooding, landslides, and mudslides
04/14	Kansas	Severe storms, tornadoes, and straight line winds
04/13	Oklahoma	Severe storms and tornadoes
04/12	Arkansas	Severe storms and tornadoes
04/05	Missouri	Severe storms, tornadoes, and flooding
04/06	Tennessee	Severe storms and tornadoes
03/28	Illinois	Tornadoes and severe storms
03/20	Oregon	Severe storms, flooding, landslides, and mudslides
03/16	Missouri	Severe storms, tornadoes, and flooding
02/27	Idaho	Severe storms and flooding
02/03	Nevada	Severe storms and flooding
02/03	California	Severe storms, flooding, mudslides, and landslides

(Continued)

Table 4–2—Cont'd

01/26	Nebraska	Severe winter storm
01/26	Kansas	Severe winter storm
01/20	South Carolina	Severe ice storm
01/11	Texas	Extreme wildfire threat
01/10	Oklahoma	Severe wildfire threat
01/04	Minnesota	Severe winter storm
01/04	North Dakota	Severe winter storm

Critical Thinking

Should there be more strict guidelines about what events the president can declare a disaster? Why or why not?

Federal Response Plan and National Response Plan

In 1992 the Federal Emergency Management Agency developed the Federal Response Plan (FRP). FEMA defined the FRP as a

> *Signed agreement among 27 Federal departments and agencies, including the American Red Cross, that: Provides the mechanism for coordinating delivery of Federal assistance and resources to augment efforts of State and local governments overwhelmed by a major disaster or emergency, Supports implementation of the Robert T. Stafford Disaster Relief and Emergency Assistance Act, as amended (42 U.S.C. 5121, et seq.), as well as individual agency statutory authorities and Supplements other Federal emergency operations plans developed to address specific hazards.*

The fundamental goal of the FRP was to maximize available federal resources in support of response and recovery actions taken by state and local emergency officials.

□ □ □ ▬▬▬▬▬▬▬▬▬▬▬▬▬▬▬▬▬▬▬▬▬▬▬▬▬▬▬

Types of Federal Assistance Available

The Federal Response Plan made available the following types of assistance:

To deliver immediate relief:

- Initial response resources, including food, water, emergency generators.
- Emergency services to clear debris, open critical transportation routes, provide mass sheltering and feeding.

To speed return to normal and reduce damage from future occurrences:

- Loans and grants to repair or replace damaged housing and personal property.
- Grants to repair or replace roads and public buildings, incorporating to the extent practical hazard-reduction structural and nonstructural measures.
- Technical assistance to identify and implement mitigation opportunities to reduce future losses.
- Other assistance, including crisis counseling, tax relief, legal services, job placement.

Source: FEMA, 1999.

Following the absorption of FEMA into the Department of Homeland Security, on February 18, 2003, President Bush signed Presidential Directive 5 (HSPD-5) "to enhance the ability of the United States to manage domestic incidents by establishing a single, comprehensive national incident management system." This action authorized the design and development of a National Response Plan to "align Federal coordination structures, capabilities, and resources into a unified, all-discipline, and all-hazards approach to domestic incident management." The Department of Homeland Security writes,

> (From the NRP Letter of Agreement) *The NRP is an all-discipline, all-hazards plan that establishes a single, comprehensive framework for the management of domestic incidents. It provides the structure and mechanisms for the coordination of Federal support to State, local, and tribal incident managers and for exercising direct Federal authorities and responsibilities. The NRP assists in the important homeland security mission of preventing terrorist attacks within the United States; reducing the vulnerability to all natural and manmade hazards; and minimizing the damage and assisting in the recovery from any type of incident that occurs.*

The NRP was designed according to the template of the National Incident Management System (released March 1, 2004) to ensure that a consistent doctrinal framework exists for the management of incidents at all jurisdictional levels, regardless of the incident cause, size, or complexity. NIMS was created to integrate effective practices in emergency preparedness and response into a comprehensive national framework for incident management. NIMS enables responders at all levels to work together more effectively and efficiently to manage domestic incidents no matter what the cause, size, or complexity, including catastrophic acts of terrorism and disasters.

The Department of Homeland Security lists the benefits of the NIMS system to be

- Standardized organizational structures, processes, and procedures.
- Standards for planning, training, and exercising and personnel qualification standards.
- Equipment acquisition and certification standards.
- Interoperable communications processes, procedures, and systems.

- Information management systems.
- Supporting technologies—voice and data communications systems, information systems, data display systems, and specialized technologies.

Consistent with the model provided in the NIMS, the NRP can be partially or fully implemented in the context of a threat, anticipation of a significant event, or the response to a significant event. Selective implementation through the activation of one or more of the system's components allows for flexibility in meeting the unique operational and information-sharing requirements of the situation at hand and enabling effective interaction among various federal and nonfederal entities.

The NRP provides the framework for federal interaction with state, local, and tribal governments; the private sector; and NGOs in the context of domestic incident prevention, preparedness, response, and recovery activities. It describes capabilities and resources and establishes responsibilities, operational processes, and protocols to help protect the nation from terrorist attacks and other natural and human-made hazards; save lives; protect public health, safety, property, and the environment; and reduce adverse psychological consequences and disruptions. Finally, the NRP serves as the foundation for the development of detailed supplemental plans and procedures to effectively and efficiently implement federal incident management activities and assistance in the context of specific types of incidents.

The NRP establishes mechanisms to

- Maximize the integration of incident-related prevention, preparedness, response, and recovery activities.
- Improve coordination and integration of federal, state, local, tribal, regional, private-sector, and nongovernmental organization partners.
- Maximize efficient utilization of resources needed for effective incident management and critical infrastructure/key resources (CI/KR) protection and restoration.
- Improve incident management communications and increase situational awareness across jurisdictions and between the public and private sectors.
- Facilitate emergency mutual aid and federal emergency support to state, local, and tribal governments.
- Facilitate federal-to-federal interaction and emergency support.
- Provide a proactive and integrated federal response to catastrophic events.
- Address linkages to other federal incident management and emergency response plans developed for specific types of incidents or hazards.

The NRP covers the full range of complex and constantly changing requirements in anticipation of, or in response to, threats or acts of terrorism, major disasters, and other emergencies. The NRP also provides the basis to initiate long-term community recovery and mitigation activities. The NRP establishes interagency and multijurisdictional mechanisms for federal government involvement in, and DHS coordination of, domestic incident management operations. This includes coordinating structures and processes for incidents requiring:

- Federal support to state, local, and tribal governments.
- Federal-to-federal support.

- The exercise of direct federal authorities and responsibilities, as appropriate under the law.
- Public- and private-sector domestic incident management integration.

The NRP distinguishes between incidents that require DHS coordination, termed *incidents of national significance*, and the majority of incidents occurring each year that are handled by responsible jurisdictions or agencies through other established authorities and existing plans.

In addition, the NRP

- Recognizes and incorporates the various jurisdictional and functional authorities of federal departments and agencies; state, local, and tribal governments; and private-sector organizations in domestic incident management.
- Details the specific domestic incident management roles and responsibilities of the secretary of homeland security, attorney general, secretary of defense, secretary of state, and other departments and agencies involved in domestic incident management as defined in HSPD-5 and other relevant statutes and directives.
- Establishes the multiagency organizational structures and processes required to implement the authorities, roles, and responsibilities of the secretary of homeland security as the principal federal official for domestic incident management.

The NRP is applicable to all federal departments and agencies that may be requested to provide assistance or conduct operations in the context of actual or potential incidents of national significance. This includes the American Red Cross, which functions as an emergency support function (ESF) primary organization in coordinating the use of mass care resources in a presidentially declared disaster or emergency. The NRP is applicable to incidents that may occur at sites under the control of the legislative or judicial branches of the federal government.

Based on the criteria established in HSPD-5, incidents of national significance are those high-impact events that require a coordinated and effective response by an appropriate combination of federal, state, local, tribal, private-sector, and nongovernmental entities to save lives, minimize damage, and provide the basis for long-term community recovery and mitigation activities.

The NRP bases the definition of incidents of national significance on situations related to the following four criteria set forth in HSPD-5:

1. A federal department or agency acting under its own authority has requested the assistance of the secretary of homeland security.
2. The resources of state and local authorities are overwhelmed and federal assistance has been requested by the appropriate state and local authorities. Examples include
   a. Major disasters or emergencies as defined under the Stafford Act.
   b. Catastrophic incidents.
3. More than one federal department or agency has become substantially involved in responding to an incident. Examples include
   a. Credible threats, indications or warnings of imminent terrorist attack, or acts of terrorism directed domestically against the people, property, environment, or political or legal institutions of the United States or its territories or possessions.

    b. Threats or incidents related to high-profile, large-scale events that present high-probability targets such as national special security events (NSSEs) and other special events as determined by the secretary of homeland security, in coordination with other federal departments and agencies.

4. The secretary of homeland security has been directed to assume responsibility for managing a domestic incident by the president. Additionally, since incidents of national significance typically result in impacts far beyond the immediate or initial incident area, the NRP provides a framework to enable the management of cascading impacts and multiple incidents as well as the prevention of and preparation for subsequent events. Examples of incident management actions from a national perspective include

- Increasing nationwide public awareness.
- Assessing trends that point to potential terrorist activity.
- Elevating the national Homeland Security Advisory System (HSAS) alert condition and coordinating protective measures across jurisdictions.
- Increasing countermeasures such as inspections, surveillance, security, counterintelligence, and infrastructure protection.
- Conducting public health surveillance and assessment processes and, where appropriate, conducting a wide range of prevention measures to include but not be limited to immunizations.
- Providing immediate and long-term public health and medical response assets.
- Coordinating federal support to state, local, and tribal authorities in the aftermath of an incident.
- Providing strategies for coordination of federal resources required to handle subsequent events.
- Restoring public confidence after a terrorist attack.
- Enabling immediate recovery activities, as well as addressing long-term consequences in the impacted area.

Signatory Partners

There are 32 signatory partners in the NRP. Each of these partners serves as a primary agency or support agency in one or more of the 15 emergency support functions in the NRP. FEMA defines primary and support agencies as follows.

Primary Agencies.   A federal agency designated as an ESF primary agency serves as a federal executive agent under the federal coordinating officer (or federal resource coordinator for non-Stafford Act incidents) to accomplish the ESF mission. When an ESF is activated in response to an incident of national significance, the primary agency is responsible for

- Orchestrating federal support within its functional area for an affected state.
- Providing staff for the operations functions at fixed and field facilities.
- Notifying and requesting assistance from support agencies.
- Managing mission assignments and coordinating with support agencies, as well as appropriate state agencies.
- Working with appropriate private-sector organizations to maximize use of all available resources.

- Supporting and keeping other ESFs and organizational elements informed of ESF operational priorities and activities.
- Executing contracts and procuring goods and services as needed.
- Ensuring financial and property accountability for ESF activities.
- Planning for short-term and long-term incident management and recovery operations.
- Maintaining trained personnel to support interagency emergency response and support teams.

Support Agencies.   When an ESF is activated in response to an incident of national significance, support agencies are responsible for

- Conducting operations, when requested by DHS or the designated ESF primary agency, using their own authorities, subject-matter experts, capabilities, or resources.
- Participating in planning for short-term and long-term incident management and recovery operations and the development of supporting operational plans, standard operating procedures, checklists, or other job aids, in concert with existing first responder standards.
- Assisting in the conduct of situational assessments.
- Furnishing available personnel, equipment, or other resource support as requested by DHS or the ESF primary agency.
- Providing input to periodic readiness assessments.
- Participating in training and exercises aimed at continuous improvement of prevention, response, and recovery capabilities.
- Identifying new equipment or capabilities required to prevent or respond to new or emerging threats and hazards or to improve the ability to address existing threats.
- Nominating new technologies to DHS for review and evaluation that have the potential to improve performance within or across functional areas.
- Providing information or intelligence regarding their agency's area of expertise.

The signatory partners are provided below.

□ □ □ ▬▬▬▬▬▬▬▬▬▬▬▬▬▬▬▬▬▬▬▬▬

National Response Plan Signatory Partners

American Red Cross
Central Intelligence Agency
Corporation for National and Community Service
Department of Agriculture
Department of Commerce
Department of Defense
Department of Education
Department of Energy

(Continued)

Department of Health and Human Services
Department of Homeland Security
Department of Housing and Urban Development
Department of the Interior
Department of Justice
Department of Labor
Department of State
Department of Transportation
Department of the Treasury
Department of Veterans Affairs
Environmental Protection Agency
Federal Bureau of Investigation
Federal Communications Commission
General Services Administration
National Aeronautic and Space Administration
National Transportation Safety Board
National Voluntary Organizations Active in Disaster
Nuclear Regulatory Commission
Office of Personnel Management
Small Business Administration
Social Security Administration
Tennessee Valley Authority
U.S. Agency for International Development
U.S. Postal Service

Source: www.dhs.gov.

Emergency Support Functions

The NRP applies a functional approach that groups the capabilities of federal departments and agencies and the American Red Cross into emergency support functions to provide the planning, support, resources, program implementation, and emergency services that are most likely to be needed during incidents of national significance. The federal response to actual or potential incidents of national significance typically is provided through the full or partial activation of the ESF structure as necessary.

The ESFs serve as the coordination mechanism to provide assistance to state, local, and tribal governments or federal departments and agencies conducting missions of primary federal responsibility. ESFs may be selectively activated for both Stafford Act and non-Stafford Act incidents where federal departments or agencies request DHS assistance or under other circumstances as defined in HSPD-5.

Each ESF is composed of primary and support agencies. The NRP identifies primary agencies on the basis of authorities, resources, and capabilities. Support agencies are assigned based on resources and capabilities in a given functional area. The ESF structure provides a structure within which to mobilize the components necessary to best address the requirements of each incident. For example, a large-scale natural disaster or massive terrorist event may require the activation of all ESFs. A localized flood or tornado might require activation only of a select number of ESFs.

The scope of each ESF is summarized as follows.

□ □ □ ▬▬▬▬▬▬▬▬▬▬▬▬▬▬▬▬▬▬▬

Scope of Each ESF

ESF #1—Transportation
- Federal and civil transportation support.
- Transportation safety.
- Restoration and recovery of transportation infrastructure.
- Movement restrictions.
- Damage and impact assessment.

ESF #2—Communications
- Coordination with telecommunications industry.
- Restoration and repair of telecommunications infrastructure.
- Protection, restoration, and sustainability of national cyber and information technology resources.

ESF #3—Public Works and Engineering
- Infrastructure protection and emergency repair.
- Infrastructure restoration.
- Engineering services, construction management.
- Critical infrastructure liaison.

ESF #4—Firefighting
- Firefighting activities on federal lands.
- Resource support to rural and urban firefighting operations.

ESF #5—Emergency Management
- Coordination of incident management efforts.
- Issuance of mission assignments.
- Resource and human capital.
- Incident action planning.
- Financial management.

ESF #6—Mass Care, Housing, and Human Services
- Mass care.
- Disaster housing.
- Human services.

ESF #7—Resource Support
- Resource support (facility space, office equipment and supplies, contracting services, etc.).

(Continued)

ESF #8—Public Health and Medical Services
- Public health.
- Medical.
- Mental health services.
- Mortuary services.

ESF #9—Urban Search and Rescue
- Life-saving assistance.
- Urban search and rescue.

ESF #10—Oil and Hazardous Materials Response
- Oil and hazardous materials (chemical, biological, radiological, etc.) response.
- Environmental safety and short- and long-term cleanup.

ESF #11—Agriculture and Natural Resources
- Nutrition assistance.
- Animal and plant disease and pest response.
- Food safety and security.
- Natural and cultural resources and historic properties protection and restoration.

ESF #12—Energy
- Energy infrastructure assessment, repair, and restoration.
- Energy industry utilities coordination.
- Energy forecast.

ESF #13—Public Safety and Security
- Facility and resource security.
- Security planning and technical and resource assistance.
- Public safety and security support.
- Support to access, traffic, and crowd control.

ESF #14—Long-Term Community Recovery and Mitigation
- Social and economic community impact assessment.
- Long-term community recovery assistance to states, local governments, and the private sector.
- Mitigation analysis and program implementation.

ESF #15—External Affairs
- Emergency public information and protective action guidance.
- Media and community relations.
- Congressional and international affairs.
- Tribal and insular affairs.

Source: www.dhs.gov.

Roles and Responsibilities

The NRP also defines the roles and responsibilities of public, private, and nonprofit parties involved in incident management at the local, state, and national levels.

Governor.   As a state's chief executive, the governor is responsible for the public safety and welfare of the people of that state or territory. The governor

- Is responsible for coordinating state resources to address the full spectrum of actions to prevent, prepare for, respond to, and recover from incidents in an all-hazards context to include terrorism, natural disasters, accidents, and other contingencies.
- Under certain emergency conditions, typically has police powers to make, amend, and rescind orders and regulations.
- Provides leadership and plays a key role in communicating to the public and helping people, businesses, and organizations cope with the consequences of any type of declared emergency within state jurisdiction.
- Encourages participation in mutual aid and implements authorities for the state to enter into mutual aid agreements with other states, tribes, and territories to facilitate resource sharing.
- Is the commander-in-chief of state military forces (National Guard when in state active duty or Title 32 status and the authorized state militias).
- Requests federal assistance when it becomes clear that state or tribal capabilities are insufficient or have been exceeded or exhausted.

Local Chief Executive Officer.   A mayor or city or county manager, as a jurisdiction's chief executive, is responsible for the public safety and welfare of the people of that jurisdiction. The local chief executive officer

- Is responsible for coordinating local resources to address the full spectrum of actions to prevent, prepare for, respond to, and recover from incidents involving all hazards including terrorism, natural disasters, accidents, and other contingencies.
- Dependent on state and local law, has extraordinary powers to suspend local laws and ordinances, such as to establish a curfew, direct evacuations, and in coordination with the local health authority, order a quarantine.
- Provides leadership and plays a key role in communicating to the public and helping people, businesses, and organizations cope with the consequences of any type of domestic incident within the jurisdiction.
- Negotiates and enters into mutual aid agreements with other jurisdictions to facilitate resource sharing. Requests state and, if necessary, federal assistance through the governor of the state when the jurisdiction's capabilities have been exceeded or exhausted.

Tribal Chief Executive Officer.   The tribal chief executive officer is responsible for the public safety and welfare of the people of that tribe. The tribal chief executive officer, as authorized by tribal government,

- Is responsible for coordinating tribal resources to address the full spectrum of actions to prevent, prepare for, respond to, and recover from incidents involving all hazards including terrorism, natural disasters, accidents, and other contingencies.

- Has extraordinary powers to suspend tribal laws and ordinances, such as to establish a curfew, direct evacuations, and order a quarantine.
- Provides leadership and plays a key role in communicating to the tribal nation and helping people, businesses, and organizations cope with the consequences of any type of domestic incident within the jurisdiction.
- Negotiates and enters into mutual aid agreements with other tribes and jurisdictions to facilitate resource sharing. Can request state and federal assistance through the governor of the state when the tribe's capabilities have been exceeded or exhausted.
- Can elect to deal directly with the federal government. (Although a state governor must request a presidential disaster declaration on behalf of a tribe under the Stafford Act, federal agencies can work directly with the tribe within existing authorities and resources.)

Secretary of Homeland Security.   Pursuant to HSPD-5, the secretary of homeland security

- Is responsible for coordinating federal operations within the United States to prepare for, respond to, and recover from terrorist attacks, major disasters, and other emergencies.
- Serves as the "principal federal official" for domestic incident management. The secretary also is responsible for coordinating federal resources utilized in response to or recovery from terrorist attacks, major disasters, or other emergencies if and when any of the following four conditions applies:
  - A federal department or agency acting under its own authority has requested DHS assistance.
  - The resources of state and local authorities are overwhelmed and federal assistance has been requested.
  - More than one federal department or agency has become substantially involved in responding to the incident.
  - The secretary has been directed to assume incident management responsibilities by the president.

Attorney General.   The attorney general is the chief law enforcement officer in the United States. In accordance with HSPD-5 and other relevant statutes and directives, the attorney general has lead responsibility for criminal investigations of terrorist acts or terrorist threats

- By individuals or groups inside the United States.
- Directed at U.S. citizens or institutions abroad.

Generally acting through the FBI, the attorney general, in cooperation with other federal departments and agencies engaged in activities to protect national security, coordinates the activities of the other members of the law enforcement community. Nothing in the NRP derogates the attorney general's status or responsibilities.

Secretary of Defense.   The DoD has significant resources that may be available to support the federal response to an incident of national significance. The secretary of defense authorizes the defense department support of civil authorities (DSCA) for domestic incidents as directed by the president or when consistent with military readiness operations and appropriate under the circumstances and the law. The secretary of defense retains command of military forces under DSCA, as with all other situations and operations. Nothing in the NRP impairs or otherwise affects the authority of the secretary of defense over the DoD.

Secretary of State.   The secretary of state is responsible for coordinating international prevention, preparedness, response, and recovery activities relating to domestic incidents and for the protection of U.S. citizens and U.S. interests overseas.

Nongovernmental Organizations.   NGOs collaborate with first responders, governments at all levels, and other agencies and organizations providing relief services to sustain life, reduce physical and emotional distress, and promote recovery of disaster victims when assistance is not available from other sources.

Private Sector.   DHS and NRP primary and support agencies coordinate with the private sector to effectively share information, form courses of action, and incorporate available resources to prevent, prepare for, respond to, and recover from incidents of national significance. The roles, responsibilities, and participation of the private sector during incidents of national significance vary based on the nature of the organization and the type and impact of the incident. Private-sector organizations may be involved as

- **An Impacted Organization or Infrastructure.** Private-sector organizations may be affected by direct or indirect consequences of the incident. Examples of privately owned elements of infrastructure include transportation, telecommunications, private utilities, financial institutions, and hospitals.
- **A Response Resource.** Private-sector organizations may provide response resources (donated or compensated) during an incident, including specialized teams, equipment, and advanced technologies.
- **A Regulated or Responsible Party.** Owners and operators of certain regulated facilities or hazardous operations may bear responsibilities under the law for preparing for and preventing incidents from occurring and responding to an incident once it occurs. For example, federal regulations require owners and operators of Nuclear Regulatory Commission–regulated nuclear facilities to maintain emergency (incident) preparedness plans, procedures, and facilities and perform assessments, prompt notifications, and training for a response to an incident.
- **Members of State and Local Emergency Organizations.** Private-sector organizations may serve as an active partner in local and state emergency preparedness and response organizations and activities.

Citizen Involvement.   Strong partnerships with citizen groups and organizations provide support for incident management prevention, preparedness, response, recovery, and mitigation. The U.S. Citizen Corps brings these groups together and focuses efforts of individuals through education, training, and volunteer service to help make communities safer, stronger, and better prepared to address the threats of terrorism, crime, public health issues, and disasters of all kinds.

The National Response Plan Coordinating Structures

- **Incident Command Post (ICP).** The field location at which the primary tactical-level, on-scene incident command functions are performed. The ICP may be collocated with the incident base or other incident facilities and normally is identified by a green rotating or flashing light.
- **Area Command (Unified Area Command).** An organization established (1) to oversee the management of multiple incidents each of which is being handled by an ICS organization or (2) to oversee the management of large or multiple incidents to which several incident management teams have been assigned. Area command has the responsibility to set overall strategy and priorities, allocate critical resources according to priorities, ensure that incidents are properly managed, and ensure that objectives are met and strategies followed. Area command becomes unified area command when incidents are multijurisdictional. Area command may be established at an EOC facility or at some location other than an ICP.
- **Local Emergency Operations Center (EOC).** The physical location at which the coordination of information and resources to support local incident management activities normally takes place.
- **State Emergency Operations Center (EOC).** The physical location at which the coordination of information and resources to support state incident management activities normally takes place.
- **Homeland Security Operations Center (HSOC).** The primary national hub for domestic incident management operational coordination and situational awareness. The HSOC is a standing 24/7 interagency organization fusing law enforcement, national intelligence, emergency response, and private-sector reporting. The HSOC facilitates homeland security information sharing and operational coordination with other federal, state, local, tribal, and nongovernmental EOCs.
- **Interagency Incident Management Group (IIMG).** The IIMG is a federal headquarters-level multiagency coordination entity that facilitates federal domestic incident management for incidents of national significance. The secretary of homeland security activates the IIMG based on the nature, severity, magnitude, and complexity of the threat or incident. The secretary of homeland security may activate the IIMG for high-profile, large-scale events that present high probability targets, such as NSSEs, and in heightened-threat situations. The IIMG is composed of senior representatives from DHS components, other federal departments and agencies, and nongovernmental organizations, as required. The IIMG membership is flexible and can be tailored or task organized to provide the appropriate subject-matter expertise required for the specific threat or incident.
- **National Response Coordination Center (NRCC).** The NRCC is a multiagency center that provides overall federal response coordination for incidents of national significance and emergency management program implementation. FEMA maintains the NRCC as a functional component

of the HSOC in support of incident management operations. The NRCC monitors potential or developing incidents of national significance and supports the efforts of regional and field components. The NRCC resolves federal resource support conflicts and other implementation issues forwarded by the joint field office (JFO). Those issues that cannot be resolved by the NRCC are referred to the IIMG.

- **Regional Response Coordination Center (RRCC).** The RRCC is a standing facility operated by FEMA that is activated to coordinate regional response efforts, establish federal priorities, and implement local federal program support. The RRCC operates until a JFO is established in the field or the principal federal officer, federal coordinating officer, or federal resource coordinator can assume his or her NRP coordination responsibilities. The RRCC establishes communications with the affected state emergency management agency and the National Response Coordination Center, coordinates deployment of the emergency response team-advance element (ERT-A) to field locations, assesses damage information, develops situation reports, and issues initial mission assignments.

- **Strategic Information and Operations Center (SIOC).** The FBI SIOC is the focal point and operational control center for all federal intelligence, law enforcement, and investigative law enforcement activities related to domestic terrorist incidents or credible threats, including leading attribution investigations. The SIOC serves as an information clearinghouse to help collect, process, vet, and disseminate information relevant to law enforcement and criminal investigation efforts in a timely manner. The SIOC maintains direct connectivity with the HSOC and IIMG. The SIOC, located at FBI headquarters, supports the FBI's mission in leading efforts of the law enforcement community to detect, prevent, preempt, and disrupt terrorist attacks against the United States. The SIOC houses the National Joint Terrorism Task Force (NJTTF). The mission of the NJTTF is to enhance communications, coordination, and cooperation among federal, state, local, and tribal agencies representing the intelligence, law enforcement, defense, diplomatic, public safety, and homeland security communities by providing a point of fusion for terrorism intelligence and by supporting joint terrorism task forces (JTTFs) throughout the United States.

- **Joint Field Office (JFO).** The JFO is a temporary federal facility established locally to coordinate operational federal assistance activities to the affected jurisdiction(s) during incidents of national significance. The JFO is a multiagency center that provides a central location for coordination of federal, state, local, tribal, nongovernmental, and private-sector organizations with primary responsibility for threat response and incident support. The JFO enables the effective and efficient coordination of federal incident-related prevention, preparedness, response, and recovery actions. The JFO utilizes the scalable organizational structure of the NIMS incident command system (ICS). The JFO organization adapts to the magnitude and complexity of the situation at hand and incorporates the NIMS principles regarding span of control and organizational structure: management, operations, planning,

(Continued)

logistics, and finance/administration. Although the JFO uses an ICS structure, the JFO does not manage on-scene operations. Instead, the JFO focuses on providing support to on-scene efforts and conducting broader support operations that may extend beyond the incident site.

- **Joint Operations Center (JOC).** The JOC branch is established by the senior federal law enforcement officer (SFLEO) (e.g., the FBI senior agent-in-charge during terrorist incidents) to coordinate and direct law enforcement and criminal investigation activities related to the incident. The JOC branch ensures management and coordination of federal, state, local, and tribal investigative/law enforcement activities. The emphasis of the JOC is on prevention as well as intelligence collection, investigation, and prosecution of a criminal act. This emphasis includes managing unique tactical issues inherent to a crisis situation (e.g., a hostage situation or terrorist threat). When this branch is included as part of the joint field office, it is responsible for coordinating the intelligence and information function (as described in NIMS), which includes information and operational security, and the collection, analysis, and distribution of all incident related intelligence. Accordingly, the intelligence unit within the JOC branch serves as the interagency fusion center for all intelligence related to an incident.

Field-Level Organizational Structures: JFO Coordination Group

The field-level organizational structures and teams deployed in response to an incident of national significance, include the following potential members of the JFO coordination group:

- **Principal Federal Official (PFO).** The PFO is personally designated by the secretary of homeland security to facilitate federal support to the established incident command system (ICS) unified command structure and to coordinate overall federal incident management and assistance activities across the spectrum of prevention, preparedness, response, and recovery. The PFO ensures that incident management efforts are maximized through effective and efficient coordination. The PFO provides a primary point of contact and situational awareness locally for the secretary of homeland security.
- **Federal Coordinating Officer (FCO).** The FCO manages and coordinates federal resource support activities related to Stafford Act disasters and emergencies. The FCO
  - Assists the unified command or the area command.
  - Works closely with the principal federal official, senior federal law enforcement official, and other senior federal officials.

In Stafford Act situations where a PFO has not been assigned, the FCO provides overall coordination for the federal components of the JFO and works in partnership with the state coordinating officer (SCO) to determine and satisfy state and local assistance requirements.

- **Senior Federal Law Enforcement Official (SFLEO).** The SFLEO is the senior law enforcement official from the agency with primary jurisdictional responsibility as directed by statute, presidential directive, existing federal policies, or the attorney general. The SFLEO directs intelligence and investigative law enforcement operations related to the incident and supports the law enforcement component of the unified command on-scene. In the event of a terrorist incident, this official normally is the FBI senior agent-in-charge.
- **Federal Resource Coordinator (FRC).** The FRC manages federal resource support activities related to non-Stafford Act incidents of national significance when federal-to-federal support is requested from DHS by another federal agency. The FRC is responsible for coordinating the timely delivery of resources to the requesting agency. In non-Stafford Act situations when a federal department or agency acting under its own authority has requested the assistance of the secretary of homeland security to obtain support from other federal departments and agencies, DHS designates an FRC. In these situations, the FRC coordinates support through interagency agreements and memoranda of understanding (MOUs).
- **State, Local, and Tribal Official(s).** The JFO coordination group also includes state representatives, such as
  - The **State Coordinating Officer (SCO)**, who serves as the state counterpart to the FCO and manages the state's incident management programs and activities.
  - The **Governor's Authorized Representative**, who represents the governor of the impacted state.
  - Possibly, local area representatives with primary statutory authority for incident management.
- **Senior Federal Officials (SFOs).** The JFO coordination group may also include representatives of other federal departments or agencies with primary statutory responsibility for certain aspects of incident management. SFOs utilize existing authorities, expertise, and capabilities to assist in management of the incident working in coordination with the PFO, FCO, SFLEO, and other members of the JFO coordination group. When appropriate, the JFO coordination group may also include U.S. attorneys or other senior officials or their designees from Department of Justice (DOJ) to provide expert legal counsel.

Field-Level Organizational Structures: JFO Coordination Staff

The JFO structure normally includes a coordination staff. The JFO coordination group determines the extent of this staffing based on the type and magnitude of the incident. The roles and responsibilities of the JFO coordination staff are summarized below:

(Continued)

- **Chief of Staff.** The JFO coordination staff may include a chief of staff and representatives providing specialized assistance, which may include support in the following areas: safety, legal counsel, equal rights, security, infrastructure liaison, and other liaisons.
- **External Affairs Officer.** The external affairs officer provides support to the JFO leadership in all functions involving communications with external audiences. External affairs includes public affairs, community relations, congressional affairs, state and local coordination, tribal affairs, and international affairs, when appropriate. Resources for the various external affairs functions are coordinated through ESF #15. The external affairs officer also is responsible for overseeing operations of the federal joint information center (JIC) established to support the JFO. The JIC:
  - Is a physical location where public affairs professionals from organizations involved in incident management activities work together to provide critical emergency information, crisis communications, and public affairs support.
  - Serves as a focal point for the coordination and dissemination of information to the public and media concerning incident prevention, preparedness, response, recovery, and mitigation.
- **Defense Coordinating Officer (DCO).** If appointed by DoD, the DCO serves as DoD's single point of contact at the JFO. With few exceptions, requests for Defense Department support of civil authorities originating at the JFO are coordinated with and processed through the DCO. The DCO may have a defense coordinating element (DCE) consisting of a staff and military liaison officers to facilitate coordination and support to activated emergency support functions. Specific responsibilities of the DCO (subject to modification based on the situation) include processing requirements for military support, forwarding mission assignments to the appropriate military organizations through DoD-designated channels, and assigning military liaisons, as appropriate, to activated ESFs.

Field-Level Organizational Structures: JFO Sections

The role of each JFO section is presented below:

- **Operations Section.** The operations section coordinates operational support to on-scene incident management efforts. Branches may be added or deleted as required, depending on the nature of the incident. The operations section also is responsible for coordination with other federal command posts that may be established to support incident management activities. The operations section may include the following elements:

- The **Response and Recovery Operations Branch** coordinates the request and delivery of federal assistance and support from various special teams. This branch is composed of four groups: emergency services, human services, infrastructure support, and community recovery and mitigation.

- The **Law Enforcement Investigative Operations Branch/Joint Operations Center (JOC)** is established by the senior federal law enforcement official (e.g., the FBI senior agent-in-charge during terrorist incidents) to coordinate and direct law enforcement and criminal investigation activities related to a terrorist incident. The JOC branch ensures management and coordination of federal, state, local, and tribal investigative and law enforcement activities. The emphasis of the JOC is on prevention as well as intelligence collection, investigation, and prosecution of a criminal act. This emphasis includes managing unique tactical issues inherent to a crisis situation (e.g., a hostage situation or terrorist threat).

- For national special security events, a third branch, the **Security Operations Branch**, or **Multiagency Command Center (MACC)**, may be added to coordinate protection and site security efforts. In these situations, the operations section chief is designated by mutual agreement of the JFO coordination group based on the agency with greatest jurisdictional involvement and statutory authority for the current incident priorities. The agency providing the operations section chief may change over time as incident priorities change.

- **Planning Section.** The planning section provides current information to the JFO coordination group to ensure situational awareness, determine cascading effects, identify national implications, and determine specific areas of interest requiring long-term attention. The planning section also provides technical and scientific expertise. The planning section is composed of the following units: situation, resources, documentation, technical specialists, and demobilization. The planning section also may include an information and intelligence unit (if not assigned elsewhere) and an HSOC representative, who aids in the development of reports for the HSOC and IIMG.

- **Logistics Section.** The logistics section coordinates logistics support that includes
  - Control and accountability for federal supplies and equipment.
  - Resource ordering.
  - Delivery of equipment, supplies, and services to the JFO and other field locations.
  - Facility location, setup, space management, building services, and general facility operations.
  - Transportation coordination and fleet management services.
  - Information and technology systems services, administrative services such as mail management and reproduction, and customer assistance.

    The logistics section may include coordination and planning, resource management, supply, and information services branches.

(Continued)

- **Finance and Administration Section (Comptroller).** The finance and administration section is responsible for the financial management, monitoring, and tracking of all federal costs relating to the incident and the functioning of the JFO while adhering to all federal laws, acts, and regulations. The position of the financial and administration chief is held exclusively by a comptroller, who serves as the senior financial advisor to the team leader (e.g., FCO) and represents the coordinating agency's chief financial officer (CFO) as prescribed by the CFO Act of 1990.

Field-Level Organizational Structures: Response Teams

Various teams are ready to deploy in response to threats or incidents. These teams include the following:

- **ERT Advance Element (ERT-A).** The ERT-A conducts assessments, and initiates coordination with the state and initial deployment of federal resources. It is headed by a team leader from FEMA and composed of program and support staff and representatives from selected ESF primary agencies. Each FEMA region maintains an ERT ready to deploy during the early stages of an incident to
  - The state EOC or to other locations to work directly with the state to obtain information on the impact of the event and identify specific state requests for federal incident management assistance.
  - The affected area to establish field communications, locate and establish field facilities, and set up support activities.
- **National Emergency Response Team (ERT-N).** The ERT-N deploys for large-scale, high-impact events or as required. An ERT-N may predeploy based on threat conditions. The secretary of homeland security determines the need for ERT-N deployment, coordinating the plans with the affected region and other federal agencies. The ERT-N includes staff from FEMA headquarters and regional offices as well as other federal agencies.
- **Federal Incident Response Support Team (FIRST).** The FIRST is a forward component of the ERT-A that provides on-scene support to the local incident command or area command structure to facilitate an integrated interjurisdictional response. The FIRST is designed to be a quick and readily deployable resource to support the federal response to incidents of national significance. The FIRST deploys within 2 hours of notification, to be on-scene within 12 hours of notification. FEMA maintains and deploys

the FIRST. On the subsequent deployment of an emergency response team (ERT), the FIRST integrates into the operations section of the JFO.

- **Domestic Emergency Support Teams (DEST).** The DEST may be deployed to provide technical support for management of potential or actual terrorist incidents. Based on a credible threat assessment, the attorney general, in consultation with the secretary of homeland security, may request authorization through the White House to deploy the DEST. The PFO and a small staff component may deploy with the DEST to facilitate their timely arrival and enhance initial situational awareness. On arrival at the JFO or critical incident location, the DEST may act as a stand-alone advisory team to the FBI special agent-in-charge providing required technical assistance or recommended operational courses of action.

Field-Level Organizational Structures: Other Federal Response Teams

Numerous special teams are available to support incident management and disaster response and recovery operations. Examples include

- Damage assessment teams.
- The nuclear incident response team (NIRT).
- Disaster medical assistance teams (DMATs).
- HHS secretary's emergency response team.
- DOL/OSHA's specialized response teams.
- Veterinarian medical assistance teams (VMATs).
- Disaster mortuary operational response teams (DMORTs).
- National medical response teams (NMRTs).
- Scientific and technical advisory and response teams (STARTs).
- Donations coordination teams.
- Urban search and rescue (US&R) task forces and incident support teams.
- Federal type 1 and type 2 incident management teams (IMTs).
- Domestic animal and wildlife emergency response teams and mitigation assessment teams.

Incident Management Actions

- **Notification and Assessment.** Federal, state, local, tribal, private-sector, and nongovernmental organizations report threats, incidents, and potential incidents using established communications and reporting channels. The Homeland Security Operations Center receives threat and operational

(Continued)

information regarding incidents or potential incidents and makes an initial determination to initiate the coordination of federal information sharing and incident management activities. When notified of a threat or an incident with possible national-level implications, the HSOC assesses the situation and notifies the secretary of homeland security accordingly.

- **Reporting.** Federal, state, tribal, private-sector, and nongovernmental emergency operations centers report incident information to the HSOC. In most situations, incident information is reported using existing mechanisms to state or federal operations centers, which in turn report the information to the HSOC. Information regarding potential terrorist threats normally is reported initially to a local or regional joint terrorism task force and, subsequently, from the FBI Strategic Information and Operations Center to the HSOC if the FBI deems the threat to be credible.

- **Activation.** For actual or potential incidents of national significance, the HSOC reports the situation to the secretary of homeland security or a senior staff member, as delegated by the secretary, who then determines the need to activate components of the NRP to conduct further assessment of the situation, initiate interagency coordination, share information with affected jurisdictions, or initiate deployment of resources. Concurrently, the secretary also determines whether or not an event meets the criteria established for a potential or actual incident of national significance as defined in the NRP. When the secretary declares an incident of national significance, federal departments and agencies are notified by the HSOC (as operational security considerations permit) and may be called on to staff the interagency incident management group and National Response Coordination Center. The affected state(s) and tribes also are notified by the HSOC using appropriate operational security protocols. In the preincident mode, such notification may be conducted discreetly, on a need-to-know basis, to preserve the operational security and confidentiality of certain law enforcement and investigative operations. The NRCC and RRCC deploy, track, and provide incident-related information until the JFO is established.

- **Response.** Once an incident occurs, the priority shifts to immediate and short-term response activities to preserve life, property, the environment, and the social, economic, and political structure of the community. Actions also are taken to prevent and protect against other potential threats. Examples of response actions include immediate law enforcement, fire, and emergency medical service actions; mass care, public health, and medical services; emergency restoration of critical infrastructure; control of environmental contamination; and responder health and safety protection. During the response to a terrorist event, law enforcement actions to collect and preserve evidence and apprehend perpetrators are critical. These actions take place simultaneously with response operations necessary to save lives and protect property.

- **Recovery.** Recovery involves actions needed to help individuals and communities return to normal when feasible. The JFO is the central coordination point among federal, state, local, and tribal agencies and voluntary organizations for delivering recovery assistance programs. Long-term environmental recovery may include cleanup and restoration of public facilities, businesses, and residences; reestablishment of habitats and prevention of subsequent damage to natural resources; protection of cultural or archeological sites; and protection of natural, cultural, and historical resources from intentional damage during other recovery operations.

- **Mitigation.** Hazard mitigation involves reducing or eliminating long-term risk to people and property from hazards and their side effects. The JFO's community recovery and mitigation branch is responsible for coordinating the delivery of all mitigation programs within the affected area, including hazard mitigation for
  - ○ Grant programs for loss reduction measures (if available).
  - ○ Delivery of loss reduction building-science expertise.
  - ○ Coordination of federal flood insurance operations.
  - ○ Community education and outreach necessary to foster loss reduction.
- **Demobilization.** When a centralized federal coordination presence no longer is required in the affected area, the JFO coordination group implements the demobilization plan to transfer responsibilities and close out the JFO. After the JFO closes, long-term recovery program management and monitoring transition to individual agencies' regional offices or headquarters, as appropriate.
- **Remedial Actions and After-Action Reports.** DHS formally convenes interagency meetings, called *hotwashes*, to identify critical issues requiring headquarters-level attention, lessons learned, and best practices associated with the federal response to incidents of national significance. Hotwashes typically are conducted at major transition points over the course of incident management operations and should include state, local, and tribal participation. Identified issues are validated and promptly assigned to appropriate organizations for remediation. Following an incident, the JFO coordination group submits an after-action report to DHS headquarters detailing operational successes, problems, and key issues affecting incident management. The report includes appropriate feedback from all federal, state, local, tribal, nongovernmental, and private-sector partners participating in the incident.

Source: FEMA Emergency Management Institute.

Two of the US&R task forces have agreements with the U.S. Agency for International Development (USAID) to provide search and rescue services overseas. These two task forces are Metro-Dade Fire Department in Florida and the Fairfax County Fire and Rescue in Virginia. A full list of US&R task forces is presented in Table 4–3.

Other FEMA Response Resources

FEMA manages a cadre of nearly 4,000 temporary disaster assistance employees (DAEs), who support FEMA response and recovery activities in the field in areas such

Table 4–3   FEMA Urban Search and Rescue Task Forces

State	Number	Organization
Arizona	AZ-TF1	Phoenix, Arizona
California	CA-TF1	LA City Fire Dept.
	CA-TF2	LA County Fire Dept.
	CA-TF3	Menlo Park Fire Dept.
	CA-TF4	Oakland Fire Dept.
	CA-TF5	Orange Co. Fire Authority
	CA-TF6	Riverside Fire Dept.
	CA-TF7	Sacramento Fire Dept.
	CA-TF8	San Diego Fire Dept.
Colorado	CO-TF1	State of Colorado
Florida	FL-TF1	Metro-Dade Fire Dept.
	FL-TF2	Miami Fire Dept.
Indiana	IN-TF1	Marion County
Maryland	MD-TF1	Montgomery Fire Rescue
Massachusetts	MA-TF1	City of Beverly
Missouri	MO-TF1	Boone County Fire Protection District
Nebraska	NE-TF1	Lincoln Fire Dept.
Nevada	NV-TF1	Clark County Fire Dept.
New Mexico	NM-TF1	State of New Mexico
New York	NY-TF1	NYC Fire and EMS, Police
Ohio	OH-TF1	Miami Valley Urban Search and Rescue
Pennsylvania	PA-TF1	Commonwealth of Pennsylvania
Tennessee	TN-TF1	Memphis Fire Dept.
Texas	TX-TF1	State of Texas Urban Search and Rescue
Utah	UT-TF1	Salt Lake Fire Dept.
Virginia	VA-TF2	Fairfax Co. Fire and Rescue Dept.
		Virginia Beach Fire Dept.
Washington	WA-TF1	Puget Sound Task Force

Source: FEMA, www.fema.gov.

as logistics, facility management, public affairs, community relations, and customer service (see Figures 4–3 and 4–4). FEMA manages a mobile operations capability that provides communications and logistical support to state and local emergency officials.

Critical Thinking

- What are the strengths and weaknesses of the National Response Plan?
- Would disaster response be more efficient if the federal government had the authority to assume power over any disaster response, regardless of the ability of local response agencies? Why or why not?

FIGURE 4–3 New York, New York, September 27, 2001. FEMA, New York firefighters and the urban search and rescue teams worked very closely throughout the cleanup effort at the World Trade Center. Photo by Bri Rodriguez/FEMA News Photo.

FIGURE 4–4 Malibu, California, 1996. A California Department of Forestry official watches the wildfire as it burns up a hillside. FEMA News Photo.

The DAE Experience

By Pat Glithero, FEMA Region V

Whenever the Federal Emergency Management Agency responds to a disaster, local and staff officials encounter and work with numerous FEMA staff members, many of them women and men of FEMA's disaster assistance employee (DAE) program. DAEs respond as needed to presidentially declared emergencies and disasters across the nation and territories and remain until the disaster field office (DFO) closes. They then return home to resume their lives as officials, businessmen, professionals, retirees, and in a myriad of other jobs.

DAEs join the cadre for many reasons. Some have benefited from FEMA programs in disasters and want to share their gratitude. Many believe strongly in programs designed to help fellow citizens. To many retirees, the DAE program allows a continued work opportunity alongside colleagues with whom they have worked for many years on a full-time basis. Some just appreciate working a job that uses their skills and allows them to feel they make a difference. Working in various geographic parts of the United States at a state or local level is a positive by-product of disaster deployment. FEMA offers many opportunities for training classes and learning that otherwise might not be available in the private sector.

At the beginning, or end, of any DFO, though, what means most to many DAEs is the sense of camaraderie and family that DAEs share with each other and other FEMA staff. With a total workforce of less than 2,500 nationwide, FEMA DAEs and staff become part of a community that comes together as needed, does the job, and then parts officially until the next call.

Source: FEMA, www.fema.gov.

FEMA'S Operations Capability

Disasters may require resources beyond the capabilities of the local or state authorities. In response to regional requests for support, FEMA provides mobile telecommunications, operational support, life support, and power generation assets for the on-site management of disaster and all-hazard activities. This support is managed by the Response and Recovery Directorate's Mobile Operations Division (RR-MO).

The Mobile Operations Division has a small headquarters staff and five geographically dispersed mobile emergency response support (MERS) detachments and the mobile air-transportable telecommunications system (MATTS) to

- Meet the needs of the government emergency managers in their efforts to save lives, protect property, and coordinate disaster and all-hazard operations.

- Provide prompt and rapid multimedia communications, information processing, logistics, and operational support to federal, state, and local agencies during catastrophic emergencies and disasters for government response and recovery operations.

The MERS and MATTS support the disaster field facilities. They support the federal, state, and local responders, not the disaster victims.

Available Support

Each MERS detachment can concurrently support a large disaster field office and multiple field operating sites within the disaster area. MERS is equipped with self-sustaining telecommunications, logistics, and operations support elements that can be driven or airlifted to the disaster location. MATTS and some of the MERS assets can be airlifted by C-130 military cargo aircraft.

The MERS and MATTS are available for immediate deployment. As required, equipment and personnel deploy promptly and provide

- Multimedia communications and information processing support, especially for the communications section, emergency support function (ESF) #2 of the Federal Response Plan.
- Operational support, especially for the information and planning section, ESF #5 of the FRP.
- Liaison to the federal coordinating officer.
- Logistics and life support for emergency responders.
- Automated information and decision support capability.
- Security (facility, equipment, and personnel) management and consultation.

Most equipment is preloaded or installed on heavy-duty, multiwheel drive trucks. Some equipment is installed in transit cases.

Source: FEMA, www.fema.gov.

Communications among Responding Agencies

General

Overlapping responsibilities and unclear delineation makes communications among responding agencies crucial. Responding agencies to a disaster event may include emergency management agencies from all levels of government, nongovernmental organizations, other responding government agencies, such as law enforcement and public health, the medical and scientific communities, and even businesses. Communications among these agencies is recognized as a current Achilles heel in the emergency management field. Issues of authority and structure are difficult to resolve, and operations are often performed in an ad hoc fashion; however, improvement in this area is becoming a point of emphasis, and technological advancements are facilitating better communications as well.

The costs of poor coordination and communication can be high. A slow or ineffective initial disaster response disproportionately increases human losses. Also, poorly coordinated and perceived response efforts can damage political careers and the reputations of agencies. After Hurricane Andrew in Florida in 1992, it became apparent early in relief efforts that there were communications and coordination problems between FEMA, the state emergency management system, local agencies, and the governor's office. Many political analysts feel that the poor public perception of the response cost President George H. W. Bush votes in the 1992 presidential election.

National Response Plan

The NRP is the major coordination mechanism for the various responding federal agencies during a major disaster. Emergency support function #5 within the NRP outlines responsibilities for emergency management. FEMA has the lead role for this activity but is supported by most other partner agencies in this respect. Individuals performing this function collect, analyze, process, and disseminate information about a disaster or emergency to facilitate the federal government assistance activities. The response is coordinated at the federal, field, regional, and headquarters levels. Daily information updates are provided to the various elements of the operation. The overall purpose of the function is to provide a central collection point where situation information can be compiled, analyzed, and prepared for use by decision makers.

The NRP also includes a communications function (ESF #2), which basically deals with the telecommunications infrastructure and technology. The lead agency for this function is the National Communications System. Its job is to ensure the provision of federal telecommunications support to federal, state, and local response efforts, and to serve as the planning point for use of national telecommunications assets and resources.

FIGURE 4–5 Hurricane Andrew, Florida, August 24, 1992. Volunteer assistance was received from volunteer organizations, including the American Red Cross and Salvation Army. One million people were evacuated and 54 died in this hurricane. FEMA News Photo.

FEMA Operations Center

The FEMA Operations Center (FOC) serves as the site of overall coordination and situation assessment operations for major disasters. It maintains a 24-hour capability to monitor all sources of information. Regional operation centers (ROCs) are the initial coordinating point for federal response efforts, however. The FEMA director serves as the federal coordinating officer (FCO) of the FOC and assumes coordination responsibilities, working with the state coordinating officer and local officials.

Joint Information Center

The joint information center also is a valuable tool for getting emergency management partners on the same page. In disasters of catastrophic or nationally significant proportions, a JIC is established to coordinate the dissemination of information about all disaster response and recovery programs. Public affairs officers (PAOs) representing all the federal, state, local, and voluntary agencies providing response or recovery services are invited to collocate and be a part of JIC operations. Interagency coordination is one of the central functions of the JIC, and teamwork is a key to implementing successful public information and media affairs programs. JICs involve coordination among the FCO, the lead state PAO, the congressional liaison, community relations and disaster assistance program managers, and other public agency PAOs.

Command and Control versus Coordination

It is generally agreed that some type of mechanism is needed to facilitate coordination and communications among responding partners. What is not agreed on is the structure of such a mechanism. The argument pits the clear, hierarchical "command and control" model against the more flexible, ad hoc "coordination" model.

The command and control model was adopted from the incident command system (ICS) used by fire departments across the United States and has clear lines of authority and responsibility. The coordination model is less rigid and more collaborative. In general, the coordination model is becoming more popular than the traditional command and control structure. For one thing, the new breed of emergency manager typically is more of a recovery coordinator than a field general. Also, command and control structures sometimes hamper communications. The commanding organization may have a value system and technical language that is distinct from those of partner organizations or the victims. The coordination model takes this variability into account and focuses on providing an open communications forum. The coordination model also often is better for negotiating turf battles among agencies and nongovernmental organizations providing overlapping services.

Technology

There are many examples of technology improving communications among partners. The use of the Internet as such a tool is an obvious trend. The city of Seattle recently integrated its Web site into its emergency communications plan. The site now provides immediate access to information for members of other departments, such as police and transportation. The site also contains a database of press releases and space for current news, which have been coordinated through an information control system. One lesson

FIGURE 4–6 West Palm Beach, Florida, October 1999. An inside view of Palm Beach County's state-of-the-art emergency operations center, which enables local, state, and federal emergency management teams to coordinate interagency disaster response. Photo by Ty Harrington/FEMA News Photo.

learned from Seattle's experience is to ensure that staff members who update the site are centrally located with emergency responders within the EOC.

Many communities are now using wireless systems to improve communications. The city of San Francisco recently developed a wireless voice and data communications system for its public safety agencies. The system overcomes the limited coverage of radio systems and the problem of various departments using incompatible systems. Mobile and portable radios now are in use at the city's fire, police, and emergency agencies. The Departments of Public Health, Public Works, Water, and the mayor's EOC also use the system. Officials indicate that it will go a long way toward helping the city handle the almost 4,000 emergency 911 calls it receives daily.

Wireless communications sometimes have their own limitation, however. After the terrorist attacks of September 11, 2001, cellular phone use overwhelmed wireless networks and prevented some local police and officials from making critical calls. In response, the White House plans to give emergency crews and government officials priority on the nation's cellular telephone system. Already in the United States, about 800 public institutions with emergency communications systems are given priority over regular users during an emergency. A similar effort is being initiated in Japan. After the 1995 Great Hanshin earthquake, incoming calls to Japan increased 50-fold and swamped the network.

Conclusion

Responding to disaster events is the most visible activity that any federal, state, or local emergency management agency conducts. The politicians, the media, and the general public rate the success of an emergency management organization by how well it functions in the response phase of a disaster. A successful disaster response at any level of government requires a strong command and control system, clear lines of communication, and coordination of numerous agencies from multiple jurisdictions. Local first responders—fire, police, and emergency medical technicians—are on the scene first. Local and state emergency managers coordinate resources and assess the damage and the capacity of their jurisdictions to respond effectively. For major disaster events, a presidential disaster declaration activates the NRP that delivers the full resources of the federal government in support of local and state authorities.

The key to the success of the emergency management system in the United States is the commitment of this country's elected officials to use the government to come to the aid of its citizens when a crisis occurs. The response process as described in this chapter ensures that government at all levels is capable of fulfilling this commitment.

CASE STUDIES

The Space Shuttle *Columbia* Disaster

On February 1, 2003, as the Space Shuttle *Columbia* reentered the earth's atmosphere following a successful space mission, it suddenly began to break apart, showering debris over an area of hundreds of square miles in East Texas and western Louisiana. President Bush issued emergency declarations for Texas and Louisiana, in the absence of requests for assistance from either governor, as the shuttle craft was considered federal property. Within hours, federal and state agencies had deployed teams to the disaster area to assist local fire, law enforcement, and emergency management authorities already on site. More than 60 agencies, including public and private groups, responded with personnel, supplies, and equipment. Disaster field offices were opened at Barksdale Air Force Base in Los Angeles and in Lufkin, Texas, and a satellite DFO was established in Fort Worth. The Lufkin DFO was the regional center of all search-related operations. This was the first major response performed by the newly created Department of Homeland Security.

As a federally declared disaster, FEMA was in charge of FRP coordination and coordinated the response and recovery operations. NASA, with the assistance of the Texas Forest Service (TFS), the U.S. Forest Service (USFS), the Environmental Protection Agency, and many others, supervised the search for shuttle material. The EPA's role was to assist FEMA and NASA by conducting environmental monitoring and assisting in the cleanup of hazardous materials from the Space Shuttle *Columbia*. EPA experts from across the country were mobilized to help local, county, and state officials protect public health and the environment, as well as to assist officials in recovering materials from communities and providing for safe transport of these materials to secure locations.

From the onset, the agencies' priorities were threefold: ensure public safety, retrieve evidence pieces of the shuttle that ultimately could determine the cause of the tragedy, and reimburse expenses of state and local governments and private citizens who may have sustained property damage as a result of the accident and search. NASA quickly identified potential hazardous materials, such as tanks

(Continued)

CASE STUDIES—Cont'd

containing toxic substances or unexploded pyrotechnic devices, and once found, the EPA secured the material. The EPA also worked with state and local authorities to clear school campuses and public access areas and tested air and water samples taken along the flight path for shuttle contaminates. Using the resources of the emergency response and removal service contractors and the U.S. Coast Guard (USCG), Gulf Strike Team, the EPA found no evidence of hazardous material in the atmosphere or drinking water supplies. Early in the recovery effort, teams from NASA, the FBI, National Guard, urban search and rescue organizations, the Department of Public Safety, and others conducted a successful search in East Texas to recover and bring home the bodies of *Columbia*'s crew.

Three days after the accident, local fire, police, volunteers, Texas Department of Public Safety (DPS) officers, Louisiana State Police, and EPA, USFS, TFS, and National Guard units from Texas, Louisiana, Oklahoma, and New Mexico began clearing shuttle debris in high-traffic areas. A one-page set of guidelines prepared by the state of Texas, NASA, and EPA enabled the teams to collect, document, tag, and transport nonhazardous debris without prior EPA or NASA clearance. These initial teams ended their search operations on February 17. The TFS, under the direction of NASA, now assumed responsibility for search activities in the field, which involved extensive air and ground searches in a 10-mile by 240-mile corridor along the projected shuttle flight path. The TFS, through the Texas Interagency Coordination Center, called on experienced management and firefighting crews from across the nation and Puerto Rico. The air operations, managed by TFS, included up to 36 helicopters and 10 fixed-wing aircraft. Also involved in the air search, but not managed by TFS, were motorized para gliders, an ER-2 (similar to the U-2), a specially equipped DC-3, and the Civil Air Patrol (CAP), among others. Volunteers put in more than 800 search-days of flying in the weeks just after the accident and covered the flight corridor area west of Fort Worth to the New Mexico border. The USFS, Bureau of Indian Affairs, Bureau of Land Management, National Park Service, U.S. Fish and Wildlife Service, along with state forestry organizations and contractors, provided the greatest number of crews, drawing from their expertise in wildland firefighting. More than 4,000 people at a time searched 12 hours a day, seven days a week. Camp crews were stationed at sites near Hemphill, Nacogdoches, Palestine, and Corsicana, with a goal of finding as much material as possible before spring vegetation growth made the search more difficult.

The U.S. Navy supervised the water search activities in Lake Nacogdoches and Toledo Bend Reservoir, located at the eastern end of the 2,400 square-mile search area. Beginning on February 22, 60 divers from the Navy, USCG, EPA, DPS, Houston and Galveston police and fire departments, and Jasper County Sheriff's Department combed the lakes using sophisticated sonar-equipped boats to help identify shuttle material. As in any operation of this magnitude, the hazards for all the searchers were challenging. Ground crews slogged though mud, dense vegetation, and rocky areas; faced wild hogs, snakes, and other vermin; and dealt with the ever-changing weather. Divers reckoned with the murky waters of the East Texas lakes, along with underwater forests, and various submerged hazards.

Ground and air operations covered over 1.5 million acres, mostly in Texas, with searches also conducted in Louisiana, California, Utah, Nevada, and New Mexico. A total of 82,500 shuttle items were recovered and processed by the Kennedy Space Center in Florida, weighing 84,800 pounds, and amounted to almost 40 percent of the total weight of the *Columbia*. The total cost of the search and recovery operation amounted to $161,945,000. These funds include costs associated with the ground, air, and water search operations, equipment, and personnel. FEMA public assistance, working through Texas and Louisiana, reimbursed the two states approximately $4.5 million for their efforts. FEMA turned over control of the recovery operation to NASA on April 30. The same day, NASA opened the Columbia Recovery Operation office at the Johnson Space Center in Houston. FEMA closed the disaster field office in Lufkin, Texas, on May 10.

Source: www.fema.gov.

CASE STUDIES

Oklahoma City

On April 19, 1995, an explosion rocked the federal plaza in Oklahoma City. The Alfred P. Murrah Federal Building was destroyed after a bomb, which was placed in a rental truck next to the building, was detonated. On arriving in the area, first responders witnessed smoke and fire coming from the Water Resource Building. Believing that it was a natural gas explosion, it was not until EMS personnel entered this building that they noticed the gaping hole in the Murrah Building. The fire chief's first step was to have a single command center, which incorporated all buildings and victims within a one-mile radius. Thirty-three fire stations, with at least 1,000 firefighters and 52 pieces of rescue apparatus responded to the scene.

Within 45 minutes after notification from the Oklahoma Department of Civil Emergency Management, FEMA deployed staff to Oklahoma City. FEMA coordinated the federal response to the Oklahoma City bombing and later worked closely with state and local officials on recovery efforts. The president signed an emergency declaration within eight hours of the occurrence. This was the first time Section 501(b) of the Stafford Act, granting FEMA the primary federal responsibility for responding to a domestic consequence management incident, was ever used. The president subsequently declared a major disaster on April 26, 1995. Because the disaster site was also a federal crime scene, FEMA appointed a liaison to the FBI to coordinate site access, support requirements, public information, and other issues. The coordinated work among federal agencies in Oklahoma City led to the further clarification of agency and department roles in crisis and consequence management.

(Continued)

CASE STUDIES—Cont'd

Harsh lessons were learned in Oklahoma City. A situation arose when local radio stations requested that all medical personnel should respond to the disaster area. A nurse who answered the call was killed by falling debris while trying to rescue victims in the building. A term constantly used after the bombing was the *Oklahoma standard*. Oklahoma had personnel on the scene within 30 minutes. Federal officials were notified within minutes of the disaster. Volunteer services were immediate, and because this was a local disaster, everyone took responsibility to do whatever they could to help. Hospital personnel established an effective and efficient triage system. Phone numbers, Internet sites, and briefings were launched within hours of the disaster. The American Red Cross, as in all disasters, was quick to respond with personnel and supplies to help family members of those who were injured or killed in the bombing. The Salvation Army responded within hours with food and supplies. By the end of the day, the Salvation Army had deployed seven units to provide services to the workers and the victims. Law enforcement and EMS personnel had up-to-date training. Oklahoma had excellent coordination with the Public Works Department, the National Weather Service, and the National Guard. The Department of Public Safety also had a predetermined disaster plan in place.

FIGURE 4–7 Aurora, Illinois, July 1993. Illinois flood victim gets food from the Salvation Army. Photo by Liz Roll/FEMA News Photo.

Although there were some initial problems with communication, this was resolved within an hour as a result of support from Cellular One and Southwest Bell. They were able to clear lines, reconfigure their systems, and dispatch cell phones to personnel on scene. But most important was that the Oklahoma Highway Patrol could talk directly with personnel from federal agencies that were on the scene. A Department of Safety technician was able to program radios within 45 minutes of the disaster. Like most major cities, Oklahoma is equipped with 800-MHz radios that can be linked with systems throughout the region. In any disaster, communication is the first line of defense in a successful response. It is essential that hospitals, rescue personnel, site commanders, and law enforcement officials have the ability to talk to one another. This was necessary to update the disaster field office about the status of the response as well as obtain needed personnel and supplies throughout the response. The only glitch was that the police were limited to those with whom they could communicate.

CASE STUDIES

Hurricane Floyd

On September 14, 1999, FEMA began mobilizing federal resources in preparation for possible landfall by Hurricane Floyd. Although, in previous years, states had to wait for the disaster to strike before obtaining FEMA assistance, in the case of Hurricane Floyd, FEMA took a proactive stance by activating emergency response teams, allocating funds to local communities for law enforcement, and working with the Tropical Predication Center to monitor Hurricane Floyd's track. The regional operations center was put into action three days before the actual landfall of Hurricane Floyd.

On September 16, 1999, Hurricane Floyd made landfall near Cape Fear, North Carolina. The Category 2 hurricane had sustained winds of 110 miles per hour, but unlike Hurricane Andrew, the local first responders in coordination with FEMA were better prepared to handle this disaster. Emergency materials, generators, sheeting, tarp, bottled water, blankets, and clothing were identified and available for immediate delivery. Disaster medical assistance teams had been placed on alert to provide medical services. Public works, including engineers, electricians, phone company employees, and public work personnel also were prepared for deployment to the area. Although forecasters thought that Floyd would hit Florida or Georgia, FEMA officials were mobile as the hurricane continued to track farther north. On September 15, 1999, President Clinton signed emergency declarations for North and South Carolina to fund law enforcement officials to help evacuate the areas. More than 2,100 employees were prepared to respond to the disaster. FEMA urban search and rescue teams from Indiana, Maryland, and Pennsylvania were activated. On the hurricane reaching land, FEMA's mobile emergency response system provided communication support to the affected communities.

(Continued)

CASE STUDIES—Cont'd

FEMA's proactive response before landfall ensured that those affected by the hurricane would have the needed materials and services to help in the recovery phase. While the rain was still falling, FEMA established their toll-free service line. Within days, people were receiving financial aid to help them through the disaster. Although FEMA took some flack from certain areas of North Carolina and Virginia because of the long-lasting flooding, lives were saved and damage was reduced because of FEMA's and the 27 agencies' response to the hurricane.

CASE STUDIES

Hurricane Andrew

On August 24, 1992, Hurricane Andrew, a Category 4 hurricane, made landfall over Dade County, Florida. For everything that went right during the response for Hurricane Floyd, the opposite was true for Hurricane Andrew. "When Hurricane Andrew was approaching Florida and the advance element of the federal emergency response team deployed to the state emergency operations center in Tallahassee, it was evident that the state lacked sufficient space and resources to coordinate an operation to handle a disaster caused by a major hurricane like Andrew" (FEMA, 1993). In a postdisaster audit of FEMA's disaster management performance after Hurricane Andrew, the inspector general noted that "state officials acknowledged that their initial assessment of requirements for federal assistance were too low, and that at first they were resistant to the idea of a massive flood of federal resources into south Florida" (FEMA, 1993, p. 41). Other problems noted by the inspector general included a failure on the part of the state to request certain federal services because the state was reluctant to incur its 25 percent cost share and the lack of awareness of certain services by both state and local officials.

What became evident in the first weeks after Andrew was that FEMA and the overall federal response as well as the Florida response were uncoordinated, confused, and often inadequate (FEMA, 1993). FEMA requested its inspector general to conduct a postdisaster audit, and Governor Chiles issued an executive order (92–242) establishing the governor's Disaster Planning and Response Review Committee "to evaluate current state and local statutes, plans and programs for natural and human-made disasters, and to make recommendations to the governor and the State Legislature" no later than January 15, 1993 (FEMA, 1993). The national emergency management system was acknowledged as being broken, and both the federal government and the state wanted to know why and what should be done to improve it.

The one key factor was that FEMA had yet to obtain clarification about its authority to supersede all other government agencies during a disaster. The inspector general's report tasks each area that FEMA failed to perform. From preparation to response and recovery, FEMA and federal officials dropped the ball. If it had not been for DoD intervention, people would have been left to their own devices in seeking medical assistance, shelter, food, and water. Because federal agencies had to have a formal declaration, they were slow in responding and providing assistance to the people of Florida.

Without electricity, FEMA was unable to disseminate the needed information to the communities. Telephone lines, radio, and TV stations were disrupted for the first few days. People were not aware of the services available to them until days after the hurricane had struck. Although there was a FEMA employee at the emergency operations center, he lacked the resources and the communication capabilities to get the needed response. The defense coordinating officer who was assigned to the emergency response team was continually being drawn away from his assignment and also had his role continually expanded or changed during the response (FEMA, 1993).

The inspector general's 200-page report took every aspect of the response and recovery phase into account and discussed in detail what needed to be done by local, state, and federal agencies for future catastrophic events. The report took into account the duplication of efforts by volunteer organizations and the lack of communication among the multiple federal agencies that had responded to Florida. Most consider President Bush's election loss to be partly attributable to the federal government's inability to manage domestic disasters.

With the inspector general's report in hand, FEMA director James Witt moved forward on his goal to make FEMA the lead agency in emergency and disaster management. With the Federal Response Plan rewritten and clarification made, FEMA has moved forward successfully in using the FRP as a foundation that can be used during all disasters.

IMPORTANT TERMS

- First responders
- Emergency manager
- Emergency response plan
- Incident command system
- Unified command

- Incident commander
- National Response Plan
- Emergency support function
- National incident management system

Self-Check Questions

1. How is the National Guard deployed to assist in response to a disaster?
2. What is the role of first responders when a routine, "minor disaster" occurs in a local community?
3. What drives the actions of local first responders?
4. Where can you find a detailed description of the roles and responsibilities of first responders in your community?

5. Who usually is in charge of developing and maintaining the community emergency plan?

6. Where does the emergency management office reside at the state level? Give three examples.

7. What is the principal source of funding for state emergency management offices?

8. What kinds of things do volunteer organizations provide for victims in the aftermath of a disaster?

9. What is the incident command system, and why was it originally developed?

10. What are the five major management systems within the incident command system?

11. What is the role of the incident commander?

12. What are the basic steps involved in a presidential disaster declaration at each level of government?

13. At whose discretion is the decision to make a disaster declaration?

14. What is the National Response Plan?

15. What are some of the reasons why communications among responding agencies is crucial?

Out of Class Exercises

1. Contact your State National Guard office. Find out what kinds of resources they can offer to assist local communities in the event of a disaster and what kind of training and exercise they conduct to prepare their members for disaster response.

2. What is the primary difference between the command and control and the coordination response models?

3. Contact your local ham radio organization and take a certification course. Use your certification to get involved in local response. You can get more information from the Amateur Radio Relay League (ARES, http://www.arrl.org).

4. Take a community emergency response team (CERT) course. To find a course being provided near you, visit the Citizen Corps CERT Web site (https://www. citizencorps.gov/cert).

The Disciplines of Emergency Management: Recovery

What You Will Learn

- How the National Response Plan guides disaster recovery operations.
- The recovery programs administered by FEMA to fuel individual and community recovery operations.
- How federal agencies other than FEMA contribute to disaster recovery.
- The role of national voluntary relief organizations.
- Tools that are available for community recovery planning.

Introduction

There is often a theoretical debate over when the response function ends and the recovery function begins. For this book, the response function is classified as the immediate actions to save lives, protect property, and meet basic human needs. The recovery function is not so easily classified. This function often begins in the initial hours and days following a disaster event and can continue for months and, in some cases, years, depending on the severity of the event.

Unlike the response function, where all efforts have a singular focus, the recovery function or process is characterized by a complex set of issues and decisions that must be made by individuals and communities. Recovery involves decisions and actions relative to rebuilding homes, replacing property, resuming employment, restoring businesses, and permanently repairing and rebuilding infrastructure. The recovery process requires balancing the more immediate need to return the community to normalcy with the longer-term goal of reducing future vulnerability. The recovery process can provide individuals and communities with opportunities to become more economically secure and improve the overall safety and quality of life.

Because the recovery function has such long-lasting effects and usually high costs, the participants in the process are numerous. They include all levels of government, the business community, political leadership, community activists, and individuals. Each of these groups plays a role in determining how the recovery will progress. Some of these roles are regulatory, such as application of state or local building ordinances, and some, such as the insurance industry, provide financial support. The goal of an effective recovery is to bring all the players together to plan, finance, and implement a recovery strategy that will rebuild the disaster-affected area safer and more secure as quickly as possible.

As noted in the previous chapter, the precipitating event for an area affected by a disaster is the presidential declaration of disaster under the Stafford Act. Recovery activities begin immediately after a presidential declaration, as the agencies of the federal government collaborate with the state in the affected area in coordinating the implementation of recovery programs and the delivery of recovery services.

In the period 1990–1999, FEMA spent more than $25.4 billion for declared disasters and emergencies, compared to $3.9 billion in current dollars for 1980–1989. For the 1990–1999 period, more than $6.3 billion was provided in grants for temporary housing, home repairs, and other disaster-related needs for individuals and families. An additional $14.8 billion went to states and local governments for cleanup and restoration projects, including more than $1.37 billion for mission-assigned work undertaken by other federal agencies. In the 1990s, a total of 88 declarations were issued for hurricanes and typhoons, for which FEMA obligated more than $7.78 billion for disaster costs. The most costly to FEMA was Hurricane Georges in 1998, followed closely by Hurricane Andrew in 1992.

The most frequently declared disaster type was flooding resulting from severe storms, with more than $7.3 billion committed by FEMA for response and recovery costs. The most costly were the Midwest floods in 1993 and the Red River Valley floods in 1997.

By December 2001, the disaster assistance provided by FEMA, the Small Business Administration, and the state of New York for the September 11, 2001, World Trade Center event had reached $700 million. Recovery costs for this disaster as of December 5, 2001, included the following:

- More than $344 million in public assistance funds to help New York City repair damaged infrastructure, restore critical services, and remove, transport, and sort debris.
- More than $196 million in individual assistance approved in the form of grants and loans. This assistance includes temporary disaster housing assistance, mortgage and rental assistance, disaster food stamps, individual and family grants, and SBA low-interest loans to homeowners and businesses.
- More than $151 million provided through other agencies, including the U.S. Army Corp of Engineers, disaster medical assistance teams from the Department of Health and Human Services, and FEMA's urban search and rescue task force.

Hurricane Katrina has become the costliest disaster in U.S. history. The federal government expects to provide in excess of $100 billion in disaster relief to individuals and communities affected by Katrina along the Gulf Coast and to communities around the country that hosted the over 250,000 persons displaced by Katrina. The White House report on Katrina, "The Federal Response to Hurricane Katrina: Lessons Learned," estimated damage to housing at $67 billion, business property suffered $20 billion in damages, and government property an estimated $3 billion in damages (Townsend,

2006). More details concerning federal recovery costs in Katrina are included in *Katrina: A Case Study.*

Without a doubt, the federal government plays the largest role in providing the technical and financial support for recovery. For that reason, this chapter focuses on the federal role in the disaster recovery function. It discusses the structure and the various programs available to assist individuals and communities in the postdisaster environment. The various national voluntary organizations that provide some assistance for recovery are briefly referenced, and several case studies are included to demonstrat e the different types of recovery.

As noted earlier, the decisions during recovery are driven predominantly by local government. At the end of the chapter is a listing of potential planning tools for the recovery process. This, along with a more encompassing discussion of the complexities of recovery and roles and responsibilities of the various players in it, can be found in a book prepared for FEMA by the American Planning Association, *Planning for Post-Disaster Recovery and Reconstruction.*

The National Response Plan for Disaster Recovery Operations

Issued in 2005, the National Response Plan outlines how the federal government implements the Robert T. Stafford Disaster Relief and Emergency Assistance Act, as amended, to assist state and local governments when a major disaster or emergency overwhelms their ability to respond effectively. The NRP describes the policies, planning assumptions, concept of operations, response and recovery actions, and responsibilities of 32 federal departments and agencies, including the American Red Cross, that guide federal operations following a presidential declaration of a major disaster or emergency.

The NRP is built on the template of the National Incident Management System, which provides a consistent doctrinal framework for incident management at all jurisdictional levels, regardless of the cause, size, or complexity of the incident. The activation of the NRP and its coordinating structures and protocols—either partially or fully—for specific incidents of national significance provides mechanisms for the coordination and implementation of a wide variety of incident management and emergency assistance activities. Included in these activities are federal support to state, local, and tribal authorities; interaction with nongovernmental, private donor, and private-sector organizations; and the coordinated, direct exercise of federal authorities, when appropriate.

A fundamental assumption in the NRP is that recovery is a cooperative effort among federal, state, and local governments; voluntary agencies; and the private sector in partnership. A principal federal official is designated by the secretary of homeland security to facilitate federal support to the established ICS unified command structure and to coordinate overall federal incident management and assistance activities.

The Response and Recovery Operations Branch coordinates the request and delivery of federal assistance and support from various special teams. This branch is composed of four groups: emergency services, human services, infrastructure support, and community recovery and mitigation.

When established in coordination with state and local jurisdictions, a disaster recovery center (DRC) is a satellite component of the joint field office, which includes the federal coordinating officer, state coordinating officer, and other senior federal officials, and provides a central facility where individuals affected by a disaster can obtain information on disaster recovery assistance programs from various federal, state, local, tribal, private-sector, and voluntary organizations.

The JFO is the central coordination point among federal, state, local, and tribal agencies and voluntary organizations for delivering recovery assistance programs. The JFO Operations Section includes the Human Services Branch, the Infrastructure Support Branch, and the Community Recovery and Mitigation Branch. The Human Services and Infrastructure Support Branches of the JFO Operations Section assess state and local recovery needs at the outset of an incident and develop relevant time frames for program delivery. These branches ensure federal agencies that have relevant recovery assistance programs are notified of an incident and share relevant applicant and damage information with all involved agencies as appropriate, ensuring that the privacy of individuals is protected. A brief summary of these branches is presented below.

Human Services Branch.   The Human Services Branch coordinates assistance programs to help individuals, families, and businesses meet basic needs and return to self-sufficiency (see Figure 5–1). This branch also coordinates with volunteer organizations, is involved in donations management, and coordinates the need for and location of DRCs with local and tribal governments. Federal, state, local, tribal, voluntary, and nongovernmental organizations staff the DRCs, as needed, with knowledgeable personnel to provide recovery and mitigation program information, advice, counseling, and related technical assistance.

Infrastructure Support Branch.   The Infrastructure Support Branch coordinates public assistance programs authorized by the Stafford Act to aid state and local governments and eligible private nonprofit organizations with the cost of emergency protective services and the repair or replacement of disaster-damaged public facilities and associated environmental restoration.

Community Recovery and Mitigation Branch.   The Community Recovery and Mitigation Branch works with the other operations branches and state and local officials to assess the long-term impacts of an incident of national significance, define available resources, and facilitate the development of a course of action to most efficiently apply available resources to restore and revitalize the community as well as reduce the impacts from future disasters.

These branches coordinate actions with one another to identify appropriate agency assistance programs to meet applicant needs, synchronizing assistance delivery and encouraging incorporation of hazard mitigation measures where possible. Hazard mitigation measures are identified in concert with congressionally mandated, locally developed plans. Hazard mitigation risk analysis; technical assistance to state, local, and tribal governments, citizens, and business; and grant assistance are included within the mitigation framework.

Additionally, these branches work in tandem to track overall progress of the recovery effort, particularly noting potential program deficiencies and problem areas. Long-term environmental recovery may include cleanup and restoration of public facilities, businesses, and residences; reestablishment of habitats and prevention of subsequent damage to natural resources; protection of cultural or archeological sites; and protection of natural, cultural, and historical resources from intentional damage during other recovery operations.

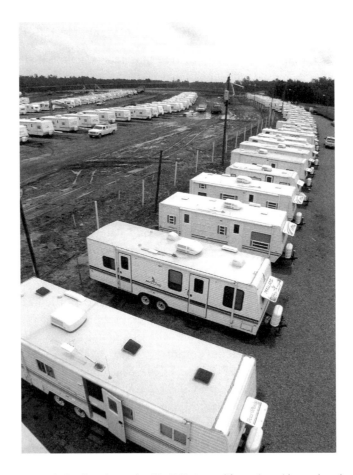

FIGURE 5–1 Rocky Mount, North Carolina, September 29, 1999. A new life awaits residents whose homes were flooded by the rains from Hurricane Floyd. These manufactured homes, located near Rocky Mount, North Carolina, housed more than 300 families. Photo by Dave Saville/FEMA News Photo.

Emergency Support Function #14.　ESF #14, long-term community recovery and mitigation, provides a framework for federal government support to state, regional, local, and tribal governments; nongovernmental organizations; and the private sector designed to enable community recovery from the long-term consequences of an incident of national significance. This support consists of available programs and resources of federal departments and agencies to enable community recovery, especially long-term community recovery, and to reduce or eliminate risk from future incidents, where feasible.

Federal disaster assistance available under a major disaster falls into three general categories: individual assistance, public assistance, and hazard mitigation assistance. Individual assistance is aid to individuals, families, and business owners. Public assistance is aid to public and certain private nonprofit entities for emergency services and the repair or replacement of disaster-damaged public facilities. Hazard mitigation assistance is funding available for measures designed to reduce future losses to public and private property. A detailed description of the first two types of assistance follows. More information on hazard mitigation assistance can be found in Chapter 3.

FEMA's Individual Assistance Recovery Programs

Individual assistance programs are oriented to individuals, families, and small businesses; and the programs include temporary housing assistance, individual and family grants, disaster unemployment assistance, legal services, and crisis counseling. The disaster victim must first register for assistance and establish eligibility. Three national centers provide centralized disaster application services for disaster victims. FEMA's National Processing Service Centers (NPSCs) are located in Denton, Texas; Berryville, Virginia; and Hyattsville, Maryland.

Since the first national center opened in 1994, more than 4 million applications have been processed and over 4.5 million calls taken, for more than 300 major disasters. These NPSCs house an automated teleregistration service, through which disaster victims apply for disaster housing and the Individual and Family Grant program and through which their applications are processed and their questions answered.

This automated system provides automatic determination of eligibility for about 90 percent of disaster housing cases, usually within 10 days of application. The other 10 percent of cases, which may need documentation, take a little longer. Cases also are automatically referred to the state for possible grant assistance if the applicant's needs exceed the Disaster Housing Program and the individual cannot qualify for a disaster loan from the Small Business Administration.

Following the September 11 events, FEMA was concerned that many individuals and businesses had not sought help in the aftermath of the attack. Working with the Advertising Council, and a volunteer ad agency, Muezzin Brown & Partners, a public service advertising campaign was developed to let viewers know that assistance was available by calling FEMA's toll-free registration number. The advertisements were distributed to electronic and media outlets in New York, New Jersey, Connecticut, Pennsylvania, and Massachusetts.

Disaster Housing Program

The Disaster Housing Program assures that people whose homes are damaged by disaster have a safe place to live until repairs can be completed. These programs are designed to provide funds for expenses that are not covered by insurance and are available to home-owners and renters who are legal residents of the United States and were displaced by the disaster.

- *Lodging expenses reimbursement* provides a check for reimbursement for the cost of short-term lodging such as hotel rooms, incurred because of damage to a home or an officially imposed prohibition against returning to a home.
- *Emergency minimal repair assistance* provides a check to help repair a home to a habitable condition.
- *Temporary rental assistance* provides a check to rent a place for the predisaster household to live.
- *Mortgage and rental assistance* provides a check to pay the rent or mortgage to prevent evictions or foreclosure. To qualify, the applicant must be living in the same house before and after the disaster and have a documented disaster-related financial hardship that can be verified by FEMA.

FIGURE 5–2 South-facing Long Beach on Oak Island, North Carolina, September 17, 1999. Hurricane Floyd brought a devastating 15 feet of storm surge that damaged or destroyed hundreds of houses along this community's oceanfront and flattened its frontal sand dunes. Here, even elevation failed to save this home. Additional strapping, upgraded mitigation work, might have helped. Photo by Dave Gatley/FEMA News Photo.

Individuals and Households Program

The Individuals and Households Program (IHP), formerly the Individual and Family Grant Program, provides funds for the necessary expenses and serious needs of disaster victims that cannot be met through insurance or other forms of disaster assistance. The IHP is not designed to cover all of a victim's losses (home, personal property, household goods) that resulted from the disaster, nor is it intended to restore damaged property to its condition before the disaster. Also, the IHP does not cover any business-related losses that resulted from the disaster. By law, the IHP cannot provide any money for losses that are covered by insurance.

The following list illustrates the assistance available through the IHP:

- *Temporary housing (a place to live for a limited period of time).* Money is available to rent a different place to live or a government-provided housing unit when rental properties are not available.
- *Repair.* Money is available to homeowners to repair damage from the disaster that is not covered by insurance. The goal is to make the damaged home safe, sanitary, and functional.
- *Replacement.* Money is available to homeowners to replace their home destroyed in the disaster that is not covered by insurance. The goal is to help the homeowner with the cost of replacing his or her destroyed home.
- *Permanent housing construction.* Direct assistance or money for the construction of a home. This type of help occurs only in insular areas or remote locations specified by FEMA, where no other type of housing assistance is possible.

- *Other needs.*   Money is available for necessary expenses and serious needs caused by the disaster. This includes medical, dental, funeral, personal property, transportation, moving and storage, and other expenses that are authorized by law.

The IHP covers only repair or replacement of items that are damaged as a direct result of the disaster that are not covered by insurance. Repairs or rebuilding may not improve a victim's home above its predisaster condition unless such improvements are required by current building codes.

Housing Needs.   Money to repair a home is limited to making the home "safe and sanitary" so the victim can continue to live there. IHP will not pay to return a home to its condition before the disaster. Grants may be used for housing needs to repair

- Structural parts of the home (foundation, outside walls, roof).
- Windows, doors, floors, walls, ceilings, cabinetry.
- Septic or sewage system.
- Well or other water system.
- Heating, ventilating, and air conditioning system.
- Utilities (electrical, plumbing, and gas systems).
- Entrance and exit ways from the home, including privately owned access roads.
- Blocking, leveling, and anchoring of a mobile home and reconnecting or resetting its sewer, water, electrical and fuel lines, and tanks.

Other than Housing Needs.   Money to repair damaged personal property or to pay for disaster-related necessary expenses and serious needs is limited to items or services that help prevent or overcome a disaster-related hardship, injury, or adverse condition. Grants may be used to pay for

- Disaster-related medical and dental costs.
- Disaster-related funeral and burial cost.
- Clothing, household items (room furnishings, appliances), tools (specialized or protective clothing and equipment) required for a job, necessary educational materials (computers, school books, supplies).
- Fuels for primary heat source (heating oil, gas, firewood).
- Cleanup items (wet/dry vacuum, air purifier, dehumidifier).
- Disaster damaged vehicle.
- Moving and storage expenses related to the disaster (moving and storing property to avoid additional disaster damage while disaster-related repairs are being made to the home).
- Other necessary expenses or serious needs as determined by FEMA.

Money received from IHP for housing and other than housing needs must be used for eligible expenses only, as identified by FEMA. A grantee who does not use the money for the reasons defined in the grant application may not be eligible for any additional help and may have to return any grant money provided. Grant money

- Is usually limited to up to 18 months from the date the president declares the disaster.
- Does not have to be repaid.
- Is tax free.

- Is not counted as income or a resource in determining eligibility for welfare, income assistance, or income-tested benefit programs funded by the federal government.
- Is exempt from garnishment, seizure, encumbrance, levy, execution, pledge, attachment, release, or waiver.
- May not be reassigned or transferred to another person.

FEMA pays 100 percent of the housing portion of the grant, and 75 percent of the other needs portion. The state pays the remaining 25 percent of the other needs portion. The states may administer only the other needs portion of the grant. The total maximum amount of grant assistance for each family or individual in fiscal year 2005 is $25,000, and this amount is broken down further into the various types of assistance provided. For example, although up to $25,000 may be provided for home repairs, a maximum of $10,000 will be provided for replacement of "owner occupied private residences."

Although some money often is made available through the IHP, most disaster aid from the federal government is provided in the form of loans from the Small Business Administration, which must be repaid. Applicants to IHP may be required to seek help from SBA first, before being considered for certain types of IHP help.

The SBA can provide three types of disaster loans to qualified homeowners and businesses to repair or replace homes, personal property, or businesses that sustained damages not covered by insurance:

- *Home disaster loans* provide funds to homeowners and renters to repair or replace disaster-related damages to home or personal property.
- *Business physical disaster loans* provide funds to business owners to repair or replace disaster-damaged property, including inventory, and supplies.
- *Economic injury loans* provide capital to small businesses and small agricultural cooperatives to assist them through the disaster recovery period. If the SBA determines that the individual is ineligible for a loan or if the loan amount is insufficient to meet the individual's needs, then the applicant is referred to the Individual and Family Grant Program.

Source: www.fema.gov.

Disaster Unemployment Assistance

The Disaster Unemployment Assistance (DUA) Program provides unemployment benefits and reemployment services to individuals who have become unemployed because of major disasters and who are not eligible for disaster benefits under regular unemployment insurance programs.

Legal Services

The Young Lawyers' Division of the American Bar Association, through an agreement with FEMA, provides free legal assistance to low-income disaster victims. The assistance that the participating lawyers provide is for insurance claims; counseling on landlord/ tenant problems; assistance in consumer protection matters, remedies, and procedures; and replacement of wills and other important legal documents destroyed in a major disaster. This assistance is intended for individuals who are unable to secure legal services adequate to meet their needs as a consequence of a major disaster.

Special Tax Considerations

Taxpayers who have sustained a casualty loss from a declared disaster may deduct that loss on the federal income tax return for the year in which the casualty occurred or through an immediate amendment to the previous year's return. Businesses may file claims with the Bureau of Alcohol, Tobacco, and Firearms for payment of federal excise taxes paid on alcoholic beverages or tobacco products lost, rendered unmarketable, or condemned by a duly authorized official under various circumstances, including where a major disaster has been declared by the president.

Crisis Counseling

The Crisis Counseling Assistance and Training Program is designed to provide short-term crisis counseling services to people affected by a presidentially declared disaster. The purpose of the crisis counseling is to help relieve any grieving, stress, or mental health problems caused or aggravated by the disaster or its aftermath. These short-term services are provided by FEMA as supplemental funds granted to state and local mental health agencies. The American Red Cross, the Salvation Army, and other voluntary agencies as well as churches and synagogues also offer crisis counseling services.

Cora Brown Fund

Cora C. Brown of Kansas City, Missouri, died in 1977 and left a portion of her estate to the United States to be used as a special fund solely for the relief of human suffering caused by natural disasters. The funds are used to assist victims and survivors of presidentially declared major disasters for disaster-related needs that have not or will not be met by government agencies or other organizations.

Critical Thinking

- Do you think that FEMA's individual grant programs provide enough assistance to individuals and families that are affected by disasters?
- Should federal assistance programs be available to all disaster victims regardless of their income or net worth? Why or why not?

FEMA's Public Assistance Grant Programs

FEMA, under the authority of the Stafford Act, administers the Public Assistance Grant Program, which provides federal assistance to state and local governments and to certain private nonprofit (PNP) organizations. These grants allow them to recover from the impact of disasters and implement mitigation measures to reduce the impacts from future disasters. The grants are aimed at governments and organizations with the final goal to help a community and its citizens recover from devastating major disasters. The federal share of assistance is no less than 75 percent of the eligible cost for emergency measures and permanent restoration. The state determines how the nonfederal share is split with the applicants.

Eligible applicants include the states, local governments, and any other political subdivision of the state, Native American tribes, Alaska Native Villages, and certain PNP organizations. Eligible PNP facilities include educational, utility, irrigation, emergency, medical, rehabilitation, temporary or permanent custodial care facilities, and other PNP facilities that are open to the public and provide essential services of a governmental nature to the general public. The work must be required as the result of the disaster, be located within the designated disaster area, and be the legal responsibility of the applicant. PNPs that provide critical services such as power, water, sewer, wastewater treatment, communications, or emergency medical care may apply directly to FEMA for a disaster grant. All other PNPs first must apply to the SBA for a disaster loan. If the loan is declined or does not cover all eligible damages, the applicant may reapply for FEMA assistance.

Work that is eligible for supplemental federal disaster grant assistance is classified as either emergency work or permanent work:

- *Emergency work* includes debris removal from public roads and rights of way as well as from private property when determined to be in the public interest. This also may include protective measures performed to eliminate or reduce immediate threats to the public.
- *Permanent work* is defined as work required to restore an eligible damaged facility to its predisaster design. This effort can range from minor repairs to replacement. Some categories for permanent work include roads, bridges, water control facilities, buildings, utility distribution systems, public parks, and recreational facilities. With extenuating circumstances, the deadlines for emergency and permanent work may be extended.

As soon as possible after the disaster declaration, the state, assisted by FEMA, conducts the applicant briefings for state, local, and PNP officials to inform them of the assistance available and how to apply for it. A request for public assistance must be filed with the state within 30 days after the area is designated eligible for assistance. A combined federal, state, and local team works to design and deliver the appropriate recovery assistance for the communities. In determining the federal costs for the projects, private or public insurance can play a major role. For insurable buildings within special flood hazard areas (SFHAs) and damaged by floods, the disaster assistance is reduced by the amount of insurance settlement that would have been received if the building and its contents had been fully covered by a standard NFIP policy. For structures located outside of an SFHA, the amount is reduced by the actual or anticipated insurance proceeds.

In 1998, FEMA redesigned the Public Assistance Program to provide money to applicants more quickly and make the application process easier. The redesigned program was approved for implementation on disasters declared after October 1, 1998. This redesigned program placed new emphasis on people, policy, process, and performance. The focus of the program also was modified to provide a higher level of customer service for disaster recovery applicants and to change the role of FEMA from inspection and enforcement to an advisory and supportive role.

Other Federal Agency Disaster Recovery Funding

Other federal agencies have programs that contribute to social and economic recovery. Most of these additional programs are triggered by a presidential declaration of a major disaster or emergency under the Stafford Act; however, the secretary of agriculture and the administrator of the SBA have specific authority relevant to their constituencies to declare a disaster and provide disaster recovery assistance. All the agencies are part of the structure of the NRP. This section does not provide a complete list of all disaster recovery programs available after a disaster declaration but provides a summary of many of the federal agencies in addition to FEMA that provide disaster recovery programs. These agencies include the following:

- U.S. Army Corps of Engineers.
- Department of Housing and Urban Development.
- Small Business Administration.
- U.S. Department of Agriculture.
- Department of Health and Human Services.
- Department of Transportation.
- Department of Commerce.
- Department of Labor.

A more comprehensive list is available in the *Catalog of Federal Domestic Assistance* (CFDA), available through the Federal Assistance Programs retrieval system. Each automated edition is revised in June and December.

FIGURE 5–3 New York, New York, October 30, 2001. FEMA/NY State Disaster Field Office personnel meet to coordinate federal, state, and local disaster assistance programs. Photo by Andrea Booher/FEMA News Photo.

U.S. Army Corps of Engineers

In a typical year, the Corps of Engineers responds to more than 30 presidential disaster declarations plus numerous state and local emergencies. Under the NRP, the Army has the lead responsibility for public works and engineering missions. For example, after the events of September 11, 2001, the Army provided technical assistance for the debris removal operation. By December 2001, more than 661,430 tons of debris had been moved to the Staten Island landfill.

Department of Housing and Urban Development

The Department of Housing and Urban Development provides flexible grants to help cities, counties, and states to recover from presidentially declared disasters, especially in low-income areas, subject to availability of supplemental appropriations. When disasters occur, Congress may appropriate additional funding for the Community Development Block Grant and HOME programs to rebuild the affected areas and bring crucial seed money to start the recovery process. Because it can fund a broader range of recovery activities than most other programs, CDBG disaster recovery assistance supplements recovery assistance from FEMA and helps communities and neighborhoods that otherwise might not recover because of limited resources.

The CDBG program funds have been especially useful to communities that are interested in incorporating mitigation into their recovery process. These funds have been combined with FEMA assistance to remove or elevate structures from the floodplain and to relocate residents and businesses to safer areas.

The HOME Program helps expand the supply of decent, affordable housing for low- and very low-income families by providing grants to states and local governments. Funds can be used for acquisition, new construction, rehabilitation, and tenant-based rental assistance. HOME disaster recovery grants are an important resource for providing affordable housing to disaster victims.

Small Business Administration

The SBA Disaster Loan Program offers low-interest loans to assist in long-term recovery efforts for those who are trying to rebuild their homes and businesses in the aftermath of a disaster. Disaster loans from SBA help homeowners, renters, businesses of all sizes, and nonprofit organizations fund rebuilding efforts. The SBA Disaster Loan Program reduces federal disaster costs compared to other forms of assistance, such as grants, because the loans are repaid to the U.S. Treasury. The SBA can approve loans only to applicants who have a reasonable ability to repay the loan and other obligations from earnings. The terms of each loan are established in accordance with each borrower's ability to repay. Generally, more than 90 percent of the SBA's disaster loans are made to borrowers without credit available elsewhere and have an interest rate of around 4 percent. The disaster loans require borrowers to maintain appropriate hazard and flood insurance coverage, thereby reducing the need for future disaster assistance.

The SBA is authorized by the Small Business Act to make two types of disaster loans: physical disaster loans and economic injury disaster loans. Physical disaster loans are a primary source of funding for permanent rebuilding and replacement of uninsured disaster damages to privately owned real and personal property. Economic injury disaster loans provide necessary working capital until normal operations resume after a physical disaster.

In 2000, the SBA approved 28,218 loans for $1.028 billion. Since the inception of the program in 1953, the SBA has approved more than 1.5 million disaster loans for more than $28.5 billion. In 2001, after the September 11 events, the SBA approved more than $161 million in low-interest loans to more than 2,000 applicants for home repairs, business loans, and loans to assist small businesses suffering economic injury as a result of losses caused by the disaster.

U.S. Department of Agriculture

The U.S. Department of Agriculture (USDA) Farm Service Agency (FSA) provides low-interest loan assistance to eligible farmers and ranchers to help cover production and physical losses in counties declared as disaster areas by the president or designated by the secretary of agriculture. The emergency loans can be used to restore or replace essential physical property, pay all or part of production costs associated with the disaster year, pay essential family living expenses, reorganize the farming operation, and refinance debts.

Department of Health and Human Services

The Department of Health and Human Services is the lead federal agency responsible for implementing the health and medical portion of the NRP. Its activities provide support to individuals and communities affected by disasters, state and local mental health administrators, and other groups that respond to those affected by human-caused disasters (such as school violence). The Center for Mental Health Services (CMHS) within the DHHS works with FEMA to implement the Crisis Counseling Assistance and Training Program discussed earlier in this chapter.

The DHHS also provides disaster assistance for older Americans through its Administration on Aging (AoA). Older people often have difficulty obtaining necessary assistance because of progressive physical and mental impairments and other frailties that often accompany aging. Many older people, who live on limited incomes and sometimes are alone, find it impossible to recover from disasters without special federal assistance service. The AoA's national aging network assists older persons by providing critical support such as meals and transportation, information about temporary housing, and other important services on which older adults often rely.

Department of Transportation

Congress authorized a special program from the Highway Trust Fund for the repair or reconstruction of federal-aid highways and roads on federal lands that have suffered serious damage as a result of natural disasters or catastrophic failures from an external cause. The Department of Transportation Federal Highway Administration (FHWA) administers the Emergency Relief Program, which supplements the commitment of resources by states, their political subdivisions, or other federal agencies to help pay for damages resulting from disasters. The applicability of the program to a natural disaster is based on the extent and intensity of the disaster.

Department of Commerce

Within the Department of Commerce, the Economic Development Administration administers programs and provides grants for infrastructure development, business incentives, and other forms of assistance designed to help communities alleviate conditions of substantial and persistent unemployment in economically distressed areas and regions. The EDA provides postdisaster economic assistance for communities affected by declared natural disasters. Funding for this program has been a problem over the years.

Department of Labor

The Department of Labor Disaster Unemployment Assistance Program provides financial assistance to individuals whose employment or self-employment has been lost or interrupted as a direct result of a major disaster and who are not eligible for regular state unemployment insurance. Funding for this program comes from FEMA. The DUA is administered by the state agency responsible for providing state unemployment insurance.

The Workforce Investment Act of 1998 authorizes the U.S. secretary of labor to award national emergency grants to assist any state that has suffered an emergency or major disaster to provide disaster relief employment. These funds can be used to finance the creation of temporary jobs for workers dislocated by disasters to clean up and recover from the disaster and to provide employment assistance to dislocated workers. Interestingly, in creating this program, Congress expanded eligibility beyond people affected by the disaster to dislocated workers and certain civilian Department of Defense employees affected by downsizing and certain recently separated members of the armed forces.

National Voluntary Relief Organizations

Numerous voluntary organizations and nongovernmental organizations are involved in disaster recovery. These organizations help individuals to get back on their feet in the immediate aftermath of a disaster event by providing food, shelter, medicine, and clothing. These groups also provide long-term assistance in many areas such as housing repair and rebuilding, child care, and assistance in accessing government relief. In Hurricane Katrina, a voluntary agency provided case management services to individual Katrina victims. For the most part, voluntary agencies and NGOs address the needs of individuals that government relief programs do not cover. A list of voluntary agencies and NGOs active in the Katrina recovery efforts is included in *Katrina: A Case Study*.

National Voluntary Organizations Active in Disaster

National Voluntary Organizations Active in Disaster coordinates planning efforts by many voluntary organizations responding to disaster in order to provide more effective service to people affected by disaster. Members include 34 national voluntary organizations active in disaster mitigation and response, 52 state and territorial chapters (VOADs), and dozens of local organizations. Once a disaster occurs, NVOAD or an affiliated state VOAD encourages members and other voluntary agencies to convene on site. The member organizations provide a wide variety of disaster relief services, including emergency distribution services, mass feeding, disaster child care, mass or individual shelter, comfort kits, supplementary medical care, cleaning supplies, emergency communications, stress management services, disaster assessment, advocacy for disaster victims, building or repair of homes, debris removal, mitigation, burn services, guidance in managing spontaneous volunteers, and victim and supply transportation. NVOAD maintains a close relationship with FEMA and encourages the state and local affiliates to work closely with the state and local emergency management agencies.

The American Red Cross

Although the American Red Cross is not a government agency, its authority to provide disaster relief was formalized when, in 1905, the Red Cross was chartered by Congress to "carry on a system of national and international relief in time of peace and apply the same in mitigating the sufferings caused by pestilence, famine, fire, floods, and other great national calamities, and to devise and carry on measures for preventing the same." Red Cross disaster relief focuses on meeting people's immediate emergency disaster-caused needs and provides disaster assistance to individuals to enable them to resume their normal daily activities independently. The Red Cross provides shelter, food, and health and mental health services to address basic human needs. The Red Cross also feeds emergency workers, handles inquiries from concerned family members outside the disaster area, provides blood and blood products to disaster victims, and helps those affected by disaster to access other available resources.

The Red Cross is one of the nongovernmental organizations included in the NRP and is designated a support agency for ESF #6, mass care, housing, and human services. The Red Cross helps coordinate the use of federal mass care resources in a presidentially declared disaster or emergency and works closely in support of state and local efforts to meet the mass care needs of victims of a disaster. This federal assistance supports the delivery of mass care services of shelter, feeding, and emergency first aid to disaster victims; the establishment of systems to provide bulk distribution of emergency relief supplies to disaster victims; and the collection of information to operate a disaster welfare information system to report victim status and assist in family reunification.

Recovery Planning Tools

Despite the pressures on politicians and community leaders to return to a period of normalcy as quickly as possible and because of federal incentives, public interest, and insurance retractions, more and more communities are looking at ways to reduce their future vulnerability. As disasters repeat themselves and the public sees the emotional and financial benefits of mitigation, communities are making the long-term investment in mitigation. For example, the devastating 1993 Midwest floods that occurred again in some areas in 1995 had a minimal impact in those towns where buyout and relocation programs were undertaken after the 1993 flood. The following is a partial list of policy areas and tools that should be considered by decision makers as they develop their recovery plan:

- *Land-use planning techniques*, including acquisition, easements, annexation, stormwater management, and environmental reviews.
- *Zoning*, including special-use permits, historic preservation, setbacks, density controls, wetlands protection, floodplain, and coastal zone management.
- *Building codes*, including design controls, design review, height and type, and special study areas (soil stability ratings).

- *Financial incentives*, including special districts, tax exemptions, special bonds, development rights, property transfer, or use change fees.
- *Information and oversight*, including public awareness and education, regional approaches and agreements, global information systems, town hall meetings, and public hearings.

Critical Thinking

Why is the recovery period often called a "risk reduction window of opportunity"? What kinds of risk reduction measures are easier to perform during recovery than other times, and why are they easier?

Conclusion

As this chapter demonstrates, the federal government plays a significant role in initiating and funding the disaster recovery process. But for recovery to be effective, the planning and decision making must be done at the local level. With a disaster comes disruption and tragedy but in the aftermath comes opportunity. Changes to FEMA's Stafford Act now require communities and states to have mitigation plans approved before the disaster. These plans, developed in the calm before an event happens, can become the blueprint for facilitating recovery and making communities less vulnerable in the postdisaster environment. Communities should strive to integrate preevent recovery and mitigation planning into their ongoing planning efforts. Such integration allows the political process to work, to include citizen participation, and to garner support for changes that will make their communities safer and more secure.

CASE STUDIES

Economic Recovery in New York City after September 11, 2001

Prior to September 11, the World Trade Center was the heart of a vibrant downtown business district. The massive complex consisted of seven buildings, including the twin World Trade Center Towers. These 110 story skyscrapers, built in 1970 by the New York Port Authority, contained nearly an acre of space on each floor. Combined, they represented 12 million square feet of office space— 14 percent of the office space in downtown Manhattan—and were the home to 50,000 employees. Together with the other buildings destroyed or damaged on that date, over 25 percent of the commercial office space in lower Manhattan was immediately uninhabitable.

The economic impact of the attack was immediate and severe. In addition to their physical space, many companies lost all or a large percentage of their workforce and operational equipment. The transportation system on which employees depended was destroyed. The nation's financial system shut down, and air travel was suspended. Shipping ground to a halt, and companies that relied on just-in-time products for production were left without many necessary parts. TV and radio stations lost advertising revenue as reports of the attack went commercial free for days. Consumer spending and confidence were devastated and did not return for weeks. And the insurance industry, heavily invested in the city, realized the costliest single event in its history.

(Continued)

CASE STUDIES—Cont'd

The exact financial impact figures related to the attack are still hard to obtain, as the means to measure them is not standardized. The human casualty figure, in flux for months, was finally set at 2,749. The economic figures are much more amorphous, for a number of reasons. First, the economy is dynamic and was affected by several other factors, such as the recession that was ongoing and various scandals (Enron, WorldCom), among other issues. Second, the recovery effort is still under way, and costs related to it will likely remain open until as late as 2015, when all the World Trade Center construction is scheduled to be completed. Insurance payments are still outstanding, and the federal government still has money yet to be allocated.

The economic recovery from the World Trade Center attacks started immediately. To limit the immediate impact on shareholder confidence, the New York financial markets were shut for a period of several days. The Federal Reserve bolstered the system by preparing to inject liquidity into the system to prevent defaults, and interest rates for short-term borrowing were lowered. The Federal Reserve also ensured the availability of U.S. dollars overseas, and Congress supported U.S. airlines with $10 billion in guaranteed loans. After electricity and communication were restored, just a few days later, the markets were ready to open and begin returning to normal operations.

These initial actions, however, were superficial, intended to limit the extent of damage that already had been sustained. It was apparent from the start that a much greater amount of recovery actions would be needed in the years to follow. Numerous organizations, government agencies, and other groups have participated in this recovery, several of which are profiled next.

FEMA

The response to the attacks on the World Trade Center marked a significant change in the way in which FEMA allocated funds. In a "normal" disaster, FEMA first determines the needs as defined by established eligibility criteria, then distributes funds from its general disaster relief fund. Congress does not give money for a specific disaster; rather, it allocates money to this pool, from which FEMA operates. There is no predefined upper limit for the disaster; as a result, disaster funding projects can be open for years after the event occurs (events related to the Northridge earthquake, for example, were still being funded nearly 10 years after the event).

In this incident, however, the amount of money that was to be allocated was established early in the process. FEMA received $8.80 billion of the $20 billion in federal funds allocated by Congress, and FEMA was given enhanced flexibility in determining how the money should be used. This strategy allowed FEMA to establish an early closeout process, forcing the city and state to establish priorities early on. It also allowed FEMA to distribute funds in ways that normally would not have been possible under the Stafford Act, such that all of the $8.80 billion would be allocated. This flexibility has been vital to the economic recovery of the area. It went beyond simply getting people back on their feet, to helping lower Manhattan reestablish itself as core of the New York City economy. FEMA funds have been used to assist owners with the cleaning of World Trade Center dust from their private residences, reimburse the city from losses associated with a reduction in tourism, pay for increased security as a result of the attacks, and fund cost-of-living allowances for the beneficiaries of the pensions of the firemen and police officers killed in the attack.

HUD

The Department of Housing and Urban Development is responsible for the second largest allocation of funds to the World Trade Center site. HUD funds were used to reimburse utility companies for emergency repairs immediately after the attacks. They assisted both individuals and businesses with compensation for disaster-related losses, through mortgage and rental insurance, crisis counseling, grants for disaster-related expenses, and businesses recovery grants and loans. HUD also has been instrumental in both the infrastructure and economic recovery of the World Trade Center site. It spent $568 million to not only return the utility infrastructure of the site to normal but to improve it. HUD's Community Development Block Grant has been used to fund several programs, among them the Small Firm Attraction and Retention Grant Program, the Job Creation and Retention Program, the Employee Training and Assistance Program, and the Business Recovery Loan Fund. These funds have been vital to retaining the businesses that make up the economic heart of lower Manhattan.

DOT

The U.S. Department of Transportation has been involved with the effort to rebuild and improve the transportation systems damaged and destroyed at the World Trade Center site. Because of the large number of workers that commute there, having a robust and efficient system is vital to the economic recovery of the site. DOT has been involved in restoring operation to the transportation systems and providing temporary repairs to the roads during the response phase. It is now involved in the permanent replacement of the Port Authority Trans-Hudson (PATH) terminal and improvements to the Fulton Street Transit Center and South Ferry Subway Station.

IRS

As part of the $20 billion package allocated for New York City, Congress approved the Liberty Zone tax benefit, worth approximately $5 billion. This amount is not money provided by the government; rather, it is a tax break targeted specifically to companies surrounding the World Trade Center site in lower Manhattan, deemed the Liberty Zone. Among its provisions are a business employee credit, special depreciation allowance, tax-exempt private activity bonds (Liberty Bonds), and increased expensing. Some of these breaks have already expired, whereas others will continue on for several more years. The $5 billion figure is an estimate, and the IRS is not tracking the actual usage of these benefits.

(Continued)

CASE STUDIES—Cont'd

State and Local: Empire State Development Corporation

The state of New York's economic development corporation is aiding in the economic recovery of the region through its NY Incentives Program, designed to help small business owners realize the benefits of doing business in the area by assisting with the various economic incentive programs.

Lower Manhattan Development Corporation

The Lower Manhattan Development Corporation is a state-city corporation designed to oversee the redevelopment and improvement of the World Trade Center site and the entire lower Manhattan area. Created shortly after the attack by Mayor Giuliani and Governor Pataki, it consists of eight board members appointed by the state and eight appointed by the city. It consults with citizen groups on issues such as transportation and infrastructure, residential and commuter concerns, economic development, tourism and the arts, and memorial planning. It approved the plans for the rebuilding of the World Trade Center site and the included memorial site. Most important, it is in charge of channeling the funds received from the federal government.

Port Authority

The Port Authority of New York and New Jersey was founded in 1921 to enhance regional commerce and transportation in the New York City metropolitan area. It has a 12-member board, with 6 members appointed by the governor of each state. The Port Authority built the World Trade Center in 1970 and owned it until July 2001, when it leased it to a private party. It owns the land today and is working closely with the Lower Manhattan Development Corporation to rebuild the World Trade Center and its transportation infrastructure.

Other Agencies

Numerous other agencies are involved in the rebuilding of the World Trade Center site and lower Manhattan. Among them are the Metropolitan Transit Authority, NYC Planning Commission, NYC DOT, NYC Department of Environmental Protection, and NYC Economic Development Corporation. Local community groups, arts societies, architects, and regional planning associations are also involved.

Insurance

Many of the insurance claims from the World Trade Center attack have yet to be settled. Estimates of actual payout range from $30 to $70 billion, depending on the estimate source and date. The two World Trade Center towers, each insured for $3.5 billion, were reimbursed for only $3.5 billion total because the two attacks were considered to be part of a single event. For the insurance industry as a whole, this attack was a watershed event. Insurance companies normally operate with thin profit margins and a reliance on actuary tables to determine the likelihood of events, but acts of terrorism are potentially bankrupting and nearly impossible to predict. The answer from the U.S. government has been the passage of the Terrorism Risk Insurance Act of 2003, which provides federal sharing of public and private compensation for insurance of commercial property.

Charitable Contributions

Although charity is present at most disasters, it was especially prevalent in the World Trade Center disaster, especially in regards to funds collected for victims and victims' families. An estimated 600 charities registered with the IRS with the explicit intention of collecting funds related to the disaster. The top 35 of these funds had collected nearly $2.7 billion by October 2002. The largest of these, the American Red Cross Liberty Fund, had collected over $1 billion dollars. (In addition to the funds collected, the American Red Cross served an estimated 11.5 million meals and provided 50,423 disaster workers in the first two months of the disaster.)

Of the money collected by the charities, over 70 percent had been distributed by October 2002. Much of the money went to victims' families, in an effort to recoup lost salaries. The GAO reports that the average nonuniformed victims' families received $90,000 in cash assistance, and uniformed families, because of charities established especially for them, received an average assistance of $715,000 (Port Authority police), $905,000 (NYC police), and $938,000 (NYC firefighters). Other examples of areas where charities donated money to help include mental health counseling, health-care provision, employment assistance, and legal and financial help.

Sources

Civic Alliance to Rebuild Downtown New York. 2002. "Listening to the City." February 7, 2002.

Cooper, J. C., and K. Madigan. "Consumers Have Done Their Part. Now, Businesses Will Have to Pitch in as Faster Recovery Requires More Capital Spending and Hiring," *BusinessWeek,* September 16, 2002, p. 19.

Fiscal Policy Institute. "Economic Impact of the September 11 World Trade Center attack, Preliminary Report." September 2001.

GAO. "Review of Studies of the Economic Impact of the September 11, 2001, Terrorist Attacks on the World Trade Center." GAO-02-700R, May 2002.

GAO. "More Effective Collaboration Could Enhance Charitable Organizations' Contributions in Disasters." GAO-03-529, December 2002.

GAO. "Overview of Federal Disaster Assistance to the New York City Area." GAO-04-72, October 2003.

Kadlec, D., B. Baumohl, M. Sieger, and A. Zagorin. "Up from the Ashes," *Time,* September 24, 2001, pp. 80–82.

Lenain, P., M. Bonturi, and V. Keon. "The Fallout from Terrorism: Security and the Economy," OECD [Organisation for Economic Cooperation and Development.] *Observer,* May 2002, pp. 9–13.

Loomis, C. J. "Insurance after 9/11," *Fortune,* June 10, 2002, pp. 110–115.

Lowenstein, Ronnie. "Federal Aid to New York City in the Aftermath of September 11th: How Much, and for What?" February 11, 2002. Testimony of Ronnie Lowenstein, director, New York City Independent Budget Office before the Joint Hearing of the City Council Finance, Lower Manhattan Redevelopment, and State and Federal Legislation Committees.

Malik, A. 2002. "World Trade Center," *GBER 2,* no. 1: 5–10.

New York Senate Finance Committee. "Financial Impact of the World Trade Center Attack." January 2002.

(Continued)

CASE STUDIES— Cont'd

"New York City Expected to Recoup Most Losses of Sept. 11," *Wall Street Journal*, November 16, 2001, p. A2.

Office of the State Comptroller. "The Impact of the World Trade Center Tragedy on the Metropolitan Transit Authority." Report 9–2002, 2002.

Ratajczak, D. "Will Insurance Be a Buffer or a Drag to the Economy during This Recovery?" *Journal of Financial Service Professionals,* 56, no. 3, May 2002, pp. 18–20.

"Rescue and Recovery Effort after the September 11, 2001 Attacks," available at www.wikipedia.com.

Starkman, D., and A. Frangos. "Before Ground Zero Rebuilding, $1.3 Billion Has Already Been Spent," *Wall Street Journal,* February 25, 2004, p. A1.

"United States: Two Years on; New York City," *The Economist,* September 13, 2003.

"Working Together to Accelerate New York's Recovery: Update of the NYC Partnership's Economic Impact Analysis of the September 11th Attack on New York City," New York City Partnership and Chamber of Commerce, February 11, 2002.

"World Trade Center Assistance: Aid Received, Aid to Come." In New York City Independent Budget Office, *Inside the Budget,* p. 117. New York: New York City Independent Budget Office, July 31, 2003.

"World Trade Center Disaster: Tracking Federal Aid for Cleanup and Rebuilding." In New York City Independent Budget Office, *Inside the Budget,* p. 89. New York: New York City Independent Budget Office. September 28, 2001.

"World Trade Center Memorial and Cultural Program, Amended General Project Plan." New York: Lower Manhattan Development Corporation, September 16, 2003.

"WTC Business Assistance Report." New York: New York City Economic Development Corporation and New York State Empire State Development Corporation, February 13, 2003.

CASE STUDIES

Federal Action Plan for the Red River Valley Floods

In April 1997, the Red River flooded its banks, displacing more than 60,000 people and affecting communities especially hard in Grand Forks, North Dakota, and East Grand Forks, Minnesota. On April 7 and 8, a presidential disaster was declared for severe spring storm conditions in North Dakota, South Dakota, and Minnesota. Following an April 22 visit to these communities, the president announced that all emergency measures and costs of debris removal under the Stafford Act would be covered 100 percent by the federal government so that the state and local governments could concentrate their resources on response and recovery efforts. The president also announced the formation of an interagency task force to develop a long-term recovery plan for the affected states. James Lee Witt, the director of FEMA at that time, chaired the effort.

The Federal Action Plan for Recovery identified three priorities for federal long-term recovery efforts: mitigation of flood hazards, housing, and reestablishing community sustainability. In conjunction with state and local governments, the action plan detailed a wide range of grants, loans, and technical assistance that the federal government would provide to ensure that community recovery needs were addressed. The president also ordered several federal departments to implement efforts to make the communities more disaster resistant. He directed the U.S. Army Corps of Engineers to aggressively pursue the development and implementation of structural and nonstructural flood protection works for the cities of Grand Forks and East Grand Forks.

FEMA and HUD were directed, in partnership with the states, to implement an accelerated program to purchase flood-damaged residences in the most severely devastated areas. FEMA, HUD, the Army Corps, the Economic Development Administration, and the SBA were directed to use all available authorities to support state and local rebuilding efforts and to incorporate mitigation to make the communities disaster resistant. The president also asked the affected communities to vigorously pursue mitigation and manage development wisely to avoid future flooding events. He encouraged the residents of these communities to purchase and maintain flood insurance.

To address the issue of immediate and long-term housing availability and maintain community continuity during the recovery process, the president directed FEMA to continue providing temporary housing on an expedited basis by providing emergency home repair grants, travel trailers to be sited next to unlivable damaged residences under repair, mobile homes for those facing longer-term displacement, and rental assistance. HUD, the Department of Commerce, the EDA, the USDA, and the SBA were directed to establish a recovery office in Grand Forks to help the communities create new housing resources through planning and design assistance, infrastructure funding, and continued low-interest loans to homes and businesses.

The Recovery Action Plan also addressed the challenge of reestablishing the sustainability of the community through preserving historic downtown and residential areas, attracting and retaining a workforce, building and repairing infrastructure and housing, and capitalizing small businesses. To help meet these challenges, the president directed HUD, the EDA, the SBA, the Army Corps, the USDA, FEMA, and the Department of Energy (DOE) to provide short-term and long-term planning and technical assistance to the communities most affected. The SBA, HUD, the EDA, the USDA, and FEMA were directed to continue to make low-interest loans and targeted grants to support development of new business facilities, assist in relocation of businesses away from highly hazardous areas, stimulate private-sector investment, and address reestablishment and relocation of critical facilities, including water treatment plants. HUD, the SBA, the USDA, and the EDA also were directed to actively seek innovative solutions to the short-term capitalization of businesses, in particular small businesses.

The president directed FEMA to provide temporary classroom and administration facilities for schools and support the communities' efforts in the design and siting of new construction of schools away from high-risk areas. FEMA was also directed to continue the repair, restoration, and mitigation of damaged

(Continued)

infrastructure, including roads, bridges, hospitals, and other public and private nonprofit facilities.

Other agencies also helped address the immediate disaster recovery needs of these three states after the floods. The Department of Labor made nearly $10 million available under the Job Training Partnership Act Title III Program to provide temporary jobs for disaster-affected workers in the three states. The Centers for Disease Control and Prevention (CDC) of the DHHS provided emergency assistance to the affected areas on environmental health, disease and injury surveillance, worker safety, and water quality. The Federal Highway Administration allocated emergency funds to repair highways. The Environmental Protection Agency provided technical assistance to the states on solid waste, pesticides, household hazardous waste, air monitoring, and underground storage tank issues.

In regard to these actions, James Lee Witt stated: "The Long Term Recovery Task Force developed recommendations that transcend our usual disaster programs. This innovative effort demonstrates the federal government's true commitment to the long-term recovery of communities in the three states deluged by the Red River of the North. In addition to helping these communities recover, we are committed to assisting state and local governments with the task of rebuilding safer and smarter to reduce future flood risks."

Long-Term Recovery Action Plan for Hurricane Georges

On September 21, 1998, Hurricane Georges, sustaining winds as high as 150 miles per hour, struck Puerto Rico and dumped more than two feet of rain on the island. More than 100,000 residences were damaged or destroyed, and 31,500 people were forced to seek refuge in shelters. This was the worst natural disaster to hit Puerto Rico in 70 years, and a major disaster was declared for all 78 of Puerto Rico's municipalities. In response to the severity and scope of the destruction, the president activated the Long-Term Recovery Task Force composed of 15 federal departments, agencies, and offices, and headed by then FEMA director James Lee Witt. The president directed the group to develop an action plan to facilitate the coordination and delivery of federal recovery assistance to Puerto Rico.

The purpose of the task force is to coordinate and target the diverse disaster programs of more than a dozen federal agencies to ensure the greatest level of effective federal support. The task force worked in collaboration with representatives of the government of Puerto Rico to identify five long-term recovery priorities: mitigation, housing, economic revitalization and sustainability, energy, and transportation.

The government of Puerto Rico identified **mitigation** as one of the core elements of its vision for long-term recovery. Federal mitigation actions emphasized three areas: building codes, planning and coordination, and floodplain management. FEMA provided technical assistance for developing long-term strategies to reduce losses in future disasters and provided funding under the Hazard Mitigation Grant Program. The federal government also worked with Puerto Rico to acquire property and elevate structures in the floodplain. The U.S. Army Corp of Engineers worked with Puerto Rico to identify funding for and expedite construction of flood control projects.

Federal assistance for **housing** focused on repairing existing homes, addressing long-term shelter needs, replacing destroyed homes, restoring public housing, and providing technical assistance and training. FEMA provided funding assistance under the Disaster Housing Assistance Program and the Individual and Family Grant Program. Additional funding was provided through the SBA Home Disaster Loans and the USDA Rural Housing Service. HUD provided disaster funds through the Community Development Block Grant Program. FEMA collaborated with Puerto Rico on improved housing design plans for low-income residents and provided technical assistance and funding for the development of long-term sheltering options.

The federal government worked with Puerto Rico to put in place improvements to achieve the long-term benefits of **economic revitalization and sustainability**. In the agricultural sector this was accomplished through financial assistance for crop and physical losses, expanding agricultural insurance and coverage, and financial and technical assistance for conservation measures to reduce flooding and erosion. The USDA Risk Management Agency provided funding for crop loss insurance claims. The USDA Natural Resources Conservation Service provided financial and technical assistance to address flooding and soil erosion problems.

In the nonagricultural sector, the federal government provided community development planning assistance, supported small business recovery, encouraged new investment, proposed fiscal assistance, provided unemployment assistance, and promoted flood insurance for homeowners, renters, and businesses. HUD made available technical assistance for economic development strategies and financial packaging. The EDA provided a community planning grant to the University of Puerto Rico's Economic Development University Center and committed funds to Puerto Rico's Economic Development Bank for a revolving loan fund assistance program. The DOL provided funding to create temporary jobs to assist in the immediate and long-term cleanup and recovery efforts. The DOL also provided unemployment assistance.

Hurricane Georges caused 100 percent of the electrical service in Puerto Rico to be disrupted. Its failure crippled other basic services such as water and sewage treatment, telephone service, transportation, and local commerce. Federal assistance for the **energy** sector included providing resources for repairing electrical transmission and distribution lines and recommendations for design improvements, emergency generators, and assistance for developing a more reliable electrical system. The cost for repairing the island's electrical system was paid by a combination of Puerto Rico's self-insurance coverage and funding through FEMA's

(Continued)

public assistance program. Electric utility workers, trucks, and equipment were flown to the island to assist local crews. Emergency generators were provided to keep critical facilities operational, and plans were developed to keep some of the generators in place to provide backup power during future disasters. The Department of Energy, FEMA, and Puerto Rico examined mitigation measures to improve the disaster resistance of the electrical system through enhanced generation/transmission relationships, better power line placement, and placing poles deeper in the ground.

Key **transportation** issues addressed included repairing damaged roads and bridges, developing a reliable power source for the Tren Urbano project, and dredging harbors. The Army Corps removed tons of debris from roadways, installed four temporary bridges, and provided financial assistance for critical dredging activities to maintain safe harbor channels. The FHA and FEMA provided financial assistance for rebuilding the island's damaged transportation system. Mitigation measures were incorporated into road and bridge repairs to reduce the risk of such severe damage in the future. The Federal Transit Authority and FEMA worked with the government of Puerto Rico to explore funding options to establish a reliable power source for the Tren Urbano, a San Juan metro-area mass transit system. The governor of Puerto Rico, Pedro Rosselló, stated: "From the President on down, the federal government mobilized all of the resources at its disposal—even before the hurricane struck—and has earned the eternal gratitude of Puerto Rico's 3.9 million people for its role in helping us cope with this catastrophe. The scope of the response is illustrated by the fact that the President's Long-Term Recovery Task Force is rarely activated."

University of Houston O'Quinn Law Library
Tropical Storm Allison formed on Wednesday evening, June 6, 2001, in the Gulf of Mexico southeast of Galveston, Texas, and eventually exited the United States on Sunday night, June 17, after passing through Florida and proceeding up the East Coast. Allison proved to be the most destructive tropical storm in U.S. history, costing 43 lives and nearly $5 billion in damages. The storm hit Houston, Texas, especially hard, dumping between 30 and 40 inches of rain and causing an estimated $1 billion in damage. On June 9, 2001, President Bush declared a major disaster for the state of Texas, with 28 counties eligible for public assistance. The University of Houston O'Quinn Law Library was flooded with eight feet of water after the heavy rains from Tropical Storm Allison.

The lower floor of the library filled nearly to the 12-foot ceilings with a mixture of water, oil, asbestos, and other pollutants. The 35,000 square feet of space in the lower level were equal to nearly two floors of a typical downtown skyscraper. The metal shelves were destroyed, partly by the tremendous weight of waterlogged books and partly by being literally exploded as the wet books began swelling and exerting tremendous sideways pressure. The library lost between 200,000 and 500,000 books, and damages were estimated at $30 million.

Through the Public Assistance Program, FEMA approved $21.4 million for the replacement of 174,000 copies of law books and microfiche storage collection. The funding approved by FEMA was for two separate projects: one project in the amount of $1,204,600 was for the microfiche collection, and the other project in the amount of $27,295,196 was for law book replacement. FEMA provided 75 percent of the cost, with the remaining 25 percent coming from local sources. "With the support of all our communities, and major assistance from FEMA, not only have we recovered, but we're putting in place an even stronger and more secure resource for our law center faculty and students as well as the community," said University of Houston president Arthur K. Smith.

IMPORTANT TERMS

- Recovery
- National Processing Service Center
- Disaster recovery center
- Joint field office
- Federal coordinating officer
- State coordinating officer
- Land-use planning
- Zoning
- Building codes

Self-Check Questions

1. Who plays the largest role in providing the technical and financial support for recovery?
2. What is a disaster recovery center?
3. Which office is the central coordination point among federal, state, local and tribal agencies and voluntary organizations for delivering recovery assistance programs?
4. What is the purpose of the National Processing Service Centers in Texas, Virginia, and Maryland?
5. What are the four types of assistance provided by the Disaster Housing Program?
6. What is covered under the Individual and Households Program?
7. What is the minimum federal share for FEMA public assistance grants?
8. What entities are eligible for public assistance grant funding?
9. What is the difference between emergency work and public work?
10. What federal agencies in addition to FEMA provide recovery assistance, and what kind of assistance does each provide?
11. What is a VOAD, and what does it do?
12. Name some examples of policy areas and tools that should be considered by decision makers as they develop their recovery plan. Explain why each should be considered.

Out of Class Exercises

1. Visit the NVOAD Web site, and find out what organizations are members of your state VOAD (http://www.nvoad.org/membersdb.php?members=State).
2. Contact your state office of emergency management, and ask if your state has any active recovery operations related to presidentially declared disasters. Find out how much money was granted the state, where it went, and what kinds of recovery and mitigation measures it covered.

6

The Disciplines of Emergency Management: Preparedness

What You Will Learn

- Why preparedness is considered the building block of emergency management.
- The difference between mitigation and preparedness.
- How FEMA's Community and Family Preparedness Program educates the public about disasters.
- Why evacuation planning is important.
- Why special consideration must be made for certain populations when planning for emergencies and disasters.
- How the Emergency Management Institute promotes community-level disaster preparedness.
- The types of exercises, and what each involves.
- How training and equipment helps first responders prepare.
- How businesses and nongovernmental organizations prepare for emergencies.

Introduction

Preparedness within the field of emergency management can best be defined as a state of readiness to respond to a disaster, crisis, or any other type of emergency situation. Preparedness is not only a state of readiness but also a theme throughout most aspects of emergency management. If you look into the history of the United States, you see the predecessors of today's emergency managers focusing on preparedness. The fallout shelters of the 1950s and the air raid wardens were promoting preparedness for a potential nuclear attack from the Soviet Union. An early 1970s study prepared by the National Governor's Association talked about the importance of preparedness as the first step in emergency management.

After the Three Mile Island Nuclear Power Plant incident in 1979, preparedness around commercial nuclear power plants became a major issue for continued licensing of these plants. The increased emphasis on preparing the public for a potential event through planning and education and preparing local responders through required exercises caused an increased focus on preparedness. The Nuclear Regulatory Commission's licensing requirements required local emergency plans, exercise of those plans, and evaluation of the exercises.

The process had a profound impact on the discipline of emergency management. This off-site preparedness planning process became the model for future emergency response plans. The required exercises were some of the first such activities. They brought a legitimacy and level of public and political exposure to the emergency management profession. Most people agree that the radiological emergency preparedness program initiated in the aftermath of Three Mile Island that became part of the newly created Federal Emergency Management Agency was the start of modern emergency management discipline.

Since that time, preparedness advanced significantly, and its role as a building block of emergency management continues. No emergency management organization can function without a strong preparedness capability built through planning, training, and exercising. Preparedness activities have led to an increased professionalism within the discipline of emergency management. Throughout the 1990s, FEMA was focused on supporting and enhancing these efforts, not just at the federal level but also throughout government and into the private sector.

All organizations in the private, public, and government sectors are susceptible to the consequences of a disaster and must consider preparedness. For example, preparedness focuses not only on getting essential government services, such as utilities and emergency services, functioning at predisaster levels but also on assisting businesses in quickly reopening to the public. Both these key functions of preparedness help minimize the required time for the affected population to return to predisaster life. Business contingency planning has emerged as a profitable offshoot of government preparedness efforts.

This chapter discusses the preparedness cycle from a systems approach, preparedness programs, hazard preparedness, training programs, and exercise programs. The focus is on federal efforts, predominantly FEMA, and best practices are highlighted through several case studies.

Preparedness: The Building Block

Within the National Response Plan, there are 15 emergency functions, each of which relies on a level of preparedness: transportation; communications; public works and engineering; firefighting; emergency management; mass care, housing, and human services; resource support; public health and medical services; urban search and rescue; oil and hazardous materials response; agriculture and natural resources; energy; public safety and security; long-term community recovery and mitigation; and external affairs. Each functional area must ensure its own preparedness to establish a systemwide posture that is ready to respond in an emergency.

All 15 functions depend on each other. For example, the functions of emergency communications must be prepared to establish emergency telecommunications support for the firefighters, who must be prepared with the equipment and training to extinguish the fires, to know where to go and coordinate their work with the urban search and rescue teams that locate and rescue victims, each of which must be provided timely transportation to reach the disaster scene.

Preparedness therefore is defined more fully by FEMA as the leadership, training, readiness, exercise support, and technical and financial assistance to strengthen citizens; communities; state, local, and tribal governments; and professional emergency workers as they prepare for disasters, mitigate the effects of disasters, respond to community needs after a disaster, and launch effective recovery efforts (www.fema.gov).

Mitigation Versus Preparedness

Preparedness has been defined, and it has been mentioned that preparedness encompasses various aspects of response, but how does mitigation play into the equation? Mitigation is the cornerstone of emergency management. It is the ongoing effort to lessen the impact disasters have on people and property. Mitigation involves keeping homes away from floodplains, engineering bridges to withstand earthquakes, creating and enforcing effective building codes to protect property from hurricanes—and more.

Preparedness deals with the functional aspects of emergency management, such as the response to and recovery from a disaster, whereas mitigation attempts to lessen these effects through predisaster actions, as simple as striving to create "disaster-resistant" communities.

A Systems Approach: The Preparedness Cycle

As an academic field as well as an applied practice in the public and private sector, emergency management was established just recently. For this reason, thus far it has drawn on the fields of emergency medicine, fire suppression, and law enforcement for many of its foundations. Although these are tried-and-tested specialties, they also are steeped in tradition, relying less on academic or analytic processes. Without a foundation that ties academia and structured analytic methodologies with tradition, the extreme complexity of emergency management, often requiring coordination among tens to hundreds of individual agencies and organizations, will not be managed effectively. Therefore, a systematic approach must be established for emergency management as a whole and specifically the steps necessary to reach preparedness.

The diagram depicted in Figure 6–1, used in terrorism planning, depicts the planning process, beginning with assessing the threats to a jurisdiction or business, be they natural or human-made, and working in a systematic approach toward a cyclical process to establish preparedness. This systematic and cyclical approach is specified by the continual evolution of the phases on the exterior ring: assessment, planning, preparation, and evaluation.

In this depiction, the interior ring shows each of the steps that organizations must work toward to be prepared. The first step is to identify what types of disasters or threats a jurisdiction, business, or any entity faces. Next, assessing the current vulnerability or level of preparedness leads toward determining the shortfalls between current preparedness and the requirements to meet an improved preparedness posture. This improved posture may be determined through industrial standards set forth by organizations such as the National Fire Protection Association, which sets fire safety standards, or the International Standards Organization (ISO), one of the largest developers of standards and certifications. Local, state, and federal laws also can statutorily specify a required level of preparedness.

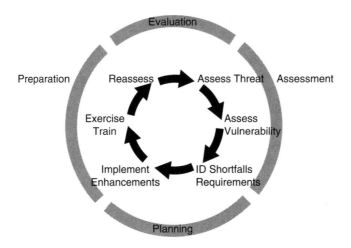

FIGURE 6–1 Preparedness planning cycle.

Implementing enhancements or revamping complete systems corrects these identified shortfalls. Exercises and training then can be used to test whether the enhancements or new systems, in fact, meet the standards determined in earlier stages. If they do, then the goal of readiness or preparedness regarding a particular threat such as terrorism or floods is met.

The cyclical nature of this system is the fundamental aspect of the successive steps to be taken after determining whether a jurisdiction or any type of entity is prepared. Whether or not those standards are met, the entity must reexamine its threats because both natural and technological threats change constantly. The important realization that preparedness is a dynamic state and can either improve or diminish in a short time must be understood by the emergency management professional. Using a systems approach ensures that an overall emergency management system is prepared and, more important, each functional area is prepared.

The importance and diversity of this vital aspect of preparedness planning can be demonstrated through the other types of assessment processes available. Another example available to emergency managers is provided by FEMA in its Capability Assessment for Readiness (CAR) Program.

□ □ □ ▬▬▬▬▬▬▬▬▬▬▬▬▬▬▬▬▬▬▬▬▬▬▬▬▬▬▬▬▬▬▬▬▬▬▬▬

FEMA'S Capability Assessment Programs

FEMA and the National Emergency Management Association (NEMA) joined together in partnership in 1997 to develop an emergency management readiness and capability assessment program for state and local emergency managers. The effort first resulted in the development of the Capability Assessment for Readiness (CAR) program. This initiative was developed to strengthen the effectiveness of the Emergency Management Performance Grant (EMPG) Program—which provides federal financial assistance to state and local governments—by providing state and local governments with a baseline readiness index from which they could measure their improvement efforts. Imbedded in the CAR were the standard minimum "ingredients" developed by the National Fire Protection Association termed Emergency Management Standards (NPFA 1600 Standard on Disaster/Emergency Management and Business Continuity Programs, 2004). The CAR process provided for the assessment component of the EMPG process, which continues to evolve as the program advances.

Unfortunately, only a handful of states completed the CAR during the first assessment period in May and June of 2000. In the years that followed, few others were added to this list. In response to the poor levels of participation, FEMA developed the National Emergency Management Baseline Capacity Assessment Program (NEMB-CAP), in 2003, to replace the CAR. The NEMB-CAP was similar to the CAR program except that it was based on the new Emergency Management Accreditation Program (EMAP) readiness standards and in that reporting could be done online.

EMAP was developed by twelve national organizations working together to further evolve the accreditation of state and local emergency management entities. The organizations included: the National Emergency Management Association, International Association of Emergency Managers, FEMA, U.S. Department of Transportation, Association of State Flood Plain Managers, Institute for Business and Home Safety, International Association of Fire Chiefs, National Association of Counties, National Association of Development Organizations, National Conference of State Legislatures, National Governors Association, National League of Cities, and the U.S. Environmental Protection Agency. EMAP is a nonprofit organization, overseen by an independent commission whose ten members are appointed by FEMA, IAEM, and NEMA.

For state and local emergency management programs, EMAP provided an opportunity to be recognized for compliance with national standards, to demonstrate accountability, and to focus attention on areas and issues where work or resources are needed. The purpose of EMAP was to evaluate and improve the delivery of emergency management services to the public through accreditation of government emergency management programs. Specifically, the program's purposes include:

- To establish and maintain standards for emergency management programs
- To administer an accreditation process that encourages an applicant to bring its program into compliance with those standards
- To oversee or conduct a process of self-assessment, documentation, and on-site assessment of the applicant's compliance with established standards
- To formally acknowledge compliance of a program by issuance of a certificate of accreditation
- To accept fees, grants, gifts, bequests, and other contributions that support the purposes of the commission
- To develop and maintain close working relationships with national, regional, state, and local associations and agencies in the emergency management and related fields for mutual growth and benefit
- To educate legislative and executive branches of government and the public on the importance of fully capable emergency management programs at all levels of government based upon high standards
- To ensure that the business affairs and the programs of the commission and its affiliates are conducted on a nondiscriminatory basis

(Continued)

- To promote the concept of voluntary self-regulation inherent in the accreditation process
- To cooperate with other private and public agencies in a manner that will lead to the improvement in the accreditation program and the delivery of emergency management services

The goal of EMAP was, and continues to be, to provide a meaningful, voluntary accreditation process for state, territorial, and local programs. The intent of its voluntary accreditation process is to encourage self-examination of strengths and weaknesses, the pursuit of corrective measures, and communication and planning among different sectors of government and the community. The accreditation process includes: application: self-assessment and documentation of compliance, on-site assessment by a team of trained EMAP assessors culminating in an assessment report, committee review of compliance with the EMAP Standard, commission decision of accreditation, and re-accreditation every five years.

Under this new program, forty states completed the process by the end of 2004. Of this number, only two states met all of the planning criteria, only five were compliant with most or all standards, and only two were fully compliant in all fourteen functional areas. The process served to highlight the importance of ensuring that roles and responsibilities are not only well understood by emergency management agencies, but that they are also made operational at the State and local levels. By August of 2007, EMAP had fully accredited thirteen programs, including:

- The State of Arizona
- The Consolidated City/County of Jacksonville/Duval (Florida)
- The District of Columbia
- East Baton Rouge Parish (Louisiana)
- The State of Florida
- The State of Illinois
- The Commonwealth of Massachusetts
- The State of Montana
- The State of New York
- The State of North Dakota
- The Commonwealth of Pennsylvania
- The State of Utah
- The Commonwealth of Virginia

Several programs have also achieved conditional accreditation, which means they have nine months to attain compliance in a number of deficient areas, at which point they will be re-reviewed for accreditation. These programs include:

- The State of Alabama
- The State of Georgia
- The State of Louisiana
- The State of Missouri
- The County of San Diego, CA
- The State of Tennessee

In August of 2007, EMAP completed their latest update to the standards by which programs are accredited, and they presented them to the public for a period of review. These standards can be viewed online at: http://www.emaponline.org/?342 More information on the EMAP accreditation process can be found online at: http://www.emaponline.org/?180

Source: EMAP, FEMA.

□ □ □

Preparedness Programs

Preparedness is everyone's job. Not just government agencies but all sectors of society: Service providers; businesses, civic, and volunteer groups; industry and neighborhood associations; as well as every individual citizen should plan ahead for disaster. As such, preparedness programs are developed to target each audiences to educate, promote, and test preparedness.

One of these public education programs is the Community and Family Preparedness Program operated by FEMA, which educates the general public about disaster awareness and preparedness. The core message of the Community and Family Preparedness Program is the Family Disaster Plan, four basic steps people can take to prepare for any type of disaster:

1. *Find out what types of disasters are most likely to occur in your community and how to prepare for them.* Contacting the local emergency management office or American Red Cross chapter for information and guidelines is a good way to get started.
2. *Create a family disaster plan.* Hold a family meeting to talk about the steps the family members will take to be ready when disaster happens in the community.
3. *Take action.* Each family member, regardless of age, can be responsible for helping the family be prepared. Activities can include posting emergency telephone numbers, installing smoke detectors, determining escape routes, assembling disaster supply kits, and taking first aid or CPR courses.
4. *Practice and maintain the plan.* The final step emphasizes the need to practice the plan on a regular basis so family members will remember what to do when disaster strikes.

As just one of the many preparedness programs sponsored by FEMA and other public and private disaster response and emergency management organizations, the Community and Family Preparedness Program highlights the foundation of a disaster program that is applicable to a wide range of disasters. Many more programs look specifically at preparedness regarding one type of disaster and can be obtained through agencies such as FEMA, the American Red Cross, and state and local offices of emergency management.

□ □ □ ▬▬▬▬▬▬▬▬▬▬▬▬▬▬▬▬▬▬▬▬▬▬▬

American Red Cross Hurricane Preparedness Tips

Here is what one can do to prepare for such an emergency.

Know What Hurricane Watch and Warning Mean

- *Watch:* Hurricane conditions are *possible* in the specified area of the watch, usually within 36 hours.
- *Warning:* Hurricane conditions are *expected* in the specified area of the warning, usually within 24 hours.

Prepare a Personal Evacuation Plan

- Identify ahead of time where to go if told to evacuate. Choose several places—a friend's home in another town, a motel, or a shelter.
- Keep the telephone numbers of these places handy as well as a road map of your locality. You may need to take alternative or unfamiliar routes if major roads are closed or clogged.
- Listen to NOAA Weather Radio or local radio or TV stations for evacuation instructions. If advised to evacuate, do so immediately.

Assemble a Disaster Supplies Kit Including the Following Items

- First-aid kit and essential medications.
- Canned food and can opener.
- At least three gallons of water per person.
- Protective clothing, rainwear, and bedding or sleeping bags.
- Battery-powered radio, flashlight, and extra batteries.
- Special items for infants, elderly, or disabled family members.
- Written instructions on how to turn off electricity, gas, and water if authorities advise to do so (remember, a professional is needed to turn them back on).

Prepare for High Winds

- Install hurricane shutters or purchase precut ½-inch outdoor plywood boards for each window of your home. Install anchors for the plywood and predrill holes in the plywood so that you can put it up quickly.
- Make trees more wind resistant by removing diseased and damaged limbs, then strategically removing branches so that wind can blow through.

*Know What to Do When a Hurricane **Watch** Is Issued*

- Listen to NOAA Weather Radio or local radio or TV stations for up-to-date storm information.
- Prepare to bring inside any lawn furniture, outdoor decorations or ornaments, trash cans, hanging plants, and anything else that can be picked up by the wind.
- Prepare to cover all windows of your home. If shutters have not been installed, use precut plywood as described previously. Note: Tape does not prevent windows from breaking, so taping windows is not recommended.
- Fill the car's gas tank.

- Recheck manufactured home tiedowns.
- Check batteries and stock up on canned food, first-aid supplies, drinking water, and medications.

Know What to Do When a Hurricane **Warning** Is Issued
- Listen to the advice of local officials, and leave if told to do so.
- Complete preparation activities.
- If not advised to evacuate, stay indoors, away from windows.
- Be aware that the calm "eye" is deceptive; the storm is not over. The worst part of the storm happens once the eye passes over and the winds blow from the opposite direction. Trees, shrubs, buildings, and other objects damaged by the first winds can be broken or destroyed by the second winds.
- Be alert for tornadoes. Tornadoes can happen during a hurricane and after it passes over.
- Remain indoors, in the center of the home, in a closet or bathroom without windows.
- Stay away from floodwaters. If coming upon a flooded road, turn around and go another way.
- If caught on a flooded road and waters are rising rapidly, get out of the car and climb to higher ground.

Know What to Do After a Hurricane Is Over
- Keep listening to NOAA Weather Radio or local radio or TV stations for instructions.
- If evacuated, return home when local officials say it is safe to do so.
- Inspect the home for damage.

Source: American Red Cross, www.redcross.org.

Evacuation Planning

For many communities, one of the most important planning considerations is how to evacuate citizens in the event of a major disaster. For disasters where advance notice of a hazard event is possible (e.g., hurricanes or tsunamis) or for situations where it is essential that all citizens be removed from the affected area as soon as possible after an event has occurred (e.g., terrorist attacks involving weapons of mass destruction), advance planning is required to determine, among other things, activation procedures, the determination of adequate and effective routes, methods of transportation, destinations for those evacuated, security precautions for homes and belongings, adherence by citizens to evacuation orders, and facilitation of the evacuation itself.

While many communities have conducted some form of evacuation planning as part of the basic emergency operations plan, few have been able to conduct a full-scale test that provides them with an idea of how the plan works in a real-life situation. The difficulties that were experienced by local emergency managers in the evacuations from

Hurricanes Katrina and Rita in 2005 highlight the both the need for evacuation planning and the shortfalls that often lie in existing plans. In the Katrina evacuation, the largest in U.S. history, resulting in the displacement of over 1.3 million people, failure to consider how the evacuation would affect people of lower economic standing resulted in thousands refusing to or being unable to leave. In Hurricane Rita, as determined by a University of Texas study, a strong majority of the deaths (90 of the 113) associated with that storm were a result of the poorly planned evacuation itself.

Since these events, the U.S. Department of Transportation conducted a study of the evacuation plans in the Gulf Coast region, where hurricanes are most likely to strike. This study looked at each of the five Gulf Coast states (Alabama, Florida, Mississippi, Louisiana, and Texas) and 58 of the counties and parishes in these states to strengthen any weaknesses in those plans and learn from any best practices that exist. According to this study, seven key elements can be used to measure the comprehensive nature of a plan:

1. Decision making and management.
2. Planning.
3. Public communication and preparedness.
4. Evacuation of people with special needs.
5. Operations.
6. Shelter considerations.
7. Mass evacuation training and exercises.

The study found that, while most of the plans were effective in terms of creating standard operating procedures, conducting exercises, and drafting after-action reports, updating plans, and defining evacuation direction and control, they were often weak in the following areas:

- Keeping evacuees informed during the evacuation.
- Provisions for evacuating persons with various special needs.
- Returning evacuees to their homes.
- Using contraflow (reversed lane) operations.
- Provisions for the care and protection of animals.

Special Needs Populations

Traditionally, emergency planning has looked at a homogenous population thought of collectively as the "community." However, communities are made up of distinct individuals and groups, each with unique conditions that define their lives, their interactions, and their abilities. Some of these individuals have special needs that must be considered by emergency planners in the drafting of emergency operations plans and other emergency procedures in the community. In the absence of such consideration, plans are likely to fail these individuals as their provisions are irrelevant or inappropriate.

No set criteria places a person in a special needs population. Likewise, no standard set of special needs populations exist in all communities. Each community must assess its own population to determine what special needs exist and how those needs must be addressed in the emergency plan, if it is to adequately protect all of the community's citizens equally. Examples of special needs populations that might exist include (but are not limited to)

- Children.
- The elderly.

- The disabled.
- Immigrant populations.
- Transient populations (tourists, students).
- Non-English-speaking populations.
- Minorities.
- The poor.
- The illiterate.
- The mentally ill.
- Prisoners.
- The homeless.

In considering these populations, planners have to work with representatives from each group (or, as in the case of children, the mentally ill, and other groups, they must work with experts with knowledge about those groups). By including these key stakeholders, the planners are better able to adjust existing policies or create new policies that allow for the safety and security of these groups before, during, and after emergency events. Consideration of special needs groups is something that must be addressed in all four phases of emergency management. Examples of the kinds of considerations that must be made include

- Foreign language training and materials.
- Registry of special needs individuals locations and emergency requirements.
- Special emergency equipment and forms of transportation.
- Special communications equipment or methods.
- Alternate (nontraditional) warning media and procedures.
- Special protection measures at shelters and during evacuations.
- Inclusion of certain prescription drugs and physical support devices in shelters and other emergency facilities.
- Special education measures targeting newcomers and transient populations.
- Special transportation and holding facilities for incarcerated evacuees or victims.
- Training for emergency responders in special-needs care.

In many, if not all of the recent disasters that occurred in the United States, there have been cases of certain special needs populations exhibiting a greater degree of vulnerability and, as result, experiencing a higher proportional impact, than other groups affected by the same event. Two specific examples include the 1995 heat wave in Chicago, in which almost all of the 600 victims were elderly and poor, and Hurricane Katrina, where it was found that most of the residents who failed to evacuate (and died as a result) were among the urban poor. In the recovery phase of Katrina (as well as many other recent major disaster), the illegal immigrant population, afraid to register for services for fear of deportation, suffered to a greater degree. To an increasing degree, however, campaigns advocating for increased consideration of special needs populations in emergency planning, initiated primarily by activist groups representing the individual groups, have accelerated the acceptance by emergency planners of the planning need throughout the United States.

Critical Thinking

Why is evacuation planning so difficult? What kinds of things can go wrong during an actual evacuation? What do you think can be done to minimize these potential setbacks?

Education and Training Programs

Since its inception in 1979, FEMA has become a leader in developing and teaching courses in emergency management. FEMA manages the Emergency Management Institute and the National Fire Academy (NFA), which are collocated on a former college campus in Emmitsburg, Maryland. Thousands of firefighters, fire officers, and emergency managers have been trained by FEMA. Additionally, FEMA helped establish degree programs in junior colleges, colleges, and universities across the country. Currently, FEMA is expanding its training and education capacities through long-distance learning programs.

Emergency Management Institute

Through its Emergency Management Institute, FEMA administers a nationwide training program of resident and nonresident courses whose primary objective is to enhance emergency management practice in the United States (and abroad, through a program that allows foreign students to participate on a case-by-case basis). At present, approximately 10,000 students are enrolled in the resident courses held at the Emmitsburg facilities. Nonresident courses, which are administered by the states through their emergency management agencies (under cooperative agreement with FEMA), see an additional 100,000 students each year. Emergency management exercises supported by the EMI draw over 150,000 participants annually, and through the range of Independent Study Program courses administered through the institute's Web site, several hundred thousand other individuals receive training.

The 2006–2007 EMI catalogue of courses lists 77 resident courses offered at the Emmitsburg campus and 76 nonresident courses in the following subject areas:

- Mitigation.
- Preparedness and technology.
- Professional development.
- Disaster operations and recovery.
- Integrated emergency management.

The EMI also offers 59 independent study courses in the 2006–2007 period. Examples of the independent study courses offered include

- The emergency manager.
- Animals in disaster.
- Introduction to the incident command system.
- Leadership and influence.
- Effective communication.
- Anticipating hazardous weather and community risk.
- Retrofitting flood-prone residential buildings.
- Community hurricane preparedness.
- Public assistance operations.
- The professional in emergency operations.
- Radiological emergency response.
- Multihazard emergency preparedness for schools.

Three EMI programs of note are the integrated emergency management courses (IEMC), the disaster-resistant jobs course, and a wide range of train-the-trainer courses available in several subject areas. The IEMC is a set of courses for public officials that covers all aspects of the community emergency management function. Community officials from Oklahoma City participated in the IEMC just months before the Alfred P. Murrah Federal Building terrorist bombing in 1995 and credit the lessons they learned through the program with helping them respond quickly and effectively in the aftermath of that event. The disaster-resistant jobs course, developed in cooperation with the Economic Development Administration of the U.S. Department of Commerce, is designed to "help small and medium-sized communities protect the economy from the effects of catastrophic events." This course was developed in response to the devastating impact the 1997 floods had on the city of Grand Forks, North Dakota. The EDA and FEMA recognized that more economic development planning could be done to reduce the impacts of future disasters on local economies.

The Integrated Emergency Management Course

Protecting the population is a primary responsibility of government, and fulfilling this responsibility depends on the abilities of emergency personnel to prepare for, respond to, recover from, and mitigate against disaster. It means developing and maintaining a high standard of readiness and an ability to function effectively under crisis conditions. Emergency personnel can attain readiness through either managing emergencies or participating in exercises. Clearly, exercises are the preferred method of gaining the necessary expertise.

The IEMC curriculum addresses emergency response activities for the total community, from the chief elected official to professional staff members, both paid and volunteer, within the emergency response organizations, and addressing such needs as fire, emergency management, planning, finance, personnel, public health, transportation and public works, and information technology. The IEMC stresses the integration of functions, resources, organizations, and individuals in all phases of emergency management.

IEMCs are designed to immerse course participants in the practical application of the various functions associated with the management of disaster response. Each course begins with presentations, discussions, and small group workshops, to familiarize participants with the specific response functions addressed. This is followed by emergency drills and exercises, presented in increasing levels of complexity, which allow participants to apply their new skills and knowledge within the high-stress but controlled environment of a simulated disaster. Participants develop emergency policies, plans, and procedures to ensure an effective response. The IEMCs even can be tailored to address the needs of a specific community (although the number of courses conducted annually in this fashion is limited).

Current IEMCs include IEMC/all hazards: preparedness and response; IEMC/all hazards: recovery and mitigation; IEMC/hurricane: preparedness and response; IEMC/hurricane: recovery and mitigation; IEMC/earthquake: preparedness and response; IEMC/earthquake: recovery and mitigation; IEMC/homeland security; IEMC/food and agriculture terrorism; and IEMC/state, IEMC/hazardous materials: preparedness and response; IEMC/metropolitan medical response system.

Source: Training.FEMA.gov.

Disaster-Resistant Jobs and Train-the-Trainer Courses

All too often, communities that experienced major disasters lost a large portion of their economic base. Studies have shown that, after a disaster, 60 percent of small- and medium-sized businesses fail within two years. Many never return to business once they are closed for even a few days because of a disastrous event. The community suffers not only from the immediate effects of the hazard but also, in the long run, from job losses and a reduction in the tax base that helps fuel recovery.

The EDA and FEMA developed the disaster-resistant jobs course to help small- and medium-sized communities protect the economy from the effect of catastrophic events. The topics of this course are as follows:

- The importance of disaster-resistant jobs.
- Creating disaster-resistant jobs.
- Recognizing the impact.
- What about mitigation?
- The disaster-resistant economic development planning process.
- Business recovery.

The purpose of train-the-trainer (TTT) courses is to develop a cadre of trainers who can raise awareness in their own localities. Participants must have the desire and ability to speak before the emergency services and other community groups (including local economic development agencies, chambers of commerce, service clubs, businesses, and other venues) to address the issue of protecting the community from the effects of disasters. Participants are provided materials that can be used to conduct presentations once they arrive back in their communities. Examples of EMI's TTT courses include

- Managing floodplain development through the National Flood Insurance Program.
- Multihazard emergency planning for schools.
- Homeland security planning for local governments.
- Radiological series.
- Incident command system.
- Continuity of operations.
- Emergency management assistance compact.
- Hospital emergency response training for mass casualty incidents.

Source: Training.FEMA.gov.

FEMA's EMI Higher Education Project works to establish and support emergency management curriculum in junior colleges, colleges, and universities. The project developed a prototype curriculum for an associate degrees in emergency management. Currently, for emergency management, FEMA lists seven doctoral programs, 39 masters degree programs, 15 bachelors degree programs, 20 bachelors-level emergency management concentrations and minors,

36 associates-level programs, 50 stand-alone certificate programs, and 46 additional programs offering one or more courses. For homeland Security, EMI lists 3 doctoral programs, 20 masters programs, 7 bachelors programs, 9 bachelors-level homeland security concentrations and minors, 9 associates degree programs, and 44 certificate programs.

☐ ☐ ☐ ▬▬▬▬▬▬▬▬▬▬▬▬▬▬▬▬▬▬▬▬▬

Community Emergency Response Team

Following a major disaster, first responders who provide fire and medical services will be unable to meet the demand for these services. Factors such as number of victims, communication failures, and road blockages will prevent people from accessing emergency services they have come to expect at a moment's notice through dialing 9-1-1. People will have to rely on each other for help in meeting their immediate lifesaving and life-sustaining needs.

If it can predict that emergency services will not meet immediate needs following a major disaster, especially if there is no warning, as in an earthquake, and people will spontaneously volunteer, what can government do to prepare citizens for this eventuality?

1. Present citizens with the facts about what to expect following a major disaster in terms of immediate services.
2. Give the message about their responsibility for mitigation and preparedness.
3. Train them in needed lifesaving skills with emphasis on decision-making skills, rescuer safety, and doing the greatest good for the greatest number.
4. Organize teams so that they are an extension of first responder services offering immediate help to victims until professional services arrive.

The Community Emergency Response Team (CERT) concept was developed and implemented by the Los Angeles City Fire Department (LAFD) in 1985. The Whittier Narrows earthquake in 1987 underscored the areawide threat of a major disaster in California. Further, it confirmed the need for training civilians to meet their immediate needs. As a result, the LAFD created the Disaster Preparedness Division to train citizens and private and government employees.

The training program that the LAFD initiated makes good sense and furthers the process of citizens understanding their responsibility in preparing for disaster. It also increases their ability to safely help themselves, their families, and their neighbors. FEMA recognizes the importance of preparing citizens. The EMI and the National Fire Academy adopted and expanded the CERT materials, believing them to be applicable to all hazards.

The CERT course benefits any citizen who takes it. This individual is better prepared to respond to and cope with the aftermath of a disaster. Additionally, if a community wants to supplement its response capability after a disaster, civilians can be recruited and trained as neighborhood, business, and government teams that, in essence, are auxiliary responders. These groups can provide immediate assistance to victims in their area, organize spontaneous volunteers who have not had the training, and collect disaster intelligence that will assist professional responders with setting priorities and allocating resources following a disaster. Since 1993, when

(Continued)

this training was made available nationally by FEMA, communities in 28 states and Puerto Rico have conducted CERT training.

The CERT course is delivered in the community by a team of first responders who have the requisite knowledge and skills to instruct the sessions. It is suggested that the instructors complete a CERT train-the-trainer course conducted by their state Training Office for Emergency Management or the Emergency Management Institute to learn the training techniques used successfully by the LAFD.

The CERT training for community groups usually is delivered in two-and-a-half-hour sessions, one evening per week over a seven-week period. The training consists of the following:

- Disaster preparedness.
- Disaster fire suppression.
- Disaster medical operations.
- Light search and rescue.
- Disaster psychology and team organization.
- Course review and disaster simulation.

Source: FEMA, www.fema.gov.

National Fire Academy

The mission of the National Fire Academy is this: "Through its courses and programs, the National Fire Academy works to enhance the ability of fire and emergency services and allied professionals to deal more effectively with fire and related emergencies."

Since its inception in 1975 as the delivery mechanism for fire training for the congressionally mandated U.S. Fire Administration (USFA), the NFA estimates it has trained more than 1.4 million students. The NFA delivers courses at its Emmitsburg, Maryland, campus, which it shares with the EMI, and across the nation in cooperation with state and local fire training organizations and local colleges and universities.

U.S. Fire Administration

As an entity of FEMA, the mission of the USFA is to reduce life and economic losses caused by fire and related emergencies through leadership, advocacy, coordination, and support. It serves the nation independently, in coordination with other federal agencies, and in partnership with fire protection and emergency service communities. With a commitment to excellence, the USFA provides public education, training, technology, and data initiatives.

□ □ □ ▬▬▬▬▬▬▬▬▬▬▬▬▬▬▬▬▬▬▬▬▬▬▬▬▬▬

USFA Programs

USFA programs to prevent and mitigate the consequences of fire are divided into four basic areas:

1. **Public education.** It develops and delivers fire prevention and safety education programs in partnership with other federal agencies, the fire and emergency response community, the media, and safety interest groups.
2. **Training.** It promotes the professional development of the fire and the emergency response community and its allied professionals. To supplement and support state and local fire service training programs, the NFA and the EMI develop and deliver educational and training courses with a national focus.
3. **Technology.** It works with the public and private groups to promote and improve fire prevention and life safety through research, testing, and evaluation. It generates and distributes research and special studies on fire detection, suppression, and notification systems, and on fire and emergency responder health and safety.
4. **Data.** It assists state and local entities in collecting, analyzing, and disseminating data on the occurrence, control, and consequences of all types of fires. The National Fire Data Center describes the nation's fire problem, proposes possible solutions and national priorities, monitors resulting programs, and provides information to the public and fire organizations.

The U.S. Fire Administration has a training program focused on the response to terrorist events. The courses, all titled Emergency Response to Terrorism, may be taken at the Emergency Management Institute in Emmitsburg, at the state level, or online (select courses). Terrorism courses include

- Emergency response to terrorism—basic concepts.
- Emergency response to terrorism tactical considerations—company officer.
- Emergency response to terrorism tactical considerations—emergency medical services.
- Emergency response to terrorism tactical considerations—hazardous materials.
- Emergency response to terrorism strategic considerations for command officers.
- Emergency response to terrorism self study.

Source: FEMA, www.fema.gov.

▬▬▬▬▬▬▬▬▬▬▬▬▬▬▬▬▬▬▬▬▬▬▬▬ □ □ □

The NFA's on-campus programs target middle- and top-level fire officers, fire service instructors, technical professionals, and representatives from allied professions. Any person with substantial involvement in fire prevention and control, emergency medical services, or fire-related emergency management activities is eligible to apply for academy courses. The NFA also delivers courses using CD-ROMs, their simulation laboratory, and the Internet. For those interested in pursuing degrees, the Degrees at a Distance Program extends the NFA's academic outreach through a network of seven colleges and universities. Fire service personnel who cannot attend college because of work hours and locations are able to earn a degree in fire technology and management through independent study.

□ □ □ ▬▬▬▬▬▬▬▬▬▬▬▬▬▬▬▬▬▬▬▬▬▬▬▬▬▬

Curriculum Offered at the National Fire Academy

- Arson.
- Emergency medical services.
- Emergency response to terrorism.
- Executive development.
- Fire prevention: Management.
- Fire prevention: Public education.
- Fire prevention: Technical.
- Hazardous materials.
- Incident management.
- Management science.
- Planning and information management.
- Training programs.

Source: FEMA, www.fema.gov.

▬▬▬▬▬▬▬▬▬▬▬▬▬▬▬▬▬▬▬▬▬▬▬▬ □ □ □

Other FEMA Education and Training Resources

FEMA provides other education and training resources such as curriculum and activities for teachers to use in the schools, school safety, and fire safety materials and information on how to talk to kids about terrorism. FEMA has built an award-winning Web site for children, FEMA for KIDS, that has such features as becoming a disaster action kid, the disaster area, the disaster connection: kids to kids, homework help, games and quizzes, and about FEMA.

Exercises

Once a plan is developed and personnel trained to the plan, the next step is exercising the plan. Exercises provide an opportunity to evaluate the efficiency and effectiveness of the plan and its components and to test the systems, facilities, and personnel involved in implementing the plan. Exercises are conducted at all levels of government and in the private sector.

FEMA defines an *exercise* as "a controlled, scenario-driven, simulated experience designed to demonstrate and evaluate an organization's capability to execute one or more assigned or implicit operational tasks or procedures as outlined in its contingency plan." Four types of exercises are identified by FEMA: full scale, partial scale, functional, and tabletop. Full descriptions of these exercise types are provided.

□ □ □ ▬▬▬▬▬▬▬▬▬▬▬▬▬▬▬▬▬▬▬▬▬▬▬▬▬▬

Emergency Management Exercise Types

Exercises are generally categorized by their scope:

- **Full scale.** This exercise is used to evaluate the operational capabilities of emergency management systems over an extended period. Usually, most or all of the organization's plan are tested. The full-scale exercise usually is conducted in conditions as close to an actual event as possible. Field teams and crews deploy and demonstrate their procedures. The full-scale exercise is designed to stress the organization's ability to accomplish its mission under realistic conditions.
- **Partial scale.** This is an exercise with limited goals, with a portion of the organization participating; the scope generally is less than that of a full-scale exercise. It may be conducted to evaluate a limited number of objectives or it may be used to evaluate the organization's capability to execute newly developed procedures. Some teams may be deployed to actual field sites, whereas some procedures may be demonstrated under simulated conditions. Partial-scale exercises generally are shorter than full-scale exercises.
- **Functional.** This exercise allows the evaluation of various procedures that are similar to one another, such as medical treatment or communications. It is limited to activities within a specific functional category of the organization. Activities are scenario driven, as with the full-scale exercise.
- **Tabletop.** This exercise usually involves senior staff members and elected or appointed officials in an informal setting. Using a hazard-specific scenario, supporting documentation, and injected messages simulating field-derived information, the participants discuss anticipated actions while in a controlled environment. With a facilitator to keep the discussions focused, the products derived from a tabletop exercise may include emerging policy, plan revisions, and conceptualization of new procedures.

Source: FEMA Comprehensive Exercise Program, July 1995.

▬▬▬▬▬▬▬▬▬▬▬▬▬▬▬▬▬▬▬▬▬▬▬▬▬▬ □ □ □

FEMA manages the Comprehensive Exercise Program (CEP). The goal of the CEP is to develop, implement, and institutionalize a comprehensive, all-hazard, risk-based exercise program. Exercises conducted under the auspices of FEMA's CEP are used to test and evaluate emergency management plans, policies, procedures, systems, and facilities developed to mitigate against, prepare for, respond to, and recover from the effects of all types of emergencies. The CEP exercises include extensive involvement of state and local officials as well as representatives from other federal agencies. The CEP program provides five categories of exercises.

Comprehensive Exercise Program Exercise Categories

1. **State and local all-hazard exercises.** These exercises serve as the focal point for all state and local emergency management exercise activity addressing natural, technological, and human-made disasters as well as national security hazards. They are designed to test and evaluate the operational readiness and capability of emergency management systems, identify systemic deficiencies and efficiencies, and define corrective actions needed to ensure readiness and emergency operations proficiency. Emergency management functions rather than specific scenarios are examined.

2. **FEMA-sponsored FRP exercises.** The concept of operations, policies, and procedures set forth in the FRP for providing a federal response to state and local governments under the authorities of the Stafford Act are tested and validated in these exercises. Ideally, detailed headquarters and regional plans and procedures to implement the FRP also are tested and validated. State and local governments are encouraged to participate, so their EOPs may be similarly tested and validated. The ultimate goal of these exercises is to achieve a seamless federal, state, and local response to and recovery from disasters of all types.

3. **Legislatively mandated exercises supported by FEMA.** These exercises focus on plans developed at the state and local levels based on guidance and requirements established by the federal government. Federal involvement in the state and local planning process is required to ensure that established standards are met and maintained. This involvement also ensures that incorporation of hazard-specific material into the jurisdiction's single EOP is accomplished in a manner consistent with the plans of federal departments and agencies responsible for incident response.

4. **FEMA-supported national and international security exercises.** National and international security exercises are designed to improve the capability of organizations and individuals to execute emergency management responsibilities and familiarize members of the federal government with the issues that might be encountered during a major emergency, including national security emergencies requiring the invocation of emergency authorities. These exercises also provide opportunities to validate and identify for subsequent correction national security emergency management plans, policies, procedures, and systems. Sponsorship of these exercises usually is by the DoD or the North Atlantic Treaty Organization. For these types of exercises, FEMA coordinates federal civil government counterpart exercise activities.

5. **Special and extraordinary event exercises sponsored or supported by FEMA.** These exercises focus on events for which overall planning rests primarily at the federal level, with other government jurisdictional elements brought in as necessary. These exercises provide opportunities to evaluate system interoperability for communications, automated data processing, and other electronic media. Exercises in this category are designed to deal with a wide

range of contingencies: nuclear, chemical, and biological terrorism; continuity of government; satellite reentry; VIP visits; presidential inaugurations; Olympic Games support; and regional events such as large-scale civil disturbances. These exercises provide the opportunity to evaluate the effectiveness of memorandums of understanding between various federal departments and agencies as well as other plans, policies, and procedures designed to guide the interaction between them. They also provide opportunities to explore issues and requirements for the management of emergencies for which there are no plans, policies, procedures, or MOUs.

Source: FEMA, www.fema.gov.

Office for Domestic Preparedness

The Office for Domestic Preparedness (ODP) is the principal component of the Department of Homeland Security responsible for preparing the United States for acts of terrorism. In carrying out its mission, the ODP is the primary office responsible for providing training, funds for the purchase of equipment, support for the planning and execution of exercises, technical assistance, and other support to assist states and local jurisdictions to prevent, plan for, and respond to acts of terrorism.

Training

The ODP provides tailored training to enhance the capacity of states and local jurisdictions to prevent, deter, and respond safely and effectively to incidents of terrorism involving weapons of mass destruction. This includes reaching multiple disciplines through training at the awareness, performance, and planning/management levels and employing the most appropriate mediums and vehicles for the particular audience:

- Direct delivery.
- Train the trainer.
- Computer-based training.
- Web-based training.
- Video teleconferencing.

Training and Data Exchange Group

A significant component of the validation process for ODP courses is the Training and Data Exchange (TRADE) Group, a federal interagency group that reviews member courses for consistency, avoidance of unnecessary duplication, and use of the most up-to-date information and protocols available. The TRADE Group is composed of the following agencies:

- United States Fire Administration's National Fire Academy.
- Federal Bureau of Investigation.

- Department of Justice.
- Federal Emergency Management Agency.
- Environmental Protection Agency.
- Department of Energy.
- Department of Health and Human Services.
- Centers for Disease Control and Prevention.
- Emergency Management Institute.
- Federal Law Enforcement Training Center.
- Department of Homeland Security.

Equipment

The terrorist attacks of September 11, 2001, demonstrated that response to an incident of terrorism can rapidly deplete local supplies and equipment. To further enhance the capability of state and local government agencies to prevent, deter, respond to, and recover from incidents of terrorism involving the use of chemical, biological, radiological, nuclear, and explosive weapons and cyber attacks, the ODP administers several equipment programs supported by ODP grant funding.

The ODP equipment programs provide a means of direct support to first responders to enable them to purchase additional, specialized equipment as well as to acquire the necessary training and technical assistance on that equipment. These programs seek to prepare state and local governments to meet the challenges presented by the terrorist threat and strengthen the capabilities of first responders to safely and effectively prepare for and respond to terrorist incidents.

The various equipment programs of the ODP include

- Information Technology and Evaluation Program.
- The Responder Knowledge Base.
- Equipment Purchase Assistance Program.
- Homeland Defense Equipment Reuse Program.
- Domestic Preparedness Equipment Technical Assistance Program.
- Prepositioned Equipment Program.
- *Interoperable Communications User's Handbook.*
- System Assessment and Validation for Emergency Responders Program.

Technical Assistance

The ODP's Homeland Security Preparedness Technical Assistance (TA) Program provides direct assistance to state and local jurisdictions to improve their ability to prevent, respond to, and recover from threats or acts of terrorism involving chemical, biological, radiological, nuclear, or explosive (CBRNE) weapons. The TA programs provide a process to help resolve a problem or create innovative approaches. All TA services are available to eligible recipients at no charge.

The TA programs in place or currently under development within ODP include

- **The Homeland Security Assessment and Strategy Technical Assistance Program** assists states and local jurisdictions with the assessment process, ability to conduct assessments, and development of a comprehensive homeland security strategy.

- **The Initial Strategy Implementation Plan (ISIP) Technical Assistance Program** assists states with completing the ISIP template. Workshops address developing a list of projects based on the state or urban area homeland security strategy and enhancing understanding of how to complete the ISIP template and the process for ISIP submission.
- **The Domestic Preparedness Equipment Technical Assistance Program** provides equipment-specific training on CBRNE detection, decontamination, and personal protection equipment.
- **The Terrorism Early Warning Group Replication Program replicates the program** that enhances capabilities for analyzing strategic and operational information needed to respond to terrorism and protect critical infrastructure.
- **The Interoperable Communication Technical Assistance Program** enhances public safety communications interoperability with regard to CBRNE terrorism threats.
- **The Port and Mass Transit Planning Technical Assistance Program** assesses the needs of port and mass transit agencies to prepare for and counter post-9/11 terrorist threats.
- **The Rapid Assistance Team Technical Assistance Program** deploys teams on short notice to support targeted projects, such as identifying equipment needs or equipment procurement plans.
- **The General Technical Assistance Program** provides specialized assistance to enhance state and local strategies to prevent, respond to, and recover from CBRNE terrorism.
- **The Prevention Technical Assistance Program** provides new initiatives to facilitate terrorism prevention efforts, such as collaboration, information sharing, risk management, threat recognition, and intervention.
- **The Plans and Planning Synchronization Technical Assistance Program** provides planning support for multijurisdictional terrorism response using innovative software tool.

Exercises

The ODP's goal is to help states, cities, towns, and villages gain an objective assessment of their capacity to prevent or respond to and recover from a disaster so that modifications or improvements can be made before a real incident occurs. This is conducted primarily through three mechanisms: the Homeland Security Exercise and Evaluation Program; the National Exercise Program; and the Models, Simulations, and Games Review Program.

- **Homeland Security Exercise and Evaluation Program.** The Homeland Security Exercise and Evaluation Program (HSEEP) includes both doctrine and policy for designing, developing, conducting, and evaluating exercises. HSEEP is a threat- and performance-based exercise program that includes a cycle, mix, and range of exercise activities of varying degrees of complexity and interaction. HSEEP includes a series of four reference manuals to help states and local jurisdictions establish exercise programs and design, develop, conduct, and evaluate exercises (each of which can be downloaded from the ODP Web site):
  - Volume I. *Overview and Doctrine.*
  - Volume II. *Exercise Evaluation and Improvement.*

- ○ Volume III. *Exercise Program Management and Exercise Planning Process.*
- ○ Volume IV. *Sample Exercise Documents and Formats.*
- **National Exercise Program.** The National Strategy for Homeland Security directed the establishment of a National Exercise Strategy. Homeland Security Presidential Directive #8 directed Secretary Tom Ridge to establish a National Exercise Program (NEP). Secretary Ridge charged ODP to develop a program that identifies and integrates national level exercise activities to ensure those activities serve the broadest community of learning. In addition to full-scale, integrated national-level exercises, the NEP provides for tailored exercise activities that serve as the DHS's primary vehicle for training national leaders and staff members. The NEP enhances the collaboration among partners at all levels of government for assigned homeland security missions. National-level exercises provide the means to conduct "full-scale, full-system tests" of collective preparedness, interoperability, and collaboration across all levels of government and the private sector. The cornerstone of national performance-based exercises is the top officials (TOPOFF), biennial exercise series. TOPOFF included a functional exercise in 2000 (TOPOFF I) and a full-scale exercise in 2003 (TOPOFF II). TOPOFF III, Exercising National Preparedness, was hailed as "the most comprehensive terrorism exercise ever conducted in the United States." TOPOFF III involved a two-year cycle of seminars, planning events, and exercises that culminated in a full-scale exercise from April 4 to 8, 2005, that simulated a coordinated terrorist attack involving biological and chemical weapons.
- **Models, Simulations, and Games.** One hundred models, simulations, and games have been reviewed for their ability to support domestic preparedness training and exercising (T&E). For each product, the review considered the product's functionality from a T&E perspective, its hardware and software requirements, and cost. Product functionality was compared to key T&E attributes that were summarized from over 1,100 T&E requirements.

Grant Programs

The ODP's grant programs are designed to provide the funding necessary to enhance state and local jurisdictions' capacities to prevent, respond to, and recover from incidents of terrorism involving chemical, biological, radiological, nuclear, or explosive weapons and cyber attacks. The ODP's grant programs began in 1998 and currently enjoy participation by agencies in all 50 states, the District of Columbia, the commonwealth of Puerto Rico, American Samoa, the commonwealth of Northern Mariana Islands, Guam, and the U.S. Virgin Islands.

The FY 2006 ODP grant programs include

- Infrastructure Protection Program, which is made up of the following:
  - ○ Transit Security Program (more than $136 million).
  - ○ Buffer Zone Protection Program (about $48 million).
  - ○ Chemical Sector Buffer Zone Protection Program ($25 million).
  - ○ Intercity Passenger Rail Security Program (more than $7.2 million).
  - ○ Trucking Security Program ($4.9 million).
  - ○ Port Security Program (more than $168 million).
  - ○ Intercity Bus Security Program ($9.5 million).
- The Citizen Corps Support Program, broken down into the following programs:
  - ○ Fire Corps Program ($750,000).

- ○ Mayoral Participation Program ($120,000).
- ○ Emergency Managers Citizen Collaboration Program ($350,000).
- ○ Volunteer Liability Research Program ($75,000).
- Competitive Training Program ($28.8 million).
- Homeland Security Training Program.
- Homeland Security Grant Program ($1.7 billion).
- Emergency Management Performance Grant ($179.5 million).

The FY 2007 ODP grant programs include

- Infrastructure Protection Program, which will total approximately $445 million and is made up of the following programs:
  - ○ Transit Security Program.
  - ○ Port Security Program.
  - ○ Intercity Bus Security Program.
  - ○ Trucking Security Program.
  - ○ Buffer Zone Protection Program.
- Homeland Security Grant Program (approximately $1.66 billion).
- Emergency Management Performance Grant ($194 million).

The FY 2007 Homeland Security Grant Program integrates the State Homeland Security Program, the Urban Areas Security Initiative Program, the Law Enforcement Terrorism Prevention Program, the Metropolitan Medical Response System, and the Citizen Corps Program.

Source: www.ojp.usdoj.gov/odp.

Critical Thinking

Why do you think that the ODP focuses its preparedness efforts on terrorism? Should preparedness activities funded by ODP be for all hazards? Why or why not?

Business Continuity Planning and Emergency Management

Business continuity planning (BCP) provides focus-driven preparedness for businesses. At its simplest, BCP involves setting up a plan to ensure the survival of an organization. Since the early concern with the restoration of computer data, the concept of continuity has evolved in response to a changing environment. Major events have demanded that BCP encompass a growing number of concerns. The severe consequences of September 11 raised many implications about how BCP will evolve in response to the disaster. How BCP evolves directly influences business as a whole.

The implications of BCP are

1. Terrorism must be considered as a real threat to the survival of business.
2. BCP will expand to include concern for the physical safety of employees.
3. BCP may involve the decentralization of business operations.
4. BCP may have to expand its sphere of concern to include the regional impacts of a disaster (including economic) to the area where a business is located.

5. The human relationships that a business depends on for its survival should be a major concern.
6. The recovery time is zero.
7. There is renewed importance to critical data backup systems.
8. Physical security concerns are included.
9. There is increased importance of and pressure on business continuity planners.

The events of September 11 raised awareness that the survival of business depends on many external factors. External factors such as infrastructure and public safety authorities play a key role in whether BCP ultimately is successful. After September 11, infrastructure vital to business has even come under the control of public safety authorities. In this case, BCP is doubly dependent on public safety authorities. This awareness has led to attempts at greater communication between business and government since the attacks. In early March 2002, the newly created Office of Homeland Security unveiled its Homeland Security Advisory System.

Business immediately responded with its own proposal, the Critical Emergency Operations Link, which is intended to be a direct, two-way communication link to government at all levels. Business demands interaction with government so that it can anticipate how to react in the event of not only terrorist attacks but any catastrophe that threatens its survival. The attempt at greater communication and interaction by business is a proactive effort to turn its reliance on public safety authorities into an opportunity to ensure the success of BCP.

This approach suggests that business will demand a more extensive role for emergency management in BCP. The connection between emergency management and BCP is natural, because emergency management is the authority that has the responsibility of public safety planning. By demanding that emergency management play an extensive role in BCP, businesses can interact with government to ensure their survival. Emergency management should meet this demand with an outstretched arm, because it represents a great opportunity for the field. If emergency management sincerely cooperates, then business may demand that government at all levels allocate more resources to emergency management to ensure that it can provide effective assistance. Ultimately, with business as its advocate, emergency management may gain the influence it needs to assume a greater role in leading the local and national public safety agenda.

Conclusion

Preparedness consists of three basic elements: preparing a plan, training to the plan, and exercising the plan. Preparedness planning at the community level is critical to reducing the effects of disaster events. FEMA sponsors numerous planning, training, and education activities designed to assist communities and states in developing effective preparedness plans and training personnel to implement these plans. Through its Comprehensive Exercise Program, FEMA helps local and state governments exercise these plans. After-action evaluation of these exercises refines the plans.

Business continuity planning is a significant growth area for the emergency management community. The devastating impacts of September 11 resulted in increased coordination and cooperation between business and emergency managers. It is hoped that the emergency management community will exploit this opportunity and get businesses more active in supporting the other phases of emergency management, particularly mitigation.

CASE STUDIES

How Were Businesses Affected by the September 11 Attacks?

Six months later, how has BCP been affected by the attacks? The severe destruction at the World Trade Center led to many significant implications that are redefining BCP. To look at these implications, this case study first lists the latest damage estimates for businesses in the World Trade Center and the lower Manhattan area:

- **Death toll.** According to a February 16, 2002, *Washington Post* article, "A Towering Task Lags in New York," the attacks killed more then 2,800 people (Powell and Haughney, 2002).
- **Estimated dollar amount of damage.** As of February 1, 2002, Chris Hawley writes in "Globalization and Sept. 11 Are Pushing Wall Street off Wall Street," that the attacks caused an estimated $83 billion in damage, and only about $50 billion will be covered by insurance. Taxpayers may have to cover some of the rest (Hawley, 2002).
- **Displaced tenants of the World Trade Center.** According to Gary Stock of the Unblinking Web site, the final tally of World Trade Center tenants has not been completed because many sources of information contained outdated tenant lists. On the day of the attacks, the number of tenants ranged from 435 to 500. By October 19, the number increased to at least 700 (Stock, 2002).
- **Estimated job losses.** As of February 1, 2002, analysts predicted Manhattan would lose about 125,000 jobs after the attacks. Nearly 53,000 financial services jobs were expected to move out of lower Manhattan (the Wall Street district) and 19,000 jobs had already left the city completely (Hawley, 2002). By February 16, 2002, one in four jobs in downtown Manhattan had disappeared, a job loss total that is thousands more than analysts had predicted immediately after September 11 (Powell and Haughney, 2002).
- **Estimated loss of office space.** As of March 11, 2002, according to the article "Return to Downtown," the destruction of office space caused by the attacks equaled about 12 million square feet at the World Trade Center and damage to another 20 million square feet in the surrounding area (Wax and Diop, 2002).
- **Communication infrastructure damage.** On October 29, 2001, in the article "Back Online, Despite Its Losses, Verizon Went Right back to Work Restoring Communication Services," John Rendleman writes that, on the day of the attacks, a Verizon switching center was destroyed by the collapse of the World Trade Center. This caused telecom service failure to 14,000 businesses and thousands of residential customers in lower Manhattan (Rendleman, 2001). According to the article "Out of the Ashes," Verizon shared its infrastructure with some 40 competitive local exchange carriers whose services were similarly affected (Gilbert, 2002). By October 29, 2001, 90 percent of the service was restored.
- **Cleanup concerns.** As of March 11, 2002, the cleanup of the Ground Zero site was expected to be complete by the end of May. Plans to reopen the No. 1 and No. 9 subway line stops were expected to be completed later in 2002. The reopening of the first downtown retailer was completed two weeks earlier (Wax and Diop, 2002).

(Continued)

CASE STUDIES—Cont'd

A significant issue that has been raised by the devastation to office space concerns the relocation of employees. Since the attacks, 55 percent of businesses displaced by September 11 have indicated that they will return (Wax and Diop, 2002). Wax and Diop add that, "Businesses that aren't returning have largely relocated to midtown, New Jersey, and elsewhere" (Wax and Diop, 2002). The issue of relocation is important given the number of employees that have moved out of the affected area. In "Consultants Push Wall Street to Leave," Stephen Gandel writes that, "In all, 39,610 financial services jobs have been relocated from downtown in the last six months. More than half, 24,376 of those employees, have been moved to midtown" (Gandel, 2002). In "Seeking Safety, Downtown Firms Are Scattering," Charles V. Balgi adds, "that another 144,000 jobs are in jeopardy in a second wave of departures" (Balgi, 2002).

Chimacum High School Earthquake Preparedness Program

Program description. This program involves high school students teaching elementary school students about earthquake preparedness. Each class designs its own project for communicating this information. School staff members see the value of such peer education. For example, the class of 1997 designed a community service project. One element of the project was to participate in the school district's earthquake preparedness committee and provide input from the students. The students also researched the needs of classroom teachers, purchased supplies, and stocked each classroom with a "teacher's kit." They also researched and prepared personal "kid kits," which are sold for $7. The kid kits are a voluntary purchase. In addition, the students prepared an earthquake preparedness course script based on information from FEMA "Earthquake Dudes" and FEMA literature, a videotape, and an earthquake simulation with sound effects, which is available on request. Each class restocks the teacher's kit. High school students have taken American Red Cross courses, so shelters could be opened in high schools if needed.

Evaluation information. Formal evaluation forms are completed after every class session by the regular classroom teacher and class students. All forms are on file. There are increased signs of school and community concern and awareness as elementary students discuss what they have learned with their parents and siblings.

Annual budget. The school district budgeted $800 to $1,000 to purchase supplies for the teacher's kits.

Sources of funding. The Chimacum School District and Chimacum class of 1997 fundraising.

Program type. Teaching earthquake preparedness.

Target population. Chimacum elementary school students.

Setting. Rural western Washington Olympic Peninsula, in a community located near a newly documented, active earthquake fault line.

Project startup date. 1993.

Source: FEMA, *Partnerships in Preparedness, a Compendium of Exemplary Practices in Emergency Management,* vol. II, 1997.

CASE STUDIES

Neighbors for Defensible Space

Program description. A grassroots volunteer program, Neighbors for Defensible Space developed out of a need to reduce the risk of uncontrolled wildfire in and around the fire-dependent district of Lake Tahoe, which has prevented catastrophic wildfires for more than 90 years.

Such a wildfire situation has three basic components: weather, topography, and fuels. Fuels are the one element Neighbors for Defensible Space can control, and the program relies on its ability to either reduce, remove, or modify fuels. The North Lake Tahoe District program is a model in public education and cooperative efforts in this area and has been able to demonstrate that both fire protection and environmental concerns can be addressed when dealing with wildfires. Neighbors for Defensible Space is in its second year of a five-year plan of "prescribed burning," a program that returns low-intensity fire to the forest system. In addition, the community is in the process of adopting a joint long-range master plan with its Incline Village General Improvement District, which provides water, sewage, water treatment, recreational facilities, and sanitation.

The U.S. Forest Service owns more than 650 parcels of land in the community and has obtained approximately $900,000 in congressional funds to manage the land. In 1991, the community's taxes paid to selectively harvest 750 acres of dead and dying timber at a cost of approximately $1 million. Of the property owners, 48 percent have involved their private lands in the effort (approximately 3,500 parcels).

Evaluation information. Neighbors for Defensible Space was recognized by the National Commission on Wildfire Disasters (a congressional committee) as a model of public education and cooperative efforts that produce results in reducing wildfire risk to urban interface communities. Their publications are used by other fire and forestry agencies.

Annual budget. $5,584 in 1995 from donations.

Sources of funding. Primarily donations and outside agencies' earmarked funds. Local taxes, congressional funds, state forest stewardship funds, community donations, and property owners provide additional monies.

Program type. Wildfire mitigation for the Reno/Lake Tahoe/Carson City region.

Target population. 10,000 district residents.

Setting. Within and surrounding the Reno/Lake Tahoe/Carson City, Nevada, region.

Project startup date. 1986.

Source: FEMA, *Partnerships in Preparedness, a Compendium of Exemplary Practices in Emergency Management,* vol. II, 1997.

CASE STUDIES

Special Needs Awareness Program (SNAP)

Program description. After flooding occurred in areas of southeast Texas in October 1994, students in the Community Problem Solving class of Austin Middle School, Beaumont, Texas, responded to stories they had heard about people having difficulty during emergency evacuations. The students originated the idea for SNAP and established a pilot program in their community.

The goal of SNAP is to identify those persons, such as the elderly, mentally and physically challenged, or homebound, who would have difficulty in an emergency evacuation. These residents are given special SNAP signs for display only during an emergency. SNAP also notifies police, fire, and emergency management personnel that they should look for the SNAP signs to determine where assistance is needed in an evacuation.

SNAP distributes information on the program to civic organizations, churches, and government agencies in the area through letters, speaker's bureaus, and videotapes. The program has spread throughout the United States and internationally via the Internet and magazine articles.

Evaluation information. Information on the program has been requested by agencies in 31 states, the Dominican Republic, and Australia. Three magazines, *Natural Hazard Observer*, *Wanted Magazine*, and *D.E.M. Digest*, featured articles on the program. The 41 SNAP students from Beaumont Middle School who originated the program won first place in the intermediate division in the 1995 International Future Problem Solving (Community Problem Solving) Competition in Providence, Rhode Island.

Annual budget. $1,200.

Sources of funding. Beaumont Public Schools Foundation, Inc., FAD (Falcons against Drugs), funds raised by SNAP team members, and personal donations.

Source for additional information. Mrs. Lynne Buchwald, Austin Middle School, Beaumont, Texas (409-866-8143).

Program type. Emergency evacuation assistance.

Target population. Elderly, physically and mentally challenged, and homebound residents who would require special assistance during an emergency.

Setting. Any residential area in any state; the SNAP program originated in Beaumont, Texas.

Project startup date. 1994.

Source: FEMA, *Partnerships in Preparedness, a Compendium of Exemplary Practices in Emergency Management,* vol. II, 1997.

CASE STUDIES

Arcadia Chamber of Commerce Emergency Preparedness Committee
for Business Owners

Program Description. The Arcadia Chamber of Commerce Emergency Preparedness
Committee for Business Owners provides local business owners with a disaster
identification packet. The informational packet contains instructions for self-
assessment of damage by the owner, along with color-coded placards that
correspond to the level of need (e.g., major, moderate, or minor/no damage).
Immediately following a disaster, a business owner, using the guidelines provided in
the packet, would determine the extent of help needed and display the appropriate
color placard. Emergency service units surveying the city instantly would be able to
identify areas that required immediate assistance and thus focus available resources
on those areas with the greatest need. Instructions also are provided on what
supplies are needed and what activities to perform after an earthquake.

     Evaluation information. Other cities and counties requested information
about the disaster identification packet and indicated an interest in replicating the
program. Following a presentation to the Arcadia Coordinating Committee, the PTA
expressed an interest in adapting the program for use in schools.

     Annual budget. None. Projects are funded individually.

     Sources of funding. Funds come from the Chamber of Commerce and the fire
department; printing companies and manufacturers have donated printing and
materials.

     Program type. Emergency preparedness information to help businesses
identify their extent of need following a disaster.

     Target population. Arcadia business owners.

     Setting. Arcadia, California.

     Project startup date. 1992.

Source: FEMA, *Partnerships in Preparedness, a Compendium of Exemplary Practices
in Emergency Management,* vol. II, 1997.

CASE STUDIES

Pacific Grove, a Model for Small City Disaster Preparedness

Program description. In 1990, Pacific Grove, California (60 miles from the epicenter
of the 1989 Loma Prieta earthquake), decided to prepare a comprehensive
earthquake and disaster plan, following a study that showed the likelihood of
a complete loss of utilities, sewer systems, and telephone services, as well as an
overload of cellular systems and damage to streets and highway overpasses during
an earthquake. City employees were sent to earthquake preparedness training
courses given at the Governor's Office of Emergency Services' California Specialized

(Continued)

CASE STUDIES—Cont'd

Training Institute in San Luis Obispo. A disaster coordinator was hired to update the city's disaster plan. A Volunteers in Preparedness Program was formed to train neighborhood emergency response teams, which include amateur radio operators and Boy Scouts, in earthquake preparedness, disaster medicine, how and when to turn off the gas, how to rescue victims trapped under earthquake debris, and firefighting. Lacking funding, the disaster coordinator enlisted retirement homes, volunteer organizations, public utilities, and emergency service agencies to join in the state's "duck, cover, and hold" earthquake drill.

Evaluation information. In 1994 Pacific Grove was cited as the only city (of 12) in Monterey County having an emergency planner and the only city to hold earthquake drills regularly. Pacific Grove received the Institute of Local Self Government's California Cities Helen Putnam Award for Excellence (honorable mention, public safety) in 1995. The city's preparedness programs have received innumerable media mentions.

Annual budget. $28,000 (FEMA, $11,000 toward the disaster coordinator's salary; $14,000 from the city's fire department budget; and $3,000 from the city budget).

Sources of funding. FEMA and city budgets.

Program type. Disaster preparedness.

Target population. Residents of Pacific Grove (17,000).

Setting. Pacific Grove, California.

Project startup date. 1990.

Source: FEMA, Partnerships in Preparedness, a Compendium of Exemplary Practices in Emergency Management, vol. II, 1997.

CASE STUDIES

Delaware City, Community Awareness and Emergency
Response Committee

Program description. The Delaware City, Community Awareness and Emergency Response Committee (DC-CAER), comprising representatives of the chemical industry; volunteer organizations; and public, state, and local governments, addresses mutual concerns involving a chemical plant complex near Delaware City. Formed voluntarily in 1985, the DC-CAER strives to meet three goals: to enhance emergency response capabilities, test and evaluate these capabilities, and foster knowledge about chemical-related hazards and protective measures. The DC-CAER maintains a comprehensive emergency response plan to deal with chemical emergencies at the plant; conducts training programs for emergency responders; coordinates annual field emergency response exercises and tabletop drills; conducts community outreach programs to disseminate emergency information; makes presentations about its programs to community, government, and professional organizations throughout Delaware and in other states; and produced a video that is distributed to Delaware's Extremely Hazardous Substance facilities.

Evaluation information. The county has received awards from the Chemical Manufacturers Association, National Coordinating Council on Emergency Management, and U.S. Environmental Protection Agency. There have been actual emergencies without injuries.

Annual budget. None, but special projects have received more than $12,000 since 1985.

Sources of funding. Shared among 11 chemical plants.

Program type. Chemical emergency preparedness planning.

Target population. 6,000 residents, emergency responders, and employees and visitors of 11 chemical plants.

Setting. Suburban environment with one small town.

Project startup date. 1985.

Source: FEMA, *Partnerships in Preparedness, a Compendium of Exemplary Practices in Emergency Management*, vol. II, 1997.

CASE STUDIES

Arlington County Emergency Management System

Program description. Arlington County's (Virginia) Emergency Management System was designed to provide the ability to respond to natural and technological disasters in a rapid and efficient manner. The system has three basic components: the emergency management team (EMT), the emergency planning team (EPT), and six functional task group teams. The EMT is composed of the directors of police, fire, public works, public affairs, and the county manager's office; it is the core of the system and the decision-making body. The EPT is the think tank that anticipates future issues and makes recommendations to the EMT. The EPT and task groups brief the EMT hourly in the early stages of an incident (less frequently as the incident diminishes). During normal business, the EPT reviews the emergency operations plan to ensure that it is current. The EPT includes personnel from departments throughout the county, such as the police, sheriff, fire department, public works, public affairs, county manager's office, parks and recreation, schools, technology and information services, and Department of Human Services. Each of the six functional task group teams has a different area of responsibility: shelters, communications, resources, routing and traffic control, employee support, and

(Continued)

recovery. Members also include personnel from outside county government who have special expertise. Any of the EMT members can convene the entire team. Through the chain of command, fire and police chiefs would invoke the system. The emergency communications center would call system members, who would assemble in the emergency operations center. Each team is in a separate area of the EOC. They can communicate in person or by 800 MHz radio. As an incident unfolds, the task groups monitor it on primary radio channels to anticipate resource needs and so on.

Evaluation information. The program has undergone independent evaluation and received feedback from participants in the program. Two Air Force Reserve officers, both individual mobilization augmentees, reviewed the program and participated in annual disaster exercises in which the program is evaluated. Both commented that Arlington's emergency management system is extraordinarily well developed and considerably ahead of most jurisdictions in emergency management. After each exercise, participants fill out a critique to assess their knowledge of the exercise. Results indicate a high knowledge and comfort range.

Annual budget. No funds were specifically allocated for this program. The staff assistant to the fire chief was responsible for maintaining the program, so that the only outlay was a portion of his annual salary. Currently, there are only ancillary costs: printing of manuals and documents and a portion of personnel expenses.

Sources of funding. Arlington County Fire Department budget.

Program type. Disaster preparedness and emergency management.

Target population. All workers and residents of the county.

Setting. Countywide.

Project startup date. 1992.

The TsunamiReady Program

TsunamiReady is an initiative that promotes tsunami hazard preparedness as an active collaboration among federal, state, and local emergency management agencies; the public; and the National Weather Service (NWS) tsunami warning system. This collaboration functions to support better and more consistent tsunami awareness and mitigation efforts among communities at risk. Through the TsunamiReady program, NOAA's National Weather Service gives communities the skills and education needed to survive a tsunami before, during, and after the event. TsunamiReady was designed to help community leaders and emergency managers strengthen their local tsunami operations (NOAA, n.d.).

The TsunamiReady program is based on the NWS StormReady model (which can be viewed by accessing http://www.stormready.noaa.gov). The primary goal of

TsunamiReady is the improvement of public safety during tsunami emergencies. As just stated, TsunamiReady is designed for those coastal communities that are at known risk of the tsunami hazard (tsunami hazard risk maps can be seen by accessing http://www.pmel.noaa.gov/tsunami/time).

Traditionally, tsunami hazard planning along the U.S. West Coast and Alaska has been widely neglected because of the statistically low incidence of tsunamis. As result of that perceived "rarity," many individuals and communities have not worked to become as "tsunami aware" as they could and should be. Among those communities that are considered to be prepared, that level of exhibited preparedness varies significantly (NWS, n.d.).

However, as is true with the earthquakes and other rare events that generate tsunamis, avoidable casualties and property damage will continue to rise unless these at-risk communities become better prepared for tsunamis. As previously mentioned, readiness involves two key components: *awareness* and *mitigation*. Awareness involves educating key decision makers, emergency managers, and the public about the nature (physical processes) and threat (frequency of occurrence, impact) of the tsunami hazard; mitigation involves taking steps before the tsunami occurs to lessen the impact (loss of life and property) of that event when it does occur. As is true with earthquakes, there is no question tsunamis will strike again.

The National Weather Service TsunamiReady program was designed to meet both of the recognized elements of a useful readiness effort: it is designed to educate local emergency management officials and their public and to promote a well-designed tsunami emergency response plan for each community.

Program Objectives

TsunamiReady promotes tsunami hazard readiness as an active collaboration among federal, state, and local emergency management agencies, the public, and the NWS tsunami warning system. This collaboration supports better and more consistent tsunami awareness and mitigation efforts among communities at risk. The main goal is improvement of public safety during tsunami emergencies. To meet this goal, the following objectives need to be met by the community:

- Create minimum standard guidelines for a community to follow for adequate tsunami readiness.
- Encourage consistency in educational materials and response among communities and states.
- Recognize communities that have adopted TsunamiReady guidelines.
- Increase public awareness and understanding of the tsunami hazard.
- Improve community preplanning for tsunami disasters.

Program Methodology

The processes and guidelines used in the TsunamiReady program were modeled to resemble those of the National Weather Service StormReady program. TsunamiReady established minimum guidelines for a community to be awarded the TsunamiReady recognition, thus promoting minimum standards based on

(Continued)

CASE STUDIES—Cont'd

expert knowledge rather than subjective considerations. Communities that accept the challenge to become TsunamiReady and are deemed to have met these requirements set by the NWS TsunamiReady program are designated as *TsunamiReady communities*. Guidelines to achieve TsunamiReady recognition are given in Table 6–1 and discussed in detail below. Four community categories (based on the population of the community and provided in the table's heading) are used to measure tsunami readiness.

Note that Guideline 3 has been skipped, as it refers exclusively to the StormReady program, which shares these guidelines with the TsunamiReady program. This is a key factor to consider, as it ensures by default that all communities that are StormReady also are TsunamiReady (as of 2002). As such, all communities certified TsunamiReady also must pass all StormReady criteria. StormReady requires access to local weather monitoring equipment (Guideline 3) and some further administrative requirements (Guideline 6). Other than that, the requirements are identical.

Guideline 1. Communications and Coordination Center. It is well known that key to any effective hazards management program is effective communication. This could not be truer when considering tsunami-related emergencies, since the arrival of the giant waves can occur within minutes of the initial precipitating event. These so-called short-fused events, therefore, require an immediate but careful, systematic, and appropriate response. To ensure such a proper response, TsunamiReady requires that communities establish the following:

1. **24-Hour Warning Point.** The NWS, not the community, determines that a tsunami threat exists. Therefore, to receive recognition under the TsunamiReady Program, an applying agency needs to establish a 24-hour warning point (WP) that can receive NWS tsunami information in addition to providing local reports and advice to constituents. Typically, the functions of this type of facility merely are incorporated into the existing daily operation of a law enforcement or fire department dispatching (emergency communications center) point. For cities or towns without a local dispatching point, a county agency could act in that capacity. In Alaska, where there may be communities that have populations of less than 2,500 residents and no county agency to act as a 24-hour warning point, the community is required to designate responsible members of the community who are able to receive warnings 24 hours per day and have the authority to activate local warning systems. Specifically, the warning point is required to have

   ○ 24-hour operation.
   ○ Warning reception capability.
   ○ Warning dissemination capability.
   ○ Ability and authority to activate local warning system(s).

Table 6–1   Guidelines to Becoming a TsunamiReady Community

Guidelines	Population			
	<2,500	2,500–14,999	15,000–40,000	>40,000
1. Communications and coordination				
24-hour warning point (WP)	X	X	X	X
Emergency operations center (EOC)		X	X	X
2. Tsunami warning reception				
Number of ways for EOC/WP to receive NWS tsunami messages (if in range, one must be NOAA Weather Radio (NWR) with tone-alert; NWR- specific area message encoding is preferred)	3	4	4	4
4. Warning dissemination				
Number of ways for EOC/WP to disseminate warnings to public	1	2	3	4
NWR tone-alert receivers in public facilities (where available)	X	X	X	X
For county/borough warning points, county/borough communication network ensuring information flow between communities	X	X	X	X
5. Community preparedness				
Number of annual tsunami awareness programs	1	2	3	4
Designate/establish tsunami shelter/area in safe zone	X	X	X	X
Designate tsunami evacuation areas and evacuation routes and install evacuation route signs	X	X	X	X
Provide written, locality-specific, tsunami hazard response material to public	X	X	X	X
In schools, encourage tsunami hazard curriculum, practice evacuations, and provide safety material to staff and students	X	X	X	X
6. Administrative				
Develop formal tsunami hazard operations plan	X	X	X	X
Yearly meeting/discussion by emergency manager with NWS	X	X	X	X
Visits by NWS official to community at least every other year	X	X	X	X

(Continued)

2. **Emergency Operations Center.** Agencies serving jurisdictions larger than 2,500 people are required to have the ability to activate an emergency operations center. It must be staffed during tsunami events to execute the warning point's tsunami warning functions. The following list summarizes the tsunami-related roles required of the EOC:

   ○ Activate, based on predetermined guidelines related to NWS tsunami information or tsunami events.
   ○ Staff with emergency management director or designee.
   ○ Establish warning reception and dissemination capabilities equal to or better than the warning point.
   ○ Maintain the ability to communicate with adjacent EOCs and warning points.
   ○ Maintain the ability to communicate with local NWS office or Tsunami Warning Center.

Guideline 2. Tsunami Warning Reception. Warning points and EOCs each need multiple ways to receive NWS tsunami warnings. TsunamiReady guidelines to receive NWS warnings in an EOC/WP require a combination of the following, based on population:

- NOAA Weather Radio receiver with tone alert. Specific area message encoding (SAME) is preferred. Required for recognition only if within range of transmitter.
- NOAA Weather Wire drop: Satellite downlink data feed from NWS.
- Emergency Managers Weather Information Network (EMWIN) receiver: Satellite feed or VHF radio transmission of NWS products.
- Statewide telecommunications system: Automatic relay of NWS products on statewide emergency management or law enforcement system.
- Statewide warning fan-out system: State authorized system of passing message throughout warning area.
- NOAA Weather Wire via Internet NOAAport Lite: Provides alarmed warning messages through a dedicated Internet connection.
- Direct link to NWS office; for example, amateur or VHF radio.
- E-mail from Tsunami Warning Center: Direct e-mail from Warning Center to emergency manager.
- Pager message from Tsunami Warning Center: Page issued from Warning Center directly to EOC/WP.
- Radio/TV via Emergency Alert System: Local radio/TV or cable TV.
- U.S. Coast Guard broadcasts: WP/EOC monitoring of USCG marine channels.
- National Warning System (NAWAS) drop: FEMA-controlled civil defense hotline.

Guideline 4. Warning Dissemination

1. On receipt of NWS warnings or other reliable information suggesting a tsunami is imminent, local emergency officials must be able to communicate this threat information with as much of the population as possible. This is fundamental to making the preparedness program effective. As such, receiving TsunamiReady recognition requires that communities have one or more of the following means of ensuring timely warning dissemination to their citizens (based on population, as described in Table 6–1):

   ○ A community program that subsidizes the purchase of NWR (NWR receiver with tone alert, SAME is preferred, required for recognition only if within range of transmitter).
   ○ Outdoor warning sirens.
   ○ Television audio/video overrides.
   ○ Other locally controlled methods; for example, local broadcast system or emergency vehicles.
   ○ Phone messaging (dial-down) systems.

2. It is required that at least one NWR, equipped with a tone alert receiver, be located in each critical public access and government-owned building and include 24-hour warning point, EOC, school superintendent's office, or equivalent. Critical public access buildings are defined by each community's tsunami warning plan. Locations recommended for inclusion by the NWS include all schools, public libraries, hospitals, fairgrounds, parks and recreational areas, public utilities, sports arenas, Departments of Transportation, and designated shelter areas. (SAME is preferred, this is required for recognition only if the community exists within range of a transmitter.)

3. Counties/boroughs only. A county- or boroughwide communications network ensuring the flow of information among all cities and towns within those administrative borders. This would include provision of a warning point for the smaller towns and fanning out of the message as required by state policy.

Guideline 5. Community Preparedness. Public education is vital in preparing citizens to respond properly to tsunami threats. An educated public is more likely to take the steps required to receive tsunami warnings, recognize potentially threatening tsunami events when they exist, and respond appropriately to those events. Therefore, communities seeking recognition in the TsunamiReady Program must be able to

- Conduct or sponsor tsunami awareness programs in schools, hospitals, fairs, workshops, and community meetings (the actual number of talks that must be given each year is based on the community's population).

(Continued)

CASE STUDIES—Cont'd

- Designate tsunami evacuation areas and evacuation routes and install evacuation route signs.
- Designate a tsunami shelter/area outside the hazard zone.
- Provide written tsunami hazard information to the populace, including
  - Hazard zone maps.
  - Evacuation routes.
  - Basic tsunami information.

These instructions can be distributed through mailings (utility bills, for example), within phone books, and posted at common meeting points located throughout the community, such as libraries, supermarkets, and public buildings. Local schools must meet the following guidelines:

- Encourage the inclusion of tsunami information in primary and secondary school curriculums. The NWS will help identify curriculum support material.
- Provide an opportunity biennially for a tsunami awareness presentation.
- Schools within the defined hazard zone must have tsunami evacuation drills at least biannually.
- Provide written safety material to all staff members and students.
- Have an earthquake plan.

Guideline 6. Administrative. No program can be successful without formal planning and a proactive administration. The following administrative requirements are necessary for a community to be recognized in the TsunamiReady Program:

1. A tsunami warning plan must be in place and approved by the local governing body. This plan must address the following:
   - Warning point procedures.
   - EOC activation guidelines and procedures.
   - Warning point and EOC personnel specification.
   - Hazard zone map with evacuation routes.
   - Procedures for canceling an emergency for those less-than-destructive tsunamis.
   - Guidelines and procedures for activation of sirens, cable TV override, and local system activation in accordance with state Emergency Alert System plans, and warning fan-out procedures, if necessary.
   - Annual exercises.
2. Yearly visits or discussions with local NWS Forecast Office warning coordination meteorologist or Tsunami Warning Center personnel. This can include a visit to the NWS office, a phone discussion, or e-mail communication.
3. NWS officials will visit accredited communities, at least every other year, to tour EOCs and warning points and meet with key officials.

Administration of the TsunamiReady Program

Oversight of the TsunamiReady Program is accomplished within the NWS by the National StormReady Board. The board is responsible for changes in community recognition guidelines. Direct proposed guideline changes to the board for action. The board consists of the NWS Regional Warning coordination meteorologist program leaders, the National WCM program manager, a Federal Emergency Management Agency representative, a National Emergency Management Association representative, and an International Association of Emergency Managers representative.

Oversight of the TsunamiReady Program at the local level is provided by the appropriate local StormReady board. The local StormReady board has the authority to enhance TsunamiReady to fit regional situations. At a minimum, this board consists of

- NWS Weather Forecast Office's meteorologist-in-charge.
- NWS Weather Forecast Office's warning coordination meteorologist.
- State emergency service director or designee.
- Local emergency management association president or designee.
- Tsunami Warning Center's geophysicist-in-charge.
- Tsunami Hazard Mitigation Program representative.

The local StormReady board is responsible for all steps leading to the recognition of the TsunamiReady community. This includes implementing procedures for site verification visits and application review.

Benefits of the TsunamiReady Program

The benefits of participation in the TsunamiReady Community Program include

- The community is better prepared for the tsunami hazard.
- Regularly scheduled education forums increase public awareness of existing dangers.
- Contact with experts (emergency managers, researchers, NWS personnel) is increased and, likewise, enhanced.
- Community readiness resource needs are identified.
- Positioning to receive state and federal funds is improved.
- Core infrastructure to support other community concerns is enhanced.
- The public is allowed the opportunity to see firsthand how its tax money is being spent in hazard programs.

Conclusion

Through the TsunamiReady Program, NOAA's National Weather Service gives communities the skills and education needed to survive a tsunami before, during, and after the event. TsunamiReady helps community leaders and emergency managers strengthen their local tsunami operations. TsunamiReady communities are better prepared to save lives from the onslaught of a tsunami through better planning, education, and awareness. Communities have fewer fatalities and property damage if they plan before a tsunami arrives. No community is tsunami proof, but TsunamiReady can help communities save lives.

(Continued)

CASE STUDIES—Cont'd

Sources

FEMA. "Fact Sheet: Tsunamis," available at http://www.govexec.com/dailyfed/1104/ 111804h1.htm, 2004.

Folger, Tim. "Waves of Destruction," *Discover Magazine*, May 1994, pp. 69–70.

NOAA (National Oceanic and Atmospheric Administration). *The National Tsunami Hazard Mitigation Program* brochure, available at http://wcatwc.arh.noaa.gov/ tsunamiready/trbrochure.pdf, n.d.

NTHMP (National Tsunami Hazard Mitigation Program). "Frequently Asked Questions," available at http://www.pmel.noaa.gov/tsunami-hazard/tsunami_faqs.htm, 2003.

NWS (National Weather Service). "TsunamiReady; The Readiness Challenge," available at http://www.prh.noaa.gov/ptwc/tsunamiready/tsunami_ready_full_ document.pdf, n.d.

IMPORTANT TERMS

- Preparedness
- Warning
- Watch
- Community emergency response team
- Continuity of Operations Plan

- Functional exercise
- Full-scale exercise
- Partial-scale exercise
- Tabletop exercise
- Business continuity planning

Self-Check Questions

1. What kinds of organizations must consider disaster preparedness?
2. What is the difference between mitigation and preparedness?
3. What are the steps involved in the preparedness cycle?
4. According to the Family Disaster Plan of the Community and Family Preparedness Program, what four basic steps can people take to prepare for any type of disaster?
5. What seven key elements can be used to measure the comprehensive nature of an evacuation plan?
6. Name five special needs populations, and describe what makes their disaster planning needs unique.
7. Why is it important to involve representatives from all stakeholders in the disaster planning process?
8. What kinds of training opportunities are provided by the federal government? What agencies provide these courses, workshops, and other programs?

9. What are the four types of disaster exercises. What does each involve?
10. Name the five ways that the Office of Domestic Preparedness assists states and local jurisdictions in planning for and responding to acts of terrorism.

Out of Class Exercises

1. Create an individual or family plan using the guidance provided in FEMA's "Are You Ready" publication (http://www.fema.gov/areyouready). Did you find any shortfalls in this program? What did you learn by using the publication?
2. Contact your local office of emergency management, and find out if there is an evacuation plan for your local community. What must occur for an evacuation to be ordered? Who has the authority to issue that order?
3. Determine what special needs populations exist in your community. Select one, and find out whether or not special preparedness and emergency planning considerations have been made to accommodate their unique needs.
4. Assist a local small business or nonprofit organization in identifying their hazards and mitigating their risk (often called a *business continuity plan* or *continuity of operations plan*). Several resources are available to help you carry out this exercise, including
   ○ Ready.Gov Business: http://www.ready.gov/business.
   ○ Institute for Business and Home Safety "Open for Business" guide: http://www.ibhs.org/publications/view.asp?cat=84&id=556.
   ○ Volunteer Florida Continuity of Operations Planning Guide: http://www.volunteerflorida.org/publications/New%20ESF-15/COOPCBOs.pdf.

The Disciplines of Emergency Management: Communications

What You Will Learn

- The mission and four assumptions of an effective disaster communications strategy.
- What audiences, or customers, receive disaster communications.
- How communications relates to the four phases of emergency management: response, recovery, preparedness, and mitigation.
- Risk communication concerns and obstacles.
- How to work with the media.
- Communications means and products.

Introduction

Communications has become an increasingly critical function in emergency management. The dissemination of timely and accurate information to the general public, elected and community officials, and the media plays a major role in the effective management of disaster response and recovery activities. Communicating preparedness, prevention, and mitigation information promotes actions that reduce the risk of future disasters. Communicating policies, goals, and priorities to staff members, partners, and participants enhances support and promotes a more efficient disaster management operation. In communicating with the public, establishing a partnership with the media is key to implementing a successful strategy.

This chapter examines the mission of an effective disaster communications strategy, outlines four critical assumptions that serve as the foundation for such a strategy, and identifies the various audiences or customers for disaster communications. The requirements for establishing a disaster communications infrastructure are specified, the difficulties in communicating risk are explored, and a strategy for communicating disaster mitigation and preparedness messages is discussed. Essential to any communications strategy is a practical guide to working with the media, which is also provided. Throughout the chapter, FEMA and the FEMA public affairs experiences are used as the principal example. In exploring the elements of a crisis communications infrastructure used during the disaster response and recovery, the public affairs operations of FEMA are used as a model.

Mission

The mission of an effective disaster communications strategy is to provide timely and accurate information to the public in all four phases of emergency management:

1. *Mitigation*—to promote implementation of strategies, technologies, and actions that will reduce the loss of lives and property in future disasters.
2. *Preparedness*—to communicate preparedness messages that encourage and educate the public in anticipation of disaster events.
3. *Response*—to provide to the pubic notification, warning, evacuation, and situation reports on an ongoing disaster.
4. *Recovery*—to provide individuals and communities affected by a disaster with information on how to register for and receive disaster relief.

Assumptions

The foundation of an effective disaster communications strategy is built on the following four critical assumptions:

1. Customer focus.
2. Leadership commitment.
3. Inclusion of communications in planning and operations.
4. Media partnership.

Customer Focus

An essential element of any effective emergency management system is a focus on customers and customer service. This philosophy should guide communications with the public and all partners in emergency management. A customer service approach includes placing the needs and interests of individuals and communities first, being responsive and informative, and managing expectations. The FEMA emergency information field guide illustrates the agency's focus on customer service and its strategy of getting messages out to the public as directly as possible. The introduction to the guide states the following:

> As members of the Emergency Information and Media Affairs team, you are part of the frontline for the agency in times of disaster. We count on you to be ready and able to respond and perform effectively on short notice. Disaster victims need to know their government is working. They need to know where and how to get help. They need to know what to expect and what not to expect. Getting these messages out quickly is your responsibility as members of the Emergency Information and Media Affairs team. (FEMA, 1998)

The guide's mission statement reinforces this point further:

> To contribute to the well-being of the community following a disaster by ensuring the dissemination of information that:
> * Is timely, accurate, consistent, and easy to understand
> * Explains what people can expect from their government

Demonstrates clearly that FEMA and other federal, state, local and voluntary agencies are working together to provide the services needed to rebuild communities and restore lives. (FEMA, 1998)

The customers for emergency management are diverse. They include internal customers, such as staff members, other federal agencies, states, and other disaster partners. External customers include the general public, elected officials at all levels of government, community and business leaders, and the media. Each of these customers has special needs, and a good communications strategy considers and reflects their requirements.

Leadership Commitment

Good communications starts with a commitment by the leadership of the emergency management organization to sharing and disseminating information both internally and externally. The director of any emergency management organization must openly endorse and promote open lines of communications among the organization's staff, partners, and public to communicate effectively. The leader must model this behavior to clearly illustrate that communications is a valued function of the organization.

In the 1990s, FEMA Director James Lee Witt embodied FEMA's commitment to communicating with the FEMA staff and partners, the public, and the media. Director Witt was a strong advocate for keeping FEMA staff members informed of agency plans, priorities, and operations. Director Witt characterized a proactive approach in communicating with FEMA's constituents. His accessibility to the media was a significant departure from previous FEMA leadership. Director Witt exhibited his commitment to effective communications in many ways:

- He held weekly staff meetings with FEMA's senior managers and required that his senior managers hold regular staff meetings with their employees.
- He published an internal newsletter to employees, *Director's Weekly Update*, which was distributed to all FEMA employees in hard copy and on the agency electronic bulletin board that updated employees on agency activities.
- He made himself and his senior staff available to the media on a regular basis, especially during a disaster response, to answer questions and provide information.
- During a disaster response, he held media briefings daily and sometimes two to three times a day.
- He held special meetings with victims and their families.
- He led the daily briefings among FEMA partners during a disaster response.
- He devoted considerable time to communicating with members of Congress, governors, mayors, and other elected officials during both disaster and nondisaster times.
- He met four to five times per year with the state emergency management directors, FEMA's principal emergency management partners.
- He gave speeches all over this country and around the world to promote better understanding of emergency management and disaster mitigation.

Through his leadership and commitment to communications, FEMA became an agency with a positive image and reputation. Communications led to increased success in molding public opinion and garnering support for the agency's initiatives in disaster mitigation.

Inclusion of Communications in Planning and Operations

The most important part of leadership's commitment to communications is inclusion of communications in all planning and operations. This means that a communications specialist is included in the senior management team of the emergency management organization. It means that communications issues are considered in the decision-making processes and a communications element is included in all organizational activities, plans, and operations.

In the past, communicating with external audiences, or customers, and in many cases internal customers, was not valued or considered critical to a successful emergency management operation. Technology has changed that equation. In today's world of 24-hour television and radio news and the Internet, the demand for information is never ending, especially in an emergency response situation. Emergency managers must be able to communicate critical information in a timely manner to their staff members, partners, the public, and the media.

To do so, the information needs of the various customers and how best to communicate with these customers must be considered at the same time that planning and operational decisions are being made. For example, a decision process on how to remove debris from a disaster area must include discussion of how to communicate information on the debris removal operation to community officials, the public, and the media.

During the many major disasters that occurred in the 1990s, FEMA Director Witt assembled a small group of his senior managers who traveled with him to the sites of disasters and worked closely with him in managing FEMA's efforts. This group always included FEMA's director of public affairs. Similarly, when planning FEMA's preparedness and mitigation initiatives, Director Witt always included staff members from public affairs in the planning and implementation phases. Every FEMA policy, initiative, or operation undertaken during this time included consideration of the information needs of the identified customers and a communications strategy to address these needs.

Media Partnership

The media plays a primary role in communicating with the public. No government emergency management organization could ever hope to develop a communications network comparable to those networks already established and maintain by television, radio, and newspaper outlets across the country. To effectively provide timely disaster information to the public, emergency managers must establish a partnership with their local media outlets.

The goal of a media partnership is to provide accurate and timely information to the public in both disaster and nondisaster situations. The partnership requires a commitment by both the emergency manager and the media to work together, and it requires a level of trust between both parties.

Traditionally, the relationship between emergency managers and the media has been tenuous. There often has been a conflict between the need of the emergency manager to respond quickly and the need of the media to obtain information on the response so it can report it just as quickly. This conflict sometimes resulted in inaccurate reporting and tension between the emergency manager and the media. The loser in this conflict always is the public, which relies on the media for its information.

It is important for emergency managers to understand the needs of the media and the value it brings to facilitating response operations. An effective media partnership provides the emergency manager with a communications network to reach the public with vital information. Such a partnership provides the media with access to the disaster site, to emergency managers and their staff, and to critical information for the public that informs and ensures the accuracy of their reporting.

An effective media partnership helps delineate the roles of the emergency management organizations, manage public expectations, and boost the morale of the relief workers and the disaster victims. All these factors can speed the recovery of a community from a disaster event and promote preparedness and mitigation efforts designed to reduce the loss of life and property from the next disaster event.

Critical Thinking

- Is the primary concern of the media of a private, nongovernmental organization its publicity ratings or helping the public with disasters?
- Does the media have a responsibility to warn the public about disasters?
- Should members of the media be required to have training in emergency management? Why or why not?

Audiences and Customers

To effectively communicate disaster information, emergency managers must clearly identify their various audiences and customers. Included in many of these audiences are both partners and stakeholders. Basic emergency management audiences include the following:

- *General public.* The largest audience, of which there are many subgroups, such as the elderly, the disabled, minority, low income, youth, and so on; and all are potential customers.
- *Disaster victims.* Those individuals affected by a specific disaster event.
- *Business community.* Often ignored by emergency managers but critical to disaster recovery, preparedness, and mitigation activities.
- *Media.* An audience and a partner critical to effectively communicating with the public.
- *Elected officials.* Governors, mayors, county executives, state legislators, and members of Congress.
- *Community officials.* City and county managers, directors of public works, department heads.
- *First responders.* Those in the police, fire, and emergency medical services.
- *Volunteer groups.* American Red Cross, Salvation Army, the NVOADs, and so on that are critical in first response to an event.

Communications with some of these customers, such as the first responders, is accomplished principally through radio and phone communications, as described in

Chapter 4. Communicating with most of the other audiences is accomplished through briefings, meetings, provision of background materials, and in some instances, one-on-one interviews. Communications strategies, plans, and operations should be developed to meet the information needs of each of these customers and staffed and funded accordingly.

Crisis Communications: Response and Recovery

Communicating with the public in the midst of a disaster response and recovery effort can be difficult. Often there are conflicting reports on casualties and damages and usually some level of confusion among responders. Add to this situation the expectation of the public to get information almost instantaneously and the demands made by the new 24-hour news culture.

The provision of timely and accurate information directly to the public and the media is critical to the success of any response and recovery effort. An effective communications strategy allows emergency managers and community officials at all levels of government to provide information and comfort to disaster victims and, at the same time, manage expectations. Regular communications with the public and the media helps ensure that accurate information is being disseminated and reduces the chances for misinformation and rumors. Monitoring direct communications with victims and media reports helps identify potential problems with misinformation and rumors and allows emergency officials to address these issues before they become too widespread and damaging.

In the 1990s, FEMA built a communications infrastructure designed to disseminate critical information to the public and the media and to monitor and correct misinformation during FEMA's disaster response and recovery operations. The two key elements of FEMA's crisis communications infrastructure are staff support and technology.

Staff Support

FEMA's Office of Public Affairs (which for a time was called the Office of Emergency Information and Media Affairs) was responsible for managing day-to-day communications activities for the agency and, during a disaster, for managing a cadre of public affairs disaster assistance employees. The Office of Public Affairs staff was responsible for establishing and managing joint information centers, both at FEMA headquarters and in the field, and working cooperatively with FEMA's community relations staff.

Public Affairs Officers

The individuals primarily responsible for carrying out this mission are the FEMA public affairs officers. PAOs develop and implement strategies to instill confidence in the community that all levels of government are working in partnership to restore essential services and help individuals begin to put their lives back together. They manage expectations so that disaster victims have a clear understanding of all disaster response, recovery, and mitigation services available to them. An overarching goal is to provide authoritative information to the public to combat misinformation.

Joint Information Center

The structure FEMA uses to implement public affairs activities after a disaster is the joint information center. FEMA determines the need for a JIC, and if one is established it becomes the central point for coordination of emergency public information, public affairs activities, and media access to information about the latest developments. The JIC is a physical location where PAOs from involved agencies come together to coordinate the release of accurate and consistent information to the media and the public. For a major disaster, a JIC may be established at both FEMA headquarters and on the disaster site. The on-site JIC preferably is collocated with the disaster field office. The chief spokesperson for headquarters JIC is the FEMA director of public affairs, and the chief spokesperson at the on-site JIC is the lead FEMA PAO.

Community Relations

A partner in FEMA's public affairs operation is the community relations staff. The community relations function typically is performed jointly by federal and state personnel but may include locally hired people who know the community well. Field officers are organized into teams and deployed into affected communities to gather and disseminate information about the response and recovery operation that becomes part of the communications process. They work closely with affected states to identify community leaders and neighborhood advocacy groups to assist in disseminating information and identifying unmet needs.

Technology

A valuable means of communications in postdisaster scenarios is the toll-free number, which has become a core element of FEMA recovery initiatives. The toll-free number is used to inform victims about the type of assistance they may be available to receive and allows them to apply for such assistance. The toll-free number is included in all forms of information and communication generated by the disaster event. An example of its usage is that during the first month after the terrorist events of September 11, 2001, more than 20,000 people called the toll-free FEMA number.

The Internet has become an increasingly popular and effective method of disseminating information to the public, and this trend will continue. FEMA's Web site traffic has grown from an average of 20,000 people per week to more than 3 million. This includes users from more than 50 countries. During major disasters, the Office of Public Affairs immediately posts a special section and keeps it updated. Real-time situation reports, maps, graphics, and links to other Internet sites are posted. In addition, nearly 6,000 clients receive FEMA updates via e-mail. The interactive nature of the Internet has not yet been completely harnessed by the emergency management community and provides an opportunity to expand relationships with the public in the future.

During the 1990s, the FEMA Office of Public Affairs developed several innovative ways of disseminating information to the public. These methods have now been used in more than 200 disasters, including the Midwest floods, the Northridge earthquake, the Oklahoma City bombing, and record hurricane seasons. FEMA credits the new methods with improving its ability to get vital information out to the public and helping rebuild the agency's credibility and the nation's comfort level with its emergency management system. Some of the information dissemination methods are described as follows:

- The Recovery Channel provides television coverage of briefings and interviews with experts in multiple languages. Using portable satellite dishes, the signal is beamed into shelters. Network and local television news use this material.

Cable television has cooperated, and a network of cable systems is committed to live Recovery Channel coverage. After the Northridge earthquake, Recovery Channel programming reached 680,000 victims on 125 cable systems in Los Angeles, with an additional potential audience of 4 million.

- The *Recovery Times* combines the latest desktop publishing technology with electronic transmission of stories and images to one printing contractor for all disasters. Prepackaging information has enabled quick publication and distribution of emergency information in an extraordinary community outreach effort. During the Midwest floods, FEMA published and distributed *Recovery Times* newspapers in nine states.

- FEMAFAX/Spectrafax uses the latest computerized facsimile system. Technology, comprehensive databases, and 48 telephone lines allow rapid, targeted information distribution. The system also has a fax-on-demand service. Clients select from more than 2,000 documents and material is transmitted automatically.

- The FEMA Radio Network (FRN) is a digitized audio production and distribution system. Radio stations can record sound bites and public service announcements with disaster officials and scientific experts. The state-of-the-art studio supports news conferences and interviews. Stations reach all this through a toll-free number.

- The Recovery Radio Network distributes live broadcasts of emergency public information. It uses the Emergency Alert System (EAS) network to provide a pool feed to local radio stations that are still operating.

- The FEMA Automatic Internet Emergency News and Situation Report Distribution Service sends subscribers news releases and disaster situation reports via e-mail.

More information on these programs can be obtained on the FEMA Web site: www.fema.gov/about/eima.htm.

Communicating Preparedness and Mitigation Messages

The objective of communicating preparedness and mitigation messages to the public is to educate, inform, raise awareness, and promote support for taking action before a disaster strikes.

Risk communication and public awareness programs can be undertaken in the wake of disasters or during times of normalcy. Communication of risk is an area of growing interest in the field and is discussed in more length later in this section. Public awareness is needed to gain approval for any type of emergency management measure. To implement programs, the public has to agree that a hazard exists, it should be reduced, and the proposed program is an appropriate measure. To achieve this consensus, the public must be involved as a partner in the process. In today's political climate, new programs usually are negotiated with the public, not decreed from officials. The case study on FEMA's Project Impact, at the end of this chapter, illustrates this type of approach well.

Communicating Risk

Most emergency management professionals believe that a more concerted effort to define and communicate risk to the public needs to be made. The value of warning and evacuation systems have been proven time and again but still often are underused. Knowledge of risk does not help if the public is not informed of the danger and the actions they can take to reduce it. Bridging this knowledge gap between the scientific community and the public at large is a major area of emergency management study today.

Risk Communication Theory

The book *Disasters by Design* by Dennis Mileti provides some valuable information on risk communication. Mileti breaks information sources for hazard awareness programs into three categories: authorities, news media, and peers. Obviously, official sources provide the most credibility. Research has shown that hazard awareness campaigns are most effective when they rely on a mix of techniques and information sources. Typically, radio and television are best for initiating or maintaining awareness, and printed materials may be best at providing detailed information.

▢ ▢ ▢ ━━━━━━━━━━━━━━━━━━━━━━━━━━━━━━

Severe Weather Watches and Warnings Definitions

Flood watch. High flow or overflow of water from a river is possible in the given time period. It can also apply to heavy runoff or drainage of water into low-lying areas. These watches generally are issued for flooding that is expected to occur at least six hours after heavy rains have ended.

Flood warning. Flooding conditions actually are occurring or imminent in the warning area.

Flash flood watch. Flash flooding is possible in or close to the watch area. Flash flood watches generally are issued for flooding that is expected to occur within six hours after heavy rains have ended.

Flash flood warning. Flash flooding actually is occurring or imminent in the warning area. It can be issued as a result of torrential rains, a dam failure, or an ice jam.

Tornado watch. Conditions are conducive to the development of tornadoes in and close to the watch area.

Tornado warning. A tornado actually has been sighted by spotters or indicated on radar and is occurring or imminent in the warning area.

Severe thunderstorm watch. Conditions are conducive to the development of severe thunderstorms in and close to the watch area.

Severe thunderstorm warning. A severe thunderstorm actually has been observed by spotters or indicated on radar and is occurring or imminent in the warning area.

Tropical storm watch. Tropical storm conditions with sustained winds from 39 to 73 mph are possible in the watch area within the next 36 hours.

Tropical storm warning. Tropical storm conditions are expected in the warning area within the next 24 hours.

(Continued)

Hurricane watch. Hurricane conditions (sustained winds greater than 73 mph) are possible in the watch area within 36 hours.

Hurricane warning. Hurricane conditions are expected in the warning area in 24 hours or less.

Source: FEMA, www.fema.gov.

Different message characteristics include the amount of material, speed of presentation, number of arguments, repetition, style, clarity, ordering, forcefulness, specificity, consistency, accuracy, and extremity of position advocated. Information characteristics should be tailored for the communications goal (i.e., awareness or adoption) and the target audience. For example, the Red Cross publishes awareness guides and manuals specific to targeted groups, such as schools, hospitals, corporations, city managers, emergency managers, and the media.

Message types vary as well. Some programs focus on content, such as scientific data or technical information about a hazard, but such information generally is processed and obtained by a small number of people. Conversely, practical instructions focus on the protective response, not the hazard itself. The simplest form of practical instruction is the "prompt," a sign that defines a single contingency and action, such as "pull lever in case of fire." Prompts are more likely to attract attention, be readily comprehended, and retained for future use. Other message styles, such as "attribute portrayal strategy," emphasize the advantages of a proposed hazard adjustment, and "fear appeals" describe the potential negative consequences of not taking the desired risk-reduction action.

Risk communication theory is based on the assumption that people leave themselves vulnerable because they are uninformed or unconvinced about the consequences of their actions. Providing accurate, helpful information would change people's beliefs about a hazard and lead to an adoption of appropriate mitigation strategies. This is a bit of an oversimplification, because many other factors and obstacles are involved, but it illustrates the general principle. The major obstacles to communicating risk and changing people's behavior include competing demands for attention, complacency, denial, and conflicts with existing beliefs.

Mileti breaks the risk communication and new behavior adoption process into the following eight steps:

1. Hearing the warning.
2. Believing that it is credible.
3. Confirming that the threat exists.
4. Personalizing the warning and confirming that others are heeding it.
5. Determining whether protective action is needed.
6. Determining whether protective action is feasible.
7. Determining what protective action to take.
8. Taking the protective action.

The field is still evolving to determine how best to influence people at each stage of the process. Most public awareness campaigns have been designed to improve disaster preparedness for near-term, high-probability threats. Less is known about what it takes to motivate people to prepare for longer-term, lower-probability events during times of normalcy. This will be an important area of study in the future.

Risk Communication Concerns

One risk communications dilemma is how to get accurate risk information to the public when there are so many competing, and possibly conflicting, information sources. The government has no control over what unofficial sources say because it cannot regulate talking heads, so-called experts, and Web sites. Partnering with the media to provide a steady stream of consistent and accurate information from responsible authorities is the best way to overcome this obstacle.

Other major issues affecting risk communication programs are when to warn the public and how much information to provide. The hurricane scenario provides the ideal model: Forecasters identify the storm, watches and warnings are issued, time frames and probabilities are provided, and the public is given clear instructions on when and how to take protective action. Communicating the risk of other hazards is not always so clear-cut, however. In the wake of the September 11, 2001, terrorist attacks, several general and unspecified terrorism threats were issued by the federal government. Weighty issues to be considered by public officials were (1) with hundreds of tips pouring in, at what point is the risk considered legitimate enough to pass on to the public and (2) how much information on the threats should be shared.

With the first issue, officials must balance the duty to warn citizens of impending danger with concerns about unnecessarily panicking people and disrupting society. There are political and economic concerns as well. Too many false warnings could lead to a loss of credibility and public inattention to future warnings. With the second issue, officials must balance concerns about frightening the public with unthinkable rumors, and perhaps compromising important information sources, against the need to provide practical, helpful information. General, unspecified warnings may protect intelligence channels, but they do not do much to help the public prepare for the event. These are delicate issues, and a consensus on how best to responsibly educate the public about risk without unnecessarily alarming them has yet to be reached. The case study on earthquake risk in Parkfield, California, at the end of the chapter, explores these issues as well.

Critical Thinking

- Other than the media and risk managers, where do individuals get their information about hazards, risks, and disasters?
- How can individuals determine the credibility of the information they receive? Is it wise to assume that recipients of "official" risk communication messages believe what they hear simply because it is coming from a government source? What can be done to improve the credibility of an official message?

Working with the Media

General

The media always has been naturally drawn to disasters and emergencies because of the compelling human interest stories and dramatic footage. With the advent of 24-hour news stations and near real-time coverage via the Internet, the role of the media in disaster response is magnified. In the response phase, the media often provides the most effective and efficient means for providing timely and accurate information to disaster victims and the general public. In addition, the media can play a critical role in communicating recovery information and building support for preparedness and mitigation activities.

The biggest development in the media world over the last 15 years is the 24-hour news cycle. Between CNN, the major networks' all-news stations, their respective Web sites, and the emergence of other independent reporting mechanisms, there is simply more air time and copy to be filled. This translates into increased coverage of disasters and emergencies and creates a demand for timely information. These pressures are likely to grow in the future. As television becomes increasingly specialized and the number of cable channels expands, it would not be surprising within the foreseeable future to see the advent of a 24-hour Disaster News Network, replete with "hurricane-cams" and "on-the-fault" reporting.

The media can make a strong contribution to emergency management. Effective warnings broadcast through the media are widely credited with reducing casualties from hurricanes, tornadoes, and floods. There is often no better or quicker way to get warning messages out. The media also can facilitate assistance to disaster-stricken areas and provide reassurance to the public about the welfare of victims. Further, good science reporting can inform the public about hazards and educate them on hazard-reduction behaviors.

Media as a Partner

Working with the media provides both a challenge and an opportunity. As discussed, the media can be a valuable element of emergency operations, disseminating important information and calling attention to urgent issues, or it can be a thorn in the emergency management official's side, distributing misleading information and misguided criticism. The key to a beneficial and productive relationship is to view the media as an important partner and treat it as such.

A great example of this approach is FEMA of the 1990s. In the early 1990s, FEMA was an agency under fire, with legislators pondering its abolishment and the media producing a steady stream of criticism after a series of poorly perceived disaster response efforts. When James Lee Witt was appointed FEMA director in 1992, he recognized communications as a key area for improvement and took appropriate measures to establish a more open and productive relationship with the media.

As a precursor to this step, the communications staff was provided the tools and equipment needed to get the job done. Press veteran Morrie Goodman was brought on board, the office began identifying actions it could take to better partner with the media, and a host of new practices were implemented. FEMA provided the media with flyover pictures and videos from closed sites. It posted transcripts and audio of news conferences on the Internet. It created an on-site press and studio room. It provided press conferences via satellite link. It partnered with *USA Today* to include FEMA informational inserts in certain editions of the paper. The press was even provided an area in the emergency operations center at major crises. FEMA in turn used the press to promote key information to the public, such as toll-free numbers for victims to call to apply for assistance. Director Witt made it a point to constantly thank the media for its role in helping to get important messages out.

As a result of this open, collaborative approach, the public was better informed, FEMA received better press, and this translated into more support from Capitol Hill, the administration, and the public at large. Much of FEMA's success during the Clinton years can be attributed to the agency's improved ability to deal well with the press.

☐ ☐ ☐ ▬▬▬▬▬▬▬▬▬▬▬▬▬▬▬▬▬▬▬▬▬▬▬▬▬▬▬

Making Information Public and Working with the Media

Established credibility and productive working relationships with representatives of the media is critical. In most instances, the media is cooperative in publishing important disaster recovery information. In an ideal world, the media simply would use all news releases as issued; however, sometimes media outlets, especially in major media markets, do not view disaster recovery information as important news after the initial stories about the event. It is important to try to make the news media understand the important public service role they play in the recovery effort. Use the following guidelines concerning media relationships:

- Be aware of and sensitive to media deadlines.
- Respond promptly to all media inquiries. Always answer requests for information, even if only to report that the information is not available or will not be available until a given time in the future.
- Reply to questions thoroughly and accurately. Do not provide more information than is requested.
- Be honest and open. If you do not know, say so and get back to the reporter as quickly as possible with the correct answer. Ask about deadlines.
- Do not go into in-depth discussions with reporters about the programs of other agencies.
- Always be diplomatic. Especially if a request seems unreasonable, deal with it tactfully.

Source: FEMA, *Emergency Information Field Guide* (condensed), 1998.

▬▬▬▬▬▬▬▬▬▬▬▬▬▬▬▬▬▬▬▬▬▬▬▬▬▬▬ ☐ ☐ ☐

This practice extends to nongovernmental organizations as well. The action of the American Red Cross in the immediate aftermath of the World Trade Center terrorist attacks in 2001 provides a good example. Within a half-hour of the first plane crash, the Red Cross deployed a 35-member rapid-response team to the World Trade Center with a mission to work with the media to inform the public of what was happening and what they could do to help. The Red Cross then called in a 65-member volunteer force to their offices in New York, Washington, D.C., and Pennsylvania to assist with media calls. Although their persistent solicitation of aid and their subsequent plans for aid distribution eventually came under criticism, the Red Cross's immediate actions illustrate how NGOs are able to partner with the press to get important messages out.

Managing Information

Beyond the general philosophy of treating the media as a partner, basic communications protocols must be followed. Information management is the most basic competency that must be developed. Managing information means developing a coordinated, consistent message to prevent confusion and maintain credibility. The release of information should be coordinated with responding partners, such as emergency management officials from other levels of government, law enforcement officials, and public health officials.

As noted earlier, FEMA achieves this through its joint information center. A variation on this approach is now used by most emergency management organizations in all disaster events.

Organizations Telling Their Own Story

Although the careful management of information flows is a critical element of any communications strategy, the desire to distribute perfect, accurate, and coordinated information must be balanced with the need to get information out quickly. The object is to tell the organization's story before someone else tells it. This goal goes hand in hand with partnering with the media, because the better the relationship with the media is, the more likely one will have this opportunity.

This was another focus of FEMA under Witt. In prior years, during major crises such as Hurricanes Iniki and Andrew and the Loma Prieta earthquake, FEMA generally attempted to shield itself from the press while it coordinated and undertook its response and recovery activities. The resulting vacuum of information left an opening for the media to portray the FEMA response as it perceived it, and coverage of these events was generally negative toward FEMA. Conversely, during major incidents of the Witt years, such as the Midwest floods, the Northridge earthquake, and the Oklahoma City bombing, FEMA made itself as accessible to the media as possible and distributed a constant stream of information on what activities were under way and what victims could do to receive assistance. Rather than reporting on perceived deficiencies, the press shared the information with the public and FEMA's public image improved.

Another excellent example of this strategy in action is New York City mayor Rudy Giuliani after the World Trade Center attacks. Giuliani generally is perceived as the hero of the tragedy, largely because of his effective communications via the media. He made himself constantly accessible to press, provided continual updates on the status of response and recovery efforts, and reassured citizens that the city would rebound. By putting himself in front of the camera and articulating the story, he built public confidence and goodwill and was able to rally people together toward recovery. Even though he did not always have all the answers, he was open, honest, and forthcoming, which fostered trust as well as good press.

The point is that, if not provided with good information from good sources, the press will continue to look elsewhere. The information reporters find may not be accurate or fair, so it is critical to seize the communications agenda and get the correct story in front of the public.

Message Objectives

The objectives of the message obviously vary depending on the situation, but in general a media partnership can help educate, inform, reassure, and rally the public. The media can help garner support and lay the groundwork for future emergency management measures. In times of normalcy, the media partnership can educate the public on disaster mitigation issues, although exposure may be difficult to obtain. Unfortunately, media interest in disasters usually is short-lived and does not last long into the recovery phase. Nevertheless, the media is one means of promoting mitigation with the public.

In times of a crisis or emergency, the media partnership can communicate situation reports regarding the nature and scope of the incident, the estimated human and economic damages, and what recovery measures are under way. This provides the public a perspective of the incident and lets it know what to expect. Public officials can go on the airwaves to reassure citizens that the government is taking action and soothe the public psyche with recovery updates. Most important, the media partnership can mobilize the public to action—whether the instruction is to call a toll-free number, evacuate homes, or open mail with gloves, there is no better way to rally the public than through the media.

Communications Means and Products

Media Lists and Contacts

FEMA's core media list consists of the following: newspapers, city and regional magazines, local trade and business publications, state bureaus of national wire services, local radio and television stations, local cable stations, public broadcasting stations, and public information officers at military bases. The specific contacts that an emergency management agency typically deals with are metro desk and city reporters, public affairs reporters, business reporters, news assignment editors, and public service announcement directors.

Press Releases

The press release is perhaps the most fundamental communications product. A press release can take the form of news releases, daily summaries, media advisories, feature articles, fact sheets, public service announcements, or other written materials. FEMA describes the objectives of its press releases as to demonstrate that FEMA and its partners are working to provide critical disaster response, recovery, and mitigation programs and to provide victims with accurate and timely information about the availability, details, and limits of these programs. FEMA press releases are routed through an established approval process.

The FEMA emergency information field guide offers some basic tips on preparing press releases. One point of emphasis for standard press releases is to never assume that information in previous disasters is appropriate for the current disaster, always review generic releases for accuracy, timeliness, and appropriateness for each specific disaster. Also, releases and advisories should be kept brief and to the point to increase the likelihood that it will be used in its entirety. An example of a FEMA press release follows. It is notable for its brevity, as it concisely lists essential information such as the who, what, when, and how of victim assistance.

FEMA Press Release: Federal Disaster Aid Ordered for Mississippi Storms

Washington, D.C., December 7, 2001. The head of the Federal Emergency Management Agency (FEMA) announced today that federal disaster aid has been made available for Mississippi families and businesses victimized by tornadoes and other extreme weather that struck the state late last month.

FEMA director Joe M. Allbaugh said the assistance was authorized under a major disaster declaration issued for the state by President Bush. The declaration covers damage to private property from the severe storms, tornadoes, and flooding that began November 24.

Immediately after the president's action, Allbaugh designated the following 10 counties eligible for federal funding to help meet the recovery needs of affected residents and business owners: Bolivar, DeSoto, Hinds, Humphreys, Madison, Panola, Quitman, Sunflower, Tate, and Washington.

The assistance, to be coordinated by FEMA, can include grants to help pay for temporary housing, minor home repairs, and other serious disaster-related expenses. Low-interest loans from the U.S. Small Business Administration also will be available to cover residential and business losses not fully compensated by insurance.

Allbaugh said federal funds also will be available to the state on a cost-shared basis for approved projects that reduce future disaster risks. He indicated that additional designations may be made later if requested by the state and warranted by the results of further damage assessments.

Gracia Szczech of FEMA was named by Allbaugh to coordinate federal relief operations. Szczech said residents and business owners who sustained losses in the designated counties can begin the disaster application process by calling 1-800-621-FEMA, or 1-800-462-7585 (TTY) for the hearing and speech impaired. The toll-free telephone numbers will be available starting Saturday, December 8 from 8 AM to 6 PM seven days a week until further notice.

Source: FEMA, www.fema.gov, updated December 7, 2001.

Press Conferences

Press conferences allow information to be directly relayed to the media and the public. They provide officials with an opportunity to inform the public, reassure them, and mobilize them toward action. It is expected that in the aftermath of major crises and emergencies, elected or appointed officials will come out and show the flag via a press conference and help calm public fears. This is an important step toward recovery and a return to normalcy.

Press Inquiries

In contrast to press releases and press conferences, press inquiries involve the media taking the communications initiative. For this reason, a dose of caution should be used when responding. The FEMA emergency information field guide provides the following general tips for interviews with the press:

- Listen to the entire question before responding.
- Avoid answering questions that call for speculation on your part.
- Be aware of false assumptions and erroneous conclusions.
- Avoid answering hypothetical conclusions.
- Be alert to multiple questions.

FEMA also has standard operating procedures to be used in receiving, responding to, and monitoring inquiries in the field. Key points of emphasis include the following:

- Never discuss program specifics or policy issues. Questions about FEMA policies or programs must always be referred to the public affairs officer to be answered by the appropriate designated spokesperson.

FIGURE 7–1 FEMA director James Lee Witt addresses the media's questions at the site of the Laguna Canyon mudflows, which led to at least one death and caused a great deal of damage (February 26, 1998). Photo by Dave Gatley/FEMA.

- Ask the media to help FEMA help the disaster victims.
- Be sure to tell the media about the JIC, the single source of accurate, up-to-date, official information about the disaster.

Web Sites

Web sites related to emergency management have become ubiquitous. From a media communications perspective, Web sites provide easy access to a repository of press releases, situation reports, general news, fact sheets, and general organizational and programmatic information. Diligence must be made to keep the site current, accurate, and easily navigable; or it loses its value as a resource. The FEMA policy for its Web site (www.fema.gov) is to keep news items on the site for 30 days. The same coordination and information management practices used for press releases apply to information posted on the Internet.

Situation Reports

Situation reports are used to provide basic information and statistics regarding emergency response efforts. The reports provide the press with facts that can be used in articles and stories and inform partner response agencies of the status of operations. FEMA produces a steady stream of situation reports in the aftermath of major events. This is consistent with the objectives of telling its story before the press does and partnering with the press by being sensitive to its need for hard data. Situation reports typically are posted on the Internet or distributed by e-mail.

FIGURE 7–2 New York City, October 2, 2001. FEMA community relations worker answers questions from victims of the World Trade Center incident. Photo by Andrea Booher/FEMA News Photo.

□ □ □ ▬▬▬▬▬▬▬▬▬▬▬▬▬▬▬▬▬▬▬▬▬▬▬▬▬

FEMA Situation Report

From the Federal Emergency Management Agency (FEMA) "National Situation Update" for Tuesday, October 09, 2001 (www.fema.gov/emanagers/natsitup.htm):

World Trade Center Update (as of October 7, 2001)
The city reported that, as of yesterday, 393 bodies have been recovered from the World Trade Center (WTC). Of those, 335 have been identified. The number of injured is 8,786 (415 remain hospitalized) and 4,979 persons are registered as missing.

As of yesterday, 206,831 tons of debris had been removed from the WTC site (not including steel) to a landfill on Staten Island. The official estimate for total debris at the WTC is 1.4 million tons.

4,776 New Yorkers have registered for housing assistance. $9.8 million in housing assistance payments have been approved for disbursement.

3,426 New Yorkers have registered for Individual and Family Grants. $32,624 has been approved for disbursement to eligible registrants.

The Small Business Administration has approved $16,984,300 in low-interest loans to businesses and individuals.

$126,325,305 has been obligated as the federal share for Public Assistance (as of October 8). (Manhattan DFO)

Source: FEMA, www.fema.gov.

▬▬▬▬▬▬▬▬▬▬▬▬▬▬▬▬▬▬▬▬▬▬▬▬▬ □ □ □

An example of a typical situation report issued by FEMA during disaster response and recovery efforts is provided. Reliefweb (www.reliefweb.int/w/rwb.nsf) is an excellent source for situation reports on international crises and emergencies posted by the United Nations and other international organizations. The U.S. Office of Foreign Disaster Assistance (www.usaid.gov/hum_response/ofda) also does a great job of providing situation reports on its assistance programs around the globe.

Spokespeople

Spokespeople can lend credibility to a message, but their words must be coordinated with the rest of the communications strategy to avoid multiple or contradictory messages. For this reason, it is often wise to select a single spokesperson to deliver information to the press. The lead local official often is the best person to assume this role, because he or she will be best informed on the local response and the community's needs.

The FEMA press information guide for its Project Impact initiative, a case study at the end of the chapter, provides some valuable pointers for spokespeople:

- Repeat information to reinforce key message points.
- Correct inaccuracies, otherwise they will be accepted as fact.

- Pair use of statistics with stories or case studies that bring them to life.
- Stay out of other people's business. Let other emergency agencies answer their own questions.
- Always be honest. If you do not know an answer to a question, say so and offer to find the answer or refer the reporter to someone who can.

Conclusion

Whether dealing with the media, the public, or partners, effective communication is a critical element of emergency management. Media relations should be open and cooperative, the information stream must be managed to provide a consistent, accurate message, and officials need to be proactive about telling their own story before it is done for them. A customer service approach is essential to communicating with the public, a collaborative approach should be taken to promoting programs, and great care should be given as to how and when risk is communicated to citizens. Multiple agencies and unclear lines of responsibility make communications among partners a challenge; political skill and acumen are needed to overcome such hurdles, and efforts are under way to improve communications in this area.

CASE STUDIES

Project Impact

FEMA's promotion of Project Impact provides an excellent example of how to sell disaster mitigation programs to the public. The FEMA public affairs team engaged and involved the public and explained the program in terms people could understand and value, partnered with the media to get its message out, and made effective use of policy windows.

Project Impact is a community-based mitigation initiative, facilitated and partially funded by FEMA. It includes getting local businesses to partner with the local government and community organizations to prepare for and reduce the effects of future disasters. Preliminary surveys had indicated that communities were interested in reducing risk, so Project Impact was born.

The communications team's first challenge was to frame the program in terms that the public could understand. Although the program is a mitigation initiative, the team wanted to move away from emergency management jargon and describe the program in a manner with which the public would be more familiar. The slogan "put FEMA out of business" was developed. The term *mitigation* was replaced with *disaster resistant*, and then *prevention*, and finally *risk reduction*. The slogans "prevention pays" and "prevention power" were used to reinforce the message.

A public affairs campaign was launched, both at the grassroots level within target communities and through the print and television media when possible. The communications model employed was based on the following guidelines:

- *Keep the message simple and understandable.* Literature was developed at the fourth-grade level. A "three little pig's analogy" was used to help explain the difference between preparedness and prevention.
- *Stick to the message or point.* Spokespeople used a "remember three things" tactic, whereby three main points are repeatedly mentioned in straight, clear language. Also, the Project Impact pamphlet was reduced to one page, containing five simple prevention tips.
- *Explain what is in it for the public.* The selling point to the public was that Project Impact would result in fewer losses from future disasters.
- *Educate the media on mitigation.* A media partner guide was developed to help Project Impact proponents explain to the media why mitigation is a story, why it is important, and how the media could help spread the message.
- *Involve partners.* The Salvation Army and Red Cross were solicited as partners in promoting Project Impact.
- *You are the message.* Project Impact hats and T-shirts were provided to team members.

From a media standpoint, articles were placed in the *USA Today* Op/Ed section and *Parade* magazine, and Al Roker of the Today Show did a spot on Project Impact. The team also took advantage of policy windows by sneaking prevention messages into interviews during major disaster operations. Spokespeople such as FEMA's Kim Fuller promoted Project Impact in interviews during Hurricanes Irene and Floyd. An animated video on mitigation steps was provided to the networks and displayed during the interviews. Also, pre-prepared press releases on how people could rebuild better for the future were provided to the media.

Source: Interview with Kim Fuller, October 2001.

CASE STUDIES

Risk Communication—Parkfield, California

One of the issues facing emergency managers is when to notify the public of a disaster risk. A desire to protect citizens must be weighed against concerns about unnecessarily alarming people, disrupting the economy, and upsetting public officials. The tension between the sheriff and the beach town mayor in the movie *Jaws* exemplifies this issue well. Even though the sheriff warned the mayor of the continuing risk of shark attacks, the mayor would have none of such talk during the busiest tourist weekend of the season and kept the information from the public.

(Continued)

CASE STUDIES—Cont'd

A real-life scenario with a different end result, to date anyway, involved a U.S. effort at earthquake prediction in Parkfield, California, a town adjacent to the San Andreas fault. In 1985, a U.S. Geological Survey analysis of previous earthquakes on a particular fault section indicated a strong likelihood of a repeat event by the end of the decade. The director of the USGS issued a formal public broadcast of the quake warning in April 1985 stating there was a 90 percent probability of a magnitude 5.5 to magnitude 6.0 earthquake some time between 1985 and 1993 in the Parkfield area. It also stated that a 10 percent probability existed for a magnitude 7.0 quake. By November 1988, the National Earthquake Prediction Evaluation Council (NEPEC) and the California Earthquake Prediction Evaluation Council had endorsed the prediction.

The release of the information became a national media event and precipitated a media campaign in central California involving newspapers, radio, and television that lasted years. In 1988, the California Governor's Office of Emergency Services published a detailed brochure and mailed it to 120,000 households considered at risk. It covered information about the earthquake hazard, the prediction, a possible short-term warning, and how to take action.

But the expected earthquake has not occurred. Further analysis showed that, although the successive repetition of similar but not identical quakes might be expected on individual fault sections, the amount of time between them may be highly variable. Also, confidence in predictors based on estimates of recurrence intervals has decreased in the scientific community. This case raises the issue of what to do with risk information. The duty to warn and protect the public must be balanced with fears about disrupting society with potentially unreliable risk information. It remains to be seen whether the correct decision was made for Parkfield, California.

Source: Mileti, *Disasters by Design*, 1999.

CASE STUDIES

Federal Government Communications during the Anthrax Crisis

The anthrax outbreak in October 2001 provides some important communications lessons, both from the perspective of media relations and communicating risk to the public. It highlights the importance of providing a consistent, coordinated message through a single spokesperson and the need to balance a desire to reassure the public with the need to be accurate and credible.

Two main challenges were involved with the crisis. First, medical and public health officials had more questions than answers. Anthrax is a very rare disease in humans, and anthrax spores spread via the mail was basically an unknown commodity altogether. Second, multiple responding agencies from various levels of government were involved and no protocol was established for distributing information.

As a result, the public was given conflicting messages about the nature of the anthrax and misinformation about the true risk. Media criticism of the public response ensued, but it should be pointed out that, in November 2001, a *USA Today* survey found that 77 percent of U.S. citizens were confident that the government could handle a major anthrax outbreak and a Harris interactive poll showed the Center for Disease Control's approval rating at 79 percent. Apparently, the public was in a forgiving mood or perhaps just still confused.

The first problem with the anthrax communications was that there was no clear spokesperson. A sole authority was needed to provide uniformity and consistency to the message and reduce fears. After the early conflicting messages, Tom Ridge was appointed the quasi-spokesperson for anthrax and terrorism threats, as part of his duties with the newly created Office of Homeland Security.

Beyond the issue of who should have been providing the message, there were questions about what information should have been provided. The case illustrates a classic communications conundrum. Officials were under pressure to provide current information to the public, which was seeking reassurances, while there was still much uncertainty about the true nature of the threat. Marc Shannon, director of Ketchum's Washington, D.C., health-care practice, summed up the dilemma well: "If you don't get out enough information you're accused of being secretive. And if you give too much information you are criticized for stirring up anxiety." As Shannon points out, a key to communications in these instances in not to be afraid to say I do not know.

Tommy Thompson of the Department of Health and Human Services might be accused of erring in this respect. During an interview on *60 Minutes* early in the crisis, he said, "We've got to make sure that people understand that they're safe, and that we're prepared to take care of any contingency, any consequence that develops from any kind of bioterrorism attack." After new cases of anthrax continued to be reported and two D.C. postal workers and a Connecticut woman later died of inhalation anthrax, it became apparent that this was a case of an official going too far in trying to assuage public fears. These remarks were in contrast to those of New York City mayor Rudy Giuliani, who after the death of the Connecticut woman said words to the effect that the government cannot guarantee that every single person will be completely safe from anthrax, and that individuals need to exercise a certain amount of due diligence. Although these remarks may not have been completely comforting, they were accurate, practical, and fostered public trust.

Source: Houston, 2001.

IMPORTANT TERMS
• Disaster communications strategy • Press release • Media partnership • Press conference • Crisis communications • Press inquiry • Risk communications • Situation report • Joint information center

Self-Check Questions

1. What is the mission of an effective disaster mitigation strategy?
2. What are the four critical assumptions of an effective disaster communications strategy?
3. What are some of the ways FEMA director James Lee Witt exhibited his commitment to effective communications?
4. What is the goal of a media partnership?
5. Name and describe six basic emergency management audiences.
6. What are the two key elements of FEMA's crisis communications infrastructure?
7. For what is the joint information center used?
8. Describe two information dissemination methods used by FEMA.
9. What is the objective of communicating preparedness and mitigation messages to the public?
10. What eight steps are involved in behavior adoption identified by Dr. Mileti?
11. What are some of the issues and dilemmas facing risk communicators?
12. What has been the biggest development in the media world over the last 15 years?
13. How can the media serve as a partner to emergency managers?
14. Describe the following communications means and products and what they contribute to the management of emergencies: media lists and contacts, press releases, press conferences, press inquiries, Web sites, situation reports.

Out of Class Exercises

1. Using the Internet, library, or other information source, print out three articles that describe the same disaster event. Compare the three articles to determine which provides the most useful information to the reader in terms of immediate response and recovery information.
2. Go to your state office of emergency management's Web site. Print out disaster preparedness and mitigation guidance provided on that site. Critique this information with regards to how useful it is to you personally, and to the members of your community.

8

International Disaster Management

What You Will learn

- How developing nations are affected by disasters.
- Why and how national, international, and nongovernmental organizations assist countries that are affected by major disasters.
- Important issues that influence how international disasters are managed.
- How several of the United Nations components respond to disasters.
- The nongovernmental response to international disasters.
- Assistance provided by the United States government to other nations affected by disasters.
- Involvement of the international financial institutions, including the World Bank and the International Monetary Fund, in funding disaster response, relief, and reconstruction.

Introduction

People of all nations face risks associated with the natural and technological hazards described throughout this book, and almost all nations eventually become victim to disaster. Throughout history, civilizations have adapted to their surroundings in the hopes of increasing the likelihood of survival. As societies became more organized, complex systems of response to these hazards were developed on local, national, and regional levels. The capacity to respond achieved by individual nations can be linked to several factors, including propensity for disaster, local and regional economic resources, organization of government, and availability of technological, academic, and human resources; however, it is becoming increasingly common that the response ability of individual nations is insufficient in the face of large-scale disaster and outside assistance must be called upon. Disasters that affect whole regions are not uncommon and require these same international response mechanisms.

This chapter introduces the conglomeration of agencies, including the U.S. government, international organizations, nongovernmental organizations, and financial institutions, that prepare for and respond to the natural, technological, and complex humanitarian emergencies (CHEs) that overwhelm the capacity of any one sovereign nation. The mission and goals of each of these entities and groups is described (although their performance is not detailed). In conclusion, a comprehensive case study is presented on the international response to the Gujarat, India, earthquake of January 26, 2001.

Disasters in Developing Nations

Disasters of all kinds strike every nation of the world, although these events do not occur with uniformity of distribution. The developing nations suffer the greatest impact of nature's fury, and these nations also most often are subject to the internal civil conflict that leads to CHEs. Further, the greatest incidence of natural disasters occurs within developing countries, with 90 percent of disaster-related injuries and deaths sustained in countries with per-capita income levels below $760 per year (UNICEF).

Although disaster preparedness and mitigation are widely accepted by international development agencies to be integral components in the overall development process, it comes as no surprise that countries ranking lower on development indices have placed disaster management very low in budgetary priority. These nations' resources tend to be focused on more socially demanded interests, such as education and base infrastructure, or on their military, instead of on projects that serve a preparatory or mitigative need, such as retrofitting structures with hazard-resistant construction. Because disasters are chance events and therefore not guaranteed to happen, disaster management programs in poor countries tend to be viewed as superfluous. Delegating disaster management responsibilities to the military also commonly is seen, even in countries with a moderate level of development, although these agencies rarely are trained to carry out the necessary response tasks required. To compound the situation, poverty and uncontrolled urbanization often force large populations to concentrate in perilous, high-risk urban areas that contain little or no defense against disasters.

International Involvement

A disaster requires the involvement of the international community of responders when a nation's capability to respond has become overwhelmed. This threshold is determined by many factors, including the availability of economic resources, the level of local responder training, the resilience of the infrastructure, the public opinion of the government's ability to manage the crisis, and the availability of specialized assets, among many others. Of course, this threshold is crossed much earlier in the poorer countries. It must be recognized, however, that even the wealthiest nations regularly find themselves in need of help from the international community, whether for supplies, personnel, money, or a specific skill or asset that cannot be found locally. Appeals for assistance are made in many ways and often are met simultaneously with unsolicited offers of aid and support. With the global interconnectivity brought about through television and the Internet (the so-called CNN effect), news of a disaster can circle the globe within minutes, stirring the machine of response into action.

Three types of emergencies normally involve an international humanitarian response: natural disasters, technological disasters, and complex humanitarian emergencies. The first two are clearly defined; however, the CHEs have been subject to diverse interpretations and changing standards, and so, for the purposes of this book, are characterized by the definition established by the United Nations (UN). The UN classifies a CHE to be a "humanitarian crisis in a country or region where there is total or considerable breakdown of authority resulting from the internal and/or external conflict and which requires an international response that goes beyond the mandate or capacity of any single agency" (DoD CCRP, n.d.). Andrew Natsios, director of the U.S. Agency for International Development (USAID), identifies five characteristics most commonly seen in CHEs in varying degrees of intensity (Natsios, 1997):

1. Civil conflict, rooted in traditional ethnic, tribal, and religious animosities (usually accompanied by widespread atrocities).
2. Deteriorated authority of the national government such that public services disappear and political control dissolves.
3. Mass movements of population to escape conflict or search for food, resulting in refugees and internally displaced people (IDPs).
4. Massive dislocation of the economic system, resulting in hyperinflation and the devaluation of the currency, major declines in gross national product, skyrocketing unemployment, and market collapse.
5. A general decline in food security, often leading to severe malnutrition and occasional widespread starvation.

Although these emergencies are fundamentally different from natural and technological disasters in regards to their generally political and intentional sources, they share many characteristics in terms of their requirements for response and recovery. In accordance, many of the organizations and entities described in this chapter respond to all three types of disasters indiscriminately.

Important Issues Influencing the Response Process

Several issues must be addressed when responding to international disasters. The first, *coordination*, is a vital and immediate component because of the sheer numbers of responding agencies that almost always appear. It is not uncommon in larger disasters to see several hundred local and international NGOs, each with a particular skill or service to offer. Successful coordination and cooperation can lead to great success and many lives saved, but infighting, turf battles, and nonparticipation can lead to confusion and even cause a second disaster (Pan American Health Organization, n.d.).

The UN has become widely recognized as the central coordinating body, with specialized UN agencies handling the more specific needs associated with particular disaster consequences. Most often, the UN capitalizes on long-standing relationships with the host country to form a partnership in which they establish joint control. In addition to the UN, several organizations and associations have come up with standards of conduct, such as the Red Cross Code of Conduct (www.ifrc.org/publicat/conduct/index.asp), the Sphere Project Humanitarian Charter and Minimum Standards in Disaster Response (www.sphereproject.org/handbook_index.htm), and the Oxfam Code of Conduct for NGOs (www.oxfam.org).

The second issue is that of *sovereignty of the state*. State sovereignty is based on the recognition of political authority characterized by territory and autonomy. Accordingly, a foreign nation or organization cannot intercede in domestic matters without the prior consent of the ruling government. This can be a major hurdle in CHEs that resulted from civil war, such as the peacekeeping mission in Somalia, where no official government was in place with which to work. Although not as commonly seen, sovereignty also has been an issue in matters of natural and technological disasters, particularly when a nation does not want to be viewed as weak or unable to take care of its people. Examples of such behavior include Japan's refusal to allow access to international agencies for several days after the earthquake in Kobe and the actions of the former Soviet Union following the nuclear power plant accident in Chernobyl.

The third issue is *equality in relief distribution*, and it applies to any type of disaster. Situations often arise where, for any number of cultural or political reasons, certain groups in need of aid are favored over others. The first example of this discrimination is the result of gender bias, which is found most commonly in societies where gender roles are strictly defined and women are traditionally tasked with duties related to the home and children (which tend to be increased in times of crisis). In these cultures, the men are more likely to have opportunity to wait in relief lines for supplies, and the women (as well as children and the elderly) become even more dependent on them for survival. This situation is exacerbated if a woman is a widow or single parent and has no ability to compete for distributed aid.

The second form of inequality in relief is that of class bias. Although most obvious in social systems explicitly based on caste identity, underlying ethnic and racial divides often present similar problems. Avoiding these forms of bias is difficult because the agencies involved must be aware of the discrimination to counteract its influence. Often, host-country nationals are "hired" by humanitarian agencies to assist in relief distribution, and inadvertent hiring of specific ethnic or social groups can lead to unfair distribution along those same ethnic or social lines. At the same time, humanitarian agencies are quick to focus on those groups most visibly affected by a CHE, such as IDP populations, causing an inordinate percentage of aid to be directed to them, while other needy groups go unnoticed.

Many of the international response agencies are continuously developing systems of relief and distribution that work to counteract the complex problems associated with these biases; however, the difficult nature of this issue is highlighted in the fact that targeting specific groups, such as women or children, can lead to reverse discrimination. Any of these biases can lead to a decline in perceived legitimacy or impartiality of the assisting agency or result in exacerbation of the needs being addressed (Maynard, n.d.).

A fourth issue is the importance of *capacity building* and *linking relief with development*. Responding agencies have an obligation to avoid using a bandage approach in assisting the affected country. Disasters almost always present a window of opportunity to rebuild old, ineffective structures and develop policy and practice in a way that leaves behind a more empowered, resilient community. Because these goals mirror those of most traditional development agencies, linking relief and development should not be a major deviation from either type of agencies' missions. These opportunities are greatest in situations that require the complete restoration of infrastructure and basic social services and are found equally in disaster and CHE scenarios. In the reconstruction phase, it is vital that training and information exchanges occur and that local risk is fully incorporated to mitigate for repeat disasters. These repeat disasters often contribute greatly to a nation's lag in development and therefore fully addressing them is vital to increasing the nation's likelihood of being developed sustainably.

Critical Thinking

- Do problems associated with equality in distribution of relief occur only in developing countries or can they occur in any country? Can you find any examples of times when there has been inequality in relief distribution in the United States?
- Why is it imperative that relief be linked with development? Do you think that disaster relief makes recipient nations more dependent or more independent? Explain your answer.

The United Nations System

The UN began in 1945, when representatives from 51 countries met in San Francisco to establish the United Nations charter as a commitment to preserve peace in the aftermath of World War II. Later that year, the charter was ratified by the five permanent members—China, France, the Soviet Union, the United Kingdom, and the United States—as well as several other countries. Today, 189 countries are members of the UN, and the charter (which is similar to a sovereign state's constitution and establishes the rights and responsibilities of member states) is amended as is necessary to reflect the changing needs of current world politics.

The UN itself is not a government body nor does it write laws; however, the autonomous member states have the ability through the UN to resolve conflict and create international policy. No decision or action can be forced on a sovereign state, but as global ideals are naturally reflected through these collaborative policies, they usually are given due consideration.

Through the major UN bodies and their associated programs, the UN has established a presence in most countries throughout the world and fostered partnerships with member state governments. Although more than 70 percent of UN work is devoted to development activities, several other issues are central in their mission, including disaster mitigation, preparedness, response, and recovery. In the event of a disaster, the UN is quite possibly the organization best equipped to coordinate disaster relief and work with the governments to rehabilitate and reconstruct. This is especially true in the case of the developing countries, where regular projects are ongoing and must be adjusted to accommodate for damages to infrastructure and economy caused by recurrent disasters and where disasters quickly exhaust the response capabilities.

At the onset of a disaster, the UN responds immediately and on an ongoing basis by supplying aid in the form of food, shelter, medical assistance, and logistical support. The UN emergency relief coordinator heads the international UN response to crises through a committee of several humanitarian bodies, including the UN Children's Fund (UNICEF), the UN Development Programme (UNDP), the World Food Programme (WFP), the UN high commissioner for refugees (UNHCR), and other associates as deemed necessary in accordance with the problems specific to the event. Each of these agencies, as shown in this section, fulfills a specific need presented by most humanitarian emergencies, be they natural or human-made.

The UN also promotes prevention and mitigation activities through its regular development projects. By encouraging the building of early warning systems and the conducting monitoring and forecasting routines, it works to increase local capacity to adequately boost local and regional preparedness. In conclusion of the International Decade for Natural Disaster Reduction of the 1990s (which strove to focus on a shift from disaster response–oriented projects to disaster mitigation), the UN adopted its International Strategy for Disaster Reduction (ISDR) to promote the necessity of disaster reduction and risk mitigation as part of its central mission. This initiative seeks to enable global resilience to the effects of natural hazards to reduce human, economic, and social losses, through the following mechanisms:

- Increasing public awareness.
- Obtaining commitment from public authorities.
- Stimulating interdisciplinary and intersectoral partnership and expanding risk-reduction networking at all levels.
- Enhancing scientific research on the causes of natural disasters and the effects of natural hazards and related technological and environmental disasters on societies.

These strategies are carried out through the country offices and local governments in the most vulnerable communities. Mitigation and preparedness strategies are implemented at all levels of society via public awareness campaigns, secured commitment from public authorities, intersectoral cooperation and communication, and technical knowledge transfer.

The United Nations Development Programme

The UNDP was established in 1965 during the UN Decade of Development to conduct investigations into private investment in developing countries, explore the natural resources of those countries, and train the local population in development activities (such as mining and manufacturing). As the concept and practice of development expanded, the UNDP assumed much greater responsibilities in host countries and in the UN as a whole.

The UNDP was not originally considered an agency on the forefront of international disaster management and humanitarian emergencies, because while it addressed national capacities, it did not focus specifically on the emergency *response* systems (previously considered to be the focal point of disaster management). However, as mitigation and preparedness received their due merit, the UNDP gained increased recognition for its vital risk reduction role. Capacity building has always been central to the UNDP's mission in terms of empowering host countries to be better able to address issues of national importance, eventually without foreign assistance.

International disaster management gained greater attention as more disasters affected larger populations and caused greater financial impacts. Developing nations, where the UNDP worked, faced the greatest inability to prepare for and respond to these disasters. The UNDP's projects have shifted toward activities that indirectly fulfill mitigation and preparedness roles. For instance, projects seeking to strengthen government institutions also improve those institutions' capacities to respond with appropriate and effective policy, power, and leadership in the wake of a disaster.

The UNDP now recognizes that disaster management must be viewed as integral to its mission in the developing world, as well as to civil conflict and complex humanitarian emergency scenarios. As excerpts from the UNDP mission show, there are implicit similarities between UNDP ideals and those of agencies whose goals specifically aim to mitigate and manage humanitarian emergencies. For instance,

- The UNDP "is committed to the principle that development is inseparable from the quest for peace and human security and that the UN must be a strong force for development as well as peace."
- The "UNDP's mission is to help countries in their efforts to achieve sustainable human development by assisting them to build their capacity to design and carry out development programs in poverty eradication, employment creation and sustainable livelihoods, the empowerment of women and the protection and regeneration of the environment, giving first priority to poverty eradication."
- The "UNDP strives to be an effective development partner for the UN relief agencies, working to sustain livelihoods while they seek to sustain lives. It acts to help countries to prepare for, avoid and manage complex emergencies and disasters."
- The "UNDP supports [development] cooperation by actively promoting the exchange of experience among developing countries."

The UNDP links disaster vulnerability to a lack of or weak infrastructure, poor environmental policy, land misuse, and growing populations in disaster-prone areas. When disasters occur, a country's national development, which the UNDP serves to promote, can be set back years, if not decades. Even small- to medium-size disasters in the least developed countries can "have a cumulative impact on already fragile household economies and can be as significant in total losses as the major and internationally recognized disasters" (Southern African Regional Poverty Network, n.d.). The UNDP's objective is to "achieve a sustainable reduction in disaster risks and the protection of development gains, reduce the loss of life and livelihoods due to disasters, and ensure that disaster recovery serves to consolidate sustainable human development" (UNDP, "Vulnerability Reduction and Sustainable Development," n.d.).

In 1995, as part of the UN's changing approach to humanitarian relief, the Emergency Response Division (ERD) was created within the UNDP, augmenting the organization's role in disaster response. Additionally, 5 percent of the UNDP budgeted resources were allocated for quick response actions in special development situations by ERD teams, thus drastically reducing bureaucratic delays. The ERD was designed to create a collaborative framework among the national government, UN agencies, donors, and NGOs that immediately respond to disasters; provide communication and travel to disaster management staff members; and distribute relief supplies and equipment. It also will deploy ERD teams to disaster-affected countries for 30 days to create a detailed response plan on which the UNDP response will be based.

In 1997, under the UN Programme for Reform, the mitigation and preparedness responsibilities of the Office for the Coordination of Humanitarian Affairs emergency relief coordinator were formally transferred to the UNDP. In response, the UNDP created the Disaster Reduction and Recovery Programme (DRRP) within the ERD. Soon after, the UNDP again reorganized, creating a Bureau of Crisis Prevention and Recovery (BCPR) with an overarching mission of addressing a range of non-response-related issues:

- Natural disaster reduction.
- Recovery.
- Mine action.
- Conflict prevention and peace building.
- Justice and security sector reform.
- Small arms and demobilization.

The BCPR helps the UNDP country offices prepare to activate and provide faster and more effective disaster response and recovery. It also works to ensure that the UNDP plays an active role in the transition between relief and development. The UNDP's disaster management activities focus primarily on the development-related aspects of risk and vulnerability and on capacity-building technical assistance in all four phases of emergency management. It emphasizes

- Incorporating long-term risk reduction and preparedness measures in normal development planning and programs, including support for specific mitigation measures where required.
- Assisting in the planning and implementation of postdisaster rehabilitation and reconstruction, including defining new development strategies that incorporate risk reduction measures relevant to the affected area.
- Reviewing the impact of large settlements of refugees or displaced persons on development and seeking ways to incorporate the refugees and displaced persons in development strategies.
- Providing technical assistance to the authorities managing major emergency assistance operations of extended duration (especially in relation to displaced persons and the possibilities for achieving durable solutions in such cases).

The UNDP created the Disaster Reduction Unit (DRU) within the BCPR, which includes a team of seven Geneva-based officials and four regional disaster reduction advisors located in Bangkok, Nairobi, New Delhi, and Panama. The DRU works to reduce disaster risk and increase sustainable recovery in countries where the UNDP operates. It strengthens national and regional capacities by ensuring that new development projects consider known hazard risks, disaster impacts are mitigated and development gains protected, and risk reduction is factored into disaster recovery. The DRU provides the UNDP country offices with technical assistance and financial support for the design and implementation of disaster reduction strategies and capacity-building programs to carry out these goals. The DRU focuses support to developing countries in the following areas:

- Increasing capacity for disaster risk reduction.
- Mainstreaming disaster risk reduction into development.
- Increasing investment in disaster risk reduction.

The UNDP Recovery Unit

Following conflict, crises, and disasters, countries eventually (and as quickly as possible) must make the transition from response to recovery. Many countries are unable to manage the difficult and diverse needs of recovery on their own, as they may have experienced widespread loss of infrastructure and services. Displaced persons and refugees may have little to return to, and economies may be damaged or destroyed. The Recovery Unit (under the BCPR) operates during the period when the response or relief phase of the disaster has ended but recovery has not fully commenced (sometimes referred to as the *early recovery period*).

The Recovery Unit addresses problems normally encountered in this postcrisis period through its Transition Recovery Programme. This program works to restore government and community capacities to rebuild and recover to prevent a return to a crisis situation. Sustainable risk reduction as a component of recovery is central to this mission. The UNDP recognizes that local expertise in risk management and reduction may not be available and the technical assistance it provides may be the only option these communities have to increase their resilience to future disasters. This program has proven effective in many recovery operations, including Cambodia after three decades of civil war, Afghanistan after the 2001 conflict, and Gujarat, India, after the 2001 earthquake. Specific activities of the UNDP Recovery Unit include

- Performing early assessments of recovery needs and designing integrated recovery frameworks.
- Planning and assistance in area-based development and local governance programs.
- Developing comprehensive reintegration programs for former IDPs, returning refugees, and ex-combatants.
- Supporting economic recovery both at the local and national levels.
- Supporting in-country capacity building, UN system coordination, resource mobilization, and partnerships.

To meet these recovery priorities, five support services have been developed within the Recovery Unit to assist the UNDP country offices and other UNDP and UN agencies identify areas where the BCPR and the Recovery Unit can provide assistance. These support services include

1. *Early assessment of recovery needs and the design of integrated recovery frameworks.* This includes assessing development losses caused by conflict or natural disaster, the need for socioeconomic and institutional recovery, identification of local partners, and the need for capacity building and technical assistance.
2. *Planning and assistance in area-based development and local governance programs.* Area-based development and local governance programs play key roles in recovery from conflict because they tailor emergency, recovery, and development issues across a country area by area, based on differing needs and opportunities. Area-based development helps bring together different actors at the operational level, promoting enhanced coordination, coherence, and impact at the field level. Area-based development is often seen as the core mechanism that most benefits reintegration.
3. *Developing comprehensive reintegration programs for internally displaced persons, returning refugees, and ex-combatants.* Internally displaced people, returning refugees, and demobilized former combatants create a huge need for in-country capacity building on different levels. Protection and security becomes a serious issue, and efforts to sustainably reintegrate these populations into their host communities are critical. The Recovery Unit provides expertise on

reintegration of IDPs, returnees, and ex-combatants, including capacity building benefiting both the returnees and formerly displaced as well as their host communities through activities such as income generation, vocational training, and other revitalization activities.

4. *Supporting economic recovery and revitalization.* One main characteristic of disasters and conflict is their devastating impact on the local and national economies. Livelihoods are destroyed through insecurity, unpredictability, market collapse, loss of assets, and rampant inflation. For recovery to achieve success, these issues need to be well understood from the outset and addressed accordingly.

5. *Supporting capacity building, coordination, resource mobilization, and partnerships.* Protracted conflict and extreme disasters tend to create political stressors that temporarily exceed the capacities of UN country offices and NGO partners. However, many recovery needs must be addressed right away to ensure that recovery sets out on a sustainable course. The Recovery Unit offers several services to accommodate the needs of this intense phase through the provision of surge capacity and short- to medium-term staff members, assistance in resource mobilization within specific fund-raising and coordination frameworks (such as the consolidated appeals process), and partnership building.

When required to assist in recovery operations, the Recovery Unit may deploy a special transition recovery team to supplement the UNDP operations in the affected country. The focus of these teams varies according to specific needs. For instance, when neighboring countries have interlinked problems (such as cross-border reintegration of ex-combatants and displaced persons), the transition recovery team may support a sub-regional approach to recovery.

It is important to note that the UNDP has no primary role in the middle of a CHE peacekeeping response; rather it fulfills a supportive role by ensuring development is tied to relief. During recovery and reconstruction, together with others, it takes the lead. In addition to the aforementioned roles and responsibilities, the UNDP leads several interagency working groups. One such group (which consists of representatives from the World Food Programme, the World Health Organization, the Food and Agriculture Organization, the UN Populations Fund, and the UN International Children's Emergency Relief Fund) develops principles and guidelines to incorporate disaster risk into the common country assessment and the UN development assistance framework. The International Strategy for Disaster Reduction Working Group on Risk, Vulnerability and Disaster Impact Assessment sets guidelines for social impact assessments. The UNDP also coordinates a Disaster Management Training Programme in Central America, runs the conference "The Use of Microfinance and Micro-Credit for the Poor in Recovery and Disaster Reduction," and created a program to elaborate financial instruments to enable the poor to manage disaster risks.

The UNDP has several reasons for its success in fulfilling its roles in the mitigation, preparedness, and recovery for natural and human-made disasters. First, as a permanent in-country office with close ties to most government agencies, activities related to coordination and planning, monitoring, and training are simply an extension of ongoing relationships. The UNDP works in the country before, during, and long after the crisis. It is able to harness vast, firsthand knowledge about the situations leading up to a crisis and the capacity of the government and civil institutions to handle a crisis and can analyze what weaknesses must be addressed by the responding aid agencies. In addition, its neutrality dispels fears of political bias.

Second, the UNDP functions as a coordinating body of the UN agencies concerned with development, so when crisis situations appear, there is an established, stable platform from which it may lead. From this leadership vantage, (theoretically) it can assist in stabilizing incoming relief programs of other responding UN bodies, such as the World Food Programme, the UN International Children's Emergency Fund, the Department of Humanitarian Affairs, and the UN high commissioner for refugees. Once the emergency phase of the disaster has ended and the Office for the Coordination of Humanitarian Affairs prepares to leave, the UNDP is in a prime position to facilitate the transition from response efforts to long-term recovery.

Third, the UNDP has experience dealing with donors, be they foreign governments or development banks, and therefore can handle the outpouring of aid that usually results during the relief and recovery period of a disaster. This contributes greatly to reducing levels of corruption and increasing the cost-effectiveness of generated funds. In several recent events, the UNDP established formalized funds to handle large donor contributions, which have been used for long-term postdisaster reconstruction efforts.

When a major disaster operation requires extended efforts, the UNDP may accept and administer special extra-budgetary contributions to provide the national government with both technical and material assistance, in coordination with the Office for the Coordination of Humanitarian Affairs and other agencies involved in the UN disaster management team (DMT). An example of such assistance includes the establishment and administration of a UN DMT Emergency Information and Coordination Support Unit. Special grants of up to $1.1 million also may be provided, allocated from special program resources funds for technical assistance to recovery efforts following natural disasters.

The United Nations Office for the Coordination of Humanitarian Affairs

Prior to 1991, the UN disaster relief coordinator managed natural disasters, and special representatives of the UN secretary general coordinated CHEs. However, UN Resolution 46/182, adopted in December 1991, merged these two roles to reside in the emergency relief coordinator (ERC). The Department of Humanitarian Affairs was created soon after, with the ERC elevated to the status of undersecretary general for humanitarian affairs. The UN Office for the Coordination of Humanitarian Affairs (OCHA) replaced the Department of Humanitarian Affairs under the UN Secretary General's Program for Reform in 1998. OCHA was established to accommodate the needs of victims of disasters and emergencies, with its specific role in disaster management the coordination of assistance provided by the UN system (in emergencies that exceed the capacity and mandate of any individual agency). OCHA response to disasters can be categorized under three main groupings:

1. Coordinating the international humanitarian response.
2. Providing support and policy development to the humanitarian community.
3. Advocating for humanitarian issues to ensure that the overall direction of relief reflects the general needs of recovery and peace building.

OCHA operations are carried out by a staff of approximately 860 people in New York, Geneva, and in the field. OCHA's 2005 budget was $110,551,973, of which only slightly more than 10 percent was from the regular UN budget. The remaining 90 percent is from "extra-budgetary resources," primarily donations from member states and donor organizations.

As head of OCHA, the undersecretary general for humanitarian affairs/UN emergency relief coordinator is responsible for the coordination of UN response efforts through the Inter-Agency Standing Committee (IASC). The IASC consists of UN and outside humanitarian organization leaders and analyzes crisis scenarios to formulate joint responses that maximize effectiveness and minimize overlap. The ERC works to deploy appropriate personnel from throughout the UN to assist UN resident coordinators and lead agencies to increase on-site coordination. In September 2003, the secretary general appointed Jan Egeland of Norway to replace Kenzo Oshima of Japan as undersecretary general for humanitarian affairs/UN emergency relief coordinator.

OCHA's Disaster Response System monitors the onset of natural and technological disasters. This system includes training assessment teams before disasters strike as well as conducts postdisaster evaluations. When a disaster is identified, the OCHA activates a response and generates a situation report to provide the international response community with detailed information (including damage assessment, actions taken, needs assessment, and current assistance provided). If necessary, OCHA may then deploy a UN disaster assessment and coordination team to assist relief activity coordination and assess damages and needs.

If a disaster appears inevitable or is already significant, the ERC in consultation with the IASC may designate a humanitarian coordinator (HC), who becomes the most senior UN humanitarian official on the ground for the emergency. The HC is directly accountable to the ERC, thereby increasing the likelihood that the humanitarian assistance provided is quick, effective, and well coordinated. The HC appointment generally signals that the event merits a long-term humanitarian presence. The criteria used by the ERC in deciding whether to appoint an HC is based on recognition of a need for

- Intensive and extensive political management, mediation, and coordination to enable the delivery of humanitarian response, including negotiated access to affected populations.
- Massive humanitarian assistance requiring action by a range of participants beyond a single national authority.
- A high degree of external political support, often from the UN Security Council.

An On-Site Operations Coordination Center may be set up in the field to assist local first response teams to coordinate the often overwhelming number of responding agencies. Finally, the OCHA can set up communications capabilities if they have been damaged or do not exist at an adequate level, as required by the UN responding agencies. The OCHA generally concludes its responsibilities when the operation moves from response to recovery.

Overall, the OCHA coordinates humanitarian affairs to maximize response and recovery operations and minimize duplications and inefficiencies through established structures and policies set forth by the IASC (adapted from OCHA, 2005):

- **Developing common strategies.** The OCHA recognizes that humanitarian assistance is most effective when those involved set common priorities, share goals, agree on tactics, and jointly monitor progress. The OCHA works with both internal and external partners to develop a common humanitarian action plan and establish clear divisions of responsibility.
- **Assessing situations and needs.** Throughout a crisis, the OCHA is responsible for identifying overall humanitarian needs, developing a realistic plan of action for meeting these needs (avoiding duplication), and monitoring progress. It must adjust its response if necessary and analyze any resulting changes. Ongoing analysis of political, social, economic, and military environments and assessing humanitarian needs help response and recovery agencies to better understand disasters' causes and effects.
- **Convening coordination forums.** In its role as coordinator, the OCHA holds a wide range of meetings to bring together the various disaster management players for planning and information exchange. These meetings help the participants to more accurately analyze the overall status of humanitarian relief efforts as well as network and share lessons learned and best practices.
- **Mobilizing resources.** Through the consolidated appeals process, the OCHA is able to raise humanitarian assistance funds cost-effectively. Allocation of funds has been found to be more efficient within this centralized system.
- **Addressing common problems.** Because every crisis is unique, both new and old problems are bound to arise. These issues may affect several agencies and NGOs but also might exist outside of any particular agency's mandate. As coordinator, the OCHA analyzes and addresses problems common to humanitarian actors, such as negotiating with warring parties to gain access to civilians in need or working with UN security officials to support preparedness and response measures in changing security situations.
- **Administering coordination mechanisms and tools.** The OCHA and the UN in general have several tools with which they can better address the humanitarian needs of disaster victims. These include the IASC; rapid-response tools, such as the UN disaster assessment and coordination teams and the International Search and Rescue Advisory Group; and smaller forums such as the geographic information support team. The OCHA also assists with civil/military cooperation, ensuring a more efficient use of military and civil defense assets in humanitarian operations.

The Field Coordination Support Unit in Geneva manages the human, technical, and logistical resources the OCHA uses. These resources are primarily provided by the Danish and Norwegian Refugee Councils, the Danish Emergency Management Agency, the Swedish Rescue Services Agency, and the emergency logistics management team of the United Kingdom Overseas Development Administration.

The Emergency Relief Coordinator

The undersecretary general for humanitarian affairs/emergency relief coordinator advises the UN secretary general on disaster-related issues, chairs the Executive Committee on Humanitarian Affairs, and leads the IASC. The coordinator is assisted by a deputy emergency relief coordinator, who is responsible for key coordination, policy, and management issues.

The Inter-Agency Standing Committee

The IASC was established in 1992 under UN Resolution 46/182. It serves as a platform within which the broad range of UN and non-UN humanitarian partners (including UN humanitarian agencies, the International Organization for Migration, three consortia of major international NGOs, and the Red Cross movement) may come together to address the humanitarian needs resulting from a disaster. The IASC's primary role is to formulate humanitarian policy that ensures a coordinated and effective response to all kinds of disaster and emergency situations. The primary objectives of the IASC are to (OCHA, 2005)

- Develop and agree on systemwide humanitarian policies.
- Allocate responsibilities among agencies in humanitarian programs.
- Develop and agree on a common ethical framework for all humanitarian activities.
- Advocate common humanitarian principles to parties outside the IASC.
- Identify areas where gaps in mandates or lack of operational capacity exist.
- Resolve disputes or disagreements about and between humanitarian agencies on systemwide humanitarian issues.

IASC members (both full members and standing invitees) include

- Food and Agriculture Organization.
- InterAction.
- International Committee of the Red Cross.
- International Council of Voluntary Agencies.
- International Federation of Red Cross and Red Crescent Societies.
- International Organization for Migration.
- Office for the Coordination of Humanitarian Affairs.
- Office of the High Commissioner for Human Rights.
- Office of the Special Representative of the Secretary General on Internally Displaced Persons.
- Steering Committee for Humanitarian Response.
- The World Bank.
- United Nations Children's Fund.
- United Nations Development Fund.
- United Nations High Commissioner for Refugees.
- United Nations Population Fund.
- World Food Programme.
- World Health Organization.

The Executive Committee on Humanitarian Affairs

The Executive Committee on Humanitarian Affairs (ECHA) was created by the UN secretary general to enhance coordination among UN agencies working on humanitarian affairs issues. ECHA meets on a monthly basis in New York to add a political and peacekeeping dimension to humanitarian consultations. Its members include

- United Nations Development Program.
- United Nations Children's Fund.

- United Nations High Commission for Refugees.
- World Food Programme.
- Office of the High Commissioner for Human Rights.
- Department of Peacekeeping Operations.
- Department of Political Affairs.
- United Nations Relief and Works Agency for Palestine Refugees in the Near East.
- Office of the Special Representative of the Secretary General for Children and Armed Conflicts.
- World Health Organization.
- Food and Agriculture Organization.

The OCHA Donor Relations Section

The OCHA Donor Relations Section, separated from the consolidated appeals process in 2003, is the focal point for all relations with donors, particularly for funding-related issues. It advises the senior management team on policy issues related to interaction with donors and resource mobilization. In addition, it plays a key role in facilitating the interaction of all OCHA entities with donors, both at headquarters and in the field level.

The Coordination and Response Division

The Coordination and Response Division was created in 2004 by joining the former New York–based Humanitarian Emergency Branch and the Geneva–based Response Coordination Branch. It is responsible for providing disaster-related direction, guidance, and support to the ERC, the UN resident/humanitarian coordinators, and OCHA's field offices (including the deployment of extra personnel as necessary or emergency cash grants).

The OCHA Emergency Services Branch

Based in Geneva, the OCHA Emergency Services Branch was created to expedite the provision of international humanitarian assistance. The branch develops, mobilizes, and coordinates the deployment of OCHA's international rapid response "toolkit"—the expertise, systems, and services that aim to improve humanitarian assistance in support of disaster-afflicted countries. Its humanitarian response activities include the coordination of disaster response and assessment, the setting of international urban search and rescue standards, and the establishment of on-site operations coordination centers. The branch supports OCHA field offices through the following:

- Surge capacity and standby partnerships.
- Military and civil liaison and mobilization of military and civil defense assets.
- Dispatch of relief supplies and specialized assistance in environmental emergencies.
- Dissemination of disaster-related information by means of ReliefWeb, the Central Register of Disaster Management Capacities, and the Virtual On-Site Operations Coordination Center. Within the ESB are three sections, established to manage particular aspects of disaster response:

○ Field Coordination Support Section.
○ Military and Civil Defense and Logistics Support Section.
○ Environmental Emergencies Section.

The **Field Coordination Support Section** was established within the Emergency Services Branch in 1996 to support national governments and the UN resident coordinators in developing, preparing, and maintaining "standby capacity" for rapid deployment to sudden-onset emergencies to conduct rapid needs assessments and coordination. The section manages several programs and offices to improve international disaster coordination and cooperation, including

- **The United Nations Disaster Assessment and Coordination Team.** The team is made up of disaster management specialists selected and funded by the governments of UN member states, OCHA, UNDP, and operational humanitarian UN agencies (such as WFP, UNICEF, and WHO). It provides rapid needs assessments and supports national authorities and the UN resident coordinator in coordinating international relief. These teams are on permanent standby status so that they can deploy within hours.
- **The International Search and Rescue Advisory Group.** This is an intergovernmental network within the UN that manages urban search and rescue and related disaster response issues. It promotes information exchange, defines international urban search and rescue standards, and develops methodologies for international cooperation and coordination in earthquake response.
- **The Virtual On-Site Operations Coordination Center.** The Internet has made it possible for humanitarian relief agencies to share and exchange disaster information continuously and simultaneously and between any locations where Internet access can be obtained. The virtual On-Site Operations Coordination Center is a central repository of information maintained by OCHA that facilitates this exchange of information with NGOs and responding governments. The information is stored on an interactive Web-based database, where users can comment on existing information and discuss issues of concern with other stakeholders.
- **The Surge Capacity Project (including the Emergency Response Roster).** OCHA's Surge Capacity Project seeks to ensure that OCHA always has the means and resources to rapidly mobilize and deploy staff members and materials to address the needs of countries affected by sudden-onset emergencies. The Emergency Response Roster, which became active in June 2002, aims to rapidly deploy OCHA staff members to sudden-onset emergencies to conduct assessments and establish initial coordination mechanisms. Staff members included in the roster are deployable within 48 hours of a request for their services through a deployment methodology based on the UN disaster and coordination model. Staff members serve on the roster for two months at a time.

Established by the IASC in 1995, the **Military and Civil Defense Unit** supports humanitarian agencies by providing military and civil defense assets. The unit conducts civil/military coordination courses and coordinates UN participation in major humanitarian emergency exercises. The unit also maintains the UN's central register, a database of noncommercial, government, and other resources that may be called on for humanitarian response and includes a full range of equipment and supplies, teams of experts, and disaster response contacts.

The **Logistics Support Unit** manages stocks of basic relief items that can be dispatched immediately to disaster- or emergency-stricken areas. The stockpile, which is located at the UN Humanitarian Response Depot in Brindisi, Italy, includes nonfood, nonmedical relief items (such as shelter, water purification and distribution systems, and household items) donated by UN member governments. The unit also is involved in other logistical challenges, such as designing contingency plans for the rapid deployment of emergency relief flights and providing interface on logistical matters with other humanitarian agencies (such as World Food Program, WHO, UNHCR, and the International Red Cross). The unit participates in the operation of a UN Joint Logistics Center and has cosponsored an effort to adopt a UN-wide system for tracking relief supplies and common procedures for air operations. Finally, the unit contributes information to the Cognizant Regional Representative (CRR) related to stockpiles and customs facilitation agreements (which helps speed up the delivery of relief items).

The **Environmental Emergencies Section,** or the Joint UN Environmental Programme/OCHA Environment Unit, serves as the integrated UN emergency response mechanism that provides international assistance to countries experiencing environmental disasters and emergencies. The joint unit can rapidly mobilize and coordinate emergency assistance and response resources to countries facing environmental emergencies and natural disasters with significant environmental impacts. The unit performs several key functions geared toward facilitating rapid and coordinated disaster response, including

- **Monitoring.** The unit performs continuous monitoring and ongoing communication with an international network of contacts and permanent monitoring of news services and Web sites for early notification of environmental occurrences.
- **Notification.** When disasters strike, the unit alerts the international community and issues information and situation reports to a comprehensive list of worldwide contacts.
- **Brokerage.** The unit is able to quickly establish contact between the affected country and donor governments ready and willing to assist and provide needed response resources.
- **Information clearinghouse.** The unit serves as an effective focal point to ensure information on chemicals, maps, and satellite images from donor sources and institutions are channeled to relevant authorities in the affected country.
- **Mobilization of assistance.** The unit mobilizes assistance from the international donor community when requested by affected countries.
- **Assessment.** The unit can dispatch international experts to assess an emergency's impacts and make impartial and independent recommendations about response, cleanup, remediation, and rehabilitation.
- **Financial assistance.** In certain circumstances, the unit can release OCHA emergency cash grants of up to $50,000 to meet immediate emergency response needs.

OCHA Preparedness and Mitigation Measures

Although OCHA's efforts focus primarily on coordinating humanitarian emergency response, the agency also serves a risk-reduction function. For instance, OCHA representatives work with operational humanitarian agencies to develop common policies aimed at improving how the humanitarian response network prepares for and responds to disasters. It also works to promote preparedness and mitigation efforts in member states to decrease vulnerability. The Coordination and Response Division and Emergency Services Branch work closely with the UN Development Programme, other UN programs as necessary, and outside organizations on various projects and activities to increase working relationships with national governments and apply lessons learned from completed disaster responses.

OCHA's Geneva offices continually monitor geologic and meteorological conditions, as well as major news services, for early recognition or notification of emerging disasters. Working with UN resident coordinators, country teams, and regional disaster response advisers, OCHA maintains close contact with disaster-prone countries in advance of and during disaster events. OCHA's regional disaster response advisers work with national governments to provide technical, strategic, and training assistance. They also provide this assistance to other UN agencies and regional organizations to improve international disaster management capacity.

OCHA Information Tools and Services

Clearly, information is key to disaster management, and information must be timely and accurate to be useful. This is especially true in the case of early warning and disaster prevention initiatives. OCHA maintains several information management activities in support of its humanitarian efforts and provides systems to collect, analyze, disseminate, and exchange information. These functions are performed jointly by the Early Warning and Contingency Planning Unit, the ReliefWeb project, the Field Information Support Project, and the Integrated Regional Information Networks.

Department of Economic and Social Affairs (DESA)

The Department of Economic and Social Affairs (DESA) is another component within the secretariat that addresses disaster management, primarily in regard to predisaster capacity building. The DESA addresses a full range of issues under three general areas:

1. It compiles, generates, and analyzes a wide range of economic, social, and environmental data and information from which member states draw to review common problems and evaluate policy options.
2. It facilitates the negotiations of member states in many intergovernment bodies on joint courses of action to address ongoing or emerging global challenges.
3. It advises national governments on translating UN-developed policy frameworks into country-level programs and, through technical assistance, helps build national capacities.

The final area where DESA addresses disaster management activities is within its Division for Sustainable Development. As part of this effort, DESA launched a plan of action during the 2002 World Summit on Sustainable Development in Johannesburg, South Africa, that included commitments to disaster and vulnerability reduction.

The UN Centre for Regional Development is another component of DESA that addresses disaster management issues. Through its headquarters in Nagoya, Japan, and its regional offices in Nairobi, Kenya, and Bogotá, Colombia, the center supports training and research on regional development issues and facilitates information dissemination and exchange. It maintains a Disaster Management Planning Office in Hyogo, Japan, that studies and develops community-based, sustainable projects for disaster management planning and capacity building in developing countries. The Hyogo office also runs the Global Earthquake Safety Initiative, designed to improve risk recognition and reduction in 21 cities around the world, and the Patanka New Life Plan, which provides affordable risk reduction means for the earthquake-stricken communities in Gujarat, India (where an earthquake killed over 20,000 people in 2001).

The Regional Commissions

Five regional economic commissions are part of the Economic and Social Council. The secretariats of these regional commissions are part of the UN secretariat and perform many of the same functions (including the disaster management functions listed previously). The five commissions promote greater economic cooperation in the world and augment economic and social development. As part of their mission, they initiate and manage projects that focus on disaster management. While their projects deal primarily with disaster preparedness and mitigation, they also work in regions that have been affected by a disaster to ensure that economic and social recovery involves adequate consideration of risk reduction measures. The five regional commissions are

- The Economic and Social Commission for Asia and the Pacific—www.unescap.org.
- The Economic Commission for Latin America and the Caribbean—www.eclac.cl.
- The Economic Commission for Europe—www.unece.org.
- The Economic Commission for Africa—www.uneca.org.
- The Economic and Social Commission for Western Asia—www.escwa.org.lb.

The United Nations Children's Fund

Like most other major UN agencies, the UN Children's Fund (UNICEF, formerly known as the United Nations International Children's Emergency Fund) was established in the aftermath of World War II. Its original mandate was to aid the children suffering in postwar Europe, but its mission has been expanded to address the problems that affect poor children throughout the world. UNICEF is mandated by the General Assembly to serve as an advocate for children's rights, ensure that each child receives at least the minimum requirements for survival, and increase their opportunities for a successful future. Under the Convention on the Rights of the Child, a treaty adopted by 191 countries, the UNHCR holds wide-reaching legal authority to carry out its mission.

Before the onset of disasters, it is not uncommon for UNICEF to have established itself as a permanent in-country presence, with regular budgetary resources. In the situations of disaster or armed conflict where this is the case, UNICEF is well poised to serve an immediate role as aid provider to its specific target groups. This rapid response is important because young mothers and children often are the most marginalized groups in terms of aid received. UNICEF works on a regular basis to ensure that children have access to education, health care, safety, and protected child rights. In the response and recovery periods of humanitarian emergencies, these roles are merely expanded to suit the rapidly extended requirements of victims. In countries where UNICEF has not yet established a permanent presence, the form of aid is virtually the same; however, the timing and delivery are affected and reconstruction is not nearly as comprehensive.

UNICEF maintains that humanitarian assistance should include programs aimed specifically for child victims. Relief projects generally work to provide a rapidly needed response in the form of immunizations, water and sanitation, nutrition, education, and health. Women are recipients of this aid as well because UNICEF considers them to be vital in the care of children. UNICEF also works through recovery and reconstruction projects, providing for the basic rights of children. UNICEF is currently working in 161 countries.

The World Food Programme

The World Food Programme is the arm of the UN tasked with reacting to hunger-related emergencies throughout the developing world. The WFP was created late in 1961 by a resolution adopted by the UN General Assembly and the UN Food and Agriculture Organization. Chance enabled the program to prove the necessity of its existence when the WFP provided relief to more than 5 million people several months before they were deemed officially operational in 1963. In the year 2000 alone, the WFP fed 83 million people through its relief programs. Over the course of its existence, the WFP has provided more than 43 million metric tons of food to countries worldwide.

Because food is a necessity for human survival, it is a vital component of development. The WFP works throughout the world to assist the poor who do not have sufficient food to survive "to break the cycle of hunger and poverty." Hunger alone can be seen as a crisis because more than 800 million people across the globe receive less than the minimum standard requirement of food for healthy survival. Hunger often is associated with other crises, including drought, famine, and human displacement.

In rapid-onset events such as natural disasters, the WFP is activated as a major player in the response to the immediate nutritional needs of the victims. Food is transported to the affected location and delivered to storage and distribution centers. The distribution is carried out according to preestablished needs assessments performed by OCHA and the UNDP. The WFP distributes food through contracted NGOs, which have vast experience and technical skills required to plan and implement such projects of transportation, storage, and distribution. The principal partners in their planning and implementation are the host governments (which must request the aid of the WFP to begin with, unless the situation is a CHE where there is no established government and the UN secretary general makes the request). The WFP works closely with all responding UN agencies to coordinate an effective and broad-reaching response because food requirements are so closely linked to every other vital need of disaster victims.

In the aftermath of disasters, during the reconstruction phase, it often is necessary for the WFP to remain an active player through continued food distribution. Rehabilitation projects are implemented in a way that fosters increased local development and include providing food aid to families, who as a result have extra money to use in rebuilding their lives, and food for work programs, which break the chains of reliance on aid as well as provide an incentive to rebuild communities.

The World Health Organization

The idea for the World Health Organization (WHO) was proposed during the original meetings to establish the UN system in San Francisco in 1945. In 1946, at the United Health Conference in New York, the WHO constitution was approved, and on April 7 (World Health Day), it was signed and made official. Like the WFP, the WHO proved its value by responding to an emergency (a cholera epidemic in Egypt) months before it was an officially recognized organization.

The WHO was established to serve as the central authority on sanitation and health issues throughout the world. It works with national governments to develop medical capabilities and health care and assist in the suppression of epidemics. The WHO supports research for the eradication of disease and provides expertise on these subjects when requested. It provides training and technical support and develops standards for medical care.

In the event of a disaster, the WHO responds in several ways that address the health of victims. Most important, it provides ongoing monitoring of diseases traditionally observed within the unsanitary conditions of disaster aftermath. The WHO also provides technical assistance to the responding agencies and host governments that are establishing disaster medical capabilities and serves as a constant source of expertise as needs arise.

Since its inception, regional offices have been established. These offices, which make up the 191 separate member states of WHO, focus on the health issues most directly related to each regional area's needs and concerns. These regions include the following:

- African Regional Office.
- Pan American Health Organization.
- South-East Asia Regional Office.
- Regional Office for Europe.
- Eastern-Mediterranean Regional Office.

Critical Thinking

Is the United Nations the organization best suited to coordinate the response to international disasters? Why or why not? If not, who do you believe should be tasked with coordination?

Nongovernmental Organizations

The number of nongovernmental organizations focusing on international humanitarian relief has grown exponentially in the past few decades. These organizations have come to play a vital role in the response and recovery to disasters, filling gaps left by national and multilateral organizations. They significantly improved the ability of international relief efforts to address the needs of victims with a diverse range of skills and supplies. Some of the larger NGOs, like the International Committee of the Red Cross (ICRC), established an international presence similar to that of the UN and developed strong local institutional partnerships and a capacity to respond almost immediately with great effectiveness. These grassroots-level organizations are so successful in their activities that the major funding organizations, such as USAID, OFDA, and the UN, regularly arrange for relief projects to be implemented by them rather than their own staff.

There are several classifications of humanitarian organizations, and for the purpose of clarification, they are described as follows. The following broad categorical definitions are widely accepted among the agencies of the international relief community. These are not definitive categories into which each organization will fit neatly, but they have become part of standardized nomenclature in disaster response:

- *Nongovernmental organization.* The general term for an organization made up of private citizens, with no affiliation with a government of any nation other than the support from government sources in the form of financial or in-kind contributions. These groups are motivated by greatly varying factors, ranging from religious belief to humanitarian values. NGOs are considered national if they work in one country, international if they are based out of one country but work in more than four countries, and multinational if they have partner organizations in several countries. Oxfam and the ICRC are examples of multinational NGOs. NGOs can be further defined according to their functionality. Examples of these would be the religious groups, such as the Catholic Church; interest groups, such as Rotary International; residents' organizations; occupational organizations; educational organizations; and so on.
- *Private voluntary organization (PVO).* An organization that is nonprofit, tax-exempt, and receives at least a part of its funding from private donor sources. PVOs also receive some degree of voluntary contributions in the form of cash, work, or in-kind gifts. This classification is steadily being grouped together under the more general NGO classification. It should be mentioned that, although all PVOs are NGOs, the opposite is not true.
- *International organization (IO).* An organization with global presence and influence. Although both the UN and ICRC are IOs, only the ICRC could be considered an NGO. International law provides a legal framework under which these organizations can function.
- *Donor agencies.* Private, national, or regional organizations whose mission is to provide the financial and material resources for humanitarian relief and subsequent rehabilitation. These donated resources may go to other NGOs, other national governments, or to private citizens. Examples of donor agencies are USAID, the European Community Humanitarian Organization, and the World Bank.
- *Coordinating organizations.* Associations of NGOs that coordinate the activities of hundreds of preregistered member organizations to ensure response with maximized impact. They can decrease the amount of overlap and help distribute need to the greatest range of victims. Also, they have the ability to analyze immediate needs assessments and recommend which member organizations would be most effective in response. Examples of coordinating organizations include InterAction and the International Council for Voluntary Agencies.

NGOs bring to the field several resources. First, they are well regarded as information-gathering bodies and thus are vital in establishing accuracy in the development of damage and needs assessments. They tend to provide a single skill or group of specific technical skills, such as the medical abilities of Medicin sans Frontiers (Doctors without Borders) or Oxfam's ability to address nutritional needs. The sheer number of helping bodies that are provided by the involvement of NGOs allows for a greater capability to reach a larger population in less time. Finally, the amount of financial support provided as result of the fund-raising abilities of NGOs brings about much greater cash resources to address the needs of victims.

These organizations can be characterized by several commonly seen characteristics (Center for Disaster Management and Humanitarian Assistance, n.d.):

1. *They value their independence and neutrality.* In situations of civil conflict, being perceived as independent is vital to safety and success because they could become targets if associated with an enemy group or denied access to victims located in territory under the control of a certain warring faction. For this reason, there often is great reluctance on the part of NGOs to share all information with involved governments, be seen as assisting one group over another, or report observed war crimes to international tribunals. This independence is advantageous in situations where one national government does not want to be seen as needing the assistance of another national government but is willing to accept the help of autonomous bodies.
2. *They tend to be decentralized in their organizational structure.* For instance, they tend to work without definitive hierarchy and succeed through greater field-level management.
3. *They are committed.* NGOs often are involved not only in the disaster relief but also in the long-term recovery efforts that follow for months or years. NGO employees are often so dedicated as to repeatedly put themselves in harm's way to deliver aid to victims.
4. *They are highly practice oriented.* They tend to improvise in the field as necessary and provide on-site training as part of their regular procedures. They rarely use field guides to direct their work, relying rather on the individual experience of employees and volunteers.

Perhaps the most well-known and most widely established NGO is the Red Cross, which is discussed below.

The International Red Cross

The International Red Cross/Red Crescent Movement consists of the International Federation of Red Cross and Red Crescent Societies (IFRC) and the International Committee of the Red Cross. The concept of the Red Cross was initiated by Henry Dunant in 1859, following a particularly brutal battle in Italy that he witnessed. Dunant gathered a local group to provide care for the battle wounded through medical assistance, food, and ongoing relief. On returning to Switzerland, he began the campaign that led to the International Committee for Relief of the Wounded in 1863 and eventually the ICRC. The committee, and its symbol of a red cross on a white background, has become the standard of neutral wartime medical care of wounded combatants and civilians.

The IFRC was founded in 1919 and has grown to be the world's largest humanitarian organization. After World War I, American Red Cross War Committee president Henry Davison proposed a creation of a League of Red Cross Societies, so that the expertise of the millions of volunteers from the wartime efforts of the ICRC could be used in a broader scope of peacetime activities. Today, the IFRC includes 195 member societies, a secretariat in Geneva, and more than 60 additional delegations dispersed throughout the world.

The IFRC conducts complex relief and recovery operations in the aftermath of disasters throughout the world. Its four areas of focus include promoting humanitarian values, disaster response, disaster preparedness, and health and community care. Through its work, it seeks to "improve the lives of vulnerable people by mobilizing the power of humanity," as stated in its mission. These people include those who are victims of natural and human-made disasters and postconflict scenarios.

Like the UN, the IFRC is well established in most countries throughout the world and is well poised to assist in the event that disaster strikes. Volunteers are continuously trained and utilized at the most local levels, providing a solid knowledge base before a major need presents itself. Cooperation among groups, through the federation, provides an enormous pool of people and funds from which to draw when local resources are exhausted.

When a disaster strikes and the local capacity is exceeded, an appeal by that country's national chapter is made for support to the federation's secretariat. As a coordinating body, the secretariat initiates an international appeal for support to the IFRD and many other outside sources and provides personnel and humanitarian aid supplies from its own stocks. These supplies, which can be shipped in if not locally available, pertain to needs in the areas of health, logistics and water specialists, aid personnel, and relief management.

The appeal for international assistance is made an average of 30 times per year, and these assistance projects can continue for years. Long-term rehabilitation and reconstruction projects, coupled with the goal of sustainable development and increased capacity to handle future disasters, have become the norm in regards to major disasters in the poorer countries. The following is how the IFRC responds to international disasters.

Depending on the complexity of the required response, a field assessment and coordination team may be deployed to assist the local chapter in determining the support needs for the event. The teams, which are deployable to any location with only 24 hours' notice, consist of Red Cross/Red Crescent disaster managers from throughout the IFRC, bringing with them skills in relief, logistics, health, nutrition, public health, epidemiology, water and sanitation, finance, administration, and psychological support. The team works in conjunction with local counterparts and host-government representatives to assess the situation and determine of what the IFRC response will consist. An international appeal is drafted then launched by the secretariat in Geneva. The teams stay in-country to coordinate the initiation of relief activities. Once the effort has stabilized and has become locally manageable, the team concedes its control to the local Red Cross headquarters.

In 1994, following a spate of notably severe disasters (i.e., the Armenian earthquake, the Gulf War Kurdish refugee problem, and the African Great Lakes Region crisis), the IFRC began to develop an Emergency Response Unit program to increase disaster response efficiency and efficacy. These units are made up of preestablished supplies, equipment, and personnel, who respond on a moment's notice and are prepared to handle a much wider range of scenarios than before. This concept, similar to the UNDP Emergency Response Division, already proved effective in making IFRC response faster and better, through several deployments, including Hurricane Mitch in Honduras. The teams, on completion of their response mission, remained in-country to train the locals in water and sanitation issues, further ensuring the sustainability of their efforts. Emergency Response Unit teams are most effective in large-scale, sudden-onset, and remote disasters.

Finally, the IFRC is heavily engaged in disaster preparedness and identified several strategies toward mitigation it hopes to achieve by 2010. These activities, which relate to reducing the impact of disasters whenever possible and working toward better prediction and prevention methods, are becoming a fundamental component of local Red Cross/Red Crescent Society programs. The IFRC has recognized the following four points of action as most vital:

1. Reducing the vulnerability of households and communities in disaster-prone areas and improving their ability to cope with the effects of disasters.
2. Strengthening the capacities of national societies in disaster preparedness and postdisaster response.
3. Determining a role and mandate for national societies in national disaster plans.
4. Establishing regional networks of national societies that will strengthen the federation's collective impact in disaster preparedness and response at the international level.

It plans to increase local capacity to handle disasters, thus decreasing the magnitude of international assistance required on disaster onset. This increase in capacity eventually will result in a decreased loss of life and property, as each country becomes more developed and better able to prevent catastrophe. The IFRC aims to accomplish these results through its regular local capacity-building projects, performed in conjunction with research and analysis, which include the following:

- Hazard prediction.
- Risk and vulnerability assessment of individual groups or regions.
- Assessment of local strength and capacity in disaster response.
- Response network development.
- Assessing the national society's disaster mitigation and response capacity.
- Assessing the national government's preparedness and response plans.

According to the Geneva Mandate on Disaster Reduction, which was adopted in 1999, the IFRC declared:

> *We shall adopt and implement policy measures at the international, regional, sub-regional, national and local levels aimed at reducing the vulnerability of our societies to both natural and technological hazards through proactive rather than reactive approaches. These measures shall have as main objectives the establishment of hazard-resilient communities and the protection of people from the threat of disasters. They shall also contribute to safeguarding our natural and economic resources, and our social well being and livelihoods.*

Critical Thinking

- Should nongovernmental organizations be required to adhere to the UN or other governmental coordination system that is in place during the response to international disasters? Why or why not?
- What are the major risks for an NGO that refuses to participate in the coordination mechanism in place in the disaster-affected country or region? What does it gain, and what does it lose by choosing to participate?

Assistance Provided by the U.S. Government

U.S. Agency for International Development

The United States has several means by which it provides assistance to other nations requiring such aid in the aftermath of a disaster, accident (nuclear, biological, or chemical), or conflict. The U.S. agency tasked with providing development aid to other countries, the U.S. Agency for International Development, also has been tasked with coordinating the U.S. response to international disasters. The USAID was created in 1961 through the Foreign Assistance Act, which was drafted to organize U.S. foreign assistance programs and separate military and nonmilitary assistance. One branch of USAID, the Bureau for Humanitarian Response (BHR), manages the various mechanisms with which the United States can respond to humanitarian emergencies of all types. The office under BHR that most specifically addresses the needs of disaster and crisis victims by coordinating all nonfood aid provided by the government is the Office of U.S. Foreign Disaster Assistance (OFDA) (see Figure 8–1).

Office of Foreign Disaster Assistance

The OFDA is divided into four distinct subunits: Disaster Response Division; Prevention, Mitigation, Preparedness, and Planning; Operations Support; and Program Support (see Figure 8–2). The Disaster Response Division handles the U.S. assistance reponding to foreign disasters. Prevention, Mitigation, Preparedness, and Planning assists foreign nations with assistance to develop their ability to mitigate and prepare for disasters. The Operations Support Division handles the technical and logistical support of all OFDA projects, and the Program Support Division works with the OFDA financial and accounting systems.

The administrator of USAID holds the title of president's special coordinator for international disaster assistance. When a disaster is declared in a foreign nation by the resident U.S. ambassador (or by the Department of State, if one does not exist), the USAID administrator is appealed to for help. This can be done when the magnitude of the disaster has overwhelmed a country's local response mechanisms, the government has requested assistance or at least will accept it, and it is in the interest of the U.S. government to assist. The OFDA is authorized to immediately disburse $25,000 in emergency aid to the U.S. Embassy to be spent at the discretion of the ambassador for immediate relief. The OFDA also can immediately send regional advisors with temporary shelter and medical aid supplies from one of four OFDA stockpiles in Guam, Italy, Honduras, and the United States.

If the disaster is considerable in size, a disaster assistance response team (DART) is deployed to the country to assess the damages and recommend the level of assistance that should be made by the U.S. government. DARTs work quickly to develop a strategy to coordinate U.S. relief supplies; provide operational support; coordinate with other donor countries, UN agencies, NGOs, and the host government; and monitor and evaluate projects carried out with U.S. funds. In the largest of disasters, response management teams (RMTs) may be established in both Washington, D.C., and the disaster site to coordinate and offer administrative assistance and communication for the several DARTs that would be deployed.

The OFDA recently developed a technical assistance group (TAG) to increase its capabilities in planning and programming. TAGs consist of scientists and specialists

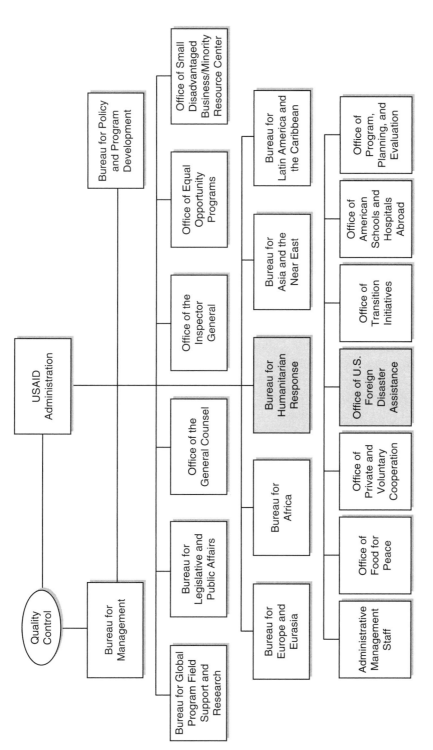

FIGURE 8–1 USAID organizational chart.

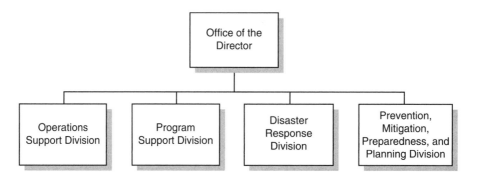

FIGURE 8–2 OFDA organizational chart.

in agriculture and food security, emergency and public health, water and sanitation, geoscience, climate, urban planning, contingency planning, cartography, and so on. TAGs work with DARTs and RMTs in response, as well as USAID development missions in preparation and mitigation for future disasters.

In addition to the direct aid and logistical and operational support offered, the OFDA provides grants for relief assistance projects. These projects are carried out primarily by PVOs and NGOs, as well as international organizations, the UN, and other various organizations (such as a pilots' club that is hired to transport supplies). Not all this monetary aid goes to response, however. Prevention, Mitigation, Preparedness, and Planning works to facilitate projects to reduce the impact of disasters before they happen again. These types of projects seek to empower national governments to make them less likely to need international assistance in subsequent events. All these organizations are monitored carefully by the OFDA to ensure that they are working efficiently and are spending monetary resources sensibly.

Other USAID Divisions

Under the USAID BHR, several other offices provide humanitarian aid. The Office of Food for Peace handles all the U.S. government's food assistance projects (U.S. food aid is categorized as Title II or Title III, with the first having no repayment obligations and the second considered a bilateral loan). The Office of Transition Initiatives works in postconflict situations to help sustain peace and establish democracy. The Department of State Bureau for Population, Refugees, and Migration provides monetary grants to NGOs, PVOs, international organizations, and the UN to respond to emergency refugee emergencies. A good portion of this assistance goes directly to the UN HCR. Last, the Department of Defense responds through its Office of Peacekeeping and Humanitarian Affairs. It is important to note that the developed nations of the world are highly unlikely to receive U.S. assistance on the level that is provided to the developing nations.

The U.S. Military

The U.S. military often is involved in relief efforts of natural and technological disasters and CHEs. The involvement of the military, a well-funded and equipped force whose primary function is national defense, brings about an entirely new perspective to the area of operations. It often is argued that nobody is better equipped to handle disasters than the military, with their wide assortment of heavy equipment, enormous reserve of trained personnel, and common culture of discipline and mission-oriented standard operation; however, it is also said that the military is a war agency, not a humanitarian assistance agency, and that these two organizational ideals are too fundamentally and diametrically opposed in practice to allow for effective military involvement.

The assistance of the military normally is requested by USAID/OFDA through the DoD Office of Political/Military Affairs. The chain of command for military operations begins with the president of the United States and the secretary of defense, collectively referred to as the National Command Authority. The National Command Authority, which directs all functions of the U.S. military, is advised by the Joint Chiefs of Staff of the Army, Navy, Air Force, and Marines. The entire military force is divided into five geographic areas of responsibility and two functional commands, as follows:

- U.S. Atlantic Command, Norfolk, Virginia, headquarters.
- European Command, Stuttgart, Germany, headquarters.
- Pacific Command, Honolulu, Hawaii, headquarters.
- Central Command, Tampa, Florida, headquarters.
- Southern Command, Miami, Florida, headquarters.
- Special Operations Command, in command of special operations, including the special forces, civil affairs, and psychological operations; Tampa, Florida, headquarters.
- Transportation Command, provides management for all air/sea/land transportation; Scott Air Force Base, Illinois, headquarters.

The U.S. military is heavily involved in the response to international disasters through organized operations termed *foreign humanitarian assistance* or *humanitarian assistance operations*. Foreign humanitarian assistance is authorized by the DoD Office of Political/ Military Affairs at the request of the OFDA (the president, as commander-in-chief, gives final authorization for any support operation). Assistance may be provided in the form of physical or technical support, such as logistics, transportation, communications, relief distribution, security, and emergency medicine. In emergencies of natural or human-made origin that do not involve conflict, the role of the military is to provide support, rather than leadership, to the national government and the overall relief community.

The military is known for its self-contained operational abilities, arriving on-scene with everything it needs, so to speak. Usually, it provides more than adequate personnel and supplies for the mission on which it was called to act. Once in-country, it works under the strict guidelines of force protection (enforced security of all military and civilian personnel, equipment, and facilities associated with the mission) and rules of engagement (a structured, preestablished guideline of "circumstances and limitations under which the military will initiate or continue combat engagement"). The rules of engagement dictate military action in both peacekeeping and disaster operations.

If a particular command unit is tasked with assisting a relief operation, it may deploy a humanitarian assistance survey team (HAST) to conduct a needs assessment, which relates to the specific functions the military is suited to address. These assessments occasionally are much different than those generated by more humanitarian-based organizations, such as the UN or OFDA, because the military operates in such a fundamentally different fashion.

The concerns of the HAST tend to focus on the military support requirements and the logistical factors involving deployment of troops. A joint task force (JTF) is established soon after to handle the management and coordination of military personnel activities, with a commander for the JTF designated as the person in charge of the operation on-site; however, if an operation involves only one military service, or is minimal in size, a JTF may not be needed.

One of the main roles of the JTF is to establish a civil/military operations center (CMOC). This center effectively functions to coordinate the military support capabilities in relation to the overall response structure involving all other players involved. The CMOC mobilizes requests for assistance from OFDA, the UN, NGOs, and the host government. All intermilitary planning is conducted through this center, including those operations involving cargo transportation and food logistics. This center is the primary node of information exchange to and from the JTF. CMOCs have taken on expanded responsibility in the past, including the reestablishment of government and civil society and the repair or rehabilitation of critical infrastructure.

Critical Thinking

- The Posse Comitatus Act limits the involvement of the U.S. military in domestic operations but not international disasters. Do you believe that the U.S. military would be better equipped than DHS to lead the federal response to domestic disasters? Why or why not?
- What aspects of the military makes it so effective overseas?
- Why do you think OFDA is a component of the U.S. Department of State and not DHS?

The International Financial Institutions

The international financial institutions provide loans for development and financial cooperation throughout the world. They exist to ensure financial and market stability and increase political balance. These institutions are made up of member states, arranged on a global or regional basis, which work together to provide financial services to national governments through direct loans or projects. In the aftermath of disasters, it is common for nations with low capital reserve to request increased or additional emergency loans to fund the expensive task of reconstruction and rehabilitation. Without these financial institutions, most developing nations would have no means with which to recover. The largest of these, The World Bank, and one of its subsidiaries, the International Monetary Fund, are detailed here. Other regional financial institutions with similar functions include the Inter-American Development Bank, which works primarily in Central and South America, and the Asian Development Bank, based in Manila, the Philippines, which works throughout the Asian continent.

The World Bank

The World Bank was created in 1944 to rebuild Europe after World War II. In 1947, France received the first World Bank loan of $250 million for postwar reconstruction. Financial reconstruction assistance has been provided regularly since that time in response to countless natural disasters and humanitarian emergencies.

Today, the World Bank is one of the largest sources of development assistance. In the 2004 fiscal year, it provided more than $20.1 billion in loans, funding 245 projects in scores of developing countries. The World Bank is owned collectively by 184 countries and based in Washington, D.C. It comprises several institutions referred to as the World Bank Group:

- International Bank for Reconstruction and Development.
- International Development Association.
- International Finance Corporation.
- Multilateral Investment Guarantee Agency.
- International Centre for Settlement of Investment Disputes.

The World Bank's overall goal is to reduce poverty, specifically, to "individually help each developing country onto a path of stable, sustainable, and equitable growth, [focusing on] helping the poorest people and the poorest countries" (World Bank, 2000). As disasters and CHEs take a greater and greater toll on the economic stability of many financially struggling countries, the bank is taking on a more central role in mitigation and reconstruction.

Developing nations, which are more likely to have weak disaster mitigation or preparedness capacity and therefore little or no affordable access to disaster insurance, often sustain a total financial loss. In the period of rehabilitation that follows the disaster, loans are essential to the success of programs and vital to any level of sustainability or increased disaster resistance. The bank lends assistance at several points along this cycle.

First, for regular financial assistance, the bank ensures that borrowed funds are applied to projects that give mitigation a central role during the planning phase. It utilizes its privilege as financial advisor to guide planners, who otherwise might forego mitigation measures in an effort to stretch the loaned capital as far as possible. Ensuring that mitigation is addressed increases systems of prediction and risk analysis in World Bank–funded projects.

Since its inception, the World Bank has been heavily involved in national reconstruction efforts. Over time, these postdisaster programs have not only grown in number and scope but also shifted in focus from that of postconflict scenarios to that of a more diverse hazard portfolio, with natural disasters emerging as the prominent instigating factor. The bank established and adjusted its policy on managing the postdisaster needs of member nations through successive policy adjustments that point to an evolution in thinking about how the bank assists its "customers" facing disasters.

Over time, the range of disaster events the bank has addressed through various response and reconstruction programs has grown over time. All bank policy stipulates that postdisaster projects concentrate on restoring assets and productivity levels, thereby focusing on reconstruction (with explicit specification that relief and consumption cannot be financed, under the guiding theory that lending should be reserved for economically productive activities, thereby leaving relief managed by local groups, affected governments, bilateral relief programs, NGOs, and specialized relief organizations).

Bank policy, in fact, restricts the bank from participating in the financing of any of the following:

- Temporary shelter.
- Search and rescue.
- Evacuation.
- Health care.
- Food and water distribution.
- Temporary sanitation.
- Restoration of access to transport.

Within the framework of these restrictions, the bank is able to offer effective assistance to disaster-affected nations through a range of loan and technical assistance instruments. The current policy describes five forms of bank emergency assistance: emergency recovery loans and credits, loan reallocation, the redesign of pipeline projects, new free-standing mitigation projects, and assessments. These, and other related capabilities, are grouped into the categories of lending instruments, coordination, and technical assistance.

World Bank Lending Instruments

Since 1984, the Executive Board of the World Bank approved 528 projects involving natural disasters in some capacity. Through these projects, a total of $26.281 billion of bank lending (representing 9.4 percent of all bank loan commitments in the same period) was provided. Among these projects, the amount of disaster-related support ranges from a few thousand to a half billion dollars. While some projects were entirely devoted to natural disasters, such as the emergency recovery loans (described next), more than two thirds involved disasters as a component of more comprehensive development goals. The value of the projects dedicated entirely to disasters totals $12.2 billion. The various disaster-related loan instruments follow:

- *The Emergency Recovery Loan Program.* The emergency recovery loan (ERL) is a loan designed to reduce the time required to complete the project appraisal process in order to meet the disaster-affected borrower's urgent needs. The goal of an ERL is to implement the funded emergency projects within a period of two to three years. Borrower nations are limited in how they can use ERL funds for reconstruction. Projects funded must be limited to the rapid restoration of physical structures and productive activities. Policy discourages the creation of permanent new institutions for project implementation, but limited changes, such as those that reduce vulnerability, are advocated. ERLs are not intended to address long-term economic problems that require major policy adjustments. They also are not intended for projects addressing broad sectoral, structural, or institutional goals. ERLs, as a disaster response instrument, are designed for more rare disasters, rather than recurrent or longer-term events such as flooding and drought (which are better managed through the use of more traditional development loan programs). ERLs must make every effort to incorporate policy and action that result in an overall reduction in vulnerability from the hazard encountered. Bank policy calls for detailed study, planning, and preparation in advance of and during the implementation of funded projects to ensure overall risk is reduced.

- *Retroactive financing.* Bank policy normally restricts financing for payments made by borrowers for a project before the date of a loan agreement. However, the disaster policies allow up to 20 percent of loans to retroactively pay for emergency recovery operation expenditures, as long as they occurred after the occurrence of the disaster and within four months before the expected date of loan signing. And, in extraordinary circumstances, exceptions to the 20 percent limit may be granted.

- *Loan reallocations.* When a government requests postdisaster assistance, the bank country staff begins by examining the existing country portfolio to identify loans for which reallocation for reconstruction is possible. Because not all emergency situations demand ERLs, the bank often uses the reallocation of existing loans to quickly provide smaller amounts of funding, as appropriate, or to supplement ERLs in larger disasters. Reallocation works so quickly because the source projects already are approved; therefore, funds can be very quickly rededicated to disaster-specific needs (often within the broad sector into which they were originally dedicated). Reallocations are most appropriate in situations where the relevance of the original project has been reduced or eliminated by the disaster. Over the past 20 years, funds from 217 projects have been reallocated. In total, almost $3.05 billion has been made available for disaster response through loan reallocation.

- *Redesign of projects not yet approved.* Another way to make funds available to a disaster-affected government is to redesign projects that have not yet been approved. In doing so, newly acquired data about the country's disaster profile, and thus its vulnerability reduction needs, can be incorporated, as can new project components that contribute to postdisaster reconstruction that was not part of the original project design.

- *Balance of payment support.* Balance of payment support is designed to provide quick disbursement of funds to meet the most pressing financial needs of affected countries. Designed to provide quick inputs to stabilize macroeconomic conditions and facilitate recovery following a calamity, this kind of support is not very common; only 15 loans have been made for balance of payment support following natural disasters.

- *Free-standing investment projects for mitigation.* After a disaster occurs, when new hazard risk information is acquired through assessment and study, disaster mitigation projects can be designed in a way that more effectively limits risk. In this context, the bank offers another lending instrument, the free-standing mitigation project loan, that nations may use to reduce their long-term risk. Although mitigation and risk analysis are considered essential components of regular loan programs, free-standing mitigation loans designed specifically to help prevent foreseeable disasters from occurring or limiting their destructive impact allow for a more targeted outcome.

- *Disaster lending instruments under development.* The bank has been developing promising alternatives to these lending instruments. For instance, increasing the amount of lending for existing projects, which is already in use for non-disaster-related projects, is being explored in the disaster context. Another specialized form of development policy lending, the contingent hazard recovery and management loan, currently is in development. It is hoped that these alternatives will help avoid the diversion of funds from their original purposes, as occurs with reallocation.

World Bank Coordination

The bank is one of a large number of institutions that governments can call on to offer coordination assistance following a disaster. Bank policy states that it is within both the ability and interest of the bank to assist disaster-affected borrowers in the coordination of overall donor efforts, especially as they relate to the gathering of damage assessment information. The policy requires that, following a disaster, the bank should facilitate collaboration between the government, the bank, multilateral and bilateral donors, and NGOs to develop a common recovery strategy. Coordination can help ensure that prevention and mitigation activities are incorporated in all reconstruction projects, bank funded or otherwise, and that neither duplication nor omission of coverage occurs.

The bank has and continues to work with other donors in postdisaster situations on several levels: cofinancing bank-supported projects, cofinancing others' projects, donors working on related projects of their own, or by performing joint damage assessments. At present, the bank fulfills this coordination role through a partnership with the UNDP and other international agencies, bilateral donors, and local nongovernmental organizations as appropriate and possible.

The bank's coordination role in the immediate aftermath of disasters has been somewhat limited. However, it has maintained a more prominent role in longer-term reconstruction efforts. The bank typically concentrates on infrastructure and housing during the reconstruction, given its comparative advantage in that area. However, the bank also has considerable experience with disaster recovery, as well as an important role in assisting with coordination that ensures that country needs are met with as few overlaps and conflicts of priorities as possible.

World Bank Technical Assistance

The World Bank assists countries in managing their disaster risk or facing an actual disaster through the provision of several technical assistance programs. These programs include

- **Analytical work.** Through the generation of publications, working papers, articles, and reports on natural disaster topics, the bank continues to advance the study of and knowledge about disasters and their management. These publications explore a range of topics that include risk management and financing mechanisms.
- **Application of the country assistance strategy.** The bank's country assistance strategy is designed to synthesize the country situation, government priorities, bank group strategy, and bank partner activities into a coherent program for future work together. In countries with significant disaster-related issues, the country assistance strategy has been used to incorporate a hazard risk component to elevate the importance of disasters in overall development strategy planning.
- **The hazard risk management team.** In 1999, in response to an increase in disaster-related lending, the disaster management facility was established, which later became the hazard management unit. This office provided bank task managers with disaster-specific technical assistance, thereby allowing them to provide a more strategic and rapid response. In 2005, this unit was drastically modified to reflect a decentralized structure and given the new title of hazard risk management team

(within the Urban Unit). The hazard risk management team, which is considered the anchor for the much larger hazard risk management thematic group (which consists of more than 100 bank staff members in the various organizational units with a particular interest in hazard risk management) works to facilitate greater adherence to prevention and mitigation objectives in bank-funded development projects. The hazard risk management team provides technical support to bank operations in promoting capacity building and establishing partnerships with the international and scientific communities working on disaster issues. The specific objectives of the hazard risk management team are

○ To improve the management of disaster risk in member countries and reduce vulnerability in the World Bank portfolio.
○ To promote sustainable projects and initiatives that incorporate effective prevention and mitigation measures.
○ To promote the inclusion of risk analysis in World Bank operations, analysis, and country assistance strategies.
○ To promote training in the areas of disaster prevention, mitigation, and response.
○ To identify policy, institutional, and physical interventions aimed at reducing catastrophic losses from natural disasters through structural and nonstructural measures, community involvement, and partnerships with the private sector.

The hazard risk management team operates by employing a combination of education, training, support, and partnerships. Key functions of the hazard risk management team include the following:

—Providing technical support and guidance to member countries and World Bank staff members in operations on lending and the preparation of country assistance strategies and economic and sector work to reduce risks from natural and technological disasters.
—Forming and fostering partnerships with the international and scientific communities to promote dialogue on disaster management issues, collaborate on activities, and receive input into World Bank activities.
—Examining the bank's disaster assistance portfolio to extract lessons for future operations.
—Identifying and disseminating World Bank and other agencies' good practices in disaster management.
—Training in the areas of disaster prevention, mitigation, and response.

• **Disaster damage and needs assessment assistance.** Bankwide experience has shown it is important to identify local vulnerabilities and determine how to reduce them in ways that lead to durable solutions. With increasing frequency, the bank has helped borrowers to assess disaster damages and develop a recovery strategy. Almost three quarters of all the disaster assessments (23 out of 32) in which the bank was involved led to a more rapid granting of an ERL.

• **Emergency preparedness studies.** Disaster projects often have a studies component related to the achievement of an important project objective. These studies may be used to increase disaster resilience for the project goals. Because so many disaster projects either have experienced or are expected to face repeat or new disasters in the future, disaster studies are necessary for proper hazard risk consideration to be incorporated.

- **Institutional development.** Through its disaster-related projects, the bank has worked in member countries to strengthen hazard management institutions and stress the importance of strengthening countries' institutional capacity for long-term disaster prevention and mitigation, both on its own and in cooperation with other agencies. Over the past 20 years, the bank formulated institutional development components for 160 completed projects, which have included project management, disaster management, general research, early warning improvements, disaster-specific training programs, engineering studies, and legal and policy reform.

The International Monetary Fund

The International Monetary Fund (IMF) was established in 1946 and has grown to a current membership of 183 countries. Its goals are to promote international monetary cooperation, exchange stability, and orderly exchange arrangements; foster economic growth and high levels of employment; and provide temporary financial assistance to countries to help ease balance of payments adjustment. It carries out these functions using loans, monitoring, and technical assistance.

In the event of an international disaster or CHE in a member country, the IMF utilizes its emergency assistance specific facility to provide rapid financial assistance. In these situations, it is not uncommon for a country to have severely exhausted its monetary reserves. The IMF's goals are to rebuild government capacity and return stability to the local economy. In the event of a natural disaster, funding is directed toward local recovery efforts and any economic adjustment that may be needed. In a postconflict situation, its aim is to "reestablish macroeconomic stability and the basis for long-term sustainable growth" (IMF, 2001). The IMF lends assistance only if a stable governing body is in place that has the capacity for planning and policy implementation and can ensure the safety of IMF resources. After stability has been sufficiently restored, increased financial assistance is offered, which is used to develop the country in its postemergency status.

A country that wishes to request emergency assistance must submit a detailed plan for economic reconstruction and ensure that it will not create trade restrictions or intensify exchange. If the country already is working under an IMF loan, then assistance can come in the form of a reorganization within existing arrangements. Separate emergency assistance loans also are offered, which do not involve the regular criteria under which the countries must normally operate. These loans, although normally available only up to 25 percent of a country's preestablished lending quota, have been created in quantities reaching 50 percent of quota; however, this funding is provided only when the member country is "cooperating with the IMF to find a solution to its economic problems." These loans are required to be repaid within five years.

A country often requires technical assistance or policy advice because it is in a situation for which it has no experience or expertise. This is common in postconflict situations where a new government has been established and partnerships are being created for the first time. The IMF offers assistance in building capacity to implement macroeconomic policy. This can include tax and government expenditure capacity; the reorganization of fiscal, monetary, and exchange institutions; and guidance in the use of aid resources.

Critical Thinking

- Should the international financial institutions be concerned with disaster management, or do you think that they should let the UN OCHA and the other UN agencies handle all disaster-related concerns? Explain your answer.
- What is the risk of allowing a disaster-affected country to reprogram a regular development loan, such as one that covers the construction of a new hospital, to be used for disaster relief? Under what circumstances does this practice make sense and in what cases should it be avoided?

Conclusion

As global populations converge into more concentrated urban settlements, their collective hazard risks amplify. Loss of life and property caused by the realization of these hazard risks overwhelm the response and recovery capacities of individual sovereign nations to an ever-increasing degree. Many of these disasters, particularly in the lesser-developed nations, contribute to existing development obstacles and regional instability unless trends toward increased multilateral cooperation in disaster assistance are recognized more widely for their importance. The capabilities and organizational capacities of the international disaster management agencies listed in this chapter—national governments, nonprofit organizations, international organizations, and the international financial institutions—are vital for both the preparation and mitigation of hazard risks and the response and recovery of actualized disasters.

CASE STUDY

The Gujarat, India, Earthquake

In Calcutta, India, as citizens were just starting to celebrate their country's 52nd Republic Day, high-rise apartment buildings began to shake at a barely perceptible intensity. Little did anybody in that city know, they were not experiencing a weak local tremor but the far-reaching effects of the second most deadly earthquake to hit the country in recorded history taking place more than *1,900 kilometers away* in the state of Gujarat. In fact, the massive temblor, which struck at 8:46 AM on January 26, 2001, also was felt in Pakistan and Nepal.[1] This event, the worst earthquake to hit the state of Gujarat in 200 years and the most devastating disaster to hit the country of India in the past 50, struck an unprepared nation.

This case study discusses the origins and disaster history for the affected region and the damage inflicted by the Gujarat earthquake (also referred to as the Bhuj earthquake because of the epicenter's proximity to that city). Also examined is the response that followed by institutions including the national government of India and the state government of Gujarat, the government of the United States, the United Nations, and the multilateral lending institutions. Three nonprofits (the Red Cross, CARE, and Catholic Relief Services) are discussed in relation to their assistance, as a sample of the hundreds of agencies that responded.

(Continued)

CASE STUDY—Cont'd

The Earthquake: Origins, Geology, Disaster History

Gujarat's location in the west of India, bordering Pakistan, lies within the Himalayan collision zone, where two surface plates (the Indo-Australian and the Eurasian) are slowly crashing together to form the world's youngest and tallest mountain chain at a pace of about two centimeters per year.[2] This movement is but one peril in a land that faces many natural challenges.

Cyclones, floods, drought, and earthquakes characterize Gujarat's history.[3] In the past 25 years, more than 3,000 people and 350 livestock have been killed and more than 1 million houses destroyed by almost yearly cyclones. Floods inundate an average of 300,000 hectares of land, damage an average of 37,000 houses, kill 135 people, and affect 2 million human lives in each average one-year span.[4] The district of Kuchchh, which is the largest in the state, is surrounded by a peculiar swamp called the Rann of Kuchchh, which floods annually and isolates the region from the rest of the Gujarat.[5] Drought is almost a yearly occurrence, with a particularly long three-year drought, which led up to and further complicated events discussed in this case.[6]

In terms of earthquakes, there have been many, with incidents measuring over 6.0 or greater on the Richter scale occurring in 1819 (8.3), 1903 (6.0), 1940 (6.0), and 1956 (7.0). Although the high vulnerability to these disasters has been long established as fact, no formalized government management plan existed to mitigate, prepare, or respond when the Gujarat quake struck. As a result, the government was totally unprepared to handle the mass casualty events that ensued.[7] Ironically, this earthquake struck surprisingly close in location to the one that had occurred in 1819 along the same fault line, in which many fewer lives were lost. A dramatic increase in development in that region with little or no building code enforcement is blamed for the much higher level of casualty even with a lower intensity of shaking.

Scope of the Quake

This was the largest earthquake to occur in India since an 8.5 magnitude event hit the state of Assam in 1950.[8] The Indian Meteorological Department recorded a Richter magnitude of 6.9, with location northeast of Bhuj, although the U.S. Geological Survey maintains that the magnitude was 7.9 and the epicenter lay north of Bachau, in a location 50 kilometers from the Indian Meteorological Department site.[9] The depth of the earthquake, also disputed, was eventually confirmed as approximately 20 kilometers, and resulting aftershocks with an unusual depth of 30 kilometers give the impression that the earthquake may have severed the lithosphere.[10] There was little surface deformation because of the depth, with no clearly discernible cracks on the surface, such as those seen with more shallow quakes; however, the liquefaction phenomenon was widespread because of the intensity,[11] and in some cases, rivers that had been dry for more than a century became activated.[12]

Most of the communication infrastructure was immediately destroyed, and a good portion of the transportation infrastructure was damaged. The local government had no immediate means to alert the central government of its imminent needs. This resulted in the lack of an initial assessment, and urban search and rescue teams were not sent in time to be fully effective in their missions. The bulk of the initial rescue missions were carried out by neighbors helping neighbors, digging with their bare hands and personal tools.[13] Nobody outside the state could have guessed the magnitude of damage they would find in the coming days, and the character of the first response reflected this knowledge gap; however, when the rescue teams reached the relatively easily accessible city of Ahmedabad and observed the damage, they immediately knew they were going to confront worse conditions in Kuchchh, where the epicenter was located. They moved relief material and volunteers to that region without preassessment.[14]

The earthquake caused damage in 7,904 villages in 21 of the state's 25 districts.[15] The district of Kuchchh sustained the bulk of the damage, with more than 400 villages affected. The towns that suffered most significantly were Bhuj, Bachhau, Anjar, Rapar, and Gandhidham, where virtually 100 percent of the buildings were damaged.[16] This district sustained 90 percent of the deaths and 78 percent of the injuries reported overall and contained 257,000 of the houses damaged or destroyed.[17] Three hundred kilometers from the epicenter, however, in the city of Ahmedabad, 179 buildings were destroyed.[18]

In many of the areas that were isolated, there was no food or medical relief for up to five days, and people began looting what they could in desperation.[19] In Bachhau, where 30,000 people of 40,000 were cut off from the relief, armed gangs formed and began attacking survivors for money or food.[20] These problems ceased almost immediately on the arrival of assistance, illustrating the effect a timely response can have on the security of an affected region.

Damage Caused

The damage resulting from this earthquake is a good indicator of the extent to which megahazards will affect nations financially in the twenty-first century because sustained losses repeatedly exceeded $1 billion. The following list summarizes these damages:

- In pure asset losses, the World Bank and Asian Development Bank estimate that India's losses will exceed $2.1 billion.
- The official government death toll, based on family registration of death and most likely severely underestimated as result, is 20,005 people; 166,812 were injured, about 20,000 seriously.[21]
- Almost 16 million people, or one in three in the state of Gujarat, were affected in some way by the January 26 events.[22]
- About 400,000 structures collapsed, and an additional 500,000 to 800,000 were damaged. In the Kuchchh district alone, 300 primary health-care centers and 1,300 child nutrition centers were lost.
- The damage to the state's infrastructure, administration, and communications was extensive and remained a major burden on resources in the reconstruction phase.[23] Several of the sustained damages follow:

(Continued)

CASE STUDY—Cont'd

○ The main telecommunications link with Kuchchh snapped and 147 exchanges were damaged in the initial tremor, confounded further by 82,000 damaged phone lines.[24] The remaining open lines were quickly flooded.

○ Most power facilities were damaged to some extent, and 925 villages lost power.[25]

○ Drinking water and irrigation systems were affected in 1,340 villages, with 1,100 of those villages reporting severe damages.

○ Of 240 damaged reservoir dams that supply the water for these irrigation and domestic needs, 20 needed to be completely rebuilt.[26]

○ More than 100 kilometers of roads were severely damaged, several railroad lines needed repair, and 5 of 10 piers at Kandla Port (the major shipping port in the state) were destroyed.[27]

○ Approximately 9,600 primary schools, 2,040 secondary schools, and 140 technical institutions needed to be rebuilt.[28]

○ The handicraft industry in Kuchchh suffered the loss of more than 3,000 artisans, and in Dhamadka village, almost 70 percent of the workers in this industry were lost. More than 3,000 small-scale and cottage industries and 20 medium to large-scale enterprises were affected.[29]

Because the impact of this event was not initially communicated to the government of India, a resulting underestimation of its severity was conveyed to the world community of responders.[30] Much of the initial response was further hampered by the fact that many of the responders (e.g., fire, police, health) were either dead, injured, or attending to family emergencies, which diverted their attention away from the greater relief effort.[31] The scope of rehabilitation required is close to inconceivable, and 18 months later many anxious people still slept in the open or under plastic sheeting.

The Participants

The State- and National-Level Governments of India. This event was "the biggest challenge Gujarat has ever faced."[32] By most accounts, the initial response by the state government was nonexistent, primarily because of the complete lack of emergency preparedness and resultant chaos that ensued. Police and fire brigades, the personnel that traditionally respond first in these situations, were occupied with duties related to security and logistics for flag-raising ceremonies and parades.[33] Most government personnel were taking advantage of the long weekend and were not prepared to suddenly return to work.[34]

The government of Gujarat immediately airlifted a team of five officials headed by the additional chief secretary, which arrived in Bhuj within six hours of the first tremors.[35] This team, although experienced in the management of engineering and medical response, was much too small to handle an event of this magnitude. To increase the rescue staff available, all government officials were officially called off vacation and an appeal for volunteers was made to doctors, engineers, retired government officials, and others with applicable skills.[36] Schools and colleges were uniformly closed to ensure that students would be available for the relief and rescue efforts.[37] A state control room was made functional on the first day, and its effectiveness increased once the communication lines were repaired on day 2.[38] Ham radio, satellite, and cell phone stations were established for both public and private use.[39] It was not until the third day, however, that the state government diverted heavy equipment used for irrigation, roads, and construction to the search, rescue, and food distribution operations.[40]

The government of India, on the other hand, took charge almost immediately and responded to an event that would have challenged even the most developed nations. It is important to note that, even though Prime Minister Vajpayee never formally requested international assistance, he did let it be known that offers of aid were welcome and would be accepted gladly.[41]

Because of the communication infrastructure problems, the initial government of India response was small and mounted only in Ahmedabad, where reports of damage could be broadcast.[42] The government of India had no formal disaster management plan that defined the responsibilities of the separate government agencies, so the approach was centralized. Assets had not been inventoried, and their mobilization was not as rapid as it could have been.[43] Other than these initial issues, the government response was to be commended.

The Krishi Control Room was set up to coordinate the central government response and provide constant communications and updates.[44] The chief secretary began holding twice-daily meetings to review the progress and planning of the relief efforts, and a hotline was set up between the prime minister and the state governor to facilitate communication.[45] Local emergency operation control rooms of varying capability and equipment were set up in tents or structures that had not collapsed, in the localities that suffered the worst damage. These centers acted as information nodes and assisted in the central government coordination to the sites.[46] Two major locations were established as collection, tracking, and distribution centers, at Gujarat College and at a town hall, for the tremendous flow of donated goods.[47]

Doctors and nurses were sent to each region with appropriate medical equipment and vehicles.[48] Fifteen thousand Gujarat Electricity Board personnel and 30 truckloads of equipment were dispatched to repair the electrical power in the affected regions.[49] A government survey team was created and examined the status of the buildings that remained standing to determine their safety.[50] Fifteen thousand Indian military service personnel and significant heavy equipment were deployed to provide transportation and distribution support to relief operations and to repair the airports and bridges that had been damaged.[51] The government sent out a request to businesses that operate cranes, gas cutters, and construction equipment to volunteer their services.[52]

When the temperature began to fall at night, temporary shelters were provided as quickly as possible.[53] The water supply, which was already deficient because of the drought, was supplemented by tankers in Kuchchh. Various foods

(Continued)

CASE STUDY—Cont'd

and cooking supplies were distributed, including the allotment of 20 kilograms of wheat and 5 kilograms of rice for each family. For the many families who lost food ration cards (prequake government subsidies), replacements were given.[54] One month's worth of grass was distributed to cattle owners in the region's hardest hit areas.[55] Public service announcements were taped and announced on radio and television instructing people not to enter damaged buildings, which could collapse.[56] Customs and excise taxes on all goods imported or manufactured for the relief efforts was waived, and the ban on foreign technology and foreign aid that was in effect was suspended as well.[57] To show government support and sympathy, Prime Minister Vajpayee visited the area and is said to have foregone regular security and stayed longer than originally planned to convey his message.[58]

The Empowered Group of Central Ministers was created to coordinate the emergency response and met for the first time on January 30, 2001. It consists of representatives from the Departments of Home Affairs, Railways, Textiles, Consumer Affairs, Information and Broadcasting, Defense, Finance, Civil Supplies, Health, Rural Development, Housing, Agriculture, Communications, and Power.[59] Their purpose was to do the following:

1. Consider the report of the Crisis Management Group and give such directions as considered appropriate.
2. Decide on all action necessary to provide immediate relief to the victims.
3. Consider measures necessary for relief and rehabilitation of the affected.
4. Consider long-term institutional and organizational measures that are necessary for management and mitigation of such natural disasters.[60]

For the restoration efforts, the Gujarat Earthquake Rehabilitation Fund was created to raise money. Grants were distributed according to the extent of financial and physical damage. The government of Gujarat State Disaster Management Authority was created to better enable these reconstruction efforts, heralding $1 billion in aid to assist more than 300,000 families according to level of village damage, distance from the epicenter, and the original house value.[61] A national Department of Earthquake Relief also was created, as part of the Department of General Administration.[62] Finally, a plea was made to ban all public celebrations until February 28 and ask that "those celebrating marriage and other social programs [be] modest and austere."[63]

The U.S. Government. The U.S. government, one of the largest donors in the relief effort, provided aid through the Department of Defense and the USAID Office of Foreign Disaster Assistance. Between the two agencies, the United States contributed $13.1 million to the response effort. The DoD provided airlifts for all the donated goods, a 2.5-ton truck, two forklifts, two 400-gallon tankers, 10,000 blankets, 1,500 sleeping bags, and 92 50-person tents. A six-person military assessment team, consisting of experts in communications, logistics, and technical support, was provided to advise the government responders.[64] The OFDA provided assistance through donated commodities and grants via organizations such as CARE, Catholic Relief Services, and the World Food Programme. Three airlifts by the OFDA (valued at $2,426,463), which carried technical equipment, shelters, blankets, sleeping bags, water and sanitation equipment, and other goods, supplied relief to more than 450,000 people.[65] Grant programs that OFDA dollars facilitated included water sanitation, disease surveillance, emergency shelters, relief distribution, medical support, trauma counseling, and food assistance. In addition to these projects, a USAID disaster assistance response team of 11 people was dispatched to conduct emergency needs assessments and coordinate the distribution of all relief supplies donated by the U.S. government.[66] Finally, $100,000 was given to the prime minister's Gujarat Rehabilitation Relief Fund.

The United States remained active in the recovery and rehabilitation of Gujarat. The USAID developed the Gujarat Earthquake Recovery Initiative, which is aimed at families in the poorest communities. An allocation of $10 million has been granted, and the funds come from existing USAID budget resources to be used by various NGOs and multilateral organizations like the UN. The funds will be used in four areas:

1. Cash, for work and other NGO programs to help repair roads, wells, water systems, homes, workplaces, and other infrastructure needed to restart economic activities.

2. Cash, for work and other NGO programs to clear away debris and rubble and repair public facilities such as health clinics and child nutrition centers.

3. Survey support, to assess damaged (but still standing) buildings, to determine whether they can be repaired and retrofitted or if they need to be demolished and rebuilt.

4. Support, to municipalities and local NGOs to develop community renewal plans that will help reconstruct devastated communities.[67]

The United States was just one of many countries that responded, providing a total of about $90 million to support the relief and reconstruction of Gujarat.[68] Other nations that assisted include Australia, Austria, Belgium, Canada, Denmark, Finland, France, Germany, Greece, Hungary, Ireland, Israel, Italy, Japan, Luxembourg, Monaco, Nepal, the Netherlands, New Zealand, Norway, Oman, Poland, Russia, Singapore, Spain, Sweden, Switzerland, Taiwan, Turkey, and the United Kingdom.[69]

The Nongovernmental Organizations. More than 200 NGOs engaged in the response and relief effort in India, creating a daunting task of cooperation and coordination.[70] Initially, there was no built-in government mechanism to organize the relief. Under these chaotic circumstances, the organizations worked out a system of coordination on their own, which attempted to create an optimal working arrangement for the disaster and increase the effectiveness of response to the greatest number of those in need. It is reported that this was the first time coordination efforts such as these had taken place in India, and they were primarily successful.[71] Three of these organizations' responses, those of CARE, Catholic Relief Services, and the Red Cross, are described next.

(Continued)

CASE STUDY—Cont'd

CARE. CARE (Cooperative for Assistance and Relief Everywhere) mobilized the morning after the quake to perform an initial assessment of the Kuchchh district. It provided an immediate supply of medical equipment, food, blankets, tarps, tents (10,000 family-sized), and water-purification tablets. CARE emergency medical teams provided treatment and trauma counseling to survivors in the hard-to-reach areas of Anjar, Bachau, Rapar, and Bhuj.[72] With the help of a USAID grant, it was able to provide food and survival kits to assist 50,000 people and encourage them to remain in their home areas rather than become displaced.[73]

CARE's work in India lasted through the end of February, helping more than 175,000 people in the remote villages where they felt need was the greatest.[74] In this time, it helped build at least 118 community service facilities (e.g., schools, health centers, government offices) and 105 water systems (locally managed for sustainability), increased access to employment and training for 6,000 people, and rebuilt damaged irrigation systems and watershed management schemes. Overall, CARE's goal was to increase the general capacity of the earthquake victims through many self-help initiatives.

Catholic Relief Services. Catholic Relief Services (CRS), like CARE, was the recipient of a large portion of the USAID grants. In addition, it committed $650,000 in private funds, as well as its Africa-based emergency technical unit and staff from various locations including Bosnia.[75] Initial cash resources were designated for the installation of temporary shelter and to meet the personal hygiene needs of more than 65,000 people in 73 villages. Mental health units were established to provide trauma counseling for the injured, their families, and the most vulnerable groups (e.g., women, children, lower-caste members, elderly, and minorities).[76] One year later, CRS was still working on follow-up projects to increase the likelihood of program success and are creating village resource maps to maximize the overall target population size.[77]

American Red Cross. The American Red Cross is one of the most experienced organizations in responding to international disasters of every type. It was one of the first organizations on the ground in Gujarat, working with a team of 11 American experts trained in logistics, communication, mental health, and family tracing. This team supported the overall International Red Cross team of more than 120 people. The Red Cross distributed almost $2 million in supplies to nearly 100,000 victims. Included in this aid were 13,000 five-gallon buckets, 550 rolls of plastic sheeting, 15,000 kitchen sets, 25,000 tarps, 15,000 blankets, and 5,000 tents. It purchased and distributed emergency health kits from the World Health Organization, which included medicine, intravenous fluids, surgical tools, and other medical supplies.[78]

The Red Cross plans to assist the state of Gujarat in the reconstruction as well. Its current projects aim to do the following:

1. Help rebuild community infrastructure to provide safe, clean water, including the repair and installation of water collection, storage, and sanitation.
2. Develop a trained network of Indian mental health professionals, who will provide mental health counseling for this and other disasters.
3. Provide community health education programs to improve access to basic health care and prevent the spread of communicable diseases.[79]

These efforts complement the $15 million in aid provided by the International Federation of Red Cross/Red Crescent Societies, of which a portion was used to construct a 310-bed, high-tech emergency hospital in Bhuj.[80]

The United Nations. The UN agencies responded immediately, having access to all government information through their established in-country presence. The UN Development Programme was coordinator, assisting in responses of the World Food Programme, the UN Children's Fund, the Office of the Coordination of Humanitarian Affairs, the International Labor Organization, and the World Health Organization. The accomplishments of each of these agencies is described.

UN Development Programme. The UNDP deployed its disaster response team, whose responsibility was to coordinate the entire emergency response until the UNDP could formally assume that role.[81] In addition, supported by $2.75 million from the governments of the United States, Britain, and Italy, the UNDP coordinated the UN body needs assessments, activity identification, project proposal design and implementation, monitoring, and quality control.[82] The UNDP and the UN volunteers it oversees worked to address the issue of the houses destroyed in the quake. Using "roaming teams," it worked with local communities to develop and fund projects for the distribution of building materials and the construction of temporary shelters. These teams also monitored the progress of the projects. The UNDP provided $100,000 for immediate relief through a project in partnership with two of the leading women's organizations in Gujarat: the Self-Employed Women's Association and the NGO Kutch Mahila Vikas Sangthan, which put together survival kits for families in addition to helping with general housing issues.[83] The UNDP sent 35 UN volunteers into several regions where no other NGOs had initiated work or provided assistance and plans eventually to have 5,000 volunteers working on the overall recovery effort.[84]

The UNDP continues to be the UN coordinating body for reconstruction, and this is to be a long and arduous task. It continued to work with the central government of India and the state government of Gujarat in implementing plans to provide permanent housing to the homeless, using construction design that is resistant to the many risks encountered in that region.[85] All these projects are merely in addition to those the UNDP already conducts throughout India.

The World Food Programme. The World Food Programme launched a $4.14 million project that provided relief food rations to 300,000 people for four months. Most of these people received packages of wheat flour and lentils, to help them survive the months following the earthquake. They specifically targeted a group of 178,000

(Continued)

children below the age of five and pregnant and nursing mothers, providing them with highly nutritious biscuits and a fortified blended food called Indiamix. A special joint logistics center was initiated in Bhuj on February 11, with a $2.3 million budget, to coordinate the overall relief efforts for the victims and airlift the relief material from a UN humanitarian response depot in Brindisi, Italy, to Bhuj.[86]

UN Children's Fund. Just two days after the earthquake struck, UNICEF sent a team of 15 members based in Gujarat to distribute 15,000 blankets, 1 million chloroquine tablets to purify drinking water, and medical supplies that could help 30,000 people for three months. In the next 72 hours, it provided an additional $600,000 in medical equipment. Over the course of the next few weeks, during the response phase, UNICEF supplied 83 mobile water tankers, countless medical supplies of every type, 75,000 blankets, measles vaccine to more than 400,000 children, water supply systems, 700 large tents (to act as temporary classrooms and health-care centers), school supplies, vitamin A for 1 million children, 1 million oral rehydration packets, refrigerators, generators, and 106,000 family survival kits.[87] UNICEF is continuing to work with the government of Gujarat to rebuild many of the schools that were damaged or destroyed and is helping the communities in the state prepare emergency preparedness plans. UNICEF contributed more than $21 million to relief and reconstruction.

Office of the Coordination of Humanitarian Affairs. The OCHA sent a five-member UN disaster assessment and coordination team on January 27 to assist the UNDP in the response phase of the disaster.[88] It provided an emergency grant of $150,000 from its own resources and from prepositioned funds from the governments of Denmark and Norway to purchase tents and blankets. Together with the WFP, the OCHA organized the three relief flights from the UN humanitarian response depot in Brindisi, Italy. Periodically during the response phase, the OCHA issued situation reports to keep the international community informed and raise support for the affected population.[89]

International Labor Organization. The ILO's activities were aimed at creating short-term work opportunities in cleanup, rebuilding the infrastructure and housing, and "protecting vulnerable groups such as young women and children."[90] It established programs that addressed aspects of disaster recovery relating to its main concern of labor issues. These projects sought to gather statistics relating to the effect on the job market from losses in employees and employment, migration flows, and the skills of the victims. Using what it refers to as "labor-intensive methods," it provided immediate employment opportunities to stimulate local markets and provide people with self-reliance. It concentrated on the most vulnerable groups, such as women and children, and worked with other agencies (such as UNICEF) to curb the disaster effects that lead to child labor, child trafficking, and sexual exploitation.[91]

World Health Organization. The WHO sent a team of nine public health experts to Gujarat to perform a rapid health assessment of the region. A disease surveillance desk was established in the main emergency operations center in Bhuj to monitor the possible outbreak of disease (which often appears in mass-casualty events).[92]

Experts from the WHO provided technical advice to the state government and health officials on public health issues. They also provided emergency health materials, including trauma kits, emergency health kits, and other essential medical supplies, all within the first days of the disaster. What was most needed, however, was the rehabilitation of the damaged and destroyed health-care facilities, and the WHO was working with the experience it acquired in the same region after the 1999 cyclone that caused similar destruction.[93]

The International Development Banks

It is important to mention the international development banks that worked with the government of India to finance reconstruction loans that are essential to the recovery of the state. Although these institutions played a vital role in establishing the preliminary and final assessments of the damages and reconstruction needs resulting from the quake, they do not perform any duties related specifically to the response. Their involvement in the reconstruction is essential because they provide the capital, without which nothing could be rebuilt, and work with the government of India in developing a reconstruction plan that will be able to better sustain the types of natural disasters that afflict the area on a regular basis.[94]

Notes

1. Government of Gujarat, India, *Earthquake in Gujarat* (n.d.) http://gujaratindia. com/preliminary.html, retrieved October 30, 2001, p. 1.

2. World Bank and Asian Development Bank, *Gujarat Earthquake Recovery Program: Assessment Report,* March 14, 2001, p. 10.

3. Ibid., p. 6.

4. Ibid., p. 9.

5. Krishna Vatsa, *The Bhuj Earthquake, District of Kutch, State of Gujarat (India) January 26, 2001* (World Institute for Disaster Risk Management, March 16, 2001), p. 1.

6. U.S. House of Representatives, *The Earthquake in India: The American Response* (Washington, DC: U.S. Government Printing Office, , March 1, 2001), p. 10.

7. Earthquake Engineering Research Institute (EERI), *EERI Preliminary Government Response Report, Earthquake in Gujarat, India, January 26, 2001,* (n.d.) www.eeri. org/earthquakes/reconn/bhuj_india/pgovtrest.html, retrieved October 29, 2001, p. 1.

8. USAID, *India—Earthquake, Fact Sheet #14 (FY 2001),* February 8, 2001, www. usembassy.state.gov/posts/in1/wwwhguj.html, p. 1.

9. Ravi Sinha and Rajib Shaw, *The Bhuj Earthquake of January 26, 2001: Consequences and Future Challenges,* April 26, 2001, p. 1.

10. CIRES, 26 *January 2001 Bhuj Earthquake, Gujarat, India,* August 2001, University of Colorado, http://cires.Colorado.edu/~bilham/gujarat2001.html, p. 3.

11. World Bank and Asian Development Bank, Bangkok, Thailand, *Gujarat Earthquake Recovery Program,* p. 2.

12. Cooperative Institute for Research in Environmental Sciences at the University of Colorado (CIRES), 26 *January 2001.*

13. Sinha and Shaw, *The Bhuj Earthquake,* p. 4.

14. Ibid., p. 11.

15. Ibid., p. 4.

(Continued)

CASE STUDY—Cont'd

16. Vasta, *The Bhuj Earthquake*, p. 6.

17. U.S. House of Representatives, *The Earthquake in India.*

18. Government of Gujarat, India, *Earthquake in Gujarat.*

19. Ibid., p. 3.

20. "Food Riots Hamper Quake Relief Work in Gujarat," *Times of India* (January 30, 2001).

21. U.S. House of Representatives, *The Earthquake in India.*

22. Government of India, *The Government of India's Official Website on the Gujarat Earthquake,* (n.d.) http://gujarat-earthquake.gov.in/mainpage.htm, p. 3.

23. Ibid., p. 2.

24. Ibid., pp. 1–9.

25. Ibid., p. 14.

26. World Bank and Asian Development Bank, *Gujarat Earthquake Recovery Program,* p. 1.

27. Government of India, *The Government of India's Official Website,* pp. 11–13.

28. World Bank and Asian Development Bank, *Gujarat Earthquake Recovery Program,* p. 1.

29. Ibid.

30. Government of Gujarat, India, *Earthquake in Gujarat,* p. 2.

31. Government of India, *The Government of India's Official Website,* p. 1.

32. Government of Gujarat, India, *Earthquake in Gujarat,* p. 11.

33. *EERI Preliminary Government Response Report.*

34. Government of Gujarat, India, *Earthquake in Gujarat.*

35. Ibid.

36. Ibid., p. 1.

37. Ibid., p. 3.

38. Ibid., p. 6.

39. Ibid., p. 3.

40. U.S. House of Representatives, *The Earthquake in India,* p. 11.

41. Sinha and Shaw, *The Bhuj Earthquake,* p. 9.

42. Ibid.

43. Government of India, *The Government of India's Official Website,* p. 5.

44. Government of Gujarat, India, *Earthquake in Gujarat,* pp. 5, 7.

45. Sinha and Shaw, *The Bhuj Earthquake,* p. 10.

46. Government of Gujarat, India, *Earthquake in Gujarat,* p. 7.

47. Ibid., p. 6.

48. Vasta, *The Bhuj Earthquake,* p. 7.

49. Government of Gujarat, India, *Earthquake in Gujarat,* p. 7.

50. USAID, *India—Earthquake,* p. 8.

51. Government of Gujarat, India, *Earthquake in Gujarat,* p. 6.

52. Ibid., p. 4.

53. Ibid., p. 9.

54. Ibid., p. 11.

55. Ibid., p. 6.

56. Ibid., pp. 33, 36.

57. Ibid., p. 4.

58. Government of India, *The Government of India's Official Website*, p. 5.

59. Government of India, "The Central Government's Relief Efforts," 2001, http://www.gujarat-earthquake.gov.in/ministry-wise.htm, last accessed May 2003.

60. Vasta, *The Bhuj Earthquake*, p. 9.

61. Government of Gujarat, *India, Earthquake in Gujarat*, p. 11.

62. Ibid.

63. USAID, *India—Earthquake*, p. 3.

64. Ibid.

65. Ibid.

66. USAID, *Summary of U.S. Government Assistance for the Victims of the Gujarat Earthquake* (Washington, DC: USAID, February 12, 2001), p. 1.

67. U.S. House of Representatives, *The Earthquake in India*, pp. 14–15.

68. Ibid., p. 39.

69. USAID, *India—Earthquake*, p. 3.

70. "Gujarat Tragedy: Could Be a Blessing in Disguise," *The Statesman* [India] (April 23, 2001), http://web.lexis-nexis.com.

71. Sinha and Shaw, *The Bhuj Earthquake*, p. 4.

72. U.S. House of Representatives, *The Earthquake in India*, p. 23.

73. USAID, "USAID Awards $2.2 Million in Contracts for Indian Earthquake," USAID Press Release, February 5, 2001, p. 1.

74. U.S. House of Representatives, *The Earthquake in India*, p. 23.

75. Ibid., p. 16.

76. Ibid., pp. 13–19.

77. Interaction, *Earthquake in India*, June 2001, www.interaction.org/india00/index.html, p. 6.

78. American Red Cross, *India Quake Relief 2001*, (n.d.), www.redcross.org/news/in/0101bhuj/india.html, p. 2.

79. Ibid., p. 3.

80. Sinha and Shaw, *The Bhuj Earthquake*, p. 12; World Bank and Asian Development Bank, Gujarat Earthquake Recovery Program, p. 3.

81. Ibid., p. 1.

82. Madhu Nainan, "Quake-Proof Houses Set the Model for Gujarat Reconstruction," *Agence France-Presse* (March 13, 2001), p. 5.

83. UNDP, "UN Steps up Relief Operations in Gujarat," United Nations Press Release, February 3, 2001, p. 2.

84. Ibid., p. 6.

85. World Bank and Asian Development Bank, *Gujarat Earthquake Recovery Program*, p. 45.

86. UN India, *The UN System Response to the Gujarat Earthquake*, August 2, 2001, www.un.org.in/dmt/guj/unresguj80201c.htm, retrieved October 9, 2001, p. 6.

87. UNICEF, *India: Earthquake, Complete Emergency Report* (n.d.), www.unicefusa.org/alert/emergency/indiaeq/archive.html, p. 6.

(Continued)

CASE STUDY—Cont'd

88. World Bank and Asian Development Bank, *Gujarat Earthquake Recovery Program*, p. 3.
89. UN India, *The UN System Response*, p. 7.
90. UNDP, "UN Steps up Relief Operations," p. 2.
91. UN India, *The UN System Response*, p. 7.
92. World Bank and Asian Development Bank, *Gujarat Earthquake Recovery Program*, p. 3.
93. UNDP, "UN Steps up Relief Operations," p. 2.
94. World Bank and Asian Development Bank, *Gujarat Earthquake Recovery Program*, p. 4.

IMPORTANT TERMS

- Complex humanitarian emergency
- International organization
- Sovereignty
- Developing nation
- Coordination
- International financial institution
- Nongovernmental organization
- Private voluntary organization
- Donor agency
- Coordinating organization

Self-Check Questions

1. What percentage of all disaster-related injuries and deaths are sustained in countries with per-capita income levels below $760 per year?
2. Why do poor nations often place disaster management so low in terms of budgetary priority?
3. When does a disaster require international involvement?
4. How are complex humanitarian emergencies different than those caused by natural or technological disasters?
5. What four important issues that influence the response process are listed in this chapter? Describe each.
6. What was the goal of the International Decade for Natural Disaster Reduction?
7. How does the United Nations Development Programme contribute to international disaster management?
8. What is the purpose of the UNDP Recovery Unit?
9. What are the three main groupings of disaster response performed by the UN OCHA?
10. How does the UN OCHA help nations mitigate and prepare for disasters?
11. Name the various classifications of nongovernmental organizations and describe each.
12. What four characteristics are shared by the NGOs?

13. How does the United States government provide assistance to disaster-affected nations?

14. Name one international financial institution, and describe how it assists in the aftermath of an international disaster.

Out of Class Exercises

1. Visit the UN consolidated appeals process Web site (http://ochaonline.un.org/cap). View the current emergencies by clicking on the tab of that name. Make a list of each emergency, and determine what percentage of the appeal has been funded. From this list, try to determine why some countries' appeals are fully funded, while others fall very far short of their request. Is this an issue of inequality in relief distribution or is it something else?

2. Visit the Interaction Web site (www.interaction.org). Select an organization from the member list, and go to that organization's Web site. Investigate what that organization does in response to disasters. In what countries around the world is that organization working in right now? If a disaster happened in the United States, would that organization respond? Why or why not?

9

Emergency Management and the New Terrorist Threat

What You Will Learn

- How the government's focus on the terrorism hazard has adjusted to new risk.
- The events of September 11, 2001, the consequences of those events, and how the government responded.
- How the Department of Homeland Security was formed, the components that make it up, its role in the emergency management and counterterrorism efforts, and its accomplishments.
- How the federal government funds first responders.
- How the U.S. government communicates terrorist threat information to the public.
- Why the 911 Commission was formed, and what was found as a result of its investigation.
- How state and local governments manage the risk of terrorism.
- How Hurricane Katrina affected terrorism preparedness and response.

Introduction

The terrorist attacks of September 11 prompted dramatic changes in emergency management in the Untied States. These attacks and the subsequent anthrax scare in Washington, D.C., in October 2001, have been the impetus for a reexamination of the nation's emergency management system, its priorities, funding, and practices. These changes are ongoing and will continue for the foreseeable future.

Prior to September 11, the Nunn-Lugar legislation provided the primary authority and focus for domestic federal preparedness activities for terrorism. Several agencies, the Federal Emergency Management Agency, Department of Justice, Department of Health and Human Services, Department of Defense, and the National Guard, were involved and jockeyed for leadership of the terrorism issue. Some attempts were made at coordination but, in general, agencies pursued their own agendas. The biggest difference among the agencies was the level of funding available, with DoD and DOJ controlling the most funds. State and local governments were confused, felt unprepared, and complained of the need to recognize their vulnerability and needs should an event happen. The Top Officials Terrorism Exercise, held in 1999, reinforced these concerns and vividly demonstrated the problems that could arise in a real event. The events of September 11, unfortunately, validated their concerns and visibly demonstrated the need for changes in the federal approach to terrorism.

The changes fall into five general categories: (1) first responder practices and protocols, (2) preparing for terrorist acts, (3) funding the war on terrorism, (4) creation of the Department of Homeland Security, and (5) the shift in focus of the nation's emergency management system to the war on terrorism. This chapter explores these categories, identifies issues, and discusses the implications of this new direction for emergency management. Where appropriate, a historic perspective to these changes is provided.

Changes in Emergency Management and the War on Terrorism

Five groups must be fully engaged in the nation's war on terrorism: the diplomats, the intelligence community, the military, law enforcement, and emergency management.

FIGURE 9–1 Oklahoma City, April 26, 1995. Scene of the devastation following the Oklahoma City bombing. FEMA News Photo.

The principal goal of the diplomats, intelligence, military, and law enforcement is to reduce if not eliminate the possibility of future terrorist attacks on American citizens inside our borders and abroad.

The goal of emergency management should be to be prepared and reduce the future impacts in terms of loss of life, injuries, property damage, and economic disruption caused by the next terrorist attack. As President Bush and many of his advisors have repeatedly informed the nation, it is not a question of if but rather when the next terrorist attack occurs. Therefore, it is incumbent on emergency managers to apply the same diligence to preparing for the next bombing or biochemical event as they do for the next hurricane, flood, or tornado. The focus of emergency management in the war on terrorism must be on reducing the danger to first responders, the public, the business community, the economy, and our way of life from future terrorist attacks. This change must occur at all levels of the emergency management system—federal, state, and local.

The war on terrorism resulted in unprecedented funding resources being made available to the emergency management community. The federal government recognized the role that state and local first responders played in limiting further harm from the September 11 and other previous terrorist attacks, and now, for the first time in memorable history, vast sums of money from the federal government are available for first responder equipment and training, for planning and exercises, and for the development of new technologies. Funding for the Federal Emergency Management Agency has increased, as has the amount of funds FEMA delivers to state and local emergency management organizations.

Historically, FEMA distributed about $175 million annually to its state and local emergency management partners. Since 2001, the amount of money granted these agencies is measured in the billions of dollars, with the FY 2008 budget request for such items and activities set at almost $3.2 billion. New federal funding sources for emergency managers from the Departments of Defense, Justice, and Health and Human Services also opened up to fund contingency plans, technology assessment and development, and bioterror equipment and training. These changes in funding for emergency management have been felt most significantly at the state and local levels.

The creation of the Department of Homeland Security represented a landmark change for the federal community, especially for emergency management. The consolidation of all federal agencies involved in fighting the war on terrorism follows the same logic that first established FEMA in 1979. At that time, then-President Carter, at the request and suggestion of the nation's governors, consolidated all the federal agencies and programs involved in federal disaster relief, preparedness, and mitigation into one single federal agency, FEMA.

The director of the new agency, FEMA, reported directly to the president. However, now that FEMA is a component of DHS, the FEMA director no longer reports directly to the president but rather to the DHS secretary. The impact of this change was not fully understood until Hurricane Katrina struck the Gulf Coast with devastating impact in 2005. This was the first post-9/11 emergency where there was a need for a strong voice leading emergency management, and that voice did not exist. While further changes to the emergency management system are under way, coming as a direct result of these events, it is highly unlikely that FEMA will soon be independent from DHS, a primarily terrorism-focused agency.

At the request of President George W. Bush, FEMA established the Office of National Preparedness in 2001 to focus attention on the then undetermined terrorist threat and other national security issues. This was the first step in the refocusing of FEMA's mission and attention from an all-hazards approach to emergency management embraced by the Clinton administration. The shift in focus was accelerated by the events of September 11 and has been embraced by state and local emergency management operations across the country. A similar shift of focus in FEMA occurred in 1981 at the beginning of the Reagan administration. Then the shift of focus was from disaster management to planning for a nuclear war. For the remaining years of the Reagan administration and the four years of President George H. W. Bush's administration, FEMA resources and personnel focused their attention of ensuring continuity of government operations in the event of a nuclear attack. Little attention was paid to natural hazard management and FEMA was left unprepared to deal with a series of catastrophic natural disasters starting with Hurricane Hugo in 1989 and culminating with Hurricane Andrew in 1992.

But 2005 demonstrated how quickly history can be repeated when the lessons of the past go unheeded. The rapid change in focus away from the diversified, comprehensive risk management approach of the 1990s is undoubtedly what resulted in a dramatic weakening of FEMA's natural disaster management capabilities. And, while the lessons of Hurricane Katrina are still being assessed, it seems clear that the current disproportional treatment of the terrorism risk will likely give way to a more balanced, all-hazard emergency management capacity in the years to come.

Summary of September 11 Events

Measuring the far-reaching impacts of the events of September 11 on emergency management can be done in a wide variety of ways. In the following sections of this chapter, we discuss some of the organizational, funding, technology, and operational changes that these events initiated. We also examine how the focus of emergency management in this country shifted because of these events. In this section, we examine the size and breadth of these events through an examination of some of the financial costs, principally spending by FEMA and other federal government agencies, in responding to and assisting in the recovery from these events.

When considering the impacts of the events of September 11, the first impact that must be considered is the horrific loss of life in New York City, Virginia, and Pennsylvania. After years of painstaking research to determine who actually was present at each of the three attack locations, a final tally of 2,973 fatalities was determined. Of this amount, 184 died at the Pentagon, 40 in Pennsylvania, and the remaining 2,749 at the World Trade Center (25 people remain classified as missing).

The attacks on the World Trade Center and the Pentagon together arguably could be considered the first national disaster event, outside of wartime, in the history of the United States. It is the first disaster event in this country that affected all citizens of this country and left all citizens and communities with an uneasy sense of vulnerability. However, the economic consequences of these attacks felt in all parts of the country and, in fact, around the world is what makes this disaster event truly national in scope. Measuring the economic impacts of such an event is daunting and some measures will

FIGURE 9–2 New York City, September 27, 2001. The remaining section of the World Trade Center is surrounded by a mountain of rubble following the September 11 terrorist attacks. Photo by Bri Rodriguez/FEMA News Photo.

take years to complete, but a quick review of some the economic impacts measured to date clearly illustrate the breadth and width of this disaster's impact on the economic well-being of the people of the United States.

☐ ☐ ☐ ▬▬▬▬▬▬▬▬▬▬▬▬▬▬▬▬▬▬▬▬▬▬

Partial List of Economic Losses Caused by September 11 Events as of December 2001

The Airline Industry

Prior to September 11, 2001, the airline industry was facing financial troubles due to internal organizational difficulties, low ridership, rising labor costs, a failing economy, and subsequent unexpectedly low profits. The September 11 attacks, which directly targeted the airline industry, was a blow that appeared to be potentially fatal. To avoid a full collapse of the industry, Congress passed the Air Transportation Safety and Stabilization Act (P.L. 107–42) in the weeks immediately following the attacks. This legislation provided $5 billion in direct compensation to the airlines, over 90 percent of which was disbursed in the first year, and $10 billion in guaranteed loans.

A major reduction in the demand levels for the industry spurred the airlines to reduce their operations by 20 percent and eliminate almost 100,000 jobs. Unfortunately, passenger demand dropped faster than even these conservative estimates could accommodate, falling to 66 percent of capacity by the end of

(Continued)

2001's fourth quarter. The immediate financial losses were grave, with the industry as a whole losing a net $7.7 billion, despite the benefits they had received from the Stabilization Act. In 2002, the trend continued, with losses exceeding even the most pessimistic estimates at over $10 billion. The year 2002 was the worst in the industry's history, although 2003 showed a moderate gain in business, with approximately $8.6 billion in losses. However, 2004 showed the best returns since 2000, with net losses of only around $5 billion, blamed mostly on the rising costs of fuel experienced during the military operations in Iraq.

The outlook for 2005 was sour, but actually saw a marked improvement over the previous four years, with estimates of net losses totaling between $1 and $3 billion by various analysts. There are signs that ridership had risen to pre-September 11, 2001, levels. The key factor to all this information, though, is that obvious winners and losers emerged within the industry. Although these industrywide numbers are negative, some airlines posted high positive profits, which indicates that others posted great net losses, resulting in an overall negative figure. The result is expected to come in the form of several bankruptcies, layoffs, and buyouts as the trend toward recovery continues.

Sources: Tom Ramstack, "Airline Traffic at Pre-September 11th Totals," *Washington Times* (July 29, 2004); U.S. Subcommittee on Aviation, Hearing on Financial Condition of the Airline Industry, 2002.

The Insurance Industry

The September 11 terrorist attacks resulted, at the time, in the second greatest amount of insured losses on record, at a total of $37 billion (the greatest being 1992, when Hurricanes Andrew and Iniki caused $38 billion in insured losses). The events led to a full reorganization of the industry, and the passage of the Terrorism Risk Insurance Act of 2003. The Act, which requires that private insurance companies operating in the United States offer insurance against acts of international terrorism events, reinsures the industry against the losses that might occur from such events. In the years that followed the 2001 attacks, there have been no attacks on U.S. soil, and as a result, no additional losses. With increased premiums, and new premiums collected on terrorism-based policies, the events eventually will cause industrywide profits in the absence of future attacks.

In an unexpected turn of events, 2004 brought about insurance claims that broke the 1992 record for the internationally based insurance industry's payouts by $4 billion, with $42 billion in losses posted. This time, however, natural disasters resulted in the bulk of losses, including the succession of hurricanes that struck the United States and the 10 typhoons that struck Asia. The catastrophic tsunami events will not have a great impact on the industry as most of the structures in the affected regions were uninsured.

Source: Arthur Poon, "Insurers Worldwide Pay Out Record $69 Billion This Year," *Straits Times* [Singapore], (December 29, 2004).

Costs Associated with Federal and State Disaster Assistance

The cost to the federal government for the response and recovery of the World Trade Center was formally estimated to be $20 billion, although other informal measures are more difficult to assess and likely raise this figure significantly. FEMA provided 42 percent of the federal share, with $8.8 billion in aid. HUD gave the second largest share, $2.48 billion, or 17 percent of the total share, and DOT ranked third at $2.37 billion (11.5 percent). All other federal agencies contributed a total of $820 million, which amounted to 4 percent of the total federal share. Also included in the federal figures of aid are the tax benefits associated with the New York City Liberty Zone, an area of the city where new tax incentives resulted in over $5 billion in indirect economic aid to the city and its residents. The exact amount of aid resulting from this program will never be known, and as such, the exact figure of federal aid will remain an estimate.

Since September 11, the costs associated with securing the nation from future acts of terrorism have eclipsed this $20 billion figure, through the creation of the Department of Homeland Security, the costs of airport security, police and fire department overtime, special events security, equipment and training grants, technology grants, port security—the list is extensive. The combined cost of all these measures, across the four years since the terrorist attacks, amounts to several hundred billion dollars and will likely continue to rise for many years to come.

U.S. Unemployment

Immediately following the September 11 attacks, specific industries laid off hundreds of thousands of workers, including the food and beverage industry (42,000 workers), hotels (46,000 workers), and the airline industry (over 100,000 workers). The economic downturn that existed before the attacks and increased in severity following them resulted in economywide losses in jobs, with the

(Continued)

unemployment rate rising from 4.0 percent in 2000, to 4.8 percent in 2001, 5.8 percent in 2002, 6 percent in 2003, and finally falling to 5.5 percent in 2004. Although many factors affect the rise and fall of unemployment, it was irrefutably proven that the attacks had a direct, significant impact on these numbers and affected specific industries more severely than others. However, the rise in security-related jobs has offset these negative figures, and moreover, as of the beginning of 2005, unemployment rates appear to be falling further away from their recent 2003 low, to 5.2 percent.

Sources: DRI-WEFA. 2001. "Greatest U.S. Employment Loss in 20 Years," DRI-WEFA economic briefing, November 2, 2001; CBS News, "Unemployment Rate Dips, But ..." CBSNews.com, February 4, 2005.

Another measure of the size of these events is the costs to the federal government in providing disaster relief. As of the end of 2004, FEMA had disbursed over $8.8 billion to the city and state of New York for emergency and recovery work. This total represents only FEMA's expenditures on this disaster and does not include expenditures by other federal agencies, insurance companies, and the private sector. According to FEMA records, this total places the World Trade Center disaster above all disasters on FEMA's list of Top 10 Natural Disasters presented in Table 9–1. (FEMA does not have a comparable list for technological disasters that could be used to compare the events of September 11, so the natural disaster list is used.) Summaries of selected FEMA costs associated with the World Trade Center disaster follow.

Table 9–1   Top Ten Natural Disasters Ranked by FEMA Relief Costs, 1900–2007

Event	Year	FEMA Funding
Hurricane Katrina (AL, LA, MS)	2005	$7.2 billion
Northridge Earthquake (CA)	1994	$6.961 billion
Hurricane Georges (AL, FL, LA, MS, PR, VI)	1998	$2.251 billion
Hurricane Ivan (AL, FL, GA, LA, MS, NC, NJ, NY, PA, TN, WV)	2004	$1.947 billion
Hurricane Andrew (FL, LA)	1992	$1.813 billion
Hurricane Charley (FL, SC)	2004	$1.559 billion
Hurricane Frances (FL, GA, NC, NY, OH, PA, SC)	2004	$1.425 billion
Hurricane Jeanne (DE, FL, PR, VI, VA)	2004	$1.407 billion
Tropical Storm Allison (FL, LA, MS, PA, TX)	2001	$1.375 billion
Hurricane Hugo (NC, SC, PR, VI)	1989	$1.307 billion

Source: www.fema.gov.

□ □ □ ▬▬▬▬▬▬▬▬▬▬▬▬▬▬▬▬▬▬▬▬▬▬▬▬▬▬▬▬▬▬

Federal Disaster Expenditures for the World Trade Center Disaster

Federal disaster assistance committed to New York City following the September 11 terrorist attacks:

Initial Response to the Attacks: $2.55 billion

- FEMA—$2.2 billion.
- DOT—$100 million.
- HUD—$250 million.

Numerous assistance programs are included in this grouping, such as search and rescue operations, debris removal operations, emergency transportation measures, and emergency utility service repair. FEMA provided the bulk of the federal funds for initial response efforts ($2.20 billion) and DOT and HUD provided the bulk of the remaining funds.

Highlights:
- Search and rescue—$22 million (largest in U.S. history).
- Debris removal—$1.7 billion ($1 billion of which will be used to establish an insurance company to cover the city and any contractors from potential claims that may arise).
- Emergency transportation measures—$299 million.
- Other response assistance (health monitoring, EPA cleanup, etc.)—$285 million.
- Emergency and temporary utility service—$250 million (to be disbursed).

Compensation for Losses: $4.81 billion

- FEMA—$3.84 billion.
- HUD—$960 million.

This funding, provided by FEMA and HUD, compensated state and local organizations, individuals, and businesses for disaster-related costs, such as mortgage and rental assistance to individuals and grants to businesses to cover economic losses.

Highlights:
- New York Police and Fire Department benefits, wages, and other reimbursement—$643 million.
- Other public assistance to New York City, New York state, and other organizations—$847 million.
- Nontraditional assistance—$1 billion.
- FEMA Hazard Mitigation Grant Program—$377 million.
- Mortgage and Rental Assistance Program—$200 million.
- Crisis counseling—$99 million.
- Individual and Family Grant Program—$110 million.
- Other FEMA assistance—$34 million.
- HUD Residential Grant Program—$106 million.
- HUD Business Assistance Program—$510 million.

(Continued)

Infrastructure Restoration: $5.57 billion

- FEMA—$2.75 billion.
- DOT—$2.24 billion.
- HUD—$580 million.

The majority of this funding is a combination of FEMA and DOT funds to rebuild and enhance the lower Manhattan transportation system, including the construction or repair of roads, subways, ferries, and railroads. HUD is funding efforts to improve utility infrastructure.

Highlights:
- Projects planned to restore and enhance the lower Manhattan transportation system—$4.55 billion.
- Permanent utility infrastructure repairs and improvements—$750 million.
- Short-term capital projects—$68 million.

Economic Revitalization: $5.54 billion

- HUD—$520 million.
- Liberty Zone—$5.03 billion.

Efforts to revitalize the economy in lower Manhattan include the Liberty Zone tax benefit plan (a congressionally created tax benefit plan in lower Manhattan)—an estimated benefit of $5.03 billion—and $515 million in HUD funding for business attraction and retention programs. Once the city, state, and HUD finalize plans for the remaining $1.16 billion, these funds most likely will be directed to infrastructure restoration and improvements or economic revitalization:

Highlights:
- Liberty Zone tax benefits—approximately $5 billion but expected to grow.
- HUD Business Assistance Programs and planning for rebuilding and permanent memorial—$515 million.

Assistance by Agencies to New York City

- FEMA—$8.8 billion (42.9 percent).
- Liberty Zone Tax Benefits—$5.03 billion (24.5 percent).
- HUD—$3.48 billion (17 percent).
- DOT—$2.37 billion (11.5 percent).
- Other agencies—$820 million (4 percent).

Source: U.S. General Accounting Office, Report GAO-03–1174T.

On May 1, 2003, FEMA closed its application assistance center located in lower Manhattan. In its one year and seven months of operation, the center's staff assisted over 190,000 individuals and small business owners, who were applying for grants and assistance with temporary housing, mortgage and rental assistance, and low-interest disaster assistance loans.

First Responder Evaluation

In July and August 2002, two September 11–related after-action reports were released: "Improving NYPD Emergency Preparedness and Response" prepared by McKinsey & Company for the New York City Police Department (NYPD) and "Arlington County After-Action Report on the Response to the September 11 Terrorist Attack on the Pentagon" prepared for Arlington County, Virginia, by Titan Systems Corporation. Both reports are based on hundreds of interviews with event participants and reviews of organizational plans. These reports provide lessons learned and present hundreds of recommendations.

The NYPD report did not pass judgment on the success or failure of the NYPD on September 11 but rather assessed the NYPD's response objectives and instruments in order to identify 20 improvement opportunities for the NYPD of which 6 merited immediate action (McKinsey & Company, 2002):

- Clearer delineation of roles and responsibilities of NYPD leaders.
- Better clarity in the chain of command.
- Radio communications protocols and procedures that optimize information flow.
- More effective mobilization of members of the service.
- More efficient provisioning and distribution of emergency and donated equipment.
- A comprehensive disaster response plan, with a significant counterterrorism component.

The Arlington County After-Action Report declared the response by the county and others to the Pentagon terrorist attack a success that "can be attributed to the efforts of ordinary men and women performing in extraordinary fashion" ("After-Action Report," 2002). The terrorist attack on the Pentagon sorely tested the plans and skills of responders from Arlington County, Virginia, other jurisdictions, and the federal government. "Notable Facts about Sept. 11 at the Pentagon" compiled in the report are provided next.

□ □ □   ▬▬▬▬▬▬▬▬▬▬▬▬▬▬▬▬▬▬▬▬▬▬▬▬▬

Notable Facts about September 11 at the Pentagon

- The first Arlington County emergency response unit arrived at the crash site less than three minutes after impact.
- Lieutenant Robert Medarios was the first Arlington County Police Department command-level official on-site. He made a verbal agreement with a representative of the Defense Protective Service that Arlington County would lead the rescue efforts of all local and federal agencies.
- Over 30 urban search-and-rescue teams, police departments, fire departments, and federal agencies assisted Arlington's police and fire personnel in the rescue. Some of these important partners included the FBI, the Federal Emergency Management Agency, U.S. Park Police, Defense Protective Service, the Military District of Washington, the Metropolitan Washington Airport Authority, the Virginia Department of Emergency Management, and USAR teams from Albuquerque, New Mexico; Fairfax

(Continued)

County, Virginia; Montgomery County, Maryland; and Memphis,
Tennessee.

- Captain Dennis Gilroy and the team on Foam Unit 161 from the Fort Meyer
  Fire Station were on-site at the Pentagon when Flight 77 crashed into the
  building. Firefighters Mark Skipper and Alan Wallace, who were next to the
  unit, received burns and lacerations but immediately began helping Pentagon
  employees, who were trying to escape from harm's way, out of the first-floor
  windows.
- Captain Steve McCoy and the crew of Engine 101 were on their way to fire
  staff training in Crystal City when they saw the plane fly low overhead and
  an explosion from the vicinity of the Pentagon. McCoy was the first person
  to call Arlington County's Emergency Communications Center to report the
  plane crash.
- The Arlington County American Red Cross Chapter coordinated support
  from the Red Cross. The chapter had 80 trained volunteers at the time
  of the attack, but the organization's mutual-aid arrangements with other
  chapters garnered nearly 1,500 volunteers, who helped support the
  emergency services personnel, victims, and their families.
- Business supporters set up temporary food service on the Pentagon parking
  lot for rescue workers. Over 187,940 meals were served to emergency
  workers. Many other businesses brought phones for rescuers to call home,
  building materials, and other vital necessities.
- Over 112 surgeries on nine burn victims were performed in three weeks.
  One of the nine burn victims died after having over 60 percent of her body
  burned. That day, 106 patients reported to area hospitals with various
  injuries.
- In all, 189 people died at the Pentagon—184 victims and five terrorists.
- On the morning of September 11, 1941, exactly 60 years before the terrorist
  attacks of 2001, the original construction on the Pentagon began.

Source: "After-Action Report on the Response to the September 11 Terrorist Attack on the
Pentagon," prepared for Arlington County, Virginia, by Titan Systems, Inc., 2002.

The Arlington County report contains 235 recommendations and lessons learned.
Of these many recommendations, the report highlights examples of lessons learned
in two categories: things that worked well and contributed to the overall success
of the response and challenges encountered and overcome by responders that could
serve as examples for other jurisdictions in the future. These lessons learned are
presented next.

□ □ □ ▬▬▬▬▬▬▬▬▬▬▬▬▬▬▬▬▬▬▬▬▬▬▬▬

Lessons Learned at the Pentagon

The Arlington County After Action Report contains 235 recommendations and lessons learned, each of which must be understood within the context and setting of the Pentagon response. Some apply specifically to a particular response element or activity. Others address overarching issues that apply to Arlington County and other jurisdictions, particularly those in large metropolitan areas. They have not been weighted nor have priorities been set. This is a task best left to those with operational responsibilities and budgetary authority.

▬▬▬▬▬▬▬▬▬▬▬▬▬▬▬▬▬▬▬▬▬▬▬▬ □ □ □

□ □ □ ▬▬▬▬▬▬▬▬▬▬▬▬▬▬▬▬▬▬▬▬▬▬▬▬

Capabilities Others Should Emulate

1. **Incident command system and unified command.** The primary response participants understood the ICS, implemented it effectively, and complied with its provisions. The Arlington County Fire Department, an experienced ICS practitioner, established its command presence within minutes of the attack. Other supporting jurisdictions and agencies, with few exceptions, operated seamlessly within the ICS framework. For those organizations and individuals unfamiliar with the ICS and unified command, particularly the military, which has its own clearly defined command and control mechanisms, the incident commander provided explicit information and guidance early during the response and elicited full cooperation.

2. **Mutual aid and outside support.** The management and integration of mutual-aid assets and the coordination and cooperation of agencies at all government echelons, volunteer organizations, and private businesses were outstanding. Public safety organizations and chief administrative officers of nearby jurisdictions lent their support to Arlington County. The response to the Pentagon attack revealed the total scope and magnitude of support available throughout the Washington metropolitan area and across the nation.

3. **Arlington County Community Emergency Management Plan (CEMP).** The CEMP proved to be what its title implies. It was well thought out, properly maintained, frequently practiced, and effectively implemented. Government leaders were able to quickly marshal the substantial resources of Arlington County in support of the first responders, without interfering with tactical operations. County board members worked with counterparts in neighboring jurisdictions and elected federal and state officials to ensure a rapid economic recovery, and they engaged in frequent dialogue with the citizens of Arlington County.

4. **Employee Assistance Program (EAP).** At the time of the Pentagon attack, Arlington County already had in place an aggressive, well-established

(Continued)

EAP offering critical incident stress management services to public safety and other county employees. In particular, the Arlington County Fire Department embraced the concept and encouraged all its members to use EAP services. Therefore, it is not surprising that the EAP staff was well received when members arrived at the incident site within three hours of the attack. During the incident response and in follow-up sessions weeks afterward, the EAP proved invaluable to first responders, their families, and the entire county support network. This is a valuable resource that must be incorporated in response plans.

5. **Training, exercises, and shared experiences.** The Arlington County Office of Emergency Management has long recognized the possibility of a weapons of mass destruction terrorist attack in the Washington metropolitan area and pursued an aggressive preparedness program for such an event, including its pioneering work associated with the Metropolitan Medical Response System. In preparation for anticipated problems associated with the arrival of Y2K, Arlington County government thoroughly exercised the CEMP. In 1998, the FBI Washington field office established a fire liaison position to work specifically with area fire departments. Washington metropolitan area public safety organizations routinely work together on events of national prominence and shared jurisdictional interests, such as presidential inaugural celebrations, heads of state visits, international conferences such as the periodic International Monetary Fund conference, and others. They also regularly participate in frequent training exercises including those hosted by the Pentagon and Military District of Washington (MDW). All this and more contributed to the successful Pentagon response.

Challenges That Must Be Met

1. **Self-dispatching.** Organizations, response units, and individuals proceeding on their own initiative directly to an incident site, without the knowledge and permission of the host jurisdiction and the incident commander, complicate the exercise of command, increase the risks faced by bona fide responders, and exacerbate the challenge of accountability. WMD terrorist event response plans should designate preselected and well-marked staging areas. Dispatch instructions should be clear. Law enforcement agencies should be familiar with deployment plans and quickly establish incident site access controls. When identified, self-dispatched resources should be immediately released from the scene, unless incorporated into the incident commander's response plan.

2. **Fixed and mobile command and control facilities.** Arlington County does not have a facility specifically designed and equipped to support the emergency management functions specified in the CEMP. The conference room currently used as the emergency operations center does not have

adequate space and is not configured or properly equipped for that role. The notification and recall capabilities of the emergency communications center are constrained by equipment limitations, and there are no protected telephone lines for outside calls when the 9-1-1 lines are saturated. The ACED does not have a mobile command vehicle and relied on the use of vehicles belonging to other organizations and jurisdictions. The Arlington County Police Department mobile command unit needs to be replaced or extensively modernized.

3. **Communications.** Almost all aspects of communications continue to be problematic, from initial notification to tactical operations. Cellular telephones were of little value in the first few hours and cellular priority access service is not provided to emergency responders. Radio channels initially were oversaturated and interoperability problems among jurisdictions and agencies persist. Even portable radios that otherwise are compatible were sometimes preprogrammed in a fashion that precluded interoperability. Pagers seemed to be the most reliable means of notification when available and used, but most firefighters are not issued pagers. The Arlington County EOC did not have an installed radio capacity and relied on portable radios coincidentally assigned to staff members assigned duties at the EOC.

4. **Logistics.** Arlington County, like most other jurisdictions, was not logistically prepared for an operation of the duration and magnitude of the Pentagon attack. The ACED did not have an established logistics function, a centralized supply system, or experience in long-term logistics support. Stock levels of personal protective equipment, critical high-demand items (such as batteries and breathing apparatus), equipment for reserve vehicles, and medical supplies for EMS units were insufficient for sustained operations. These challenges were overcome at the Pentagon with the aid of the more experienced Fairfax County Fire and Rescue Department logistics staff. A stronger standing capacity, however, is needed for a jurisdiction the size of Arlington County.

5. **Hospital coordination.** Communications and coordination were deficient between EMS control at the incident site and area hospitals receiving injured victims. The coordination difficulties were not simple equipment failures. They represent flaws in the system present on September 11. Regional hospital disaster plans no longer require a clearinghouse hospital or other designated communications focal point for the dissemination of patient disposition and treatment information. Therefore, hospitals first learned of en route victims when contacted by transporting EMS units, and EMS control reconstructed much of the disposition information by contacting hospitals after the fact. Although the number of victims of the Pentagon attack were fewer than many anticipated, they were not insignificant. An incident with more casualties would have seriously strained the system.

Source: "After-Action Report on the Response to the September 11 Terrorist Attack on the Pentagon," prepared for Arlington County, Virginia, by Titan Systems, Inc., 2002.

The events at the World Trade Center and the Pentagon varied significantly in size and impact but, from a responder's perspective, they were similar in terms of surprise and challenges. There are striking similarities between the "improvement opportunities" listed in the NYPD report and the "lessons learned" in the Arlington County report.

Although the specifics vary, both responses identified issues in five key areas: command, communications, coordination, planning, and dispatching personnel.

Many of the actions taken after September 11 by government officials and emergency managers at the federal, state, and local levels reflect the need for changes to prepare for the next terrorist event.

Critical Thinking

Do you feel that the recommendations of the Arlington County report are relevant to small communities or do they apply only to large metropolitan areas? Explain your answer.

FIGURE 9–3 New York City, October 4, 2001. A New York firefighter chief at the site of the World Trade Center. Photo by Andrea Booher/FEMA News Photo.

Federal Government Antiterrorism Activity

For FEMA and its partner agencies in the National Response Plan (NRP, formerly the Federal Response Plan, see Chapter 4), the most significant actions taken by the federal government to combat terrorism were the creation of the Department of Homeland Security and the global war on terrorism (which involves direct military action in both Afghanistan and Iraq in addition to the diplomatic and other nonmilitary actions throughout the rest of the world).

For state and local emergency managers, the most significant result of federal government actions since September 11 has been the increased funding and additional funding agencies providing support for first responders and emergency management terrorism planning and prevention activities and the fundamental shift in funding from more traditional hazard management to management of the terrorist threat.

For the American people, the most significant impacts of federal government activities to combat terrorism is the confusion resulting from the terrorism threat warnings being issued by public officials, an uncertainty regarding individual risk presented by the terrorist threat, and the effects resulting from the nation's participation in a major overseas conflict (alteration in social program funding, increased security measures at public events and in transportation, and the displacement of reservist family members, employees, and business owners—many of whom are first responders—and changes in social programs that the federal government influenced). All three perspectives are discussed in this section.

The Department of Homeland Security

On November 25, 2002, President Bush signed into law the Homeland Security Act of 2002 (P.L. 107–296) and announced that former Pennsylvania governor Tom Ridge would become secretary of a new Department of Homeland Security, to be created through this legislation. This act, which authorized the greatest federal government reorganization since President Harry Truman joined the various branches of the armed forces under the Department of Defense, was charged with a threefold mission of protecting the United States from further terrorist attacks, reducing the nation's vulnerability to terrorism, and minimizing the damage from potential terrorist attacks and natural disasters.

The sweeping reorganization into the new department, which officially opened its doors on January 24, 2003, joined together over 179,000 federal employees from 22 existing federal agencies under a single, cabinet-level organization. The legislation also included several changes within other federal agencies that were only remotely affiliated with the DHS.

The creation of the DHS was the culmination of an evolutionary legislative process that began largely in response to criticism that increased federal intelligence interagency cooperation could have prevented the September 11 terrorist attacks. Both the White House and Congress recognized that a homeland security czar would require a staff and a large budget to succeed and so began deliberations to create a new cabinet-level department that would fuse many of the security-related agencies dispersed throughout the federal government.

For several months during the second half of 2002, Congress jockeyed between different versions of the Homeland Security bill in an effort to establish legislation that

FIGURE 9–4 New York City, November 1, 2001. FEMA's Disaster Field Office in New York was ground zero for the agency's operations in the aftermath of the World Trade Center tragedy. Photo by Larry Lerner/FEMA News Photo.

was passable yet effective. Lawmakers were particularly mired on the issue of the rights of employees—an issue that prolonged the legal process considerably. Furthermore, efforts to incorporate many of the intelligence gathering and investigative law enforcement agencies—namely, the National Security Agency, the FBI, and the CIA—into the legislation failed.

Despite these delays and setbacks, after the 2002 midterm elections, the Republican seats gained in both the House and Senate gave the president the leverage he needed to pass the bill without further deliberation (H.R., 299–121 on November 13, 2002; Senate, 90–9 on November 19, 2002). Although the passage of this act represented a significant milestone, the implementation phase presented a tremendous challenge, a concern expressed by several leaders from the agencies that were to be absorbed. On November 25, 2002, President Bush submitted his Reorganization Plan (as required by the legislation), which mapped out the schedule, methodology, and budget for the monumental task.

Beginning March 1, 2003, almost all the federal agencies named in the act began their move, whether literally or symbolically, into the new department. Those remaining followed on June 1, 2003, with all incidental transfers completed by September 1, 2003. Although a handful of these agencies remained intact after the move, most were fully incorporated into one of four new directorates: Border and Transportation Security, Information Analysis and Infrastructure Protection, Emergency Preparedness and Response, and Science and Technology. A fifth directorate, Management, incorporated parts of the existing administrative and support offices within the merged agencies.

Secretary Ridge was given exactly one year to develop a comprehensive structural framework for DHS and name new leadership for all five directorates and other offices created under the legislation.

In addition to the creation of the Department of Homeland Security, the HS Act made several changes to other federal agencies and their programs and created several new programs. A list of the most significant follows:

- Established a National Homeland Security Council within the Executive Office of the President, which assesses U.S. objectives, commitments, and risks in the interest of homeland security, oversees and reviews federal homeland security policies, and makes recommendations to the president.
- Transferred the Bureau of Alcohol, Tobacco, and Firearms from the Department of the Treasury to the Department of Justice.
- Explicitly prohibited both the creation of a national ID card and the proposed Citizen Corps "Terrorism Information and Prevention System" (Operation TIPS, which encouraged transportation workers, postal workers, and public utility employees to identify and report suspicious activities linked to terrorism and crime). The act also reaffirmed the Posse Comitatus Act, which prohibits the use of the Armed Forces in law enforcement activities except under constitutional or congressional authority (the Coast Guard is exempt from this Act).
- Incorporated the Arming Pilots against Terrorism Act into the HS Act, which allows pilots to defend aircraft cockpits with firearms or other "less-than-lethal weapons" against acts of criminal violence or air piracy and provides antiterrorism training to flight crews.
- Incorporated the Critical Infrastructure Information Act (2002) into the HS Act, which exempts certain components of critical infrastructure from Freedom of Information Act regulations.
- Created the Johnny Michael Spann Patriot Trusts to provide support for surviving spouses, children, or dependent parents, grandparents, or siblings of various federal employees who die in the line of duty as result of terrorist attacks, military operations, intelligence operations, or law enforcements operations.

On November 30, 2004, following the presidential elections, DHS Secretary Ridge announced his resignation. After an initial nomination of NYPD commissioner Bernard Kerik for the position, which was withdrawn due to questions about an undocumented immigrant he employed at his home, Federal Judge Michael Chertoff was named to lead the agency.

Homeland Security Department Subcomponents and Agencies

The Department of Homeland Security is a massive agency, with many responsibilities in a staggeringly wide range of program areas, approximately 180,000 employees, a massive multibillion dollar budget, and an ambitious list of tasks and goals. The department leverages resources within federal, state, and local governments, coordinating the transition of multiple agencies and programs into a single, integrated agency focused on protecting the American people and their homeland. More than 87,000 different government jurisdictions at the federal, state, and local levels have homeland security responsibilities.

The following list comprises the major components that make up the Department of Homeland Security.

Office of the Secretary

The staff members in the Office of the Secretary oversee activities with other federal, state, local, and private entities as part of a collaborative effort to strengthen the U.S. borders, provide for intelligence analysis and infrastructure protection, improve the use of science and technology to counter weapons of mass destruction, and create a comprehensive response and recovery division. Within the Office of the Secretary are multiple offices that contribute to the overall homeland security mission:

- The Privacy Office.
- Office for Civil Rights and Civil Liberties.
- Office of the Inspector General.
- Citizenship and Immigration Services Ombudsman.
- Office of Legislative and Intergovernmental Affairs.
- Office of Recovery and Rebuilding of the Gulf Coast Region.
- Office of the General Counsel.
- Office of Counter Narcotics Enforcement.
- Office of Public Affairs.
- Executive Secretariat.
- Military Advisor's Office.

The National Protection and Programs Directorate (NPPD)

The National Protection and Programs Directorate works with state, local, and private sector partners to identify threats, determine vulnerabilities, and target resources where risk is determined to be the greatest. Particular focus is placed on safeguarding borders, seaports, bridges, highways, and critical information systems. The components of the directorate include the following:

- The **Office of Infrastructure Protection** identifies risks, threats and vulnerabilities to critical infrastructure and develops methods to mitigate them. The office helps strengthen the first line of defense against attacks on critical infrastructure and provides real-time monitoring and response to incidents of national significance.
- The **Office of Cyber Security and Communications** focuses on both cybersecurity and emergency and interoperable communications, identifying cyber vulnerabilities and threats, and helps protect against and respond to cyber-based attacks, including performing analysis on the potential consequences of a successful attack.
- The **Office of Risk Management and Analysis** focuses on the protection, prevention, and mitigation of homeland security risks ranging from physical critical infrastructure to cybersecurity and other risk analysis arenas.
- The **Office of Intergovernmental Programs** provides the department-level focal point for coordinating related communications and policies with departmental leadership and ensures consistent and coordinated component level interactions.
- The **US-VISIT** is a program that guides the nonimmigrant travel of foreigners to the United States, applying security measures that begin overseas and continue through a visitor's arrival in and departure from the United States. It incorporates eligibility determinations made by both the Departments of Homeland Security and State.

The Directorate of Science and Technology

The Directorate of Science and Technology serves as the primary research and development arm of homeland security, using the nation's scientific and technological resources to provide federal, state, and local officials with the technology and capabilities to protect the homeland. The focus is on catastrophic terrorism, threats to security that could result in large-scale loss of life and major economic impact. S&T's work is designed to counter those threats, both by evolutionary improvements to current technological capabilities and development of revolutionary, new technological capabilities. S&T contains several programmatic divisions, including the following:

- The **Explosives Division** focuses on the detection, mitigation, and response to explosives such as improvised explosive devices and suicide bombers.
- The **Chemical and Biological Division** conducts analyses for better characterization and priority setting of the threat, develops detection systems to provide early warning of a possible attack so as to minimize exposure and speed treatment of victims, conducts forensic analyses to support attribution, and works with federal partners who have lead responsibilities in decontamination and restoration, agrodefense, and food security.
- The **Border and Maritime Security Division** develops, evaluates, and demonstrates technologies and tools for better securing land and maritime ports of entry.
- The **Command, Control, and Interoperability Division** focuses on operable and interoperable communications for emergency responders, security and integrity of the Internet, and development of automated capabilities that are better able to recognize potential threats.
- The **Human Factors Division** applies the social and behavioral sciences to
  - Improve detection, analysis, and understanding of threats posed by individuals, groups, and radical movements.
  - Support the preparedness, response, and recovery of communities affected by catastrophic events.
  - Advance national security by integrating human factors into homeland security technologies.
- The **Infrastructure/Geophysical Division** focuses on identifying and mitigating the vulnerabilities of the nation's critical infrastructure and key assets.

The Directorate for Management

The Directorate for Management is responsible for the budget, appropriations, expenditure of funds, accounting and finance, procurement, information technology systems, facilities, property, equipment, other material resources, and the identification and tracking of performance measurements relating to the responsibilities of homeland security.

The Office of Policy Directorate

The Office of Policy Directorate is DHS's primary policy formulation and coordination component, providing a centralized, coordinated focus to the development of departmentwide long-range planning to protect the country.

The Federal Emergency Management Directorate

FEMA prepares the nation for hazards, manages the federal response and recovery efforts following major declared disasters (incidents of national significance), and administers the National Flood Insurance Program. Offices and functions administered by FEMA also include the following:

- The **Fire Administration** seeks to reduce deaths and economic losses from fires and related emergencies through public education, training for fire protection personnel, and enhanced technology.
- The **Office of Grant Programs** assists states, local communities, regional authorities, and tribal jurisdictions in preventing, deterring, and responding to terrorist and other security threats through a range of funding, training, and exercise programs.
- The **Chemical Stockpile Emergency Preparedness Division.**
- The **Radiological Emergency Preparedness Program.**
- The **Office of National Capital Region Coordination** oversees and coordinates federal programs for and relationships with the national capital region to ensure adequate planning, information sharing, training, and execution of domestic preparedness activities.

The Office of Intelligence and Analysis

The Office of Intelligence and Analysis is responsible for using information and intelligence from multiple sources to identify and assess current and future threats to the United States.

The Office of Operations Coordination

Operations Coordination is responsible for monitoring national security on a daily basis and coordinating activities within the DHS and with governors, homeland security advisors, law enforcement partners, and critical infrastructure operators in all 50 states and more than 50 major urban areas nationwide.

The Domestic Nuclear Detection Office

The Domestic Nuclear Detection Office works to enhance the nuclear detection efforts of federal, state, territorial, tribal, and local governments, and the private sector and to ensure a coordinated response to such threats.

The Transportation Security Administration

The Transportation Security Administration A protects the nation's transportation systems to ensure freedom of movement for people and commerce.

United States Customs and Border Protection

The United States Customs and Border Protection is responsible for protecting national borders for the purpose of preventing terrorists and terrorist weapons from entering the United States, while continuing to facilitate the flow of legitimate trade and travel.

United States Immigration and Customs Enforcement

United States Immigration and Customs Enforcement is the DHS's largest investigative arm, responsible for identifying and mitigating vulnerabilities in the nation's border, economic, transportation, and infrastructure security.

The Federal Law Enforcement Training Center

The Federal Law Enforcement Training Center provides career-long training to law enforcement professionals to help them fulfill their responsibilities safely and proficiently.

United States Citizenship and Immigration Services

The United States Citizenship and Immigration Services is responsible for the administration of immigration and naturalization adjudication functions and establishing immigration services policies and priorities.

The United States Coast Guard

The United States Coast Guard protects the public, the environment, and U.S. economic interests in the nation's ports and waterways, along the coast, on international waters, or in any maritime region as required to support national security.

The United States Secret Service

The United States Secret Service is responsible for the protection of the president, the nation's leaders, as well as the country's financial and critical infrastructures. It is a crucial component of homeland security. The Secret Service is organized into two major components, one focused on protection and the other focused on investigation.

Office of Health Affairs

The Office of Health Affairs is led by the chief medical officer, who carries the title of assistant secretary for health affairs and chief medical officer. The Office of Health Affairs has three main divisions:

- **Weapons of Mass Destruction and Biodefense** is led by a deputy assistant secretary who administers the department's biodefense activities, including the Bioshield and BioWatch Programs and the National Biosurveillance Integration System.
- **Medical Readiness** oversees contingency planning, readiness of medical first responders, WMD incident management support, and medical preparedness grant coordination.
- **Component Services** provides policy, standards, requirements, and metrics for the department's occupational health and safety programs and provides protective and operational medical services within the department.

Critical Thinking

Do you think that the Department of Homeland Security can ever have a true risk-based all-hazards focus or will its focus always be terrorism? Explain your answer.

Select Strategic Goals for Protection and Response from the U.S. Department of Homeland Security Strategic Plan

Strategic Goal 1. Awareness

Identify and understand threats, assess vulnerabilities, determine potential impacts, and disseminate timely information to our homeland security partners and the American public.

- Objective 1.1. Gather and fuse all terrorism-related intelligence; analyze and coordinate access to information related to potential terrorist or other threats. Intelligence and information analysis is an integral component of the nation's overall efforts to protect against and reduce the vulnerability to terrorism. The DHS will receive, assess, and analyze information from law enforcement, the intelligence community, and nontraditional sources (e.g., state and local governments, private sector) to increase situational awareness of terrorist threats and specific incidents. It will review and, as necessary, work to improve policies for law enforcement and intelligence information sharing within the federal government and between state and local authorities. Data collection and analysis capabilities are supported through investment in and development of leading-edge information analysis, data mining, data warehousing, and threat/vulnerability mapping applications and tools, and recruiting, training, and retaining human analysts.

- Objective 1.2. Identify and assess the vulnerability of critical infrastructure and key assets. The DHS will conduct and sustain a complete, current, and accurate assessment of the nation's infrastructure sectors and assets. It will use modeling, simulation, and risk-based analytic tools to set priorities for work with an emphasis on critical infrastructure and key resources that could be catastrophically exploited. By establishing this understanding of the full array of critical infrastructure facilities and assets, how they interact, and the interdependencies across infrastructure sectors, the DHS will be in a position to anticipate the national security, economic, and public safety implications of terrorist attacks and assign priorities on protective measures accordingly.

- Objective 1.3. Develop timely, actionable, and valuable information based on intelligence analysis and vulnerability assessments. The DHS will integrate intelligence, threat, and infrastructure vulnerability information to provide national leaders, decision makers, and the owners and operators of critical infrastructure and key assets with the increasingly targeted and actionable information necessary in the post-9/11 threat environment. It will build an intelligence analysis structure that coordinates with the rest of the federal government as well as state, local, and tribal governments; the private sector; and international partners. The national imperative is to improve the sharing, analysis, integration of all-source threat, risk, and infrastructure vulnerability information so appropriate preventative and protective actions can be taken.

- Objective 1.4. Ensure quick and accurate dissemination of relevant intelligence information to homeland security partners, including the public. Securing the homeland is a joint effort of the federal government; state, local, and tribal governments; the private sector; international partners; and the public. Therefore, the DHS will work to empower those partners by disseminating relevant intelligence and threat information to them accurately and as quickly as possible. It will work with partners to remove roadblocks to information sharing. It will administer the Homeland Security Advisory System, including the issuance of public advisories and coordination of warning information with other agencies. It will deploy and operate tools and secure communications channels to analyze and disseminate information to relevant agencies as quickly and efficiently as possible.

Strategic Goal 2. Prevention

Detect, deter, and mitigate threats to the United States.

- Objective 2.1. Secure the U.S. borders against terrorists, means of terrorism, illegal drugs, and other illegal activity. The DHS interdicts terrorist activities by targeting unlawful migration of people, cargo, drugs, and other contraband, while facilitating legitimate migration and commerce. The department will enforce border security in an integrated fashion at ports of entry, on the borders, on the seas, and before potential threats can reach these borders. Through the continued deployment of the appropriate balance of personnel, equipment, and technology, the DHS will create "smart borders." Not only will it create more secure United States borders, but in conjunction with international partners, it will extend the zones of security beyond the United States' physical borders, identifying, setting priorities on, and interdicting threats to the nation before they arrive. It will develop and provide resources for a cohesive, unified enforcement capability that makes border security effective, smarter, and stronger.
- Objective 2.2. Enforce trade and immigration laws. The DHS will enforce all applicable laws in an integrated fashion while facilitating free commerce and the flow of legal immigration and travel into the United States. It will interdict smuggling and stop other illegal activities that benefit terrorists and their supporters. It will build a unified, cohesive enforcement capability to actively conduct and coordinate law enforcement operations.
- Objective 2.3. Provide operational end users with the technology and capabilities to detect and prevent terrorist attacks, means of terrorism, and other illegal activities. The nation's technical superiority in science and technology is key to securing the homeland. The DHS will use leverage, and enhance the vast resources and expertise of the federal government, private sector, academic community, nongovernmental organizations, and other scientific bodies. It will develop new capabilities to facilitate the sharing of information and analysis; test and assess threats and vulnerabilities; counter various threats, including weapons of mass destruction and illegal drugs; and mitigate the effects of terrorist attacks. It also will focus our efforts on

(Continued)

developing technology to detect and prevent the illicit transport of chemical, biological, radiological, and nuclear materials. It will develop and deploy the capabilities, equipment, and systems needed to anticipate, respond to, and recover from attacks on the homeland.

- Objective 2.4. Ensure national and international policy, law enforcement, and other actions to prepare for and prevent terrorism are coordinated. The DHS will effectively coordinate and communicate with other federal agencies; state, local, and tribal governments; the private sector; and the American people. Increasing and coordinating information sharing between law enforcement, intelligence, and military organizations will improve the ability to counter terrorists everywhere. It will coordinate training and education across multiple levels, both national and international, ensuring common standards and approaches to recognizing key indicators of future terrorist actions.

- Objective 2.5. Strengthen the security of the nation's transportation systems. Transportation systems have the unique ability to be either a means of delivering weapons of terror or the target of a direct terrorist attack. The U.S. domestic transportation system is intertwined inextricably with the global transportation infrastructure. Safety and security are two sides of the same coin. The DHS will strengthen the security of the transportation network while it works to remove all threats or barriers to the safe movement of commerce and people. It will coordinate with federal, state, local, and tribal agencies, as well as international and private sector partners, to ensure the transportation system remains a safe and vital economic link, while preventing terrorists from using transportation conveyances or systems to deliver implements of destruction.

- Objective 2.6. Ensure the security and integrity of the immigration system. The DHS will ensure that immigrants and nonimmigrants comply with laws and security mandates to prevent persons who seek to exploit the economic and social benefits of immigration or engage in illegal activities from obtaining lawful status. It will strengthen legal protections and design programs appropriately to create a more secure immigration system. It will make decisions in a timely and efficient manner by applying technology and allocating resources to provide actionable and accurate information. It will ensure that those persons entitled to benefits receive them through verification services and encouraging employers to verify status. It will refer illegal aliens to enforcement entities for prosecution or removal from the United States.

Strategic Goal 3. Protection

Safeguard the American people and their freedoms, critical infrastructure, property, and the economy of our nation from acts of terrorism, natural disasters, or other emergencies.

- Objective 3.1. Protect the public from acts of terrorism and other illegal activities. The DHS must not let the threat of terrorism alter the American way of life. It will identify and disrupt terrorists and criminals before they threaten the well-being of American citizens. Its investigative efforts will focus on identifying the tools and conveyances used by terrorists and criminals and apprehending suspect individuals. Through partnerships with other agencies and its own efforts, the DHS will coordinate and apply knowledge and skills acquired through years of practical use in drug interdiction and airspace security to remain at the forefront of global law enforcement and counterterrorism efforts. It will ensure that the nation's shipping routes do not become avenues of entry for terrorists, their weapons, or supplies. It will conduct national and international investigations to gather evidence of violations of United States laws and prevent terrorist groups from obtaining sensitive weapons of United States origin.

- Objective 3.2. Reduce infrastructure vulnerability from acts of terrorism. The DHS will lead and coordinate a national effort to secure America's critical infrastructure. Protecting America's critical infrastructure is the shared responsibility of federal, state, local, and tribal governments, in active partnership with the private sector, which owns approximately 85 percent of the nation's critical infrastructure. Using the results of modeling, simulation, and analytic tools to rank its efforts, the DHS will implement standardized and tiered protective measures that are rapidly adjustable to counter various levels of threat. It will coordinate the implementation of a comprehensive integrated national plan to protect both the physical and cyber infrastructure and significantly reduce vulnerabilities, while ensuring that government at all levels enables and does not inhibit the private sector's ability to carry out its protection responsibilities.
- Objective 3.3. Protect against financial and electronic crimes, counterfeit currency, illegal bulk currency movement, and identity theft. A principal component of homeland security is economic security, including protection of the nation's currency and financial payment systems. The Department of Homeland Security participates in task forces and other joint operations with the financial community and federal, state, local, and tribal law enforcement partners to investigate crimes targeting the stability, reliability, and security of financial systems. To prevent, detect, and investigate various forms of electronic crimes, the DHS will operate a nationwide network of Electronic Crimes Task Forces. It will maintain an overseas investigative presence where criminal groups engage in the counterfeiting United States currency and other financial crimes targeting the homeland. International drug traffickers steal $20 to $30 billion annually from the United States economy. Much of these illegal funds are shipped out of the United States as bulk currency. This weakens our economy and strengthens the ability of the international drug traffickers to destabilize the governments of their countries by bribery or to finance terrorist activities. The DHS will investigate, identify, and seize outbound shipments to take away this ability to fund illegal activities.

(Continued)

- Objective 3.4. Secure the physical safety of the president, vice president, visiting world leaders, and other protectees. The DHS will protect the nation's leaders and visiting dignitaries from all threats, including terrorists and other criminals; natural, technological, and human-made emergencies; and preventable accidents. It will coordinate with military, federal, state, local, and tribal law enforcement organizations to ensure their safety. It will evaluate information received from law enforcement and intelligence agencies and other sources to investigate, apprehend, and prosecute, if appropriate, those who pose a threat. It will ensure that protectees have a safe environment in which to continue their operations in the event of any threat contingency.

- Objective 3.5. Ensure the continuity of government operations and essential functions in the event of crisis or disaster. The DHS will partner with other federal departments and agencies to ensure the continuous operation of the federal government and secure the survival of an enduring constitutional government in times of attack, national emergency, or disaster. It will provide alternative facilities, equipment, and communications capabilities to ensure that the federal government is capable of performing its essential functions and the nation will continue to be governed as set forth in the United States Constitution.

- Objective 3.6. Protect the marine environment and living marine resources. The DHS will partner with other nations; federal agencies; state, local, and tribal governments; and responsible sectors of the maritime industry, to ensure the quality of U.S. marine resources are protected. It will encourage, pursue, and enforce bilateral and regional agreements with other governments to ensure that the world's living marine resources are properly maintained and managed. The ability to use unpolluted waters for transportation and recreation is vital to the safety of the citizens and the economy of the United States; it will work to ensure compliance with existing regulations and consider others that may be required to protect the marine environment. It will maintain an uncompromising commitment to the stewardship of the national living marine resources through the highest caliber enforcement of fisheries laws and regulations supporting the national policy.

- Objective 3.7. Strengthen nationwide preparedness and mitigation against acts of terrorism, natural disasters, or other emergencies. The best way to protect against the effects of harmful incidents is to be prepared. Preparedness and mitigation are important elements in reducing the impacts of acts of terror and other disasters. The DHS will ensure all levels of public safety and emergency management are capable of rapid and effective response by establishing a unified, capabilities-based preparedness strategy incorporating all-hazard assessments, training, exercises, and assistance for federal, state, tribal, and local governments; first responders; and communities. It will establish, implement, and evaluate capabilities through a system of national standards, mutual aid systems, and credentialing protocols and supply technologies for rapid and interoperable communications, personal protection, and incident management. It will implement and sustain a national citizen preparedness movement that includes private sector involvement. It will expand the nation's community risk management capabilities and reduce the nation's vulnerability to acts of terrorism and other disasters through effective vulnerability assessments and risk management programs.

Strategic Goal 4. Response

Lead, manage, and coordinate the national response to acts of terrorism, natural disasters, or other emergencies.

- Objective 4.1. Reduce the loss of life and property by strengthening nationwide response readiness. The nation must have a vigorous capability to respond when disaster strikes. The DHS will strengthen the national capability to respond to disasters of all types, including terrorism, through the integration of Department of Homeland Security response systems and teams and the completion of catastrophic all-hazard plans for the nation's most vulnerable communities and geographic areas, including tactical elements to ensure coordinated response operations, logistics, and support. It will provide health and medical response readiness through integrated planning and surge capacity to address health and medical emergencies or acts of terrorism and develop the logistical capacity to provide intermediate emergency housing to large displaced populations following major disasters.
- Objective 4.2. Provide scalable and robust all-hazard response capability. The nation will know it can rely on the DHS to respond in time of need. It will provide and coordinate a quick and effective response when state, local, and tribal resources are overwhelmed by disasters and emergencies. It will bring the right people and resources to bear where and when they are needed most, including medical, urban search and rescue, and incident management capabilities, and assist all mariners in peril. It will provide integrated logistical support to ensure a rapid and effective response and coordinate among Department of Homeland Security and other federal, state, and local operations centers consistent with national incident command protocols. It will work with partners to create and implement a National Incident Management System and a single, all-discipline National Response Plan that will strengthen the nation's ability to respond to catastrophic events of all types, including terrorism.
- Objective 4.3. Provide search and rescue services to people and property in distress. Mariners operate in an unforgiving and often remote environment that increases the risk of injury, loss of life, and property. The DHS will continue to use its maritime expertise, assets, and around-the-clock, on-call readiness to conduct search and rescue missions to save lives and property. It also will continue to partner with other nations; federal, state, local agencies; the maritime industry and professional mariners; commercial providers; and volunteer organizations to assist mariners in distress and protect property in imminent danger. A number of projects are under way

(Continued)

that will improve the ability to respond to maritime distress incidents. Recapitalization of aviation, surface, command, and control architecture and supporting logistic and personnel systems, as well as the procurement of specialized boats and attainment of additional search planning tools will greatly enhance the ability to assist mariners in distress.

Strategic Goal 5. Recovery

Lead national, state, local, and private sector efforts to restore services and rebuild communities after acts of terrorism, natural disasters, or other emergencies.

- Objective 5.1. Strengthen nationwide recovery plans and capabilities. The DHS will work with partners to ensure the nation's capability to recover from multiple or simultaneous disasters, including terrorist use of weapons of mass destruction, other human-made hazards and natural disasters, through the development and maintenance of short- and long-term plans and capabilities.
- Objective 5.2. Provide scalable and robust all-hazard recovery assistance. The DHS will lead the nation's recovery from the impacts of disasters and emergencies. It will deliver timely and appropriate assistance to individuals and families following acts of terrorism, natural disasters, and other emergencies, acknowledging the unique requirements of recovery from catastrophic disasters and weapons of mass destruction events. It will provide help to restore services and public facilities and provide states and other partners with professional, readily deployable, trained, and certified leaders and staff to manage all levels and types of disasters. It will make assistance available to states and local governments for the management, mitigation, and control of local hazards and emergencies that threaten to become major disasters.

Source: U.S. Department of Homeland Security Strategic Plan.

Secretary Chertoff's Six-Point Agenda

On July 13, 2005, DHS Secretary Michael Chertoff released a six-point agenda to reorganize the department. The agenda followed an initial review that Chertoff initiated immediately on assuming his leadership position. The review was designed to closely examine the department to discover ways in which leadership could better manage risk in terms of threat, vulnerability, and consequence; set priorities on policies and operational missions according to this risk-based approach; and establish a series of preventive and protective steps that would increase security at multiple levels. The resulting agenda brought about several changes that led to the present design and focused on

- Increasing overall preparedness, particularly for catastrophic events.
- Creating better transportation security systems to move people and cargo more securely and efficiently.

- Strengthening border security and interior enforcement and reforming immigration processes.
- Enhancing information sharing (with partners).
- Improving financial management, human resource development, procurement, and information technology within the department.
- Realigning the department's organization to maximize mission performance.

Several new policy initiatives were included in the proposed overhaul of the department, including

- A new approach to securing borders through additional personnel, new technologies, infrastructure investments, and interior enforcement, coupled with efforts to reduce the demand for illegal border migration by channeling migrants seeking work into regulated legal channels.
- Restructuring the current immigration process to enhance security and improve customer service.
- Reaching out to state homeland security officials to improve information exchange protocols, refine the Homeland Security Advisory System, support state and regional data fusion centers, and address other topics of mutual concern.
- Investing in DHS personnel by providing professional career training and other development efforts.

One of the most significant changes that occurred as result of the six-point agenda was an organizational restructuring of the department. Chertoff asserted that these changes were made to increase the department's ability to prepare, prevent, and respond to terrorist attacks and other emergencies. Changes included

- The creation of the Directorate of Policy, which centralized and improved policy development and coordination.
- The creation of a new Office of Intelligence and Analysis, to strengthen intelligence functions and information sharing. This office was created to ensure that information is gathered from all relevant field operations and other parts of the intelligence community, is analyzed with a mission-oriented focus, is informative to senior decision makers, and is disseminated to the appropriate federal, state, local, and private sector partners. Led by a chief intelligence officer who reports directly to the secretary, this office comprises analysts within the former Information Analysis Directorate and draws on the expertise of other DHS components with intelligence collection and analysis operations.
- The creation of a new Office of Operations Coordination, to improve operational coordination and efficiency. This office works to enable the DHS to more effectively conduct joint operations across all organizational elements, coordinate incident management activities, and utilize all resources within the department to translate intelligence and policy into immediate action. The Homeland Security operations center, which serves as the nation's nerve center for information sharing and domestic incident management on a full-time basis, was moved into this new office.
- The renaming of the Information Analysis and Infrastructure Protection Directorate to the Directorate for Preparedness, and the consolidation of

preparedness assets from across the department under it. The Directorate for Preparedness now facilitates grants and oversees nationwide preparedness efforts supporting first responder training, citizen awareness, public health, and infrastructure and cyber security and ensure proper steps are taken to protect high-risk targets.

- The moving of FEMA so that it reports directly to the DHS secretary. As a result of the new DHS reorganization, FEMA now focuses on response and recovery activities rather than all four phases of emergency management.
- The moving of the Federal Air Marshal Service from the Immigration and Customs Enforcement bureau to the Transportation Security Administration to increase operational coordination and strengthen efforts to meet the common goal of aviation security.
- The creation of the Office of Legislative and Intergovernmental Affairs, which merged certain functions among the Office of Legislative Affairs and the Office of State and Local Government Coordination. This was done to streamline intergovernment relations efforts and better share homeland security information with members of Congress, as well as state and local officials.
- The moving of the Office of Security under the direction of the undersecretary for management to better manage information systems, contractual activities, security accreditation, training, and resources.

The Post-Katrina Emergency Management Reform Act

To correct the emergency management shortfalls highlighted in the inadequate response to Hurricane Katrina, Congress passed the Post-Katrina Emergency Management Reform Act, which was signed into law by President Bush on October 4, 2006. The act established new leadership positions within the department, created additional functions that were assumed by FEMA, created and reallocated functions to other components within the DHS, and amended the Homeland Security Act in ways that directly and indirectly affect the organization and functions of various entities within the DHS. These changes, which also included nonmandated actions, include transferring (with the exception of certain offices) the functions of the Preparedness Directorate to the new FEMA, including

- The United States Fire Administration.
- The Office of Grants and Training.
- The Chemical Stockpile Emergency Preparedness Division.
- The Radiological Emergency Preparedness Program.
- The Office of National Capital Region Coordination.

According to the Act, the director of FEMA is now referred to as the FEMA administrator and is supported by two deputy administrators. The first is the deputy administrator and chief operating officer (the principal deputy, with overall operational responsibilities at FEMA), and the other is a deputy administrator for national preparedness, a new division within FEMA.

The National Preparedness Division includes existing FEMA programs and several legacy Preparedness Directorate programs. Its focus is policy, contingency planning, exercise coordination and evaluation, emergency management training and hazard mitigation with respect to the Chemical Stockpile Emergency Preparedness and Radiological

Emergency Preparedness Program. National Preparedness oversees two divisions: Readiness, Prevention and Planning and the National Integration Center. Readiness, Prevention and Planning is now the central office within FEMA handling preparedness policy and planning functions. The National Integration Center maintains the National Incident Management System, the National Response Plan, and coordinates activities with the U.S. Fire Administration.

The Office of Grants and Training was moved to the new FEMA and renamed the Office of Grant Programs. The Training and Systems Support Divisions of the Office of Grants and Training were transferred to the National Integration Center. The Office of the Citizen Corps within the Office of Grants and Training was transferred into the FEMA Office of Readiness, Prevention and Planning.

Additional headquarters positions created at FEMA by the post-Katrina act include a disability coordinator, residing in the FEMA Office of Equal Rights, a small state and rural advocate, a law enforcement advisor to the administrator, and a National Advisory Council. The National Advisory Council, which was created in early 2007, advises the FEMA administrator on all aspects of emergency management to ensure better coordination. Members of the council are appointed by the FEMA administrator, representing a geographic and disciplinary cross section of officials from emergency management and law enforcement, and include homeland security directors, adjutants general, emergency response providers from state, local, and tribal governments, private sector, and nongovernmental organizations.

Funding for First Responders and Emergency Management

For state and local government, the events of September 11 (see Table 9–2) resulted in an extraordinary increase in funding for first responders—fire, police, and emergency medical technicians—and emergency management activities. Also, the number of federal government agencies and programs now providing funds for these activities has increased significantly. In the first responder community, historically, only the police have received significant funding from the federal government. Fire departments across the country traditionally raised the majority of their funding from local sources. Emergency medical technicians are often private contractors paid for by local and state government sources.

Properly training and equipping of firefighters responding to a biochemical terrorist attack has been a concern among the fire services community and FEMA since the early 1990s. Passage of the Fire Prevention and Assistance Act in 2000 was the first effort by Congress to support the nation's paid and volunteer fire departments. In spring 2001, FEMA initiated a new Fire Grant Program that provided $100 million in small grants to local fire departments for equipment, protective gear, training, and prevention programs. In 2002, the amount available for FEMA fire grants increased to $300 million. By 2004, that amount had risen to over $700,000 (although these totals have fallen every year since). In addition to the annual fire grants, the bulk of the $3 to $3.5 billion spent on first responders each year has been designated for equipping and training first responders for future terrorist events (see proposed 2008 budget figures in Table 9–2).

FEMA is not the only source of antiterrorism funding for state and local government. The Department of Justice, through a variety of programs, is making funding available for the acquisition of equipment and technology. The Department of Health and

Table 9–2 Local First Responder Funding Figures: 2006–2008 (dollars in millions)

Funding Area	FY 2006, Enacted	FY 2007, Enacted	FY 2008, Proposed	Change, FY 2007–FY 2008
State Homeland Security Grant Program	$545	$525	$187	($338)
Urban Area Security Initiative	$740	$770	$800	$30
UASI Infrastructure Subgrants	$415	$459	$459	$0
Law Enforcement Terrorism Prevention Grants	$400	$375	$0	($375)
Assistance to Firefighters Grant Program	$655	$547	$300	($247)
Emergency Management Performance Grants	$183	$200	$200	$0
Citizen Corps	$20	$15	$15	$0
Metropolitan Medical Response System	$33	$32	$0	($32)
Public Safety Interoperable Communications Grant	$0	$0	$1,000	$1,000
Staffing for Adequate Fire and Emergency Response	$110	$115	$0	($115)
First Responder Training, Exercise, and Assistance	$346	$352	$229	($123)
Total	$3,447	$3,390	$3,190	($200)

Human Services is making available substantial funding to state and local government to address the threat of biochemical terrorist attacks. The Centers for Disease Control is providing funding for public health planning and capacity building and bolstering the national pharmaceutical stockpile. The Department of Defense currently provides funding for emergency management training for military personnel and community officials.

Communicating Threat Information to the American People

As noted earlier, in Objective 1.4 of the DHS Strategic Plan,

> *Securing the homeland is a joint effort of the federal government; state, local and tribal governments; the private sector; our international partners; and the public. Therefore we will work to empower those partners by disseminating relevant intelligence and threat information to them accurately and as quickly as possible. We will work with our partners to remove roadblocks to information sharing. We will administer the Homeland Security Advisory System, including the issuance of public advisories and coordination of warning information with other agencies. We will deploy and operate tools and secure communications channels to analyze and disseminate information to relevant agencies as quickly and efficiently as possible.*

The Homeland Security Advisory System was borne out of Homeland Security Presidential Directive 3 (HSPD-3), issued on March 11, 2002, which stated that

> *The nation requires a Homeland Security Advisory System to provide a comprehensive and effective means to disseminate information regarding the risk of terrorist acts to federal, state, and local authorities and to the American people. Such a system would provide warnings in the form of a set of graduated "Threat Conditions" that would increase as the risk of the threat increases.*

At each Threat Condition, federal departments and agencies would implement a corresponding set of "Protective Measures" to further reduce vulnerability or increase response capability during a period of heightened alert.

This system is intended to create a common vocabulary, context, and structure for an ongoing national discussion about the nature of the threats that confront the homeland and the appropriate measures that should be taken in response. It seeks to inform and facilitate decisions appropriate to different levels of government and to private citizens at home and at work.

There are three components of the system, which is designed to combine threat information with vulnerability assessments and provide communications to public safety officials and the public. They are as follows:

- **Homeland Security threat advisories** contain actionable information about an incident involving or a threat targeting critical national networks or infrastructures or key assets. For example, they could relay newly developed procedures that, when implemented, would significantly improve security or protection. They could also suggest a change in readiness posture, protective actions, or response. This category includes products formerly named *alerts, advisories,* and *sector notifications.* Advisories are targeted to federal, state, and local governments; private sector organizations; and international partners.
- **Homeland Security information bulletins** communicate information of interest to the nation's critical infrastructures that do not meet the timeliness, specificity, or significance thresholds of warning messages. Such information may include statistical reports, periodic summaries, incident response or reporting guidelines, common vulnerabilities and patches, and configuration standards or tools. It also may include preliminary requests for information. Bulletins are targeted to federal, state, and local governments; private sector organizations; and international partners.
- **Color-coded threat level system** is used to communicate with public safety officials and the public at-large through a threat-based, color-coded system so that protective measures can be implemented to reduce the likelihood or impact of an attack. Raising the threat condition has economic, physical, and psychological effects on the nation; so, the Homeland Security Advisory System can place specific geographic regions or industry sectors on a higher alert status than other regions or industries, based on specific threat information.

Figure 9–5 provides suggestions for public action in accordance with the five color codes of the Homeland Security Advisory System. The following information, based on the same color-coded chart, provides DHS recommendations to federal departments and agencies.

Guidance for Federal Departments and Agencies

The following threat conditions represent an increasing risk of terrorist attacks. Beneath each threat condition are some suggested protective measures, recognizing that the heads of federal departments and agencies are responsible for developing and implementing appropriate agency-specific protective measures:

 **READY**.GOV
From The U.S. Department of Homeland Security.

Citizen Guidance on the Homeland Security Advisory System

Risk of Attack	Recommended Actions for Citizens
GREEN Low Risk	➡ Develop a family emergency plan. Share it with family and friends, and practice the plan. Visit www.Ready.gov for help creating a plan. ➡ Create an "Emergency Supply Kit" for your household. ➡ Be informed. Visit www.Ready.gov or obtain a copy of "Preparing Makes Sense, Get Ready Now" by calling 1-800-BE-READY. ➡ Know how to shelter-in-place and how to turn off utilities (power, gas, and water) to your home. ➡ Examine volunteer opportunities in your community, such as Citizen Corps, Volunteers in Police Service, Neighborhood Watch or others, and donate your time. ➡ Consider completing an American Red Cross first aid or CPR course, or Community Emergency Response Team (CERT) course.
BLUE Guarded Risk	➡ *Complete recommended steps at level green.* ➡ Review stored disaster supplies and replace items that are outdated. ➡ Be alert to suspicious activity and report it to proper authorities.
YELLOW Elevated Risk	➡ *Complete recommended steps at levels green and blue.* ➡ Ensure disaster supply kit is stocked and ready. ➡ Check telephone numbers in family emergency plan and update as necessary. ➡ Develop alternate routes to/from work or school and practice them. ➡ Continue to be alert for suspicious activity and report it to authorities.
ORANGE High Risk	➡ *Complete recommended steps at lower levels.* ➡ Exercise caution when traveling, pay attention to travel advisories. ➡ Review your family emergency plan and make sure all family members know what to do. ➡ Be Patient. Expect some delays, baggage searches, and restrictions at public buildings. ➡ Check on neighbors or others that might need assistance in an emergency.
RED Severe Risk	➡ *Complete all recommended actions at lower levels.* ➡ Listen to local emergency management officials. ➡ Stay tuned to TV or radio for current information/instructions. ➡ Be prepared to shelter-in-place or evacuate, as instructed. ➡ Expect traffic delays and restrictions. ➡ Provide volunteer services only as requested. ➡ Contact your school/business to determine status of work day.

Developed with input from the <u>American Red Cross</u>.

FIGURE 9–5 Homeland Security Advisory System. *Source:* www.dhs.gov.

1. **Low condition (green).** Declared when there is a low risk of terrorist attacks. Federal departments and agencies should consider the following general measures in addition to the agency-specific protective measures they develop and implement:

○ Refining and exercising as appropriate preplanned protective measures.

○ Ensuring personnel receive proper training on the Homeland Security Advisory System and specific preplanned department or agency protective measures.

○ Institutionalizing a process to assure that all facilities and regulated sectors are regularly assessed for vulnerabilities to terrorist attacks, and all reasonable measures are taken to mitigate these vulnerabilities.

2. **Guarded condition (blue).** Declared when there is a general risk of terrorist attacks. In addition to the protective measures taken in the previous threat condition, federal departments and agencies should consider the following general measures in addition to the agency-specific protective measures that they will develop and implement:

○ Checking communications with designated emergency response or command locations.

○ Reviewing and updating emergency response procedures.

○ Providing the public with any information that would strengthen its ability to act appropriately.

3. **Elevated condition (yellow).** Declared when there is a significant risk of terrorist attacks. In addition to the protective measures taken in the previous threat conditions, federal departments and agencies should consider the following general measures in addition to the protective measures that they will develop and implement:

○ Increasing surveillance of critical locations.

○ Coordinating emergency plans as appropriate with nearby jurisdictions.

○ Assessing whether the precise characteristics of the threat require the further refinement of preplanned protective measures.

○ Implementing, as appropriate, contingency and emergency response plans.

4. **High condition (orange).** Declared when there is a high risk of terrorist attacks. In addition to the protective measures taken in the previous threat conditions, federal departments and agencies should consider the following general measures in addition to the agency-specific protective measures that they will develop and implement:

○ Coordinating necessary security efforts with federal, state, and local law enforcement agencies or any National Guard or other appropriate armed forces organizations.

○ Taking additional precautions at public events and possibly considering alternative venues or even cancellation.

○ Preparing to execute contingency procedures, such as moving to an alternate site or dispersing their workforces.

○ Restricting threatened facility access to essential personnel only.

5. **Severe condition (red).** Reflects a severe risk of terrorist attacks. Under most circumstances, the protective measures for a severe condition are not intended to be sustained for substantial periods of time. In addition to the protective measures in the previous threat conditions, federal departments and agencies also should consider the following general measures in addition to the agency-specific protective measures that they will develop and implement:

○ Increasing or redirecting personnel to address critical emergency needs.

○ Assigning emergency response personnel and prepositioning and mobilizing specially trained teams or resources.

○ Monitoring, redirecting, or constraining transportation systems.
○ Closing public and government facilities.

The Department of Homeland Security also helps citizens and business owners prepare for future acts of terrorism through its Ready.gov campaign. The Web-based public education campaign provides a "common sense framework designed to launch a process of learning about citizen preparedness."

The DHS urges citizens to stay informed about how to react to various disaster scenarios. These include biological, chemical, explosive, nuclear, radiological, and natural disasters. Ready.gov states:

> Terrorists are working to obtain biological, chemical, nuclear, and radiological weapons, and the threat of an attack is very real. Here at the Department of Homeland Security, throughout the federal government, and at organizations across America we are working hard to strengthen our nation's security. Whenever possible, we want to stop terrorist attacks before they happen. All Americans should begin a process of learning about potential threats so we are better prepared to react during an attack. While there is no way to predict what will happen, or what your personal circumstances will be, there are simple things you can do now to prepare yourself and your loved ones.
>
> Some of the things you can do to prepare for the unexpected, such as assembling a supply kit and developing a family communications plan, are the same for both a natural or man-made emergency. However, as you will see throughout the pages of Ready.gov, there are important differences among potential terrorist threats that will impact the decisions you make and the actions you take. With a little planning and common sense, you can be better prepared for the unexpected.

The supplements at the companion Web site for this book include the recommendations for citizens to stay prepared provided by Ready.gov. (See the URL for the companion Web site in the *Introduction.*) More detailed recommendations for each step are provided at www.Ready.gov.

Critical Thinking

Since its creation, the Homeland Security Advisory System has been raised to orange eight times and to red one time. During these periods of elevated status, there were no attacks. Do you think that the absence of attacks makes citizens ignore future threats? Why or why not?

Accomplishments of the Department of Homeland Security

Accomplishments Since 2001

- The DHS has hired over 5,700 new border patrol agents and acquired nearly 7,800 new detention beds.
- The DHS provided over $22 billion to state, local, and tribal governments to enhance first responder preparedness, including $16.3 billion in support related to terrorism and catastrophic preparedness events.

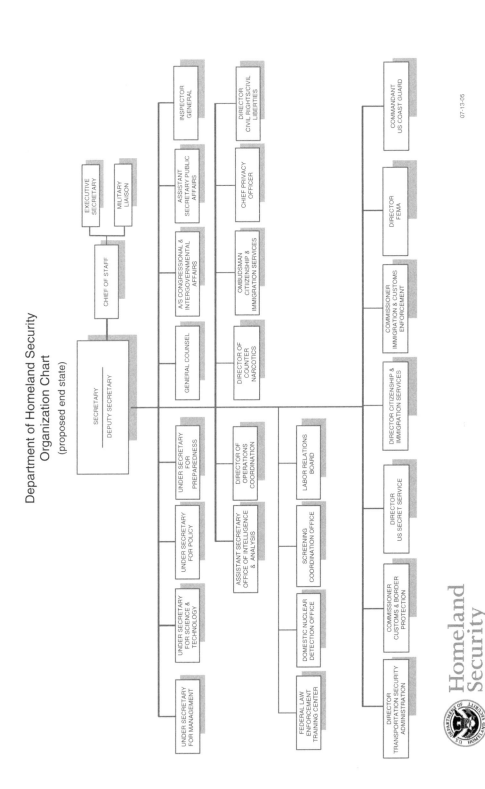

FIGURE 9-6 Organizational chart for the Department of Homeland Security. *Source:* www.dhs.gov.

- The DHS created the Domestic Nuclear Detection Office to detect, identify, and track down the origins of nuclear and radiological materials.
- The DHS hired a workforce and deployed sufficient technology to electronically screen 100 percent of airline passengers and checked baggage.
- The DHS strengthened marine transportation systems and the cargo supply chain through the Container Security Initiative, Customs Trade Partnership against Terrorism and the Maritime Transportation Security Acts.
- The DHS awarded more than $700 million in port security grants to enhance the physical security of the nation's seaports.

Accomplishments for 2006

Securing the nation's transportation system—the Transportation and Security Administration:

- **Liquid explosive threat response.** In response to the foiled terror plot in England, the Transportation and Security Administration (TSA) trained its 43,000 security officers to address the threat of liquid explosives in a matter of hours.
- **Air cargo security strengthened.** In fall 2006, the TSA issued two security directives requiring inspection of 100 percent of high risk cargo and packages tendered to airlines at the ticket counters. The TSA also expanded the use of explosives detection canine teams and added 100 air cargo inspectors.
- **Screening of port workers.** The TSA conducted more than 700,000 name-based security threat assessments on port workers.
- **Freight rail security.** The TSA worked with freight rail stakeholders to mitigate the greatest vulnerability in freight rail transportation, the standing toxic inhalation hazard rail car. These efforts provide for minimizing the occurrence of unattended toxic inhalation hazard cars in high threat urban areas, and if they are present, lowering the cars' standstill times and providing protection or surveillance.
- **Baseline security evaluations for mass transit and passenger rail systems.** One hundred surface transportation inspectors reviewed implementation of 17 security and emergency management action items that the TSA and the Department of Transportation's Federal Transit Administration jointly developed, in coordination with the Mass Transit Sector Coordinating Council.

Strengthening border security—Customs and Border Protection:

- **Deployment of the National Guard to the border.** Under Operation Jumpstart, the Customs and Border Protection (CBP) deployed up to 6,000 National Guard personnel to the southwest border. In addition to the National Guard deployment, border patrol staffing increased by 8 percent, from 11,265 to 12,349.
- **Increased border security at and between the nation's ports of entry.** CBP border patrol agents reduced the number of apprehensions at the borders by more than 8 percent in fiscal year 2006. As a result of targeted coordinated enforcement efforts, CBP border patrol reduced non-Mexican illegal alien apprehensions by 35 percent. In FY 2006, the CBP border patrol seized more than 1.3 million pounds of marijuana and 11,900 pounds of cocaine between the ports of entry. CBP officers at the nation's ports of entry seized more than 644,000 pounds of

marijuana, arrested more than 23,000 suspected criminals, and interdicted more than 209,000 inadmissible aliens and 1.628 million agricultural interceptions.

- **Radiation portal monitors deployed at land and sea ports.** The CBP deployed 280 new radiation portal monitors throughout the nation's ports of entry, bringing the number of radiation portal monitors to 881 at the nation's land and sea ports of entry.
- **CSI expanded.** The CBP expanded the Container Security Initiative, increasing participating ports to 50 in fiscal year 2006. It now covers more than 80 percent of U.S.-bound maritime containers.
- **Processed 61 repatriation flights.** During the evacuations from Lebanon, the DHS facilitated the processing of 61 civilian and military repatriation flights for 11,287 U.S. citizens.
- **Capability to secure the northern border increased.** CBP Air and Marine opened its third of five air branches planned for the U.S. northern border.
- **Ports of entry inspections.** CBP officers inspected 422 million travelers, more than 132 million cars, trucks, buses trains, vessels. and aircraft.

Protecting national security and upholding public safety—Immigration and Customs Enforcement:

- **"Catch and return" replaces "catch-and-release" along the borders.** In 2006, Immigration and Customs Enforcement (ICE) reengineered the detention and removal process to effectively end the practice of "catch and release."
- **New record set for work site enforcement.** More than 4,300 arrests were made in ICE work site enforcement cases, more than seven times the arrests the Immigration and Naturalization Service made in 2002.
- **New record set for compliance enforcement.** ICE completed 5,956 compliance enforcement investigations resulting in the administrative arrest of 1,710 overstay and status violators, a 75 percent increase over FY 2005.
- **New record set for alien removals.** ICE removed a record 189,670 illegal aliens from the country this fiscal year, a 12 percent increase over the number of removals during FY 2005.
- **Number of fugitive operations teams tripled.** ICE nearly tripled the number of fugitive operations teams deployed nationwide from 18 to 50. These teams locate, apprehend, and remove fugitive aliens, nearly one third of whom have criminal histories.
- **One of the world's most powerful drug cartels dismantled.** ICE concluded a 15-year probe into Colombia's Cali drug cartel, once responsible for 80 percent of the world's cocaine supply, with guilty pleas by its leaders and a $2 billion forfeiture settlement.
- **Transnational gangs targeted.** Through Operation Community Shield, ICE arrested roughly 2,290 violent gang members nationwide in 2006, of which 1,073 had convictions for violent crimes.

Protecting the public, the environment, and U.S. economic interests—the U.S. Coast Guard:

- **First new high endurance cutter in over 35 years christened.** The U.S. Coast Guard christened the cutter *Bertholf*, the first new high endurance cutter to be built in more than 35 years and the first national security cutter in its deepwater acquisition program.

- **National capital region air defense implemented.** The USCG officially assumed responsibility for air intercept operations in the nation's capital from U.S. Customs and Border Protection.
- **U.S. Coast Guard arrests "Tijuana cartel" drug lord.** With federal drug agents, the USCG arrested Mexican drug lord Francisco Javier Arellano-Felix, leader of the Tijuana cartel.
- **Record set for drug seizures and arrests.** Counterdrug boardings from U.S. and Royal Navy vessels resulted in all-time records for seizures and arrests. The 93,209 pounds of drugs that were seized was more than the combined amount seized in the previous two years.

Preventing or mitigating the effects of catastrophic terrorism—Science and Technology

- **Air cargo explosives detection pilot program launched.** The $30 million program, designed to capture vital information associated with enhanced air cargo screening and inspection, was launched at San Francisco and Seattle-Tacoma International Airports.
- **National interoperability baseline survey results announced.** The Office for Interoperability and Compatibility's SAFECOM program released the final results of its National Interoperability Baseline Survey, helping policy makers and emergency response leaders make informed decisions about strategies for improving interoperability and target resources.
- **Rail security explosives detection pilot programs conducted.** These programs were conducted in Baltimore, Maryland, and Jersey City, New Jersey, to test and evaluate security equipment and operating procedures.
- **Ground broken for the national biodefense analysis and countermeasures center.** The facility will cover roughly 160,000 square feet with a concentration of research and associated space. It will support a staff of approximately 120 and house two centers, the Biological Threat Characterization Center and the National Bioforensic Analysis Center.
- **Contracts to support emerging counter-MANPADS technologies awarded.** Science and Technology completed Phase II of a multiphase program to migrate onboard military countermeasures technology to commercial aircraft to protect against shoulder-fired, antiaircraft missiles, known as the Man-Portable Air Defense Systems (MANPADS). Under Phase III of the program, Science and Technology and its industry partners are collecting operations, support, and performance data. Additionally, three firms were selected to receive $7.4 million in combined contract awards to assess alternative methods to counter the MANPADS threat.

Keeping America's doors open while ensuring national security—U.S. Citizenship and Immigration Services:

- **Backlog eliminated.** The U.S. Citizenship and Immigration Services (USCIS) eliminated case backlogs of applications for immigration services and benefits, reducing the backlog from 3.8 million cases in January 2004 to less than 10,000 at the end of September 2006.

- **National Security and Records Verification Directorate established.** To combat fraud and criminal activity, the USCIS established the National Security and Records Verification Directorate.
- **Employers enrolled in pilot employment eligibility verification program.** The USCIS enrolled more than 12,500 employers and businesses in the Basic Pilot Employment Eligibility Verification Program, which verifies the work authorization of more than 1 million new hires a year at 47,000 hiring sites.
- **Electronic filing expanded.** The USCIS expanded opportunities for customers to file service or benefit applications electronically, then track the status of their cases online through the USCIS.gov Web site.

Establishing a nimble, effective emergency response system—FEMA:

- **Rebuilding FEMA as the preeminent emergency management agency for the nation.** FEMA concentrated its efforts on improving core competencies, in such areas as incident management, operational planning, disaster logistics, emergency communications, public communication, and customer service.
- **Disaster coordination teams predesignated.** In preparation for the 2006 hurricane season, the DHS predesignated five teams to coordinate the federal government's role in support of state and local governments preparing for and responding to major natural disasters. In total, 27 federal officials were appointed, each with unique expertise and experience.
- **FEMA achieved key developments in assisting disaster victims.** FEMA increased registration capability to 200,000 a day through its toll-free registration number, online registration process, registering individuals in shelters and using mobile units; increased home inspection capacity to 20,000 a day; activated a contract to assist in identity verification in future disasters; and tightened processes to speed up delivery of needed aid while simultaneously reducing waste, fraud, and abuse.
- **FEMA strengthened logistics management capabilities.** FEMA implemented the Total Asset Visibility Program to provide enhanced visibility, awareness, and accountability over disaster relief supplies and resources. It assisted in both resource flow and supply chain management.
- **FEMA improved communications and situational awareness.** FEMA already achieved real-time information sharing. To improve on existing systems, the DHS has initiated technological advances and elevated the standard by using satellite imagery, upgrading radios, and employing frequency management. The new National Response Coordination Center at FEMA is now operable. In addition, mobile registration intake centers, logistics supply systems, and total asset visibility programs have been implemented.
- **FEMA enlisted a seasoned leadership team.** In addition to the confirmation of Director R. David Paulison, FEMA built a strong team of leaders across the organization, each of whom brings more than 20 years of experience in emergency management or applicable fields.

Building a culture of preparedness—Emergency Preparedness:

- **The DHS awarded $2.6 billion for preparedness.** Included in this total, approximately $1.7 billion in Homeland Security Grant funds has been awarded to state and local governments for equipment, training, exercises, and various other measures designed to increase the level of security in communities across the nation. Another $400 million in grants was awarded to strengthen the nation's ability to prevent, protect against, respond to, and recover from terrorist attacks, major disasters, and other emergencies that could affect this country's critical infrastructure. Almost $300 million was distributed in grants to fire departments and EMS organizations to enhance their response capabilities to more effectively protect the health and safety of the public and emergency response personnel with respect to fire and all other hazards.

- **The DHS reviewed 131 state and local emergency plans.** By reviewing state and local disaster plans, collocating decision makers, and predesignating federal leadership, the DHS improved coordination across all levels of government. Through the nationwide plan review, the DHS completed visits to 131 sites (50 states, six territories, and 75 major urban areas) and reviewed the disaster and evacuation plans for each.
- **The DHS completed National Infrastructure Protection Plan.** The National Infrastructure Protection Plan is a comprehensive risk management framework that clearly defines critical infrastructure protection roles and responsibilities for all levels of government, private industry, nongovernmental agencies, and tribal partners.
- **The DHS received new authority to enhance chemical security.** The DHS was given authority by Congress to implement risk-based security standards for chemical facilities that present high levels of security risk.

Transforming U.S. border management and immigration systems—US-VISIT Program:

- **The DHS and DOJ began to establish interoperability.** The DHS and the Department of Justice began the initial phase of establishing interoperability between the US-VISIT program's Automated Biometric Identification System and the FBI's Integrated Automated Fingerprint Identification System fingerprint databases. This interoperability increases the DHS and State Department's ability to screen travelers, increase accuracy of matching, and provide greater ability to match against latent prints.
- **The DHS tests biometric verification at sea.** The U.S. Coast Guard and US-VISIT began a pilot program to collect biometric information (digital fingerprints and photographs) from migrants interdicted while attempting to unlawfully enter U.S. territory through the Mona Passage, the body of water between the Dominican Republic and Puerto Rico.
- **US-VISIT deployed e-passport readers to 33 airports.** US-VISIT completed deployment of e-passport readers to 33 U.S. airports so that ports of entry can compare and authenticate data in e-passports issued by Visa Waiver Program countries.

Protecting the nation from dangerous goods—the Domestic Nuclear Detection Office

- **The DNDO awarded over $1 billion for next generation nuclear detection devices.** The Domestic Nuclear Detection Office (DNDO) announced the award of Advanced Spectroscopic Portal program contracts totaling $1.15 billion to enhance the detection of radiological and nuclear materials at the nation's ports of entry.

- **The DNDO established the Nuclear Forensics Center.** The DNDO established the National Technical Nuclear Forensics Center to collect and analyze material evidence to identify and ultimately prosecute those responsible for any potential act of nuclear terrorism.

Training the Front Line Officers—the Federal Law Enforcement Training Center

- **The training center.** Over 51,000 federal, state, local, tribal, campus, and international law enforcement agents and officers were trained by the Federal Law Enforcement Training Center on topics including border security and the prevention and detection of nuclear, radiological, or biological attacks.

Establishing policy to protect the nation—the DHS Policy Office

- **The DHS renegotiated passenger name record data.** The DHS successfully renegotiated an interim agreement regarding passenger name record data with the European Union, allowing the department to make full use of passenger data as needed to protect national borders.
- **Secure freight initiative launched to begin screening at foreign ports.** The DHS and Department of Energy announced the first phase of the Secure Freight Initiative, an unprecedented effort to build on existing port security measures by enhancing the federal government's ability to scan containers for nuclear and radiological materials overseas and better assess the risk from inbound containers.
- **Improvements to the Visa Waiver Program.** The administration announced its intention to work with Congress to reform the Visa Waiver Program, to strengthen security and facilitate international allies' ability to join the program.

Always Be Ready—the Ready campaign:

- **Ad Council deemed Ready one of the most successful campaigns.** The Ad Council declared the Ready campaign one of the most successful campaigns in its more than 60-year history. The campaign generated more than $593 million in donated media support. The Web site received more than 1.9 billion hits, the toll-free number received more than 272,000 calls, and more than 9.7 million Ready materials have been requested or downloaded.
- Ready Kids launched. Ready Kids, an extension of the Ready campaign, was launched as a tool to help parents and teachers educate children ages 8–12 about emergencies and how they can help get their family prepared.
- The DHS and the Ad Council launched new ads. Together with the Ad Council, the DHS released new television, radio, print, outdoor, and Internet public service announcements to support the Ready campaign.

Preparing for and responding to incidents of medical significance—the Office of the Chief Medical Officer:

- **The DHS coordinated pandemic influenza activities.** The Office of the Chief Medical Officer coordinated the department's pandemic influenza preparedness activities.

Shaping the intelligence network—Intelligence and Analysis

- **Fusion centers facilitated flow of information.** Intelligence and Analysis (I&A) began embedding DHS analysts at state and local fusion centers across the nation, deploying personnel to five centers and providing over $380 million in support of these centers.
- **DHS enhanced information sharing with government and private partners.** I&A analysts produced and distributed nearly 450 intelligence products that provided actionable information to help its partners protect their communities and critical infrastructure.
- **Installation began on the Homeland Security data network.** While an interim capability had been in use for several years, I&A began installing the Homeland Security data network, a classified network to allow the advanced, real-time communications capability to exchange information up to the secret level with partners at the federal, state, and local level.

Integrating and unifying all aspects of the screening process—the Office of Screening Coordination:

- **The Office of Screening Coordination created.** The DHS started the Office of Screening Coordination to integrate the department's terrorist- and immigration-related screening efforts, create unified screening standards and policies, and develop a single redress process for travelers.

Strengthening and unifying DHS operations and management—the DHS management:

- **Chief Human Capital Office moved forward with performance management goals.** The DHS deployed its performance management program and its automated system to approximately 10,000 employees in multiple components and trained 350 senior executives and more than 11,000 managers and supervisors in performance leadership.
- **The Office of Security completed HSPD-12 goals.** The Office of Security met all Homeland Security Presidential Directive (HSPD) 12 requirements by deploying an HSPD-12 compliant credentialing system and associated policy and procedures.
- **The Chief Procurement Office exceeded small business goals.** The DHS awarded approximately 34 percent of DHS prime contracts to small businesses, exceeding the goal by 4 percent.

Countering the drug threat to the United States—Counternarcotics Enforcement

- **National Southwest Border Counternarcotics Implementation Plan closed gaps.** On August 18, 2006, the DHS and Department of Justice, serving as cochairs and represented by the Office of Counternarcotics Enforcement and the Office of the Deputy Attorney General, respectively, submitted a National Southwest Border Counternarcotics Strategy and Implementation Plan to the International Drug Control Policy Coordinating Committee.

Protecting America and preserving its freedoms—civil rights and civil liberties

- **The Office for Civil Rights and Civil Liberties implemented new training through the Civil Liberties University.** The Office for Civil Rights and Civil Liberties, working with component offices throughout the DHS, developed a number of useful training products and posters for DHS personnel, including an hour-long training on the introduction to Arab American and Muslim American cultures; on-line training that emphasizes the core elements of the National Detention Standards developed by the Immigration and Customs Enforcement Detention and Removal Office; two posters that provide guidance on how to screen and, if necessary, search individuals who wear common Muslim and Sikh head coverings; and an educational poster on how to screen those of the Sikh faith who carry a *kirpan*, a ceremonial religious dagger.

- **The Office for Civil Rights and Civil Liberties implemented effective processing of EEO complaints.** The Equal Employment Opportunity Program has developed an effective process for issuing final actions by hiring subject-matter experts, having a multitier quality control process, utilizing contractor support, and exercising strong project management controls. The first priority has been addressing the oldest cases received from the DHS's legacy organizations. The oldest case predate the DHS by 16 years. As of December 1, 2006, the Office for Civil Rights and Civil Liberties received over 3,812 EEO complaints of discrimination for final agency action and over 3,576 decisions have been issued.

- **The DHS cosponsored the Working Conference on Emergency Management and Individuals with Disabilities and the Elderly.** The Office for Civil Rights and Civil Liberties, in partnership with the Department of Health and Human Services, cosponsored a working conference that brought together governor-appointed state teams to connect state emergency management officials with key disability and aging experts to work toward integration of efforts within their jurisdiction's emergency management framework, facilitate cooperative planning with senior officials of the FEMA regions, and identify and institute measurable outcomes and systems for tracking results.

- **The Office for Civil Rights and Civil Liberties continued engagement with American Arab, Muslim, Sikh, South Asian, and other ethnic and religious communities.** The Office for Civil Rights and Civil Liberties actively led or participated in regularly scheduled meetings with representatives from the American Arab, Muslim, Sikh, and South Asian communities in Houston, Los Angeles, Detroit, Chicago, Buffalo, and Washington, D.C. The office also established working relationships with immigration advocacy groups concerned with border security and naturalization policies and leaders of the disability community to discuss emergency preparedness issues, particularly in the context of natural disasters.

Source: www.dhs.gov.

The DHS Budget

The White House proposed a budget for fiscal year 2008 that requests a total of $46.4 billion for the Department of Homeland Security. This amount is an increase of 8 percent over what was funded by Congress in FY 2007 (excluding funds provided in emergency supplemental funding). The FY 2008 budget request targets five areas:

1. Protecting the nation from dangerous people.
2. Protecting the nation from dangerous goods.

3. Protecting critical infrastructure.
4. Rebuilding the nation's emergency response system and creating a culture of preparedness.
5. Strengthening DHS operations and management.

The 2008 budget provides more than $3.5 billion for the border patrol (an increase of 27 percent over the 2007 enacted level), including funding for 3,000 new agents. This would bring the total number of agents to 17,819, almost double pre-2001 levels. This funding also supports border fencing, technology, and other related infrastructure (including the Secure Border Initiative). The 2008 budget includes $2.2 billion in detention and removal resources to continue the "catch and release" program and support a total of 28,450 detention beds across the country that house apprehended illegal aliens.

To improve coordination and provide assistance to state and local law enforcement officials, the FY 2008 budget expands the 287(g) program, which provides state and local law enforcement officials with guidance and training in immigration law. The 2008 budget includes an increase of $26 million for this program and the Law Enforcement Support Center, including the training of an additional 250 state and local law enforcement officers, detention beds for apprehended illegal aliens, and personnel to assist state and local law enforcement when they encounter aliens. It also includes an increase of $29 million to identify criminal aliens in federal, state, and local prison facilities and remove those aliens from the United States.

The 2008 budget provides $30 million to support the Basic Pilot Program, which allows employers to better verify the employment eligibility of prospective employees and avoid hiring unauthorized workers. In addition, the budget includes an increase of $5 million to improve work site enforcement through cooperative agreements with private employers.

The 2008 budget also includes increases for investigating smuggling and border criminal activity ($13 million) and identifying, apprehending, prosecuting, and removing aliens involved in gang activities ($5 million). The ongoing US-VISIT program will receive $462 million, including $228 million to deploy fingerprint collection at all of the nation's land, air, and sea ports of entry and for interoperability with the FBI's fingerprint system, the Integrated Automated Fingerprint Identification System.

The Domestic Nuclear Detection Office, which coordinates nuclear detection efforts, would receive $562 million under this budget (its budget has grown more than 400 percent since its 2005 establishment). Another $25 million would be provided to regulate security at high-risk chemical facilities. This funding provides the DHS with the capability to develop and refine vulnerability assessment tools, review site security plans submitted by high-risk chemical facilities, and inspect facilities for compliance with chemical facility security regulations.

The FY 2008 budget provides $100 million to implement changes to FEMA resulting from the Katrina experience. With these funds, the DHS will attempt to strengthen FEMA's core capabilities, competencies, and capacities; expand regional preparedness and response activities; strengthen partnerships with the states; and professionalize the national emergency management system. These changes are aimed at allowing FEMA to establish better program analysis and project management capabilities by reshaping its workforce and becoming more results and performance oriented. The DHS will continue to ensure the integration of federal plans and planning efforts. FEMA will hire dedicated operational planners who will form partnerships with states and localities to develop operational disaster response plans and incident-specific catastrophic plans. This funding will allow FEMA to improve its ability to deliver disaster assistance to individuals and communities by increasing registration speed and capacity and expanding mobile registration intake centers to make it easier for people to register for the Individual Assistance Program. Some of this money will be used to fund any ongoing Katrina recovery efforts.

FY 2008 DHS Budget Highlights

The FY 2008 DHS budget revolves around five major themes: protecting the national from dangerous people, protecting the nation from dangerous goods, protecting critical infrastructure, building a nimble and effective emergency response system and culture of preparedness, and strengthening and unifying DHS operations and management.

Protecting the Nation from Dangerous People

The DHS will strive to protect the United States from dangerous people by strengthening border security; developing fraud resistant identification and biometric tools; creating an interoperable architecture for the Transportation Worker Identification Credential Program, the Western Hemisphere Travel Initiative, and Real ID requirements; and achieving full database interoperability among the DHS, the FBI, and the Department of State.

- $1 billion will support the deployment of the SBInet (Secure Border Initiative) Program and create an integrated infrastructure and technology solution for effective control of the border that includes fencing and virtual barriers to prevent illegal entry into the United States.
- $778 million will allow 3,000 additional border patrol agents to be hired, as well as facilities to house the agents, support personnel, and equipment necessary to gain operational control of national borders.
- $252 million is requested for implementation of the Western Hemisphere Travel Initiative at land ports of entry, which is designed to ensure that all people arriving at U.S. ports of entry have a valid and appropriate means of identification and can be processed in an efficient manner.
- An increase of $146.2 million for the Unique Identity Initiative will establish the foundational capabilities to improve identity establishment and verification with the transition to interoperability of the 10-Print and Automated Biometric Identification System and the Integrated Automated Fingerprint Identification System. The funding will provide the capability

(Continued)

to biometrically screen foreign visitors requesting entry to the United States through the collection of 10-print capture, rather than the current 2, at enrollment. US-VISIT, along with the Departments of State and Justice, will be able to continue efforts to develop interoperability between the DHS and Justice Department systems.

- An increase of $224.2 million in funding will support the Transportation Security Administration's screening operations. This includes the transportation security officers, document checkers, a Career Progression Program, and procurement and installation of checkpoint support and explosives detection systems. In FY 2007 and FY 2008, the Transportation Security Administration plans to assume responsibility for document checking.

- An increase of $38 million in funding will support development and initial operating capability for the Secure Flight system. This includes funding for hardware procurement, operations ramp-up and training, and network interface engineering between the Secure Flight and U.S. Customs and Border Protection's Advanced Passenger Information System network. Secure Flight will strengthen watch list screening and vet all domestic air travelers.

- An increase of $28.7 million for the Immigration and Customs Enforcement Criminal Alien Program, which would fund the addition of 22 investigation teams. These teams will continue the mission of identifying and removing incarcerated criminal aliens so they are not released back into the general population.

- An increase of $16.5 million in funding will support the Transportation Worker Identification Credential Program, which establishes an integrated, credential-based, identity verification program through the use of biometric technology. To gain unescorted access to the secure areas within the nation's transportation system, transportation workers who need access to these areas will go through identity verification, a satisfactory background check, and be issued a biometrically verifiable identity card to be used with local access systems.

- An increase of $788.1 million for the Coast Guard's Integrated Deepwater System. This funding will complete the acquisition of four national security cutters, fund engineering and design costs for the replacement patrol boat, and purchase four additional maritime patrol aircraft. These upgrades to its fleet will strengthen the Coast Guard's ability to safeguard U.S. seaports from terrorists seeking to enter the country or transport dangerous weapons or materials.

- Total funding of $30 million for the Employment Eligibility Verification Program, to sustain the expansion of the program to provide increased interior enforcement of U.S. immigration laws and more robust work site enforcement.

□ □ □ ▬▬▬▬▬▬▬▬▬▬▬▬▬▬▬▬▬▬▬▬▬▬

Protecting the Nation from Dangerous Goods

The DHS seeks to improve maritime cargo security, including enhancing domestic and overseas container scanning. In addition, the department is funding technology improvements and reducing costs of the BioWatch Program.

- $178 million will provide for the procurement and deployment of radiation portal monitors, including next generation advanced spectroscopic portal systems. The requested resources will assist the department in achieving its goal of screening 98 percent of all containers entering the United States by the end of FY 2008.
- An increase of $15 million is requested for the Secure Freight Initiative, which is designed to maximize radiological and nuclear screening of U.S.-bound containers from foreign ports. Secure Freight includes a next generation risk assessment screening program and an overseas detection network, while merging existing and new information regarding containers transiting through the supply chain to assist customs and screening officials in making security and trade decisions.
- An increase of $47.4 million is requested for the Acceleration of Next-Generation Research and Development Program, which increases funding for several research, development, and operations program areas.

▬▬▬▬▬▬▬▬▬▬▬▬▬▬▬▬▬▬▬▬▬ □ □ □

□ □ □ ▬▬▬▬▬▬▬▬▬▬▬▬▬▬▬▬▬▬▬▬▬▬

Protecting Critical Infrastructure

Central to the DHS mission is the support of effective critical infrastructure security investments at the federal, state, and local levels. The 2008 presidential budget requests funding for initiatives that continue to support strengthening national chemical plant security, protecting high-risk rail shipments, and cultivating mutually beneficial partnerships with industry owners and operators.

- An increase of $30 million will provide for the Securing the Cities Implementation Initiative. The DHS will begin the implementation of strategies developed through analysis conducted in FY 2006 and 2007 in support of the initiative in the New York region. Activities included in the development of regional strategies include analyses of critical road networks, mass transit, maritime, and rail vulnerabilities. The Domestic Nuclear Detection Office will engage state and local partners in additional urban areas beginning in FY 2008 to tailor strategies and lessons learned from the New York region to meet requirements specific to these regions.

(Continued)

- An increase of $21.9 million will support the newly formed Science and Technology Office of Innovation to provide increases to program development and "leap-ahead" technologies that address some of the highest priority needs of the department. The technologies being developed seek to create a resilient electric grid, to protect critical infrastructure sites, detect cross-border tunnels, defeat improvised explosive devices, and utilize high-altitude platforms or ground-based systems for detection and engagement of MANPADS to offer alternative solutions to installing systems on aircraft.
- An increase of $15 million (for a total of $25 million) to improve chemical site security and regulate security of chemical plants. The funding will be used to manage training of inspector staff and assist desk personnel and other administrative staff. Funds will also be spent on assisting chemical facilities with vulnerability assessments.
- An increase of $3.5 million will expand the Transportation Security Administration's National Explosive Detection Canine Team Program by approximately 45 teams to support the nation's largest passenger transportation systems in both mass transit and ferry systems.
- An increase of $35.6 million for the presidential campaign to enable the U.S. Secret Service to provide the appropriate level of resources to adequately protect the candidates and nominees during the 2008 presidential campaign while sustaining other protective programs.

Build a Nimble and Effective Emergency Response System and Culture of Preparedness

The DHS must remain in a state of readiness to deter and respond to acts of terror or other disasters. The following funding requests are designed to strengthen the department's ability to build an effective emergency response system and culture of preparedness.

- An increase of $100 million to fund FEMA's Vision Initiatives, which are designed to enable the agency to intensify and speed the development of core competencies central to achieving disaster readiness, response, and recovery. A combination of staffing increases, new technologies, and investment in equipment and supplies is being made increase FEMA's mission capacity in the areas of incident management, operational planning, continuity programs, public disaster communications, hazard mitigation, disaster logistics, and service to disaster victims. In addition, the requested increase will support FEMA's plan to transform its approach to business operations and project management, enabling the development and integration of information systems, policies, internal controls, and processes necessary to effectively build, manage, and support the agency's core competencies.

- A total of $3.2 billion will be available in FY 2008 for state and local preparedness expenditures as well as assistance to firefighters. Of this amount, $2.2 billion is requested for the DHS to fund grant, training, and exercise programs. In addition, in coordination with its State Preparedness Grant Program, the DHS will coadminister the $1.0 billion Public Safety Interoperable Communications Grant Program, in partnership with the Department of Commerce. Funds requested through these programs will provide critical assistance to state and local homeland security efforts, support resources available through other federal assistance programs that center on first responder terrorism preparedness activities, and deliver ample support to all state and local first responder organizations to obtain the equipment, training, and other resources required to protect the public in the event of a terrorist attack or other major incident.
- A realignment of $132.7 million in base resources will establish a Deployable Operations Group and strengthen the Coast Guard's overall response capability. The alignment of Coast Guard's deployable specialized forces under a single command will improve and strengthen Coast Guard's ability to perform day-to-day operations and respond to maritime disasters and threats to the nation.
- A total of $48 million is requested to further professionalize FEMA's disaster workforce by converting the cadre of on-call response employee positions with four-year terms into permanent full-time positions. This transition will stabilize the disaster workforce, allowing for the development and retention of employees with needed program expertise and increased staffing flexibility to ensure critical functions are maintained during disaster response surge operations.
- An increase of $12 million for the Nationwide Automatic Identification System will continue funding for this vital project that significantly enhances the Coast Guard's ability to identify, track, and exchange information with vessels in the maritime domain, especially those vessels that may threaten the nation.

Strengthen and Unify DHS Operations and Management

The DHS is continuing to strengthen departmental operations to improve mission success. A variety of critical investments have been initiated to help it accomplish that goal.

- An increase of $139 million in premium processing fees will transform and improve the USCIS business processes and outdated information technology systems. This will support automation of the USCIS operations and improve processing times, increase security and fraud detection, improve customer service, and replace paper-based processes and antiquated technology.

(Continued)

Additionally, $124 million in anticipated application fee revenue will be committed to upgrade and maintain the USCIS information technology environment.

- $17 million in new funding within U.S. Immigration and Customs Enforcement and Customs and Border Protection will help improve the internal oversight of personnel.
- An increase of $120 million for the DHS Consolidated Headquarters Project to further consolidate executive program leadership of the department in a secure setting. This is being done to foster a unified-DHS culture and enhance the flow of information, while optimizing prevention and response capabilities across all operations.
- An increase of $9.6 million for the Office of the Chief Procurement Officer will establish the staffing requirements necessary to properly award and administer departmentwide acquisition programs to ensure effective delivery of services and proper procurement and contracting procedures in compliance with all federal laws and regulations governing procurements.
- $99.1 million for the inspector general to continue serving as an independent and objective inspection, audit, and investigative body promoting economy, efficiency, and effectiveness in the DHS programs and operations.

Source: Department of Homeland Security, "DHS Proposed 2008 Budget," www.DHS.gov, 2007.

The 911 Commission

In late 2002, in an effort to "prepare a full and complete account of the circumstances surrounding the terrorist attacks that occurred on September 11, 2001," the National Commission on Terrorist Attacks upon the United States (more commonly known as the 911 Commission) was formed. This commission set out to determine the shortfalls and the lessons learned from the preparedness for and response to international terrorism within the United States and to formulate recommendations for activities that would help improve these systems in case of future threats and attacks.

The commission, which consisted of five Republicans and five Democrats, interviewed over 1,200 people from 10 countries, including several past and present government officials at the federal, state, and local levels, and studied millions of pages of documentation to accurately assess the events. On July 22, 2004, the 911 Commission released its long-awaited report. Although there was initial criticism of earlier commission reports and its members, including claims of bias, difficulty in attaining cooperation from White House officials, partisanship, among others, the final report's findings generally have been met with approval and acceptance for their recommendations.

The report found many opportunities that could have been exploited by the federal government to stop the terrorists who attacked in 2001, including

- Not watchlisting future hijackers Hazmi and Mihdhar, not trailing them after they traveled to Bangkok, and not informing the FBI about one future hijacker's U.S. visa or his companion's travel to the United States.
- Not sharing information linking individuals in the *Cole* attack to Mihdhar.
- Not taking adequate steps in time to find Mihdhar or Hazmi in the United States.
- Not linking the arrest of Zacarias Moussaoui, described as interested in flight training for the purpose of using an airplane in a terrorist act, to the heightened indications of attack.
- Not discovering false statements on visa applications.
- Not recognizing passports manipulated in a fraudulent manner.
- Not expanding no-fly lists to include names from terrorist watchlists.
- Not searching airline passengers identified by the computer-based CAPPS screening system.
- Not hardening aircraft cockpit doors or taking other measures to prepare for the possibility of suicide hijackings.

The report also identified failures on the part of U.S. government policy that could have prevented the attacks, including

- **Imagination.** The commission saw this as the most important failure. They do not believe leaders understood the gravity of the threat or that terrorist danger from Bin Ladin and al Qaeda was a major topic for policy debate among the public, the media, or in the Congress. Al Qaeda's new brand of terrorism presented challenges to U.S. government institutions that they were not well-designed to meet. Although top officials told the commission that they understood the danger, the commission believed there was uncertainty among them as to whether this was just a new and especially venomous version of the ordinary terrorist threat the United States had lived with for decades or it was indeed radically new, posing a threat beyond any yet experienced.
- **Policy.** The commission felt that terrorism was not the overriding national security concern for the U.S. government under either the Clinton or the pre-9/11 Bush administration. The policy challenges were linked to this failure of imagination. Officials in both the Clinton and Bush administrations regarded a full U.S. invasion of Afghanistan as practically inconceivable before 9/11.
- **Capabilities.** Before 9/11, the United States tried to solve the al Qaeda problem with the capabilities it had used in the last stages of the Cold War and its immediate aftermath. The commission claims these capabilities were insufficient. The CIA had minimal capacity to conduct paramilitary operations with its own personnel, and it did not seek a large-scale expansion of these capabilities before 9/11. The CIA also needed to improve its capability to collect intelligence from human agents.

At no point before 9/11 was the Department of Defense fully engaged in the mission of countering al Qaeda, even though this was perhaps the most dangerous foreign enemy threatening the United States. NORAD itself was barely able to retain any alert bases at all. Its planning scenarios occasionally considered the danger of hijacked aircraft being guided to American targets, but only aircraft that were coming from overseas.

The commission saw the most serious weaknesses in agency capabilities in the domestic arena. The FBI did not have the capability to link the collective knowledge of agents in the field to national priorities. Other domestic agencies deferred to the FBI. FAA capabilities were weak. Any serious examination of the possibility of a suicide hijacking could have suggested changes to fix glaring vulnerabilities—expanding no-fly lists, searching passengers identified by the CAPPS screening system, deploying federal air marshals domestically, hardening cockpit doors, alerting air crews to a different kind of hijacking possibility than they had been trained to expect. Yet the FAA did not adjust either its own training or training with NORAD to take account of threats other than those experienced in the past.

- **Management.** The commission reported that the missed opportunities to thwart the 9/11 plot were also symptoms of a broader inability to adapt the way government manages problems to the new challenges of the twenty-first century. Action officers should have been able to draw on all available knowledge about al Qaeda in the government. Management should have ensured that information was shared and duties were clearly assigned across agencies and across the foreign/domestic divide. There also were broader management issues with respect to how top leaders set priorities and allocated resources. The U.S. government did not find a way of pooling intelligence and using it to guide the planning and assignment of responsibilities for joint operations involving entities as disparate as the CIA, the FBI, the State Department, the military, and the agencies involved in homeland security.

In addition to these general findings, the commission also reported a description of several specific findings they claim resulted in the inability of the government to thwart the attacks and its ability to respond once they occurred, including

- Unsuccessful diplomacy.
- Lack of military operations.
- Problems with the intelligence community.
- Problems in the FBI.
- Permeable borders and immigration controls.
- Permeable aviation security.
- Terrorist financing.
- The lack of an improved homeland defense.
- Problems with emergency response systems.
- The poor response of Congress to the terrorist threat.

The 911 Commission made recommendations that fell into two general categories: what to do and how to do it. The following information comes directly from the Executive Summary of the 911 Commission Report.

What to Do? A Global Strategy

The enemy is not just "terrorism." It is the threat posed specifically by Islamist terrorism, by Bin Ladin and others who draw on a long tradition of extreme intolerance within a minority strain of Islam that does not distinguish politics from religion and distorts both.

The enemy is not Islam, the great world faith, but a perversion of Islam. The enemy goes beyond al Qaeda to include the radical ideological movement, inspired in part by al Qaeda, that has spawned other terrorist groups and violence. Thus our strategy must match our means to two ends: dismantling the al Qaeda network and, in the long term, prevailing over the ideology that contributes to Islamist terrorism.

The first phase of our post-9/11 efforts rightly included military action to topple the Taliban and pursue al Qaeda. This work continues. But long-term success demands the use of all elements of national power: diplomacy, intelligence, covert action, law enforcement, economic policy, foreign aid, public diplomacy, and homeland defense. If we favor one tool while neglecting others, we leave ourselves vulnerable and weaken our national effort.

What should Americans expect from their government? The goal seems unlimited: Defeat terrorism anywhere in the world. But Americans have also been told to expect the worst: An attack probably is coming; it may be more devastating still.

Vague goals match an amorphous picture of the enemy. Al Qaeda and other groups are popularly described as being all over the world, adaptable, resilient, needing little higher-level organization, and capable of anything. It is an image of an omnipotent hydra of destruction. That image lowers expectations of government effectiveness.

It lowers them too far. Our report shows a determined and capable group of plotters. Yet the group was fragile and occasionally left vulnerable by the marginal, unstable people often attracted to such causes. The enemy made mistakes. The U.S. government was not able to capitalize on them.

No president can promise that a catastrophic attack like that of 9/11 will not happen again. But the American people are entitled to expect that officials will have realistic objectives, clear guidance, and effective organization. They are entitled to see standards for performance so they can judge, with the help of their elected representatives, whether the objectives are being met.

We propose a strategy with three dimensions: (1) Attack terrorists and their organizations, (2) prevent the continued growth of Islamist terrorism, and (3) protect against and prepare for terrorist attacks.

Attack Terrorists and Their Organizations

- Root out sanctuaries. The U.S. government should identify and give priority to actual or potential terrorist sanctuaries and have realistic country or regional strategies for each, utilizing every element of national power and reaching out to countries that can help us.
- Strengthen long-term U.S. and international commitments to the future of Pakistan and Afghanistan.
- Confront problems with Saudi Arabia in the open and build a relationship beyond oil, a relationship that both sides can defend to their citizens and includes a shared commitment to reform.

Prevent the Continued Growth of Islamist Terrorism

In October 2003, Secretary of Defense Donald Rumsfeld asked if enough was being done "to fashion a broad integrated plan to stop the next generation of terrorists." As part of such a plan, the U.S. government should

- Define the message and stand as an example of moral leadership in the world. To Muslim parents, terrorists like Bin Ladin have nothing to offer their children but visions of violence and death. America and its friends have the advantage—our vision can offer a better future.
- Where Muslim governments, even those that are friends, do not offer opportunity, respect the rule of law, or tolerate differences, then the United States needs to stand for a better future.
- Communicate and defend American ideals in the Islamic world, through much stronger public diplomacy to reach more people, including students and leaders outside of government. Our efforts here should be as strong as they were in combating closed societies during the Cold War.
- Offer an agenda of opportunity that includes support for public education and economic openness.
- Develop a comprehensive coalition strategy against Islamist terrorism, using a flexible contact group of leading coalition governments and fashioning a common coalition approach on issues like the treatment of captured terrorists.
- Devote a maximum effort to the parallel task of countering the proliferation of weapons of mass destruction.
- Expect less from trying to dry up terrorist money and more from following the money for intelligence, as a tool to hunt terrorists, understand their networks, and disrupt their operations.

Protect against and Prepare for Terrorist Attacks

- Target terrorist travel, an intelligence and security strategy that the 9/11 story showed could be at least as powerful as the effort devoted to terrorist finance.
- Address problems of screening people with biometric identifiers across agencies and governments, including our border and transportation systems, by designing a comprehensive screening system that addresses common problems and sets common standards. As standards spread, this necessary and ambitious effort could dramatically strengthen the world's ability to intercept individuals who could pose catastrophic threats.
- Quickly complete a biometric entry/exit screening system, one that also speeds qualified travelers.
- Set standards for the issuance of birth certificates and sources of identification, such as driver's licenses.
- Develop strategies for neglected parts of our transportation security system. Since 9/11, about 90 percent of the nation's $5 billion annual investment in transportation security has gone to aviation, to fight the last war.
- In aviation, prevent arguments about a new computerized profiling system from delaying vital improvements in the "no-fly" and "automatic selectee" lists. Also, give priority to the improvement of check-point screening.
- Determine, with leadership from the president, guidelines for gathering and sharing information in the new security systems that are needed, guidelines that integrate safeguards for privacy and other essential liberties.
- Underscore that as government power necessarily expands in certain ways, the burden of retaining such powers remains on the executive to demonstrate the

value of such powers and ensure adequate supervision of how they are used, including a new board to oversee the implementation of the guidelines needed for gathering and sharing information in these new security systems.

- Base federal funding for emergency preparedness solely on risks and vulnerabilities, putting New York City and Washington, D.C., at the top of the current list. Such assistance should not remain a program for general revenue sharing or pork-barrel spending.
- Make homeland security funding contingent on the adoption of an incident command system to strengthen teamwork in a crisis, including a regional approach. Allocate more radio spectrum and improve connectivity for public safety communications, and encourage widespread adoption of newly developed standards for private-sector emergency preparedness—since the private sector controls 85 percent of the nation's critical infrastructure.

How to Do It? A Different Way of Organizing Government

The strategy recommended is elaborate, even as presented here very briefly. To implement it will require a government better organized than the one that exists today, with its national security institutions designed half a century ago to win the Cold War. Americans should not settle for incremental, ad hoc adjustments to a system created a generation ago for a world that no longer exists.

These detailed recommendations are designed to fit together. Their purpose is clear: to build unity of effort across the U.S. government. As one official now serving on the front lines overseas put it to us: "One fight, one team."

We call for unity of effort in five areas, beginning with unity of effort on the challenge of counterterrorism itself:

- Unifying strategic intelligence and operational planning against Islamist terrorists across the foreign/domestic divide with a National Counterterrorism Center.
- Unifying the intelligence community with a new national intelligence director.
- Unifying the many participants in the counterterrorism effort and their knowledge in a network-based information sharing system that transcends traditional governmental boundaries.
- Unifying and strengthening congressional oversight to improve quality and accountability.
- Strengthening the FBI and homeland defenders.

Unity of Effort: A National Counterterrorism Center

The 9/11 story teaches the value of integrating strategic intelligence from all sources into joint operational planning, with *both* dimensions spanning the foreign/domestic divide.

- In some ways, since 9/11, joint work has gotten better. The effort of fighting terrorism has flooded over many of the usual agency boundaries because of its sheer quantity and energy. Attitudes have changed. But the problems of coordination have multiplied. The Defense Department alone has three unified commands (SOCOM, CENTCOM, and NORTHCOM) that deal with terrorism as one of their principal concerns.

- Much of the public commentary about the 9/11 attacks has focused on "lost opportunities." Although characterized as problems of "watchlisting," "information sharing," or "connecting the dots," each of these labels is too narrow. They describe the symptoms, not the disease.
- Breaking the older mold of organization stovepiped purely in executive agencies, we propose a National Counterterrorism Center (NCTC) that would borrow the joint, unified command concept adopted in the 1980s by the American military in a civilian agency, combining the joint intelligence function alongside the operations work.
- The NCTC would build on the existing Terrorist Threat Integration Center and would replace it and other terrorism "fusion centers" within the government. The NCTC would become the authoritative knowledge bank, bringing information to bear on common plans. It should task collection requirements both inside and outside the United States.
- The NCTC should perform joint operational planning, assigning lead responsibilities to existing agencies and letting them direct the actual execution of the plans.
- Placed in the Executive Office of the President, headed by a Senate-confirmed official (with rank equal to the deputy head of a cabinet department) who reports to the national intelligence director, the NCTC would track implementation of plans. It would be able to influence the leadership and the budgets of the counterterrorism operating arms of the CIA, the FBI, and the Departments of Defense and Homeland Security.
- The NCTC should *not* be a policy-making body. Its operations and planning should follow the policy direction of the president and the National Security Council.

Unity of Effort: A National Intelligence Director

Since long before 9/11—and continuing to this day—the intelligence community is not organized well for joint intelligence work. It does not employ common standards and practices in reporting intelligence or training experts overseas and at home. The expensive national capabilities for collecting intelligence have divided management. The structures are too complex and too secret.

- The community's head—the director of central intelligence—has at least three jobs: running the CIA, coordinating a 15-agency confederation, and being the intelligence analyst-in-chief to the president. No one person can do all these things.
- A new national intelligence director should be established with two main jobs: to oversee national intelligence centers that combine experts from all the collection disciplines against common targets, like counterterrorism or nuclear proliferation, and to oversee the agencies that contribute to the national intelligence program, a task that includes setting common standards for personnel and information technology.
- The national intelligence centers would be the unified commands of the intelligence world—a long-overdue reform for intelligence comparable to the 1986 Goldwater-Nichols law that reformed the organization of national defense.

The home services—such as the CIA, DIA, NSA, and FBI—would organize, train, and equip the best intelligence professionals in the world and would handle the execution of intelligence operations in the field.

- This national intelligence director (NID) should be located in the Executive Office of the President and report directly to the president, yet be confirmed by the Senate. In addition to overseeing the National Counterterrorism Center described earlier (which will include both the national intelligence center for terrorism and the joint operations planning effort), the NID should have three deputies:
  - For foreign intelligence (a deputy who also would be the head of the CIA).
  - For defense intelligence (also the undersecretary of defense for intelligence).
  - For homeland intelligence (also the executive assistant director for intelligence at the FBI or the undersecretary of homeland security for information analysis and infrastructure protection).
- The NID should receive a public appropriation for national intelligence, should have authority to hire and fire his or her intelligence deputies, and should be able to set common personnel and information technology policies across the intelligence community.
- The CIA should concentrate on strengthening the collection capabilities of its clandestine service and the talents of its analysts, building pride in its core expertise.
- Secrecy stifles oversight, accountability, and information sharing. Unfortunately, all the current organizational incentives encourage overclassification. This balance should change; and as a start, open information should be provided about the overall size of agency intelligence budgets.

Unity of Effort: Sharing Information

The U.S. government has access to a vast amount of information. But it has a weak system for processing and using what it has. The system of "need to know" should be replaced by a system of "need to share."

- The president should lead a governmentwide effort to bring the major national security institutions into the information revolution, turning a mainframe system into a decentralized network. The obstacles are not technological. Official after official has urged us to call attention to problems with the unglamorous "back office" side of government operations.
- No agency can solve the problems on its own; to build the network requires an effort that transcends old divides, solving common legal and policy issues in ways that can help officials know what they can and cannot do. Again, in tackling information issues, America needs unity of effort.

Unity of Effort: Congress

Congress took too little action to adjust itself or to restructure the executive branch to address the emerging terrorist threat. Congressional oversight for intelligence—and counterterrorism—is dysfunctional. Both Congress and the executive branch need to do more to minimize national security risks during transitions between administrations.

- For intelligence oversight, we propose two options: either a joint committee on the old model of the Joint Committee on Atomic Energy or a single committee in each house combining authorizing and appropriating committees. Our central message is the same: The intelligence committees cannot carry out their oversight function unless they are made stronger and thereby have both clear responsibility and accountability for that oversight.
- Congress should create a single, principal point of oversight and review for homeland security. There should be one permanent standing committee for homeland security in each chamber.
- We propose reforms to speed up the nomination, financial reporting, security clearance, and confirmation process for national security officials at the start of an administration and suggest steps to make sure that incoming administrations have the information they need.

Unity of Effort: Organizing America's Defenses in the United States

We have considered several proposals relating to the future of the domestic intelligence and counterterrorism mission. Adding a new domestic intelligence agency will not solve America's problems in collecting and analyzing intelligence within the United States. We do not recommend creating one.

- We propose the establishment of a specialized and integrated national security workforce at the FBI, consisting of agents, analysts, linguists, and surveillance specialists who are recruited, trained, rewarded, and retained to ensure the development of an institutional culture imbued with a deep expertise in intelligence and national security.

At several points we asked: Who has the responsibility for defending us at home? Responsibility for America's national defense is shared by the Department of Defense, with its new Northern Command, and by the Department of Homeland Security. They must have a clear delineation of roles, missions, and authority:

- The Department of Defense and its oversight committees should regularly assess the adequacy of Northern Command's strategies and planning to defend against military threats to the homeland.
- The Department of Homeland Security and its oversight committees should regularly assess the types of threats the country faces to determine the adequacy of the government's plans and the readiness of the government to respond to those threats.

We call on the American people to remember how we all felt on 9/11, to remember not only the unspeakable horror but how we came together as a nation—one nation. Unity of purpose and unity of effort are the way we will defeat this enemy and make America safer for our children and grandchildren. We look forward to a national debate on the merits of what we have recommended, and we will participate vigorously in that debate.

Source: 911 Commission Final Report.

Follow-up Report

In December 2005, the 911 Commission released a follow-up report that graded the Bush administration and Congress's handling of the commission's recommendations. The findings, issued in the form of a report card, assigned letter grades to the 41 key recommendations. The grades were as follows (with I signifying Incomplete).

Homeland Security and Emergency Response

- Radio spectrum for first responders—F
- Incident command system—C
- Risk-based allocation of homeland security funds—F
- Critical infrastructure assessment—D
- Private sector preparedness—C
- National strategy for transportation security—C–
- Airline passenger prescreening—F
- Airline passenger explosive screening—C
- Checked bag and cargo screening—D
- Terrorist travel strategy—I
- Comprehensive screening system—C
- Biometric entry/exit screening system—B
- International collaboration on borders and document security—B
- Standardization of secure identifications—B–

Intelligence and Congressional Reform

- Director of national intelligence—B
- National Counterterrorism Center—B
- FBI national security workforce—C
- New missions for CIA director—I
- Incentives for information sharing—D
- Governmentwide information sharing—D
- Northern Command planning for homeland defense—B–
- Full debate on the Patriot Act—B
- Privacy and civil liberties oversight boards—D
- Guidelines for government sharing of personal information—D
- Intelligence oversight reform—D
- Homeland security committees—B
- Unclassified top-line intelligence budget—F
- Security clearance reform—B

Foreign Policy and Nonproliferation

- Maximum effort to prevent terrorists from acquiring WMD—D
- Afghanistan—B
- Pakistan—C+
- Saudi Arabia—D
- Terrorist sanctuaries—B
- Coalition strategy against Islamist terrorism—C
- Coalition detention standards—F
- Economic policies—B+

- Terrorist financing—A
- Clear U.S. message abroad—C
- International broadcasting—B
- Scholarship, exchange, and library programs—D
- Secular education in Muslin countries—D

In early 2007, the new Democratic House presented for its first vote of the session a bill, Implementing the 9/11 Commission Recommendations Act of 2007 (H.R. 1), which would fund all the remaining unfulfilled recommendations of the 911 Commission. The bill easily passed by a vote of 299–128. However, the cost of implementing these remaining recommendations, estimated to be over $21 billion between 2007 and 2012, drew considerable fire from opponents, who claimed the bill's provisions were misguided. The Senate introduced its own bill, Improving America's Security Act of 2007, which was still being considered in committee as this text went to press.

Critical Thinking

Do you agree with the findings of the 911 Commission or do you think that the findings go too far? Explain your answer.

State Government Antiterrorism Activity

Governors, and the states they govern, are recognized for the critical role they play in Homeland Security. State and local law enforcement and health personnel provide the first line of defense in protecting critical infrastructure and public health and safety. Should an incident occur, state and local personnel are the first to respond to an emergency and the last to leave the scene. Governors, with the support of the federal government, are responsible for coordinating state and local resources to effectively address natural disasters, accidents, and other types of major emergencies, including terrorist incidents.

The national effort to protect the nation from acts of terrorism has been conducted with equal strength at the state level as at the federal level. As the recipients of a bulk of the homeland security funding distributed by the Department of Homeland Security and other federal agencies, the states have the ability to administer new statewide programs aimed at bringing preparedness and prevention to every community.

State Homeland Security entities were created to ensure that the states are preparing for the wide range of terrorist attacks identified by the DHS and other entities. The state offices accomplish this by facilitating the interaction and coordination needed among each state's governor's office, the homeland security director, the state emergency management office, other state agencies, local governments, the private sector, volunteer organizations, and the federal government.

Following the attacks of September 11, the governors designated individuals from various backgrounds in state government to serve as their state homeland security directors. Among the states and territories, there is no common model; however, in several states, the homeland security director serves as an advisor to the governor in addition to coordinating state emergency management, law enforcement, health, and related public safety functions. In other models, governors designated the state's adjutant general as homeland security advisor. Although governors generally opted not to create unique cabinet-level positions with oversight over all state agencies, they formed homeland security task forces. The task forces typically consist of executive office staff members and agency heads from law enforcement, fire and rescue, public health, National Guard, transportation, public works, and information technology.

☐ ☐ ☐ ▬▬▬▬▬▬▬▬▬▬▬▬▬▬▬▬▬▬▬▬▬▬▬▬▬▬▬▬▬▬

State Offices of Homeland Security Have Been Placed in All of the Following State Government Agencies Since 2001, in Order of Most to Least Common

- Governor's office
- Military/adjutant general
- Emergency management
- Public safety
- Law enforcement
- Attorney general
- Lieutenant governor
- Land commissioner

Source: National Emergency Management Association, 2002; National Governors Association, 2007.

▬▬▬▬▬▬▬▬▬▬▬▬▬▬▬▬▬▬▬▬▬▬▬▬▬▬▬▬▬▬ ☐ ☐ ☐

In August 2002, the Center for Best Practices of the National Governors Association released "States' Homeland Security Priorities." A list of 10 "major priorities and issues" was identified by the NGA center through a survey of states' and territories' state homeland security offices. (NGA Center for Best Practices, 2002). A list of these priorities follows.

☐ ☐ ☐ ▬▬▬▬▬▬▬▬▬▬▬▬▬▬▬▬▬▬▬▬▬▬▬▬▬▬▬▬▬▬

List of States' Homeland Security Priorities
- Coordination must involve all levels of government.
- The federal government must disseminate timely intelligence information to the states.
- States must work with local governments to develop interoperable communications among first responders, and adequate wireless spectrum must be set aside to do the job.
- State and local governments need help and technical assistance to identify and protect critical infrastructure.
- Both the states and federal government must focus on enhancing bioterrorism preparedness and rebuilding the nation's public health system to address twenty-first century threats.

(Continued)

- The federal government should provide adequate federal funding and support to ensure that homeland security needs are met.
- The federal government should work with states to protect sensitive security information, including restricting access to information available through "freedom of information" requests.
- An effective system must be developed that secures points of entry at borders, airports, and seaports without placing an undue burden on commerce.
- The National Guard has proven itself to be an effective force during emergencies and crises. The mission of the National Guard should remain flexible, and guard units should remain primarily under the control of the governor during times of crises.
- Federal agencies should integrate their command systems into existing state and local incident command systems rather than requiring state and local agencies to adapt to federal command systems.

Source: NGA Center for Best Practices, Issue Brief, August 19, 2002.

Local Government Antiterrorism Activity

The Counties

Emergency preparedness, mitigation, response, and recovery all occur at the local community level. This is true for terrorism preparedness, mitigation, response, and recovery activities. It is at the local level that the critical planning, communications, technology, coordination, command, and spending decisions matter the most. The priorities of groups such as the National Conference of Mayors and the National Associations of Counties (NACo) represent what matters at the local community level in the fight against terrorism. The fight against terrorism has spawned a series of new requirements in preparedness and mitigation planning at the local level.

The NACo created a "Counties and Homeland Security: Policy Agenda to Secure the People of America's Counties." This policy paper states, "Counties are the first responders to terrorist attacks, natural disasters and major emergencies" (NACo, 2004). The NACo established a 43-member NACo Homeland Security Task Force that, in July 2004, reaffirmed a set of 21 recommendations concerning homeland security issues. The 21 NACO recommendations are presented next.

NACo Homeland Security National Objectives and Funding Recommendations for Counties and Homeland Security

1. **National Strategies for the Nation.** A national long-term strategy for homeland security should be developed to guide federal, state, and local

preparedness efforts. Input from local and state stakeholders must be included in the development of this strategy and funding must be consistent with national goals and objectives.

2. **Sustained Funding for Homeland Security.** Congress must provide sustained funding for homeland security to enhance the ability of local governments to protect their communities. Funding for federal public safety programs that existed prior to September 11 should not be supplanted by recent homeland security funding.

3. **Base Level of Preparedness for All Communities.** Federal funding allocations for homeland security should ensure a base level of preparedness to all states and regions to ensure that all citizens are protected from the threat of terrorism.

4. **High Threat Funding to Most Critical Areas.** Federal funding to the nation's high threat urban areas (cities, counties, contiguous counties, and mutual aid partners) must be provided. These areas of high visibility, heightened threat and risk, vulnerable critical infrastructure, and population density have a heightened sense of vulnerability to terrorist attacks.

5. **Expediting Assistance at All Levels of Government.** Federal and state assistance for homeland security, public health, "all hazards," and safety must reach first responders in an expedited fashion. As a result, all levels of government should work together to ensure the timely distribution of assistance to first responders. In the event that federal, state, and local government legal, procedural, or procurements processes delay the expenditure of funds, efforts must be made to establish an expedited authorization and appropriation process.

Public Health

6. **Fund Local Public Health Emergency Preparedness.** Congress should continue to provide adequate funding for HHS cooperative agreements with the states for public health emergency preparedness and give strong direction to the states to ensure that (1) no less than 80 percent of the funds are used to improve local preparedness and local infrastructure and (2) county public health agencies are consulted and concur with the state plans for expenditures of these funds.

7. **Ensure an Adequate Supply of Vaccines and Antibiotics.** The federal government should ensure an adequate supply of appropriate antibiotics, vaccines, and other relevant medications and medical supplies are made available to counties and other local communities in a timely manner as part of the stockpiled push packages administered by the CDC. Also, the federal government must continue to build an advanced surveillance system for the detection and identification of biological and other harmful agents.

8. **Train Health Personnel.** Public and private sector health personnel should receive adequate training to manage public health emergencies, in cooperation with federal, state, and local governments. Although specific training relative to bioterrorism is needed, general competency building in public health also is needed to assure that the workforce is fully prepared.

(Continued)

9. **Ensure That Adequate Medical Surge Capacity Exists.** The federal government, in cooperation with state and local governments, should ensure that the medical surge capacity needs associated with events of mass casualties and large outbreaks of infectious diseases can be met, particularly in communities that serve as regional medical centers.

Information Sharing and Critical Infrastructure Security

10. **Sharing of Intelligence.** The federal government must develop an efficient and comprehensive system for the sharing, analysis, and dissemination of intelligence between federal, state, and local public safety agencies in concert with local governments.

11. **Balance Heightened Border Security with Economic Activity.** Improve border security operations to enhance the nation's ability to restrict the movement of weapons, weapons components, or potential terrorists into the country and eliminate their ability to operate within our borders, in such a way that heightened security does not impede the ability to continue active cross-border commerce.

12. **Securing Critical Infrastructure.** The federal government should provide assistance to counties for enhancing critical infrastructure and key resources. Enhanced coordination between local governments and the private sector is critical for ensuring the preparedness of states and localities and for protecting vital physical and economic infrastructure. State and local intelligence information should be utilized in the development and continued refinements of the DHS's national critical infrastructure protection list.

13. **Help Localities Secure Public Utilities and a Safe Water Supply.** Congress should authorize funds for drinking water systems and other public utilities (large and small) to conduct physical vulnerability assessments, emergency planning, and security enhancements. Additional research should be conducted into the threats to water and sewer systems and other public utilities and the development of methods and technologies to prevent and respond to such attacks.

14. **Reimburse Counties for Costs Incurred on Behalf of the Federal Government.** The federal government should reimburse counties for the local public safety and law enforcement costs associated with requests to provide security to federal installations and federally owned infrastructure within their jurisdictions and for the federal use of county facilities and other federally mandated expenses incurred during an emergency or a heightened sense of alert.

Emergency Planning and Public Safety

15. **Assist Counties to Develop Evacuation Capacity.** Support assistance to counties for the evaluation of transportation and other infrastructure systems and evacuation planning, including developing capacity at the local level to facilitate evacuations.

16. **Train County Elected and Appointed Officials to Prepare for and Respond to Acts of Terror.** Federal, state, and local governments should collaborate to train first responders to respond to acts of terror, utilizing and expanding on existing training facilities and opportunities to their fullest extent. Curricula also should be established for the specific purpose of training elected county officials and other representatives of general-purpose local governments. A standard core set of competencies should be developed and cross-discipline training must be encouraged.

17. **One-Stop Clearinghouse.** The federal government should create a "one-stop" clearinghouse for grants, training programs, and other disaster preparedness assistance for state and local governments and public safety agencies.

18. **Assist Public Safety Communications Interoperability and Interference Issues.** The federal government should assist counties to provide the broadest possible interoperability between public safety agencies across voice, data, and geo-data and wireless technologies. The federal government also should assist counties in obtaining additional spectrum as soon as possible to address interoperability and dead zone problems created by congestion and interference with commercial services. In the event of a disaster or terrorist attack, all first responders should have access to a common set of frequencies that can be used to communicate among agencies. Manufacturers should expand their commitment to producing standards-compliant communications infrastructure. Equally important, the public safety community should be made aware of standards-compliant equipment, and the importance of public safety participation in standards development efforts should be emphasized. Working with the first responder's community, a common standard "language" for interoperability communication needs to be established so that responders from various agencies can act on specific instructions without mistake or delay.

19. **Establish a Public Communication Network.** A communication network capable of delivering information in a timely manner between the federal government, state and local governments, and the general public should be established.

20. **Urge the Release of Federal Research to Assist Counties.** The federal government should make its research and information available to counties at the earliest possible time—including declassifying such information as appropriate—to facilitate their use by counties to prepare for and respond to acts of terrorism and other emergencies.

21. **Provide Immunity to Encourage Mutual Aid and Support.** The federal government and state governments, where applicable, should provide legal immunity from civil liability for counties and other local governments responding collaboratively to emergencies outside their primary jurisdiction. Also, the federal and state governments should allow reimbursement under the Public Assistance Program for assistance rendered by mutual aid partners.

Source: NACo Homeland Security Task Force, July 2004.

As previously mentioned, the global war on terrorism has caused various hardships at the state and local levels. One particular hardship that has been endured is the loss of critical employees serving as military reservists on deployment in Afghanistan, Iraq, and elsewhere. The NACo performed a survey of county governments, "How Has the Deployment of Reserves Affected Your County?" to assess these hardships, the results of which are summarized next.

□ □ □ ▬▬▬▬▬▬▬▬▬▬▬▬▬▬▬▬▬▬▬▬▬▬▬▬▬▬▬▬▬▬▬▬

Effects of Military Reservists' Deployment on County Governments

Counties were asked if county employees who are members of the reserves have been called up for duty. Of the 164 responding counties, 43 percent reported that employees have been called up. Of these counties that had employees called up, 76 percent had fewer than five employees called to the military. Twelve percent had between 5 to 10 employees called up, and 8 percent had more than 20.

Departmental Distribution

Counties were asked to list the departments most affected by the call up. Seventy-four percent report that police and sheriff departments were affected. This was followed by 28 percent stating other departments, and 18 percent reporting fire and emergency medical departments and public works departments also were affected. Nine percent report that transit and transportation as well as administration departments were among those affected.

Benefits for the Military

Counties were asked about the benefits their county employees received while serving on active duty in the military. Forty-three percent report that benefits stopped in accordance with the time period required by federal law. However, 35 percent of the responding counties indicate that they established policy that continues benefits to the military beyond those required by federal law. Sixteen percent of responding counties report continuing to extend benefits to the military based on state law.

Hardships Caused by Deployment

Counties are coping with missing employees in several ways. Fifty-nine percent reallocated other staff members to fill the positions of missing employees, and 46 percent hired temporary staff members. More than 14 percent indicate that they had to cut back on service delivery while these employees are deployed.

Counties are making do, with 52 percent reporting that their counties have not experienced a hardship while these employees are on active duty. Examining this response by population size however, paints a different picture. Sixty-nine percent of counties with populations below 10,000 reported the deployment created a hardship for them.

Of the 48 percent of counties reporting hardships caused by the current deployment, several provided the following anecdotes:

- *We have a very tight budget and hiring temporary help has placed an additional burden on the county. We have had a large murder trial in the last month that has taxed the Sheriff's Office and they have needed all personnel.*
- *Temporary employees are not certified as police officers so they are still understaffed.*
- *It is difficult to recruit, hire, and train Juvenile Probation Counselors when you don't know for how long they'll be hired. Training is expensive and takes about two years.*
- *With one of seven deputies on staff, the other six had to take up his shifts because we couldn't find another deputy since we were paying his salary and benefits in his absence.*
- *Especially for 24/7 operations such as sheriff deputies, we have to pay overtime to backfill the shifts while picking up the pay difference for the employee.*
- *The Sheriff's Department has had to reduce service in some instances when part-time staff could not fill the empty slot.*
- *We have been forced to use overtime to compensate for the absent staff. Additionally, this has caused us to prioritize duties and not accomplish some that we would normally desire to accomplish.*
- *Sheriff's office has had to adjust to using lesser-trained personnel.*
- *When you are short a deputy sheriff it puts a greater burden on the other law enforcement officials by working longer hours, which may cause more accidents.*
- *Cut back on services due to vacancies.*

Source: www.NACo.org.

Cities and Towns

Other than the largest cities, most local communities do not have specially designated offices of homeland security or any other terrorism-specific government office or agency. In general, local communities rely on the skills and training of their teams of first responders, who include the fire, police, emergency management, emergency medical, and other officials that live within their jurisdictions.

However, these first responders are the heart of the system that the nation depends on for the protection from and response to terrorist attacks. Local communities are instructed that they may have to manage the aftermath of a terrorist attack for a full 24 to 48 hours on their own before state or federal backup arrives. As should be obvious by the levels of funding that have been described in copious detail throughout this text, the federal government has recognized and responded to such facts.

Local first response still has much catching up to do to be able to fulfill the preparedness and response needs of the federal government. Interoperable communication, the condition where all responders and emergency management within and without each community can talk to each other, still is not possible. Many communities lack the equipment and training necessary to respond to attacks involving weapons of mass destruction. Efforts to vaccinate health-care workers from biological weapons such as smallpox have failed, and there are still questions about whether communities could handle an outbreak of one of these diseases even if sufficient vaccines were available to them.

In the larger communities, where the training and equipment are better funded and considered adequate, other issues presented themselves. Large ports still are not passing minimum security requirements to keep out potential weapons of mass destruction, financial woes are sounded each time the Homeland Security Alert System is raised for specific terrorist threats due to the need for police overtime and the loss of other essential services to reassigned officials, and contentious battles over the appropriation of both federal and state funding has soured many preexisting relationships.

But, the will to prepare exists, and the growing pains are becoming less severe as more and more funds reach deeper into American communities. Cooperation and intelligence sharing has made the state and local responders a more integral part of the counterterrorism team that will be necessary to prevent or contain future terrorist attacks, whether they be internationally based or home grown. The DHS Office of State and Local Coordination was established to serve as a single point of contact for facilitation and coordination of departmental programs that affect state, local, territorial, and tribal governments. Through this office, the DHS has brought together many organizations with a long history of interaction with and support to state, local, territorial, and tribal government organizations and associations, and the office is working hard to consolidate and coordinate that support. Today, this office facilitates the coordination of DHS-wide programs that affect state, local, territorial, and tribal governments; serves as the primary point of contact within the DHS for exchanging information with state, local, territorial, and tribal homeland security personnel; identifies homeland security–related activities, best practices, and processes that are most efficiently accomplished at the federal, state, local, or regional levels; and utilizes this information to ensure that opportunities for improvement are provided to state, territorial, tribal, and local counterparts.

The events of September 11 established the security of community infrastructure as a potential target for terrorist attacks. Community infrastructure always has been vulnerable to natural and other technological disaster events. So much so that FEMA's largest disaster assistance program, Public Assistance, is designed to fund the rebuilding of community infrastructure damaged by a disaster event. Local government officials and local emergency managers must now increase the attention they give to protecting and securing community infrastructure from a terrorist attack. They must also include in these preparedness efforts the local public health system. A checklist designed for the town of Boone, North Carolina, as part of a Technological Annex developed for the town's *All-Hazards Planning and Operations Manual* in March 2002 is provided next.

☐ ☐ ☐

Goals and Questions for Local Governments Preparing to Fight Terrorism—Boone, North Carolina

The preparedness and response of terrorist events requires that local governments do the following:

- Identify the types of events that might occur in the community.
- Plan emergency activities in advance to ensure a coordinated response.
- Build the capabilities necessary to respond effectively to the consequences of terrorism.
- Identify the type or nature of an event when it does happen.
- Implement the planned response quickly and efficiently.
- Recover from the incident.

The response to terrorism is similar in many ways to that of other natural or human-made disasters Boone has prepared for already. With additions and modifications, the development of a completely separate system can be avoided. Training and public education are vital, and understanding the federal assistance available will drastically increase local capacity before and during a terrorist attack.

The following are the general types of activities that Boone must undertake to meet the objectives just mentioned:

- Strengthen information and communications technology.
- Establish a well-defined incident command structure that includes the FBI.
- Strengthen the local working relationships and communications.
- Educate the health-care and emergency response community about identification of bioterrorist attacks and agents.
- Educate the health-care and emergency response community about medical treatment and prophylaxis for possible biological agents.
- Educate the local health department about state and federal requirements and assistance.
- Maintain a locally accessible supply of medications, vaccines, and supplies.
- Address health-care worker safety issues.
- Designate a spokesperson to maintain contact with the public.
- Develop comprehensive evacuation plans.
- Become familiar with state and local laws relating to isolation and quarantine.
- Develop or enhance the local capability to prosecute crimes involving weapons of mass destruction or the planning of terrorism events.
- Develop, maintain, and practice an infectious diseases emergency response plan.
- Practice with surrounding jurisdictions and strengthen mutual agreement plans.
- Outline the roles of federal agency assistance in planning and response.
- Educate the public in recognizing events and how to respond as individuals.
- Stay current.

Source: Town of Boone, "All-Hazards Planning and Operations Manual," 2002.

☐ ☐ ☐

The Effect of Hurricane Katrina on Terrorism Preparedness and Response

The unexpected nature of the September 11 events were interpreted by both the government and the public alike to mean that too little was being done to plan for and protect the nation from the suddenly obvious terrorist threat. The resulting action included a fundamental shift in the focus of emergency management that many considered to be knee-jerk and included, among other changes, the restructuring of a significant number of U.S. government agencies and offices and a redrafting of all U.S. emergency operations plans at all levels of government. Many proponents of "all-hazards emergency management" contended that this shift was so great as to leave the country more vulnerable to the effects of natural disasters than before the changes occurred.

After a period of relatively few major disaster events, during which time the nation's focus on all accounts was the global war against terrorism, the fears of all-hazards proponents were confirmed when Hurricane Katrina (an anticipated and previously exercised natural hazard event) struck on August 29, 2005, and quickly overwhelmed response mechanisms at all government levels. As with all devastating disasters, the subsequent aftermath was rife with finger-pointing and wide denials of blame, with the federal government accusing local responders of poor decision making and the local and state officials claiming that FEMA ignored their pleas for help. On closer examination, however, the general consensus was that FEMA had been diluted too much as an effective response organization within the Department of Homeland Security, much of which came as a result of the terror focus (both programmatically and in relation to the targeting of disaster preparedness grants) and major changes would have to be made if such weaknesses were ever to be addressed.

In FY 2006, which began just one month into the yet ongoing Hurricane Katrina disaster recovery operation, the Government Accountability Office found that over 75 percent of the DHS's preparedness grants targeted state and local readiness for terrorism. These figures indicated that emergency management funds still were misaligned with the reality of risk that was much better understood by the local agency responders to be that of an all-hazards portfolio. Fortunately, since that time, changes have been made by the administration and Congress that clearly show promise that FEMA, as an emergency management organization, must focus on all hazards and not just terrorism. FEMA is steadily regaining many of its former responsibilities that were lost to other agencies more narrowly focused on terrorism, such as the Office of Domestic Preparedness and the DHS Preparedness Directorate. How far these corrective actions go ultimately depends on whether or not another major terrorist attack interrupts the steady flow of natural disasters that are guaranteed to strike in coming years.

Conclusion

Emergency management in the United States was changed forever by the events of September 11. New focus, new funding, new partners, and new concerns associated with the fight against terrorism are changing the way emergency management functions in this country every day. At the federal government level, the Department of Homeland Security was established, which includes FEMA and all the federal government disaster management programs. At the state level, governors and state emergency management directors are calling for better coordination, new communications technologies, and always more and more funding. At the local government level, terrorism is a new threat that greatly expands local facility security requirements and is added to a long list of needs and priorities. But the threat of terrorism is one that cannot be ignored. Issues of coordination, communications, and funding concern local governments as well.

The United States has taken its typical response to a new problem. It reorganized and committed huge amounts of funding to reducing the problem. The ability of the Department of Homeland Security to achieve an enhanced level of coordination is improving but still has a ways to go. Preventing future terrorism attacks remains mostly outside the purview of the DHS, residing with the intelligence community, the military, diplomatic corps, and law enforcement. What the DHS can offer is a better prepared and equipped first responder cadre, enhanced transportation and border security, and more money for emergency management programs.

But the question of cost-effectiveness remains to be seen. The likelihood of natural and technological disasters has already proven to be far greater than that of terrorist attacks. In the four years following the September 11 terrorist attacks, the United States was affected by hurricanes, floods, wildfires, chemical accidents, transportation accidents, volcanoes, ice storms, tornadoes, severe winter weather, and avalanches—the list goes on and on. The Department of Homeland Security needs to continually reassess its priorities in terms of terrorism versus other, less sinister hazards and shift funding as appropriate. The terrorist threat will never go away completely, but over time, it should require much less of the attention of the nation's first responders, state responders, and federal government preparedness and response agencies.

CASE STUDY

"Redefining Readiness: Terrorism Planning through the Eyes of the Public," a study by Roz D. Lasker of the New York Academy of Medicine (September 2004)

The Redefining Readiness Study, the first of its kind, measured how Americans might react to protective instructions in two terrorist attacks: a smallpox outbreak and the explosion of a dirty bomb. This information is considered critically important because the plans currently being developed to deal with these situations are based on expert *assumptions* about what people would be concerned about and how they would behave. If planners' assumptions about the public are wrong, as they have been in the past, the plans being developed will not work as expected, and a large number of people who should be protected will be unnecessarily harmed.

This study included confidential, in-depth conversations with government and private-sector planners and an extensive review of the literature to identify the critical assumptions about the public on which current plans are based. A diverse spectrum of community residents around the country were engaged through 14

(Continued)

CASE STUDY—Cont'd

group discussions to identify a frame of reference for thinking about terrorism preparedness planning that is meaningful to the general public. Incorporating lessons learned, the research team fielded a telephone survey of 2,545 randomly selected adult residents of households in the continental United States.

The Study

The study uses scenarios that put people in smallpox and dirty bomb situations at a place and time they would be likely to hear about the attack and be told what to do. The smallpox scenario explores how people would react to instructions to go to a public site to be vaccinated if some residents in their community and people in other parts of the country became sick with smallpox after having been exposed to the virus in an attack at a major airport. The dirty bomb scenario explores how the public would react to instructions to stay inside a building other than their own home if a dirty bomb exploded a mile from where they were and a cloud containing radioactive dust were moving in their direction. In addition to these scenarios, the study also explored people's interest in and perspectives about their community's terrorism planning activities.

Following are highlighted key findings from the study report, focusing on

- The public's reactions to the smallpox and dirty bomb situations.
- The public's redefinition of readiness in these situations.
- The public's role in future planning efforts.

The Public's Reactions to the Smallpox and Dirty Bomb Situations

Far fewer people than needed would follow protective instructions in these two terrorist attack situations:

- Only two fifths of the American people would go to the vaccination site in the smallpox outbreak.
- Only three fifths of the American people would shelter-in-place for as long as told in the dirty bomb explosion.

One reason for this lack of cooperation is that many people would be seriously worried about something *other* than what planners are trying to protect them from:

- Two fifths of the American people would be seriously worried about what government officials would say or do. This concern is even more prevalent among members of the public who are Hispanic, African-American, foreign born, have a low income, lack health insurance coverage, live in New York City, or have not attended college. People's trust in official instructions and actions is important because people who have little trust are only half as likely to cooperate in the smallpox and dirty bomb situations as are those who have more.

- Three fifths of the American people would have serious worries about the smallpox vaccine—that's *twice* as many people as would be seriously worried about catching smallpox in the outbreak situation.
- Worries about vaccine side effects would make one fifth of the American population afraid to follow instructions to go to the vaccination site. The public's worries appear to be well founded, since it is estimated that over 50 million people in this country have conditions that put them at risk of developing serious complications from the vaccine, either from being vaccinated themselves or from accidentally coming in contact with someone who has recently been vaccinated.
- Half of the American people—and two thirds of African Americans—would be seriously worried if they were told that the smallpox vaccine is investigational. More people would be seriously worried about this issue than about any other aspect of the smallpox situation. Concern about the investigational status of the vaccine would make one third of the population decide *not* to get it, even if they were at the vaccination site already.

Many people would face *conflicting* worries and trade-offs in these situations, which would make it very difficult for them to decide what the most protective course of action would be:

- Three quarters of the people who would be seriously worried about catching smallpox in the outbreak situation *also* would be seriously worried about the vaccine. People who are worried *only* about catching smallpox are three times more likely to cooperate as those who are not. But that increase in cooperation is completely *eliminated* when people are also seriously worried about the vaccine.
- Two thirds of the American people would try to avoid being in the same place with other people they do not know in the smallpox situation. But going to a public vaccination site *violates* people's inclination toward protective isolation.
- Two fifths of the population would be afraid of catching smallpox from other people at the site. One fifth would be afraid of coming in contact with people at the site who should not be exposed to anyone who recently got the vaccine. In the dirty bomb situation, many people face conflicting obligations, and assuring the safety of people who are dependent on them often is more important than assuring their own safety. One third of the people who would not cooperate fully in this situation would leave the shelter of their building to take care of their children; one quarter would leave to take care of other family members.

A substantial number of people would be able to cooperate with protective instructions if certain conditions were met, but those conditions are *not* met now:

- Three quarters of the people who said they would not fully cooperate with instructions to stay inside the building in the dirty bomb situation *would* do so if they could communicate with people they care about or if they knew that they and their loved ones were in places that had prepared in advance to take good care of them in this kind of situation. But three fifths of the American

(Continued)

CASE STUDY—Cont'd

population know only a little or nothing at all about how people would actually be cared for in those places. Overall, the American people are half as likely to cooperate in the dirty bomb situation if they do not know a lot about their building's shelter-in-place plans than if they do. And they are half as likely to cooperate if they lack confidence in their community's preparedness plans than if they do not.

Not surprisingly, considering the serious worries and trade-offs people face, many people would want more information or advice to decide what to do in these situations:

- Members of the public are looking for decision-making support not just facts, and they want to be able to talk with someone beforehand *not* just during an attack.
- For free telephone support from a trained person in the smallpox situation, considerably *more* people would find it very helpful to talk with someone who they know wants what is best for them (like their health practitioner) than to talk with someone they do not know who works for their local government.

The Public's Redefinition of Readiness in These Two Terrorist Attack Situations

These findings are cause for worry because they suggest that current plans to deal with smallpox and dirty bomb attacks will be far less effective than planners want or the public deserves. Although the study is based on a hypothetical scenario, our findings need to be taken seriously because the way the American people say they would react to instructions in the smallpox outbreak is consistent with the *actual behavior* of health-care workers in the CDC Smallpox Vaccination Program. If three fifths of the American people were reluctant to follow instructions in a smallpox outbreak, the protection of large-scale vaccination might not be achieved, even if planners worked out all of the challenging logistics involved in dispensing the vaccine. If two fifths of the American population were reluctant to shelter-in-place in a dirty bomb explosion, many people would be unnecessarily exposed to dangerous dust and radiation, and first responders would face excess traffic and congestion in getting to the scene of the explosion.

Planners have been focusing a lot of attention on public education and risk communication, but our study suggests that informing people what they should do in these terrorist attack situations will *not* be sufficient to garner their timely cooperation. On a more optimistic note, the study shows how, by addressing the public's concerns, planners can develop more behaviorally realistic approaches for dealing with smallpox and dirty bomb attacks and, as a result, protect many more people than would otherwise be possible.

The report describes what plans to deal with these two kinds of terrorist attacks would look like if they incorporated the public's perspectives. As readers will see, looking at preparedness planning through the public's eyes redefines the notion of protection.

In the smallpox situation, the public's insights emphasize the importance of developing plans that protect *everyone* at risk: not only the people who are at risk of contracting smallpox, but also the large number of people who are at risk of developing serious complications from the vaccine.

In the dirty bomb situation, the public's insights emphasize that people not only need to be protected from dangerous dust and radiation. They also need to know that they and their loved ones would be safe and cared for in whatever building they happen to be in at the time of an explosion. To make such protection possible, a broad array of places—work sites, shops, malls, schools, day care centers, hospitals, clinics, cultural institutions, recreational and entertainment facilities, government buildings, apartment buildings, and transportation terminals—have to be able to serve as safe havens for people should the need arise. The managers of these places need to recognize that it is as important to prepare to serve as a safe haven as to be able to evacuate people in the event of a fire or an explosion.

The American people's perspectives also redefine how public protection can best be achieved. To a large extent, this involves the development of community and organizational plans that address people's concerns, minimize the conflicts and trade-offs they would face, and support them in choosing the best protective action.

As the plans in the report illustrate, many of these actions need to be taken now, well before an attack occurs. Examples related to the smallpox situation include

- Strategies to enable everyone in the country to determine his or her own vaccine risk status and that of the other members of the household.
- Training health-care practitioners and other community members to provide people with decision-making support.
- Involvement by community leaders, particularly among the African-American population, in overseeing the development and testing of vaccines.

Examples related to the dirty bomb situation include the development of

- Confidence-generating safe-haven plans in the broad array of buildings and places where people frequently are.
- Backup systems that can maintain telephone and e-mail service for the general public in the event of a large-scale emergency.

The plans also involve changes in actions that would be taken *during* the crisis, as the following strategies from the smallpox plan illustrate:

- Rather than triaging or screening people at public sites, steps would be taken to make sure that anyone who is potentially infected or exposed to smallpox or who is at risk of developing serious complications from the vaccine stays home and does *not* go to any public vaccination site.

(Continued)

CASE STUDY—Cont'd

- To provide people with accurate information from people they trust, government-run telephone networks would be supplemented with a more community-embedded telephone support system.

Finally, the plans emphasize the need for communities and the nation to focus on *long-term issues*. Reflecting the public's concerns in the dirty bomb situation, for example, the plans emphasize the need to discuss and address the potential environmental, economic, and health consequences that might ensue.

The Public's Role in Future Planning Efforts

The Redefining Readiness Study documents the value of letting the American people speak for themselves rather than relying on planners' untested assumptions about what the public cares about and how the public will behave. Moreover, the study provides planners in government agencies and private-sector organizations with reliable information from the public that they can use to assess and strengthen their plans to deal with terrorist-initiated smallpox outbreaks and dirty bomb explosions. Because most of the findings in the study are generalizable, they are applicable to planning efforts throughout the country. Some of the strategies in the study's illustrative plans are also applicable to other situations, such as an outbreak of pandemic influenza or SARS, an electrical blackout, or the malfunction of a nuclear reactor.

Planners need to work with community residents directly, however, to benefit from their insights about responding to many other kinds of terrorist attacks and emergency situations. The study documents that involving people in these kinds of planning efforts can accomplish another important objective as well: It can address the trust and confidence issues that currently discourage so many members of the public from following protective instructions:

- The study shows that people are more likely to follow official instructions when they have a lot of trust in what officials tell them to do and are confident that their community is prepared to meet their needs if a terrorist attack occurs. Currently, the American people's trust and confidence levels are disturbingly low. But elected officials, government agencies, and private-sector organizations have a unique opportunity to build the public's trust, confidence, and cooperation by involving the public directly in planning. When community members are part of the planning process, they can be more confident that planners are actually aware of their concerns. When community residents play a role in developing protective strategies, they can be more trusting of officials who instruct them to follow those strategies.

Thus far, the public has had little or no direct involvement in community and organizational preparedness planning. The study documents that only a tiny fraction of the American people know very much about the plans being developed in their communities, and it paints a mostly discouraging picture about people's perceptions about current planning activities:

- Large proportions of people think their community is not prepared to deal with these kinds of terrorist attacks, that planners do not know about their concerns and information needs, that people like them cannot influence the plans being developed, and that neither they nor the people they care about would receive the help they need when they need it if a terrorist attack were to occur.
- People's perceptions about the potential benefits of planning are in stark contrast to the problems they see. Three fifths of the American population believe that the harm caused by a terrorist attack in their community could be reduced a great deal or a lot by preparing ahead of time to deal with the effects.

Fortunately for planners, the study documents that a large proportion of the American people are interested in community-level planning—not just in learning more about plans but in being actively involved in developing them:

- In New York City and Washington, D.C., where terrorism is a particularly salient issue, two fifths of the population are extremely or very interested in *personally* helping a government agency or other community organization develop plans to deal with these kinds of attacks.
- Interest levels also are high in the rest of the country, where people think much less about terrorist attacks and believe the possibility of an attack is much less likely. In those places, one third of the population has a strong personal interest in participating in planning.

The next challenge is to make it possible for government agencies and private-sector organizations to engage the public in planning efforts. This study demonstrates that, to make participation meaningful and worthwhile to community residents, the process needs to assure them considerable influence in planning and needs to focus their involvement on identifying and addressing the issues they care about a lot. We recognize that this kind of inclusive process would entail a substantial change in the way many planners currently go about their work and a variety of barriers currently make it difficult for planners to move in this direction. Nonetheless, the stakes are too high to continue the status quo. To provide planners with practical models for engaging the public in these kinds of activities, the next step is to support planning processes in selected sites around the country that demonstrate exactly how community residents can be meaningfully and feasibly engaged.

Source: Roz Lasker, "Redefining Readiness: Terrorism Planning Through the Eyes of the Public," Center for the Advancement of Collaborative Strategies in Health, The New York Academy of Medicine, September 14, 2004.

IMPORTANT TERMS

- After-action report
- Homeland Security Presidential Directive
- Homeland Security Advisory System
- Critical infrastructure
- Adjutant general

Self-Check Questions

1. What five groups must be fully engaged in the nation's war on terrorism?
2. What is the goal of emergency management in regard to the terrorism threat?
3. How much money did the federal government spend in the response and recovery to the September 11 attacks?
4. What did the two September 11–related after-action reports say about the capabilities of first responders?
5. What has been the most significant result of the September 11 attacks for state and local emergency managers?
6. What were the names of the original five DHS directorates? Which of these still exist?
7. Why did Secretary Chertoff release the Six-Point Agenda? What was the purpose of the agenda?
8. What did the Post-Katrina Emergency Management Reform Act do?
9. Other than the DHS, what federal agencies provide terrorism-based funding for first responders?
10. What was the purpose of the 911 Commission? What did the commission find?
11. How did the states respond to the terrorist threat?
12. How have military reservist's deployments affected emergency management capacity?
13. How did Hurricane Katrina affect terrorism preparedness in the United States?

Out of Class Exercises

Visit the Web site for your state homeland security office. Where in government is this office? What grants and other assistance does it provide local governments and citizens of the state? Is this office collocated with the office of emergency management or is it a separate office? What is the experience of the lead executive of the office?

□□□
□□□ 10
□□□

The Future of Emergency Management

As Americans and people around the world witnessed the despair and devastation of the victims of Hurricane Katrina and the disorder and ineffectiveness of the government's response, it was apparent that the nation's system for responding to any disaster, natural or human-made, was broken. In looking at these images, people were reminded of disaster scenes more typical in underdeveloped, Third World countries. How this chaos could be happening in the United States, the world's richest country and the supposed leader in regard to emergency management, was incomprehensible. The reasons for this shameful moment in our history have been discussed in many of the previous chapters and include the deconstruction of FEMA, the transfer of significant expertise and financial resources out of FEMA to other priorities within the Department of Homeland Security, a change at all government levels from an all-hazards focus to one that favors terrorism above all else, and a lack of political commitment and leadership to emergency management.

In previous editions of this textbook, we discussed the possible consequences of moving FEMA into the Department of Homeland Security, focusing emergency management on terrorism at the cost of natural and other hazards, and the importance of supportive political leadership, at the highest levels, including the presidency, as bellwethers for the demise of effective emergency management. We, unfortunately, predicted the failure that was evidenced in Hurricane Katrina. However, even we could not have predicted the total collapse of the system nor the subsequent string of mistakes and ineffective leadership during the recovery.

What led us to suggest the potential for a Katrina failure was an understanding of the forces that formed the discipline of emergency management in the United States, the undervalue of the day-to-day importance of emergency management, and our experience in the 1990s, when there was a strong political commitment to emergency management by the president. Finally, in spite of efforts to change, emergency management remains a discipline reactive to events and not proactive in addressing the risks and hazards that cause these events. In any discussion relative to the future of emergency management, these important issues merit inclusion. However, we would argue that simply correcting the mistakes that occurred in Katrina or creating a new, improved emergency management system modeled after the 1990s FEMA/state/local system may not be the answer. As communities face new hazards and larger portions of the population are at risk, as disasters become more frequent and severe, as global warming accelerates, and as competition for financial and human resources to address these problems increases, new thinking and new approaches must be identified as we look toward the future of emergency management.

Our goal in this chapter is to explore new models and ideas for achieving the functions of emergency management in government and nongovernmental organizations. To put the options in perspective, the following background material regarding the evolution of the discipline of emergency management may be useful.

Understanding the Past

In the 1960s, when the National Governors Association commissioned the seminal study on this discipline, comprehensive emergency management became defined as a cycle of preparedness, response, recovery, and mitigation. This cycle and its functions became what emergency managers were supposed to accomplish at the local, state, and federal levels.

At this stage, emergency management was a new discipline. Two factors were prominent at this time: First, the establishment of the discipline and its concepts was being driven by the reaction to a series of hazard events (Hurricane Betsy, the Three Mile Island accident, and the Mt. St. Helens eruption) and, second, the individuals that initially staffed state and local emergency management positions held military or civil defense backgrounds. As a result, the response function was emergency management's dominant driving force. Skills such as logistics, command and control, and search and rescue prevailed. Preparedness as a function came second and reflected the civil defense mentality of watch and warning, sheltering and evacuation. In addition, what drove the importance of preparedness was the government's reaction to the accident at the Three Mile Island nuclear power plant. In this event's aftermath, adequate off-site preparedness around commercial nuclear power plants became a condition for continued licensing by the Nuclear Regulatory Commission. Hence, this regulatory requirement led to the embrace of preparedness as an important emergency management function. This was especially true at the state level, where state emergency management organizations received funding for staff and operations from the commercial power plants to ensure that they could perform the necessary operations and exercises to attest to adequate preparedness for the licensing process.

The functions of recovery and mitigation were not widely understood nor regarded within the field, and the skill set needed to support these functions (e.g., land-use planning, building code design and enforcement, engineering, architecture, cartography, and geology) were not possessed by most emergency managers. As noted in an earlier chapter, the National Flood Insurance Program, the first major national mitigation effort, in many states, was not even part of the state emergency manager's portfolio. Instead, it often fell under either the department of natural resources or community development.

Recovery was neither well understood nor supported until the late 1980s, when a major overhaul of the legislation supporting the federal government's disaster management programs occurred. Passage of the Robert T. Stafford Act in 1988 significantly expanded the role of the federal government in disaster recovery. However, not until the 1990s, under the Clinton administration, did emergency management assume a major role in a community's recovery from a major disaster. The recovery skill set was very similar to that of mitigation, and to adequately perform either of these functions, the emergency manager was required to venture beyond his or her realm of control. State or local offices of planning, zoning, community development, natural resources, parks and recreation, public works, and the like had to be included and consulted.

There was another influential factor in this scenario, however. Unlike response and preparedness, which were regarded as fundamental to the discipline, mitigation and recovery involved more complex political processes, problematic issues that needed to be resolved, and a wide consensus among community leaders had to be reached, activities that the emergency manager may not have had the skills or the desire to pursue. From an emergency manager's vantage point, these functions may have been considered excessively risky and less than critical. As a well-respected state emergency manager once said, "I won't lose my job if I don't mitigate but I will lose my job if I don't respond."

One factor that predisposes emergency managers to embrace the response and preparedness functions is availability of or association with financial resources for each. As previously noted, funding of preparedness by private, commercial utilities supported that function on an annual basis. In fact, this private funding for off-site preparedness planning at commercial nuclear power plants provided the impetus and model for all later preparedness planning efforts.

With response, the basis of its prominence is legal in nature. Since public health and safety are a constitutional obligation of all state and local governments, a response capability would always be supported with a discrete amount of funding and resources on an annual basis.

The forces that drove mitigation and recovery were very different. For example, because the majority of recovery funding was event driven and therefore always depended on the occurrence of actual disasters (and federal declarations to support them), most states and localities rarely received discrete recovery funds. Mitigation fared even worse. Not until the Stafford Act was enacted, thereby providing a funding source for postdisaster mitigation in communities where presidential disaster declarations were made, did mitigation funding exist. And other than the Stafford Act, virtually no federal, state, or local funds were available for the practice. In fact, instead of providing funding, the National Flood Insurance Program, the only national mitigation program, mandated mitigation without any financial resources to support it, or at least to support emergency management operations. However, in return for passage of land-use ordinances that restricted development in the floodplain, the NFIP did provide low-cost, subsidized flood insurance for individual homeowners. So, in this case, mitigation supported individuals but not the emergency management organizations. Of course, there were collateral benefits to emergency managers from the NFIP, including the federal government providing a detailed map delineating NFIP communities' flood risk (which helped guide emergency planning and response operations).

To further illustrate the importance of funding to emergency managers' attitudes and priorities, one need only to look to the Project Impact initiative. As noted earlier, Project Impact was a local community mitigation program started by FEMA in the late 1990s. Seed funding was provided to communities to undertake a communitywide process that resulted in actions that increased resilience to future disasters. One of the major drivers behind this program was that many effective mitigation practices must be agreed to and implemented at the community level. The funding went directly to the community, often through the local emergency management organization but not always. Most local emergency managers embraced this program and became leaders or, at least, active partners. Many state directors of emergency management, however, were highly critical of and complained about this program. Not until FEMA agreed to provide funding to the state to ostensibly "oversee" this program did the state directors (albeit reluctantly) agree to support Project Impact and the mitigation goals it was trying to accomplish.

Another example of how funding drives the emergency management agenda can be seen in the actions taken by the emergency management community relative to the creation of the Department of Homeland Security. Emergency managers were almost universal in their support of moving FEMA into the new department in spite of the considerable loss of authority, prestige, and an advocate within the president's cabinet. What drove their stance was the accurate assumption that a substantial increase in federal funding was likely to be made available to deal with the new threats of terrorism and bioterrorism. Unfortunately, the emergency management community incorrectly assumed that the bulk of this funding would be directed to it, but in most cases the exact opposite occurred.

In a majority of states, governors established new homeland security organizations. In some cases, the state emergency management function was subsumed into these organizations, while in other cases, these new organizations became competitors for funding. So, not only did most emergency management organizations fail to get an actual increase in funds, like FEMA, they lost authority and political clout.

As noted in earlier chapters, one particularly unfortunate example of this could be seen in New Orleans, where the emergency management function was incorporated into a new Office of Homeland Security and the functional emphasis of the organization was placed on terrorism rather than the more predictable (and likely) natural hazards, including hurricanes. In addition, the office was led by a former military officer with little experience in responding to natural hazards.

The primary mission of homeland security is to prevent future acts of terrorism. This requires the inclusion and prominence of law enforcement and intelligence functions. Even in the event of an actualized terrorist act, these two functions have primacy in the immediate response. The rush by the emergency management community to follow the new terrorism money may have been shortsighted, but it is understandable because the discipline historically has been dramatically underfunded.

Reflecting on this detailed background and the disaster events of the past few years, we would like to suggest a range of emergency management models that we feel deserve consideration as the evolution of emergency management moves forward. We propose that these organizational options for establishing an effective emergency management system in the future will enhance the public health and safety of U.S. citizens from all types of risks and promote disaster resiliency in communities and individuals.

Option 1. A New FEMA

The first and most obvious option is a return to the successful model that existed in the 1990s. That would require the restoration of independent agency status to FEMA and its movement out of the Department of Homeland Security. The director of FEMA could then regain cabinet-level status (although the agency would not be a cabinet-level agency). Anyone considered for the FEMA director position would have demonstrated leadership and managerial skills at the highest level. All the functions that existed within FEMA in the 1990s would need to be restored. A governmentwide review would be undertaken to discover if any other programs or entities should be added to FEMA, as result of the many changes that occurred in the intervening years, which could enhance the FEMA mission. For example, entities in the Department of Commerce National Oceanographic and Atmospheric Administration like the National Hurricane Center, Alert and Warning Systems, could all become part of the new FEMA.

FEMA would utilize the National Response Plan mechanism to refocus its mission to coordinate and activate all the resources of the federal government in support of dealing with the consequences of any major threat or disaster, including public health disasters (such as pandemic flu or a small pox outbreak). FEMA would reassert its role as coordinator and manager of the federal resources, not the lead agency responsible for execution and delivery of the functions. FEMA, through the Disaster Relief Fund and under the Stafford Act, would become the funding agent to support other federal departments and agencies in executing the federal response to any disaster.

Under this model, state and local emergency management organizations would be full partners with FEMA. FEMA would be an advocate for state and local emergency management within the administration and Congress in support of enhanced funding and resources for their partners. Governors would be encouraged to make the state emergency director part of their cabinets and independent organizations within the state structure.

At all levels, the emergency management community would work in partnership with nongovernmental organizations and the private sector to create new coalitions and new strategic approaches to accomplish the full realm of emergency management functions. With the ever-increasing recognition of the impact of climate change on communities, it is also time that the emergency management and environmental advocacy communities join forces to deal with these impacts.

FEMA would actively encourage and support predisaster mitigation programs and work with state and local partners to implement programs for disaster resistance and community resiliency. All disaster recovery programs would support those goals and a reduction of the impact of future disasters. There would be return to an "all hazards" approach to dealing with the consequences of hazards, with communities deciding what are their greatest risks. State and local emergency management organizations would follow the federal lead.

The administration and Congress would need to commit adequate resources to the staffing and financing of FEMA programs in support of mitigation and preparedness. We worked very hard in the aftermath of Katrina to convince Congress that taking these actions would remedy many of the problems evidenced during the Hurricane Katrina response. Congress chose not to take this dramatic step; rather it passed legislation that addressed the Katrina problems on a piecemeal basis.

The positive aspects of this approach are the fact that this emergency management model can work already has been demonstrated in the FEMA and state organizations of the 1990s. Tinkering with the model to expand the partnership to include the NGOs and the private sector as full partners certainly is possible, likely necessary, and clearly has significant potential. This process was initiated during the late 1990s but was never institutionalized.

The major downfall of this model lies with its historic functional structure relative to the culture of emergency management. As has been demonstrated through history and experience, it will take a cultural change and an expanded skill base for emergency management to elevate the functions of mitigation and recovery to that of response. In previous editions of this text, we spoke to this point and believed that a new type of emergency manager was emerging from the environment of the 1990s. However, the events of September 11 clearly reversed this trend.

Concerns have been voiced that such a model may not be as effective in the present world as it was in the 1990s. The current situation includes new and different threats, which were just emerging at the close of the 1990s. Pandemic flu is but one example. Dealing with these emerging threats could overwhelm the consideration of all other risks and require a different knowledge base, even in the context of coordination and oversight. In some cases, we may not know how to mitigate these threats or what it will take as a society to recover from them. Unless enormous increases in funding are forthcoming for research and development, skill enhancement, and staff, it will become ever easier for emergency management to again focus on the preparedness and response functions.

Option 2. Nonprofit Organizations Are Emergency Management

The second option is for emergency management organizations at the federal, state, and local levels to reassess their responsibilities for preparedness, response, recovery, and mitigation and work with the nongovernmental sector (volunteer, nongovernmental, and faith-based organizations and the private business sector) to create "official" partnerships in which the nongovernmental sectors assume total responsibility for some of the functions or parts of them. Historically, NGOs partnered with emergency management agencies and played a significant role in response and recovery. The failure of all levels of government in the Katrina response activated an unprecedented response by the NGO community, which stepped in not only to support their own constituencies but to fill the void created by an incompetent government response. NGOs always played an important role in filling the gaps to support victims who cannot qualify for federal support or where federal support falls short.

Historically, the NGO response has been on an individual victim level. After Katrina, there was evidence of vast NGO participation and support expanding to cover the immediate needs, community recovery, and other requirements that normally would be handled by government entities. As the Katrina recovery slowly progresses, the NGOs are effecting the changes, not waiting for the bureaucratic red tape to clear but taking action. Most often their support comes from the private sector. In the current political environment, it is believed that the shift in the responsibility to deal with the needs of disaster victims from the government to the nongovernmental sector was a long-term goal of the Bush administration. And, while this may be true, the NGO establishment still failed to venture far beyond the immediate response and initial recovery needs as a sector. There has been no evidence that the NGO community is either interested or anxious to move into the areas of mitigation or to assume the challenges of longer-term recovery. Therefore, once again, we see a positive option for response and initial recovery with potential inroads into preparedness and long-term recovery.

A cautionary aspect of divesting emergency management functions to the NGO sector is the temporal nature of disasters. We must question how engaged NGOs will remain if we experience a period of few major disasters. NGOs are supported by fundraising; and while disasters create very positive fundraising opportunities, if these opportunities dry up, even for a short period, it is unlikely that the NGO sector could depend on the public as other more prominent issues deflect its attention and erode any capability the NGOs have developed. Could the federal government's solution to this issue be the provision of an annual stipend, provided to selected NGOs, that would be used to maintain a minimum level of capability to support emergency management?

Option 3. Recreate Emergency Management with a New Entity

The third and final option is the most radical of the three. In light of the expanding threat environment and the impact of global climate change, it may be time to take a fresh look at emergency management to better understand the limitations of the current cycle. We already discussed the historical and cultural barriers that led parts of the emergency management community not to focus on the functions of mitigation and long-term recovery. The sacred nature of the emergency management cycle of preparedness, response, recovery, and mitigation rested on the supposed connectivity of these factions. But, as we maintain, disagreement always existed as to when the mitigation function begins. Do you undertake mitigation before the disaster occurs, when the risk has been identified and delineated? Or is it only after a hazard risk has manifested and a "window of opportunity" for mitigation is opened that mitigation becomes possible? To be effective, mitigation must be part of the everyday planning and decisions in which individuals and communities participate.

After a disaster, the process of long-term recovery offers the most accessible and accommodating political environment for implementing mitigation actions. By mitigation, we speak not only about mitigation in the built environment but also measures individuals can take on a more personal level. For example, after a home is damaged in a disaster, the homeowner is more likely to purchase or retain appropriate insurance than prior to falling victim to the disaster.

Referring to the previous discussion of the different skill set and partnerships needed for effective mitigation and recovery, is it still logical or even necessary that these functions continue to be part of the emergency manager's portfolio? We would like to propose new organizational structures to address the functions of preparedness, response, recovery, and mitigation.

Consistent with the constitutional requirements for public health and safety, we propose that the functions of preparedness and response remain within the purview of the federal, state, and local government emergency management organizations. FEMA would remain within the DHS structure. To be effective, all these organizations must assess their resource requirements and a commitment must be made by the administration and Congress to commit the resources necessary to make these organizations effective at the local, state, and federal levels. As noted earlier in this chapter, FEMA would utilize the National Response Plan mechanism to refocus its mission to coordinate and activate all of the resources of the federal government in support of dealing with the consequences of any major threat or disaster, including public health disasters such as pandemic flu or a small pox outbreak. FEMA would reassert its role as coordinator and manager of the federal resources, not the lead agency responsible for execution and delivery of the functions. We would encourage FEMA and its state and local partners to engage the NGOs and the private sector in executing these functions.

The radical idea we propose is that the functions of mitigation and long-term recovery be supported by a different quasi-governmental structure. One of the strongest arguments for this approach is that the private sector is a more significant player in these functions than that of either preparedness or response. The private sector owns most of the built environment that faces the hazard risk and actually is affected in disaster events. The private sector has an enormous influence in the political environment that can support or reject certain mitigation measures, including the passage of building codes and land-use ordinances. And with regard to the insurance industry, the private sector is already in control of one of the most effective vehicles that can best be used to implement mitigation measures.

When any community recovers from a disaster, the success of its efforts depends greatly on how quickly the predominantly private sector functions are restored. Businesses provide the majority of a community's employment, critical services (such as health, child care, food supplies), and critical infrastructure (such as transportation, energy, and communications). In the event of a presidentially declared disaster, recovery of many of these functions may be supported through the federally administered Disaster Relief Fund as a part of the response, such as with public transportation systems. Unfortunately, more and more, these resources, which are critical to the facilitation of a quick recovery, are not supported by the federal programs.

To date, the emergency management community has not been extremely effective in engaging the private sector. Even in the heyday of emergency management in the 1990s, when FEMA and its state and local partners were exploring new partnership opportunities, there was a general lack of understanding about the private sector's needs in the postdisaster environment and the potential opportunities the private sector could provide. Government agencies' relations with the private sector most often occur as a regulatory requirement. In the emergency management world, this is evidenced by the relationships with the commercial nuclear industry and the flood insurance industry.

The National Institute of Building Sciences (NIBS) provides a potential model for this organizational structure. The NIBS is a nonprofit organization created by Congress and receives appropriations from Congress but is independent of the federal government. The original purpose in establishing the NIBS was to support and promote affordable options within the housing sector. The NIBS was expected to bring together representatives of government, industry professionals, and labor and consumer interests to focus on the identification and resolution of actual and potential problems hampering the construction of safe, affordable structures for housing, commerce, and industry throughout the United States. The NIBS has been successful in bringing together representatives from government agencies, regulatory agencies, legislators, and the private sector to "seek consensus solutions to problems of mutual concern."

We are not suggesting that the functions of mitigation and recovery be added to the NIBS mission, although they have been extremely effective partners with FEMA. With the NIBS, FEMA in the past promoted mitigation through the work of the Building Seismic Safety Council and the Multihazard Mitigation Council. While the NIBS mission is limited to the built environment, it has demonstrated that this type of structure can provide the vehicle for the private sector to work as equivalent partners with government to accomplish mutually beneficial goals.

We propose that the Congress establish a new entity that would bring together not just the public and private building community but also the following (selected examples):

- Private and public infrastructure representatives (e.g., lifelines, transportation, energy).
- Private and public financial and risk management industries (e.g., insurance, Fannie Mae).
- Public and private environmental community stakeholders.
- Public and private community development stakeholders.
- Construction code design and enforcement community members.
- Climate change research scientists.
- NGOs, academia, and foundations.
- Public and private emergency management community members.

Creating a new entity is difficult, and Congress usually is reluctant to interfere in what historically was considered a purely government function. However, the events of Hurricane Katrina, the competing priorities within the DHS, the changing threat environment, and the dire prospects of global climate change together require that a new, fresh look and approach be considered. This concept needs to be explored and developed with all the partners essential to accomplishing the functions of mitigation and recovery. Simply reading this list of partners can provoke an understanding of the diversity and complexity of the groups that must be involved and interconnected to implement any mitigation or recovery action. The participants that need to be included are

- The building and building code community.
- The infrastructure community.
- The financial sector.
- Other private sector groups.
- Other constituency groups (e.g., NAHB, developers, realtors).
- Environmental groups.
- Media organizations.
- Other NGOs (e.g., The National Conservancy, Habitat for Humanity).
- Local governmental constituency groups (e.g., NGA, NACo, ICMA).
- Private citizens and citizen organizations.
- Scientific community.
- Academia.
- Foundations.
- Public interest groups.
- DHS, FEMA, and state and local emergency management entities.
- Emergency management constituency groups (e.g., NEMA, IAEM).
- Congress.

Obviously, these entities are not listed in order of priority. Together, however, they illustrate the wide range of constituencies that must be included in any discussion of the functions of mitigation and recovery.

While it may be extremely difficult to understand how mitigation and recovery can become effective in the current political environment, one can identify distinct positive and negative aspects of this concept. The negative aspects are obvious. This approach would require a major change to the current governmental structure. It would require the DHS and FEMA to relinquish a level of authority, which is an anathema to bureaucratic politics; although, especially in the case of mitigation, the authority is minimal and the politics are major. It might require the DHS, FEMA, and state and local emergency management organizations to give up some of their resources. It is unlikely that this would happen, because each organization would claim that only minimal resources were attributed to these functions. It also requires a new pattern for making connections among the necessary partners, not just at the federal level but also at the state and local levels. Because of the nature of communities, the connections and cooperation at the local level may be the easiest to accomplish.

The most significant obstacle is overcoming the inertia and reluctance of Congress to create new government or quasi-government entities. Typically, only major events precipitate such congressional action. Without some external pressure or an external event, discussion and support for this option would be difficult to generate.

The primary positive aspect of this approach is twofold: (1) mitigation and the benefits of long-term recovery would be given attention equivalent to preparedness and response and (2) one of those entities most important to the implementation of mitigation (i.e., the private sector) would play a significant role in the process. As a nation, the United States cultivated, to a degree, an awareness of the need for preparedness and the necessity of response. It has not yet invested the same level of effort in mitigation and recovery. In spite of the cost/benefit analysis data and empirical evidence of the value of mitigation and its inclusion in long-term recovery, it is still a very hard sell. The "sell" often is being made by participants who do not necessarily have the expertise, skills, and comfort with the audience. It is unfair to ask current emergency management professionals to change how they operate, to change priorities when the change requires an entirely new skill set and the acceptance of considerable political risk.

To provide the opportunity for the culture of mitigation to exist, we need to engage those stakeholders who can affect this in a meaningful way and with a level of leadership that understands the risks and benefits of the process. This leadership does not exist in emergency management, and we need to find another vehicle to exercise the leadership. The usual government approaches will not work. If we are serious about reducing the impacts of future disasters and improving individual and community disaster resiliency, then we need to look at a new model.

Conclusion

What does the future hold for emergency management? It is abundantly clear that, in the ongoing aftermath of Hurricane Katrina, the status quo is no longer viable. Congress undertook this responsibility and made certain structural changes to FEMA and emergency management. While these changes are positive, in general, they are piecemeal and tend to address the problems encountered in Katrina. Katrina was a tragic event in our history. Katrina was also an event that could and should have been prevented. The failures of Katrina should not reflect on the dedication and professionalism of the emergency management community. Katrina, at its essence, was the colossal failure of political leadership at the federal, state, and local levels.

Aside from Katrina, we would argue that the world has changed and the emergency management cycle and discipline that worked in the past (and reached an exceptional level of performance during the 1990s) is no longer adequate. We believe we need to look at new and radical approaches to supporting the public health and safety of communities and to promoting disaster resiliency in communities in the future. We believe it is time for a new dialogue about the expectations of the emergency management discipline, what should constitute emergency management in the future, and what organizational structures can best support preparedness, response, recovery, and mitigation.

In this chapter, we attempted to identify several ideas and approaches that together could stimulate thought, ideas, and a much needed dialogue. The evolving threats, the realities of global climate change, and our changing social, economic, and political environment demand innovative approaches and leadership. We hope this text will motivate each reader to accept the challenge.

Katrina: A Case Study

Introduction

It is hard to imagine that anyone living in the United States and around most of the world was not aware of the human and physical tragedies that resulted along the Gulf Coast from Hurricane Katrina. Hurricane Katrina made landfall in Buras, Louisiana, on Monday, August 29, 2005. At the time it was reported as a Category 4 storm when it made landfall. The National Hurricane Center would later downgrade it to a Category 3 storm. In any event, it was considered an extremely dangerous storm by weather forecasters and the National Hurricane Center. It impacted a broad geographic area stretching from Alabama, across coastal Mississippi and southeast Louisiana, covering an estimated 90,000 square miles. As of May 2006, the death toll from the storm stood at 1,856 with another 705 individuals listed as missing.

The storm impacted over 1.5 million people and displaced more than 800,000 citizens. As of March 2007, over 200,000 individuals remain displaced from their homes and communities. The U.S. Coast Guard rescued over 24,273 people and FEMA Search and Rescue Teams rescued nearly 6,600 persons. The federal government claims disaster relief expenses will exceed $100 billion, the National Flood Insurance Program paid more than $16.1 million to over 205,000 people filing claims

related to Katrina, and the insurance losses are expected to exceed $35 billion. Forty-four States and the District of Columbia received emergency declarations to cover their expenses for sheltering the millions of evacuees that were transported out of the Gulf.

By any account, Hurricane Katrina was a massive storm, deadly and destructive. It served to expose severe cracks in the nation's emergency management system and its ability to respond to a catastrophic event. Government after action reports, which are done after most disasters, and media accounts have judged the response a failure and the recovery phase is judged to be proceeding with the same level of incompetence. Changes that had been made to Louisiana's coastal landscape, particularly the loss of wetlands and increased channelization, made New Orleans and the Louisiana coast more vulnerable to hurricanes. Design and construction decisions on the levee system and inadequate maintenance of that system contributed to the impacts of Katrina. The storm challenged the capacities and capabilities of emergency management operations at all levels of government. The lack of planning for the Superdome as the designated shelter of last resort for New Orleans and the subsequent problems that occurred in that facility provided the most visible demonstration of the failed operations. Many of the problems of the immediate response exposed the impacts of priority focus on terrorism and homeland security in recent years that may have contributed to the decrease in these capacities and capabilities.

Elected officials at all levels of government stumbled badly as they tried to provide leadership in the face of this disaster. The business community, voluntary agencies, and nongovernmental organizations (NGOs) stepped up to provide extraordinary services to storm victims. The general public, corporations, unions, and foundations donated billions of dollars for disaster relief.

We do not intend in this case study to recount everything that went wrong in the Katrina response but to highlight the most obvious systemic problems, identify potential causes, discuss various reactions and recommendations for correcting those failures, and look at the progress toward recovery. This section examines the timeline of events leading up to the moment when Hurricane Katrina made landfall, the impact of the storm, the immediate response to the storm, the ongoing recovery phase, and a review of reports evaluating the government's response and resulting recommendations for moving forward to prevent another Katrina debacle.

Hurricane Katrina Timeline

The color insert provides a verbal and visual timeline of events starting with the initial formation of Hurricane Katrina as Tropical Depression 12 through the first days following Katrina making landfall on August 29, 2007; Table 1 gives a fuller version of events. This timeline was compiled from several sources including FEMA, The Brookings Institution, CNN, and the after action report prepared by the United States Senate entitled "Hurricane Katrina: A Nation Still Unprepared."

The Impact of the Storm

Hurricane Katrina impacted different areas in different ways. Along the Mississippi Gulf Coast, Katrina generated a 25–30 foot tidal surge that swept away structures and vehicles in its path. Hotels and casinos located on the Gulf were severely damaged; in some cases entire communities disappeared. In New Orleans, the principal impact was the flooding caused by the breaches in the levees that left almost 80% of the city underwater for up to six weeks. However, some sections of the city, notably those areas closest to the river such as the French Quarter, experienced very little if any flooding. Tidal surge was only a factor in the Lower Ninth Ward section of the City which together with St. Bernard Parish experienced the tidal surge that traveled up the Mississippi River Gulf Outlet. Wind and rain caused considerable damage to homes and businesses throughout the region.
Table 2 illustrates the impact of Katrina on the Gulf Coast.

Over 1.3 million people evacuated in advance of Katrina making landfall and an estimated 800,000 persons were displaced for an extended period of time. As of February 2007, the population of New Orleans is at less than 50% of its size pre-Katrina. An estimated 200,000 city residents have yet to return to the city and are living in various temporary housing situations including in temporary housing sites built and managed by FEMA in locations in Louisiana, Mississippi, and Alabama.

Critical infrastructures such as water, power, communications, schools, hospitals, and child care were severely damaged and disrupted in all impacted areas. Government facilities and private industry suffered massive losses. The White House report on Katrina, "The Federal Response to Hurricane Katrina: Lessons Learned," estimated damage to housing at $67 billion, business property suffered $20 billion in damages, and government property an estimated $3 billion in damages (Townsend, 2006). Insured losses from Katrina are estimated to be the greatest ever in U.S. history (see Table 3).

Table 4 details the levels of assistance provided by FEMA. Over 1.3 million individuals have applied for assistance and over 1 million applications have been approved through FEMA's Individual and Household Assistance Program. Billions of dollars from FEMA's Public Assistance program have been disbursed to communities in the three states impacted by Katrina. Over $15 billion in flood insurance claims have been paid by FEMA through the National Flood Insurance Program.

Table 5 details expenses incurred by FEMA in providing temporary housing for evacuees, debris removal, crisis counseling, evacuation reimbursements to host sites, disaster unemployment assistance, and expedited assistance of more than $1.6 billion to 803,470 individuals

immediately after the storm. Large and small businesses were hit hard by the storm, and the Small Business Administration has provided over $10 billion in loans to date (see Table 6).

Voluntary agencies, nongovernmental organizations (NGOs), and the business sector made major contributions to the relief efforts and provide another measure of the impact of Katrina. Table 7 describes the activities undertaken by the American Red Cross, Table 8 identifies the large number of voluntary agencies and NGOs that responded to Katrina, and Table 9 summarizes the funds raised and spent on relief efforts by the major voluntary agencies and NGOs in Katrina.

The business community raised and contributed record sums exceeding $1 billion to the Katrina response and recovery efforts (see Table 10). Family, corporate, and community foundations gave generously to response and recovery efforts, in many cases meeting those unmet needs for individuals and communities that government relief programs do not cover (see Table 11).

The Response

By all accounts, the response to Hurricane Katrina was a failure on all levels. According to the White House Report, "the response to Hurricane Katrina fell far short of the seamless, coordinated effort that had been envisioned by President Bush when he ordered the creation of the National Response Plan in February 2003." (Townsend, 2006)

The U.S. Senate report found that "the suffering ... continues longer than it should have because of — and in some cases exacerbated by — the failure of government at all levels to plan, prepare for, and respond aggressively to the storm. These failures were not just conspicuous; they were pervasive." (Senate Committee on Homeland Security and Governmental Affairs, 2006)

The report concludes that "among the many factors that contributed to these failures, the Committee found that there were four overarching ones:

1. Long-term warnings went unheeded and government officials neglected their duties to prepare for a forewarned catastrophe;

2. Government officials took insufficient actions or made poor decisions in the days immediately before and after landfall;

3. Systems on which officials relied on to support their response efforts failed; and

4. Government officials at all levels failed to provide effective leadership." (Senate Committee on Homeland Security and Governmental Affairs, 2006)

The report prepared by the House of Representatives crafted 14 findings based on their review of the response:

• The accuracy and timeliness of National Weather Service and National Hurricane Center forecasts prevented further loss of life.

• The Hurricane Pam exercise reflected recognition by all levels of government of the dangers of a Category 4 or 5 hurricane striking New Orleans.

• Levees protecting New Orleans were not built for the most severe hurricanes.

• The failure of complete evacuations led to preventable deaths, great suffering, and further delays in relief.

• Critical elements of the National Response Plan were executed late, ineffectively, or not at all.

• DHS and the States were not prepared for this catastrophic event.

• Massive communications damage and a failure to adequately plan for alternatives impaired response efforts, command and control, and situational awareness.

- Command and control was impaired at all levels, delaying relief.

- The military played an invaluable role, but coordination was lacking.

- The collapse of local law enforcement and lack of effective public communications led to civil unrest and further delayed relief.

- Medical care and evacuations suffered from a lack of advance preparations, inadequate communications, and difficulties coordinating efforts.

- Long-standing weaknesses and the magnitude of the disaster overwhelmed FEMA's ability to provide emergency shelter and temporary housing.

- FEMA logistics and contracting systems did not support a targeted, massive, and sustained provision of commodities.

- Contributions by charitable organizations assisted many in need, but the American Red Cross and others faced challenges due to the size of the mission, inadequate logistics capacity, and a disorganized shelter process.

(Select Bipartisan Committee to Investigate the Preparation for and Response to Hurricane Katrina, 2006)

In summary, these reports found that the government response lacked leadership at the top, was unprepared, operated on poor information and situational awareness, was poorly coordinated, and was incapable of communicating among the various responding agencies and with the general public. All of these factors added up to the confusion, violence, and suffering documented in the first weeks by the media and witnessed by billions across the globe.

New Orleans, LA, February 24, 2006   FEMA contractors remove debris created by Hurricane Katrina from the lower 9th ward. Crews continue collecting wreckage throughout the neighborhood as more people return to rebuild New Orleans.
Robert Kaufmann/FEMA

The Recovery

As of March 2007, the recovery efforts have been ineffectively designed and implemented. Issues of leadership, coordination, and planning that plagued the response phase have turned the recovery into a difficult, not easily understood process that has made little progress in some areas, especially in New Orleans. Over 200,000 New Orleans residents have yet to return to the city because of lack of housing, critical services such as child care and schools, hospital beds, and in some neighborhoods basic utilities such as power, water, and telephone service.

The Brookings Institution has created the Katrina Index that reviews key social and economic indicators on how New Orleans is recovering from Hurricane Katrina on a monthly basis. Its August 2006 Special Edition of the Katrina Index on the One Year Anniversary of the storm noted some progress in housing issues, a slow rebound of the community infrastructure, a smaller labor force and the high level of federal aid to the area (see Table 12).

On the 18-month anniversary of Hurricane Katrina, the Katrina Index found that "eighteen months after the storm, residents across the region are frustrated that so many schools are still closed, police and fire stations are not repaired, and streetlights don't work, despite the large amount of committed federal assistance and significant charitable contributions, given to the area." (The Brookings Institution, 2007) Problems continue with the distribution of federal aid, housing, retention of students at local universities, infrastructure shortages in the areas of public transportation, schools, hospitals, and child care, and the economy (see Table 13).

Problems that are slowing the recovery cited often by the public include difficulties in obtaining full payment from their insurance companies on damage to their homes and businesses (this reflects the historical issue of the difference between water and wind damage and what an insurance policy covers), delays and difficulties in accessing government home rebuilding programs such as the Road Home program in Louisiana, and delays in the rebuilding of public and private infrastructures. Many businesses, small and large, have been hampered by a reduction in the workforce, soaring utility rates, and the slow return of the tourism economy.

Recovery appears to be moving more smoothly in Mississippi thanks to the leadership of the Governor and the state's Congressional delegation which has succeeded in securing ample Federal aid for state residents. The casinos have returned to operation in many areas, again generating jobs and income for area residents and tax revenues for the state. Chevron USA, working with the

Early Childhood Institute at Mississippi State University and Save the Children, has spearheaded the restoration and upgrading of child care centers across the three Gulf Coast counties, giving families a safe and secure place to leave their children as they rebuild their lives and their communities.

New Orleans, September 18, 2005 The city skyline looks over a neighborhood south of the city still flooded after three weeks. Recovery from Hurricane Katrina's aftermath will take time.
Win Henderson/FEMA

Lessons Learned

Hurricane Katrina made it very clear that the emergency management system in this country is broken. The White House report noted, "Hurricane Katrina obligates us to re-examine how we are organized and resourced to address the full range of catastrophic events—both natural and man-made. The storm and its aftermath provide us with the mandate to design and build such a system." (Townsend, 2006)

The United States Senate report noted, "Based on the weaknesses and challenges we uncovered in our investigation, we believe the core recommendations are the essential first steps in the successful construction of an effective system." (Senate Committee on Homeland Security and Governmental Affairs, 2006)

The House of Representatives report concluded, "With this report we have tried to identify where and why chaos ensued, so that even a storm the size of Katrina can be met with more order, more urgency, more coordination, and more initiative." (Bipartisan Committee, 2006)

The House report offers no recommendations on how to proceed to rebuild the nation's emergency management system but the Senate, the White House, and numerous other reports do.

The U.S. Senate report lists 7 core recommendations and 81 additional recommendations. The 7 core recommendations call for creation of a new emergency management organization, a return to the all hazards approach, better regional coordination, building a government-wide operations center, a sustained commitment to the emergency management system, strengthening of response plans and systems, and improved capacity to respond to catastrophic events. (See Table 14.)

The White House report noted, "The Lessons Learned Report confirms the imperative of integrating and synchronizing the Nation's homeland security policies, strategies, and plans across Federal, State, and local governments, as well as the private sector, nongovernmental organizations (NGOs), faith-based groups, communities, and individual citizens." (Townsend, 2006) To this end the report recommended that the nation's emergency management system be transformed and built on the following three principles:

First, we must implement a comprehensive National Preparedness System to make certain that we have a fully national system that ensures unity of effort in preparing for and responding to natural and man-made disasters;

Second, we must create a Culture of Preparedness that emphasizes that the entire nation — at all levels of government, the private sector, communities, and individual citizens — shares common goals and responsibilities for homeland security; and

Third, we must implement corrective actions to ensure we do not repeat the problems encountered during Hurricane Katrina. (Townsend, 2006)

Table 15 summarizes these recommendations.

The White House report includes 125 recommendations in 17 broad categories including:

1. **National Preparedness** (Recommendations 1–21)

2. **Integrated Use of Military Capabilities** (Recommendations 22–32)

3. **Communications** (Recommendations 33–37)

4. **Logistics and Evacuation** (Recommendations 38–43)

5. **Search and Rescue** (Recommendations 44–48)

6. **Public Safety and Security** (Recommendations 49–56)

7. **Public Health and Medical Support** (Recommendations 57–62)

8. **Human Services** (Recommendations 63–67)

9. **Mass Care and Housing** (Recommendations 68–72)

10. **Public Communications** (Recommendations 73–77)

11. **Critical Infrastructure and Impact Assessment** (Recommendations 78–85)

12. **Environmental Hazards and Debris Removal** (Recommendations 86–88)

13. **Foreign Assistance** (Recommendations 89–97)

14. **Non-Governmental Aid** (Recommendations 98–103)

15. **Training, Exercises, and Lessons Learned** (Recommendations 104–111)

16. **Homeland Security Professional Development and Education** (Recommendations 112–118)

17. **Citizen and Community Preparedness** (Recommendations 119–125)

(Townsend, 2006)

The National Emergency Managers Association (NEMA), which represents the nation's 56 state and territorial emergency management directors, produced a white paper entitled "Emergency Management Goes Back to the Future" in December 2005. The paper noted that many of the issues raised by the ineffective response to Katrina are not new "because as a society we have not made the necessary investment to build and sustain an effective national emergency management system that integrates local, state and federal resources and capabilities." (National Emergency Management Association, 2005) The NEMA white paper presents a series of recommendations that identifies the actions needed by all stakeholders to build a sustainable system (see Table 16).

Analysis

The numerous after action reports identified many factors that contributed to the failure of the response and recovery efforts in Hurricane Katrina (see Table 17). Many of these factors can be summarized below.

- Lack of Leadership — Political leaders at all levels of government did not assume leadership of the response and recovery efforts as New York Mayor Rudy Giuliani did in the aftermath of the World Trade Center attacks. The leadership of the FEMA and the State and local emergency management operations were also found lacking.

- Information — During the response, there was no clear effort made to collect, analyze, and disseminate information among the various responders. As more than one report noted, there was little if any situational awareness in the early days of the response. The media became the first source of information.

- Communications — The elected and appointed officials involved in the response failed to communicate with each other and failed to communicate effectively with the general public.

- Preparedness — DHS/FEMA, the State Office of Homeland Security and the New Orleans Office of Homeland Security were unprepared to deal with a disaster of this size and magnitude. A major contributing factor was the almost exclusive focus on homeland security and terrorism issues since September 11. These agencies and their personnel were not prepared to respond to a large natural disaster.

- Mitigation — The levee system is the principal flood mitigation mechanism in the New Orleans area and it failed. Reports indicate that the system was badly designed and poorly maintained.

- Coordination — Federal, state, and local emergency responders failed to work together and to effectively coordinate their actions. Part of this failure was the inability of the FEMA Director to marshal and direct the full resources of the federal government in support of state and local efforts. The National Response Plan failed because FEMA, as the designated leader of the plan, was unable to direct the actions of other federal agencies.

There are questions that come from the Katrina experience that must be considered as efforts are made to rebuild the nation's emergency management system:

- Role of the Military and the National Guard — With the nation at war, the resources available from the State and Federal National Guards are much more limited than in peacetime. What continuing role should

the active-duty military play in responding to future disasters?

- Voluntary Agencies, Nongovernmental Organizations (NGOs), and the Business Community — All three sectors played big roles in the response and continue to play major roles in the recovery. How can these sectors work best with the government sector in future disasters in order to fully leverage the resources that each sector can bring to the table?

- Who Is in Charge — Will the reforms proposed by all the after action reports and now being implemented within the federal government settle the key question of who is in charge at the federal level of the next major disaster?

- Vulnerable Populations — Katrina exposed the extreme vulnerability of certain populations in our society such as the elderly, the disabled, children, the economically disadvantaged, non-English speakers, etc. What can be done to revise emergency plans to address the issues that impact these special needs populations in a major disaster?

- Mitigation — With global climate change and the severity and frequency of large weather events rising, we can expect more Katrinas in the future. When will government and nongovernment leaders recognize that reducing the loss of life and the economic and environmental impacts of future disasters can be accomplished through hazard mitigation actions and provide the resources to take action across the country?

In consideration of all these factors and questions, the authors would propose consideration of the following five points that alone or in concert may contribute to rebuilding the nation's emergency management system in the wake of Hurricane Katrina:

- Move FEMA out of DHS and reestablish it as an independent executive branch agency whose director reports directly to the president.

- Elevate the FEMA director to cabinet status and invest the FEMA director with the authority to direct federal disaster response resources.

- Refocus the National Response Plan to marshal the full resources of the federal government at the direction of the FEMA director in support of state and local emergency managers in a major disaster event.

- Create a new entity (could be a new federal government agency or a quasi-governmental agency or a nonprofit organization funded by government) that focuses on building community and individual resiliency through a mix of policy/legislative initiatives and community-based programming in the areas of mitigation and preparedness—include federal government involvement from FEMA, HUD, EPA, DOE, Dept. of Education, Commerce, HHS, NOAA, etc.

- Establish an agreement with the nongovernmental sector (voluntary agencies, NGOs, and the business community) that details how government and nongovernment entities will work together in all four phases of emergency management.

Conclusion

The nation's emergency management system is broken. The failed response to and the ongoing failure of the recovery from Hurricane Katrina have made this fact abundantly clear. The nation's leaders and emergency managers must take a hard look at the Katrina experience and come together to rebuild the system that was once the best in the world.

TABLE 1

Hurricane Katrina Timeline

Tuesday, August 23	**4:00 PM**	Tropical Depression 12 develops about 200 miles southeast of Nassau in the Bahamas.
Wednesday, August 24	**2:30 PM**	Tropical Depression 12 strengthens into Tropical Storm Katrina over the Central Bahamas. Hurricane warning issued for the southeastern Florida coast.
Thursday, August 25		Tropical Storm is elevated to a Hurricane.
	4 PM	The National Hurricane Center, for the first time, reports that some models show Katrina coming ashore "between Mobile, Alabama, and Grand Isle, Louisiana." Katrina, still about 15 miles east of Florida, is expected to gradually strengthen once in the Gulf of Mexico.
	5:30 PM	Katrina makes landfall in Florida as a Category 1 hurricane with 80 mph winds. Nine people reportedly died. Governor Jeb Bush declares State of Emergency in Florida.
Friday, August 26	**10:30 AM**	Katrina, still moving westward in the Gulf of Mexico, is elevated to a Category 2 hurricane, with note that storm "could become a category or major hurricane on Saturday."
	11 AM	National Hurricane Center officials state in a video teleconference that their prediction models indicate a shift in Katrina's path west "towards New Orleans." Prior models had predicted a probable strike in the Florida panhandle.
		White House declares impending disaster area. Orders FEMA and DHS to prepare. 10,000 National Guard troops dispatched along Gulf Coast (arrival time unclear).
	1 PM	Louisiana Governor Kathleen Blanco declares a State of Emergency and activates her state's National Guard.
	Afternoon-Evening	Mississippi Governor Haley Barbour declares a State of Emergency and activates his state's National Guard.

	4 PM	NHC issues an official forecast shifting Katrina's track 170 miles west, predicting a probable Category 4 hurricane striking the Mississippi coast near the Alabama border with landfall on Monday, August 29.
	10 PM	NHC issues a forecast shifting the track farther west and predicting a probable strike at or near the Louisiana-Mississippi border, east of New Orleans, on Monday, August 29.
Saturday, August 27	**4 AM**	NHC issues a forecast stating that Katrina is a Category 3 hurricane and predicting a direct hit on New Orleans.
	6 AM	FEMA headquarters begins 24-hour operations in Washington, D.C.
	7:30 AM	National Weather Service, in teleconference, informs Louisiana state and local officials that the probable path of the storm is "smack dab through the metropolitan New Orleans area."
	9 AM	The first phase of the Louisiana Emergency Evacuation Plan begins. Under Phase I, citizens in coastal areas, south of the Intracoastal Waterway, would evacuate 50 hours before a Category 3 or stronger hurricane hits.
	10 AM	Expected Category 4 storm.
	11:41 AM	Governor Blanco requests a declaration of a federal state of emergency for Louisiana under the Stafford Act. President Bush issues the declaration later in the day.
	12 PM	Phase II of the Louisiana Emergency Evacuation Plan is initiated.
	1 PM (approximately)	New Orleans Mayor C. Ray Nagin, in a joint press conference with Governor Blanco, declares a State of Emergency, announces he will issue a voluntary evacuation order, and announces that the Superdome will open at 8 a.m. on Sunday as a special-needs shelter.
		Mississippi Gov. Haley Barbour declares a State of Emergency. A mandatory evacuation ordered for Hancock County.
	2 PM	Louisiana Emergency Operations Center in Baton Rouge goes to 24-hour operations.

4 PM	The final phase of the Louisiana Emergency Evacuation Plan is initiated and contraflow evacuation by highway begins (highways become one-way only to increase capacity during the emergency).
6 PM	National Weather Service Prediction: 45% chance that a Category 4 or 5 storm will hit New Orleans directly.
7 PM	National Weather Service advises City of New Orleans Office of Emergency Preparedness that the New Orleans levees could be overtopped.
7:25–8 PM	NHC Director Max Mayfield briefs Governor Blanco, Governor Barbour, and Mayor Nagin about Katrina's potential impact. Late evening traffic from Louisiana's evacuation into Mississippi subsides, allowing Mississippi to issue mandatory evacuations for three coastal counties — Hancock, Harrison, and Jackson.
10 PM	NHC issues first official storm-surge forecast for Katrina, predicting surge flooding of 15 to 20 feet above normal tides and locally as high as 25 feet. NHC issues Hurricane Warning for north-central Gulf Coast from Morgan City, Louisiana, eastward to the Alabama-Florida border, including the City of New Orleans. Hurricane-force winds are expected within 24 hours.
Sunday, August 28	President Bush issues federal emergency declarations for Mississippi and Alabama, and declares Florida a federal disaster area. Alabama, Mississippi, and Louisiana Governors request Presidential Major Disaster Declarations; they are signed the next day.
1 AM	NHC issues Special Advisory: "Katrina Strengthens to Category 4 with 145 mph winds."
7 AM	NHC issues Special Advisory stating that Katrina is "now a potentially catastrophic Category 5 hurricane" with maximum sustained winds near 160 mph.
	Early: DHS Secretary Chertoff and FEMA Director Brown given electronic briefings by Hurricane Center on possibility of levee break.
8 AM	Superdome opens. Allows people in.

9:30 AM	Mayor Nagin orders a mandatory evacuation of Orleans Parish. Nagin announces that Regional Transit Authority (RTA) buses will pick up people in 12 locations throughout the city to take them to places of refuge, including the Superdome. The New Orleans Comprehensive Emergency Management Plan calls for buses to evacuate citizens out of the city (this component not in effect).
10 AM	NHC increases storm-surge forecast to 18 to 22 feet above normal tide levels and locally as high as 28 feet.
11 AM	During a daily video teleconference with the President, DHS headquarters, FEMA headquarters, FEMA's regional offices, and representatives from Louisiana and Mississippi, National Hurricane Center Director Max Mayfield states, "I don't think any model can tell you with any confidence right now whether the levees will be topped or not, but that's obviously a very, very grave concern." FEMA Director Michael Brown says, "Just keep jamming those lines full as much as you can with commodities.
11 AM	Ten shelters set up for those unable to leave (Nagin referred to them as "refuges of last resort" rather than shelters). Evacuation orders posted all along coast. President Bush suggests mandatory evacuation after decision was already made but before it was reported to the public.
11:30 AM	President Bush delivers statement vowing to help those affected.
Noon	Highways packed. City activates contraflow traffic system so some highways become one-way only.
12 PM	The Superdome is opened as a "refuge of last resort" for the general population.
4 PM	NHC issues first official forecast addressing New Orleans levees which states, "Some levees in the greater New Orleans area could be overtopped."
5 PM	Contraflow highway evacuation in Louisiana ends. Gov. Blanco requests disaster relief funds (some evidence this request was on 8-27).

	3 PM	Superdome has 10,000 people inside. 150 National Guardsmen are stationed there (approximately two-thirds of them are unarmed).
	6 PM	Nagin orders a curfew of 6 PM.
	7 PM	National Weather Service predicts the levees may be "overtopped" due to storm surge.
Monday, August 29	**6:10–7 AM**	On August 29, at approximately 6:10 a.m. CT, Hurricane Katrina's eye makes landfall at Buras on the Louisiana coast between Grand Isle and the mouth of the Mississippi River. Storm surge overtops the levees on the east bank of the river, "crosses" the river, overtops the levees on the west bank, and sends additional water into neighborhoods in Plaquemines Parish. The center of Hurricane Katrina moves ashore into southeast Louisiana just east of Grand Isle.
		Catastrophic flooding begins in New Orleans resulting from massive overtopping of levees in east Orleans and St. Bernard Parishes, overtopping and breaking of the Industrial Canal levees, and breaks in the 17th Street and London Avenue Canal floodwalls. The Superdome's roof begins to leak; it loses air conditioning, plumbing in all but the first floor, and its communication system. A backup generator provides minimal lighting.
	9 AM	Lower 9th Ward Levee reportedly breached. Floodwaters 6–8 feet in this area.
	10 AM	Hurricane Katrina makes landfall in Mississippi. Storm surge reported 20 feet above normal in Biloxi area.
	11:00 AM	FEMA Director Michael Brown dispatches 1,000 employees 5 hours after landfall—gives them 2 days to arrive. Brown arrives in Baton Rouge at the State Office of Emergency Preparedness.
	Afternoon	State and local first responders' communications begin to fail in the Greater New Orleans area and Mississippi.
	Mid-afternoon	Search-and-rescue operations begin by the U.S. Coast Guard, the New Orleans Police and Fire Departments, the Louisiana National Guard, and the Louisiana Department of Wildlife and Fisheries.
	2–3 PM	Local officials in Mississippi begin search and rescue.

	2 PM	City Hall confirms 17th Street levee breach. Floods affect ≈20% of the city.
	Afternoon	FEMA issues statement asking first responders to only come to the city if there was proper coordination between the state and local officials.
	1:45 PM	President Bush declares Emergency Disaster for Louisiana and Mississippi. Frees up federal funds.
		Superdome damaged (with 10,000 people inside). Refineries damaged, and eight refineries closed. Airports close.
		Coast Guard rescues 1,200 from flood; National Guard called in.
	Evening	FEMA Director Brown assures Governor Blanco that FEMA will send 500 buses to New Orleans the next day.
	10 PM	MEMA search-and-rescue teams arrive and immediately begin life-saving operations.
Tuesday, August 30		Mayor Nagin opens the New Orleans Convention Center as a refuge for the general population.
	10:30 AM	Acting Deputy Secretary of Defense orders U.S. Northern Command to move all necessary assets to the Gulf Coast, giving blanket authority for forces to provide military assistance.
	4 PM	U.S. Army Lieutenant General Russel Honoré is designated Commander of Joint Task Force Katrina.
	Evening	Plumbing fails completely at the Superdome. Conditions at the stadium deteriorate due to the massive crowds and lack of air conditioning and sanitation. DHS Secretary Michael Chertoff declares Katrina an "incident of national significance." Chertoff designates Michael Brown as the Principal Federal Official (PFO) to manage the response and recovery operations for Hurricane Katrina.
		Second levee in New Orleans breaks. Water covers 80% of the city (20 feet high in some places).
		FEMA activates the National Response Plan to fully mobilize federal government's resources.

FEMA stops volunteer firefighters with hurricane expertise due to the insecurity of the city. Asks them to wait for National Guardsmen to secure city first.

An estimated 50,000–100,000 remain in New Orleans on roofs, the Superdome, and the convention center. The convention center was discussed as a possible option for refugees by New Orleans officials, but it was never officially chosen as a place of refuge. It was not a shelter listed in the New Orleans Comprehensive Emergency Management Plan. Unclear why it became a shelter.

	4:30 PM	Officials call for anyone with boats to help with rescue mission.
	5:50 PM	President Bush announces that he will cut vacation short.
	6:30 PM	Nagin issues urgent bulletin that waters will continue to rise—12–15 feet in some places. He reports that pumps will soon fail.
	8:10 PM	Reports suggest looting is widespread.
	8:55 PM	Army Corps of Engineers begin work on 17th Street levee.
	10:15 PM	Gov. Blanco orders an evacuation of the Superdome. She sets no timetable.
	Late evening	Governor Blanco directs the Department of Social Services to find a shelter by 6 a.m. Wednesday for at least 25,000 people.
Wednesday, August 31	6 AM	Health and Human Services Secretary Michael Leavitt declares a public-health emergency for Louisiana, Mississippi, Florida, and Alabama. Governor Blanco issues an Executive Order to commandeer school buses.
	Morning	Gov. Blanco requests more National Guardsmen from President Bush. Orders total evacuation of city.
	1:30–1:45 AM	FEMA, for the first time, mission-assigns DOT to send buses to New Orleans.

	8:30–9:30 AM	Governor Blanco calls Governor Rick Perry of Texas to request that the Houston Astrodome open to house New Orleans evacuees.
	10 AM	Texas Governor spokesperson says that Superdome refugees will be put in Astrodome.
	11 AM	Chief of the federal National Guard Bureau directs all state Adjutants General to rapidly deploy available National Guard troops to Louisiana and Mississippi.
	2:30 PM	Governor Blanco and President Bush discuss by telephone the need for military assistance and the Governor's command of the Louisiana National Guard in a unified-command structure.
	4:11 PM	President Bush holds a Cabinet meeting at the White House and speaks publicly to outline federal relief efforts.
	Evening	Some federally contracted buses arrive in New Orleans and begin evacuation of overpasses and special-needs shelter.
		Buses begin arriving to evacuate Superdome. 25,000 people in Superdome. 52,000 people in Red Cross shelters.
	12:30 PM	Refugees begin arriving in Houston at the Astrodome.
		~ Pentagon sends four Navy ships with emergency supplies. Launches search-and-rescue mission.
		~ Water level stops rising in New Orleans.
		~ Looting grows exponentially. Police forced to focus on violence/looting rather than search and rescue.
		~ London Avenue canal breached.
		~ Military transport planes take seriously ill and injured to Houston.
		~ FEMA deploys 39 medical teams and 1,700 trailer trucks.
Thursday, September 1	**10 AM**	Bus evacuation of the general population begins at the Superdome.
		Military increases National Guard deployment to 30,000. Violence, carjacking, looting continues. Military helicopters shot at while evacuating residents. FEMA water rescue operations suspended because of gunfire.

Nagin issues a "desperate SOS" for more buses.

~ President Bush appoints George H.W. Bush and Bill Clinton to fundraise for hurricane victims.

~ Halliburton awarded Navy contract for storm cleanup.

~ Sandbags arrive for levees.

~ Superdome and Convention Center now housing up to 45,000 refugees.

~ Senators return from recess to begin work on emergency aid bill.

~ DHS Secretary Chertoff states in an interview that he was not aware of the people at the convention center until recently.

8 PM	Brown states (on Paula Zahn's show) that he became aware of the convention center problem only a few hours before.
Late Evening	Colonel Terry Ebbert, New Orleans Director of Homeland Security and Public Safety, requests assistance from Louisiana National Guard commander Major General Bennett Landreneau to secure and evacuate the Convention Center in conjunction with the New Orleans Police Department.
Friday, September 2	~ President Bush tours Gulf area. Acknowledges failures of government. Calls the results "not acceptable."
Late Morning	In a private meeting, the President and Governor Blanco discuss command and control for the military response.
12–12:30 PM	1,000 National Guard forces (LA, TX, OK, NV, and AR) move toward the Convention Center and secure the building to begin relief operations.
11:20 PM	White House faxes proposal to Governor Blanco under which there would be appointed a dual-status commander who would be an active-duty military officer and who would exercise command and control on behalf of the Governor over National Guard forces and on behalf of the President over federal active-duty forces.

~ More National Guardsmen arrive; 6500 arrive in New Orleans, 20,000 by day's end in LA and MS.

~ Congress approves $10.5 billion for immediate rescue and relief efforts.

	~ U.S. and Europe tap oil and gas reserves (2 million barrels a day).
	~ Explosions at chemical storage plant in New Orleans. Scattered fires.
	~ Fifteen airlines begin flying refugees out of New Orleans to San Antonio.
Saturday, September 3	~ President Bush orders 7,200 active-duty forces to the Gulf Coast.
	~ 40,000 National Guardsmen now on Gulf Coast.
8:56 AM	Governor Blanco declines the White House proposal to appoint a dual-status commander and retains sole command of National Guard troops in Louisiana.
10 AM	Convention Center evacuation begins.
1 PM	Superdome evacuation is complete.
6:30 PM	Convention Center evacuation is complete.
	~ U.S. Labor Department announces emergency grant of $62 million for dislocated workers.
	~ New Orleans police report 200 officers have walked off the job, 2 have committed suicide.
Sunday, September 4	Superdome fully evacuated (except stragglers).
	Gov. Blanco declares State of Public Health Emergency.
	Carnival Cruise offers cruise ships for 7,000 victims.
Monday, September 5	~ Gap in levee closed. Still repairing another gap.
	~ I-10 Cloverleaf and Causeway Boulevard evacuations are complete. Coast Guard Admiral Thad Allen is appointed Deputy PFO.
	~ Bush returns to the region. 4,700 more active duty troops dispatched.
	~ Former Presidents George H.W. Bush and Bill Clinton announce hurricane fund.
	~ 500 New Orleans officers unaccounted for.
	~ Some refineries restart production.
	~ Other countries frustrated with relief efforts of their citizens (Europe, Canada, S. Korea, etc.).

Tuesday, September 6		~ Executive and legislative branches pledge separate investigations into federal response.
		~ U.S. Army Corps of Engineers begins pumping New Orleans. Now 60% underwater.
		~ Fewer than 10,000 people still in New Orleans. Streets secure. Four fires.
		~ FEMA: Victims will be given debit cards for necessities.
		~ Labor Department pledges $62 million for Louisiana, $50 million for Mississippi, $75 million for refugees in Texas, and $4 million for Alabama for dislocated workers.
	Late Evening	Mayor Nagin issued his emergency declaration authorizing police and military to remove anyone who refused to leave their homes. Unclear as to whether force will actually be used at this time (reports suggest not).
Wednesday, September 7		President Bush calls for another $52 billion in aid to supplement the $10.5 billion already approved by Congress.
Thursday, September 8		$52 billion in aid approved by Congress.

Sources: United States Senate (together with additional views), 2006, "Hurricane Katrina: A Nation Still Unprepared, Special Report of The Committee on Homeland Security and Governmental Affairs," S. Rept. 109-322, Government Printing Office, 2006.

CNN Katrina Timeline:
http://www.cnn.com/SPECIALS/2005/katrina/interactive/timeline.katrina.large/frameset.exclude.html

The Brookings Institution: Hurricane Katrina Timeline
http://www.brookings.edu/fp/projects/homeland/katrinatimeline.pdf
www.fema.gov

TABLE 2

Hurricane Katrina: Indicators of Impact

Deaths caused by Hurricane Katrina, as of May 23, 2006	1,577
Land area damaged by Hurricane Katrina	90,000 sq. miles
Homes destroyed or made unlivable by Hurricane Katrina	300,000
Estimated economic loss related to Hurricane Katrina	$125–$150 billion
Louisiana unemployment rate, August 2005	5.6 percent
Louisiana unemployment rate, September 2005	12.1 percent
Sustained-wind speed at landfall, August 29, near Buras, LA	125 miles per hour
Rainfall accumulation along Gulf Coast from Katrina	8 to 10 inches
Storm surges above normal ocean levels, various locations	20 to 30 feet
Electric customers, all types, left without power by storm	1.7 million
Number of oil spills caused by Katrina	142
Gallons of oil spilled	8 million
Estimated debris created by Hurricane Katrina	118 million cu. yds.
Number of children reported displaced/missing	5,088
Number reunited with families or guardians	5,088

Sources: United States Senate (together with additional views), 2006, "Hurricane Katrina: A Nation Still Unprepared, Special Report of The Committee on Homeland Security and Governmental Affairs," S. Rept. 109-322, Government Printing Office, 2006.

TABLE 3

Top 10 Insured Property Losses in United States
($ billions)

Rank	Date	Disaster	Losses	Losses In 2004 Dollars
1	Aug. 2005	Hurricane Katrina	$35.0*	??
2	Aug. 1992	Hurricane Andrew	15.5	20.9
3	Sept. 2001	WTC Terrorist Attacks	18.8	20.1
4	Jan. 2004	Northridge, CA Earthquake	12.5	15.9
5	Aug. 2004	Hurricane Charley	7.5	7.5
6	Aug. 2004	Hurricane Ivan	7.1	7.1
7	Sept. 1989	Hurricane Hugo	4.1	6.4
8	Aug. 2004	Hurricane Frances	4.6	4.6
9	Aug. 2004	Hurricane Jeanne	3.7	3.7
10	Sept. 1998	Hurricane Georges	2.9	3.4

*Preliminary estimate from Risk Management Solutions, Newark, California.

Source: CRS Report to Congress, September, 2005, "Hurricane Katrina: Insurance Losses and National Capacities for Financing Disaster Risk," Insurance Service Office, Property Claims Service.

New Orleans, LA, September 18, 2005 Damage to homes and property in Lower 9th Ward due to Hurricane Katrina. **Andrea Booher/FEMA**

TABLE 4

FEMA Assistance in Hurricane Katrina

Individual and Household Program Statistics (Cumulative)	
Total Approved Registrations	1,066,059 (as of 2/28/07)
Total Assistance Distributed	$5,747,777,700 (as of 2/28/07)

Individual Assistance (As of 2/28/07)		
KATRINA	Housing Assistance	Other Needs Assistance
DR-1603-LA	$3.2 billion	$1.1 billion
DR-1604-MS	$848 million	$318 million
DR-1605-AL	$90 million	$31 million

Hurricane Katrina Public Assistance (As of 2/23/07)				
KATRINA	Protective Measures	Debris Removal	Roads & Bridges	Public Buildings
DR-1603-LA	$1.65 billion	$900 million	$18 million	$1.27 billion
DR-1604-MS	$332 million	$720 million	$32 million	$424 million
DR-1605-AL	$16 million	$36 million	$2 million	$5 million

Hurricane Katrina National Flood Insurance Program (NFIP) (Actual figures as of 01/31/07)				
States Affected by Hurricane Katrina	Losses Received	Total Closed	Percentage Closed	Total $ Paid on Closed Claims
Alabama	5,741	5,628	98.0%	$275,445,207
Florida	8,428	8,397	99.6%	$115,728,003
Mississippi	19,055	18,653	97.9%	$2,418,484,220
Louisiana	176,150	173,703	98.6%	$12,851,837,022
TOTAL	209,374	206,381	98.6%	$15,661,494,451

Source: http://www.fema.gov/hazard/hurricane/2005katrina/index.shtm

TABLE 5

FEMA Expenses in Hurricane Katrina

Hotel Motel Program — 85,000 households & $650 million

- FEMA has paid more than $650 million for hotel/motel rooms to date; at its peak in October 2005, FEMA provided hotel/motel rooms for 85,000 households in need of short-term sheltering.

Housing Inspections and Repair — 1.3 million inspections

- Since Hurricane Katrina 1.3 million housing inspections have been completed in Alabama, Louisiana, and Mississippi.

Travel Trailers and Mobile Homes — 101,174 households (Currently Occupied)
*Section revised on 8/25/06

- There are 101,174 travel trailers and mobile homes serving as temporary housing for Hurricane Katrina victims, outnumbering any housing mission in FEMA's history. The following shows number of units currently occupied as of 8/17/06:

	Total	Mobile Homes	Travel Trailers
Louisiana	64,150	3,169	60,981
Mississippi	36,127	4,709	31,418
Alabama	897	0	897

Of those households occupying travel trailers and mobile homes, there are:

15,000 households in Group/Commercial Sites:

9,344 in Louisiana	5,507 in Mississippi	149 in Alabama

83,962 households in Private Sites:

52,594 in Louisiana	30,620 in Mississippi	748 in Alabama

2,212 households in Industry Sites located in Louisiana.

Travel Trailers and Mobile Homes — 121,922 households (Cumulative Leases)

- 121,922 travel trailers and mobile homes have served as temporary housing for Hurricane Katrina victims, outnumbering any housing mission in FEMA's history. The following shows the cumulative number of units used as of 8/25/06.

	Total	Mobile Homes	Travel Trailers
Louisiana	71,134	3,514	67,620
Mississippi	48,274	6,300	41,974
Alabama	2,514	0	2,514

Of those households occupying travel trailers and mobile homes, there were:

• 19,074 households in Group/Commercial Sites:		
10,976 in Louisiana	7,242 in Mississippi	856 in Alabama
• 99,959 households in Private Sites:		
57,269 in Louisiana	41,032 in Mississippi	1,658 in Alabama
• 2,889 households in Industry Sites located in Louisiana.		

Cruise Ships — Housing over 7,000 households

• For the initial six months after Hurricane Katrina, FEMA used cruise ships to house evacuees, workers from the City of New Orleans and St. Bernard Parish, and first responders and their families, totaling more than 7,000 workers and families.

Debris Clean-up — 99 million cubic yards

• Since Hurricane Katrina, more than 99 million cubic yards of debris have been removed in Alabama, Mississippi, and Louisiana, paying out $3.7 billion to date.

Crisis Counseling — $126 million

• After Hurricane Katrina, 50 States, Puerto Rico, and the District of Columbia were eligible to apply for CCP grants to serve victims in the disaster area and displaced evacuees in other locations. Currently, more than $126 million in federal crisis counseling support has been approved thus far. This funding allows states to have the flexibility to develop service programs including outreach, counseling, support groups, and public education most appropriate for the hurricane evacuees within their state. (Updated — September 8, 2006)

Evacuation Reimbursements — $735 million to evacuee host states

• FEMA public assistance reimbursed more than $735 million to 45 states and the District of Columbia for sheltering and emergency protective measures taken during the evacuation of the Gulf Coast and for ongoing sheltering initiatives directly following Hurricane Katrina. This is in addition to funds obligated to Louisiana, Mississippi, and Alabama totaling nearly $1.75 billion for emergency sheltering operations.

Expedited Assistance — $1.6 billion

• Through Expedited Assistance, FEMA's accelerated method of disbursing disaster assistance, FEMA provided more than $1.6 billion to 803,470 individuals and households to help the evacuees meet immediate emergency needs, such as housing, food, and clothing.

Disaster Unemployment Assistance — $410 million

• FEMA has obligated more than $410 million to support DUA expenditures for Hurricane Katrina victims. (Updated — September 8, 2006)

Source: http://www.fema.gov/hazard/hurricane/2005katrina/anniversary_factsheet.shtm

TABLE 6
Business Impact and
Small Business Administration Actions

Impact on Businesses

Number of businesses in Orleans Parish that closed after the storm	3400
Percentage of all businesses in Orleans Parish that closed after the storm	35%
Percentage that had up to five employees before the storm that had closed by summer 2006	42.4%
Businesses in St. Bernard Parish that closed by the first quarter of 2006	59%

Source: latimes.com, "Katrina, Rita still roil business climate." Ann M. Simmons, March 9, 2007.

Small Business Administration (SBA) Actions (as of September 2006)

The Small Business Administration (SBA) has approved more than $10.3 billion in disaster loans to homeowners, renters, and business owners in the Gulf Coast states affected by the hurricanes. SBA has completed damage assessments on 99 percent of applications submitted and it has rendered decisions on more than 99 percent of the loan applications for businesses, homeowners, and renters. More than 22,000 (of 154,000 total) loans have gone to small business owners to the tune of $2.4 billion.

- In Louisiana: 91,345 disaster loans were approved for $6.4 billion; 78,364 home loans were approved for $5 billion; 12,981 business disaster loans were approved for $1.4 billion.

- In Mississippi: 34,937 disaster loans were approved for $2.5 billion; 30,473 home loans were approved for $2 billion; 4464 business disaster loans were approved for $500 million.

Source: Department of Homeland Security, 2006. "Hurricane Katrina: What the Government Is Doing." http://www.dhs.gov/xprepresp/programs/gc_1157649340100.shtm. September 24, 2006.

TABLE 7

American Red Cross Donations and Spending in Hurricane Katrina

Amount Raised

As of March 31, 2006, the Red Cross raised $2.067 billion designated for Hurricanes Katrina, Rita, and Wilma, as well as $141 million for the Disaster Relief Fund.

How Donations Were Spent

The American Red Cross traditionally provides for the immediate emergency needs of disaster victims and this disaster was no different. As the storm approached, the Red Cross opened thousands of evacuation shelters. In the wake of the storm, sheltering became an even greater priority with more than a million families rendered homeless. The Red Cross also provided food and water for the millions left in shelters or without power to their homes. And, as the full scope of the disaster became evident, Red Cross mental health workers provided emotional support and counseling to hundreds of thousands of people suffering from the trauma of the

disaster. While the Red Cross continued to provide shelter, food, and emotional support in the days after landfall, the organization also launched a program to give survivors the financial means to purchase food, clothing, and other recovery items.

Specifically, during the 2005 hurricane season, the Red Cross opened more than 1,400 shelters, provided survivors and emergency workers with more than 68 million meals and snacks, and provided more than 800,000 people with emotional support. In addition, more than 1.4 million families received Red Cross financial assistance, totaling nearly $1.4 billion dollars.

Ongoing Programs & Services

The Red Cross continues its service to hurricane survivors through the Hurricane Recovery Program. This two year program is one of many contributors to overall recovery efforts. It offers direct services to clients and also supports the other organizations that have made this phase of disaster relief their primary focus. The Hurricane Recovery Program is focusing on four primary areas of activity for survivors still living on the Gulf Coast and those who have relocated to other areas of the country, including casework services, mental health support, information referral, and emerging needs.

Source: http://www.charitynavigator.org/index.cfm/bay/katrina.report/orgid/3277

New Orleans, LA, September 18, 2005 Damage to homes and property in Lower 9th Ward due to Hurricane Katrina. Markings on house were from the Search and Rescue teams searching for survivors following the storm – the date searched, time, who the search party was, survivors found, and animals still in the house.
Andrea Booher/FEMA

TABLE 8

Major Voluntary and Nongovernmental Organizations Responding to Hurricane Katrina

ACORN
ADRA International
Alley Cat Allies
Allied Jewish Federation of Colorado
America's Second Harvest
American Friends Service Committee
American Humane Association
American Red Cross
American Refugee Committee
American Society for the Prevention of
    Cruelty to Animals
Americares
Ananda Marga Universal Relief Team
Baptist World Aid
Best Friends Animal Society
Brother's Brother Foundation
Catholic Charities, USA
Christian Appalachian Project
Christian Reformed World Relief Committee
Christian Relief Fund
Church World Service
Convoy of Hope
Counterpart International
Direct Relief International
Episcopal Relief and Development
Food for the Hungry
Food for the Poor
Gifts In Kind International
Habitat for Humanity
Heart to Heart International
Hebrew Immigrant Aid Society
Heifer International
Humane Society of the United States
Interchurch Medical Assistance
International Aid
International Medical Corps
International Orthodox Christian Charities
International Relief and Development, Inc.
International Relief Teams
International Rescue Committee (IRC)
Islamic Relief

KaBOOM!
Kids In Distressed Situations (K.I.D.S.)
Life for Relief and Development
Lutheran World Relief
MAP International
Mercy Corps
Mercy-USA for Aid and Development
Mazon: A Jewish Response to Hunger
My Stuff Bags Foundation
National Center for Rural Early Childhood
    Learning Initiatives
National Trust for Historic Preservation
Northwest Medical Teams International
Operation Blessing
Operation USA
Oxfam America
PETsMART Charities
Presbyterian Disaster Assistance
Project HOPE
Rebuilding Together
Relief International
Salvation Army
Samaritan's Purse
Save the Children
Shelter Partnership
The Society of St. Andrew
The United Way
Trickle Up Program
Unitarian Universalist Service Committee
United Animal Nations
United Jewish Communities
United Methodist Committee on Relief
U.S. Committee for Refugees and Immigrants
United States Fund for UNICEF
Volunteers of America
World Concern
World Emergency Relief
World Help
World Hope International
World Relief
World Vision

TABLE 9

Funding for Voluntary Agencies and Nongovernmental Organizations in Hurricane Katrina

Donations to major disasters:

- 2001: September 11th 2001 Terrorist Attacks — $1.5 billion

- 2004: Asian Tsunami — over $7 billion — ($1.32 billion from U.S. private sources alone, not including $234 million in in-kind donations)

- 2005: Hurricanes Katrina and Rita — $2.96 billion

Donations for Hurricane Katrina:

$2.1 billion	American Red Cross
$363 million	Salvation Army
$146 million	Catholic Charities
$129 million	Bush–Clinton Katrina Fund
$122 million	Habitat for Humanity
$45.0 million	United Way
$34.0 million	Samaritan's Purse
$27.7 million	America's Second Harvest
$27.5 million	Baton Rouge Area Foundation
$26.0 million	United Methodist Committee Relief
$25.0 million	Help America Hear Project
$23.0 million	Humane Society U.S.
$20.0 million	Evangelical Lutheran Church in America
$17.1 million	Foundations for Recovery
$15.0 million	Hear Now Project
$15.0 million	Federal Home Loan Bank of Cincinnati
$14.0 million	Federations of North American/Partners
$12.0 million	W.K. Kellogg Foundation
$11.5 million	Americares
$10.0 million	Mercy Corps
$10.0 million	Muslim Hurricane Relief Task Force
$10.0 million	Episcopal Relief and Development
$9.0 million	Ford Foundation
$8.4 million	Southern Baptist Convention Disaster Relief
$7.3 million	World Vision
$6.5 million	Next of Kin Registry
$6.0 million	John D. and Catherine T. MacArthur Foundation
$5.0 million	Save the Children

TABLE 10

Business Donations Top $1 Billion for Katrina Victims

On October 20, the U.S. Chamber's Center for Corporate Citizenship (CCC) reported that businesses hit the $1 billion mark for donations to hurricane relief efforts. Of the $1 billion in aid, businesses donated $536 million in cash, $53 million in employee-matching contributions, $28 million in employee donations, $204 million in in-kind donations, $195 million in customer donations, and $7 million in customer-matching funds. CCC also announced that a total of 245 companies pledged at least $1 million each in cash or in-kind contributions. This is by far the largest response to a disaster by the American business community in modern history.

Source: US Chamber of Commerce — http://www.uschamber.com/publications/weekly/update/051025b.htm

TABLE 11

Sample of Foundation Grants to Hurricane Katrina

After Katrina: Big Foundation Donors	
Among the Largest Grants	Total Amount
W.K. Kellogg Foundation (Battle Creek, Mich.)	$36,300,000
Lilly Endowment (Indianapolis)	$30,000,000
Bill & Melinda Gates Foundation (Seattle)	$24,200,000
Ford Foundation (New York)	$20,000,000
Walton Family Foundation (Bentonville, Ark.)	$15,000,000
Andrew W. Mellon Foundation (New York)	$12,500,000
Southeastern Library Network (Atlanta)	$12,200,000
Robert Wood Johnson Foundation (Princeton, N.J.)	$11,500,000
American Red Cross (Washington)	$10,000,000
Rockefeller Foundation (New York)	$6,500,000
Louisiana Public Health Institute (New Orleans)	$8,800,000
Bush–Clinton Katrina Fund (Washington)	$8,000,000
Conrad N. Hilton Foundation (Reno, Nev.)	$6,000,000
H.N. & Frances C. Berger Foundation (Palm Desert, Calif.)	$5,000,000
Bush–Clinton Katrina Fund (Washington)	$5,000,000
Bush Foundation (St. Paul)	$5,000,000
Michael and Susan Dell Foundation (Austin, Tex.)	$5,000,000
Greater New Orleans Foundation	$3,500,000
Tulane University (New Orleans)	$2,500,000
Salvation Army (Alexandria, Va.)	$2,500,000
Dillard University (New Orleans)	$2,000,000
Enterprise Corporation of the Delta (Jackson, Miss.)	$1,500,000
Louisiana Rural Health Services Corporation (Hammond)	$1,250,000
Baton Rouge Area Foundation	$750,000

TABLE 11

A Sampling of Foundation Grants for Katrina Recovery

Annie E. Casey Foundation (Baltimore)

Amount: $200,000

Recipient: National Fair Housing Alliance (Washington)

Purpose: To ensure fair access to mortgage and insurance lending, provide housing counseling, and combat predatory financial practices affecting Gulf Coast residents

Chatlos Foundation (Longwood, FL)

Amount: $25,000

Recipient: New Orleans Baptist Theological Seminary

Purpose: To help rebuild its campus

Ford Foundation (New York)

Amount: $900,000

Recipient: State University of New York, Rockefeller Institute of Government

Purpose: To examine how the 2005 hurricanes affected demographic and economic conditions in 30 local jurisdictions and track how government, business, and nonprofit organizations are responding to community needs

F.B. Heron Foundation (New York)

Amount: $100,000

Recipient: Southern Mutual Help Association (New Iberia, LA)

Purpose: To support their work to rebuild rural communities affected by the storm

JEHT Foundation (New York)

Amount: $1,000,000

Recipient: Equal Justice Works (Washington)

Purpose: To pay for public-interest lawyers to provide legal services to Gulf Coast residents in need

W.K. Kellogg Foundation (Battle Creek, MI)

Amount: $749,570

Recipient: National Center on Family Homelessness (Newton Centre, MA)

Purpose: To provide training so that caregivers of children in communities affected by the hurricane can identify signs of trauma and help children cope

John S. and James L. Knight Foundation (Miami)

Amount: $250,000

Recipient: Living Cities (New York)

Purpose: To develop a plan to rebuild East Biloxi, MS, in concert with citizen, corporate, and government partners

McCormick Tribune Foundation (Chicago)

Amount: $400,000

Recipient: Mississippi Counseling Association (Brandon)

Purpose: To provide mental-health services to individuals and families affected by the hurricane

Needmor Fund (Toledo, OH)

Amount: $10,000

Recipient: Louisiana Disaster Recovery Foundation (New Orleans)

Purpose: To support a fellowship program that allows 21 community organizers in New Orleans to take a break from their work

Open Society Institute (New York)

Amount: $125,000

Recipient: Center for Social Inclusion (New York)

Purpose: To organize low-income communities affected by the storm, as well as local and national groups, to advocate policies that will encourage equity and opportunities in rebuilding efforts

Virginia G. Piper Charitable Trust (Scottsdale, AZ)

Amount: $125,000

Recipients: Archdiocese of New Orleans and the Roman Catholic Archdiocese of Mobile (AL)

Purpose: To rebuild parish schools

Andy Warhol Foundation (New York)

Amount: $100,000

Recipient: Contemporary Arts Center (New Orleans)

Purpose: To rehire staff members who were laid off after the hurricane and to support the center's visual-arts programs featuring Louisiana artists this year

Note: The New York Regional Association of Grantmakers has published the "Donors' Guide to Gulf Coast Relief & Recovery," a 70-page booklet that lists both charities working on hurricane-recovery efforts and examples of its members' grants in the region. The booklet is available free on the group's Web site at http://www.nyrag.org.

Source: Chronicle of Philanthropy, August 17, 2006, http://phil anthropy.com/premium/articles/v18/i21/21001801htm#grants

Baton Rouge, LA, September 23, 2005 The Red Cross is in Baton Rouge to provide aid to victims of Hurricane Katrina. The facility, formerly a Wal-Mart, provides a large working space to operate from and to bring relief to the victims of the storm.
Robert Kaufmann/FEMA

was to become Hurricane Katrina is first recognized as a potential hazard.

sustained winds in excess of 74 mph moves across South Florida and into the Gulf of Mexico—Katrina is now over the warm waters of the Gulf where it begins to strengthen, and early tracks by the National Hurricane Center show Katrina making landfall "between Mobile, AL and Grand Isle, FL."

COVER: NEW ORLEANS, LA, AUGUST 28, 2005
Residents begin lining up to get into the Superdome which has been opened as a hurricane shelter in advance of Hurricane Katrina.
Marty Bahamonde/FEMA

1) NEW ORLEANS, LA, AUGUST 30, 2005
Interstate ramp filled with rescue workers, people and trucks going down to the flood waters of New Orleans. New Orleans is being evacuated as a result of floods from Hurricane Katrina. Thousands of people have been rescued from the flood waters by moving to their roofs and attics.
Jocelyn Augustino/FEMA

Friday, August 26

Hurricane track shifts twice during the day, first projected to make landfall on the MS/AL border and later in the day projected to make landfall on the LA/MS border—Governors in LA and MS declare a State of Emergency and activate their state National Guards.

Saturday, August 27

Katrina, now a Category 4 or 5 storm, is expected to hit New Orleans and Governor Blanco requests a declaration of a federal state of emergency for LA which is approved that day by President Bush, New Orleans Mayor Nagin declares state of emergency, and evacuations begin in LA and MS.

2) ATLANTA, GA, AUGUST 28, 2005
A FEMA representative (right, standing) briefs the Regional Response Coordination Center (RRCC) staff on the status of his Emergency Support Function (ESF). FEMA is preparing for the landfall of Hurricane Katrina.
Mark Wolfe/FEMA

3) NEW ORLEANS, LA, AUGUST 28, 2005
Residents are bringing their belongings and lining up to get into the Superdome which has been opened as a hurricane shelter in advance of Hurricane Katrina. Most residents have evacuated the city and those left behind do not have transportation or have special needs.
Marty Bahamonde/FEMA

4) NEW ORLEANS, LA, AUGUST 28, 2005
People inside the Superdome which is being used as a shelter during Hurricane Katrina.
Marty Bahamonde/FEMA

- ## Sunday, August 28
  Mayor Nagin issues mandatory evacuation order, Superdome opened as a shelter of last resort and by the end of the day 10,000 people and 150 National Guardsmen are in the Dome; evacuation all along the Gulf Coast continues.

- ## Monday, August 29
  Katrina, now a Category 4 hurricane with 145 mph winds, makes landfall in lower Plaquemines Parish, LA, between 6–7AM CST, major disaster declarations are signed by President Bush, levees in New Orleans are breached, and floodwaters begin to fill sections of the city; the Coast Guard begins to rescue persons in New Orleans.

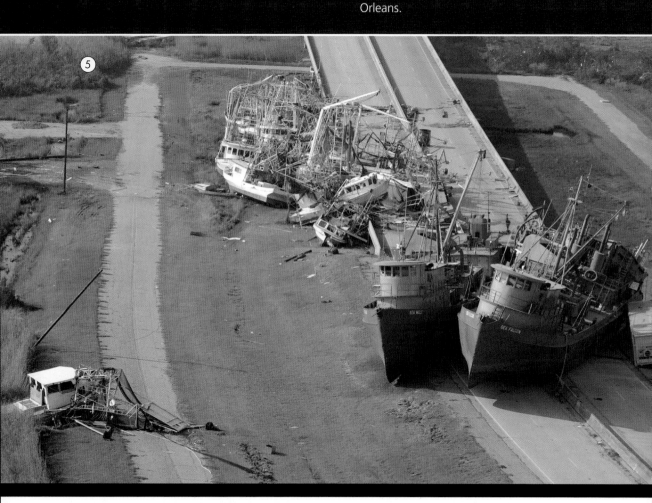

5) SOUTHERN LOUISIANA, SEPTEMBER 12, 2005
Boats tossed around by Hurricane Katrina remain lodged on dry ground.
Jocelyn Augustino/FEMA

6) WAVELAND, MS, SEPTEMBER 9, 2005
Volunteer groups pass out donated water in Waveland, MS. Hurricane Katrina destroyed the possessions of thousands of people in Mississippi.
Mark Wolfe/FEMA

- ## Tuesday, August 30
  Floodwaters cover up to 80% of the city, an estimated 50–100,000 people are trapped in the city including the Superdome and Convention Center, Governor Blanco issues order to evacuate the Superdome, Coast Guard rescues continue, and widespread looting is reported.

- ## Wednesday, August 31
  Governor Blanco and President Bush discuss military assistance and who is in charge of the National Guard, and the Houston Astrodome prepares to receive evacuees from Katrina.

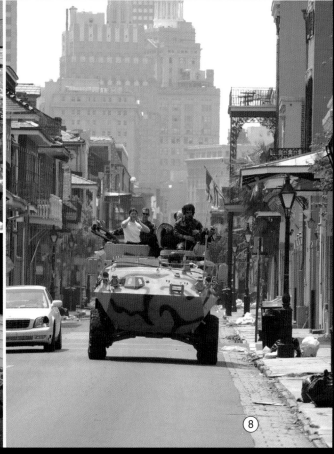

7) 9TH WARD, NEW ORLEANS, LA, MARCH 6, 2006
Wayne Buford from Search & Rescue (Jefferson, Missouri) and dog Rusty search for human remains before this house can be demolished. All homes being demolished in 9th Ward are searched by a search and recovery team that includes special search recovery dogs so that no human remains are left in houses that are being demolished.
Marvin Nauman/FEMA

8) NEW ORLEANS, LA, SEPTEMBER 10, 2005
An armored tank rolls down Bourbon Street in downtown, days after Hurricane Katrina.
Jocelyn Augustino/FEMA

- ## Thursday, September 1
  45,000 people are now housed in the Superdome and the Convention Center, bus evacuation of populations in New Orleans begins, and DHS Secretary Chertoff and FEMA Director Brown indicate they were unaware of problems at the Convention Center.

- ## Friday, September 2
  President Bush makes his first visit to disaster area meeting with governors and Mayor Nagin, number of National Guard troops deployed increases, and Congress approves $10.5 billion in immediate relief.

9) **PASS CHRISTIAN, MS, OCTOBER 4, 2005**
Aerial photo shows the only surviving home in the area that was completely destroyed by Hurricane Katrina. Foundations are all that remain of most of the neighboring homes. Surviving home was built using many FEMA standards.
John Fleck/FEMA

10) **NEW ORLEANS, LA, OCTOBER 22, 2005**
Evacuee Umberto Romero gathers food and necessities at the distribution center at the Chalmette Recovery Center following devastating Hurricane Katrina.
Andrea Booher/FEMA

11) **BILOXI, MS, OCTOBER 4, 2005**
US Army Corps of Engineers' Operation Blue Roof helps to prevent further damage to structures as a result of Hurricane Katrina. US Army Corps of Engineers installed millions of square yards of blue plastic to cover damaged structures under the Operation Blue Roof Program.
John Fleck/FEMA

- ## Saturday, September 3

  40,000 National Guardsmen are now deployed to Gulf Coast, President Bush orders 7,200 active duty military to the Gulf, and evacuation of Superdome and Convention Center is completed.

- ## Monday, September 5

  Gap in levee closed but more levee repairs are ongoing, Bush-Clinton Fund is announced, and President Bush dispatches 4,700 additional active military troops.

12) NEW ORLEANS, LA, SEPTEMBER 17, 2005
Mary Seither and Madeline Harper can only salvage a few glassware items. Most of flooded homeowners are only able to save a few items as they return to New Orleans.
Marvin Nauman/FEMA

13) CHALMETTE, LA, SEPTEMBER 17, 2005
Brian Fankhauser and John Haugh of California Task Force 2's Urban Search and Rescue from the Los Angeles County Fire Department search homes for survivors from Hurricane Katrina.
Bob McMillan/FEMA

- **Tuesday, September 6**
  US Army Corps of Engineers begins pumping water out of New Orleans, and Mayor Nagin authorizes troops and police to remove individuals from the city.

- **Thursday, September 8**
  Congress approves President Bush's request for $52 billion in additional aid.

BILOXI, MS, SEPTEMBER 3, 2005 AND AUGUST 8, 2006
Before (left) and after the process of cleaning up Biloxi Beach. Over 33,000 cubic yards of debris was left on Harrison County beaches by Hurricane Katrina.
Mark Wolfe/FEMA

TABLE 12

Brookings Institution

Special Edition of the Katrina Index:
A One-Year Review of Key Indicators of Recovery in Post-Storm New Orleans
by Amy Liu, Matt Fellowes, and Mia Mabanta

Findings

A review of dozens of key social and economic indicators on the progress of recovery in the New Orleans region since the impact of Hurricane Katrina finds that:

Housing rehabilitation, and demolition, are well underway while the housing market tightens, raising rent and home prices. Across the most hard-hit parishes in the New Orleans area, the pace of demolitions has accelerated in the last six months while the number of permits issued for rehab has nearly doubled in the city. Yet, housing is less affordable as rent prices in the region have increased by 39 percent over the year and home sale prices have spiked in suburban parishes.

Across the city, public services and infra-structure remain thin and slow to rebound. Approximately half of all bus and streetcar routes are back up and running, while only 17 percent of buses are in use, a level of service that has not changed since January. Gas and electricity service is reaching only 41 and 60 percent of the pre-Katrina customer base, respectively.

The labor force in the New Orleans region is 30 percent smaller today than one year ago and has grown slowly over the last six months; meanwhile, the unemployment rate remains higher than pre-Katrina. The New Orleans metro area lost 190,000 work-ers over the past year, with the health and education services industries suffering the

largest percentage declines. In the past six months, the region has seen 3.4 percent more jobs but much of that may reflect the rise in new job seekers. The unemployment rate is now 7.2 percent, higher than last August.

Since last August, over $100 billion in federal aid has been dedicated to serving families and communities impacted by Hurricanes Katrina, Rita, and Wilma. In the meantime, the number of displaced and unemployed workers remains high. To date, the federal government has approved approximately $109 billion in federal aid to the Gulf Coast states most impacted by the storms. Of these funds, nearly half has been dedicated to emergency and longer-term housing. In the meantime, an estimated 278,000 workers are still displaced by the storm, 23 percent of whom remain unemployed.

One year after Katrina, New Orleans is show-ing signs of early rebirth. The housing market is beginning to turn around and increased business and visitor travel have helped bolster the region's tax base and economy. But the majority of indicators are troubling, pointing to much needed progress in basic city services, infrastructure, and affordable housing for workers in order to boost market confidence and move the region's economy affirmatively forward.

Source: The Brooking Institution: http://www. brook.edu/metro/pubs/20060822_Katrina.pdf

TABLE 13

The Brookings Institution Katrina Index

Summary of findings: March 2007

Months Since Katrina Made Landfall: 18

Thousands of college students and families on Spring Break this month are coming to the Gulf Coast to volunteer their time to help with rebuilding, buoying residents' spirits. Yet, eighteen months after the storm, residents across the region are frustrated that so many schools are still closed, police and fire stations are not repaired, and streetlights don't work, despite the large amount of committed federal assistance and significant charitable contributions given to the area.

Unfortunately, red tape remains an enormous obstacle to the flow of federal funds to the area. The release of billions of federal dollars for basic repairs to essential infrastructure has stalled, in large part because complying with federal regulations for the required 10 percent local match is prohibitively complex—especially when applied to 20,000 separate projects. And, the $3.5 billion in charitable contributions given post-Katrina (while greater than for any other American disaster, including 9/11) cannot make a visible impact on recovery needs estimated at $135 billion.

Meanwhile, waterways and drainage arteries are still clogged with hurricane debris from St. Bernard to St. Tammany. And police and firemen still work out of FEMA trailers. The lack of progress on such critical projects leaves the New Orleans area vulnerable, with hurricane season less than three months away.

President Bush can hasten the recovery by waiving the need for the 10 percent match as he did after the 9/11 attacks. The new

Congress can also exercise this authority, but their legislation will take some months to complete.

In short, the March Index finds that infrastructure repair indicators remain basically stalled. Recent housing indicators are mixed. Somewhat more promising is that economic indicators suggest that the New Orleans area may be showing the first signs of increasing employment expected in a major rebuilding setting.

Housing

The number of residential properties for sale continues to inch upward from 13,385 in February to 13,609 in March, primarily in the most flooded parts of the metro area.

There has been a notable slowing in the number of Army Corps building demolitions with only 151 demolitions this month.

Residential building permits in Orleans Parish have gradually slowed since the anniversary of Katrina—down to only 1,000 building permits in the month of February.

New residential housing permits reached a new record of 725 for the metro area in January—notably higher than the 500 per month average pre-Katrina.

The Road Home contractor has still only closed on a small fraction (2.5 percent) of the 115,000 applications they have received. Despite a slight acceleration in the number of closings completed, the number of new applications received each week continues to exceed the number of closings completed in that same week.

Population

Enrollment at all reporting universities has fallen since the spring semester following Katrina, as school officials struggle to convince parents to send their freshmen to New Orleans for college.

Infrastructure

The number of operational buses and open public transportation routes has remained virtually stagnant for a year.

Only one additional public school was opened last month in Orleans Parish. Despite pressing demand, 76 school facilities remain closed.

No additional hospitals have opened in Orleans, St. Bernard, or Jefferson in the last four months despite pressing need.

Although four child care centers opened in Orleans Parish, and two opened in St. Tammany Parish, two child care centers closed in Jefferson Parish this past month. This may be the first signal that child care centers that charge low fees are financially unsustainable given demand for higher wages among child care workers due to increased housing costs.

Economy

The New Orleans metropolitan area gained more than 50,000 workers from November to January. Simultaneously the unemployment rate dropped from 5 percent to 4.5 percent and remained just below the national average of 4.6 percent.

One additional hotel opened in New Orleans this month. Now fully 91 percent of hotels are open in the city.

Louis Armstrong International Airport continued to handle a healthy volume of arriving and departing passengers in January — approximately 65 percent of pre-Katrina levels.

In sum, with hurricane season less than three months away, officials must take quick action to eliminate excessive red tape at the federal, state and local levels to ensure the flow of federal recovery dollars allocated to the Gulf Coast to date.

—The Brookings Institution Metropolitan Policy Program

Source: The Brookings Institution: http://www. gnocdc.org/KI/ESKatrinaIndex.pdf

New Orleans, LA, March 7, 2006   On day 2 of moving in, Dionne Roberts stands by her FEMA trailer giving instructions to her plumber Glen Harris about repairing leaking water pipes in her house.
Marvin Nauman/FEMA

TABLE 14

Core Recommendations from the United States Senate Report on Katrina

Core Recommendation #1
Create a New, Comprehensive Emergency-Management Organization within DHS to Prepare for and Respond to All Disasters and Catastrophes.

Hurricane Katrina exposed flaws in the structure of the Federal Emergency Management Agency (FEMA) and the Department of Homeland Security (DHS) that are too substantial to mend. We propose to abolish FEMA and build a stronger, more capable structure within DHS. The structure will form the foundation of the nation's emergency-management system. It will be an independent entity within DHS, but will draw on the resources of the Department and will be led and staffed by capable, committed individuals.

We must create a robust National Preparedness and Response Authority (NPRA) within the Department of Homeland Security. The NPRA would fuse the Department's emergency management, preparedness, and critical-infrastructure assets into a powerful new organization that can confront the challenges of natural or man-made catastrophes. It will provide critical leadership for preparedness and response by combining key federal personnel and assets, as well as federal partnerships with state and local officials and the private sector to prepare for and respond to terror attacks or natural disasters.

Core Recommendation #2
From the Federal Level Down, Take a Comprehensive All-Hazards Plus Approach to Emergency Management.

The new organization should bring together the full range of responsibilities that are core to preparing for and responding to disasters. These include the four central functions of comprehensive emergency management — preparedness, response, recovery, and mitigation — which need to be integrated. Actions in recent years that removed preparedness grants from FEMA and separated preparedness from response weakened FEMA's relationship with state officials and undermined its ability to utilize "the power of the purse," in the form of grant funding, to encourage states to improve their preparedness and response functions.

A more comprehensive approach should be restored. If NPRA is going to effectively respond to major events, for example, it needs to have been involved in the preparations for such events. The Director, moreover, must be responsible for administering and distributing preparedness grants to state and local governments and for national preparedness training, as these are key tools for ensuring a consistent and coordinated national response system.

All-Hazards Plus. NPRA would adopt an "all-hazards plus" strategy for preparedness. In preparing our nation to respond to terrorist attacks and natural disasters, NPRA must focus on building those common capabilities — for example survivable, interoperable communications and evacuation plans — that are necessary regardless of the incident. At the same time, it must not neglect to build those unique capabilities — like mass decontamination in the case of a radiological attack, or water search and rescue in the case of flooding — that will be needed for particular types of incidents.

Core Recommendation #3
Establish Regional Strike Teams and Enhance Regional Operations to Provide Better Coordination Between Federal Agencies and the States.

Most of the essential work of emergency management does not happen in Washington, D.C., but on the front lines, with state and local officials and first responders having lead responsibility in a disaster. Regional offices — building on FEMA's 10 existing regional offices — should play a key role in coordinating with and assisting states and localities in preparing for and responding to disasters. Regional offices can facilitate planning tailored to the specific risks and needs of a particular geographic area: for example, the risks faced, and the types of preparedness necessary, in Gulf Coast states may differ markedly from that of cities along the Northeast Corridor that were attacked on 9/11, or of those areas that lie along the New Madrid seismic fault in the central Mississippi Valley.

Core Recommendation #4
Build a True, Government-Wide Operations Center to Provide Enhanced Situational Awareness and Manage Interagency Coordination in a Disaster.

During Katrina, the Homeland Security Operations Center (HSOC) had difficulty maintaining accurate situational awareness and failed to ensure that those in DHS's leadership had an accurate picture of the situation on

the Gulf Coast, particularly about the failing levee system in New Orleans. Currently, a multiplicity of interagency coordinating structures with overlapping missions attempt to facilitate an integrated federal response. Three of these structures — the Homeland Security Operations Center (HSOC), the National Response Coordination Center (NRCC), and the Interagency Incident Management Group (IIMG) — should be consolidated into a single, integrated entity — a new National Operations Center (NOC).

Core Recommendation #5
Renew and Sustain Commitments at All Levels of Government to the Nation's Emergency Management System.

Commitment from State and Local Government. Although the federal government should play a more proactive role in responding to catastrophic events when state and local officials may be overwhelmed, states and localities will continue to provide the backbone of response — the first response — for all disasters, catastrophic or not. State and local officials must take responsibility for their citizens' welfare and conduct the planning, training, and exercising that will prepare them to meet this obligation.

Core Recommendation #6
Strengthen the Plans and Systems for the Nation's Response to Disasters and Catastrophes.

Despite their shortcomings and imperfections, the NRP (National Response Plan) and National Incident Management System (NIMS), including the ESF (Emergency Support Function) structure that has taken years to develop, currently represent the best approach available to respond to multi-agency, multi-jurisdictional emergencies of any kind, and should be retained and improved. Federal, state, and local officials and other responders must commit to supporting the NRP and NIMS and work together to improve the performance of the national emergency-management system. We must undertake further refinements of the NRP and NIMS, develop operational plans, and engage in training and exercises to ensure that everyone involved in disaster response understands them and is prepared to carry them out.

Core Recommendation #7
Improve the Nation's Capacity to Respond to Catastrophic Events.

As documented in this report, FEMA does not have the capacity to respond to large-scale disasters and catastrophes. The United States was, and is, ill-prepared to respond to a catastrophic event of the magnitude of Hurricane Katrina. Catastrophic events are, by their nature, difficult to imagine and to adequately plan for, and the existing plans and training proved inadequate in Katrina. Yet it is precisely events of such magnitude — where local responders may be rendered victims, where hundreds of thousands of citizens are rendered homeless and thousands may need medical attention, where normal communications systems may fail, and where the usual coordination mechanisms may not be available — that most require advance planning. As stated previously, preparation for domestic incidents must be done as robustly as that for foreign threats. We would not tolerate a DOD that was not prepared for a worst-case catastrophic attack, nor should we tolerate a FEMA that is unprepared for domestic catastrophes.

Pascagoula, MS, November 29, 2005 and August 8, 2006   Before (top) and after the elevation of a house flooded by the storm surge of Hurricane Katrina. Elevating a house is an excellent method to mitigate against flooding.
Mark Wolfe/FEMA

Source: Townsend, Francis F., 2006, "The Federal Response to Hurricane Katrina Lessons Learned," The White House, February 2006.

TABLE 15

Recommendations from The White House Report "The Federal Response to Hurricane Katrina: Lessons Learned"

Hurricane Katrina and Its Aftermath Provide Us with the Imperative to Design and Build a Unified System. The *Lessons Learned* report confirms the imperative of integrating and synchronizing the Nation's homeland security policies, strategies, and plans across federal, state, and local governments, as well as the private sector, nongovernmental organizations (NGOs), faith-based groups, communities, and individual citizens. To achieve this, the Report identifies three immediate priorities:

- First, we must implement a comprehensive National Preparedness System to make certain that we have a fully national system that ensures unity of effort in preparing for and responding to natural and man-made disasters;

- Second, we must create a Culture of Preparedness that emphasizes that the entire Nation — at all levels of government, the private sector, communities, and individual citizens — shares common goals and responsibilities for homeland security; and

- Third, we must implement corrective actions to ensure we do not repeat the problems encountered during Hurricane Katrina.

A Comprehensive National Preparedness System

- ***The Existing National Preparedness System Must Be Improved to Minimize the Impact of Disasters on Lives, Property, and the Economy.*** Pursuant to the National Strategy for Homeland Security, the President directed the creation of a comprehensive national preparedness system in Homeland Security Presidential Directive 8 (HSPD-8), starting with a national domestic all-hazards preparedness goal. In response, the Department of Homeland Security (DHS) has developed an Interim National Preparedness Goal. We must now translate this Goal into a robust preparedness system that includes integrated plans, procedures, training, and capabilities at all levels of government. The System must also incorporate the private sector, NGOs, faith-based and other grassroots groups, communities, and individual citizens. The objective of our National Preparedness System must be to achieve and sustain risk-based target levels of capability to prevent, protect against, respond to, and recover from major natural disasters, terrorist incidents, and other emergencies.

- ***The Response to Hurricane Katrina Revealed a Lack of Familiarity with Incident Management, Planning Discipline, and Field-Level Crisis Leadership.*** Going forward, the Federal government must clearly articulate national preparedness goals and objectives. It must create the infrastructure for ensuring unity of effort. The federal government must manage the National Preparedness System for measuring effectiveness and assessing preparedness at all levels of government. The *Lessons Learned* report outlines five elements that are critical for a National Preparedness System:

1. Building and integrating the federal government's operational capability for emergency preparedness and response;

2. Strengthening DHS's capacity to direct the federal response effort while providing resources to responders in the field;

3. Ensuring unity of effort and eliminating red tape and delays in providing federal assistance to disaster areas;

4. Strengthening homeland security education, exercises, and training programs; and

5. Ensuring that homeland security assessments, lessons learned, and corrective action programs are institutionalized throughout the federal government.

Creating a Culture of Preparedness

- ***The Creation of a Culture of Preparedness Will Emphasize That the Entire Nation Shares Common Goals and Responsibilities for Homeland Security.*** A Culture of Preparedness must build a sense of shared responsibility among individuals, communities, the private sector, NGOs, faith-based groups, and federal, state, and local governments. Our homeland security is built on a foundation of partnerships. The *Lessons Learned* report outlines four principles to guide the development of a Culture of Preparedness:

  1. A prepared nation will be a long-term continuing challenge;

  2. Initiative and innovation must be recognized and rewarded at all levels;

3. Individuals must play a central role in preparing themselves and their families for emergencies; and

4. Federal, state, and local governments must work in partnership with each other and the private sector.

Transforming the Federal Response to Future Emergencies

Acting on the Recommendations in the Lessons Learned Report Will Enable the Federal Government to Respond to Natural and Man-Made Disasters More Effectively and Efficiently. The lessons of Hurricane Katrina cannot be learned and put into action without change. As the federal government works to implement the near-term critical activities and 125 recommendations, state and local governments, the private sector, NGOs, faith-based and community organizations, the media, communities, and individuals should undertake a review of their respective roles and responsibilities in preparing for and responding to catastrophic events.

Together, We Will Strengthen Our Ability to Prepare for, Protect Against, Respond to, and Recover from Catastrophic Events. The lessons learned from Hurricane Katrina and the recommendations set forth in today's Report will yield preparedness dividends that transcend federal, state, and local boundaries. Their full implementation will help the entire nation achieve a shared commitment to preparedness.

Source: The White House, http://www.whitehouse.gov/news/releases/2006/02/20060223.html

TABLE 16

Recommendations from the National Emergency Management Association (NEMA)

(concerning rebuilding the emergency management system)

The Need for Effective Emergency Management

Emergency management is the discipline and the profession of applying science, technology, planning, and management to deal with extreme events that can injure or kill large numbers of people, do extensive damage to property and disrupt community life. As a process it involves preparing, mitigating, responding and recovering from an emergency. Critical functional components include planning, training, simulating drills (exercises), and coordinating activities.

In 2005 alone, 43 major disaster declarations were declared in 32 states for events that included hurricanes, a typhoon and a cyclone, floods, landslides, and severe winter storms. A total of 68 federal emergency declarations were made along with 29 fire management assistance declarations. The largest disaster in U.S. History — Hurricane Katrina — devastated the Gulf Coast in 2005. The need for a national emergency management system that effectively integrates local, state, and federal capabilities and resources has never been greater. Without question Hurricane Katrina revealed the weaknesses in our current system. The question remains whether we will learn from our failures and shortcomings and take advantage of this opportunity to rebuild and then sustain an effective national emergency management system.

Priority Recommendations for Congress

1. The role of the military should continue to be in support of civilian authorities.

Procedures should be refined for requesting assistance from the Department of Defense (DoD) in those rare and catastrophic events when assets are needed that only DoD can provide.

2. Congress should require that criteria be developed for the FEMA Director position to ensure competent leadership and provide for a direct reporting relationship with the President. Congress should allow stakeholders to have a say in the vetting process for nominees. Reduce the number of political appointments within FEMA and fill positions of authority with individuals who have requisite experience.

3. FEMA must be fully staffed and have the capability to establish and maintain stockpiles and pre-position resources and equipment, as well as establish trained cadres of personnel to provide surge capacity in large disasters.

4. The fix to the nation's emergency response challenges is not exclusively a FEMA/federal issue. The capabilities of local and state emergency management and their emergency support functions must be strengthened. Emergency operations centers at all levels of government must be adequate to the task and responsibility and they are not at this point in time.

5. Congress should support the Hazard Mitigation Grant Program (HMGP) as an effective tool to reduce the loss caused by future disasters.

Priority Recommendations for the Department of Homeland Security

1. The nation's approach to preparedness must be multi-hazard to reflect all threats and risks, natural and man-made and technological alike, including acts of terrorism.

2. Integrated planning, training, and exercise are a requirement for effective disaster response. Preparedness cannot be a separate function from disaster readiness, response and recovery.

3. Unity of effort is a prerequisite for effective disaster response. Relationships must be established and communications networks in place prior to events. The Department of Homeland Security should establish a field presence that interacts with state partners on a day-to-day basis.

4. A federal/state/local working group of experienced professionals should be convened to review the National Response Plan and make adjustments based on lessons learned from Hurricane Katrina.

5. The Robert T. Stafford Act exists to enable assistance to state and local governments.

Bureaucratic wrangling by federal lawyers gets in the way of disaster response. The public expects full and immediate implementation of authorities under the Stafford Act. Officials with these authorities should be empowered to act.

Priority Recommendations for the Federal Emergency Management Agency

1. The federal government is not nor should it be the nation's 9-1-1 for disaster response. Local government has primary responsibility for initial disaster response and when their resources are overwhelmed the state becomes the second line of response.

FEMA and the federal government is the third responder.

2. FEMA and emergency management must provide additional focus on its ability to effectively implement recovery programs for local governments, individuals, families, and businesses.

3. Debris removal continues to be one of the most challenging recovery issues for state and local governments and must be addressed.

4. There should be a trained cadre of emergency management reservists, following a military model, to assist states and/or the federal government in response to large scale disasters.

5. There is a lack of institutional knowledge for emergency management. The culture, policy, and doctrine of previous eras have been lost and public officials have no roadmap to follow. Leadership and professional development curricula are needed for state and local officials, as well as those at the federal level with responsibilities for disaster preparedness, response, and recovery. The development of future leaders is of paramount importance to professional, highly credible emergency management organizations.

Priority Recommendations for State and Local Governments

1. State and local governments should be held accountable against nationally established and agreed upon emergency management standards. The Emergency Management Accreditation Program (EMAP) was developed by and for state and local emergency management agencies and will continue to evolve to help programs meet the challenges of the future.

2. Criteria and standards should be established for emergency management professionals at each level of government.

3. Appointed and elected officials should be required to understand and exercise (drill) their emergency authorities and responsibilities in conjunction with emergency management officials. NIMS cannot function effectively if public officials don't understand how the system is intended to work in a real event.

4. All levels of government must focus on enhanced public information, crisis communications, and warning to include corresponding actions by the public.

5. Statutory incentives and regulations should be implemented that do not reward local and state governments or insurance organizations for poor public policy choices that result in inappropriate land use planning and preparedness, ineffective building code requirements, and insufficient enforcement.

Priority Recommendations for Citizens

1. The media and the general public must understand that the federal government is not a first responder. Individuals, families, and businesses have preparedness responsibilities to be self-sufficient for up to 72 hours following a disaster.

2. The nation must do a better job of integrating private sector resources during disaster response.

Source: National Emergency Management Association, December 2005, "Emergency Management Goes Back to the Future."

New Orleans, LA, October 22, 2005   Evacuee Umberto Romero gathers food and necessities at the distribution center at the Chalmette Recovery Center following devastating hurricane Katrina.
Andrea Booher/FEMA

TABLE 17

Excerpts from GAO Report on Preliminary Observations on Hurricane Response

Significant local, state, and federal resources were mobilized to respond to the Hurricane Katrina disaster, along with significant participation from charitable and private sector organizations. However, the capabilities of several federal, state, and local agencies were clearly overwhelmed in response to Hurricane Katrina, especially in Louisiana. Therefore, there was widespread dissatisfaction with the level of preparedness and the collective response. As events unfolded in the immediate aftermath and ensuing days after Hurricane Katrina's final landfall, responders at all levels of government—many victims themselves—encountered significant breakdowns in vital areas such as emergency communications as well as obtaining essential supplies and equipment.

The causes of these breakdowns must be well understood and addressed in order to strengthen the nation's ability to prepare for, respond to, and recover from major catastrophic events in the future—whether natural or man-made. Unfortunately, many of the lessons emerging from the most recent hurricanes in the Gulf are similar to those GAO identified more than a decade ago, in the aftermath of Hurricane Andrew, which leveled much of South Florida in the early 1990s. For example, in 1993, we recommended that the President designate a senior official in the White House to oversee federal preparedness for, and response to, major catastrophic disasters.

There are several key themes that, based on our current preliminary work, underpin many of the challenges encountered in the response to Hurricane Katrina and reflect certain lessons learned from past disasters. The following three key themes seem to be emerging.

Clear and Decisive Leadership

First, prior to a catastrophic event, the leadership roles, responsibilities, and lines of authority for the response at all levels must be clearly defined and effectively communicated in order to facilitate rapid and effective decision making, especially in preparing for and in the early hours and days after the event. As we recommended in 1993, we continue to believe that a single individual directly responsible and accountable to the President must be designated to act as the central focal point to lead and coordinate the overall federal response in the event of a major catastrophe. This person would work on behalf of the President to ensure that federal agencies treat the catastrophe as a top priority and that the federal government's response is both timely and effective. In cases where there is warning, such as the high probability of a major hurricane (e.g., a Category 4 or 5), the senior official should be designated prior to the event, be deployed appropriately, and be ready to step forward as events unfold. Neither the DHS Secretary nor any of his designees, such as the Principal Federal Official (PFO), filled this leadership role during Hurricane Katrina, which serves to underscore the immaturity of and weaknesses relating to the current national response framework.

Strong Advance Planning, Training, and Exercise Programs

Second, to best position the nation to prepare for, respond to, and recover from major catastrophes like Hurricane Katrina, there must be strong advance planning, both within and among responder organizations, as well as robust training and exercise programs to test these plans in advance of a real disaster. Although the NRP framework envisions a proactive national response in the event of a catastrophe, the nation does not yet have the types of detailed plans needed to better delineate capabilities that might be required and how such assistance will be provided and coordinated. In addition, we observed that the training and exercises necessary to carry out these plans were not always developed or completed among the first responder community. The leadership to ensure these plans and exercises are in place must come from DHS in conjunction with other federal agencies, state and local authorities, and involved nongovernmental organizations.

Capabilities for a Catastrophic Event

Response and recovery capabilities needed during a major catastrophic event differ significantly from those required to respond to and recover from a "normal disaster." Key capabilities such as emergency communications, continuity of essential government services, and logistics and distribution systems underpin citizen safety and security. In addition, as these capabilities are brought to bear, streamlining, simplifying, and expediting decision making must quickly replace "business as usual" approaches to doing business. The following provides examples of capabilities we have identified in our preliminary work. All of these areas require better contingency plans and the resources to carry them out.

Biloxi, MS, October 4, 2005　Mississippi Gulf Coast Highway I-90 was destroyed as a result of winds and tidal surge from Hurricane Katrina. The support columns are all that remain of this section of I-90 that connects Biloxi with Ocean Springs, MS.
John Fleck/FEMA

Source: GAO-06-365R Preliminary Observations on Hurricane Response Enclosure I: Statement by Comptroller General David M. Walker on GAO's Preliminary Observations Regarding Preparedness and Response to Hurricanes Katrina and Rita, February 1, 2006.

References

CNN Katrina Timeline: http://www.cnn.com/SPECIALS/2005/katrina/interactive/timeline.katrina.large/frameset.exclude.html.

Department of Homeland Security, 2006. "Hurricane Katrina: What the Government Is Doing." http://www.dhs.gov/xprepresp/programs/gc_1157649340100.shtm. September 24, 2006.

General Accounting Office, 2006, GAO-06-365R, "Preliminary Observations on Hurricane Response," February 1, 2006.

Lewis, Nicole, August 2006, "Beyond Relief and Recovery: The Chronicle of Philanthropy," August 17, 2006.

Lipman, Harvy, August 2006, "A Record Fund-Raising Feat: The Chronicle of Philanthropy," August 17, 2006.

Liu, Amy, Fellowes, M., and Mabanta, M., 2006, "Special Edition of the Katrina Index: A One-Year Review of Key Indicators of Recovery in Post-Storm New Orleans." The Brookings Institution, August 2006.

National Emergency Management Association (NEMA), 2005, "Emergency Management Goes Back to the Future," December 2005.

Office of Inspector General, Department of Homeland Security, March 2006, "A Performance Review of FEMA's Disaster Management Activities in Response to Hurricane Katrina."

Select Bipartisan Committee to Investigate the Preparation for and Response to Hurricane Katrina, 2006, "A Failure of Initiative: Final Report of the Special Bipartisan Committee to Investigate the Preparation for and Response to Hurricane Katrina," Government Printing Office, http://www.gpoacess.gov/congress/index.hmtl. February 15, 2006.

Senate Committee on Homeland Security and Governmental Affairs, 2006, "Hurricane Katrina: A Nation Still Unprepared," S. Rept. 109-322, Government Printing Office, May 2006.

Simmons, Ann M. 2007. "Katrina, Rita Still Roil Business Climate," latimes.com, March 9, 2007.

The Brookings Institution: Hurricane Katrina Timeline — http://www.brookings.edu/fp/projects/homeland/katrinatimeline.pdf.

The Brookings Institution, 2007, "Katrina Index: Summary of Findings." http://www.gnocdc.org/KI/ESKatrinaIndex.pdf. March 2007.

Townsend, Francis F., 2006, "The Federal Response to Hurricane Katrina: Lessons Learned," The White House, February 2006.

Appendix
Selected Acronyms

AAR	after-action report
AEC	agency emergency coordinator
AFRO	African Regional Office (WHO)
AoA	Administration on Aging
ARC	American Red Cross
ARES	Amateur Radio Emergency Services
BHR	Bureau for Humanitarian Response (USAID)
B-NICE	biological, nuclear, incendiary, chemical, and explosive (weapons)
CARE	Cooperative for Assistance and Relief Everywhere
CAT	crisis action team
CBRN	chemical, biological, radiological, and nuclear (weapons)
CBRNE	chemical, biological, radiological, nuclear, and explosive (weapons)
CCP	Crisis Counseling Assistance and Training Program
CCP	casualty collection point
CCP	Citizens Corps Program
CDBG	Community Development Block Grant
CDC	Centers for Disease Control and Prevention, U.S. Public Health Service
CDRG	Catastrophic Disaster Response Group
CEPPO	Chemical Emergency Preparedness and Prevention Office
CERCLA	Comprehensive Environmental Response, Compensation, and Liability Act
CFDA	Catalog of Federal Domestic Assistance
CHE	complex humanitarian emergency
CJTF	commander for the joint task force (DoD)
CMHS	Center for Mental Health Services
CMOC	civil/military operations center (DoD)
CMT	crisis management team
CNN	Cable News Network
CRC	Crisis Response Cell
CRM	crisis resource manager
CRS	Catholic Relief Services
DAE	disaster assistance employee
DART	disaster assistance response team (USAID)

DCE	Defense coordinating element
DCO	Defense coordinating officer
DCSA	Defense Support of Civil Authorities
DEA	Drug Enforcement Agency
DEST	domestic emergency support team
DFO	disaster field office
DHHS	Department of Health and Human Services
DHS	Department of Homeland Security
DMAT	Disaster medical assistance team
DMORT	Disaster mortuary response team, National Disaster Medical System
DMTP	Disaster Management Training Programme
DoD	Department of Defense
DOJ	Department of Justice
DOL	Department of Labor
DOT	Department of Transportation
DRC	Disaster Recovery Center
DRD	Disaster Response Division
DRRP	Disaster Reduction and Recovery Programme
DUA	Disaster Unemployment Assistance
EAS	Emergency Alert System
EC	emergency coordinator
ECHO	European Community Humanitarian Organization
ECS	emergency communications staff
EDA	Economic Development Administration
EGOM	Empowered Group of Ministers (India)
EICC	Emergency Information and Coordination Center
EMPG	Emergency Management Performance Grants
EMRO	Eastern-Mediterranean Regional Office (WHO)
EMS	emergency medical services
EOC	emergency operations center
ERC	emergency response coordinator (UN)
ERCG	Emergency Response Coordination Group, Public Health Service/Centers for Disease Control and Agency for Toxic Substances and Disease Registry
ERD	Emergency Response Division (UNDP)
ERL	emergency recovery loan (World Bank)
ERT	emergency response team
ERT-A	emergency response team advance element
ERT-N	national emergency response team
ERU	Emergency Response Unit (IFRC)
ESF	emergency support function
EST	emergency support team
EUCOM	European Command (DoD)
EURO	Regional Office for Europe (WHO)
FAA	Federal Aviation Administration
FACT	field assessment and coordination team (IFRC)
FAO	Food and Agriculture Organization

FBI	Federal Bureau of Investigation
FCO	federal coordinating officer
FECC	federal emergency communications coordinator
FEMA	Federal Emergency Management Agency
FERC	FEMA emergency response capability
FESC	federal emergency support coordinator
FHA	Foreign Humanitarian Assistance (DoD)
FHWA	Federal Highway Administration
FIRST	federal incident response support team
FOC	FEMA Operations Center
FRC	federal resource coordinator
FRERP	Federal Radiological Emergency Response Plan
FRN	FEMA Radio Network
FRP	Federal Response Plan
FSA	Farm Service Agency
GSN	Global Seismographic Network
HAST	humanitarian assistance survey team (DoD)
HAZUS	Hazards US (FEMA Consequence Modeling System)
HET-ESF	Headquarters Emergency Transportation Emergency Support Function
HHS	Department of Health and Human Services
HSAS	Homeland Security Advisory System
HSEEP	Homeland Security Exercise and Evaluation Program (ODP)
HSOC	Homeland Security Operations Center
HSPD	Homeland Security Presidential Directive
HUD	Department of Housing and Urban Development
IAEM	International Association of Emergency Managers
IASC	Inter-Agency Standing Committee
IBRD	International Bank for Reconstruction and Development (World Bank)
ICPAE	Interagency Committee on Public Affairs in Emergencies
ICRC	International Committee of the Red Cross
ICP	incident command post
ICS	incident command system
IDA	International Development Association (World Bank)
IDNDR	International Decade for Natural Disaster Reduction (UN)
IDP	internally displaced persons
IFC	International Finance Corporation (World Bank)
IFG	Individual and Family Grant
IFRC	International Federation of Red Cross/Red Crescent Societies
IHP	Individuals and Households Program
IIMG	Interagency Incident Management Group
IMD	Indian Meteorological Department
IMF	International Monetary Fund
IMT	Incident Management Team
INS	Immigration and Naturalization Service
IO	international organization
ISCID	International Centre for Settlement of Investment Disputes (World Bank)
ISDR	International Strategy for Disaster Reduction (UN)

JFO	joint field office
JIC	joint information center
JOC	joint operations center
JTF	joint task force (DoD)
JTTF	Joint Terrorism Task Force
MACC	Multiagency Command Center
MIGA	Multilateral Investment Guarantee Agency (World Bank)
MMRS	Metropolitan Medical Response System
MOA	memorandum of agreement
MOU	memorandum of understanding
NACo	National Association of Counties
NASA	National Aeronautics and Space Agency
NCA	National Command Authority (DoD)
NDMOC	National Disaster Medical Operations Center
NDMS	National Disaster Medical System
NDMSOSC	National Disaster Medical System Operations Support Center
NEHRP	National Earthquake Hazard Reduction Program
NEIC	National Earthquake Information Center
NEMA	National Emergency Management Association
NEP	National Exercise Program (ODP)
NEPEC	National Earthquake Prediction Evaluation Council
NGO	nongovernmental organization
NIMS	National Incident Management System
NIRT	nuclear incident response team
NIST	National Institute of Standards and Technology
NMRT	national medical response team
NOAA	National Oceanic and Atmospheric Administration
NPSC	National Processing Service Center
NRC	Nuclear Regulatory Commission
NRCC	National Response Coordination Center
NRT	National Response Team
NRP	National Response Plan
NSF	National Science Foundation
NSSE	National Security Special Event
NSEP	National Security Emergency Preparedness
NVOAD	National Voluntary Organizations Active in Disaster
OCHA	Office for the Coordination of Humanitarian Affairs
ODP	Office for Domestic Preparedness
OEP	Office of Emergency Preparedness, U.S. Public Health Service
OET	Office of Emergency Transportation
OFDA	Office of U.S. Foreign Disaster Assistance
OPA	Office of Public Affairs
OSC	on-scene coordinator
OSTP	White House Office of Science and Technology Policy
PACOM	Pacific Command (DoD)
PAHO	Pan-American Health Organization (WHO)
PAO	public affairs officer

PFO	principal federal official
PM	Office of Political/Military Affairs (DoD)
PNP	private nonprofit
PRM	Bureau of Population, Refugees, and Migration (USAID)
PSA	public service announcement
PVO	private voluntary organization
QIP	Quick Impact Project (UNHCR)
RACES	Radio Amateur Civil Emergency Services
RDD	radiological dispersion device
REACT	radio emergency associated communication team
REC	regional emergency coordinator
RECC	regional emergency communications coordinator
RECP	Regional Emergency Communications Plan
RET	regional emergency transportation
RETCO	regional emergency transportation coordinator
RMT	response management team (OFDA)
ROC	regional operations center
ROST	regional operations support team
RRT	regional response team
SAMHSA	Substance Abuse and Medical Health Services Administration
SAC	FBI senior agent-in-charge
SBA	U.S. Small Business Administration
SCO	state coordinating officer
SEARO	South-East Asia Regional Office (WHO)
SFHA	special flood hazard areas
SFLEO	senior federal law enforcement official
SHSP	State Homeland Security Program (ODP)
SIOC	Strategic Information and Operations Center
SOCOM	Special Operations Command (DoD)
SOUTHCOM	Southern Command (DoD)
START	scientific and technical advisory and response team
TAG	Technical Assistance Group (OFDA)
TOPOFF	Top Officials Terrorism Exercise (biennial)
TRADE	ODP Training and Data Exchange Group
TRANSCOM	Transportation Command (DoD)
UASI	Urban Areas Security Initiative
UN	United Nations
UNDAC	UN Disaster Assessment and Coordination
UNDP	United Nations Development Programme
UNHCR	United Nations high commissioner for refugees
UNICEF	United Nations Children's Fund
US&R	Urban Search and Rescue
USACE	United States Army Corps of Engineers
USACOM	United States Atlantic Command (DoD)
USAID	United States Agency for International Development
USDA	United States Department of Agriculture
USGS	United States Geological Survey

VMAT   veterinarian medical assistance team
WB   World Bank
WFP   World Food Programme
WHO   World Health Organization
WMD   weapons of mass destruction
WTC   World Trade Center
ZECP   zone emergency communications planner

References

"After-Action Report on the Response to the September 11 Terrorist Attack of the Pentagon," Washington, DC: Titan Systems, Inc., July 2002.

American Red Cross. *Disaster Operations Center Visitor's Guide.*

Bagli, Charles V. "Seeking Safety, Downtown Firms Are Scattering," *New York Times*, January 29, 2002, p. A-1.

Bakhet, Omar, "Linking Relief to Development," UNDP Rwanda, June 1998.

Ballard, Mark. "Officials Urge Federal Role in Hurricane Insurance," *The Advocate Online*, February 8, 2007.

Burke, Robert. *Counter Terrorism for Emergency Responders*. Boca Raton, FL: CRC/Lewis Publishers, 2000.

Center for Disaster Management and Humanitarian Assistance. *NGOs and Disaster Response Who Are These Guys and What Do They Do Anyways?*, available at www.cdmha.org/ppt/%20presentation.ppt, n.d.

Congress Daily. "Estimated Price Tag of Security Causes Stir," *Government Executive Magazine*, Federal Briefing, February 2, 2007.

Congressional Research Service. "Federal Emergency Management Policy Changes after Hurricane Katrina, a Summary of Statutory Provisions," available at http://www.fas.org/sgp/crs/homesec/RL33729.pdf, December 15, 2006.

Coyle, David. *The United Nations and How It Works*. New York: Columbia University Press, 1969.

Department of Defense, CCRP. "The Complex Process of Responding to Crisis," available at www.dodccrp.org/ngoCh2.html, n.d.

Department of Homeland Security. "DHS Proposed Budget 2008," available at http://www.dhs.gov/xlibrary/assets/budget_bib-fy2008.pdf, 2007.

DHS Office of the Inspector General. "Audit of FEMA's Individuals and Households Program in Miami-Dade County, Florida, for Hurricane Frances" OIG-05-20, available at http://www.dhs.gov/xoig/assets/mgmtrpts/OIG_05-20_May05.pdf, 2005.

Emergency Management Institute. "2001–2002 Catalog of Activities, Emmitsburg, MD," available at www.fema.gov.

Erickson, Paul A. *Emergency Response Planning for Corporate and Municipal Managers.*

Federal Emergency Management Agency Office of the Inspector General. *FEMA's Disaster Management Program: A Performance Audit after Hurricane Andrew*. H-01-93. Washington, DC: FEMA, January 1993.

FEMA. "Report on Costs and Benefits of Natural Hazard Mitigation." Washington, DC: FEMA, March 1997.

FEMA. *Partnerships in Preparedness, a Compendium of Exemplary Practices in Emergency Management*, vol. II. Washington, DC: FEMA, May 1997.

FEMA. *FEMA Emergency Information Field Guide* (condensed). Washington, DC: FEMA, October 1998.

FEMA. *Federal Response Plan*. Washington, DC: FEMA, April 1999.

FEMA. *Partnerships in Preparedness, a Compendium of Exemplary Practices in Emergency Management,* vol. IV. Washington, DC: FEMA, January 2000.

FEMA. *International Technical Assistance Activities of the United States Federal Emergency Management Agency.* Washington, DC: FEMA, 2001.

FEMA. "Homeland Security Establishing New Advisory Council," press release, February 7, 2007.

FEMA. "Catalog," Emergency Management Institute, available at http://training.fema.gov/emiweb/emicourses/emicatalog.asp, 2007.

FEMA. Web site, www.fema.gov.

Flynn, Kevin. "After the Attack: The Firefighters; Department's Cruel Toll: 350 Comrades." *New York Times,* September 13, 2001, Section: National Desk.

Gandel, Stephen. "Consultants Push Wall Street to Leave; Downtown's Losses Are Huge, but Some Companies Shrug off Fears, Concentrate Workers in Midtown." *Crain's New York Business,* March 4, 2002, p. 1.

Gilbert, Alorie. "Out of the Ashes," *Information Week,* March 2002, available at www.informationweek.com/story/IWK20020104S0008.

Gilbert, Roy, and Alcira Kreimer. *Learning from the World Bank's Experience of Natural Disaster Related Assistance.* Washington, DC: The World Bank, 1999.

GlobalCorps. *OFDA's Evolving Role,* available at www.globalcorps.com/ofda/ofdarole.html, n.d.

Grimmett, Richard. "9/11 Commission Recommendations: Implementation Status," Congressional Research Service, Report RL33742, 2006.

Hawley, Chris. "Globalization and Sept. 11 Are Pushing Wall Street off Wall Street, Analysts Say." Associated Press State and Local Wire, February 1, 2002, State and Regional Section, in *Lexis-Nexis Universe: World Trade Center, Firm and Tenant,* March 20, 2002.

Hedges, Chris. "Monday Counting Losses, Department Rethinks Fighting Every Fire." *New York Post,* October 1, 2001.

Hollis, Mark. "Florida Calling for Catastrophe Fund," *Los Angeles Times,* February 14, 2007, part A, p. 17.

Houston, Allen. "Crisis Communications: The Readiness Is All: How the Red Cross Responded," *PR Week,* October 22, 2001, p. 13.

Houston, Allen. "Crisis Communications: Confused Messages Spur Switch to Sole Spokesman." *PR Week,* November 5, 2001, p. 11.

Intergovernmental Panel on Climate Change. "Special Issues in Developing Countries," available at www.ipcc.ch/pub/tar/wg2/340.htm, 2001.

International Monetary Fund. "IMF Emergency Assistance Related to Natural Disasters and Post-Conflict Situations: A Factsheet," www.imf.org/external/np/eexr/facts/conflict.htm, 2001.

"The Look Back at Mitch's Rampage," *USA Today,* June 8, 1999, available at www.usatoday.com/weather/news/1998/wmrmpage.htm.

Madison County, North Carolina. "Multi-Hazard Plan for Madison County."

Mancino, Kimberly. *Development Relief: NGO Efforts to Promote Sustainable Peace and Development in Complex Humanitarian Emergencies.* Washington, DC: Interaction, 2001.

Maynard, Kimberly. "Healing Communities in Conflict: International Assistance in Complex Emergencies," available at www.ciaonet.org/book/maynard/maynard07.html, n.d.

McKinsey & Company. "Improving NYPD Emergency Preparedness and Response." Author, August 19, 2002.

Mileti, Dennis S. *Disasters by Design: A Reassessment of Natural Hazards in the United States.* Washington, DC: John Henry Press, 1999.

Mitchell, James K., et al. *Crucibles of Hazard: Mega-Cities and Disasters in Transition.* New York: United Nations University Press, 1999.

National Association of Counties. "Counties and Homeland Security: Policy Agenda to Secure the People of America's Counties," available at www.naco.org/programs/homesecurity?policyplan.cfm, August 2004.

National Emergency Management Association. "White Paper on Domestic Preparedness." Washington, DC: NEMA, October 1, 2001.

National Emergency Management Association. "NEMA Reports on State Homeland Security Structures," available at www.nemaweb.org/ShowExtendedNewscfm?ID=171, June 2002.

National Fire Protection Association. "Fire Loss in the U.S. during 2005. NFPA Report," available at http://www.nfpa.org/assets/files/PDF/OS.fireloss.pdf, 2006.

National Governor's Association (NGA) 2002. Center for Best Practices. Issue Brief, August 2002.

National Governors Association (NGA). Letter to Senator Leahy and Senator Bond, February 5, 2007, available at http://www.nga.org/portal/site/nga/menuitem.cb6e7818b34088d18a278110501010a0/?vgnextoid=edd8b31eb2990110VgnVCM1000001a01010aRCRD.

Natsios, Andrew S. *U.S. Foreign Policy and the Four Horsemen of the Apocalypse*. Westport, CT: Praeger Publishers, 1997.

NOAA. "The Northeast Snowfall Impact Scale (NESIS)," available at the NOAA Web site, http://www.ncdc.noaa.gov/oa/climate/research/snow-nesis, 2006.

Office for the Coordination of Humanitarian Affairs. OCHA Organigramme, available at http://ochaonline.un.org/webpage.asp?site=organigramme, 2005.

Office for the Coordination of Humanitarian Affairs. "Information Summary on Military and Civil Defence Assets (MCDA) and the Military and Civil Defence Unit (MCDU)," available at www.reliefweb.int/ocha_ol/programs/response/mcdunet/0mcduinf.html, n.d.

Office for the Coordination of Humanitarian Affairs. "Coordination of Humanitarian Response," available at www.reliefweb.int/ocha_ol/programs/response/service.html, n.d.

Office of Domestic Preparedness. "ODP Grant Programs," available at the U.S. Department of Justice Web site, http://www.ojp.usdoj.gov/odp, 2007.

Office of Homeland Security. "State and Local Actions for Homeland Security, July 2002," available at www.whitehouse.gov/homeland/stateandlocal.

Oklahoma Department of Civil Emergency Management. "After Action Report, Alfred P. Murrah Building Bombing. Lessons Learned." Author, 1997.

Otero, Juan. "Congress, Administration Examines Emergency Communications Systems," *Nation's Cities Weekly*, October 22, 2001, p. 5.

Pan American Health Organization. "Natural Disasters: Protecting the Public's Health," PAHO Scientific Publication No. 575, n.d.

Powell, Michael, and Christine Haughney. "A Towering Task Lags in New York, City Debates Competing Visions for Rebuilding Devastated Downtown," *Washington Post*, February 25, 2002, p. A03, available at www.washingtonpost.com/ac2/.../A22040-2002Feb16?language=printe.

Ranganath, Priya. *Mitigation and the Consequences of International Aid in Postdisaster Reconstruction*. Centre d'Etude et de Cooperation Internationale, 2000.

Rendleman, John. "Back Online, Despite Its Losses, Verizon Went Right back to Work Restoring Communications Services." *InformationWeek*, available at www.informationwee.com/story/IWK20011105S0017, October 29, 2001.

Salomons, Dirk. *Building Regional and National Capacities for Leadership in Humanitarian Assistance*. New York: The Praxis Group, 1998.

Senate Committee on Homeland Security and Governmental Affairs. "Hurricane Katrina: A Nation Still Unprepared," available at http://hsgac.senate.gov/_files/Katrina/ExecSum.pdf, 2006.

Site One. "History of the Red Cross," available at www.siteone.com/redcross/anniv.htm, n.d.

Smith, Lloyd R. "Lessons Learned from Oklahoma City: Your Employees ... Their Needs, Their Role in Response and Recovery," available at www.recovery.com.

Southern African Regional Poverty Network. "Least Developed Countries of the Disaster Profiles," www.savpn.org.za/relsites.php?site=2, n.d.

Strohm, Chris. "Homeland Security Budget Generous to Customs, Border Agency," *Government Executive*, February 5, 2007.

Strohm, Chris. "Proposed Cuts to First Responder Grants Draw Fire," *Government Executive*, February 6, 2007.

Town of Boone, North Carolina. "All Hazards Planning and Operations Manual." Boone, NC: Author, July 1999.

"Tsunami Education a Priority in Hawaii and West Coast States," *Bulletin of the American Meteorological Society*, June 2001, p. 1207.

UN Rwanda. "The United Nations Development Programme in Rwanda," available at www.un.rw/UNRwa/UNDP.shtml, n.d.

United Nations Development Programme. "Further Elaboration on Follow-up to Economic and Social Council Resolution 1995/96: Strengthening of the Coordination of Emergency Humanitarian Assistance," available at www.undp.org/erd/archives/executiv.htm, March 10–14 1997.

UNDP. *Disaster Profiles of the Least Developed Countries*. New York: United Nations, May 2001.

UNDP. "About ERD," available at www.undp.org/erd/about.htm, n.d.

UNDP. "Building Bridges Between Relief and Development: A Compendium of the UNDP in Crisis Countries," available at www.undp.org/erd/archives/bridges.htm, n.d.

UNDP. "The Disaster Reduction and Recovery Program: An Introduction," available at www.undp.org/erd/archives/brochures/drrp/main.htm, n.d.

UNDP. "Reintegration and Rehabilitation," available at www.undp.org/erd/randr.htm, n.d.

UNDP. "Strengthening National Disaster Management," available at www.undp.org/erd/archives/brochures/drrp/countries/Botswana.htm, n.d.

UNDP. "The United Nations Development Programme Mission Statement," available at www.undp.org/info/discover/mission.html, n.d.

UNDP. Vulnerability Reduction and Sustainable Development, available at www.UNDP.org.in/dmweb, n.d.

UNDP. "Working for Solutions to Crises: The Development Response," available at www.undp.org/erd/archives/bridges2.htm, n.d.

United Nations. "General Assembly Economic and Social Council.," New York: United Nations, May 8, 2001.

U.S. Agency for International Development. "Rebuilding Postwar Rwanda: The Role of the International Community." available at www.usaid.gov/pubs/usaid_eval/ascii/pnaby212.txt, 1996.

U.S. Agency for International Development. *Field Operations Guide for Disaster Assessment and Response, Version 3.0*. Washington, DC: USAID, 1998.

U.S. Agency for International Development. *OFDA Annual Report 2000*. Washington, DC: USAID, 2000.

U.S. Army. "About NGOs," available at http://call.army.mil/fmso/ngos/indtroduction.html, n.d.

U.S. Conference of Mayors. "A National Action Plan for Safety and Security in America's Cities," available at www.usmayors.org/uscm/home.asp, December 2001.

U.S. Department of State. "Bureau of Population, Refugees, and Migration," available at www.state.gov/g/prm, n.d.

"VIPs, Disaster Service Calls May Get Priority," *The Daily Yomiuri* [Tokyo], The Yomiuri Shimbun, November 26, 2001, p. 1.

Walsh, Edward. "National Response to Terror; FEMA Leads Effort; Borders Tightened," *Washington Post*, September 12, 2001, p. A-1.

Waugh, William, Jr. *Living with Hazards—Dealing with Disasters: An Introduction to Emergency Management*. New York: M.E. Sharpe, 2000.

Wax, Alan J., and Julie Claire Diop. "Return to Downtown; Office Leases Are Being Signed Again, but Revival Will Take a While," *Newsday*, March 11, 2002, p. D13.

"Wireless System Improves Communications," *American City and County*, August 2001.

Whoriskey, Peter. 2007. "Florida's Big Hurricane Gamble," *Washington Post*, February 20, 2007, section A, p. A02.

World Bank. "Assistance to Post-Conflict Countries and the HIPC Framework," available at www.imf.org/external/np/hipc/2001/pc/042001.htm, April 2000.

Zevin, Rona. "Tapping Web Power in Emergencies," *American City and County*, August 2001.

Index